Case Studies in Financial Decision Making
Third Edition

Diana R. Harrington

Babson Distinguished Professor of Finance
Babson College

Kenneth M. Eades

Darden Graduate School of Business Administration
University of Virginia

The Dryden Press
Harcourt Brace College Publishers

Fort Worth Philadelphia San Diego New York Orlando Austin San Antonio
Toronto Montreal London Sydney Tokyo

Publisher   Elizabeth Widdicombe
Acquisitions Editor   Rick Hammonds
Developmental Editor   Stacey Fry
Production Manager: Marilyn Williams
Project Management   Elm Street Publishing Services, Inc.
Compositor   Weimer Graphics, Inc.
Text Type   10/12 Times Roman

Address for Editorial Correspondence:
The Dryden Press, 301 Commerce Street, Suite 3700, Fort Worth, TX 76102

Address for Orders:
The Dryden Press, 6277 Sea Harbor Drive, Orlando, FL 32887
1-800-782-4479, or 1-800-433-0001 (in Florida)

ISBN: 0-03-075479-8

Library of Congress Catalog Number 93-29962

Printed in the United States of America

3 4 5 6 7 8 9 0 1 2 066 9 8 7 6 5 4 3 2 1

The Dryden Press
Harcourt Brace College Publishers

For Will and Maya and Linda, Alison, and Mark

The Dryden Press Series in Finance

Reilly
Investment Analysis and Portfolio Management
Fourth Edition

Reilly
Investments
Third Edition

Sears and Trennepohl
Investment Management

Seitz
Capital Budgeting and Long-Term Financing Decisions

Siegel and Siegel
Futures Markets

Smith and Spudeck
Interest Rates: Principles and Applications

Stickney
Financial Statement Analysis: A Strategic Perspective
Second Edition

Turnbull
Option Valuation

Weston and Brigham
Essentials of Managerial Finance
Tenth Edition

Weston and Copeland
Managerial Finance
Ninth Edition

Wood and Wood
Financial Markets

The Harcourt Brace College Outline Series

Baker
Financial Management

Preface

More than ever, students and practitioners of finance face complex situations in an integrated and changing world. New problems in a dynamic environment challenge us all. Clear thinking, born of good skills and broad knowledge, is needed. The cases in this book attempt to provide students with an opportunity to learn and hone their skills on real problems that have confronted managers over the last decade. The cases feature a variety of economic environments inside and outside the United States that allow students to make decisions requiring an analysis of both micro and macro environments. The third edition of *Case Studies in Financial Decision Making* attempts to broaden the scope of the case issues addressed in the first two editions and to provide students with cases that introduce issues on which to learn as well as practice skills.

The Case Method

Although many in the past have mistakenly believed that cases were useful only to teach practical skills, suggest tools, and present institutional information, cases are also a good method for teaching the understanding and use of theory. Cases can and do include problems that some might label theoretical or abstract but that are in fact drawn from actual situations. By studying the factual descriptions of problems that have been faced and dealt with by managers, students can learn about the application of theory as well as gain practice in using tools and skills in realistic situations. In short, cases deal with real-world problems and managers; they contain more than simple problems involving a test of a single skill or concept. Students should find them interesting to use today and useful as they grow as financial managers or analysts.

For some students the case method is new and perhaps somewhat frightening. Fear comes from the fact that there is rarely a right and verifiable answer in each case. That is not to suggest that any approach is acceptable, however. Clearly, certain kinds of analysis are more appropriate for certain situations, and certain courses of action show more insight, skill of analysis, and probability of success than others. The challenge of case analysis is to combine the appropriate skills and tools with judgment and creativity to solve problems that are as realistic as the written word can make them. Apprehension is the last thing that the case method should engender.

Intended Market

While the basic skills and tools of financial analysis can be used in analyzing these cases, they also offer the opportunity to solve more advanced and complex problems. Thus this book can either be used as part of an introductory finance course, or the book can be used for a second course—assuming the second course follows an introductory course that teaches the basic tools and concepts of finance. For either strategy, students should have a basic finance book as a reference during the course featuring these cases.

Features of the Book

Value Creation.   The concept of value creation is the thread that connects the cases in this book, just as identifying, choosing, and implementing value-creating opportunities is the challenge facing managers. Because value is in the eye, and hand, of the shareholder, the manager or student must be concerned with the share price and the effect that the investment and financing decisions will have on the price of the shares. Thus the cases in this edition provide more data about the capital markets, and especially the market for the subject company's stock, than cases in two previous editions. In addition, a note at the end of the book, "The Business Environment: A Retrospective, 1929–1993," gives a brief overview of the business environment to emphasize the link between the macroeconomic conditions for business, corporate profitability, cash flow, and changes in shareholders' value. The link can be a difficult one to make but because the corporate objective is to create value, every student and manager must make this connection. Understanding that link comes only with practice. These cases should give current and future managers some of that practice.

International Focus.   Some of the cases are set outside the United States with non-U.S. companies or with U.S. companies in a foreign country. Still other cases feature U.S. corporations facing problems induced by doing business with foreign companies or problems caused by foreign competition. These cases are included for two reasons. First, some of the simple insights and methods we use in solving problems in U.S. domestic situations do not work elsewhere in the world. For example, determining the appropriate capital structure in a foreign country can be a very different decision than one made in the United States. Capital structure theory based on the tax deductibility of interest payments is a useful concept but only in a country where the taxing authorities allow such deductions. A student or manager who believes this theory is applicable in all situations could overestimate the attractiveness of debt financing. Second, the integrated nature of worldwide business means that most students who are in school today will, at some point in their careers, work for or with a non-U.S.-based corporation. It would be a disservice to concentrate cases in only one of the many environments in which managers may find themselves.

New to This Edition. Of the 45 case studies in the book, 15 are new to this edition. The new cases were selected primarily because they present challenging situations that occurred in the past decade. They cover a wide variety of topics including financial forecasting, capital budgeting, required rate of return (cost of capital), financing choice, and corporate governance. Most of the companies featured in the new cases are large and well-known companies such as General Motors, Procter & Gamble, Mead Corporation, AMF, PepsiCo, Colt Industries, Burlington Northern Railroad, Chausson Trading Company, and Beazer PLC.

In keeping with the objective of having an international focus, 6 of the 15 new cases are either about non-U.S.-based companies or U.S. companies facing foreign competition and/or foreign currency exposure. As businesses increasingly compete in a global marketplace and are affected by international economic forces, managers must face the reality of having to think beyond the confines of their home countries. These cases provide students with an opportunity to discuss issues including international tax law, currency risk management, and expansion into foreign markets. For example, Koppers Co. is about the purchase of a U.S. company by Beazer PLC, a British firm; the Chausson Body and Assembly case is about a joint venture between Chausson Trading Company, a French automotive designing and manufacturing firm, and a U.S. auto company; and the Dozier Industries (A) and (B) cases evaluate the effect on a U.S. company of various potential bids on a contract with a British company.

Three new required-rate-of-return cases have been added to this edition. The Procter & Gamble case covers calculating the weighted-average cost of capital for a corporation. The Mead Corporation case shows how cost of capital is constantly changing over time, and the PepsiCo case asks whether divisional costs of capital should be used in lieu of the overall corporate hurdle rate.

Three of the new cases feature the analysis of contingent-claim contracts. Burlington Northern Railroad requires that students analyze a lease-versus-buy decision that includes an option for the lessee to buy the asset at a fixed price at the termination of the lease. Dozier Industries (B) introduces students to the concept of using currency options to hedge a company's possible currency exposure. Finally, General Motors: Valuation of Class E Contingent Notes considers the potential liability of a contingent note issued in conjunction with the merger with Electronic Data Systems in 1984.

In addition to the new cases, three cases from the second edition have been updated. Financial Footprints is an introductory case that has been updated. The Metalcrafters case has been rewritten to provide the perspective of a manager in 1992 who must forecast cash flows for 1993 and beyond. Zukowski Meats, Incorporated has been updated to reflect the consequences of changing credit policy in 1992. To serve as a basic resource of analysis for all the cases, the technical note on the business environment has also been updated to include a retrospective on the period 1926 to 1993.

Computer Assistance.   Each copy of this textbook includes a computer disk with copies of *Lotus 1-2-3* files for the relevant cases. Each Lotus file contains the major exhibits of the case as they appear in the textbook. Thus, students familiar with Lotus (or Lotus-compatible software) can more quickly understand the exhibits by looking at the formulas behind the numbers and the references between the variables. The intent of the files is to eliminate the need for students to enter data from the exhibits manually into their own spreadsheets. The time saved for data entry should allow more time for students to analyze and make intelligent decisions about the problems at hand. It should be noted that the spreadsheets contain formulas and references among variables but give no guidance as to how to extend or analyze the data.

In addition to the data files, the computer disk contains four basic *Lotus 1-2-3* template files. These templates can facilitate historical analysis, forecasting, capital budgeting, and choosing among financing alternatives. Although the data for the template files must be input manually, students may find a payoff to the extra effort. The key is knowing when to invest the time and which template will provide useful information for the particular problem being analyzed.

Organization of the Book

Analyzing Corporate Performance.   The cases in this part highlight the tools needed to analyze the historical performance of a company. In Financial Footprints, the differences in how a variety of companies in different industries operate and their resulting performance at the end of 1991 can be seen. General Motors (A), (B), and (C) provide data on the U.S. and international auto manufacturers for several years. These cases feature the performance over time of the significant players in one important worldwide industry.

Forecasting Future Corporate Performance.   After students have mastered evaluation of historical performance and ratio analysis, which are necessary to understand the strategies and success of a variety of companies, we turn to the second part of the text where the cases require a forward-looking analysis of performance. Forecasting financial statements for an entrepreneurial venture in the midst of entering a new market provides the challenge in the United Telesis Corporation case. Fisher Electric, Inc. concerns the funding needs of a Canadian wholesaler with significant growth prospects. In Fantastic Manufacturing, Inc., a company that obtains much of its materials from Asia has rapid growth that requires careful management control and good forecasts. Alfred Brooks Menswear, Limited challenges the students to consider the financial management implications for a firm that is both an importer and an exporter. The case shows how managers must assess and manage foreign-currency exposure and how a working-capital loan might be structured. The case also allows the student to take the viewpoint of a bank that must identify the products that best meet a client's needs while at the same time ensuring that the portfolio of products offered to the client meets the risk and return demands of the bank. Mushrooms Division (A) and (B) describe the division of a company and its parent as the division expands into a new product. Coordinating marketing plans with financial requirements and resources is the challenge in this two-case series.

Capital Budgeting. To decide whether an investment or strategy should be pursued, one must decide whether it creates value for the firm's shareholders. To create value, the strategy's returns must exceed its costs. Deciding which costs and benefits are relevant in investing capital is the focus of the cases in this section. Metalcrafters, Inc. is a straightforward look at the process of making such investment decisions. Zukowski Meats, Incorporated considers the cash-flow impacts of a changing credit policy at a small private company. AMF requires a detailed projection of revenues and expenses for a make-or-buy decision for a new line of bowling balls. The Federal Reserve Bank of Richmond (A) features an investment decision for a public agency. Management of Polymold, a division of a much larger company, considers alternative strategies for its markets and must deal with uncertain forecasts in making a strategic investment decision. In Massalin Particulares, the investment decision is taken to an international setting. In The Jacobs Division, capital-investment forecasts must accommodate uncertainties in the product markets. The Chausson Body and Assembly case concerns an investment analysis of an international joint venture between a French company and a U.S. manufacturer. The final case in this section of the book, The Becker Corporation, provides a link between the capital-investment process, a company's cost of capital, and use of that concept in making value-creating investment decisions.

Required Return on Investment—Cost of Capital. Following the discussion of the capital budgeting process and how risk should be included in it, the Star Appliance cases directly address the best way of estimating a company's required rate of return—its cost of capital. The Federal Reserve Bank of Richmond (B) addresses the same question for a public-sector agency. Procter & Gamble provides the opportunity to estimate the cost of capital for a large consumer goods corporation. In the Mead Corporation case students see how a major corporation monitors its cost of capital over time and how that cost of capital varies with the economy. PepsiCo, Inc. asks the question whether management should use the overall corporate cost of capital or separate costs of capital for each business segment within the corporation.

Financing Capital Investments.   After management has decided to make a new investment in property, plant, and equipment or in working capital, a company must decide how to fund the project. The cases in this part deal with the financing of a corporation. New Hampshire Savings Bank Corporation focuses on whether a company is better off paying dividends or retaining the funds for future investment. Hop-In Food Stores, Incorporated examines issuing new equity. Kelly Services, Inc. and Marriott Corporation deal directly with the relative value of debt. Moving into the international capital markets is the decision that faces management in Philip Morris, Incorporated: Swiss Franc Financing. Burlington Northern Railroad Company involves a choice between an operating lease and equipment-secured debt. Bearings, Inc. and Van Dusen Air, Inc. look at the costs and relative value of equity and debt of various types. Dozier (A) concerns currency risk management that occurs as a U.S. firm bids for business from a British company. Dozier (B) and the General Motors cases deal with contingent claims analysis. In Dozier (B) the student must decide whether options can be used as an alternative to forwards and spot market transactions for currency risk management. In General Motors: Valuation of Class E Contingent Notes, students must estimate the value of a contingent liability that is coming due.

Strategic Investment and Financing Decisions.   The cases in the final part of the book call on most of the tools, skills, and concepts learned and exercised in the preceding sections. Valuing a company is the problem facing management in Superior Industries International, Omni Services, Incorporated, and Philip Morris: Seven-Up Acquisition. Omni is a closely held company while the other two are large publicly traded corporations. In Diamond Shamrock Corporation the concern is the divestiture of a division and its effect on the company. Koppers Co. describes a cross-border acquisition featuring the purchase of a U.S. company by a British conglomerate. Colt Industries and Norris Industries deal with leverage: Colt is a leveraged recapitalization; Norris is a leveraged buyout. Finally in Gaylord Container Corporation, the students examine what happens to a company after a leveraged buyout when a company is seriously impacted by an economic recession.

Technical Note. The technical note is a comprehensive retrospective on the U.S. business environment from 1929 to 1993.

Ancillary Package

Instructor's Manual. Each teaching note includes the objective of the case, a teaching plan, extensive case analysis focusing on key issues, and references to chapters in widely used textbooks and relevant journal articles that might be used in conjunction with the cases. Each teaching note is based on the authors' classroom experience with the case. To enhance the range of topics available for class use, the *Instructor's Manual* also contains four additional cases and accompanying teaching notes.

Instructor's Computer Disk. Accompanying each *Instructor's Manual* is an instructor's computer disk for IBM-compatible microcomputers. The Lotus files on this disk reveal how the important exhibits in the teaching notes were generated. Thus the instructor has the power to create his or her own personalized solution by simply changing a few assumptions or formulas within the spreadsheet.

Acknowledgments

Students at a number of business schools have used and found these cases challenging and exciting. We are indebted to these students for their enthusiasm and skill in analyzing the cases. They have not only been lively subjects on which to test this material but have contributed in no minor way to the excitement of teaching and learning with the case method.

In the gathering of the case studies, numerous managers contributed by providing material about and insight into their problems. Without willing subjects, the case method would not be possible. The corporations, in the main, are not disguised; where possible, the managers who faced the problems are identified by name. We thank Paul Weyandt at Burlington Northern Railroad Company; Phyllis Grossman at Norwest Corporation; Cheryl Harris, formerly of Mead Corporation; and Juan Munro, Chairman of the Board and President of Massalin Particulares. These managers supported this research in tangible and intangible ways.

The following colleagues gathered materials for, wrote, or supervised the writing of cases: Brent D. Wilson of Nexus Consulting Group; Robert Conroy, Robert Harris, John Colley, William Sihler, the late Robert Vandell, Richard Brownlee, Leslie Grayson, Robert F. Bruner, William Rotch, and C. Ray Smith, professors at the Darden School; James Hatch and David Shaw of Western Ontario University; and J. Peter Williamson of the Amos Tuck Graduate School of Business at Dartmouth College. In addition to contributing case study material and their case-writing talents, these persons provided helpful comments as the revision proceeded.

Numerous research assistants helped us and the other case contributors to gather, organize, and write the cases. Debra Lalor, Sharon Graham, Yvette Reyes, Eric Olsen, Matt Wilkinson, Guy Brossy, Kathy Ford-Carr, Paul Frankel, John Guertler, John MacFarlane, III, Mary McCall, Emmett McClean, Bill Miller, Emily Morgan, Casey Opitz, Louis Sarkes, Richard Swasey, Jr., and David Wellborn played major parts in the development of specific cases. To each of them we are most indebted.

For funding and supporting the case writing in other ways, we are in debt of the Darden School and the Darden Foundation.

Finally, there are a number of tireless and priceless people who made the production of this book easier than it otherwise would have been. Ginny Fisher managed the process of producing the manuscript. Her skills in typing, organizing, and supporting are without peer. The members of Darden's fine editing staff, Bette Collins, Stephen Smith, and Elaine Moran, did their job with skill and humor. The professionals at The Dryden Press provided good suggestions and skilled support. Our academic colleagues and reviewers

John Ballantine
Babson College

Thomas Berry
DePaul University

Lyle L. Bowlin
University of Northern Iowa

Neil Cohen
The George Washington University

Brent Dalrymple
University of Texas—Pan American

Philip Fanara, Jr.
Howard University

Tim Gallagher
Colorado State University

Jayat R. Kale
Georgia State University

Susan E. Moeller
Eastern Michigan University

Edgar Ortiz
University of San Diego

Paul E. Pender
Augsburg College

Jim Schallheim
University of Utah

Carl Weaver
James Madison University

provided comments and suggestions that were thoughtful and useful.

Lastly, we are grateful to our families who showed more humor, patience, and support than we had the right to expect. In many ways they made this edition possible.

Diana R. Harrington
Wellesley, Massachusetts
October 1993

Kenneth M. Eades
Charlottesville, Virginia
October 1993

About the Authors

Diana R. Harrington (D.B.A. University of Virginia, M.S.B.A. Boston University, B.A. College of William and Mary) is the Babson Distinguished Professor of Finance at Babson College in Wellesley, Massachusetts. She has also taught at the Darden Graduate School of Business Administration at the University of Virginia, the Kellogg School of Management at Northwestern University, Iowa State University, and the University of Northern Iowa after being in industry for 15 years. She is a trustee of the Landmark Funds, has taught in a variety of executive development programs, and has served as a consultant to industry. Professor Harrington has authored or co-authored other books and articles and is a trustee of the Eastern Finance Association and on the board of directors of the Financial Management Association.

Kenneth M. Eades (Ph.D. Purdue University, B.S. Electrical Engineering University of Kentucky) is Associate Professor of Business Administration at the Darden Graduate School of Business Administration at the University of Virginia in Charlottesville, Virginia. Before joining the Darden School in 1988, he taught at Purdue University, the University of Michigan, and Northwestern University. While at the Kellogg School of Management at Northwestern University, Professor Eades was voted one of the top eight instructors for the year. During his career he has published research on dividend policy and the pricing of convertible securities in some of the top academic journals. At the Darden School he received the First Wachovia Award for Excellence in Research. In addition Professor Eades has served as a consultant to industry and has taught in a variety of executive development programs.

Contents

Alphabetical List of Cases

Introduction

Welcome to the case method. To analyze a case successfully, you must do two things—put yourself in the position of the manager making the decision, and make the decision.

Within each case you must assume the role of the manager whose job it is to analyze alternatives for the company. In most instances it will be an easy task to determine who is the decision maker, since that person will be identified by name in the case and his or her position and role will be described. In the few instances where the decision maker is not identified by name, your point of view will be that of the company's top management.

Once you have identified the person or group of persons whose role you will assume, you need to gather the information that you, as the manager described in the case, would naturally have. Managers, even young analysts, have considerable knowledge about their company, the industry in which it competes, and the economic environment in which it operates. Since, as a manager, you would have that information, as the case analyst assuming the manager's role, you must acquire it.

Once you have the background necessary for your role, your task is the same as the manager in the situation would have—to identify, understand, and analyze the problems the company faces. As would the manager, you will define the problems and the available courses of action, and you will gather the information needed to determine the appropriate course. The steps you will take in assuming the manager's role and in confronting and solving problems are listed below.

I. *Assume the manager's role*
1. Understand the environment in which the company operates:
   The worldwide socioeconomic and political environment
   The domestic environment
   The industry situation
2. Know the company's history, current condition, and future prospects

II. *Solve the problem facing the company*
1. Identify the problem
2. Define the alternatives
3. Gather information about the alternatives
4. Analyze the risks and returns of the options
5. Make a decision and develop a plan of action

Assume the Manager's Role

As you develop as a case analyst, you will refine your own approach and develop a sense of the depth and breadth of analysis appropriate for the particular situation described in a case. Depending upon the situation, one or more of the areas discussed below could receive more attention than the others.

Understand the Environment in Which the Company Operates. Perhaps the best way to begin to understand the milieu in which the company operates is to investigate the general economic environment. Frequently the case analyst looks only at the domestic environment; however, with the increased integration of the world's economy, the *worldwide environment* cannot be ignored. Certainly some decisions described in this book are less affected than others by worldwide socioeconomic and political events. However, the isolation of countries and industries from events in the rest of the world has greatly diminished, and, as U.S. managers found after the oil price rises in the 1970s and early 1980s, to ignore events outside the local economy can be dangerous. Since most of the cases in this book are set in periods when events profoundly changed the nature of the environment in which all countries, industries, and companies operated—worldwide considerations are particularly relevant.

Because different factors are important at different times and to different companies, the manager, and thus you as the case analyst, should be aware of the relative robustness of the worldwide economy at the time of a particular case, and should sense what concerns for and predictions about the future might have prevailed at that time.

In cases where the company or the decision is, or can be, directly affected by worldwide events, the cases will provide information that you as the manager would have had. Because of the necessary brevity of the cases, however, some of the data you might like to have, or believe the manager would have had, may not be included. You must decide on the basis of the information you have. Some basic data about international events are contained in the last section of "The Business Environment: A Retrospective, 1929–1993."

The strength and nature of the *domestic economy* are certainly of more obvious concern, and this is an area in which managers often have more personal and professional experience. Although certain factors and events in the economy will affect some companies more than others, nevertheless there are universal touchstones of concern. The analyst should consider such things as (1) the robustness of the economy and its expansion or contraction because it can affect the company's sales, profits, and cost and availability of funds; (2) the level of unemployment because it affects the potential for strikes as well as the sales of certain products; (3)

cyclical upturns because they can increase the sales of products such as consumer durables while increasing the potential for strikes and prices of other resources; and (4) cyclical downturns because they can decrease the need for productive capacity and the likelihood of protracted strikes in many industries, can decrease resource costs, and because they hurt firms whose sales depend upon the level of consumers' disposable income.

Most cases contain a brief description of the environment in which the firm operates. For more information about the U.S. environment—the setting for the majority of the cases in this book—a background note, "The Business Environment: A Retrospective, 1929–1993," is presented in the last section of this book. The information in this note can be used in analyzing many of the cases.

While the analyst will want to understand the current state of the domestic economy and the future directions it might take, of particular interest is the effect changes in the economy have had and will have on the particular industry and company featured in the case. Just as some economies are more sensitive than others to worldwide events, some industries and companies are influenced more than others by domestic events.

Many industries seem relatively immune to ongoing economic changes, while others are so sensitive that managers spend much of their time and effort developing ways to forecast and insulate their firms from probable changes. The relationship of companies to suppliers, customers, and other companies in the industry, as well as the nature of the industry's products, seems to influence how strong an impact outside economic events have on a given industry. The sources of return and the factors that affect the predictability of that return are quite different in each industry.

Know the Company's History, Current Condition, and Future Prospects. Interestingly, most of the tools and techniques of financial analysis concentrate on the company—its past, present, and future. Moreover, this is the form of analysis with which most students of finance have some experience, and with which many case analysts start and finish their work. Clearly, it is very important; the history and current situation of the firm are of considerable interest to the practicing manager as well as the case analyst. These subjects will occupy the greatest part of the case analyst's time and skill. Keeping in mind the possible effects of changes in the environment, both domestic and worldwide, the analyst will want to review the success of the firm's past investment and financing strategies by analyzing financial statements, market share and competitive product market information, and stock and bond market results.

Typically, the analyst will look first to the way the company has managed its assets, and is likely to be able to manage them, by asking such questions as:

1. Is the company capital-intensive? Does its productive capacity come from plant and equipment, people, and/or a franchise in the market bought with product reputation and/or advertising? How expensive is it to add capacity or enhance a product's reputation? What is the lead time needed to increase or modify any factor of production? If the company is capital-intensive, how old is the equipment, and for how long will it continue to be useful? If it is not capital-intensive, what is the source of the company's productivity, and how readily available are additional resources?

2. To what degree are company assets subject to obsolescence or migration? In a capital-intensive business, do technological innovations change processes slowly or rapidly? If it is not capital-intensive, how firm a grip does the company have on its source of productive capacity? For example, genetic engineering companies with large investments in the expertise of their research staffs can suffer if those research staffs are likely to move from firm to firm.

3. How much of the firm's assets are long term and difficult to redeploy, and how much can be changed rapidly? Firms with significant investments in short-term assets often have much more flexibility in dealing with rapid changes in the economic environment and/or the industry. How well has the firm coped with changes in the recent past—has it managed to maintain control of its assets in both good and bad times—and how likely is it to be able to maintain control in the foreseeable future?

4. What opportunities for new products and processes are on the horizon? Is the company in a position to identify and take advantage of these opportunities?

Second, the analyst will consider where and how the firm has financed itself and how it will be able to finance itself in the future by asking such questions as:

1. How much of the firm's investments have been financed from profits, and how stable are its profits (do they fluctuate widely from year to year, or are they relatively steady)? Companies that have relatively stable profitablility are better insulated from the vagaries of the capital markets.

2. Do the shareholders have a call on some portion of the current profits? How important is the dividend level to the stock price, how close is the firm's current dividend policy to what is common in the industry, and how secure are dividends from fluctuations in profits (does the company raise funds to maintain its capital investment program and/or dividend payments)?

3. How much of the funds used, and those likely to be used, have been and will be raised from outside sources?

4. Are the firm's liabilities short or long term? How secure are the sources of capital? Do lenders place any restrictions on the firm by virtue of their position? Are the restrictions by custom or by contract? Is the firm able to deal easily with the restrictions and the costs of its debt?

5. Is the company's equity capital closely held or is the stock publicly traded in the capital markets? If the stock is closely held, what are the objectives and needs of the owners? If it is publicly held, are any large blocks held by individuals or groups, and what is their interest in the firm? What is the degree of institutional interest in the stock? What is the stock price, the relative level of the stock market, and the interest in trading equities in general, both in this industry and in this company? How easy would it be to sell new equity and at what price could it be sold?

Finally, the analyst will want to determine the company's unique strengths and weaknesses.

The above questions are not meant to be exhaustive, nor would the case analyst seek to answer each question or set of questions in depth for every case. They are meant solely as an indication of the form analysis may take, and as a guide to the areas in which the analyst should have an interest and in which he or she should acquire at least cursory information.

Once the company's history, current situation, strength in the industry, and current corporate goals and strategies are coupled with an analysis of the industry and the economy, the case analyst is ready to assume the role of the decision maker—the manager.

Solve the Problem Facing the Company

Identify the Problem. Obviously, the first task is to understand the situation and to identify the problem or problems facing the manager. Many cases present more than one problem, and some of the problems will be more important than others. As with any real situation, there are times when real problems are obfuscated by concerns of the company or manager that are not critical to the firm and its success. It is up to the analyst to sort through the issues described in the case and to determine which are actually important.

The decisions managers face fall into one or both of two categories. The problem may require (1) investing assets to replace old products or processes, to increase sales, or to decrease costs, and/or (2) securing funds to support the growth of the firm or to replace old processes and products.

For funding the firm, the manager has only four choices. Funds can be raised by (1) increasing the liabilities of the firm—with either short-term obligations such as accounts payable or one of a variety of long-term debt instruments; (2) increasing the equity in the firm by increasing the amount of common stock or retained earnings; (3) increasing the firm's profits or decreasing the dividends paid to its shareholders; or (4) establishing relationships with other companies. On the basis of the traditional accounting definition of the firm, the following diagram shows where decisions that change the firm can be made.

$$\text{Assets} = \text{Liabilities} + \text{Equity}$$
$$\Uparrow$$
$$\text{Equity} = \text{Common Stock} + \text{Retained Earnings}$$
$$\Uparrow$$
$$\text{Retained Earnings} =$$
$$\text{Profits} - \text{Dividends}$$

Another way to look at the same problem is to use the sustainable growth rate framework.

$$\text{Sustainable Growth Rate} =$$
$$\text{Return on Sales} \times \text{Total Asset Turnover} \times \text{Leverage} \times \text{Profit Retention}$$

$$= \frac{\text{Profit}}{\text{Sales}} \times \frac{\text{Sales}}{\text{Assets}} \times \frac{\text{Assets}}{\text{Equity}} \times \left(1 - \frac{\text{Dividends}}{\text{Net Income}} \right)$$

If changes are made in one factor, changes need to be made in at least one other factor to keep the formula in balance. Thus, for example, the firm cannot increase its assets without augmenting its profits to sustain the increase or acquiring additional outside funds.

Identifying the most important problems is often easier if the analyst has determined the objectives and goals of the corporation (or division or subsidiary, if that is the level at which the decision is being made) and of the manager. There are instances where the personal position and goals of the manager may conflict with the objectives held by the firm on behalf of its owners. The importance attached to the problems and the decisions that will be made often reflect the goals of the strongest participant rather than those of the owners. Since these conflicts arise in almost every situation, the analyst must recognize them and make decisions on the basis of that recognition.

Define the Alternatives. Once the problems have been identified, the next task the vicarious manager must undertake is to define the options—the alternative courses of action for dealing with the problem. Many of the cases in this book define some or all of the options or describe the situation so that the alternatives can be identified. In some instances the analyst may want to identify options that are not available in the particular case— options that would have been available to other managers and companies or at different times. These options, alternatives for which there is little or no information, are hard to evaluate. These courses of action often have to be relegated to the realm of "strategies that should be explored" as the case analyst proceeds with consideration of the options that *are* available for analysis.

Developing options is often the most important step in the process of making the decision about the problem the manager and company face. Untried and unidentified options often turn out, in retrospect, to have been the plans that might have spelled success. Industry and corporate custom can constrain the creativity of managers in determining possible solutions and, as a result, can limit the company's potential for success. Analysis and understanding of the current situation and future direction of the economic and industry environments can open avenues that were never available when traditional paths were followed almost without thought. Unlike textbook problems where there are few alternatives, the real world provides many alternatives, and so do case decriptions of it.

Gather Information about the Alternatives. Here the case analyst has an advantage over the manager described in the case. The case usually provides a summary of the information the manager and his or her staff gathered to analyze their options. Much of that data is summarized in the exhibits at the end of each case. One of a manager's frustrations, and one that case analysts feel as well, is the lack of certain information that would be useful in deciding on the appropriate plan. Rarely would that information be omitted from the case unless it was unavailable when the manager sought it or was deemed unnecessary by the manager in making the decision. In either case, the manager, and thus you as the vicarious manager, would have to make the decision based on the information available.

Analyze the Risks and Returns of the Options. This is the heart of the problem facing the case analyst and manager. All the information about the economic environment, the industry, the company, and the problem has to be utilized to estimate the potential risks and returns of alternative solutions to the problem. The task is to find the strategy that will create the most value for the firm's owners over the long term.

Value depends upon three things: (1) the *size* of the returns expected, (2) the *time* it takes before the returns are expected to be received, and (3) the *risk* taken to obtain the expected returns. We know that investors, and thus corporate owners and managers, prefer larger returns received sooner and with less risk. The question is what trade-offs must be made in the size, timing, and riskiness of the expected returns for each alternative course of action. Those trade-offs are presented graphically on the following page.

Value is created when the returns from a given strategy more than offset the risk being taken, that is, when the net present value of the option is positive. Value-creating investments and strategies are difficult to find. When real economic value is available (for instance, when a company has a new product, process, or product source), competitors usually follow rather rapidly and drive out excess profits—unless the firm has some franchise or barrier that keeps competitors at bay. Managers forecast unusual and sustained excess profits (unusual returns) for one of three reasons: the returns really are likely to occur because of some special circumstance, the manager has ignored competitive realities, or the manager's forecasts are simply overly optimistic. As the manager, the case analyst should examine any forecasts to make sure that when value is expected to be created, it is not because of unwarranted optimism.

Value is maintained (the net present value is zero) when the expected returns are just sufficient to compensate the investor for taking the risk inherent in the project. Typically, most investment and financing strategies provide the prospect of a fair return—a return with which the shareholder would be satisfied—that would keep the stock at its current price.

Value is destroyed when the company pays too much, gets too little, or takes too much risk relative to the returns. These are the things that the manager would like to avoid at all cost—they are investments or financing schemes for which the net present value is negative.

As hard as value-creating options are to find, suffice it to say that most managers think they can be found; they do not believe that the product markets (and perhaps capital markets) are fully efficient. Thus managers usually believe they can find real sources of value for the firm's shareholders—investment and financing plans that will increase the price of the common stock.

Make a Decision and Develop a Plan of Action.   Just as the manager must weigh all the information available and come to a decision, so must a case analyst. While it is often difficult to decide among alternative courses of action, the analyst, taking the information developed from the analysis or provided in the case, must weigh the evidence before reaching a conclusion. It is helpful if the analyst has developed the assumptions upon which the analysis rested and detailed the conditions under which each decision would be appropriate. The consistency and reality of the assumptions are critical to making a good decision.

After the decision has been made, the analyst should follow with a plan of action to implement it. The plan is usually sequential in nature and describes what must be done, by whom, and when.

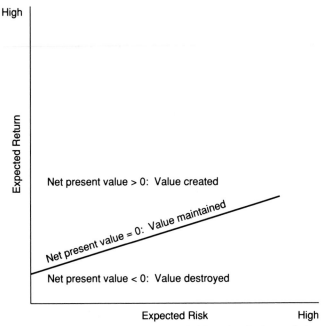

Note: For those using internal-rate-of-return methodology, the value is created when the IRR exceeds the hurdle rate, maintained when the IRR equals the hurdle rate, and destroyed when it falls short of the hurdle rate.

The goals, concepts, and theories of finance will help you, in the manager's role, to guide and focus the analysis. Using the framework of value creation to appraise the options presented in the cases in this book will help you to decide which is the appropriate course of action, given the firm, its strengths and weaknesses, its industry, and the environment in which it is likely to operate.

PART

1

Analyzing Corporate Performance

Financial Footprints (1991)

The investment, financial, and profitability characteristics of different industries vary, often significantly. For example, some industries require substantial investments in property, plant, and equipment, while in others a larger proportion of capital is invested in liquid assets such as cash and accounts receivable. Differences also frequently exist in the means of financing assets. One industry may have to rely extensively on long-term debt, while in another trade credit is readily available. Finally the way statements are analyzed can make a difference. For instance, certain measures of profitability and asset utilization will reveal significantly different results in industry comparisons. Financial statements and the ratios computed from them can be used to reflect the differences among industries and companies.

		Fiscal Year End
1	Auto Manufacturer	12/91
2	Bioengineering Company	12/91
3	Computer Manufacturer	9/91
4	Department Store Chain	1/92
5	Drugstore Chain	8/91
6	Electric Utility	12/91
7	Food Processing Company	5/91
8	Hospital Owner and Manager	8/91
9	Regional Airline	12/91
10	Regional Bank	12/91
11	Retail Jewelry Chain	3/91
12	Temporary Service Provider	12/91
13	Software Developer	10/91
14	Steel Manufacturer	12/91
15	Supermarket Chain	2/91
16	Textile Manufacturer	12/91
17	Standard and Poor's 200	12/91

Financial Footprints (1991)

EXHIBIT 1 • Balance Sheet (in percentage of assets)

	A	B	C	D	E	F
Assets						
Cash and marketable securities	6.4%	0.5%	41.8%	14.2%	5.5%	6.5%
Receivables	5.4	24.2	5.6	2.6	48.9	6.3
Inventory	34.6	19.0	4.6	1.3	5.5	43.5
Other current assets	5.8	4.0	0.8	0.5	10.5	3.2
Net property, plant and equipment	13.6	45.7	27.8	81.3	20.0	38.6
Other long term assets	34.2	6.7	19.4	0.2	9.6	1.8
Total assets	100.0%	100.0%	100.0%	100.0%	100.0%	100.0%
Liabilities and Equity						
Notes payable	12.1%	2.3%	0.1%	0.0%	0.0%	0.0%
Accounts payable	0.0	6.5	2.3	3.0	5.5	17.5
Other current liabilities	12.7	10.4	8.1	10.8	0.0	15.0
Long-term debt and leases	53.5	25.0	12.4	33.9	51.0	6.1
Other long-term liabilities	2.1	10.3	0.8	18.1	26.3	9.9
Preferred stock	0.0	0.0	0.0	0.0	0.1	0.0
Shareholders' equity	19.6	45.5	77.1	34.2	14.8	51.6
Total liabilities and equity	100.0%	100.0%	100.0%	100.0%	100.0%	100.0%

Exhibits 1 and 2 present balance-sheet percentages and selected ratios for one company chosen from each of the 17 industries listed on page 13. The company's fiscal year is also indicated. Study this information and associate each set of figures in the exhibits with a particular industry. Be prepared to explain the basis for your selections.

G	H	I	J	K	L	M	N	O	P	Q
22.8%	2.0%	0.8%	14.3%	0.7%	6.2%	47.4%	10.3%	25.6%	3.6%	47.7%
68.3	10.0	2.3	2.3	29.8	16.0	35.6	13.0	26.0	17.8	25.5
0.0	11.0	1.8	18.0	24.8	8.5	0.0	21.4	19.2	2.3	1.6
0.0	0.2	1.7	1.3	2.4	2.7	2.8	1.4	11.2	2.6	1.3
1.9	69.4	86.2	62.2	41.9	39.9	10.7	20.6	12.8	58.1	19.5
7.0	7.4	7.3	1.9	0.4	26.8	3.4	33.3	5.2	15.5	4.4
100.0%	100.0%	100.0%	100.0%	100.0%	100.0%	100.0%	100.0%	100.0%	100.0%	100.0%
7.7%	0.0%	0.0%	0.0%	6.6%	5.6%	0.0%	2.7%	4.3%	0.0%	0.2%
79.4	10.8	2.3	18.3	10.6	7.2	5.8	2.9	10.2	4.0	3.9
0.0	9.1	3.9	7.8	9.5	11.6	20.2	32.0	20.4	20.6	12.3
4.5	21.1	45.1	21.4	25.0	22.2	0.0	27.9	0.0	19.1	0.2
1.7	42.7	11.8	5.1	2.3	16.8	0.0	11.3	14.6	11.0	1.1
0.3	0.2	5.9	0.0	0.0	1.0	0.0	3.8	0.0	0.0	0.0
6.8	16.3	36.9	47.3	46.0	32.2	74.0	23.1	50.6	45.4	82.4
100.0%	100.0%	100.0%	100.0%	100.0%	100.0%	100.0%	100.0%	100.0%	100.0%	100.0%

Financial Footprints (1991)

EXHIBIT 2 • Selected Annual Ratios

	A	B	C	D	E	F
Profitability						
Return on Sales (ROS)	-4.1%	1.4%	11.6%	2.0%	-3.7%	2.9%
Return on Assets (ROA)	-3.0	2.2	3.6	1.5	-2.4	9.3
Return on Equity (ROE)	-15.5%	4.8%	4.7%	4.3%	-16.4%	18.0%
Asset Utilization						
Receivables Turnover	1378.0%	625.0%	555.0%	2765.0%	133.0%	5085.0%
Days Sales in Receivables	26	58	65	13	271	7
Inventory Turnover	216.0%	796.0%	682.0%	5702.0%	1190.0%	738.0%
Days Cost of Goods in Inventory	167	45	53	6	30	49
Inventory Method	LIFO	LIFO	FIFO	Av. Cost	LIFO	LIFO
Sales/Assets	75.0%	151.0%	31.0%	72.0%	65.0%	321.0%
Leverage						
Acid Test	47.0%	116.0%	493.0%	119.0%	148.0%	39.0%
Current Ratio	210.0	224.0	548.0	131.0	191.0	182.0
Interest Coverage Ratio	61.0	254.0	10.7	253.0	29.0	1818.0
Total Liabilities/Total Assets	80.0	55.0	23.0	66.0	85.0	48.0
Total Liabilities/Common Equity	411.0	120.0	30.0	192.0	575.0	94.0
Long-Term Debt/Equity	273.0	51.0	16.0	98.0	149.0	11.0
Total Assets/Equity	511.0	220.0	130.0	292.0	675.0	194.0
Stock Information						
Payout Ratio	N/A	77.8%	N/A%	15.7%	-22.8%	32.8%
Dividends/Market Price	N/A	4.0	—	4.0	4.4	1.6
Market Price/Book Value	N/A	110.0	325.0	316.0	90.0	363.0
Price/Earnings Ratio	N/A	1.3×	72.4×	41.0×	—	18.5×
Beta	N/A	1.30	N/A	1.25	1.00	1.10

G	H	I	J	K	L	M	N	O	P	Q
7.4%	-17.8%	13.4%	3.5%	4.3%	60.0%	2.7%	1.6%	4.9%	6.1%	25.4%
0.7	-18.6	4.3	10.1	6.7	5.3	8.4	3.3	8.9	8.0	22.4
10.7%	-115.2%	13.7%	21.4%	14.5%	12.2%	11.1%	17.1%	17.5%	17.7%	27.5%
14.0%	1044.0%	1402.0%	12540.0%	523.0%	1182.3%	11.9%	1587.0%	696.0%	743.0%	345.0%
2,622	34	26	3	69	61	43	23	52	48	104
N/A	952.0%	1793.0%	1585.0%	628.0%	1630.7%	N/A	966.0%	939.0%	5639.0%	5432.0%
N/A	38	20	23	57	41	N/A	37	38	6	7
N/A	LIFO	LIFO	LIFO	FIFO	N/A	N/A	Av. Cost	FIFO	LIFO	FIFO
9.0%	105.0%	32.0%	285.0%	156.0%	96.1%	299.9%	207.0%	181.0%	133.0%	88.0%
93.0%	53.0%	63.0%	62.0%	113.0%	87.4%	320.0%	77.0%	148.0%	86.0%	450.0%
1442.0	103.0	204.0	135.0	213.0	141.8	330.0	399.0	235.0	106.0	468.0
66.0	N/A	117.0	878.0	542.0	930.4	N/A	77.0	N/A	672.0	27035.0
1481.0	84.0	271.0	53.0	54.0	58.4	26.0	433.0	49.0	55.0	16.0
105.0	519.0	44.0	111.0	117.0	200.8	35.1	54.0	98.0	120.0	20.0
105.0	92.0	95.0	18.0	51.0	67.7	N/A	106.0	N/A	41.0	0.0
176.0	612.0	251.0	211.0	217.0	287.0	135.1	265.0	198.0	220.0	121.0
43.1%	-4.0%	53.5%	33.7%	19.3%	81.5%	56.3%	40.2%	18.3%	40.2%	N/A%
4.8	2.6	5.8	2.5	8.0	N/A	2.6	1.8	1.0	2.7	N/A
161.0	161.0	122.0	218.0	274.0	200.0	2.3	273.0	403.0	173.0	1240.0
9.1×	—	9.9×	17.6×	23.9×	20.1×	21.8×	17.6×	12.9×	13.6×	24.1×
0.95	1.45	0.75	1.00	1.25	1.00	0.95	1.30	1.25	1.15	1.65

General Motors Corporation: Macroeconomics and Competition (A)

Rebecca Shepherd began working for General Motors Corporation as a writer in the corporate finance division in June 1984. Although she had taken a couple of accounting and economics courses during her freshman and sophomore years at college, Ms. Shepherd had been hired for her communications skills, not her analytical abilities. Both she and her boss, Isaac Weaver, knew, however, that she would be of little value to the firm until she brushed some of the rust off her business skills and understood at least the rudiments of GM's position in the marketplace and how the firm was affected by the economy and competition. With this in mind, Mr. Weaver sat down with Ms. Shepherd early one morning during her first week to explain the information that he had gathered for her to study.

Mr. Weaver said he wanted her to spend some time that morning analyzing GM's financial statements for the previous four years, as shown in Exhibits 1, 2, and 3. He thought the early 1980s made a particularly good period for her to study, since the U.S. economy had reached the depths of a severe recession in 1982 and had begun to recover in 1983. Given that bit of information, he wanted her to study the way the company earned, spent, and invested its money. He asked Ms. Shepherd to see if she could detect any changes in the statements that may have come about due either to external influences or to internal changes such as management decisions. He said they would discuss what she found over lunch.

General Motors Corporation (A)
EXHIBIT 1 • Statement of Consolidated Income for the Years Ended December 31
         (dollars in millions, except per-share amounts)

	1980	1981	1982	1983
Net sales	$57,728.5	$62,698.5	$60,025.6	$74,581.6
Cost of sales and other operating charges, exclusive of items listed below	52,099.8	55,185.2	51,548.3	60,718.8
Selling, general, and administrative expenses	2,636.7	2,715.0	2,964.9	3,234.0
Depreciation of real estate, plants, and equipment	1,458.1	1,837.3	2,403.0	2,569.7
Amortization of special tools	2,719.6	2,568.9	2,147.5	2,549.9
Amortization of intangible assets	0.0	0.0	0.0	0.8
Total costs and expenses	58,914.2	62,306.4	59,063.7	69,073.2
Operating income	(1,185.7)	392.1	961.9	5,508.4
Other income less income deductions (net)	348.7	367.7	476.3	815.8
Interest expense	(531.9)	(897.9)	(1,415.4)	(1,352.7)
Income (loss) before income taxes	(1,368.9)	(138.1)	22.8	4,971.5
United States, foreign, and other income taxes (credit)	(385.3)	(123.1)	(252.2)	2,223.8
Income (loss) after income taxes	(983.6)	(15.0)	275.0	2,747.7
Equity in earnings of nonconsolidated subsidiaries and associates	221.1	348.4	687.7	982.5
Net income (loss)	$ (762.5)	$ 333.4	$ 962.7	$ 3,730.2
Dividends paid on preferred stock	$ 12.9	$ 12.9	$ 12.9	$ 12.9
Earnings (loss) on common stock	(775.4)	320.5	949.8	3,717.3
Market price				
High	$65	$58	$50.1	$75
Low	49	43.9	34	56
Close	52	44	48	75
Price/earnings (end of year)	$—	$44.3	$14.9	$5.8
Number of shares	298.1	304.8	312.4	317.7
Earnings per share	$(2.60)	$1.05	$3.04	$11.70
Dividends per share	$2.93	$2.40	$2.40	$2.80
Beta	0.95	0.85	0.90	1.00

Source: Annual Reports 1980–1983, and Value Line *Stock Guide*, various years.

General Motors Corporation (A)

EXHIBIT 2 • Consolidated Balance Sheets December 31, 1980–1983
(dollars in millions, except per-share amounts)

	1980	*1981*	*1982*	*1983*
Assets				
Cash	$ 157.2	$ 204.1	$ 279.6	$ 369.5
United States government and other marketable securities and time deposits, at cost	3,558.0	1,116.6	2,846.6	5,847.4
Total cash and marketable securities	3,715.2	1,320.7	3,126.2	6,216.9
Accounts and notes receivable (less allowances)	3,768.4	3,645.5	2,864.5	6,964.2
Inventories (less allowances)	7,295.0	7,222.7	6,184.2	6,621.5
Prepaid expenses	706.5	1,527.2	1,868.2	997.2
Total current assets	15,485.1	13,716.1	14,043.1	20,799.8
Equity in net assets of nonconsolidated subsidiaries and associates (principally GMAC and its subsidiaries)	2,899.8	3,379.4	4,231.1	4,450.8
Other investments and miscellaneous assets, at cost (less allowances)	1,147.3	1,783.5	1,550.0	1,222.5
Common stock held for the GM incentive program	125.8	71.5	35.2	56.3
Real estate, plants, and equipment, at cost	29,202.7	34,811.5	37,687.2	37,777.8
Less accumulated depreciation	15,217.1	16,317.4	18,148.9	20,116.8
Net real estate, plants, and equipment	13,985.6	18,494.1	19,538.3	17,661.0
Special tools, at cost (less amortization)	937.4	1,546.6	2,000.1	1,504.1
Total property	14,923.0	20,040.7	21,538.4	19,165.1
Total assets	$34,581.0	$38,991.2	$41,397.8	$45,694.5

continued

General Motors Corporation (A)
EXHIBIT 2 • *continued*

	1980	1981	1982	1983
Liabilities and Stockholders' Equity				
Accounts payable (principally trade)	$ 3,967.7	$ 3,699.7	$ 3,600.7	$ 4,642.3
Loans payable	1,676.5	1,727.8	1,182.5	1,255.2
Accrued liabilities, deferred income taxes, and income taxes payable	6,628.8	7,127.6	7,601.8	9,011.5
Total current liabilities	12,273.0	12,555.1	12,385.0	14,909.0
Long-term debt	1,886.0	3,801.1	4,452.0	3,137.2
Capitalized leases	172.3	242.8	293.1	384.6
Other liabilities (including GMAC and its subsidiaries of $300.0 in 1983, $876.0 in 1982, and $424.0 in 1981)	1,482.5	3,215.1	4,259.8	4,698.2
Deferred credits (including investment tax credits)	952.6	1,456.0	1,720.8	1,798.9
Stockholders' equity				
Preferred stock	283.6	283.6	283.6	283.6
Common stock: $1⅔ par value common	496.7	508.0	520.6	526.2
Capital surplus (principally additional paid-in capital)	1,297.2	1,589.5	1,930.4	2,136.8
Net income retained for use in the business	15,737.1	15,340.0	15,552.5	18,390.5
Accumulated foreign currency translation and other adjustments	—	—	—	(570.5)
Total stockholders' equity	17,814.6	17,721.1	18,287.1	20,766.6
Total liabilities and stockholders' equity	$34,581.0	$38,991.2	$41,397.8	$45,694.5
Common stock outstanding (thousands of shares)	298,054	304,804	312,364	317,711

General Motors Corporation (A)
EXHIBIT 3 • Cash Flow Statement (dollars in millions)

	1980	1981	1982	1983
Sources of Funds				
Net income	$ (762.5)	$ 333.4	$ 962.7	$ 3,730.2
Depreciation of real estate, plants, and equipment	1,458.1	1,837.3	2,403.0	2,569.7
Amortization of special tools	2,719.6	2,568.9	2,147.5	2,549.9
Net deferred income taxes, undistributed earnings of nonconsolidated subsidiaries and associates, etc.	311.5	68.0	75.8	645.5
Total funds provided by current operations	3,726.7	4,807.6	5,589.0	9,495.3
Increase in long-term debt	1,305.1	2,172.7	2,497.4 -	3,177.1
Proceeds from sale of newly issued common stock	271.9	303.6	353.5	212.0
Other, net	95.2	1,703.3	1,459.2	772.8
Total funds supplied	$ 5,398.9	$ 8,987.2	$ 9,899.1	$13,657.2
Uses of Funds				
Dividends paid to stockholders	$ 874.1	$ 730.5	$ 750.2	$ 892.2
Decrease in long-term debt	299.1	257.6	1,846.5 -	4,491.9
Expenditures for real estate, plants, and equipment	5,160.5	6,563.3	3,611.1	1,923.0
Expenditures for special tools	2,600.0	3,178.1	2,601.0	2,083.7
Increase (decrease) in other working capital items	(4,267.7)	341.2	(1,306.2)	1,142.0
Investments in nonconsolidated subsidiaries and associates	4.1	311.0	591.0	33.7
Total use of funds	4,670.1	11,381.7	8,093.6	10,566.5
Increase (decrease) in cash and marketable securities	728.8	(2,394.5)	1,805.5	3,090.7
Cash and marketable securities at beginning of year	2,986.4	3,715.2	1,320.7	3,126.2
Cash and marketable securities at end of year	$ 3,715.2	$ 1,320.7	$ 3,126.2	$ 6,216.9
Increase (Decrease) in Other Working Capital Items				
Accounts and notes receivable	$ (1,262.0)	$ (125.1)	$ (778.8)	$ 4,099.7
Inventories	(844.1)	(72.3)	(1,038.5)	437.3
Prepaid expenses and deferred income taxes	243.1	820.6	341.1	(871.0)
Accounts payable	(586.4)	268.0	99.0	(1,041.6)
Loans payable	(752.4)	(51.3)	545.3	(72.7)
Accrued liabilities	(1,065.9)	(498.7)	(474.3)	(1,409.7)
Increase (decrease) in other working capital items	$ (4,267.7)	$ 341.2	$ (1,306.2)	$ 1,142.0

General Motors Corporation: Macroeconomics and Competition (B)

Rebecca Shepherd, a new employee in General Motors Corporation's corporate finance division, had spent a couple of hours one morning analyzing the company's financial statements in order to get a feel for the structure of the firm. Isaac Weaver, her boss, wanted her to devote the rest of the day to comparing GM's financial statements against those of its major U.S. competitors, Ford and Chrysler, taking into account the impact of changes in the economy. He had organized the 1982 and 1983 financial statements of the three firms, as shown in Exhibits 1 through 5. Ms. Shepherd was to compare and contrast the financial statements to see how each company operated in that period and to see if she could detect any corporate strengths or weaknesses reflected in the statements. He thought that this was a particularly good period to study the three companies, for the U.S. economy had been in the depths of a severe recession in 1982 and had begun to recover in 1983.

The U.S. Economy

The auto industry reacted with great volatility to changes in the economy. Gross national product (GNP) growth, unemployment, interest rates, and fuel prices affected automobile sales. As shown in Exhibit 6, all of these economic variables played important roles in the early 1980s; real GNP declined in 1980 and 1982, the unemployment rate reached 9.5 percent in 1982, and the prime lending rate soared to an average of almost 19 percent in 1981. In addition, crude fuel prices (mostly oil) increased by about 20 percent each year. To compound these problems, the inflation rate was over 10 percent for three straight years. In 1983, the economy began to recover. Unemployment remained high, but fuel–price increases, inflation, and interest rates all dropped as GNP rebounded.

The Competition

U.S. automobile production fell from 12.9 million cars in 1978 to 7.0 million in 1982; in 1983, production rebounded to 9.2 million cars. All three auto companies had manufacturing facilities in Canada, and Exhibit 7 shows that about one-eighth of the three firms' total auto production took place there.

General Motors, the largest automobile company in the world, traditionally manufactured a wide variety of cars, but focused its energies on family–sized and luxury models, that is, on higher–priced cars with larger profit margins. The company was founded in 1908 by William C. Durant when Buick Manufacturing Company of Flint, Michigan; Olds Motor Works of Lansing, Michigan; Cadillac Motor Company of Detroit, Michigan; and Oakland (Pontiac) Motor Company of Pontiac, Michigan merged. In the company's first year, it manufactured 165,000 cars and 6,000 trucks. Chevrolet Motor Company of Detroit was founded in 1911 and was bought by GM in 1918.

Ford management had always pictured its company, the second largest in the industry, as being in direct competition with GM, but its niche was in the production of smaller cars such as the Mustang and Pinto. Although it made some larger cars, the company offered little competition for GM's Buick, Oldsmobile, and Pontiac models. The company was founded in Detroit in 1903 by Henry Ford. The Model A was introduced the same year. The Model T, the better known of Ford's early models, was introduced in 1908, the same year the maverick entrepreneur Ford told GM that his company would act alone rather than merge. In 1922, the firm bought Lincoln Motor Company, which had been founded in 1917. Through this company Ford competed in the luxury car market. Henry Ford II succeeded his grandfather as president of the company in 1945, and still held the office of chairman of the board in 1970 when Lee Iacocca, vice president and general manager of the company, took over as president. Since that time, both men had stepped down.

Chrysler Corporation was founded in 1925 in Detroit. The company introduced its lower-priced Plymouth line in 1928 to compete with Chevrolet and Ford, and it bought Dodge in 1935. The recent past had been difficult for Chrysler, however; as demand for small cars grew in the late 1960s, Chrysler introduced several full-sized models. To stave off losses, the company arranged to sell small, Japanese-made Mitsubishi models as it slowly introduced its own midsize cars. Larger cars came back into demand in the early 1970s, but as Chrysler began to respond to the change, the 1973 oil embargo was announced. Chrysler's costs from retooling its factories rose as its sales fell.

In 1978, Lee Iacocca left his position at Ford to become president of the financially ailing Chrysler Corporation. In 1980, the company was threatened with bankruptcy, but was granted a $1.5-billion loan guaranteed by the U.S. and Canadian governments. Before Walter Chrysler founded the corporation, he had worked for Buick and had saved two smaller automobile companies from bankruptcy. By 1983, Lee Iacocca was trying to do the same thing for Chrysler with innovative marketing techniques and his own charismatic public image. He was also trying to find a niche for the company in the small-car market.

Mr. Weaver asked Ms. Shepherd to compare the three companies' financial statements for similarities and differences, then he wanted her to analyze the statements for possible reflections of relative corporate strengths and weaknesses. Mr. Weaver looked forward to talking with her the next morning to find out how strong her analytical skills were.

General Motors Corporation (B)

EXHIBIT 1 • U.S. Auto Manufacturers—Comparative Income Statements (millions of dollars, except as noted)

	General Motors		Ford		Chrysler	
	1982	1983	1982	1983	1982	1983
Net sales	$60,025.6	$74,581.6	$37,067.2	$44,454.6	$10,044.9	$13,240.4
Costs and expenses						
Cost of goods sold	51,548.3	60,718.8	32,462.8	37,316.3	8,585.1	10,854.2
Selling and administrative	2,964.9	3,234.8	2,300.4	2,399.7	669.8	775.6
Depreciation	2,403.0	2,569.7	1,200.8	1,262.8	195.9	183.3
Amortization	2,147.5	2,549.9	955.6	1,029.3	236.7	273.9
Interest (income)	1,415.4	1,352.7	182.8	(2.0)	158.0	82.1
Other	0.0	0.0	631.2	642.8	271.7	254.7
Total costs	60,479.1	70,425.9	37,733.6	42,648.9	10,117.2	12,423.8
Operating income (loss)	(453.5)	4,155.7	(666.4)	1,805.7	(72.3)	816.6
Other income (loss)	476.3	815.8	0.0	0.0	182.2	19.8
Other expense	0.0	0.0	(6.7)	29.2	0.0	223.9
Income (loss) before taxes	22.8	4,971.5	(659.7)	1,776.5	109.9	612.5
Income taxes (credit)	(252.2)	2,223.8	256.6	270.2	0.9	401.6
Net income (loss) before extraordinary items and nonconsolidated subsidiaries	275.0	2,747.7	(916.3)	1,506.3	109.0	210.9
Extraordinary items	0.0	0.0	0.0	0.0	66.9	399.0
Nonconsolidated subsidiaries	687.7	982.5	258.5	360.6	(5.8)	90.8
Net income (loss)	$ 962.7	$ 3,730.2	$ (657.8)	$ 1,866.9	$ 170.1	$ 700.7
Preferred dividends	$ 12.9	$ 12.9	0.0	0.0	0.0	0.0
Average shares outstanding (millions)	307.4	313.9	180.6	181.4	77.7	117.8
Earnings (loss) per share of common stock	$ 3.09	$ 11.84	$ (3.64)	$ 10.29	$ 2.19	$ 5.94
Average annual stock price	$ 46.04	$ 68.67	$ 16.85	$ 34.99	$ 7.95	$ 24.72
Dividends per share	$ 2.40	$ 2.80	$ 0.0	$ 0.50	$ 0.0	$ 0.0
Automobile production (thousands)	3,507.8	4,513.9	1,387.1	1,832.2	749.9	1,010.1
Employees (thousands)	657.0	N. Av.	379.2	N. Av.	73.7	N. Av.

N. Av. = not available.

General Motors Corporation (B)
EXHIBIT 2 • U.S. Auto Manufacturers—Comparative Balance Sheets (millions of dollars, except as noted)

	General Motors 1982	General Motors 1983	Ford 1982	Ford 1983	Chrysler 1982	Chrysler 1983
Assets						
Cash	$ 279.6	$ 369.5	$ 943.7	$ 2,185.4	$ 109.7	$ 111.6
Marketable securities	2,846.6	5,847.4	611.7	966.7	787.5	957.8
Accounts receivable	2,864.5	6,964.2	2,376.5	2,767.6	247.9	291.2
Inventories	6,184.2	6,621.5	4,123.3	4,111.7	1,133.0	1,301.4
Other	1,868.2	997.2	743.7	787.7	91.0	91.8
Total current assets	14,043.1	20,799.8	8,798.9	10,819.1	2,369.1	2,753.8
Property, plant, and equipment	39,687.3	39,281.9	19,683.2	19,920.9	4,728.9	5,389.0
Less depreciation	18,148.9	20,116.8	9,546.9	10,119.0	2,255.2	2,334.0
Net property, plant, and equipment	21,538.4	19,165.1	10,136.3	9,801.9	2,473.7	3,055.0
Investments in associated companies	4,231.1	4,450.8	2,413.4	2,582.7	352.4	128.5
Other assets	1,585.2	1,278.8	613.1	665.2	1,068.3	835.0
Total assets	$41,397.8	$45,694.5	$21,961.7	$23,868.9	$ 6,263.5	$ 6,772.3
Liabilities and Equity						
Accounts payable	$ 3,600.7	$ 4,642.3	$ 4,119.6	$ 5,247.1	$ 897.8	$ 1,628.7
Short-term debt	1,182.5	1,255.2	2,265.0	942.0	100.4	416.8
Income taxes	0.0	0.0	383.0	362.1	0.0	0.0
Other	7,601.8	9,011.5	3,656.4	3,764.7	1,114.4	1,408.4
Total current liabilities	12,385.0	14,909.0	10,424.0	10,315.9	2,112.6	3,453.9
Long-term debt	4,745.1	3,521.8	2,353.3	2,712.9	2,189.0	1,104.0
Deferred credits	1,720.8	1,798.9	1,054.1	1,103.2	0.0	0.0
Other liabilities	4,259.8	4,698.2	2,052.8	2,191.6	970.8	849.1
Stockholders' equity						
Preferred stock	283.6	283.6	0.0	0.0	1,320.9	222.2
Common stock and additional paid-in capital	520.6	526.2	241.2	366.0	501.4	121.8
Retained earnings	17,482.9	19,956.8	5,836.3	7,179.3	(831.2)	1,021.3
Total equity	18,287.1	20,766.6	6,077.5	7,545.3	991.1	1,365.3
Total liabilities and equity	$41,397.8	$45,694.5	$21,961.7	$23,868.9	$ 6,263.5	$ 6,772.3
Common shares outstanding (millions)	312.4	317.7	180.6	183.0	119.2	182.7

General Motors Corporation (B)
EXHIBIT 3 • General Motors Corporation Cash Flow Statement (in millions)

	1982	*1983*
Sources of Funds		
Net income	$ 962.7	$ 3,730.2
Depreciation of real estate, plants, and equipment	2,403.0	2,569.7
Amortization of special tools	2,147.5	2,549.9
Deferred income taxes, undistributed earnings of nonconsolidated subsidiaries and associates, etc., net	75.8	645.5
Total funds provided by current operations	5,589.0	9,495.3
Increase in long-term debt	2,497.4	3,177.1
Other	1,459.2	772.8
Proceeds from sale of newly issued common stock	353.5	212.0
Total sources	$ 9,899.1	$13,657.2
Uses of Funds		
Dividends paid to stockholders	$ 750.2	$ 892.2
Decrease in long-term debt	1,846.5	4,491.9
Expenditures for real estate, plants, and equipment	3,611.1	1,923.9
Expenditures for special tools	2,601.0	2,083.7
Increase (decrease) in other working capital items	(1,306.2)	1,142.0
Investments in nonconsolidated subsidiaries and associates	591.0	33.7
Total uses	$ 8,093.6	$10,566.5
Increase (decrease) in cash and marketable securities	$ 1,805.5	$ 3,090.7
Cash and marketable securities at beginning of year	1,320.7	3,126.2
Cash and marketable securities at end of year	$ 3,126.2	$ 6,216.9
Increase (Decrease) in Other Working Capital Items		
Accounts and notes receivable	$ (778.8)	$ 4,099.7
Inventories	(1,038.5)	437.3
Prepaid expenses and deferred income taxes	341.1	(871.0)
Accounts payable	99.0	(1,041.6)
Loans payable	545.3	(72.7)
Accrued liabilities	(474.3)	(1,409.7)
Increase (decrease) in other working capital items	$ (1,306.2)	$ 1,142.0

General Motors Corporation (B)
EXHIBIT 4 • Ford Motor Company Cash Flow Statement (in millions)

	1982	1983
Cash, cash items, and marketable securities at Jan. 1	$ 2,100.0	$ 1,555.4
Funds Provided (Used) by Operations		
Net income (loss)	(657.8)	1,866.9
Items included in net income (loss) not requiring (providing) funds		
Depreciation and amortization	2,156.4	2,292.1
Deferred income taxes	91.3	49.1
Other liabilities, noncurrent	68.0	55.3
Earnings of unconsolidated subsidiaries and affiliates in excess of dividends remitted	(184.3)	(111.6)
Other	(77.1)	58.3
Changes in Working Capital That Provided (Used) Funds		
Receivables	240.8	(391.1)
Inventories	497.5	11.6
Other current assets	89.8	(44.0)
Accounts payable and accrued liabilities	233.3	1,235.8
Current payable income taxes	174.1	(20.9)
Funds provided by operations	$ 2,632.0	$ 5,001.5
Funds Provided by (Paid to) Outside Sources		
Addition of long-term debt	$ 797.4	$ 1,162.7
Reduction of long-term debt	(966.6)	(1,009.8)
Decrease in short-term debt	(99.9)	(1,116.3)
Cash dividends	0.0	(90.9)
Other	97.3	0.0
Funds provided by (paid to) outside sources	$ (171.8)	$ (1,054.3)
Other Sources (Uses) of Funds		
Net additions to property	$ (2,649.2)	$ (1,932.8)
Other	132.0	(41.7)
Total other uses of funds	(2,517.2)	(1,974.5)
Effect of changes in foreign-currency exchange rates	(487.6)	(376.0)
Net increase (decrease) in funds	(544.6)	1,596.7
Cash, cash items, and marketable securities at December 31	$ 1,555.4	$ 3,152.1

General Motors Corporation (B)
EXHIBIT 5 • Chrysler Corporation Cash Flow Statement (in millions)

	1982	*1983*
Funds Provided by (Used in) Operations		
From continuing operations:		
Earnings (loss)	$ (68.9)	$ 301.9
Depreciation and amortization	432.6	457.2
Contribution to employee stock ownership plan	40.6	40.6
Equity in (earnings) loss of unconsolidated subsidiaries	5.8	(90.8)
Other, including write-down of investment in Peugeot S. A.	(19.2)	241.5
Total funds from continuing operations	$ 390.9	$ 950.4
Changes in working capital affecting operations:		
(Increase) decrease in accounts receivable and inventories	$ 415.8	$ (211.7)
Increase (decrease) in accounts payable and accrued expenses	45.3	1,024.1
Total changes in working capital	461.1	812.4
Extraordinary item—utilization of tax loss carryforwards	66.9	399.0
Net change in noncurrent assets and liabilities	(47.2)	(40.8)
Funds provided by continuing operations	$ 871.7	$ 2,121.0
Funds Provided by (Used in) Investment Activities		
Decrease (increase) in investments and advances	$(184.9)	$ 243.0
Sale and purchase of subsidiaries, net	202.5	0.0
Sale of property, plant, and equipment	62.3	9.2
Expenditures for property, plant, and equipment	(146.8)	(642.5)
Expenditures for special tools	(227.0)	(414.5)
Other	(2.3)	(12.0)
Funds used in investment activities	$(296.2)	$ (816.8)
Funds Provided by (Used in) Financing Activities		
$311 million for purchase of warrants in 1983	$ (24.4)	$ 281.7
Proceeds from long-term borrowing	11.0	220.2
Payments on long-term borrowing	(69.9)	(1,269.4)
Purchase of U.S. government–held warrants, including related expenses	0.0	(313.9)
Proceeds from sale of common stock (exercise of public warrants)	0.0	63.1
Other changes in common stock	0.6	3.2
Funds provided by (used in) financing activities	$ (82.7)	$(1,015.1)
Cash dividends paid on preferred stock	$ 0.0	$ (116.9)
Funds Flow		
Increase during year	$ 492.8	$ 172.2
Cash, time deposits, and marketable securities at beginning of year	404.4	897.2
Cash, time deposits, and marketable securities at end of year	$ 897.2	$ 1,069.4

General Motors Corporation (B)
EXHIBIT 6 • The U.S. Economy—Selected Data

	Gross National Product		Average Prime Lending Rate	Consumer Prices		Crude Fuel Prices	
	Billions of 1982 Dollars	Percentage Change		Index	Percentage Change	Index	Percentage Change
1979	$3,192.4	2.5%	12.67%	100.0	11.3%	100.0	18.9%
1980	3,187.1	(0.2)	15.27	113.5	13.5	121.2	21.2
1981	3,248.8	1.9	18.87	125.3	10.4	148.0	22.1
1982	3,166.0	(2.6)	14.86	132.9	6.1	174.6	18.0
1983	3,277.7	3.5	10.79	137.2	3.2	183.5	5.1

	Unemployment Rate	Disposable Income (billions of 1982 dollars)	U.S. Auto Sales (billions of 1982 dollars)	U.S. Auto Production (thousands of units)	Percentage Sold in United States	Auto Imports into United States (thousands of units)
1979	5.8%	$2,092.7	$129.0	11,480	90.8	3,006
1980	7.0	2,104.9	97.9	8,010	91.2	3,248
1981	7.5	2,162.0	104.3	7,943	91.4	2,999
1982	9.5	2,180.5	97.0	6,986	92.7	3,067
1983	9.5	2,257.2	122.9	9,205	91.9	3,667

Sources: *Economic Report of the President*, February 1986; and *Motor Vehicle Facts and Figures*, Motor Vehicle Manufacturers Association of the United States, Inc., 1984, p. 29.

General Motors Corporation (B)
EXHIBIT 7 • General Motors, Ford, and Chrysler: U.S. and
Canadian Auto Production (units in thousands)

	United States		Canada		Total	
	1982	*1983*	*1982*	*1983*	*1982*	*1983*
Passenger Cars						
Chrysler	601	904	149	106	750	1,010
Ford	1,104	1,547	283	285	1,387	1,832
GM	3,173	3,975	335	539	3,508	4,514
Trucks and Buses						
Chrysler	122	148	96	141	218	289
Ford	712	925	114	134	826	1,059
GM	890	1,125	232	263	1,122	1,388

Source: *Motor Vehicle Facts and Figures*, Motor Vehicle Manufacturers Association, Inc., 1984, pp. 8–9.

General Motors Corporation: Macroeconomics and Competition (C)

Rebecca Shepherd, a new employee in General Motors' corporate finance division, had spent a day in June 1984 analyzing GM's financial statements and then comparing them to those of Ford and Chrysler. She was now ready to move on to the more complex analysis that Isaac Weaver, her boss, had prepared for her: a comparison of GM's financial condition and operations against those of nine worldwide competitors over three years, in light of the world economy.

American cars of the 1950s and 1960s reflected and typified, at least in part, the American auto industry of the time; they were large, solid, somewhat ponderous, occasionally glorified, and fairly inefficient. With few exceptions, European imports were either funny looking, very expensive, or exotic, and Japanese imports were derided as cheap little rattle-traps. "But then," said Mr. Weaver, "two events conspired against the U.S. auto industry. The OPEC countries discovered that they could make a bundle by hiking up the price of oil, and at the same time the Japanese work ethic and their goal of zero-defects began to pay off. Suddenly, Japanese cars began to look like good alternatives to the big, gas-guzzling American models," and the young, affluent buyer was attracted to the luxurious European "sport sedans."

The Economy

Due to its size and importance, the U.S. economy strongly influenced the state of the world economy. Exhibit 1 provides some details on the U.S. economy between 1970 and 1983. Crude fuel (primarily oil) prices had almost doubled between 1973 and 1976, and had tripled by 1979. OPEC's initial price increases hastened and deepened the worldwide recession of the mid-1970s and caused consumer prices to rise sharply. U.S. gross national product declined and unemployment rose in 1974 and 1975.

Prices rose by more than 20 percent over the same period. A modest recovery in the late 1970s did not last long, and by 1982, GNP had fallen almost 1 percent from its 1979 level, unemployment had risen to almost double-digit levels, and prices had risen by an average of over 10 percent per year for four years. Finally in 1983, although unemployment remained high, GNP improved by 3.5 percent, the consumer price index rose only 3.2 percent (its smallest increase in over 10 years), and lending rates began to fall. The effect of the recession on the economies of Europe and Japan can be seen in Exhibit 2, which provides production, inflation, and employment data for Japan, Germany, Sweden, the United Kingdom, and France.

The auto industry reacted with great volatility to the state of the economy. Exhibits 3, 4, and 5 provide information on world auto production and exports and U.S. imports and exports.

Mr. Weaver asked Ms. Shepherd to compare GM's balance sheets and operating ratios with those of nine competitors from the United States, Japan, and Europe to determine similarities and differences, strengths and weaknesses. Exhibits 6, 7, and 8 show the financial information he had gathered for Ms. Shepherd's analysis. It presented financial data from 1980 to 1982 for three U.S., two Japanese, and five European auto manufacturers. (Complete 1983 data were not yet available.) Before leaving, Mr. Weaver also gave her a verbal sketch of each foreign company grouped by country.

The Industry

Japan.   Nissan (Datsun) was the world's fifth largest and Japan's second largest automobile company, having produced 2.4 million cars in 1979. The company first entered the U.S. market in 1965 and began to flourish in the 1970s when consumers began to demand the company's smaller, less expensive, well-built cars. The company was also well known for its sports car, the Datsun 280Z.

Honda was the world's 12th largest auto manufacturer in terms of output. In 1979, it produced 802,000 cars; in addition, motorcycles accounted for 25 percent of the company's dollar sales and parts for 15 percent. Honda entered the U.S. market in 1970 with a tiny car called the Civic. Since that time, the company had broadened its offerings to include luxury compacts in addition to its small, less ostentatious models.

Germany.   In the 1930s, Adolph Hitler commissioned the development of a "Peoples' Car," in German a *"Volkswagen,"* that was to be inexpensive enough to be widely affordable. The plan survived World War II and two Volkswagen Beetles were imported to the United States in 1948. By 1960, 160,000 were being imported each year and it went on to become the biggest-selling car of all time. The Beetle resembled the Model T Ford of

1908 to 1927 in that it was inexpensive and its style did not change from year to year. The company halted production of the Beetle in the mid-1970s, and by 1978, Volkswagen was manufacturing the successful Rabbit model in both the United States and Europe. More recently, it had introduced several luxury and sports cars to fill out and complement the higher-priced line of cars manufactured by its Audi subsidiary.

Daimler-Benz had always manufactured high-priced luxury and sports cars. A Mercedes Benz was a status symbol and usually cost more than any of the standard American-made cars. The origins of the company dated back to 1886, when Gottlieb Daimler and Karl Benz developed their first self-propelled road vehicle. By 1888, the company held U.S. patents and by 1890, U.S. distributors of the car had been appointed.

Sweden. Volvo was founded in 1927. Its cars became increasingly popular in the United States throughout the late 1960s and early 1970s due to the company's reputation for quality. The company used an unusual manufacturing technique, in that each car was built by a team of workers, rather than on an assembly line. By 1979, Volvo was the world's 18th largest auto company, manufacturing 352,000 cars a year. The auto company was part of a conglomerate; 40 percent of Volvo's dollar sales came from cars, 44 percent from energy sales, and the rest from miscellaneous operations.

Great Britain. British Leyland manufactured a variety of cars from the small, practical Mini and Metro, and the MG, Lotus, and Triumph sport cars, to the Jaguar luxury cars. The corporation formed over a period of years after World War II. In 1952, the Austin and Morris auto companies merged to form British Motor Corporation (BMC); in 1966, BMC merged with Jaguar to form British Motor Holdings (BMH); in 1968, BMH merged with Leyland to form British Leyland.

The oil price increases of the 1970s caused demand within the United Kingdom to drop; in addition, government export policies had undermined the company's ability to sell overseas. In 1974, when the company was on the verge of bankruptcy, it was purchased by the British government. Production fell from 587,000 units in 1980 to 525,000 in 1981 and 519,000 in 1982. Over the same period, the total number of employees fell from 160,000 to 111,000.

France. Peugeot, the world's sixth largest auto company, manufactured 2.3 million cars in 1979. The firm was best known for its small, economical touring cars. The company had begun as a bicycle manufacturer and made its first car in 1890. Peugeot had made diesel powered cars as early as the 1950s and sales of its diesel models soared in the 1970s when fuel prices rose, due to their 25-percent greater fuel efficiency. Soon, Nissan, Volkswagen, Oldsmobile, and others followed suit. Peugeot bought Chrysler's European subsidiaries in 1978.

Conclusion

Mr. Weaver expected that, by the time Ms. Shepherd finished analyzing the financial statements and operating results of the ten auto makers, she would have a strong feeling for GM's relative financial strengths and weaknesses. "The best way to understand how well a company works is to see how it looks compared to its competition. Each similarity or difference in their financial statements may reflect corporate strategies or the effects of the economy or competition. I'll talk to you tomorrow morning about what you find."

General Motors Corporation (C)
EXHIBIT 1 • U.S. Economy—Selected Data

	Gross National Product (billions of 1982 dollars)	Percentage Change	Average Prime Lending Rate	Consumer Prices		Crude Fuel Prices		Unemployment Rate
				Index	Percentage Change	Index	Percentage Change	
1970	$2,416.2	(0.2)%	7.91%	116.3	5.9%	122.6	15.0%	4.8%
1971	2,484.8	2.8	5.72	121.3	4.3	139.0	13.4	5.8
1972	2,608.5	5.0	5.25	125.3	3.3	148.7	7.0	5.5
1973	2,744.0	5.2	8.03	133.1	6.2	164.5	10.6	4.8
1974	2,729.4	(0.5)	10.81	147.7	11.0	219.4	33.4	5.5
1975	2,695.0	(1.2)	7.86	161.2	9.1	271.5	23.7	8.3
1976	2,826.7	4.9	6.84	170.5	5.8	305.3	12.4	7.6
1977	2,958.6	4.7	6.83	181.5	6.5	372.1	21.9	6.9
1978	3,115.2	5.3	9.06	195.4	7.7	426.8	14.7	6.0
1979	3,192.4	2.5	12.67	217.4	11.3	507.6	18.9	5.8
1980	3,187.1	(0.2)	15.27	246.8	13.5	615.0	21.2	7.0
1981	3,248.8	1.9	18.87	272.4	10.4	751.2	22.1	7.5
1982	3,166.0	(2.6)	14.86	289.1	6.1	886.1	18.0	9.5
1983	3,277.7	3.5	10.79	298.4	3.2	931.5	5.1	9.5

Source: *Economic Report of the President*, February 1986.

General Motors Corporation (C)
EXHIBIT 2 • European and Japanese Economic Data

	Gross Domestic Product		Consumer Prices		
	Local 1980 Currency (billions)	Percentage Change	Index	Percentage Change	Unemployment Rate
Japan					
1979	¥225,085	5.2%	92.6	3.6%	2.1%
1980	235,834	4.8	100.0	8.0	2.0
1981	245,371	4.0	104.9	4.9	2.2
1982	253,569	3.3	107.7	2.7	2.4
1983	262,073	3.4	109.6	1.8	2.7
Germany					
1979	DM1,458	4.0%	94.9	4.2%	3.8%
1980	1,486	1.9	100.0	5.4	3.8
1981	1,483	(0.2)	106.3	6.3	5.5
1982	1,468	(1.0)	111.9	5.3	7.5
1983	1,487	1.3	115.6	3.3	9.1
Sweden					
1979	K516	3.8%	87.9	7.2%	2.1%
1980	525	1.7	100.0	13.8	2.0
1981	524	(0.2)	112.1	12.1	2.5
1982	528	0.8	121.7	8.6	3.2
1983	541	2.5	132.6	9.0	3.5
United Kingdom					
1979	£235	2.1%	84.8	13.5%	5.1%
1980	230	2.2	100.0	17.9	6.4
1981	227	(1.3)	111.9	11.9	10.0
1982	231	1.7	121.5	8.6	11.7
1983	238	3.0	127.1	4.6	12.4
					Unemployment (thousands)
France					
1979	FF2,741	3.3%	87.9	10.7%	1,350
1980	2,769	1.0	100.0	13.8	1,451
1981	2,782	0.5	113.4	13.4	1,773
1982	2,832	1.8	126.8	11.8	2,008
1983	2,853	0.7	139.0	9.6	2,042

Sources: *International Financial Statistics,* International Monetary Fund; unemployment data from *Main Economic Indicators, 1964–1983,* Organization for Economic Cooperation and Development, 1984.

General Motors Corporation (C)

EXHIBIT 3 • World Motor Vehicle Production (units in thousands)

	United States	Canada	United States and Canada Total	Europe	Japan	Other	World Total	United States Percentage of World Total
1983	9,205	1,524	10,729	15,813	11,112	2,053	39,727	23.2%
1982	6,986	1,276	8,262	14,929	10,732	2,190	36,113	19.3
1981	7,943	1,323	9,266	14,561	11,180	2,223	37,230	21.3
1980	8,010	1,374	9,384	15,530	11,043	2,538	38,495	20.8
1979	11,480	1,632	13,112	16,389	9,636	2,387	41,524	27.7
1978	12,899	1,818	14,717	16,205	9,269	2,108	42,299	30.5
1977	12,703	1,775	14,478	15,979	8,515	1,977	40,949	31.0
1976	11,498	1,640	13,138	15,316	7,841	2,046	38,346	30.0
1975	8,987	1,424	10,411	13,590	6,942	2,056	32,998	27.2
1974	10,071	1,525	11,596	14,513	6,552	2,073	34,733	29.0
1973	12,682	1,575	14,256	15,700	7,083	1,878	38,918	32.6
1972	11,311	1,430	12,741	14,836	6,294	1,674	35,545	31.8
1971	10,672	1,347	12,018	13,956	5,810	1,640	33,424	31.9
1970	8,284	1,187	9,471	13,154	5,289	1,352	29,267	28.3
1969	10,205	1,326	11,532	12,367	4,675	1,236	29,810	34.2
1968	10,820	1,150	11,971	11,241	4,085	1,058	28,356	38.2
1967	9,204	940	9,943	9,969	3,146	965	24,023	37.6
1965	11,138	847	11,984	9,549	1,876	858	24,267	45.9
1960	7,905	398	8,303	6,824	482	879	16,488	47.9
1955	9,204	452	9,656	3,742	68	162	13,628	67.5
1950	8,006	391	8,397	2,128	32	20	10,577	76.2
1973/1983 Percentage Change	(27.4)	(3.2)	(24.7)	0.9	56.9	9.3	2.1	N. Ap.

N. Ap. = not applicable.

Source: *Motor Vehicle Facts and Figures*, Motor Vehicle Manufacturers Association of the United States, Inc., 1984, p. 31.

General Motors Corporation (C)

EXHIBIT 4 • World Motor Vehicle Exports (in thousands)

	World Total[a]	Percentage of World Motor Vehicle Exports from								
		Japan	Belgium	France	Germany	Italy	Sweden	United Kingdom	Canada[b]	United States[b]
1982	14,595.2	38.3	6.5	12.8	16.4	3.6	1.5	2.8	7.6	3.5
1981	14,537.5	41.6	5.9	12.8	14.8	3.5	1.4	2.9	6.2	4.9
1980	15,161.7	39.4	5.8	14.6	13.7	3.9	1.3	3.2	6.2	5.3
1979	14,570.5	31.3	7.1	16.7	14.9	5.0	1.6	3.7	7.2	7.2
1978	14,598.8	31.5	7.1	15.7	14.2	4.8	1.4	4.2	9.0	6.5
1977	13,895.3	31.3	7.4	16.3	15.3	5.1	1.2	4.8	9.5	6.5
1975	10,807.2	24.8	7.3	18.0	15.3	6.6	1.8	6.4	9.3	8.0
1970	8,660.5	12.5	8.5	17.6	24.3	7.8	2.4	10.0	10.7	4.4

[a] World total includes countries with a small number of vehicle exports not shown separately. In 1982, vehicle exports from these countries totaled 1,024,200 units, 7.0 percent of world vehicle exports.

[b] Includes intercompany shipments between the United States and Canada.

Source: *Motor Vehicle Facts and Figures*, Motor Vehicle Manufacturers Association of the United States, Inc., 1984, p. 32.

General Motors Corporation (C)
EXHIBIT 5 • U.S. Automobile Trade: U.S. Imports of New, Assembled Passenger Cars by Country of Origin

	Belgium	Canada	France	Germany	Italy	Japan	Sweden	United Kingdom	Others	Total Imports
1983	5,230	836,756	212,858	330,263	5,347	2,112,011	109,494	53,284	1,780	3,667,023
1982	825	703,530	90,142	337,628	9,307	1,823,111	89,231	13,023	1,195	3,066,992
1981	66	563,943	42,477	376,327	21,635	1,911,525	68,042	12,728	1,818	2,998,561
1980	40	594,771	47,386	470,528	46,899	1,991,502	61,496	32,517	3,127	3,248,266
1979	85	677,008	27,887	495,565	72,456	1,617,328	65,907	46,911	2,376	3,005,523
1978	1,530	833,061	28,502	416,231	69,689	1,563,048	56,140	54,478	2,303	3,024,982
1975	38,176	733,766	15,647	370,012	102,344	695,573	51,993	67,106	36	2,074,653
1970	50,602	692,783	37,114	674,945	42,523	381,338	57,844	76,257	14	2,013,420
1965	332	29,135	24,941	376,950	9,509	25,538	26,010	66,565	450	559,430

1983 U.S. New Passenger Car Exports by Country of Destination, Engine Size

Country	Six Cylinders or Less		More than Six Cylinders	
	Units	Value (thousands)	Units	Value (thousands)
Arab Emirates	69	$ 688	590	$ 7,698
Belgium	371	4,083	97	1,607
Canada	438,102	2,840,622	93,936	1,013,410
Colombia	288	2,410	125	1,961
Ecuador	67	488	78	1,315
Germany, West	2,171	20,389	507	7,172
Japan	866	8,797	1,349	21,226
Kuwait	172	1,630	2,071	27,647
Mexico	60	347	206	3,007
Peru	288	2,583	150	1,858
Qatar	52	500	304	4,123
Saudi Arabia	974	8,169	9,009	119,475
Switzerland	130	1,346	412	5,544
Taiwan	166	1,504	105	1,566
Venezuela	116	1,084	79	993
Others	2,977	25,760	2,378	35,905
Total	436,869	$2,920,400	11,396	$1,254,507

Source: *Motor Vehicle Facts and Figures*, Motor Vehicle Manufacturers Association of the United States, Inc., 1984, p. 31.

General Motors Corporation (C)
EXHIBIT 6 • Automobile Industry Comparative Data, 1980

	GM	Ford	Chrysler
Balance Sheet Percentages (percentage of assets, except as noted)			
Cash and marketable securities	10.79%	10.63%	4.50%
Receivables	10.94	12.32	7.20
Inventories	21.17	21.07	28.95
Other current assets	2.05	3.47	2.59
Plant and equipment (net)	43.31	41.18	38.08
Other assets	11.74	11.35	18.68
Total assets	100.00	100.00	100.00
Accounts and notes payable	16.38	19.39	40.80
Other current liabilities	19.24	26.09	4.98
Long-term debts and leases	3.11	8.46	37.52
Other liabilities	7.60	10.32	9.76
Capital stock and surplus	5.66	3.71	25.30
Retained earnings	48.01	32.03	(18.36)
Total liabilities and stockholders' equity	100.00%	100.00%	100.00%
Total sales (millions 1982 dollars)	$52,699	$33,851	$8,421
Total assets	$31,450	$22,224	$6,041
Selected Ratios (percentage, except as noted)			
Current ratio	126.17%	104.40%	94.45%
Acid test	60.98	50.45	25.53
Inventory turnover	751%	673%	487%
Accounts and notes receivable collection (days)	48	47	62
Net sales/Total assets	167.55%	152.32%	139.40%
Cost of goods sold/Sales	97.49	98.88	105.14
Selling, general, and administrative/Sales	4.59	7.26	6.08
Net profit/Net sales	(1.32)	(4.16)	(13.17)
Net profit/Total assets	(2.21)	(6.34)	(18.36)
Total assets/Net worth	186.32	284.17	14.41
Net profit/Net worth	(4.12)	(18.01)	(264.59)
Total debt/Total assets	3.11	18.34	42.31
Long-term debt/Total capital	5.79%	24.04%	540.63%
Employees (thousands)	746.0	426.7	92.6

N. Av. = not available.

Nissan	Honda	Volkswagen	Daimler–Benz	Volvo	British Leyland	Peugeot
11.37%	10.04%	19.94%	21.64%	2.18%	0.83%	3.08%
21.93	12.22	5.89	14.41	33.33	19.08	23.38
16.42	35.29	24.26	25.59	37.99	41.62	31.77
4.85	5.57	12.35	12.54	0.00	0.00	0.00
26.68	29.59	33.36	23.58	24.49	37.90	36.49
18.75	7.29	4.20	2.24	2.01	0.57	5.28
100.00	100.00	100.00	100.00	100.00	100.00	100.00
15.26	23.68	11.55	10.67	14.11	44.11	16.81
36.65	32.57	25.61	16.93	28.01	9.50	36.89
6.20	8.47	6.69	2.39	14.97	14.49	18.46
5.40	0.73	30.89	37.10	30.64	3.41	4.91
7.97	11.16	4.80	7.77	9.55	51.83	5.85
28.52	23.39	20.46	25.14	2.72	23.34	17.08
100.00%	100.00%	100.00%	100.00%	100.00%	100.00%	100.00%
$15,104	$6,936	$13,444	$12,542	$4,291	$4,291	$11,943
$10,237	$4,040	$10,079	$ 7,059	$4,167	$4,208	$ 8,889
105.13%	112.22%	168.01%	268.70%	174.51%	106.58%	108.43%
64.14	39.58	69.49	130.56	84.31	34.48	49.27
951%	529%	638%	784%	285%	290%	432%
25	53	51	51	12	24	22
147.54%	171.70%	133.39%	177.66%	102.96%	126.57%	134.34%
77.19	65.18	N. Av.	N. Av.	N. Av.	N. Av.	N. Av.
18.04	24.41	N. Av.	N. Av.	N. Av.	N. Av.	N. Av.
2.92	5.52	0.97	1.55	0.16	(26.57)	(2.12)
4.31	9.49	1.30	2.75	0.17	(23.56)	(2.84)
274.05	289.44	395.72	303.86	813.67	351.00	436.30
11.82	65.25	5.14	8.36	1.36	(161.40)	(12.40)
25.94	26.70	25.89	8.75	28.55	25.41	43.78
16.99%	52.76%	26.47%	7.26%	121.80%	49.88%	80.54%
N. Av.	N. Av.	N. Av.	N. Av.	N. Av.	160.2	245.0

General Motors Corporation (C)
EXHIBIT 7 • Automobile Industry Comparative Data, 1981

	GM	Ford	Chrysler
Balance Sheet Percentages (percentage of assets, except as noted)			
Cash and marketable securities	3.39	9.12	6.45
Receivables	9.37	11.28	6.85
Inventories	18.56	20.17	25.52
Other current assets	3.92	3.64	2.66
Plant and equipment (net)	51.49	42.77	39.03
Other assets	13.27	13.02	19.49
Total assets	100.00	100.00	100.00
Accounts and notes payable	13.95	16.90	34.89
Other current liabilities	18.31	26.27	3.68
Long-term debt and leases	4.34	11.77	32.84
Other liabilities	18.05	13.07	16.14
Capital stock and surplus	6.11	3.34	39.42
Retained earnings	39.24	28.65	(26.99)
Total liabilities and stockholders' equity	100.00%	100.00%	100.00%
Total sales (millions 1982 dollars)	$60,744	$37,054	$6,074
Total assets	$37,706	$22,303	$9,661
Selected Ratios (percentage, except as noted)			
Current ratio	109.25%	102.38%	107.54%
Acid test	39.56	47.24	34.48
Inventory turnover	864%	783%	567%
Accounts and notes receivable collection (days)	62	50	80
Net sales/Total assets	161.10%	166.13%	159.03%
Cost of goods sold/Sales	95.04	96.23	93.93
Selling, general, and administrative/Sales	4.33	7.05	8.88
Net profit/Net sales	0.53	(2.77)	(4.77)
Net profit/Total assets	0.86	(4.60)	(7.59)
Total assets/Net worth	220.51	312.70	803.86
Net profit/Net worth	1.89	(14.40)	(60.99)
Total debt/Total assets	4.34	21.23	36.68
Long-term debt/Total capital	9.57%	36.81%	266.00%
Employees (thousands)	746.0	404.8	46.0

N. Av. = not available.

Nissan	Honda	Volkswagen	Daimler–Benz	Volvo	British Leyland	Peugeot
11.83	8.24	14.89	20.29	2.14	1.04	3.82
19.43	13.68	6.80	14.73	36.12	16.03	24.64
17.19	36.29	23.54	23.58	31.60	40.95	28.25
5.52	5.50	11.79	12.90	0.00	0.00	0.00
27.04	29.57	40.22	26.48	22.88	41.47	37.46
18.99	6.72	2.76	2.03	7.26	0.51	5.84
100.00	100.00	100.00	100.00	100.00	100.00	100.00
13.83	24.16	12.68	10.29	15.77	33.69	16.08
37.45	31.20	23.82	17.74	31.68	19.97	41.72
8.19	11.42	7.03	2.66	17.58	13.29	20.40
4.64	(0.66)	30.89	37.40	24.56	1.77	3.99
9.31	9.43	4.73	7.48	7.59	79.83	5.44
26.58	24.45	20.85	24.43	2.82	(48.55)	12.37
100.00%	100.00%	100.00%	100.00%	100.00%	100.00%	100.00%
$15,176	$7,325	$15,122	$14,636	$7,404	$4,865	$10,670
$11,499	$4,560	$10,130	$ 8,155	$5,651	$3,607	$ 8,376
105.26%	115.11%	156.18%	255.11%	147.24%	108.13%	101.25%
60.97	39.61	59.41	124.94	80.64	31.82	42.64
853%	489%	630%	789%	472%	316%	327%
26	49	87	48	17	27	18
131.98%	160.64%	149.29%	179.47%	131.03%	134.86%	127.38%
75.94	67.83	N. Av.	N. Av.	N. Av.	N. Av.	75.61
17.60	23.93	N. Av.	N. Av.	N. Av.	N. Av.	21.83
2.61	3.49	0.36	0.83	0.94	(17.32)	(2.75)
3.44	5.60	0.54	1.49	1.24	(23.37)	(3.51)
278.55	295.16	390.93	313.29	960.61	319.69	558.35
9.58	16.54	2.10	4.66	11.88	(74.70)	(19.58)
29.10	30.42	23.92	7.42	34.10	32.15	45.48
22.81%	33.71%	27.48%	8.33%	168.88%	42.49%	113.90%
N. Av.	N. Av.	246.9	188.0	76.1	130.2	231.5

General Motors Corporation (C)
EXHIBIT 8 • Automobile Industry Comparative Data, 1982

	GM	Ford	Chrysler
Balance Sheet Percentages (percentage of assets, except as noted)			
Cash and marketable securities	7.56%	7.09%	14.32%
Receivables	6.93	10.82	3.96
Inventories	14.95	18.77	18.09
Other current assets	4.52	3.39	1.45
Plant and equipment (net)	52.07	46.15	39.49
Other assets	13.97	13.78	22.69
Total assets	100.00	100.00	100.00
Accounts and notes payable	11.56	18.76	14.33
Other current liabilities	18.38	28.70	19.39
Long-term debt and leases	4.77	10.72	34.95
Other liabilities	21.16	14.14	15.50
Capital stock and surplus	6.61	3.48	40.16
Retained earnings	37.52	24.20	(24.33)
Total liabilities and stockholders' equity	100.00%	100.00%	100.00%
Total sales (millions 1982 dollars)	$60,026	$37,067	$10,045
Total assets	$41,360	$21,962	$ 6,264
Selected Ratios (percentage, except as noted)			
Current ratio	113.39%	84.41%	112.14%
Acid test	48.37	37.72	54.20
Inventory turnover	895%	846%	735%
Accounts and notes receivable collection (days)	67	54	108
Net sales/Total assets	145.12%	168.78%	160.37%
Cost of goods sold/Sales	93.46	93.40	89.77
Selling, general, and administrative/Sales	4.94	7.91	9.37
Net profit/Net sales	1.60	(1.77)	1.69
Net profit/Total assets	2.33	(3.00)	2.72
Total assets/Net worth	226.60	361.40	631.11
Net profit/Net worth	5.27	(10.82)	17.16
Total debt/Total assets	4.77	21.03	36.47
Long-term debt/Total capital	10.81%	38.74%	220.92%
Employees (thousands)	657.0	379.2	73.7

N. Av. = not available.

Nissan	Honda	Volkswagen	Daimler–Benz	Volvo	British Leyland	Peugeot
11.94%	6.01%	11.87%	20.13%	2.25%	1.92%	2.30%
16.69	15.08	6.12	15.31	36.17	18.74	19.91
12.73	32.06	21.79	21.96	30.99	37.49	28.83
5.41	6.14	12.91	12.18	0.00	0.00	0.00
32.22	33.56	44.25	28.04	20.49	41.54	38.99
21.01	7.15	3.06	2.39	10.10	0.31	9.97
100.00	100.00	100.00	100.00	100.00	100.00	100.00
12.17	22.30	13.58	9.77	14.70	35.64	17.18
35.39	28.35	24.23	17.73	31.73	12.13	40.95
12.49	12.17	5.59	3.51	18.73	23.09	23.43
4.36	0.83	33.23	37.61	23.37	1.82	4.55
8.81	10.64	4.63	6.66	8.55	84.94	5.26
26.78	25.71	18.74	24.72	2.92	(57.62)	8.63
100.00%	100.00%	100.00%	100.00%	100.00%	100.00%	100.00%
$16,345	$8,953	$15,425	$16,031	$12,035	$5,377	$11,450
12,897	5,308	10,684	9,459	7,365	4,035	8,952
98.32%	117.07%	139.35%	253.10%	149.50%	121.75%	95.36%
60.18	41.64	47.58	128.92	52.75	43.26	35.03
888%	525%	644%	789%	583%	354%	315%
27	45	83	44	18	29	17
126.73%	168.68%	144.37%	169.49%	163.42%	133.26%	127.91%
75.93	66.82	N. Av.	N. Av.	N. Av.	N. Av.	84.07
18.71	24.55	N. Av.	N. Av.	N. Av.	N. Av.	16.45
2.57	3.24	(0.80)	0.90	0.66	(9.53)	(2.85)
3.25	5.46	(1.16)	1.52	1.07	(12.71)	(3.65)
280.98	275.10	427.90	318.47	871.84	366.03	722.02
9.14	15.03	(4.89)	4.85	9.34	(46.51)	(26.36)
33.96	29.71	23.36	8.38	35.75	33.55	46.90
35.09%	33.48%	23.92%	11.18%	163.30%	84.51%	169.39%
N. Av.	N. Av.	243.0	186.8	75.6	111.0	213.0

PART

2

*Forecasting Future
Corporate Performance*

United Telesis Corporation

In early March 1985, John Cunningham, executive vice president of the San Diego–based United Telesis Corporation (UT), was debating whether to proceed with a new venture in the business of vending (owning, operating, and servicing) private coin-operated telephones. Since the divestiture of AT&T, the Federal Communications Commission (FCC) had ruled that pay telephones could be owned and operated by firms other than the regional telephone companies. The Public Utilities Commissions (PUCs) in nine states had approved the operation of such companies and had established appropriate tariff structures for access to local telephone lines. United Telesis, through a subsidiary acquired early in the industry's existence, was already gaining valuable operating experience vending pay phones in high-tariff Minnesota, and had received publicity as the "largest private coin-operated telephone (COT) operator in the country." Using Minnesota as a proving ground for its operations, UT hoped to capitalize on its industry-leading reputation by expanding services into Florida, Texas, New York, and California—all prime COT states on the verge of establishing tariffs.

The California PUC had made it illegal for a company like UT to install telephones until a tariff structure had been established. Industry analysts had advised Mr. Cunningham that they expected a tariff to be established in the near future. Originally, the California PUC had been scheduled to deliver the long-awaited tariff in early February 1985, but almost on the eve of the tariff's release, it was delayed in the courts. Having believed the February date to be accurate, Mr. Cunningham had just spent $50,000 on a 45-day marketing blitz in San Diego and had obtained 1,000 phone contracts in prime locations. Because the contracts contained a clause requiring installation of the phones by June 30, 1985, Mr. Cunningham faced a difficult question: Should he go ahead and illegally install his company's phones in anticipation of the tariff, risking an unknown fate in the courts, or should he wait for the PUC to act and risk losing his

---

signed contracts because of the installation deadline? In either case, the tariff terms could be set too high for companies like UT to operate COTs profitably in California.

Mr. Cunningham faced another question as well, one that depended in part on his current actions and their success. If he proceeded, how much external financing would UT need over the next several years?

The COT Industry

Private ownership of COTs was first permitted by the FCC on June 14, 1984. State jurisdiction called for each PUC to establish the amount a private company could charge callers and a tariff for the connection of private COT service to local lines. PUCs in most states were expected to permit private phone companies to charge 25¢ for a local phone call. Because the local (Bell) phone companies were still under the regulatory eyes of their PUCs, each company had to file a proposed tariff and price schedule for the state agencies to review and either accept or reject.

Currently, local phone companies, called regional Bell operating companies (RBOCs), installed pay phones and vended the service; they owned the equipment, installed and maintained it, and, if the phone produced over $75 revenue per month, paid the location account a commission, which averaged 3 to 6 percent of the phone's gross revenue. If the phone did not meet the minimum revenue level, the location account was charged between $28 and $50 per month per phone.

The pay-phone business represented a small portion of the local phone companies' total revenues. Many of them viewed their COT business as a public service that did not have to be profitable. Those RBOCs that were interested in profitability could not be sure their operations were breaking even, however, because of the awkward way most of them allocated overhead. As a result, now that the business was deregulated, a few were considering abandoning the COT business altogether.

The COT industry generated revenues of $1.6 to $1.8 billion in 1983. It was estimated that 62 percent of these revenues were generated by approximately 20 percent of the COTs. The COT market had three distinct but related segments:

1.   High coin/low credit card revenue: Only 6 to 25 percent of all COTs generated coin revenues over $250 a month. These COTs were generally in high-traffic locations with a large percentage of local calls such as busy bars and restaurants, gas stations at intersections, or shopping malls.

2.   Medium coin/medium credit card revenue: 75 percent of the coin market consisted of COTs with coin revenues between $50 and $250 a month. Owners of most of these locations received little commission from

the phones. Included in this segment were "semi-public" phones, typically low-revenue phones for which location accounts paid the $28 to $50 a month per phone to have this service available to their employees and customers.

3.   High credit card/low coin revenue: The credit card COT market generated annual revenues in excess of $2 billion. AT&T, MCI, Sprint, and other long-distance carriers were competing for a share of this growing market, mostly by focusing on the large transportation centers (e.g., airports and hotels). Technological advances in equipment were expected soon to allow conversion of strictly coin phones into combination coin and credit card units.

Presently, private COT companies such as UT were able to pay locations a commission only on cash revenues, because long-distance carriers such as MCI and AT&T did not pay commissions to private COT companies for providing access through their phones. Mr. Cunningham believed, however, that as UT expanded the size of its operation, long-distance carriers would begin to bid for access through UT's phones, which would enable UT to receive revenue and pay commissions on all business, coin and card.

The Company

United Telesis Corporation was founded in 1984 by two Santa Clara University classmates, John Cunningham and Ed Benkman. They had become interested in the pay-phone industry through their involvement in a small vending company called Vidcom. At the height of operations, Vidcom had placed video games and pinball machines in over 2,000 locations in 12 states. By early 1985, however, decline in public interest in video games had shrunk the business to 1,000 sites in four states (California, Ohio, New York, and Arizona). Vidcom owned 45 percent of UT's stock, current UT management and insiders owned another 35 percent, and the rest was held by the public. UT was a Nevada corporation that had been "blue-skied" in 42 states. Its stock was traded over the counter (the "pink sheets") and was currently selling at about $1 per share.

Mr. Cunningham, 28, a 1983 MBA graduate of the Darden School at the University of Virginia, had previously been an account executive and trader with Dean Witter Reynolds in Menlo Park, California. He joined UT in 1984 after a year in real estate investment banking in Seattle, Washington. Friends from school believed "John's personality, personal resources, and his ability to cultivate, develop, and utilize contacts to be perhaps his company's biggest asset."

Mr. Benkman, also 28, president of Vidcom and UT, was a 1979 graduate of the University of Santa Clara. He was a classic entrepreneur, who had only once in his life ever worked for someone other than himself (managing a hotel his first summer after school). In his first venture in the vending business, he had invented an electronic monitoring device for video games called the "Nighthawk" that remotely counted the number of coins deposited into a vending machine. He had also obtained contracts with all the Circle-K and 7–11 stores in southern California, Arizona, and Nevada. Mr. Benkman was detail oriented, operations minded, and a proven financier. By age 28, he had formed several different companies. Both he and Mr. Cunningham had high expectations for their new venture.

UT had until now been heavily financed by a group of foreign investors who had pledged $1.65 million to purchase stock in the young company. An initial $650,000 had been funded, with the remaining $1 million due in the next several months. These funds were expected to get the company set up in California, where the success of one operation could generate follow-up capital from such sources as limited partnerships, leasing companies, and private placements of stock.

The California COT Market

United Telesis was particularly interested in the California market for a number of reasons. First, the company's home office was in San Diego, a city in the southern part of the state known for its beaches and year-round perfect climate. Second, California was the second largest COT market (189,000 phones in place) in the country, and over two-thirds of the COTs in California were located in the southern part of the state. Third, because weather conditions permitted less expensive protection for outdoor phones, initial capital-investment levels in California were as much as 20 percent lower than in, for example, Minnesota, where all outdoor phones required some sort of enclosure. UT was interested in Texas (129,000 COTs) and Florida (89,000) COTs for the same reasons. Fourth, the southwest portion of the United States, known as the "sunbelt," was expected to be the fastest growing area of the country during the next 25 years, and the company wanted to take part in this growth.

UT's mode of operation was similar to that of Vidcom, the video game company. Locations such as gas stations, bars, restaurants, shopping malls, and convenience stores would be solicited to contract with UT to have phones installed. The company sought to convert current locations that were proven revenue producers to its equipment, so that once a phone was installed, it would immediately begin producing positive cash flow. In addition, installation costs were much lower at those sites, because RBOC wall mountings were already in place.

In southern California, UT obtained locations by promising the prospective account 20 percent of the COT's gross margin (total cash in the box, less the local phone company's charges). As a result, net income to the various customers' accounts was expected to be twice that of the area's RBOC (Pacific Bell)—all with no investment on the part of the accounts. After obtaining a contract at a location, UT planned to instruct Pac Bell to remove its existing equipment and then install its own. UT would collect the money from the phones and provide monthly preventive maintenance. It also guaranteed seven-day, 24-hour service, and would pay the account its commission by the 20th of each month.

The key to obtaining accounts was reaching the decision-maker at a particular location. At a local bar with one or two phones, this person was probably the owner. A sale to a restaurant or convenience-store chain with 50 to 100 phones at sites all over the state meant contacting the regional office. Obviously, UT was interested in obtaining corporate accounts, where one visit could produce a contract for hundreds of phones, but these sales often took months, sometimes years, to close, because the accounts were not as interested in higher commissions as in continued high-quality equipment and service. Thus UT was equally interested in the small, independent locations. Choice sites could be hand-picked, often for far lower commissions than the chain accounts demanded, and the decision-making process was much faster.

COT Equipment

Mr. Cunningham wanted to establish routes, each with a minimum of 3,000 pay phones, in the California, Florida, and Texas markets. Each route would have a district office, and a two-person service/collection team for every 500 phones. At this point, UT had purchased 1,000 phones manufactured by Seiscor, a division of Raytheon. Distributed by Cointel Corporation of Los Angeles, this phone model was considered attractive because it had several months of field testing behind it. Although the number of new COTs on the market was increasing and their prices were falling, none of the new phones had any performance history.

The new, privately owned COTs were termed "smart phones"; their intelligence was contained on a microchip within the phone. The intelligence included a rate table that would determine for the user exactly how much a call would cost without the assistance of an operator. Existing COTs were termed "dumb phones," because they relied on a central switching location and directory assistance for the rate information. Most smart phones also had an LCD display that indicated the number dialed, the cost of the call, the amount deposited, the time remaining at that cost, and any additional charges.

UT was already using the Cointel phone in its Minnesota test market, with mixed results. All the RBOCs in the states where United Telesis intended to compete operated "pre-pay" COTs, meaning the user picked up the hand set, deposited the coins, dialed the number, and if the party answered, could immediately begin speaking. If no one answered, the coins were returned. Over 99 percent of the COTs in the United States were pre-pay phones.

Because the answer-supervision technology required for a pre-pay system was still very expensive, the Cointel phone, like all the new phones then on the market, was a "post-pay" phone, meaning that the user picked up the hand set, dialed the number, deposited the coins, and, if the call was answered, pushed a button in order to speak; pushing the button signaled the phone to take the coins. If the party did not answer and the button was not pushed, the coins were returned. Any coins that had been inserted before the number was dialed were not returned.

Although instructions were printed clearly on the phones, this different mode of operation caused many users to have difficulty with the new phones. Most of the complaints came during the first 60 days after installation, however, and the company expected this natural resistance to change to diminish. Answer supervision, the highly desired feature that would allow the COTs to operate in a more traditional way, was expected to be available in the next generation of phones, due to be released during the next year, perhaps within three to six months. All current manufacturers' phones, including Cointel's, had other potential problems such as vulnerability to vandalism.

All the COT manufacturers were anxious for a significant industry member such as UT to make a large purchase of their phones, so they could capitalize on the publicity. Mr. Cunningham believed that, for the price ($1,395 per phone for 1,000 phones), the Cointel phone presented the best value, despite its shortcomings. As new phones with more advanced features were produced, he intended to replace the Cointel phones in the best locations with newer models and rotate the older phones to less profitable locations. His main concern now, however, was to sign up the best locations and install the phones.

Competition

Although few firms like UT currently served the California market, heavier competition was expected in the wake of the upcoming PUC decision. Mr. Cunningham expected the strongest competition in the near term to come from such established vending companies as ARA ($4 billion sales) and Canteen (owned by Trans World Corp., TWA's parent company), neither of which had yet entered the market. He expected later competition from smaller operators, from both the vending industry and new entrants. This competition was expected to reduce profit margins, forcing many of the marginal firms to go out of business or to consolidate their operations with those of other firms. Initial capital requirements were the greatest barrier to entry: a thousand phones required an investment upwards of $1.8 million.

Mr. Cunningham also believed that Pacific Bell, despite its claim that it wanted to get out of the pay-phone business, would inevitably become UT's key competitor. After all, its phones and operations were already in place; all Pac Bell needed to do was double its current commissions of between 3 and 6 percent of gross revenue (coin and card) to be competitive. He felt sure that, once Pac Bell began to examine the cost of getting out of the business, it would choose to stay.

Historically, state PUCs and established local phone companies, while sometimes adversarial, had worked closely together. Their relationships generally offered an opportunity to structure tariffs and privately owned COT regulations in favor of the phone companies. What these relationships did not give them, lobbying power did. Regardless of how you looked at it, the RBOC–PUC combination was a powerful competitor for new companies like UT. Nevertheless, Mr. Cunningham believed UT would not only be the leader among the new entrants, it could compete against giants like Pac Bell because of its low-cost operation.

UT Projections

Before establishing a pay-phone operation in California, Mr. Cunningham had examined the economies of the business. In order to determine the company's breakeven point of operation (in terms of number of phones), he assumed the average monthly revenue of a phone would be $220. He expected that the PUC's tariff would include a $30-per-month line charge, plus per-call charges of $0.08—all to be paid to Pac Bell. Tariffs ranged from $10 per month and $0.045 in Illinois to Minnesota's $57.50 per month for 200 calls, $0.10 per call for the next 200 calls, $0.08 for the next 200 calls, and $0.05 per call thereafter. Commissions at each location were projected to cost 20 percent of the phone's gross margin (total cash revenue less line charges and per-call charges).

To calculate the monthly debt service for each COT, Mr. Cunningham used an interest rate of 16 percent, a 48-month time frame, and a purchase price of $1,800 (including both phone and booth). Sales commissions would be $25 per phone to secure a location contract, and installation costs were expected to average $100 per phone. For maintenance and service, Mr. Cunningham projected costs of $20/month/COT. For projection purposes, depreciation was handled on a straight-line basis, although the ACRS depreciation schedule shown in Exhibit 1 would apply for tax purposes. An investment tax credit of 8 percent could be taken on the total cost per phone, including installation. (See Exhibit 2 for a calculation of revenues, costs, and profits per phone.) Other costs expected to be incurred by the company, including a personnel budget large enough for 3,000 phones, are shown in Exhibit 3.

Mr. Cunningham wanted to target accounts with locations that would provide at least breakeven levels of gross cash revenues. This information was to be obtained after each particular account signed a preliminary contract. With the agreement of the account, UT would submit a request to Pac Bell for the account's pay-phone revenue history, which was available under the Freedom of Information Act. If the phone revenue was high enough, a UT officer would sign the contract to activate the terms.

UT planned to operate a total of 3,000 COTs by the end of 1985, 7,000 by the end of 1986, 12,000 by 1987, and 17,000 and 22,000 by the ends of 1988 and 1989, respectively. Three-minute local calls were expected to constitute 85 percent of the total number of calls on the phones, while long-distance calls would make up the remaining 15 percent. From this information, Mr. Cunningham believed that he could generate UT's projected income statement.

Mr. Cunningham also wanted to determine his internal funding and external capital needs over the next several years. Because this industry was new and exciting, a warm investor reception was expected, but because both Mr. Cunningham and Mr. Benkman received much of their compensation in the form of stock and stock options, he naturally wanted to avoid substantial equity dilution if possible.

United Telesis Corporation
EXHIBIT 1 • Tax Depreciation Schedule
for Telephone Equipment (as of 1985)

Year of Service	Percentage of Purchase Price Depreciated
1	15%
2	22
3	21
4	21
5	21

United Telesis Corporation
EXHIBIT 2 • Average Margin per Phone per Month

Revenue	$220.00
Telephone charges	(92.40)
Gross margin	127.60
Location commission	(25.52)
Gross profit	102.08
Service and maintenance	(20.00)
Overhead	(13.42)
Depreciation[a]	(15.00)
Profit before debt service and income taxes	$ 53.66

[a]Depreciation calculation:

Installation and equipment	
COT cost	$1,400.00
Installation	100.00
Booth/enclosure	300.00
Total cost per COT	$1,800.00
Depreciable life	10 years
Annual depreciation	$180.00

United Telesis Corporation
EXHIBIT 3 • UT Projected Monthly Corporate Overhead

Operational salaries	$ 8,000
Administrative salaries	15,000
Rent and utilities	3,000
Postage	750
Travel and entertainment	2,000
Telephone	1,500
Auto	3,000
Advertising	2,000
Contingency	5,000
Total projected overhead	$40,250

Fisher Electric, Inc.

On February 5, 1989, Gerry Wilson, the manager of the main Vancouver branch of Confederation Bank, was considering an application for a C$10-million line of credit from Fisher Electric, Inc. Fisher currently conducted all of its banking activities with Pacific Bank of Canada (Pacific), a major competitor of Confederation's, and acquiring the account would be a coup for Mr. Wilson.

Michael Murray, the president of Fisher, initiated the discussions with Mr. Wilson because he believed that the credit limit of C$8.5 million imposed on Fisher by Pacific restricted the company's existing operations and its plans for continued growth and expansion. Pacific's credit manager maintained that Fisher's loan amount should stabilize in 1989 after a rapid buildup over the past five years to its current level, and he advised Mr. Murray that the maximum loan he would consider at this time was C$8.5 million.

Mr. Murray had started with Fisher in 1983 as the manager of its highly successful Vancouver branch. His uncle, who had founded the company, sold all of his shares to Mr. Murray in 1985. In 1989, 72 percent of Fisher common stock was owned by Mr. Murray and 28 percent by the four branch managers and three other key employees. Mr. Murray initiated a stock-purchase plan in 1986 in order to keep his key people and to focus their attention on the profitability of the business.

Fisher had been a Pacific Bank customer for over 35 years, and it had a record of growth and profitability over the past four years that impressed Mr. Wilson. The company's recent financial statements are presented in Exhibits 1 and 2.

Fisher, operating as a wholesaler of electrical supplies, sold to contractors of single-family and multiple-dwelling units, as well as to retailers of electrical products such as hardware stores and building-supply outlets. The firm's branches were located in the western Canadian cities of Saskatoon, Edmonton, Calgary, and Vancouver. The head office was in Vancouver.

This case was prepared by Professor David Shaw of the Western Business School. Copyright 1989, The University of Western Ontario.

Fisher's products consisted of a large variety of electrical supplies and materials generally used in residential construction. Principal items sold were wiring, all types of fixtures, breaker panels, fuse panels, switch and receptacle boxes, electric baseboard heaters, and grounded floor receptacles. Fisher was gradually expanding its line into such related products as security systems.

Each Fisher branch purchased independently from an established product list and dealt directly with approved suppliers. Mr. Murray instituted monthly meetings with the individual branch managers, during which inventory control was stressed. Each branch manager received separate financial statements for her or his operations, with key ratios such as inventory turnover, gross profit percentages, and net profit to sales highlighted. Each branch's results were discussed at each meeting.

Most manufacturers of electrical products offered volume discounts and early-payment incentives. Manufacturers typically offered a 2 percent discount for payment within 20 days. On large orders, Fisher would attempt to take advantage of these discounts. Usually, however, Fisher paid its accounts in about 60 days, which was the industry standard, although the bank loan limit sometimes forced Fisher to take a longer time to pay. All payments to creditors were made from the head office on the basis of approved invoices from the branches.

Fisher managers believed that high inventory levels provided clients with the best service and sheltered the company somewhat from price increases. The wholesale electrical-supply business was highly competitive, and Mr. Murray was convinced that Fisher would lose business to its competitors if it were caught in stock-outs. Contractors wanted supplies on demand, and they counted on Fisher to supply them—today. Electrical products had experienced inflationary price increases of roughly 3 to 4 percent in each of the last three years.

Fisher's sales were relatively stable throughout the year. Trade credit was granted to contractors and retail hardware and building-supply stores by the individual branch managers, who obtained credit reports on all new accounts and regularly updated reports on existing customers. When an account receivable exceeded 90 days outstanding and C$20,000, Fisher's credit manager at the head office became involved. The credit manager met with the branch managers quarterly to review all receivables.

Normal bad-debt losses, which were included in general expenses, amounted to about C$100,000 per year. One of Fisher's major customers went bankrupt in 1987; however, the company recovered approximately C$200,000 of C$800,000 it was owed.

Most of Fisher's recent sales growth could be attributed to the recovery in residential construction activity in the cities and surrounding suburban areas where the company operated. Exhibit 3 presents the actual levels of housing starts in each city over the past 10 years compared with the national level and provides projected levels of housing starts for 1989.

Fisher's sales dropped with the level of new housing starts in 1982, 1983, and 1984, and the company incurred small losses in each of those years. Fisher's sales and profits had increased each year for the past four years. Mr. Murray predicted that net sales for fiscal 1989 would be C$56 million.

The existing branches in the chain varied considerably in sales and earning performance. Vancouver had consistently outperformed expectations and contributed 40 percent of the total profits in 1988, while Saskatoon had been a major disappointment over the last three years and barely reached breakeven in 1988.

Fisher had undertaken an aggressive sales approach to residential electrical contractors in western Canada. The objective was to increase Fisher's market share and customer loyalty. In 1988, 55 percent of Fisher's sales were to new-housing contractors and the remaining 45 percent to retail outlets.

Frank Scully, sales manager, estimated that sales volume in 1989 would be 10 percent greater than in 1988 and 10 percent greater again in 1990 over 1989 because of the sales effort and the steadily growing new-housing market. He forecast that selling prices would increase an average of 4 percent in each year.

Mr. Murray proposed that Confederation Bank take as security for its C$10-million line of credit both a demand debenture againt Fisher, which would include a first floating charge against inventory, and a general assignment of accounts receivable. In Mr. Wilson's opinion, the realizable value of the inventory was high because it consisted of staple merchandise. Although a distress sale would probably not realize book value, Mr. Wilson estimated that value was sufficient to recover at least 50 percent of cost in a reasonably short time.

For similar accounts, Confederation Bank charged prime plus 1½ percent on loan balances. Prime was currently at 12¾ percent. In addition, the bank usually set a margin formula that, in effect, limited borrowings to 75 percent of current (less than 90 days) receivables and 50 percent of inventory.

Gerry Wilson wondered whether he should accept the account. If he did take it, was C$10 million a sufficient amount for Fisher? What would the company's future credit needs be? Was the collateral package proposed by Mr. Murray satisfactory?

Fisher Electric, Inc.

EXHIBIT 1 • Income Statement for the Years Ended December 31, 1986–88
(in thousands of Canadian dollars)

	1986	*1987*	*1988*
Gross sales	$38,254	$43,104	$49,620
Less: Discounts allowed	598	654	762
Net Sales	37,656	42,450	48,858
Cost of goods sold	29,828	33,466	38,877
Gross profit	7,828	8,984	9,981
Operating expenses			
Administrative	2,706	3,144	3,114
Selling	1,028	1,130	1,730
Warehouse	1,826	2,078	2,342
Total operating expenses	5,560	6,352	7,186
Operating income	2,268	2,632	2,795
Interest expense	753	912	1,460
Income before taxes	1,515	1,720	1,335
Income taxes	697	791	614
Income after taxes	818	929	721
Dividends	$ 640	$ 0	$ 0

Fisher Electric, Inc.

EXHIBIT 2 • Balance Sheet as of December 31, 1986–88
(in thousands of Canadian dollars)

	1986	1987	1988
Assets			
Current assets			
Cash	$ 0	$ 100	$ 94
Accounts receivable	6,212	7,582	9,104
Inventory	10,348	12,372	14,716
Prepaid expenses	490	1,082	640
Total current assets	17,050	21,136	24,554
Land	442	494	494
Building and property, net	1,056	1,314	1,402
Equipment and other fixed assets, net	1,038	1,552	1,446
Total assets	$19,586	$24,496	$27,896
Liabilities			
Current liabilities			
Bank loan	$ 6,550	$ 6,995	$ 8,200
Trade payables	5,292	7,284	7,662
Long-term debt, current portion	12	234	549
Income taxes payable	348	505	370
Total current liabilities	12,202	15,018	16,781
Five-year term loan secured by fixed assets, 14%	862	1,971	2,831
Total liabilities	13,064	16,989	19,612
Shareholders' equity			
Equity	294	350	406
Retained earnings	6,228	7,157	7,878
Total shareholders' equity	6,522	7,507	8,284
Total liabilities and shareholders' equity	$19,586	$24,496	$27,896

Fisher Electric, Inc.
EXHIBIT 3 • Residential Housing Starts in Canada and Selected Cities

Housing Starts	1978	1979	1980	1981	1982	1983	1984	1985	1986	1987	1988	1989
All Canada	178,678	151,717	125,013	142,441	104,792	134,207	110,874	165,826	199,785	215,340	189,635	185,000
Saskatoon	3,250	4,259	1,880	2,076	3,481	2,529	1,462	2,002	1,963	1,746	1,426	1,800
Calgary	15,382	12,383	11,104	15,172	9,599	4,882	1,803	2,318	2,679	3,466	3,800	4,200
Edmonton	17,065	12,298	9,967	11,999	9,738	6,543	2,384	2,528	2,561	3,608	4,133	4,500
Vancouver	12,183	12,827	16,780	15,227	9,247	12,302	9,683	11,315	13,578	17,860	17,901	18,800
Total four cities	47,880	41,767	39,731	44,474	32,065	26,256	15,332	18,163	20,781	26,680	27,260	29,300

Sources: Canada Mortgage and Housing Corporation and Statistics Canada Canadian Economic Observer.

Fantastic Manufacturing, Inc.

In late October 1980, David Rose and Pierce Turner, principals of Fantastic Manufacturing, Inc., were preparing forecasts for their rapidly growing business assembling and marketing ceiling fans. A product many had thought of as a fad, ceiling fans had instead been accepted by consumers as energy conservers, and new-home builders and homeowners were installing them in record numbers.

Fantastic Manufacturing was incorporated in late 1976 by Mr. Rose and Mr. Turner in Charleston, South Carolina. Mr. Rose had his own manufacturers' representative, Rose Sales, Inc., with annual sales of approximately $40 million to accounts around the world. He specialized in sales of building materials to mass-merchandisers.

In 1976 Mr. Rose had found many of his accounts interested in ceiling fans, and at the end of that year, he approached Mr. Turner, a tax attorney by training and head of his own manufacturing company, to discuss the possibility of importing and assembling ceiling fans. Agreeing with the idea, Mr. Turner accompanied Mr. Rose to Taiwan and Hong Kong to find parts suppliers for a new, low-priced, assemble-it-yourself fan. The men took their specifications to all the fan factories they could find in Taiwan and Hong Kong and selected exclusive suppliers.

Fantastic's first order for fans was placed in September 1977 and arrived in late November. After assembly, the fans were shipped to customers in December. By the end of the first fiscal year, which ended January 31, 1978, total sales were approximately $230,000.

Fantastic had begun operations by emphasizing sales of low-priced fans to the do-it-yourself market, selling largely through small stores. Initially, Mr. Rose and Mr. Turner had viewed the product as appealing to nostalgia, and they expected limited growth potential. The initial objective of the business was to get the product on the shelf, and the company encouraged retailers to advertise heavily. Many stores used the product initially as a faddish draw.

Studies had shown, however, that ceiling fans were economically beneficial, reducing both cooling costs in summer and heating costs in winter. As consumers began viewing ceiling fans as energy-saving devices, the growth prospects for the industry improved. Much of this improvement was expected to come from the upper end of the market, for which Fantastic Manufacturing had positioned its recently introduced Cotillion line. Their major premium-line competition came from two domestic lines, Hunter and Casablanca, both produced by Emerson Electric. Emerson had done little to promote its products.

Not much public information was available about fan sales in general, which made it difficult for Mr. Rose and Mr. Turner to estimate the potential for competition. They did know that Fantastic held a cost advantage because of its overseas sourcing. Customers were pleased with Fantastic's products and had commented positively on the high level of service and timeliness of delivery. The company's seven-year warranty on the fans had also encouraged consumer acceptance.

Fantastic's revenues increased rapidly from the beginning. In fiscal 1979 and 1980, the first two full years of operations, Fantastic had sales of $3.1 million and $9.9 million, respectively. Net profits in those years were $73,000 and $108,000, as shown in Exhibit 1. Although 1980 revenues had increased 213 percent from the prior year, net income rose only 48 percent because of substantially higher costs. Increased rent, advertising, bad debts, and interest costs had caused selling, general, and administrative costs to increase over 250 percent.

Fan sales were seasonal, with over 65 percent of revenues coming from April through September, as shown in Exhibit 2. Sales were made by salespeople working exclusively on commission. Commissions were paid in the same month the sales were made. The company served more than 100 customers, including many small accounts as well as mass-merchandisers and home-center stores such as K-Mart, J. C. Penney, Zayre, Ace Hardware, Best Products, and 84 Lumber. Two customers, however, had accounted for approximately 40 percent of total sales in 1980.

Salespeople wrote and confirmed the orders with no penalty for cancellation. Customers typically paid between 60 and 90 days after Fantastic shipped the merchandise. Accounts receivable were of good quality, although the bad debts/sales ratio was 2.1 percent in 1980 because of unpaid accounts from some small stores. Balance sheets for the period are shown in Exhibit 3.

The lead time for Fantastic's orders was 60 days—30 days for their suppliers to manufacture the fan parts once the order had been received and 30 days for shipping. Because the manufacturers had limited capacity, they could not supply highly variable quantities on short notice. As a result, Fantastic management had decided to place regular fan component orders, assemble the fans, and hold them in inventory until they were sold.

To finance the parts orders, the suppliers in Taiwan and Hong Kong required that letters of credit (L/C) be issued at the time the merchandise was ordered. A typical L/C was for 30 days, the time required to manufacture the goods and prepare them for shipment. The L/Cs were submitted for payment by the supplier when the merchandise was shipped. Because growth had been rapid, Fantastic did not keep cash available to pay for the goods when the L/C documents arrived at the bank. Thus the company typically drew a 60-day draft on the bank in the amount of the needed funds. The bank would accept the draft under an arrangement already established with Fantastic and extend the loan for a discounted amount of the draft. All Fantastic's current financing arrangements are summarized in Exhibit 4; representative short-term borrowing costs for 1978 to 1980 are in Exhibit 5.

The cost of the fans delivered at the Charleston plant had averaged 63 percent of Fantastic's final selling price. This cost varied with exchange rates shown in Exhibit 6. So far about half of the fans had been sourced from Hong Kong and half from Taiwan. Mr. Rose and Mr. Turner were satisfied with their suppliers and expected the relationships to continue.

The company's warehouse was located near Charleston in a building that had been purchased in July 1979 by a partnership owned by Mr. Rose and Mr. Turner and subsequently leased back to Fantastic. The term of the lease was 15 years, with annual payments of $185,000. The 116,000-square-foot facility was sufficient to support a sales volume of approximately $100 million. Most of the operations were simple; the company used the facility for unloading, inspecting, processing, repacking, and shipping the imported goods. The trickiest part of the operation was weighting and balancing the fan blades.

For the first half of fiscal 1981, sales were $15.8 million and profits almost $1 million. By year end, Mr. Rose and Mr. Turner expected sales to reach $30 million. Mr. Rose believed sales for 1982 would be over $71 million. He knew that this figure represented substantial growth in demand, growth that far outstripped forecasts,[1] but with Fantastic's $40-million order backlog, the forecast seemed reasonable. Furthermore, he believed that a return on sales of 9.8 percent was likely.

Up to now, Fantastic had grown more rapidly than had been expected, and planning had been lacking. Orders to suppliers had been based on forecasts of sales with a lead time of two months, and Fantastic's creditors had been willing to satisfy the growing company's capital needs on demand. Mr. Rose and Mr. Turner believed that, to continue good relationships with these two critical groups, longer range forecasts would

---

[1] The U.S. Department of Commerce had forecast little growth in retail sales of home appliances through mid-1982 and a slight decline in sales in the second half of that year.

be useful. As sales grew, suppliers would have to arrange for ways to produce more, and Fantastic would have increasing needs for funds.

Mr. Rose and Mr. Turner looked at the company's brief history, considered their forecasts for the expected demand for ceiling fans, and decided first they needed to decide for how long to forecast. So far demand had grown so rapidly that forecasts for even a few months would be rapidly outdated. On the other hand, some order needed to be brought to their relationships with their parts and capital suppliers. Good forecasts would help.

Fantastic Manufacturing, Inc.
EXHIBIT 1 • Income Statements (in thousands)

	Year Ending		Three Months Ending April 31, 1980	Six Months Ending July 31, 1980
	January 31, 1979	January 31, 1980		
Net revenues	$ 3,155	$ 9,860	$ 6,693	$ 15,818
Cost of goods sold	(2,263)	(7,306)	(4,543)	(10,310)
Gross profit	892	2,554	2,150	5,508
Salaries and payroll taxes	(252)	(308)		
Commissions	(149)	(487)		
Freight	(19)	(62)		
Rent	(0)	(128)		
Bad debts	(24)	(209)		
Interest[a]	(78)	(496)		
Other selling, general, and administrative	(278)	(709)		
Total operating expenses	(800)	(2,399)	(1,615)	(3,428)
Income before taxes	92	155	535	2,080
Taxes	(19)	(47)	(239)	(998)
Net income before extraordinary item	73	108	296	1,082
Extraordinary item (net of income tax credit)	0	0	0	(94)
Net income	$ 73	$ 108	$ 296	$ 988

[a]Includes line-of-credit charges.

Fantastic Manufacturing, Inc.
EXHIBIT 2 • Monthly Pattern of Sales, 1979 and 1980

	Proportion of Annual Sales
January	2.8%
February	5.9
March	7.8
April	9.8
May	10.8
June	11.2
July	11.7
August	12.7
September	9.8
October	7.8
November	5.8
December	3.9
	100.0%

Fantastic Manufacturing, Inc.
EXHIBIT 3 • Balance Sheet (in thousands of dollars)

	January 31, 1979	*January 31, 1980*	*April 30, 1980*	*July 31, 1980*
Assets				
Cash	$ 3	$ 1	$ 1	$ 1
Accounts receivable	387	2,045	3,898	4,568
Due from affiliates	0	160	70	317
Collateral on letters of credit	97	83	171	249
Inventory	928	2,092	2,761	1,536
Inventory in transit	478	2,690	1,414	1,864
Prepaid expenses	26	78	155	112
Insurance claims receivable	0	0	0	756
Income tax refund receivable	0	0	0	134
Note receivable	0	0	0	53
Total current assets	1,919	7,149	8,470	9,590
Net property and equipment	384	241	402	614
Deposits	0	57	65	61
Total assets	$2,303	$7,447	$8,937	$10,265
Liabilities and Shareholders' Equity				
Accounts payable	$ 294	$ 613	$ 774	$ 628
Bank overdraft	0	312	445	51
Due to banks:				
Receivables financing	252	2,046	2,682	4,493
Inventory financing	1,127	3,531	3,518	1,716
Other	0	100	100	0
Current portion of long-term debt	22	31	44	74
Due to affiliates and shareholders	43	533	719	1,161
Taxes payable	8	23	85	891
Total current liabilities	1,746	7,189	8,367	9,014
Long-term debt	360	36	53	43
Notes payable, shareholders	85	0	0	0
Total liabilities	2,191	7,225	8,420	9,057
Shareholders' equity[a]	1	1	1	1
Retained earnings	111	221	516	1,207
Net worth	112	222	517	1,208
Total liabilities and shareholders' equity	$2,303	$7,447	$8,937	$10,265

[a]Common stock, $5 par; authorized, issued, and outstanding, 100 shares.

Fantastic Manufacturing, Inc.
EXHIBIT 4 • Summary of Financing Arrangements

Lender	Amount	Use	Rate	Collateral
Congress Financial Corp.	Varied	Direct loan on eligible accounts receivable	Prime + 6%	All accounts receivable Personal guarantees Deposits by stockholders
Standard Chartered	$6 million	Letters of credit Banker's acceptances ($4.5 million limit)	Prime + 1½% Banker's acceptances + 2%	All inventory and personal guarantees Deposits by stockholders Partial guarantee by Congress Financial 10% deposit on L/Cs
Capital Bank	$1 million	Letters of credit	Prime + 1½%	Unsecured

Fantastic Manufacturing, Inc.
EXHIBIT 5 • Recent Prime and Banker's Acceptance Rates

Year/ Quarter	Average Prime Rate	Banker's Acceptance, Annual Average Rate (90 days)
1978		
1	8.0%	6.8%
2	8.5	7.3
3	9.5	8.2
4	10.5	10.1
1979		
1	11.0	10.1
2	11.5	9.9
3	12.6	10.1
4	14.9	13.4
1980		
1	17.6	14.9
2	16.0	11.8
3	11.8	9.9

Fantastic Manufacturing, Inc.
EXHIBIT 6 • Recent Exchange Rates

Hong Kong Dollars (HK$) per U.S. Dollar (US$)

March 31, 1978	4.6202	February 6, 1980	4.8616
June 30	4.6505	February 13	4.8668
July 31	4.6396	February 20	4.9221
August 30	4.7102	February 27	4.9421
December 29	4.7869	March 26	5.0751
March 30, 1979	4.9927	March 30	4.9059
June 29	5.0690	May 28	4.8898
July 26	5.1814	June 9	4.9179
September 28	4.9784	June 30	4.9300
October 17	4.9468	July 30	4.9564
December 31	4.9516	August 27	4.9481
January 30, 1980	4.8011	September 29	4.9916

New Taiwan Dollars (NT$) per U.S. Dollar (US$)[a]

June 18, 1980	36.1312	September 3, 1980	35.8680
July 2	35.9703	September 17	36.0711
July 16	36.0590	October 1	35.9891
July 30	35.5765	October 8	36.0685
August 6	35.5158	October 13	36.0000

[a]In July 1978, the NT$ was allowed to float around its fixed exchange rate of NT$38=US$1.

Source: National Westminster Bank.

Alfred Brooks Menswear, Limited

In early February 1989, Harry Lagerfeld, treasurer of Alfred Brooks Menswear, Limited (ABM), was preparing for an introductory meeting with an account manager from the Confederation Bank. ABM had been dealing for several years with the Metropolitan Bank, but when Mr. Lagerfeld told Metropolitan about ABM's plans for a large expansion over the next year, he met with a noncommittal response. Mr. Lagerfeld was surprised at Metropolitan's hesitancy and believed the time was appropriate to reassess ABM's banking relationship.

Up to now, ABM's products had largely been produced and sold in Canada. In the past year, however, Alfred Brooks had personally spearheaded a concerted selling effort to Sutton's, a large national department store in the United States, that had led to a major order. The order would cause fiscal 1989 sales to increase 80 percent over the sales for fiscal 1988, and Mr. Lagerfeld knew that additional working capital would be needed to fund this increase in sales.

At the same time, Mr. Lagerfeld and the company buyer were nearing completion of an agreement with a Hong Kong supplier, Leung Manufacturing, for the contract production of a new line of suits. Preliminary manufacturing of "unfinished" suits was to take place in Hong Kong before shipment to Toronto for "finishing." ABM had purchased fabric from abroad in the past, but in order to meet the tight cost targets on this new order, ABM had been forced to follow the strategy of other North American garment manufacturers and source more value-added production from Asia. By importing the clothing in "unfinished" form, ABM would minimize punitive duties and be able to claim Canadian content in the garments subsequently exported to the United States. The rule-of-origin interpretation for men's suits required that 50 percent of the cost be Canadian value added.

This case was prepared by Professor Jim Hatch of the Western Business School. Copyright 1989, The University of Western Ontario.

The Clothing Industry

Menswear was a major segment within the clothing-manufacturing industry, and suits/sport coats made up 12 percent of the menswear share of wardrobe dollars. Menswear had enjoyed reasonably healthy growth in the 1980s as the numbers of men in their 30s and 40s, who were the prime suit purchasers, increased. At the same time, imports took on an increasing share of the market, as can be seen in Exhibit 1.

Competition within the suit/jacket manufacturer's segment was intense in both Canada and the United States. The industry depended heavily on sales of branded and private-label menswear to discounters, general merchandise stores (Sears, Ward's Sutton's), department stores, and men's specialty retailers. Additionally, a few manufacturers had set up their own retail outlets.

In 1987, the United States and Canada signed a comprehensive Free Trade Agreement (FTA). The clothing-manufacturing industry had historically received a high degree of government protection in both countries because of the significant employment the industry generated. Government policies included duties and taxes, import quotas, and subsidies. As a result of the FTA, the duties on domestically produced clothing traded across the border were to be reduced. The duty reduction would not be applied to clothing manufactured abroad and imported into Canada or the United States for reexport, however, unless the finished garments had a significant domestic value-added component (minimum of 50 percent content). The present U.S. duty on men's suits was 77.2 cents/kilogram plus 20 percent, and it was to be reduced to zero over a 10-year period in 10 equal reductions of 10 percent.

Mr. Lagerfeld was concerned about the impact of the Free Trade Agreement. Although ABM would benefit under the FTA through lower duties on cross-border shipments of Canadian-made garments into the United States, Mr. Lagerfeld worried that competing U.S. manufacturers who possessed greater resources would soon be making significant inroads into the Canadian market. The American competitors were approximately 20 times the size of ABM in terms of sales.

Alfred Brooks Menswear Company Background

Established in 1978 by Alfred Brooks, ABM manufactured men's suits and jackets for wholesale distribution in Canada; a small portion of ABM products were wholesaled in the United States and Italy. Alfred Brooks, now 55, had started work as a tailor when he was 15 and had spent his life in the industry. Before starting ABM with the proceeds of an inheritance, he had worked for eight years as the general manager of a major Canadian men's clothier.

Alfred Brooks acted as chairman and president of the company. The senior management group included Ben Bulmer, who was the marketing manager, Denham Crawford, who was operations manager, and Harry Lagerfeld, who acted as treasurer. All three senior managers, who had varied backgrounds in the industry prior to joining the company, had been with ABM since its inception. Alfred Brooks had designed generous compensation packages for each of his senior managers to keep them motivated and loyal to the company.

ABM employed 25 full-time employees—4 managers (including Mr. Brooks), 2 office support staff, 2 buyers, 2 designers, 5 pattern makers/cutters, 3 sales people, 2 shippers, and 5 warehouse workers/inspectors. Garments were manufactured by casual employees, primarily new immigrants to Canada, who were paid on a piecework basis. Anywhere from 10 to 200 such workers were employed at any particular time. These workers were not unionized.

Manufacturing and Warehousing Facilities

ABM, located in Toronto's Spadina garment district, operated out of premises rented under a 15-year lease and was into the second year of the first five-year term with two renewal options remaining. ABM's administrative, selling, manufacturing, and warehousing operations were all located at the leased Spadina facility, although the company occasionally rented temporary warehousing space when needed.

Suit Design and Development

Alfred Brooks personally supervised all aspects of suit/jacket design and development. The preliminary design process was spearheaded by two highly experienced designers. Suit patterns were then laid out by pattern makers who were hired on free-lance contracts. Cloth bolts were cut in substantial quantities, and the cloth pieces were then sewn together by seamsters working on a piecework basis. ABM occasionally contracted some manufacturing to other Toronto clothiers.

In Alfred Brook's opinion, ABM had cultivated a quality reputation. ABM was careful about the materials it chose and picked classic patterns and colors in fabrics with a lasting feel. Mr. Brooks instinctively steered away from faddish colors or finishes. ABM produced sophisticated-looking end products with much handwork involved in the sewing, assembly, and pressing of the suit. As a result, ABM's finished product resembled European-styled suits more than American.

Markets

Over the years, Alfred Brooks had developed a good sense of who wore his suits and jackets. In his opinion, ABM's target customer was a white-collar male who wanted top-of-the-line quality but at reasonable prices. ABM's suits typically retailed in the $250-to-$300 price range, which was below the top-end quality suits at $400 plus (Holt Renfrew, Harry Rosen), but above the mass-market suits in the $150-to-$200 range (Tip Top, Moores).

ABM sold most of its suits to a client list of 48 large Canadian retail department stores and menswear chains, but roughly 10 percent of annual sales were to a mix of 11 retailers in the United States. ABM also sold a small number of suits (less than 1 percent of sales) to an Italian retailer who had been a customer for several years, and Mr. Brooks was anxious to expand his sales to other Italian retailers.

Financing and Performance

Mr. Lagerfeld provided the bank with a monthly list of accounts receivables outstanding (Exhibit 2) and a listing of the inventory on hand. Both were pledged as security for the company's loans, but Mr. Lagerfeld was annoyed that the bank excluded accounts receivable from American and Italian retailers when calculating the amount of funds available to ABM. Accounts receivable in the United States (and a few in Canada) were protected with insurance from American Credit Indemnity (ACI).

ACI was a commercial-credit insurer that established credit limits for an approved list of accounts and insured accounts receivable up to that limit. The insurance fee charged was based on the Dunn and Bradstreet ratings for the buyer firms. Although ABM had never had to make a claim under its policy, Mr. Lagerfeld had heard that obtaining a claim was difficult in certain circumstances. The insurance did not apply to trade disputes, and it carried a $100,000 deductible.

All ABM sales were made on an open-account basis. Most invoices stated terms of 2 percent, 10, net-30 days, although some of ABM's retailers stretched these terms. The large Canadian clients typically took between 45 and 60 days to pay, and ABM extended some terms up to 90 days. Additional discount terms were selectively offered to ABM's large customers. Typically, a discount/warehousing allowance ranging from 2 to 6 percent, depending on the size of the client, was offered and given in exchange for prompt payment (within 10 days). Discounts were not deducted from the monthly accounts-receivable listing; they were allowed only when payment was received. Returns were not allowed, except under special agreement.

Expansion: The Big Order

Late in 1988, Ben Bulmer of ABM had visited the menswear buyer for Sutton's in Dallas to show him the new "swatch books" (fabric samples) for the upcoming 1989 fall season. Sutton's was a potentially important account. It was a very profitable, large, national department store with over 1,000 branches and sales exceeding $9 billion. One of the company's key product lines was clothing.

Sutton's had always received positive customer feedback about the Alfred Brooks line of suits. In particular, its American clientele liked the distinctive European-style cuts of the Alfred Brooks suits together with their reasonable prices. ABM management thought that, with a little hard sell, it might be able to get Sutton's to double its previous year's purchases of C$800,000.

On Friday, February 3, 1989, ABM received the purchase order: Sutton's total order would amount to 71,130 suits at US$137.50 each for a total sale price of US$9,780,375. The exchange rate that day was C$1.1858/US$1.00, which worked out to a total order of C$11,597,568, ten times ABM Management's optimistic expectations. The order was denominated in U.S. dollars.

In February 1989, the prime interest rate charged by Canadian financial institutions was set at 12.75 percent. The prime rate in the United States was 11 percent, while the Confederation Bank set a base rate on U.S.-dollar loans of 11.5 percent. Canadian prime rates had increased from the levels of late 1987, when the rate had been set at 9.75 percent, and further increases in the prime rate were expected, as the Bank of Canada continued fighting inflation (which was exceeding 5 percent) through increases in the Bank of Canada rate. This made-in-Canada interest-rate strategy continued to keep the Canadian dollar strong relative to the U.S. dollar in spite of a worsening Canadian balance of payments. The U.S. dollar was currently trading at C$1.1858. The U.S. dollar had weakened steadily since 1987, at which time it was trading at approximately C$1.3200. During the past 12 months, the value of the U.S. dollar, quite erratic relative to the Canadian dollar, had fluctuated between C$1.2400 and C$1.1700. The forward rate for Canadian dollars for three months was $1.1883; for six months, $1.1940; and for one year, $1.2032.

The purchase order stated that 15,000 suits were to be delivered to specified U.S. warehouses on the 15th of July, August, September, and October and 11,130 suits on the 15th of November. The order specified quantities by fabrics, colors, and sizes. The agreed terms of sale were 60

---

* "Swatch books" were similar to catalogues and indicated different fabric textures, finishes, patterns, and colors.

days with an offered discount of 6 percent and 10 percent E.O.M. (end of month). There was no provision for returns, but Sutton's reserved the right to refuse shipments if the quality did not match the samples. No back orders or substitutions were allowed. Freight and duties were to be paid FOB to the specified warehouse by ABM.

The Sutton's order, taken together with the orders already on hand from other retailers, would mean a huge increase in sales from C$20.9 million in 1988 to C$37.3 million in 1989. Mr. Lagerfeld estimated that monthly sales would be as shown in Exhibit 3.

Financial Implications

Mr. Lagerfeld knew that ABM would require financial assistance to meet the cash-flow demands of the new order. In an attempt to quantify the needs, he drew up the annual financial statement forecasts and monthly cash-flow forecasts in Exhibit 4. Because banks typically loan against only a portion of inventories and account receivable, called margining, he drew up the schedule in Exhibit 5, which indicates the monthly margin position.

Key Suppliers

ABM's suppliers of fabric (primarily bolts of wool knit cloth), buttons, zippers, and thread were Canadian. Raw materials were purchased on an open-account basis. Terms varied from 2 percent, 10, net-30 to 180-day terms extended by one supplier. Ninety percent of ABM's accounts payable were owed to trade accounts, with the remaining 10 percent being other payables such as vacation pay. ABM maintained good relationships with trade creditors and kept payments in line with the terms. A schedule of outstanding accounts payable can be found in Exhibit 6.

In order to meet the cost targets for the order, the fabric and preliminary manufacturing for the Sutton's sale would be sourced from Leung Manufacturing in Hong Kong. ABM planned a gross margin of C$30 per suit, which it had based on a US$43 per-suit raw material and labor (cutting and preliminary assembly) component from Hong Kong. The unfinished suits would then be shipped to Canada for finishing: pressing, sewing on zippers, belt loops, buttonholes and buttons, and the final tailoring of pleats and pockets.

The fixed-price contract for the Hong Kong production was denominated in U.S. dollars. It specified delivery to Canada in five tranches of 15,000 suits on the 1st of May, June, July, August, and September. ABM had ordered a larger number of unfinished suits than needed for the Sutton's order and planned to sell the excess suits in Canada. Leung Manufacturing was responsible for delivering the unfinished suits to dockside in

Hong Kong. The costs of freight, insurance, and duty were to be paid by ABM.

Leung Manufacturing had been suggested to Alfred Brooks by a close friend who owned a women's outerwear manufacturing company and had used Leung previously. Mr. Brooks had made some independent inquiries and discovered that Leung had been managed by two generations of the Leung family since its inception in 1974. Annual sales were in the US$50 million range, and Leung had always been profitable.

Mr. Leung had never heard of ABM and wanted some assurance of ABM's ability to pay before he would set the production in motion. Moreover, Leung wanted to be paid within 30 days of delivery, and production would not start until the method of payment was confirmed.

Decision

ABM's financial statements for the fiscal year ending November 30, 1988, had just been received from the accountants and are shown in Exhibit 7. Mr. Lagerfeld was proud of the rebound in profitability from the depressed levels of 1987, when an aggressive effort to expand in the United States with low introductory prices had significantly reduced overall gross margin. He knew that ABM performed well in comparison with the industry, and he had put together some key industry averages (shown in Exhibit 8).

ABM had been a Metropolitan Bank client since its inception. Mr. Lagerfeld knew that ABM lacked sufficient working capital, and he wanted an expansion in its operating loan to help accommodate increased sales. Mr. Lagerfeld estimated that ABM would require an increase in its operating-loan ceiling from $8,250,000 to $12,000,000 in order to finance its expanded production and sales resulting from the Sutton's order. Mr. Lagerfeld hoped that the Confederation Bank would react more positively than Metropolitan Bank had. He had also arranged a meeting with a representative from Irving Trust.

Alfred Brooks Menswear, Limited

EXHIBIT 1 • Canadian Garment Shipments, 1981–1985
(thousands of garments)

	1981	*1982*	*1983*	*1984*	*1985*
Domestic	372,876	336,112	338,500	339,724	338,706
Less: Exports	4,383	4,606	4,426	4,998	5,137
Net domestic	368,493	331,506	334,074	334,726	333,569
Plus: Imports	165,489	166,402	202,453	237,277	247,539
Total Canadian market	533,982	497,908	536,527	572,003	581,108
Imports/Total	31.0%	33.4%	37.7%	41.5%	42.6%

Source: Government of Canada Report on Apparent Markets for Textiles and Clothing, *Financial Post*, April 20, 1987.

Alfred Brooks Menswear, Limited

EXHIBIT 2 • Accounts Receivable as of January 31, 1989
(in thousands of Canadian dollars)

	Days Outstanding				
	0–30	*31–60*	*61–90*	*Over 90*	*Total*
Canada					
Large diversified clothing retailer	C$ 144	C$ 580	C$ 241	—	C$ 965
Large national department store	—	222	395	—	615
Large national department store	—	355	—	—	355
Regional department store	—	—	292	—	292
Large men's clothing chain	—	145	—	—	145
Other retailers	62	175	220	$ 201	658
Subtotal	206	1,477	1,148	201	3,032
United States					
Sutton's	—	145	—	—	145
Northeast department store	125	—	—	—	125
Midwest department store	—	—	60	—	60
Other retailers	—	65	39	43	147
Subtotal	125	210	99	43	477
Italy					
Northern menswear chain	—	58	—	—	58
Total	$ 331	$1,745	$1,247	$ 244	$3,567

Alfred Brooks Menswear, Limited
EXHIBIT 3 • Monthly Sales December 1988–November 1989
(thousands of Canadian dollars)

Month	Sales	Month	Sales
Dec. 1988	C$2,993	June	C$2,742
Jan. 1989	1,292	July	3,728
February	2,393	August	5,903
March	1,860	September	5,644
April	308	October	4,547
May	512	November	5,378
		Total	C$37,300

Alfred Brooks Menswear, Limited
EXHIBIT 4 • Financial Statement Forecast as of November 30, 1989
(in thousands of Canadian dollars)

Assets	
Accounts receivable	C$ 9,925
Directors' advances	86
Inventory	4,655
Deposits	2
Prepaid expenses	55
Total current assets	14,723
Net fixed assets	214
Total assets	C$14,937
Liabilities and Shareholders' Equity	
Bank loans	C$ 6,443
Account payable	2,596
Income taxes payable	995
Total current liabilities	10,034
Shareholder loan	1,487
Total liabilities	C$11,521
Capital stock	C$ 339
Retained earnings	3,077
Total shareholders' equity	3,416
Total liabilities and shareholders' equity	C$14,937

Forecasted Income Statement for the Year Ending November 30, 1989
(in thousands of Canadian dollars)

Sales	C$37,300	
Cost of goods sold		
Beginning inventory	(4,558)	
Purchase and labor	(30,459)	
Available for sale	35,017	
Ending inventory	(4,655)	
	30,362	
Gross profit	6,938	
Expenses		
Selling and administrative	(3,240)	
Interest	(1,239)	
Depreciation	(61)	
Total expenses	(4,540)	
Earnings before taxes		2,398
Taxes		(995)
Net income		C$1,403

EXHIBIT 4 *continued* • Sutton Order Monthly Cash Budget for December 1988–November 1989 (thousands of Canadian dollars)

	Dec.	Jan.	Feb.	Mar.	Apr.	May
Sales						
Sutton's[a]	0	0	0	0	0	0
Other	C$2,993	C$1,292	C$2,393	C$1,860	C$ 308	C$ 512
Total sales	2,993	1,292	2,393	1,860	308	512
Opening-loan balance	(3,901)	(4,310)	(4,709)	(4,010)	(5,235)	(5,507)
Cash inflows						
Collections[b]						
Sutton's	0	0	0	0	0	0
Other	2,539	2,634	2,993	1,292	2,393	1,860
Total available	C$2,539	C$2,634	C$2,993	C$1,292	C$2,393	C$1,860
Cash Outflows						
Leung purchase[c]	0	0	0	0	0	0
Labor	C$ 530	C$ 530	C$ 530	C$ 530	C$ 530	C$ 530
Material	2,082	2,163	1,371	1,641	1,786	2,580
Administration and selling	270	270	270	270	270	270
Interest: Al Brooks[d]	17	17	17	17	17	17
Taxes	0	0	61	0	0	0
Total outflows	2,899	2,980	2,249	2,458	2,603	3,397
Inflows less outflows	(4,261)	(4,656)	(3,965)	(5,176)	(5,445)	(7,044)
Loan interest	(49)	(53)	(45)	(59)	(62)	(81)
Ending net inflow	(C$4,310)	(C$4,709)	(C$4,010)	(C$5,235)	(C$5,507)	(C$7,125)

Assumption:

[a] Exchange rate = C$1.1858/US$1.00.

[b] Paid in 60 days.

[c] Paid in 30 days.

[d] Interest at prime rate (12.75 percent) plus 1 percent.

	Jun.	Jul.	Aug.	Sept.	Oct.	Nov.	Total
	0	2,446	2,446	2,446	2,446	1,814	11,598
	C$2,742	C$ 1,282	C$ 3,457	C$ 3,198	C$ 2,101	C$ 3,564	C$25,702
	2,742	3,728	5,903	5,644	4,547	5,378	37,300
	(7,125)	(9,260)	(11,769)	(12,076)	(11,978)	(9,347)	−3,901
	0	0	0	2,446	2,446	2,446	7,338
	308	512	2,742	1,282	3,457	3,198	25,210
	C$ 308	C$ 512	C$ 2,742	C$ 3,728	C$ 5,903	C$ 5,644	C$32,548
	765	765	765	765	765	0	3,825
	C$ 530	C$ 530	C$ 530	C$ 530	C$ 530	C$ 530	C$ 6,360
	756	1,306	1,331	1,913	1,585	1,851	20,365
	270	270	270	270	270	270	3,240
	17	17	17	17	17	17	204
	0	0	0	0	0	0	61
	2,338	2,888	2,913	3,495	3,167	2,668	34,055
	(9,155)	(11,636)	(11,940)	(11,843)	(9,242)	(6,371)	(1,035)
	(105)	(133)	(136)	(135)	(105)	(72)	
	(C$9,260)	(C$11,769)	(C$12,076)	(C$11,978)	(C$ 9,347)	(C$ 6,443)	(C$ 6,443)

Alfred Brooks Menswear, Limited

EXHIBIT 5 • Loan Margin Calculation for December 1988–November 1989 (in thousands of Canadian dollars)

	Dec.	*Jan.*	*Feb.*	*Mar.*	*Apr.*
Accounts receivable	C$5,627	C$4,285	C$3,685	C$4,253	C$2,168
Inventory	4,734	6,375	6,328	6,985	9,051
Margin[a]	6,587	6,401	5,928	6,682	6,152
Operating loans	(4,310)	(4,709)	(4,010)	(5,235)	(5,507)
Surplus (deficit)	C$2,277	C$1,692	C$1,918	C$1,447	C$ 645

Assumptions:
[a]Accounts receivable @ 75 percent; inventory @ 50 percent.

May	Jun.	Jul.	Aug.	Sept.	Oct.	Nov.
C$ 820	C$3,254	C$6,470	$9,631	$11,547	$10,191	$9,925
11,744	11,563	11,129	8,950	7,564	6,743	4,746
6,487	8,222	10,417	11,698	12,442	11,015	9,817
(7,125)	(9,260)	(11,769)	(12,076)	(11,978)	(9,347)	(6,443)
(C$ 638)	(C$1,038)	(C$1,352)	(C$ 378)	C$ 464	$ 1,668	$ 3,374

Alfred Brooks Menswear, Limited
EXHIBIT 6 • Accounts Payable as of January 31, 1989
(in thousands of Canadian dollars)

Supplier (month of invoice)

Textile Supplies, Inc.	C$ 195
Canadian Worsted Knit Products, Ltd. (Dec/88)	262
Texfab Manufacturers, Ltd. (Nov/88)	542
Toronto Garment Centre, Inc. (Oct/88)	606
Sundry payables	217
Total	C$1,605

Alfred Brooks Menswear, Limited
EXHIBIT 7 • Financial Statements

AUDITORS' REPORT

We have examined the balance sheet of Alfred Brooks Menswear (Canada) Ltd. as at November 30, 1988, and the statements of income and retained earnings for the year then ended. Our examination was made in accordance with generally accepted auditing standards, and accordingly included such tests and other procedures as we considered necessary in the circumstances.

Waterhouse Ross
Chartered Accounts

Toronto, Ontario
January 29, 1989

continued

EXHIBIT 7 *continued* • Balance Sheet as of November 30, 1988 (in thousands of Canadian dollars)

	1985	*1986*	*1987*	*1988*
Assets				
Current assets				
Accounts receivable	C$3,780	C$4,079	C$ 7,860	C$ 5,173
Loans receivable, director	40	7	55	86
Inventory (note 2)	2,762	3,646	4,139	4,558
Deposits	5	2	2	2
Prepaid expenses	21	44	39	55
Income taxes refundable	0	0	97	0
Total current assets	6,608	7,778	12,192	9,874
Net fixed assets (note 3)	275	168	118	110
Total assets	C$6,718	C$7,896	C$12,360	C$10,149
Liabilities and Shareholders' Equity				
Liabilities				
Current liabilities				
Bank Loan (note 4)	C$1,518	C$2,638	C$ 6,834	C$ 3,901
Accounts payable	2,395	1,980	2,339	2,687
Income taxes payable	61	96	0	61
Total current liabilities	3,974	4,714	9,173	6,649
Long-term debt (note 5)	1,487	1,487	1,487	1,487
Total liabilities	5,461	6,201	10,660	8,136
Shareholders' equity				
Capital stock	339	339	339	339
Retained earnings	918	1,356	1,361	1,674
Total shareholders' equity	1,257	1,695	1,700	2,013
Total liabilities and shareholders' equity	C$6,718	C$7,896	C$12,360	C$10,149

EXHIBIT 7 *continued* • Income Statement for the Year Ended November 30, 1988
(in thousands of Canadian dollars)

	1985	1986	1987	1988
Sales	C$18,144	C$18,763	C$21,570	C$20,965
Cost of sales				
Inventory, beginning year	(901)	(2,762)	(3,644)	(4,139)
Purchases	(12,831)	(12,315)	(13,985)	(13,249)
Labor	(4,013)	(4,195)	(4,808)	(4,151)
Styling and designing	(233)	(35)	(74)	(68)
	(17,978)	(19,307)	(22,511)	(21,607)
Inventory, end of year	2,762	3,644	4,139	4,558
Total cost of sales	(15,216)	(15,663)	(18,372)	(17,049)
Gross profit	2,928	3,100	3,198	3,916
Expenses				
Selling (note 6)	(1,015)	(1,050)	(1,314)	(1,400)
Administrative (note 6)	(780)	(785)	(965)	(1,193)
Depreciation and amortization	(28)	(31)	(38)	(61)
Interest	(544)	(687)	(873)	(873)
Total expenses	2,367	2,553	3,190	3,527
Income before income taxes	561	547	6	388
Income taxes	(115)	(109)	(1)	(75)
Net income	C$ 446	C$ 438	C$ 5	C$ 313

EXHIBIT 7 *continued* • **Notes to Financial Statements as of November 30, 1988**

1. *Accounting Policies*
   Inventory
   Inventory is valued at the lower of cost (first-in, first-out basis) and net realizable value.

   Depreciation and amortization
   The company depreciates its fixed assets by the declining-balance method at the following rates per annum:

Machinery and equipment	20%
Furniture and fixtures	20
Truck	30
Computer equipment	30%

   Leasehold improvements are amortized by the straight-line method over the term of the lease for a period of 5 years.

2. *Inventory*
   Inventory consists of the following:

	1987	1988
Raw materials	C$ 628,127	C$2,069,144
Work in process	937,272	491,136
Finished goods	1,790,542	1,435,504
Goods in transit	1,201,631	143,462
Total inventory	C$4,557,572	C$4,139,246

3. *Fixed Assets*

	Cost	Accumulative Depreciation	Net 1987	Net 1988
Machinery and equipment	C$140,784	C$ 51,066	C$ 64,448	C$ 89,718
Furniture and fixtures	91,410	29,564	25,995	61,846
Truck	15,954	4,786	15,954	11,168
Computer	81,202	41,730	24,037	39,472
Leasehold improvements	120,050	47,383	37,670	72,667
Total fixed assets	C$449,400	C$174,529	C$274,871	C$168,104

EXHIBIT 7 *continued* • **Notes to Financial Statements as of November 30, 1988**

4. *Bank Loan*

Bank loans are secured by a registered general security agreement covering accounts receivable and inventory to the extent of C$8,250,000, and by the issuance of a C$5,500,000 debenture, which provides for a fixed and floating charge on all assets of the company.

5. *Long-Term Debt*

Long-term debt is payable to the shareholder, bearing interest at bank prime plus 1 percent per annum with no specific terms of repayment.

6. *Selling and Administrative Expenses*

Selling	1987	1988
Delivery, freight, shipping	C$ 633,465	C$ 731,564
Rent/warehousing	157,518	227,146
Travel/entertainment/promotion	523,480	441,059
Total selling expenses	C$1,314,463	C$1,399,769
Administrative		
Bad debts	C$ 29,419	C$ 33,190
Charitable donations	34,965	5,087
Computer	46,001	55,353
Insurance	89,550	68,063
Management salaries	185,644	208,845
Professional fees	39,831	113,540
Rent	7,956	45,966
Repairs and maintenance	43,920	90,852
Salaries	353,991	400,981
Taxes	63,535	67,538
Telephone	69,882	103,391
Total administrative expenses	C$ 964,694	C$1,192,806

Alfred Brooks Menswear, Limited
EXHIBIT 8 • Key Industry Ratios: Men's and Boys' Clothing
(asset size = US$1–10 million)

	Upper Quartile	Median	Lower Quartile
Gross margin		25.8%	
Operaing expenses		19.5	
Profit before taxes		5.2	
Current ratio	220%	190%	150%
Quick ratio	160%	90%	60%
Days receivable	33 days	51 days	83 days
Days inventory	39	91	122
Days payable	13 days	25 days	36 days
Sales/Working capital	290%	620%	100%
Earnings before interest and taxes/Interest	930	300	120
Debt/Equity	80	150	240
Profit before taxes/Equity	42.6	15.3	2.5
Sales/Assets	310%	200%	140%

Source: Robert Morris Associates, 1988.

Mushrooms Division (A)

Introduction

Dick Burrell, Vice President–Finance of R. G. Barry Corporation, looked at the memo he had received that morning from Barry's president, Gordon Zacks, asking for revised projections reflecting the new plan for the Mushrooms line. The day before, at the executive committee meeting, Mr. Burrell, Mr. Zacks, and the other committee members had been presented with test-market results for their new Mushrooms brand of women's shoes. Barry had recently changed its marketing strategy for Mushrooms in several markets to emphasize saturation television advertising. The television campaigns had been more successful than expected, and revised sales estimates (shown in Exhibit 1), called for doubling 1978 sales from the previous plan. The marketing manager of Mushrooms and his staff were quite confident the new strategy would succeed. The Mushrooms division manager supported the proposed changes.

Before actually accepting the new strategy, Mr. Zacks wanted to look at revised, detailed financial forecasts for the division. He had asked Mr. Burrell to make forecasts for Mushrooms.

The Footwear Industry

R. G. Barry was a producer of comfort footwear products, including slippers, sandals, moccasins, and after-ski boots. The company was a part of the $11.6 billion (1976 retail sales) footwear business in the United States. Although sales of the major footwear manufacturers had grown steadily over the years, profits were cyclical:

Sales and Profits of Major Footwear Manufacturers (dollars in millions)

	1968	1969	1970	1971	1972	1973	1974	1975	1976
Sales	$2,381	$2,263	$2,908	$3,224	$3,724	$4,149	$4,509	$5,052	$5,975
Net income	97.1	98.0	106.9	115.6	132.2	97.8	142.8	187.6	250.1
Net income/Sales	4.1%	4.3%	3.7%	3.5%	3.6%	2.4%	3.2%	3.7%	4.2%

The variation in profitability of footwear manufacturers was caused in part by the industry's basic cost structure. The major factor was the price of leather hides, the industry's principal raw material. Hide prices fluctuated widely, depending primarily on the rate of domestic cattle slaughter. Because leather typically accounted for approximately 40 percent of the industry's production costs, price changes caused significant changes in profit. In addition, the industry was labor intensive, and footwear manufacturers found it difficult at times to pass on their full labor cost increases to consumers.

The industry was fashion oriented, and the vagaries of such business heightened profit variability. Individual manufacturers experienced significant inventory markdowns when they failed to anticipate changing fashion trends correctly.

In the late 1960s, changes had begun to occur in the domestic footwear industry. Several of the leading manufacturers, in order to offset the effects of the footwear industry's cyclicality, had begun to integrate vertically into footwear retailing and to diversify into nonfootwear businesses.

Nevertheless, by the early 1970s, the industry's domestic cost structure had put it at a competitive disadvantage to foreign manufacturers. Imported footwear products had increased their share of the U.S. market from less than 25 percent of unit sales to over 45 percent. The principal beneficiaries of increased import sales were manufacturers in Taiwan, South Korea, and Spain, all lower-labor-cost producers. Some of the pressure had been reduced in mid-1977, when Taiwan and South Korea signed an orderly marketing agreement to limit their exports of footwear to the United States for the four years ending June 30, 1981. This agreement was coupled with a U.S.-government program designed to increase the mechanization of domestic manufacturers. The import-limitation agreement was expected to aid principally domestic manufacturers of low and moderately priced footwear, that segment previously supplied by Taiwanese and South Korean manufacturers.

By 1976 domestic production and distribution were fragmented and highly competitive. The largest domestic footwear manufacturers were as follows:

Producer	Total Company Sales, 1976 (in millions)	Major Brands
Interco	$1,500	Florsheim
Melville	1,200	Thom McAn
Brown Group	843	Buster Brown
U.S. Shoe	607	Red Cross, Joyce, Pappagallo, and Cobbies

In addition to these manufacturers and foreign imports were many other small domestic producers of specialty footwear products. Barry was classified in this diverse group.

Barry's principal competition for its primary product, washable slippers, came from unbranded merchandise produced by a number of manufacturers. In addition to competition from unbranded products, Daniel Green, Inc., a small, publicly held corporation with 1975 sales of $10.4 million, marketed a high-priced line of branded slippers sold primarily in shoe departments of better department stores.

R. G. Barry Corporation

R. G. Barry Corporation was established in 1945. The company's first product was Shold-a-Shams, removable shoulder pads used to achieve the square–shouldered look in women's fashions. In 1947 Barry introduced Angel Treads, its first line of foam-soled slippers. During the next two decades, Barry added other brands to its line of soft, washable slippers (Dear Foams, Snug Treds, Pim Poms); it also began to produce terry-cloth bath wraps and to manufacture pillows from the slipper operation's scrap.

Until the mid-1960s, Barry management had sought opportunities in whatever businesses seemed to have some profit potential. As a result, Barry's 1966 sales of $12.7 million came from an odd collection of profitable and unprofitable products sold in diverse markets. In the late 1960s, after an evaluation of the business, management redefined the firm's primary objective: to be a leader in every market served or entered. Strategically, Barry would innovate in the design, manufacture, and marketing of leisure footwear, selling most of its products under its own brand names. As a result of this new strategy, management wanted to identify niches in the footwear market neither served by larger manufacturers nor especially attractive to them.

Barry management began to implement this new long-range strategy with a series of acquisitions and divestitures. The pillow business, a user of scrap, was sold, and bath-wrap manufacture was suspended. The space used by those operations was easily converted for use by the still-growing slipper business. Employees were transferred to the other operations with little disturbance, and most continued to work at similar jobs at the same location. Employee reassignment was important to Barry management, which was very concerned with employee satisfaction. An operation would not be sold or suspended without a great deal of thought if such a move involved firing or laying off workers.

R. G. Barry acquired the leading producer of lingerie-matched glamour slippers, Madye's Inc., in 1967. Additional acquisitions to implement the new strategy included Bernardo, a maker of women's high-fashion sandals, in 1969, and Quoddy, a producer of moccasins and outdoor footwear, in 1971. As distribution channels for these products were developed, Barry added manufacturing capacity for its increasing sales. By 1976 Barry sales had grown to $58 million. Profits had grown at a rate of greater than 10 percent for the 10 years ending in 1976.

Mushrooms

In the early 1970s, Gordon Zacks had identified another segment of the footwear market he believed was not being adequately served by larger manufacturers. This market segment was defined as women who valued foot comfort above style, and Mushrooms were designed for their needs. Mr. Zacks believed the key to producing a really comfortable shoe was creating a soft, flexible sole. Barry staff, as well as outside consultants, had looked at materials already in use by other manufacturers and had rejected them. The materials were too heavy to provide real comfort, so inflexible that they restricted walking, or too quickly worn out. A new product was needed.

Barry management looked at a variety of different materials and processes with which to create a new sole. Eventually, polyurethane was chosen because it produced a light, soft, and flexible sole while still providing the desired durability. The sole was finally developed by an outside subcontractor, and in 1974 Barry purchased its first 100,000 pairs of polyurethane soles.

In addition to creating the sole, Barry designed the complete shoe to be comfortable yet fashionable. Low- and high-heeled sandals, clogs, and closed shoes were designed for both the spring and fall seasons. In creating the uppers, management had encouraged designers to avoid using leather and to concentrate on designs that might stay in the line for several years rather than being faddish, single-year products. The uppers were attached to the soles by a subcontractor. The first shoes were sold in test markets to selected department-store accounts under the Mushrooms brand name.

Product design and test marketing continued through 1974 and 1975, and the number of Mushrooms' test-market areas was gradually increased. During this time, the subcontractor that had developed and supplied the

Mushrooms' sole discontinued its plastics operations. Since the proprietary sole was Mushrooms' principal product advantage, Barry decided to purchase the subcontractor's sole-making equipment and produce the soles itself. The machinery was installed in a small, unused portion of one of the Barry slipper plants. Production and attachment of the uppers would continue to be subcontracted.

Sales of the Mushrooms brand in 1976 were $2.38 million.

Market Test

Because Barry did not offer a full line of women's shoes, and because its slipper lines were sold primarily in the notions and hosiery departments of department stores, Barry had experienced some difficulty in securing the desired distribution outlets in large department-store shoe departments. Barry's advertising agency thus suggested a saturation campaign, and in late 1976, Barry decided to evaluate the effect that television advertising would have on Mushrooms' sales. In part, the television campaign was intended to create product demand among consumers so that shoe-department buyers would be encouraged to stock Mushrooms. Barry decided to test the new campaign in two markets, Denver and Miami.

The results of the two advertising campaigns were better than had been expected. The results supported the advertising agency's conclusion that Mushrooms could achieve a 6- to 8-percent share of the market for moderately priced women's footwear during the first year of an intensive advertising campaign, because no one had a product to compete with Mushrooms. Based on these test-market results, the revised sales estimates appearing in Exhibit 1 had been prepared. These estimates reflected both the larger sales from increased advertising and market-share growth over time.

At the same time the advertising campaigns were underway and the results were being evaluated, Barry management had changed the way Mushrooms were produced. Barry had subcontracted production during the product-development stage to avoid brick–and–mortar investments. Problems with subcontractors, however, coupled with the change in expected demand confirmed by the test-market results, encouraged management to assume total responsibility for manufacturing the shoe. This move would ensure both product quality and availability. One additional change was made: the line was expanded to include Mushrooms' styles with leather uppers.

Although present capacity was adequate for current needs, Barry's sole-manufacturing capabilities could not service the anticipated demand. The company would need an additional sole-manufacturing plant and a shoe-assembly plant. By mid-1977 management was investigating possible plant sites and anticipated securing, equipping, and renovating two separate facilities. The estimated cost of the plants was $2.5 million. The two plants were to be leased or purchased using industrial revenue bonds issued by the county where they would be located. The facilities would be depreciated over approximately 20 years on a straight–line basis.

Projections

Working with his staff, as well as with people from the Mushrooms' marketing and operations group, Mr. Burrell had revised estimated operating costs and profits. Cost of goods sold were expected to be 63 percent of gross sales in 1977. As Barry's own production facilities began operations in 1978, cost of goods sold was expected to decline, perhaps to 58 percent. The Mushrooms' product line was expected to have larger sales adjustments and inventory markdowns than other Barry product lines. The adjustment for defective Mushrooms was expected to exceed 10 percent of sales in 1977 and 7½ percent thereafter.

Because Mushrooms were sold to different department-store buyers than other Barry products, a separate sales force was needed. That cost, coupled with the cost of the saturation television advertising, meant that projected selling expenses would be high—19 percent of 1977 gross sales and 15 percent from then on. General and administrative expenses would decline from 15 percent of gross sales the first year to the company average of 10 percent. All these figures were estimates based on the company's past experience in its other businesses.

Sales would follow the pattern shown in Exhibit 2, and accounts-receivable balances were expected to fluctuate as a function of sales. On average, management expected that sales outstanding in accounts receivable would exceed the net-30 credit terms by 30 days. Accounts payable and accruals, current liabilities, would be about 20 days of annual average days' sales.[1] Barry's work in progress usually averaged 25 days of annual average days' sales, and the Mushrooms experience was not expected to be very different. Finished-goods inventory would, of course, rise and fall during the year because of the level production schedule, a feature of Barry's strong commitment to steady employment for its workers. Once Barry's production facilities began operation in 1978, year-end finished-goods inventory was expected to be about 82 days of annual average day's sales, up from the 40 days of annual average days' sales projected for December 1977.

In addition to the Mushrooms' sales and profit projections, Mr. Burrell had made forecasts for funds needs. Mushrooms' planned plant expan-

---

[1] Barry managers used annual average days' sales in forecasting many of their current asset and liability accounts, even though the business was seasonal.

sion would require $2.35 million in 1978 and $150,000 more in 1979. As he forecasted for Mushrooms, Mr. Burrell wanted to include in his analysis a consideration of what might happen if sales actually grew faster than what had been forecasted. What if the projections were wrong? How would that affect R. G. Barry?

Mushrooms Division (A)
EXHIBIT 1 • Sales Projections (in millions)

	1977	*1978*	*1979*	*1980*	*1981*
Original dollar volume	$4.0	$ 6.0	$ 8.0	$10.0	$12.0
Revised dollar volume	$5.0	$12.6	$19.85	$28.9	$42.5
Units	0.6	1.2	1.8	2.5	3.5

Mushrooms Division (A)
EXHIBIT 2 • Projected Monthly Percentage of Total Annual Sales

Monthly Percentage	
January	7.5%
February	7.5
March	15.0
April	7.5
May	2.5
June	20.0
July	10.0
August	7.5
September	5.0
October	5.0
November	7.5
December	5.0
	100.0%

Mushrooms Division (B)

Dick Burrell, Vice President–Finance for R. G. Barry Corporation, looked once again at the memo he had received from Gordy Zachs, Barry's president. He and his staff had almost memorized the memo reproduced in Exhibit 1, as they had made financial forecasts for the Mushrooms Division over the previous few days. They had not yet concerned themselves with the last part of Zachs' request, to determine the effect of Mushrooms on R. G. Barry's financial needs over the next five years. Mr. Burrell also wanted to look at what effect, if any, doubling the sales in the Mushrooms Division would have on the future funds requirements for Barry as a whole. Because Mr. Burrell's job was to assure adequate financing, he was the logical person to make the projections, to present them, and to lay out a course of action for securing whatever funds were required.

The Footwear Industry

R. G. Barry was a producer of comfort footwear products, including slippers, sandals, moccasins, and after-ski boots. The company was a part of the $11.6 billion (1976 retail sales) footwear business in the United States.

Although sales of the major footwear manufacturers had grown steadily over the years, profits were cyclical. The impact on Barry's financial statements can be seen in Exhibits 2 and 3. In addition to the cyclicality of the footwear industry as a whole, which affected Barry to a degree, Barry's own sales were seasonal, as shown in Exhibit 4. As a consequence of this seasonality, Dick Burrell had secured seasonal financing for the company.

Current Situation

Barry's $6-million line of credit, spread evenly among three banks, was intended to finance the company's seasonal working-capital needs. Seasonal needs had been quite predictable. In terms of annual average day's sales, a shorthand measure Barry's staff used to track seasonal needs,[1] Barry's peak need came in October, as seen in Exhibit 5. That was, of course, without the new Mushrooms venture.

While Barry's business had grown rather slowly, it had needed capital. During March 1977, Barry had obtained additional permanent financing from its principal lender, a major insurance company. This insurance company loaned Barry an additional $4 million at 9⅜ percent. While the insurance company had formerly required short-term borrowings to be repaid for 60 days each year, the new covenants shown in Exhibit 6 no longer had this "clean-up" requirement. Barry also expected to pay off $900,000 of notes during 1977 and to lease some $750,000 of computer equipment.

For the $6-million line of credit, the banks charged the prime rate with compensating balances to equal 10 percent of the credit line extended. Presently, the banks did not require those loans to be repaid for any portion of the year. These covenants could, of course, be changed any time Barry sought additional financing.

Exhibit 7 shows the projected funds needed for investments and debt repayments planned by Barry management for the company, not including Mushrooms. The financing arrangements, together with the expected balances for plant and equipment, receivables, and inventory, were used to project the December 31, 1977, Balance Sheet. As Exhibit 8 shows, Barry expected to end 1977 with a comfortable cash position. In addition, the company's projected 1977 peak seasonal borrowing requirement (determined with assumptions shown in Exhibits 4 and 5) was not expected to exceed $3 million, or half of the existing credit line. Of course, more would be needed as sales grew. Exhibit 9 provides forecasted income statements through 1981.

When the additional $4 million in notes had been sold to the insurance company in early 1977, Mr. Burrell had stated that Barry would require no additional permanent financing for the next three years. Now, only a few months after that transaction had been completed, he was not so sure. Barry had already decided to acquire two new production plants,

---

[1] Balances in working-capital accounts were tracked by Barry management in annual average day's sales. They did not reflect the seasonal average day's sales. For example, in Exhibit 5, accounts receivable for October are 100 days of annual average sales of $58 million in 1976. If expressed in days of average September sales (which are 13 percent of the annual sales), accounts receivable would be only 64 days.

and sales growth for Mushrooms was projected to skyrocket. If the plants were financed by industrial revenue bonds, not considered part of long-term financing by the lenders, Mr. Burrell believed Barry might be able to avoid renegotiating the covenants.

Conclusion

As he began to evaluate Barry's financing needs, Mr. Burrell wanted to be prepared to answer several questions about Barry's future with and without the Mushrooms Division:

1. Was the present line-of-credit arrangement adequate to finance peak seasonal working-capital requirements through fiscal 1979? If not, how much should the line be increased?

2. Were the present long-term financing arrangements adequate to support projected growth over the next few years? If not, how much additional permanent financing would be required, and when?

3. If funds were needed, should they be raised through long-term debt or equity?

4. What if the present Mushrooms' sales projections were wrong? Phenomenal sales growth was anticipated over the coming five years. What if sales actually grew at an even faster rate? Mr. Burrell wondered if his plans should include some sort of reserve financing arrangements to meet such a contingency.

Mr. Burrell was sure these questions would be raised at the meeting on the 25th. It was his job to be ready with the answers.

Mushrooms Division (B)
EXHIBIT 1 • Memo Requesting a Presentation of Mushrooms' Projections

---

OFFICE OF THE PRESIDENT

TO: Dick Burrell
FROM: Gordy Zacks
DATE: May 15, 1977
RE: May 25, 1977 meeting

   Please bring your revised Mushrooms' projections to the meeting on the 25th. After presenting them you should be ready to discuss the effect the changes will have on Barry's financial needs over the next 5 years.

Mushrooms Division (B)

EXHIBIT 2 • R. G. Barry Income Statements and Selected Financial-Statement Data
(in thousands, except per-share figures and percentages)

	1967	1968	1969[a]	1970	1971	1972	1973	1974[b]	1975[a]	1976
Ten-Year Comparative Summary of Operations										
Net sales	$ 15,938	$19,404	$24,667	$28,164	$34,123	$39,162	$43,162	$49,615	$52,260	$58,008
Cost of sales	10,642	12,514	16,237	18,222	21,919	25,667	28,621	33,233	34,586	37,666
Gross profit	5,296	6,890	8,430	9,942	12,204	13,495	14,541	16,382	17,674	20,342
Selling, general, and administrative	3,887	5,104	6,672	7,481	9,264	10,012	10,784	12,429	13,735	16,117
Interest expense, net	171	142	337	282	395	549	599	723	639	789
Earnings before income taxes	1,238	1,644	1,421	2,179	2,545	2,934	3,158	3,230	3,300	3,436
Income taxes	522	831	721	1,094	1,271	1,484	1,523	1,589	1,617	1,629
Net earnings	$ 686	$ 813	$ 700	$ 1,085	$ 1,274	$ 1,450	$ 1,635	$ 1,641	$ 1,683	$ 1,807
Financial Summary										
Current assets	$ 5,192	$ 7,200	$10,004	$10,945	$12,810	$16,409	$18,312	$19,495	$19,759	$21,245
Current liabilities	1,922	2,652	5,716	3,652	3,061	3,218	3,909	4,228	3,746	3,790
Net working capital	3,270	4,548	4,288	7,293	9,749	13,191	14,403	15,267	16,013	17,455
Long-term debt	1,616	1,495	1,936	2,179	5,095	7,285	6,970	8,513	8,129	8,640
Stockholders' equity	3,208	4,743	5,356	8,074	9,403	10,865	12,462	13,957	15,634	17,093

Net property, plant, and equipment	1,317	1,466	1,771	1,682	3,343	3,372	3,500	5,743	6,069	6,661
Total assets	6,804	8,950	13,070	13,983	17,654	21,484	23,485	26,842	27,653	29,668
Capital expenditures, net	329	421	639	262	2,043	468	589	2,749	866	1,249
Depreciation and amortization	$ 228	$ 272	$ 334	$ 351	$ 382	$ 439	$ 461	$ 507	$ 540	$ 657
Additional Data										
Earnings per share	$0.41	$0.46	$0.38	$0.53	$0.61	$0.69	$0.78	$0.79	$0.81	$0.88
Market price per share, high	3.00	6.60	8.30	5.50	7.00	8.70	6.30	3.60	3.00	5.90
Market price per share, low	1.30	2.70	4.20	1.90	3.50	5.20	2.10	2.10	2.10	2.60
Book value per share	$1.91	$2.58	$2.91	$3.90	$4.49	$5.18	$5.95	$6.75	$7.54	$8.36
Annual change in net sales (percentage)	25.6%	21.1%	27.1%	14.2%	21.2%	14.8%	10.2%	15.0%	5.3%	11.0%
Annual change in net earnings (percentage)	47.5%	18.5%	(13.9%)	55.0%	17.4%	13.8%	12.8%	0.4%	2.6%	7.4%
Net earnings/Average stockholders' equity	23.9%	20.5%	13.9%	16.2%	14.6%	14.3%	14.0%	12.4%	11.4%	11.0%
Average number of shares outstanding (in thousands)	1,675	1,785	1,839	2,049	2,087	2,096	2,099	2,078	2,069	2,054
Dividends and distributions:										
Cash	$0.02	0.03	0.04	0	0	0	0	0	0	$0.09
Stock	10% and 5-for-4 split	5-for-4 split	5-for-4 split	10%	10% 3-for-2 split	5%	5%	5%	5%	0

---

[a] Fiscal year includes 53 weeks.

[b] Effective in 1974, the company changed its method of valuing a substantial portion of inventory to the last-in, first-out (LIFO) method.

Mushrooms Division (B)
EXHIBIT 3 • R. G. Barry Consolidated Balance Sheets (in thousands)

	December 31, 1975	December 31, 1976
Assets		
Cash and marketable securities	$ 3,031	$ 1,698
Accounts receivable	6,461	7,372
Inventories	9,742	11,822
Other	525	353
Total current assets	19,759	21,245
Property, plant, and equipment	10,029	10,705
Less: Accumulated depreciation	(3,960)	(4,044)
Net property, plant, and equipment	6,069	6,661
Other assets	1,825	1,762
Total assets	$27,653	$29,668
Liabilities and Stockholders' Equity		
Accounts payable	$ 2,235	$ 1,947
Accrued expenses	1,039	1,176
Income taxes	88	278
Current installments of long-term debt	384	389
Total current liabilities	3,746	3,790
Long-term debt	5,289	5,885
Capitalized lease obligations	2,840	2,755
Other	144	145
Total liabilities	12,019	12,575
Stockholders' equity		
Common stock ($1 par value)	2,072	2,043
Paid-in capital in excess of par	6,506	6,506
Retained earnings	7,056	8,544
Total stockholders' equity	15,634	17,093
Total liabilities and stockholders' equity	$27,653	$29,668

Mushrooms Division (B)

EXHIBIT 4 • Projected Monthly Percentage of Total Annual Sales, All R. G.
　　　　　　Barry Divisions *except* Mushrooms, 1978–1981

	Monthly Percentage
January	6%
February	6
March	6
April	6
May	6
June	6
July	6
August	10
September	13
October	18
November	11
December	6
	100%

Mushrooms Division (B)

EXHIBIT 5 • Projected 1978 Monthly Working-Capital Requirements, All R. G. Barry Divisions *except*
　　　　　　Mushrooms (in days of average annual sales)

	Jan.	*Feb.*	*March*	*April*	*May*	*June*	*July*	*Aug.*	*Sept.*	*Oct.*	*Nov.*	*Dec.*
Accounts receivable	38	38	38	38	38	38	35	53	74	100	88	52
Inventory												
Finished goods	49	55	61	67	73	78	84	82	71	49	44	49
Work in progress	25	25	25	25	25	25	25	25	25	25	25	25
Accounts payable	20	20	20	20	20	20	20	20	20	20	20	20

Mushrooms Division (B)

EXHIBIT 6 • R. G. Barry March 1977 Loan Repayment Schedule and Summary of Loan Covenants

The $4-million loan made in March 1977 was payable in annual installments of $225,000 from 1981 through 1986, $440,000 from 1987 through 1991, and $450,000 in 1992. The most restrictive covenants agreed to by Barry in connection with this loan included the following:

1. Consolidated net tangible assets (defined as current assets plus net property, plant, and equipment less capital lease obligations) must exceed 300 percent of senior long-term debt. Industrial revenue bonds (IRBs) would not be considered part of long-term debt for purposes of this covenant. IRB payments were considered property rental payments. Debt-service payments for IRBs could not exceed 2½ percent of consolidated net income.

2. Consolidated net tangible assets must exceed 200 percent of total long-term debt (senior long-term debt plus subordinated debentures).

3. Current assets must exceed 175 percent of current liabilities.

4. Payment of dividends, repurchase of Barry common shares, and other specified transactions must be limited to $1 million plus net income.

5. For at least one consecutive 60-day period during the year, the amount of borrowings made under short-term line-of-credit arrangements must be convertible into long-term debt and still satisfy the covenant described in (1) above.

Mushrooms Division (B)

EXHIBIT 7 • Projected Capital Expenditures and Other Funds Uses, All R. G. Barry Divisions *except* Mushrooms (thousands of dollars)

	1977	*1978*	*1979*	*1980*	*1981*
Capital investment	$1,460	$810	$1,110	$900	$1,000
Long-term debt repayments	415	690	700	705	710

Mushrooms Division (B)

EXHIBIT 8 • Projected Balance Sheet as of December 31, 1977[a] for All R. G. Barry Divisions *except* Mushrooms (in thousands)

Current Assets		Current Liabilities	
Cash	$ 2,605	Accounts payable and accrued expenses	$ 3,820
Accounts receivable	9,850	Accrued taxes	750
Finished-goods inventory	9,250	Total current liabilities[b]	4,570
Work-in-progress and raw-material inventory	4,570	Other	145
Prepaids, etc.	500	Long-term debt[c]	8,570
Total current assets	26,775	Long-term lease obligations	3,505
Property, plant, and equipment	12,165	Total long-term debt	12,075
Less: Accrued depreciation	(4,775)	Common stock	2,050
		Paid-in capital	6,500
Net property, plant, and equipment	7,390	Retained earnings	10,600
Other	1,775	Total stockholders' equity	19,150
Total assets	$35,940	Total liabilities and stockholders' equity	$35,940

[a]Includes Mushrooms' performance through 12/31/76. Mushrooms' performance (and projected performance) for 1977 is not included.

[b]Excludes debt due within 1 year.

[c]Includes $2.5 million of subordinated debentures.

Mushrooms Division (B)

EXHIBIT 9 • Five-Year Profit-and-Loss Projections for All R. G. Barry Divisions *except* Mushrooms

	1977	1978	1979	1980	1981
Sales	$64,737	$73,152	$81,920	$91,697	$104,617
Cost of goods sold	41,290	46,958	52,650	59,015	67,330
Gross profit	23,447	26,194	29,270	32,682	37,287
Selling expense	6,855	7,659	8,585	9,617	10,972
General and administrative expense	7,237	8,176	9,141	10,214	11,653
Divisional profit before corporate expenses	9,355	10,359	11,544	12,851	14,662
Corporate expense[a]	3,665	3,937	4,274	4,577	4,902
Interest expense	862	957	921	896	871
Inventory adjustments	300	350	425	500	575
Other	125	150	175	200	225
Profit before tax	4,403	4,965	5,749	6,678	8,089
Income taxes	2,166	2,443	2,829	3,285	3,979
Net income	$ 2,237	$ 2,522	$ 2,920	$ 3,393	$ 4,110

[a]Includes depreciation of $ 695 $ 755 $ 860 $ 950 $ 1,055

PART
3

Capital Budgeting

Metalcrafters, Inc.

In September 1992, Mark Chen, a new financial analyst at Metalcrafters, Inc., was preparing the analysis of four investments and two contracts that Metalcrafters' budget committee would review at the end of the week. This analysis was the first real assignment he had received from his boss, Dena Brownowski, chief financial officer at Metalcrafters, and he wanted to make a good impression.

The Company

Metalcrafters was founded in the early 1960s by two Korean War buddies who had returned home to Detroit, Michigan after the war and gone to work in the automobile industry. They had seen an opportunity to go into business producing specialized polished and anodized[1] aluminum hardware and molding parts for the auto industry, and Metalcrafters was the result. The plant was located just outside Detroit.

In the late 1960s, the company diversified in an attempt to insulate itself from the cyclicality of the auto industry. By 1992, Metalcrafters was producing parts for aluminum windows, ladders, and industrial lighting fixtures, as well as some consumer products. Of the 800 different parts produced in 1992, over half were for customers outside the auto business, accounting for about 40 percent of total revenues.

Metalcrafters management was known for its conservativism. The company expanded slowly, and large investments were carefully considered. For instance, all capital-investment proposals exceeding $5,000 were submitted to the company's budget committee. The proposal for each investment had to include a description and justification of the investment as well as detailed forecasts for costs and revenues. Ms. Brownowski and her staff had the job of reviewing the proposals and preparing a detailed

---

[1] Anodizing is a process that treats parts electromagnetically to make them corrosion resistant.

financial analysis for each. The budget committee, consisting of the company's four top officers—the president, chief financial officer, and directors of marketing and operations—relied on these analyses in making their decisions.

In September 1992, several requests were on Mr. Chen's desk. Two were for investments in new equipment—replacement of a stamping press and the purchase of an extrusion press. In addition, Ms. Brownowski had asked Mr. Chen to look at two orders for extruded parts to see whether capital-budgeting techniques could be adapted for use in deciding between them. Ordinarily the company would fill both orders, but because it currently lacked the capacity to do so, and new equipment could not be installed in time to meet the contract provisions, the company would have to choose between the orders.

The Stamping Press

Because of rapidly rising repair costs of the old machine and the greatly improved efficiency of new presses, management had decided the time had come to replace an old stamping press. The two options that had been proposed differed primarily in expected life and cost. Both machines could be purchased from the same company. The first, called the SX-65, would cost $60,000 installed and would last 5 years. At the end of its 5-year life, management believed it could be sold for about $5,000. Annual savings of $28,000 were expected from its operation.

The second press, the MD-40, was more durable. It cost $90,000 but would last 10 years. Annual savings were also expected to be $28,000, and at the end of its life, the press could be sold for an estimated $5,000. Regardless of which press management decided to purchase, the old, fully depreciated press could be sold for $1,000.

The Extrusion Press

Metalcrafters' management had been forced to turn down several contracts recently because the company lacked sufficient extrusion capacity. Management had considered two extrusion presses and engaged in considerable debate over the choice. One had a much larger capacity than the other one and a price to match.

A small press was available for $600,000 installed. The press could handle aluminum billets up to 4 inches in diameter, and it would allow Metalcrafters to fill most of the orders it currently turned away. The press was expected to produce annual sales of $750,000 for its 10-year life. Of the revenues, 65 percent would cover labor and materials. An additional 5 percent would be needed to cover marketing and administrative costs, which were typical of extrusion-press operations and would not be incurred if the sales did not materialize. At the end of 10 years, management believed that it could sell the small press for $20,000.

With the larger press, Metalcrafters could accept all the orders that it could not now take, and because the press could accept 8-inch billets, the company could consider expanding by producing larger parts used in consumer products. This press cost $1 million, would also last 10 years, and was expected to result in annual sales of $1.075 million. At the end of its life, management forecast that it could be sold for $45,000.

Some of the sales that were forecast for each of the two new extrusion presses would come from parts that would otherwise have been produced on Metalcrafters' present presses. Management estimated that about $100,000 of sales per year would have been produced without a new press. The old presses were expected to be used for only 7 more years before being scrapped.

The New Parts Orders

Because the company had limited extrusion-press capacity, management had to choose between orders from the Sawmasters and Beck companies. Once a new extrusion press was in place, they would not be confronted with the same problem, particularly if they chose the larger press. However, both Sawmasters and Beck had written in their contracts that capacity had to be in place at the time the contract was accepted. Mr. Chen was not sure that a capital-budgeting approach was the way to choose between these two projects. Neither required new capital.

Beck Electric was one of Metalcrafters' oldest and largest customers, but it had been switching from aluminum to plastic for many of its components. The result had been a decline of 15 percent in orders from Beck during the last two years. Beck urgently needed a new part that Metalcrafters could easily produce. The contract would generate sales of $50,000 each year for three years.

Sawmasters' order was for a special chain-saw part. Sawmasters had never ordered from Metalcrafters before, although it was a customer that Metalcrafters had long courted. The contract would add sales of $30,000 in the first year, $36,000 in the second, and $99,000 in the third and final contract year.

To set up the equipment and train staff to produce the parts for either order would cost $8,000. Cost of materials and labor averaged 65 percent of sales for parts of this type. New expenses associated with administering either of the projects would be 5 percent of sales.

Capital Budgeting

As Mr. Chen prepared to do his analysis, he recalled Ms. Brownowski's comments about the criteria used by the budget committee. Two of the committee members preferred payback; the other two, net present value. The committee was using a 15-percent required after-tax rate of return for all projects.

Mr. Chen had failed to ask Ms. Brownowski how to handle taxes. Currently the marginal tax rate was 34 percent, and depreciation was calculated according to MACRS (modified accelerated cost recovery system) rules passed by the U.S. Congress as part of the 1986 Tax Reform Act. The four presses were classified as 5-year MACRS property and could be depreciated as follows:

MACRS Depreciation Schedule, 5-Year-Life Equipment

Year	Proportion Depreciated
1	20%
2	32
3	19
4	12
5	12
6	5

Ms. Brownowski was on vacation until Friday, the budget committee's meeting day. Mr. Chen was to be ready on her return to brief her on his analysis and recommend which, if any, of the projects should be approved.

Zukowski Meats, Incorporated

Stanley Zukowski, president of Zukowski Meats, Inc., was confused. Sales of the company's Polish meats, kielbasa and ham, which had increased steadily over the previous years, had declined during 1987. Mr. Zukowski's son, Donald, a recent business-school graduate, suggested that his father change the credit terms on these sales to reestablish the family's market position. Mr. Zukowski thought that the idea warranted serious consideration and wanted to make the decision before the onset of the Christmas season in November, three weeks away. However, he was unsure of exactly how to analyze his son's proposal.

Company Background

The Zukowski family had been manufacturing and selling various types of German and Polish meats in the Greenpoint section of Brooklyn, New York, for over 30 years. The family had met with considerable success: their products were excellent and appealed to a wide range of consumers. Sales in 1986 were $20 million on assets of $12 million, as shown in Exhibit 1. The Zukowskis sold their meats through the numerous neighborhood butcher shops in the New York metropolitan area as well as through certain supermarkets. Over the years, their products had found a ready market in Brooklyn among the successive waves of eastern European immigrants who made Greenpoint their first stop in America, as well as the wider markets in Manhattan and Queens. The Zukowskis' products and their levels of profitability in 1991 are shown in Table 1.

Between 1986 and 1991, the company's sales had increased steadily. However, preliminary results for 1992 showed a considerable decline in the growth rates in sales of the company's Polish sausage and hams. Mr. Zukowski believed the major problem was an increase in the supply of these specialty meats. Substantial growth in the Polish population in the

TABLE 1 • Product-Line Sales and Profits, 1991 (in thousands)

	Net Sales	Profit before Tax[a]
German Meats		
Knockwurst	$ 3,700.0	$111.0
Bratwurst	3,000.0	84.0
Polish Meats		
Kielbasa	9,500.0	332.5
Polish ham	3,800.0	133.0
Total	$20,000.0	$660.5

[a]Tax rate of 34 percent expected under the 1986 Tax Reform Act.

metropolitan area, particularly in Greenpoint, had increased the demand for the products enough to encourage new producers to enter the market. Furthermore, these producers were themselves recent immigrants who were able to match the authentic quality of the Zukowski company's meat products. Mr. Zukowski realized that he would have to do something to reclaim his former market share and reestablish the company's dominant position in the market for Polish meats. Little competition had arisen in the market for German sausages, sales of which were relatively stable. Consequently, Mr. Zukowski did not believe that the new credit terms needed to be extended for those products.

Donald Zukowski's Proposal

Historically, the Zukowski company and its competitors had offered credit terms of net 30 days. While many Polish-sausage manufacturers required their accounts to pay on delivery, Zukowski sold primarily to large commercial accounts, for which credit was arranged. A few accounts were required to pay on delivery. An increase to net 45 days on all sales of kielbasa and Polish hams might, therefore, provide a significant competitive edge for the company. Donald had made several points to support his proposal. First, he argued, sales would increase as existing and new customers were attracted by the relaxed credit terms. Second, the change would improve the Zukowski family's competitive position by making the larger competitors realize that the Zukowskis intended to maintain their dominant market position in Polish meat products, while possibly even forcing some of the smaller competitors out of business. And all of this was at no cost and with no risk, Donald pointed out. The company had excess capacity available to meet the anticipated increase in sales. Thus, even if the competition did match the new credit terms, the Zukowskis would at least maintain their current market share with no additional investment. Donald was confident that this strategy would allow the family to recoup

TABLE 2 • Polish Meats—Cost Estimates

Sales (in millions)	Variable Costs/Sales	Fixed Costs/Sales	Profit before Taxes/Sales
$12.0–12.9	70.20%	26.20%	3.60%
$13.0–13.9	70.20	25.90	3.90
$14.0–14.9	70.20	25.65	4.15
$15.0–15.9	70.20	25.30	4.50
$16.0–16.9	70.20	25.10	4.70

the estimated $500,000 in sales lost so far in 1992 and to maintain the products' growth rate at 4 percent per year, the rate at which the Zukowskis currently expected their Polish meat segment to grow.

They made some preliminary cost estimates, shown in Table 2, for increased sales of their Polish meats. With increased sales, the profits were sure to rise.

Stanley Zukowski pondered his son's arguments. Although he respected Donald's ability as an "idea man," he knew his son often did not consider all of the ramifications. For instance, the Zukowskis had experienced almost no bad-debt losses with their existing clientele. However, Mr. Zukowski thought that the proposed relaxation in credit might attract customers who were a little shakier financially than current customers. Bad-debt losses might reach 1 percent of the new sales, he thought. Mr. Zukowski knew also that, for each additional sales dollar generated by the relaxed credit terms, he would have to maintain cash and inventory balances 10 cents greater than the credit he could get from his suppliers. That was in addition to the expected increase in accounts receivable resulting from the credit he would be offering his clients.

These funds would have to come out of the company's planned capital budget, Mr. Zukowski knew, because his lenders were not eager to invest more in the company at this time. The company might, therefore, have to postpone purchases necessary for its planned entry into the lunch-meat market. Mr. Zukowski had planned to make capital expenditures of about $1.5 million per year over the next five years. Roughly one-third of this amount was earmarked for annual routine machinery replacements. The remainder was to have been invested in 1993 in lunch-meat processing and packaging machines. These investments had already undergone financial analysis and had met the company's 12 percent after-tax hurdle rate. Mr. Zukowski thought it only reasonable to argue that any other use to which these funds might be put should also meet that same criterion.

Furthermore, Mr. Zukowski wasn't sure he agreed with Donald that there was no cost associated with using the excess plant capacity. For example, it seemed to him that some cost should be incorporated into the analysis to reflect the fact that increased use of the machinery would speed the need both to replace existing equipment and to expand the plant's capacity over the next five years

Conclusion

Although he had managed to keep the company growing since his father's death, Mr. Zukowski knew that his strength lay in production and marketing rather than in the financial end of the business. He decided to seek the advice of his friend Peter Zelig, a retired accountant. Mr. Zukowski gathered up all the papers he thought he and Mr. Zelig would need, stuffed a kielbasa under his arm as a gift for his friend, and left the office.

Zukowski Meats, Incorporated
EXHIBIT 1 • Balance Sheet (in thousands)

	1991
Cash	$ 1,840
Marketable securities	780
Net accounts receivable	1,600
Inventory	1,000
Other	260
Total current assets	5,480
Net property, plant, and equipment	6,000
Other	520
Total assets	$12,000
Short-term debt	$ 1,100
Accounts payable	1,800
Accruals	450
Other	250
Total current liabilities	3,600
Long-term debt	3,800
Common stock	2,000
Retained earnings	2,600
Total liabilities and owners' equity	$12,000

AMF Bowling, Inc.

In January 1989, Phil Knisely, president of AMF Bowling, Inc., decided to launch a new line of high-performance urethane bowling balls. The new line of balls would play a crucial role in Mr. Knisely's efforts to rejuvenate the company's product lines and to continue the turnaround of AMF Bowling. Although bowling balls accounted for a small portion of the company's total sales, they were flagship products that displayed the AMF name and motivated bowlers to buy other AMF products such as bags, shirts, and shoes.

Much already had been done to ensure the success of the new ball product launch: market studies had been completed; the Cobra name had been selected. Yet Knisely had not decided whether to manufacture the Cobra balls or purchase them from one of the industry's suppliers. His primary and immediate concern was whether AMF should expand its manufacturing facilities. In addition, if he decided that AMF should expand the manufacturing facility, Mr. Knisely needed to consider whether it should be financed with debt. Thus Knisely needed to balance the long-term strategic implications of the choice as well as the immediate economic effects.

Company Background

In July 1985, Minstar Corporation, controlled by Irwin Jacobs, had successfully acquired all the stock of AMF, Inc., for approximately $545 million. In June 1986, Minstar sold the Bowling Division of AMF to a group of Richmond, Virginia, investors for approximately $225 million. The division was renamed AMF Bowling in 1988. The new company moved from facilities in Ohio and New York to a modern office and production facility outside Richmond, Virginia.

Since its purchase in 1985, AMF Bowling had undergone dramatic improvements in operating efficiency. The company was organized into

This case is based on work done by Suzanne G. Barrs and was written by Martin G. King under the supervision of John L. Colley, Jr., Almand R. Coleman Professor of Business Administration. Some names, places, and figures have been disguised. Copyright © 1990 by the University of Virginia Darden School Foundation, Charlottesville, Virginia. All rights reserved.

four functional divisions. The Capital Equipment, Automatic Scoring, and Pins & Lanes Division manufactured bowling-alley equipment such as automatic pinspotters, ball returns, bowling lanes, Amflite pins, and automatic scoring and front-desk systems. Consumer Products Division purchased bowling balls, bags, shoes, shirts, and supplies from outside vendors under private-label arrangements and resold them. A sister company, Major League Lanes, owned and operated 163 bowling centers worldwide.

The Bowling Ball Industry

Bowling enjoyed a long and rich history in the United States that began when early Dutch settlers brought the game to New York. Until the mid-1950s, it was not considered family entertainment. Since then, the game had grown to become the most popular participation sport in America. The number of bowling lanes began to decline after peaking in 1976. The bowling industry responded to the decline by upgrading bowling's image: millions of dollars were spent on renovating existing bowling alleys and building new ones. As these investments started to pay off in the 1980s, there was a shift toward a slightly younger and more affluent bowler as profiled in Exhibit 1. Corporate sponsorship of bowling tournaments rose as companies recognized the spending power of the American bowler. In 1988, more than $3 million was spent to sponsor professional bowling competitions.

Bowling Ball Sales

The bowling ball industry divided sales according to the material used to make the balls. The low-priced rubber balls were primarily used as house balls (5 percent of industry unit sales), the mid-priced polyester balls (60 percent) were popular among regular but infrequent bowlers, and the high-priced urethane balls (35 percent) tended to be used by serious and more affluent bowlers. Since affluent, younger bowlers demanded urethane balls because they thought these balls would improve their performance, urethane ball sales were gradually replacing sales of polyester and rubber balls. Industry analysts expected the urethane segment of bowling ball sales to add 0.75 percent to its market share each year.

AMF had further divided the urethane ball segment into high-performance and regular-performance segments. The high-performance segment accounted for 57 percent of unit sales and was expected to grow faster, taking an additional 1 percent share of the urethane market each year. AMF forecast total 1989 ball sales at 2.1 million and expected them to grow 0.5 percent per year, mostly from higher international demand.

Most of these balls would be sold through one of three outlets: bowling pro shops, general sporting goods stores, or discount mass merchandisers. Exhibit 2 contains a breakdown of unit and dollar sales by type of outlet. The mass merchandisers tended to sell only rubber and polyester balls, while the pro shops sold mostly urethane balls. The general sporting goods stores sold a mix but favored polyester balls.

Competition

AMF Bowling faced four main competitors in the bowling ball segment of the bowling industry: Western Industries, Mercury International, Classic Enterprises, and Brunswick Corporation. Brunswick was the only other major full-line manufacturer in the bowling industry.

Western Industries

Western Industries, a privately held company, accounted for an estimated 29 percent of the bowling ball market. It was also one of AMF's two current ball suppliers. Western had traditionally sold only polyester balls but had launched a very successful urethane ball in 1986 and now held 21 percent of the high-performance, urethane ball segment. The firm was noted for the quality of its products and its responsiveness to customers. Not only did Western consistently have the best delivery record in the industry, but it also had the most depth in its research and development efforts. Finally Western's facility was the most flexible in the industry, allowing the firm to produce an adequate supply of balls for its own sales and for wholesale customers' new-product launches.

Mercury International

Mercury, AMF's other ball supplier, currently provided all the balls for AMF's aging high-performance urethane ball line, the *Angle*. AMF's contracts had contributed heavily to Mercury's plant utilization and profits. Mercury sold its own lines of low-to-medium-priced polyester and rubber balls to mass merchandisers and sporting good chains, and a urethane line to pro shops. Mercury had about 24 percent of the bowling ball market but only 10 percent of the high-performance portion of the urethane ball market. In addition, Mercury had a 300,000 ball-per-year contract with K-Mart.

Classic Enterprises

Several innovative and successful products had recently been introduced by Classic Enterprises. Because many professional bowlers used its *Crowbar* ball, it was widely recognized by the bowling public. Its *Rivet* line was successful in the regular performance portion of the urethane ball market.

Despite its technical success with these two products, bowlers criticized Classic for its uneven quality. The urethane lines suffered especially from a lack of consistency in the grade of urethane used in production. Classic's market share had steadily declined to its current 18 percent of bowling-ball unit sales.

Brunswick

Brunswick sold a full line of bowling balls, but it had been most successful with rubber balls. Brunswick's balls in the declining rubber segment continued to have sales, while its products in the growing urethane segment had not done well. As a result, Brunswick's relationships with pro shops were strained. Brunswick still had 20 percent of unit sales of bowling balls, however. Brunswick manufactured its own balls but had recently subcontracted the manufacture of the urethane ball cores to Western Industries. The age of Brunswick's manufacturing facility, and its uncharacteristic reliance on an outside supplier, led some industry analysts to speculate that the company would soon build a new ball-manufacturing facility.

Bowling Balls at AMF Bowling, Inc.

AMF's share of the bowling ball market had eroded from a high of 15 percent in 1986 to 9 percent in 1988. The primary reason for this loss of market share was AMF's failure to introduce any new bowling balls since the successful launch of the *Angle* line in 1981. The *Angle* line was the first urethane bowling ball in the industry, and professional bowlers had adopted it rapidly. The *Angle* was the first ball to break the $100 retail-price threshold as avid bowlers were willing to pay more for a high-performance urethane ball that they believed would raise their scores. Since 1981, AMF's strategy had been to expand the *Angle* line by adding slightly different balls targeted at relatively small customer segments. Although marketing expenditures had increased significantly, the *Angle* brand name was dying by 1988. Customers were no longer excited by another ball that added some modifier such as *Blue* or *Ultra* to the *Angle* name. AMF continued to market nonurethane balls, but rubber and polyester balls were declining in profitability and importance.

The marketing group at AMF was excited about the new *Cobra* line of bowling balls. They were convinced that they could repeat the success of the *Angle* line by introducing a ball that was technically superior to any other on the market. The marketing group projected that the *Cobra* line would win a 13 percent share of the high-performance portion of the urethane market during the first year of introduction. AMF management expected to add 0.5 percent each year to the initial 13 percent share. Because new product launches were notoriously difficult to predict, the marketing group estimated that initial market share could be as low as 8 percent or as high as 20 percent. The *Cobra* bowling ball would be sold by AMF to pro shops for $55. The retail price of the ball would be about $120. The price was expected to rise with inflation, estimated by management to be about 5 percent per year. Marketing expenses were projected to be 15 percent of *Cobra* sales in the year that the *Cobra* line was launched and 11 percent thereafter. Management expected the new Cobra line would be a mature, slow-growing (5 percent per year) product by 1996.

The In-House Manufacturing Option

In-house manufacturing of the new *Cobra* line of bowling balls offered several advantages: (1) AMF would have direct control over development, quality, and delivery of the balls; (2) it would earn higher margins on the sale of the balls to pro shops; (3) it would develop the technical expertise to ensure a steady supply of new bowling ball lines, preventing dramatic swings in bowling ball market share as ball lines aged; (4) it would no longer be in the vulnerable position of relying on its competitors to supply bowling balls.

AMF had no room to manufacture the new bowling balls in its Richmond, Virginia, facility. However, Mr. Knisely knew of an appropriate piece of nearby land that he estimated would cost $200,000. Construction of a facility with annual single-shift capacity of 90,000 balls would cost approximately $1.5 million. One million dollars would be spent in the first year of construction and the remainder in the second year. Equipment was an important part of the total investment in a bowling ball facility. Because standard bowling ball manufacturing equipment was available only on a limited basis, most manufacturers had their own lines of internally developed proprietary machinery: AMF would have to spend $1.5 million to purchase and modify machinery in the first year and an additional $500,000 in the second year. The final portion of the investment would be for working capital. Mr. Knisely estimated that AMF would have to have $100,000 of additional working capital in the first year of construction and another $150,000 in the second year. Thereafter, working capital would grow with sales—a constant 10 percent of sales.

The accounting department suggested that the equipment and building be depreciated using a straight-line method starting in the first year of production. The building could be depreciated over 31.5 years and the equipment over 5 years. Despite the equipment's 5-year depreciation schedule, it was expected to last indefinitely. Regular equipment maintenance expenses were included as part of other expenses.

There would be other expenses associated with the new facility as well. Incremental fixed costs would be incurred in 1989 as AMF developed the new facilities and hired managers. Salaries would be $75,000 in 1989 and $200,000 in 1990. By the 1991 launch date, salaries would be $250,000 and would rise with inflation. Other expenses would total $80,000 in 1989 and 1990, jumping to $600,000 in 1991. They would also rise with inflation. The average variable cost of the balls produced at the new facility was expected to decline as production became more efficient beginning at $25.62/unit in the first year and dropping to $23.49 by year 5 (see Exhibit 3).

AMF would continue to sell the *Angle* line during the two years it would take to complete the new facility. Knisely estimated that AMF would be able to sell 40,000 *Angle* balls each year. The selling price of $42.00 for 1989 would have to be discounted 15 percent in 1990 in order to maintain sales. It would cost AMF $27 per ball to purchase them from Mercury International. Marketing expenses would be 11 percent of sales.

There were three serious concerns Mr. Knisely had about the construction of the manufacuturing facility. First, since it would take two years to have the facility up and running, AMF's ball launch would miss two buying seasons. Second, there was overcapacity in the industry. AMF management estimated that the bowling ball industry was operating at less than 70 percent of capacity and were concerned that retail prices might be cut by the competition to stimulate demand and fill unused capacity. Finally, the company was already highly leveraged as a result of the recent acquisition and its move to Virginia. Since the debt required to make the large investment in a bowling ball facility might constrain future investments in process improvements, research and development, and the continued restructuring of the company, this had to be a high potential investment.

The Purchase Option

AMF could purchase balls from Western Industries. AMF had purchased balls from both Western Industries and Mercury International in the past. The relationship with Mercury management had deteriorated recently because of friction over delivery dates and the impending launch of the *Cobra* bowling ball. In contrast, Western had proved to be an excellent supplier and was eager to provide AMF with the new balls. Western had lobbied AMF for the new business by offering extensive technical ability and flexible capacity to fill orders for even a very successful product launch. Mr. Knisely felt that Western would be willing to supply the balls for $33 each in the first year of production. Future prices would rise with inflation. If AMF were to source the *Cobra* ball with Western, it could launch the ball in one year rather than waiting two years for the new facility.

Under the purchase option, AMF would still market the *Angle* line of balls for one year and discontinue it before the launch of the *Cobra* line.

Sales volume, sales price, purchase costs, and marketing expenses for the *Angle* in 1989 would be the same as those outlined under the manufacturing option.

Under the purchase option, fixed costs for 1989 would include $100,000 for salaries and $80,000 for other expenses. By 1990, when the ball was launched, salaries would increase to $150,000 and other expenses to $150,000. Both salaries and other expenses would rise with inflation. The only investment required would be for working capital of $20,000 in 1989 and $60,000 in 1990. Working capital would be 5 percent of increased sales.

AMF used a 15 percent discount rate and a 34 percent tax rate to analyze investment decisions.

AMF: Bowling, Inc.
EXHIBIT 1 • Demographic Profile of the Typical American Bowler

U.S. Profile	Bowlers	Population
Median adult age	33.3 yrs.	39.9 yrs.
18 to 34	40%	32%
18 to 49	59%	51%
Median household income	$25,556	$20,885
Household income > $25,000	52%	41%
Highest educational level		
Graduated/attended college	49	32
High school graduate	44	34
Employment		
Professional/managerial	30	22
Craftsman/foreman	27	13
Married	71	72
Own home	76	65
Children under 18	49%	42%
Mean household size	3.5 persons	2.7 persons

Source: Marketdata Enterprises, *The Bowling Centers, Pro Shops & Accessories Market—Strategies for the 1990s*, Lynbrook, N.Y., January 1988, reprinted from National Bowling Council, *Market Facts 1985 Survey*, U.S. Bureau of Census.

AMF: Bowling, Inc.

EXHIBIT 2 • Dollar and Unit Distribution of Bowling Ball Sales

Type of Outlet	Units	Dollars
Pro shops	48.3%	65.7%
Discount mass merchandisers	43.3	29.6
General sporting goods stores	8.4	4.7

AMF: Bowling, Inc.

EXHIBIT 3 • Average Variable Cost per New Bowling Ball

	1989	1990	1991	1992	1993
Average Variable Cost	$25.62	$24.79	$24.24	$23.82	$23.49

Federal Reserve Bank of Richmond (A)

As manager of planning at the Federal Reserve Bank of Richmond (FRBR), Reid Carter had been asked to find a way to reduce costs of savings bond processing. During late 1977, he had been working with the director of the fiscal agency department at the bank, who supervised savings bond processing, as well as with people from the bank's computer services group, to develop the three options that now lay before him. Opinions of FRBR's managers as to which of the three should be implemented differed widely. What Reid Carter needed to do now was evaluate the costs and benefits, as well as the less tangible pros and cons of each option, and make a firm recommendation that his boss, Roy Fauber, could pass on to the Federal Reserve Board of Governors for approval.

Background

The Federal Reserve System, supervised by its Board of Governors, was established in 1913 by the Federal Reserve Act. That act, plus subsequent legislation (e.g., the Banking Act of 1934), placed the Federal Reserve System in the position of responsibility for:

1. Monetary Policy. The Federal Reserve Board attempted to control the availability and cost of money and credit through its control over the reserves held by the banking system. Reserves could be influenced by:

    a. The Federal Reserve System Open Market Committee's trading of government securities. To expand credit, securities were purchased, bank reserves rose over the required limit, and the banks' funds were freed for loans. To tighten credit, securities were sold, reserves were reduced, and previously loanable funds were reduced.

    b. The rediscount rate. The Board of Governors loaned money to its member banks at a rate it controlled.

c.   The level of reserves held by member banks. All national banks were required to be members of the Federal Reserve System. State banks were allowed but not required to become members. The membership was required to maintain a percentage of their deposits in reserve.[1] A change in the level of reserves changed the percentage of deposits loanable by the bank.

2.   Supervision and Regulation. The Federal Reserve Board set maximum interest rates on time and savings deposits, examined state-chartered member banks, regulated offshore activities of U.S. banks, regulated bank holding companies, established rules for credit and repayment terms disclosure, voted on the establishment of state member branch banks, and approved bank mergers.

3.   U.S. Government Bank. The board acted as the fiscal agent for the federal government. U.S. government securities were issued, delivered, and handled by them.

4.   Bank Services for Member Banks. Activities such as collecting and cashing checks, wiring money, making loans, and holding securities for commercial banks were provided. Between 75 and 80 percent of the expenses of each of the 12 district banks resulted from executing these services.

All federal reserve activities in the Fifth District were under the jurisdiction of the Richmond Federal Reserve Bank.

Most of the services provided by the district banks were to benefit federal reserve member and nonmember banks. In general, these services were provided without charge; the reserve balances that the banks maintained with the district banks were viewed as compensation for the services provided throughout the Federal Reserve System. A district bank could, however, determine the level of the particular service it wished to provide. For instance, all district banks processed commercial bank checks, but the conditions under which credit was granted were under the district's control.

Operating decisions made by the district banks had little effect on their income, which came from the interest on U.S. government securities held as a result of monetary policy. In order to meet the system-wide goal of maximizing the surplus returned to the U.S. Treasury, the FRBR had to minimize costs rather than maximize revenue. That is why savings bond automation looked promising.

---

[1] Membership also required the purchase of stock in the Federal Reserve District Bank serving the area. The amount of stock purchased was based on the size of the national bank's capital and surplus accounts.

Capital Allocation Process

The process of making capital investments had recently become more formal at the FRBR. Based on the size of the expected expenditure, proposals were divided into three categories. Department managers could authorize expenditures of up to $5,000. For investments between $5,000 and $100,000, approval had to come from top management of the district bank, and for anything in excess of $100,000, from the Board of Governors of the Federal Reserve System in Washington, D.C.

In general, proposals that exceeded $5,000 were of two varieties. The first were investments to maintain a required level of service (e.g., to replace worn-out equipment), and little economic justification was required for their approval. The second were cost-reduction projects, and those were expected to meet certain minimum standards based on present value analysis. Controversy over those projects centered around what the minimum standard, the discount rate, should be.

The Savings Bond Automation Project

During his tenure as chairman of the Federal Reserve Board, Arthur Burns had put intense pressure on the 12 federal reserve banks to reduce their internal costs. Budgets at the FRBR had risen less than 5.5 percent annually over the past four or five years in spite of increased volume and the effects of inflation. The Richmond bank had been effective in cost cutting, but in 1977, management believed that several areas still remained where more could be done. Savings bond processing under the fiscal agency department was one of those areas. The unit costs for the process had been higher at the FRBR than those for the same function performed at other federal reserve banks. In fact, they were higher than the system-wide average by a significant margin. (See Exhibit 1.) Since the banks competed to have the lowest costs, the FRBR had an incentive to find a way to reduce the costs.

Because little of the current savings bond processing at the FRBR was automated, it remained one of the most labor-intensive operations at the bank. Even so, the rate of cost increase could have been contained if the U.S. Treasury had not been planning tighter reporting requirements, which, together with increasing volume, led to only one thing—hiring more people and higher unit costs. The vice president, Roy Fauber, and his planning staff had therefore become involved in the problem. Mr. Fauber asked Reid Carter to work with the director of fiscal agency, Harold Lipscomb, in solving the problem.

The savings bond group issued, processed, and redeemed bonds for individuals, issuing agents, and payroll accounts. Currently, the main use of the computer in the savings bond function was at the Richmond office for keeping records related to consignment accounts held by the district's issuing agents (that is, the banks), the initiation of reserve accounts, and the automated printing of savings bonds for several payroll accounts. In the first 6 months of 1977, charges for computer operations in savings bonds had been $15,057. The savings bond function had also been charged $5,570 for data system support in the first 6 months. Everything else was done manually. The reissue activity alone required 18 separate steps, all done manually. The kind of work done in the section obviously lent itself to computerization, which preliminary estimates suggested might eliminate up to 50 percent of the current staff (Exhibit 2).

A variety of alternatives for reducing the cost of handling savings bonds had been explored, and three had been considered in detail. All the suggestions involved further automating the process. Two of the proposals relied on using the excess capacity of the computer equipment already owned by the FRBR; the other required the purchase of a minicomputer system similar to that used by the New York Federal Reserve Bank.

1. Four Phase Mini-System.   As a result of a discussion with a Federal Reserve System bank-examining team, Mr. Carter and Mr. Lipscomb had learned about a new system in use at the New York district bank. The FRBNY had employed an outside consultant to install a minicomputer and provide software specifically designed for their savings bond process. Such a system would do just what the Richmond team believed was needed: it would automate the routine bookkeeping, clerical, and reporting activities; it would centralize much of the work now being done at the Charlotte and Baltimore branch banks; and it could be ready 6 months from the time the consultant was notified. Mr. Carter, Mr. Lipscomb, and the consultant had worked out some preliminary estimates of the costs involved in bringing the Four Phase system to FRBR. The hardware itself was expected to cost $285,245, although a discount might be offered. The FRBNY consultant said the software could not be directly transferred to the new FRBR system and, therefore, estimated further software development costs of $28,000, modifications costing $35,000, and conversion costs running no more than $15,000. The FRBR would provide a part-time staff member to coordinate the project, which would take between one-quarter and one-third of the person's time; a cost of $7,500 was estimated.

In addition to those start-up costs, continuing annual hardware and software maintenance would require $11,556 and $18,000, respectively. The current main computer charge for the operation was about $41,000 per year.

The real benefit of this system would come from the smaller staff needed to perform the same tasks. It appeared that, with this system, seven fewer people would be needed for savings bond processing (Exhibit 3). Intrabank transfers and normal attrition would make the effect on the people involved negligible.

2. IBM 370s. After a description of the Four Phase system had been circulated at the FRBR, the computer services and planning department responded by supplying the following information. They had the staff necessary to create similar software. The in-house computer system (dual IBM 370s) was operating at about 30 percent of capacity, and even if the backup time required for the wire transfer of funds was added, the system was committed for only 50 percent of its time. Putting the savings bond processing onto the IBM 370s would reduce the unit costs to all other users at FRBR. Furthermore, the use of the IBM 370s would meet the computer-utilization plan filed by the FRBR with the Systems Committee of the Board of Governors.

The department believed, however, that the time to create the software necessary to satisfy the savings bond needs could take up to two years (Exhibit 4). Allocation for programmers' time would be as high as $285,896 (Exhibit 5). Continuing software maintenance could cost $3,000 per year. A total of eight staff positions could be eliminated.

The Board of Governors' Systems Committee, in charge of the planning and the utilization of system-wide computer resources, had strongly suggested that everything be loaded on a district's main system. The district banks at San Francisco, Dallas, and St. Louis were involved in projects to do just that. If the FRBR waited, the committee felt sure that software adaptable for the savings bond activity would become available within the Federal Reserve System in two or three years.

3. IBM 370s with Consultant Software. The third option was to use the IBM 370 capacity, but hire the firm that had created the FRBNY minisystem to provide the software. Although language differences existed between the two systems, the consultants were familiar with the needs of the savings bond process, and their New York system had received the necessary approval of the U.S. Treasury. The consultant had estimated it would take up to 14 months to have this system ready for use.

Costs for this system included software ($250,000), its conversion ($15,000), and the in-bank coordinator ($7,500). Yearly software maintenance was estimated at $18,000. This system would also reduce the processing staff by eight people.

Each of the systems reduced the labor intensity of the operation and provided identifiable benefits. The pros and cons for the three options had been well summarized by one of the systems analysts (Exhibit 6).

Conclusion

As Mr. Carter and Mr. Lipscomb prepared to make cost and benefit estimates for each of the alternatives, Mr. Carter had several concerns: in making the estimates, they expected to treat real dollars and in-house allocations in the same way. For instance, if the FRBR chose the mini-system, they would be obligated to pay up to $285,245 for the Four Phase hardware. If, however, they used the IBM 370s, the computer charges would be allocated as in-house costs that must be borne by someone regardless of the system chosen for this project. They planned to treat both costs in the same way for in-house programming help versus the hiring of the outside consultant for development of the software. Mr. Carter wondered if all these costs and allocations should, in fact, be treated similarly. Furthermore, the payments for the Four Phase hardware and the consultant's charges would be contractual, while the in-house costs and benefits were merely estimates. Should that, he wondered, be taken into account?

Capacity provided another nagging question. The IBM 370s were not fully utilized, but in the past, whenever there had been time available, the capacity seemed to be used eventually. Right now the computer people estimated that the capacity of the 370s probably would be adequate for about three more years. The Four Phase, on the other hand, brought excess capacity with it.

The Systems Committee had encouraged the use of main systems and the system-wide standardization of software. The FRBR's computer-utilization plan, which had been filed with the committee, had covered the use of the main systems alone. Thus, there was some doubt that a proposal for mini-system investment would be welcomed by the Board of Governors.

Finally, Mr. Carter was not sure whether any of the projects should be recommended. Would they solve the savings bond processing problems at economically justifiable costs? Putting the costs and benefits together was Mr. Carter's first step.

Federal Reserve Bank of Richmond (A)

EXHIBIT 1 • Fifth District Performance Measures, Fourth Quarter, 1978

The following chart illustrates the District-wide Performance Indexes for the fourth quarter of 1978. The First Level Aggregates compare the direct, support, and allocated overhead costs associated with an activity to the system average for the same activity. Two or more activities are combined to derive the Second Level Aggregates, and all Second Level Aggregates are combined to form the Overall District Aggregate Index. The performance measures indexes cover 85 percent of the district's expenses. Major excluded functions are Monetary and Economic Policy, Supervision and Regulation, Bank and Public Relations, and several smaller functions. These performance indexes are based upon a system average index of 100. Variations above 100 indicate that unit cost is greater than the system average, and those below 100 indicate that unit cost is below system coverage.

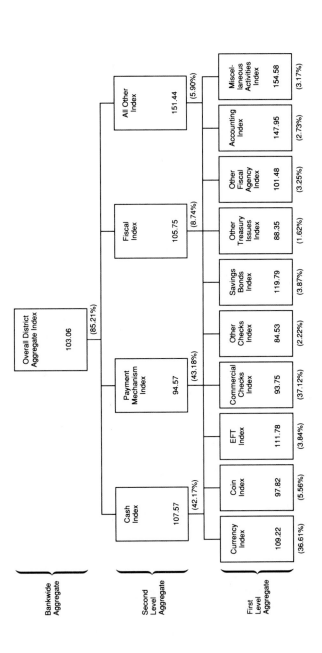

Performance Measures, 1977–1980

The following graphs illustrate the variations of the Performance Measures Indexes, by quarter between the first quarter 1977 and the fourth quarter 1980. The first graph illustrates the comparison of the district activity unit cost index and the system average unit cost index (100). The second graph for a given activity illustrates both the unit cost index and the aggregate volume index over time and compares the activity against a base index using 1977 as a base of 100.

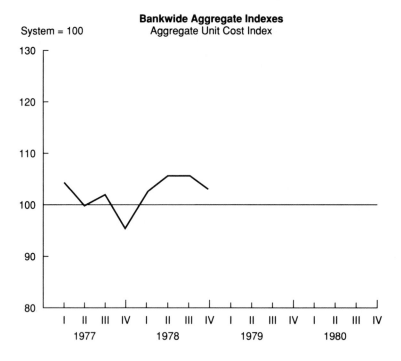

continued

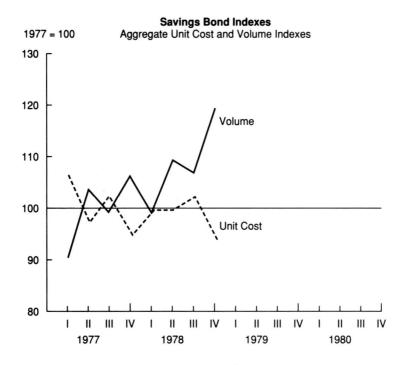

Current Savings Bond Processing Costs, 1977 Aggregate Unit Cost Calculation

Activity	Cost	Volume
Original issue	$ 178,207	1,048,351
Accounting for stock	424,610	126,667
Reissues and replacements	147,167	404,809
Direct redemptions	168,980	207,270
Processing retired bonds	180,885	325,039
	$1,099,849	2,112,136

Aggregate unit cost: $0.52

Federal Reserve Bank of Richmond (A)
EXHIBIT 2 • Project Title: Savings Bond System

Description

The Savings Bond Section plans to implement a comprehensive Automated Savings Bond System that will provide computer support in the following areas:

1. Consignment accounting
2. Vault custody
3. Original issue
4. Reissue
5. Book entry
6. Paid bonds
7. Direct redemption
8. Administration.

Benefits

The primary benefit from the system results from the elimination and/or simplification of many tasks in the savings bond area. The major areas of improvement are listed below:

1. Elimination of reissue activities at Baltimore and Charlotte. (These activities will be moved to Richmond.)
2. Elimination of original issue activities at Baltimore and Charlotte. (These activities will be moved to Richmond.)

3. Elimination of direct redemption activities.

4. Elimination of the manual recording of bond serial numbers.

5. Elimination of manually kept accounting records by fiscal agency bookkeeper.

6. Elimination of addressographing bond registrations and dating of bonds.

7. Elimination of manual preparation of checks for direct redemption.

8. Simplification of settlement procedures.

9. Simplification of mail procedures and elimination of typing of labels and mail manifests.

10. Reduction of work caused by errors.

11. Elimination of manual preparation of certain letters to issuing agents.

12. Elimination of sorting reserve and certain account entries by office.

13. Manual accumulation of certain statistics and preparation of reports.

14. Elimination of the need to enter reserve account entries into the IBM 370.

15. Specific audit trails would be produced and response to issuing agents would improve.

In addition, the system will result in the following benefits not directly related to a reduction in manual work:

1. Improved accuracy in handling of data should lead to fewer errors and their resulting complications.

2. Simplified work flow should lead to improved control of work and valuables.

3. Broader and more timely management information will contribute to the department management.

4. Future enhancements or new applications could improve operations; benefits to other fiscal agency activities could result.

Federal Reserve Bank of Richmond (A)

EXHIBIT 3 • Automation of the Savings Bond Function

	Personnel Requirements and Savings		
	Current System	Four Phase System	Savings
Richmond			
Original issue	5.8	2.5	−3.3
Accounting for stock	5.8	3.0	−2.8
Reissue	3.4	2.5	−0.9
Data entry	N.Ap.	3.0	+3.0
Total personnel	15.0	11.0	−4.0
Baltimore: See note below.			−2.0
Charlotte: See note below.			−1.0
Total district personnel			−7.0

N.Ap. = not applicable.

Note: The personnel savings at the Baltimore and Charlotte branches represent the minimum number of personnel involved with the savings bond activity who could be eliminated after automation and centralization of the activity at Richmond. The personnel savings are the same under the IBM 370 alternative with the exception that one additional individual could be eliminated in the data entry area: i.e., the Four Phase system requires an individual to control the operation of the computer system, whereas in the IBM 370 system this function would remain in the data processing department.

	Annual Cost Savings		
	Personnel	Average Wages and Benefits	Total Annual Savings
Richmond	4	$9,858	$39,432
Baltimore	2	11,172	22,344
Charlotte	1	9,858	9,858
Total			$71,634

Federal Reserve Bank of Richmond (A)
EXHIBIT 4 • Implementation Schedule

IBM 370, In-House Software	
Consignment and vault custody	10.0 months
Original issue	6.0 months
Reissue	3.0 months
Paid bonds	1.5 months
Book entry	3.0 months
Total implementation time	23.5 months
IBM 370, Consultant Software	14 months
Consultant Software on Four Phase	4–6 months

Federal Reserve Bank of Richmond (A)
EXHIBIT 5 • Savings Bond System Detailed—IBM Alternative Costs

I. Development and Implementation Costs (IBM 370)
   In-House Software

	Man Weeks		Hrs./Wk.		Rate	Cost
Analyst (1)	95	×	30	×	$32.35	$ 91,913
Programmers (3)	240	×	30	×	23.00	165,600
Operations specialist (1)	40	×	30	×	23.00	27,600
Transfer time[a]						783
Total	375					$285,896

[a]Transfer time is that time spent by computer services production support to become familiar with the system in general.

II. Computer Operations Charges (IBM 370)

	Unit/Mo.		Rate	Cost
Print lines	924,766	×	$.0007	$ 647
Characters	2,500,000	×	.00063	1,575
CPU time/Sec.	10,800	×	.17	1,836
Hardware (CRT)	2	×	70	140
Total/Month				$ 4,198
Total/Year				$ 50,376
Total/6 Years				$302,256

Federal Reserve Bank of Richmond (A)
EXHIBIT 6 • Savings Bond System Options—Intangible
Pros and Cons Unique to Alternatives Investigated

Alternative 1.   Purchase Four Phase computer and pay consultant to install New York savings bond software.

Pro

- Four Phase equipment is rated favorably by users. In *Datapro* (a trade publication), users rated the equipment 3.2 on a scale of 4 for overall satisfaction.

- Provided no unique changes must be made to the New York software for New York, Boston, or this bank, the cost advantage of software resource-sharing may be realized by these banks.

- The hardware and software have run successfully at the New York Federal Reserve Bank for over a year and a half.

- The New York system has been endorsed by the Subcommittee on Computers and Related Resources, and the reports have been endorsed by the U.S. Treasury.

- By acquiring the Four Phase hardware, excess computer capacity will be available. This excess could be used by the fiscal agency department for new applications.

- Work turnaround may be faster on a dedicated computer.

Con

- Unless a Four Phase high-speed printer is leased, potential operational and hardware interface problems may be incurred because of the requirement to use another vendor's printers (IBM or Burroughs) for high-volume reports.

- Out-of-pocket expenses will be required by the district if this alternative is chosen.

- A minicomputer creates the opportunity to add other applications to the system. However, additional problems for management arise if applications are added because the district would be less flexible in considering long-term hardware changes.

- Hardware maintenance support in the Richmond area is currently dependent upon two maintenance persons. The acquisition of replacement parts, if not stocked here in the city, may be time consuming.

- Due to the limited number of Four Phase users in the city (six at this time), off-site equipment backup may be difficult to find.

- This alternative will introduce a new device and computer vendor into the district and is in conflict with the direction of the district's approved automation plan.

- The Four Phase minicomputer uses two programming languages that are new to computer services personnel and are not widely used in the industry. They are Four Phase COBOL (Basic) and Four Phase Assembler. Training of personnel will be required. The possibility exists that, unless the personnel use the languages frequently, time will be lost in relearning the language each time software maintenance is required.

- Because the system was not developed in-house, computer services personnel may have to spend more time in learning the software. Therefore, maintenance may be more time consuming than it would be if computer services had developed the system themselves. This disadvantage is shared with Alternative 2.

- Detailed program documentation is poor. This may hinder the production support (maintenance) by increasing learning time.

- Problems with the New York consultant's support of the system:

    Distance. The consultant's office is in New York City.

    Control. The consultant will not be an employee of the Federal Reserve Bank but just another service vendor.

continued

Availability. The consultant's availability may be limited and will only be controlled by a detailed maintenance contract; e.g., the consultant could not give us a detailed estimate on Alternative 2 because he was leaving for Europe.

Inflexibility. The consultant should only make changes to the system when these changes have been approved by all federal reserve banks who use the system. If we make our own permanent changes to the software, the consultant would not support us.

Alternative 2. Consultant rewrites software to be processed on Richmond's IBM 370 computer.

Pro

- The system architecture has proved successful at the New York Federal Reserve Bank for over a year and a half.
- The New York system's reports have been endorsed by the U.S. Treasury and will be available under this alternative.
- IBM hardware support is readily available.
- Trained programmers and computer operators are already employed; this is an advantage over Alternative 1.
- The consultant, who knows the New York savings bond system well, will do the conversion. Therefore, no program logic should be lost or misinterpreted in the translation.

Con

- Production turnaround on the IBM computer(s) may be slower than on a dedicated Four Phase computer; this is a disadvantage shared with Alternative 3.
- Out-of-pocket expenses will be required by the district if this alternative is chosen.
- The New York savings bond system was not originally designed to be processed on an IBM computer. Because of the code conversion, some additional inconvenience to the user and data processing may be expected during system implementation.
- The system will not be developed in-house; therefore, computer services personnel may have to spend more time in learning the software. Program maintenance may be more time consuming than it would be if computer services personnel had developed the system themselves. This disadvantage is shared with Alternative 1.

Alternative 3. Develop the software in-house to be processed on Richmond's IBM 370.

Pro

- The system architecture has proved successful at the New York Federal Reserve Bank for over a year and a half. This software will be the basis of the new system design.
- The New York system's reports have been endorsed by the U.S. Treasury and will be available as output from this system.
- IBM hardware support is readily available.
- Trained computer operators are already employed; this is an advantage over Alternative 1.
- A full understanding of the software is guaranteed because the programs will be written by computer services personnel. Therefore, product support (maintenance) will be more timely.
- No out-of-pocket funds would be expended due to the allocation of existing resources.
- Personnel could be made available to begin this alternative in a short amount of time, whereas Four Phase approval (Alternative 1) may be time consuming.
- Programs may be written to meet specific needs of the Fifth District without approval from the New York or Boston Federal Reserve Banks.

continued

Con

■ Because of the extensive development and implementation effort required, it would be 28 months before *full* project benefits can be realized, assuming one analyst and four to five programmers are committed to the project.

■ Production turnaround on the IBM computer may be slower than on a dedicated Four Phase computer; this is a disadvantage shared with Alternative 2.

Polymold Division

The Polymold Division of Congeries Corporation was planning to purchase a computerized manufacturing and designing system known as "CAD/CAM" in January 1984. In September 1983, the manager of the Polymold Division, Joel Martin, curious to know how the CAD/CAM investment would affect Polymold's financial condition, was preparing to forecast the division's financial statements for the following five years.

The Company

Congeries Corporation was a conglomerate, divisions of which manufactured a wide variety of low- and medium-technology products ranging from small construction parts such as hinges and doorknobs to plastic injection molds. As shown in Exhibit 1, Congeries had been affected by the recent recession; in 1982 the firm lost over $1 million after posting a net income of $8.3 million in 1981. Given a $5-million loss in the first quarter, corporate management was not yet sure whether 1983 would be a profitable year.

Congeries' Polymold Division was one of the largest manufacturers of precision injection molds in the country. Exhibit 2 presents the division's financial statements from 1976 through 1982. Earnings and return on assets ranged from a high of $1.5 million and 29.9 percent, respectively, in 1980 to $679,000 and 13.2 percent in 1982. This precipitous decline was, as far as management could tell, simply the effect of the business cycle. Mr. Martin believed, however, that sales would continue to decline: if Polymold did not invest in the new computer-aided designing and manufacturing system, it would lose market share on its remaining products to its more technologically advanced competitors.

This case was prepared as a basis for class discussion rather than to illustrate either effective or ineffective handling of an administrative situation. Copyright © 1985 by the University of Virginia Darden School Foundation, Charlottesville, Virginia. All rights reserved.

The Market

The basis of Mr. Martin's fear was a change in the marketplace. Polymold manufactured high-quality precision molds with interchangeable parts. The company's largest clients produced all sorts of small plastic items, such as plastic bottles and caps, razor handles, various computer parts, and cosmetic, camera, video, and cassette cases. More customers' needs were met with multi-cavity molds (molds with more than four cavities) or single/complex molds (molds with four or fewer cavities that were more difficult to design and manufacture). Multi-molds (several molds of a single type) were also common; the one remaining category was single/simple molds.

Polymold's 1983 sales by mold type were expected to be as follows:

Multi-mold	$2.5 million
Multi-cavity	2.5
Single/complex	2.8
Single/simple	1.0
Repairs and spares	2.0
Total sales	$10.8 million

This $10.8 million represented a 5.1 percent market share. Mr. Martin was worried about Polymold's ability to retain this share for several reasons:

1. The injection-mold manufacturing industry was highly segmented and regional, but analysts believed that the greater the degree of manufacturing precision a company could attain, the more national its potential market was.

2. Some of Polymold's large competitors already had highly computerized operations that made them more efficient than Polymold.

3. Others had become vertically integrated to provide customers not only the molds, but also large presses and peripheral equipment. This integration was attractive to customers, because they could purchase more of their equipment from one source, sometimes as packages. The integrated firms had already lured customers away from small competitors.

4. Still other mold manufacturers were being bought out by large plastics companies and used exclusively as in-house suppliers.

5. Several new competitor mold shops had been established by former Polymold employees, who knew the company's organization and clients.

Mr. Martin deduced from a variety of economic projections (shown in Exhibit 3) and his knowledge of the industry that the market for injection molds would grow from a total of $210 million in 1983 to $278 million by 1987. Demand and growth were expected to be greatest for multi-cavity and single/complex molds. Exhibit 4 breaks down forecasts for total demand by type of end-user. The packaging industry, with its demand for bottles and caps, was expected to continue as the largest customer, although it required less precise molding capabilities than Polymold provided. It was followed by commercial products, home entertainment, consumer products, and medical products.

Polymold already had a strong presence in the consumer and home-entertainment segments, as shown in Exhibit 5, and Mr. Martin had been discussing new marketing efforts to attract more buyers from the commercial and medical markets. The commercial-products segment, made up of the data-storage, computer, office-products, and telecommunications industries, was expected to grow 70 percent over the next six years.

Polymold's business by industry segment in 1983 was expected to break down as follows:

Segment	Polymold Sales
Consumer	$3.7 million
Medical	0.8
Commercial	3.8
Home entertainment	1.5
Packaging	0.3
Miscellaneous	0.7
Total sales	$10.8 million

Consumer products had dominated Polymold's sales for the previous 15 years, for 5 years in conjunction with commercial products. These two markets continued to be the most important, but Mr. Martin expected the medical and home-entertainment sectors to grow.

Polymold's customers consisted of a small number of large nationally and internationally known firms. This dependency contributed to the cyclical nature of the demand for the company's products. Should even a small number of firms demand fewer molds, Polymold's sales would greatly diminish.

Despite the new marketing plans, without the use of the computer design and manufacturing, Mr. Martin considered a further loss of market share in all segments to be likely. He had supplemented his own judgment with data from a consultant's study, which pointed out, as shown in Exhibits 6 through 11, that even though Polymold's market share had increased during the recessionary period of declining sales, the company was not keeping pace with its closest competitors.[1] Furthermore, although Polymold's productivity remained higher than that of similar companies and the company was becoming increasingly capital intensive, real productivity per employee was stagnant. The study also indicated that the quality of Polymold's products, although high, was slipping dramatically when compared with its closest competitors'.

Manufacturing Technology

During the 1970s, most of Polymold's major competitors upgraded their production processes by installing numerically controlled (NC) machines. Numerically controlled equipment had been available for about 20 years, but had basically been ignored by the industry until the machines had become computerized and until the demand levels and the needs of plastics manufacturers justified the investment. Computerized NC machines, which referred to machines that were both computerized and numerically controlled, raised the capital intensity of the manufacturing process and permitted greater precision and efficiency than previously possible. The equipment carried out many functions by itself, so that less staff was required and errors were minimized.

The CAD/CAM system was the industry's latest technological advance. With the aid of CAD/CAM, injection molds could be designed and drawn on the computer rather than at the drafting table, the flow and cooling of the plastic in the mold could be analyzed, and the mold-manufacturing NC equipment could be controlled. In addition, CAD/CAM could be used to inspect the machined parts, to order materials, and to estimate the costs of production more accurately than previously possible. Using the system in both design and manufacture almost eliminated human error.

Mr. Martin saw CAD/CAM first as a time-saver, because it could remove design errors. Furthermore, the system would enhance the company's ability to expand its product line into rubber and powdered metal molds, which demanded more precision than plastics. Perhaps most importantly, because many customers designed their own molds, CAD/CAM could improve communications between the designer and the builder, especially if the customer also owned the system for its own design purposes. If both companies used CAD/CAM, designs and ideas could be readily transferred. The firms with CAD/CAM clearly would control the precision mold market.

---

[1] The consultants carried out a PIMS, or Profit Impact of Marketing Strategy, study. PIMS was a service of the Strategic Planning Institute, Cambridge, Massachusetts, which combined a company's answers to a strategy–and–marketing questionnaire with a data base outlining the characteristics and experiences of a large sample of other companies. The resulting data were used to derive a complete report on the potential impact of a strategic move.

In 1981, recognizing that it had begun to fall behind its competition technologically, Polymold had invested in two pieces of NC equipment and two programmable inspection stations. Recently, the division had also leased a small, single-station CAD/CAM unit with limited computing power, so that it could assess the equipment's benefits, train operators, and determine whether to purchase a full, four-station CAD/CAM system.

Financial Analysis

To determine the effect of CAD/CAM, Mr. Martin projected the financial positions of the division with and without the device. Specifically, he wanted to project the financial condition of the division through 1988, first assuming the CAD/CAM was not purchased, and then assuming it was purchased in January 1984 for $750,000 ($190,000 of which was the price of the software). Regardless of whether CAD/CAM was purchased, other capital investments would have to be made in the future. All would be depreciated using ACRS depreciation guidelines over five years. Mr. Martin used the economic and market projections given in Exhibit 3 as the basis for his forecasts.

Without CAD/CAM. With the division's marketing strategy but without CAD/CAM, Mr. Martin projected a slow decrease in Polymold's market share from 5.1 percent of the total in 1983 to 4.2 percent in 1988.

Total cost of goods sold (COGS) was expected to be about 73 percent of sales in 1983, rising by slightly more than four percentage points by 1988. The 4-percentage point increase would come from a combination of factors affecting the various components of cost of goods sold: labor, 34 percent of sales in 1982, was expected to rise slowly to 36 percent or more; raw materials were also expected to rise from their current level of 11 percent to 12 percent; plant administration, a component of cost of goods sold that currently consumed 2.4 percent of sales, would double by 1988, largely because of its labor component; overhead, the second largest COGS expense, was expected to decline slightly; the costs of electricity, heat, water, and maintenance were expected to change little, because no new plants would be added and no major change in operations would be made without the addition of CAD/CAM. Polymold's accountants noted that they had not included in their COGS forecasts the savings expected from a special cost-reduction program recently instituted by management. For 1983 the savings were expected to be only $37,000, but they would rise rapidly to $210,000 in 1984 and reach $391,000 by 1988.

Mr. Martin believed that the salespeople would have a hard job trying to maintain Polymold's decreasing market share without CAD/CAM. That factor, coupled with increases in other general and administrative expenses, would increase selling, general, and administrative costs by an average of 2 percentage points to 12.5 percent by 1988. This figure did not include research and engineering, usually buried in that category, which would stay at about $130,000 per year.

Depreciation, capital expenditures, and interest expense were expected to be as shown in Exhibit 12, which also shows tax credits that Polymold currently had available. Because Polymold was a division, it also paid a corporate expense assessment that rose each year. The amount would be the same regardless of whether CAD/CAM was purchased. The corporate accountants had told Mr. Martin that in 1983 this expense would be $168,000; in 1984, $176,000; and in 1985, $185,000. It had not yet been projected beyond 1985.

Even with the drop in market share, Polymold would need more working capital. Although that need had declined in the recent past, Mr. Martin believed that small increases each year would create a total increase in net working capital of about $300,000 by 1988. For convenience Mr. Martin always used a 50-percent tax rate for his projections.

With CAD/CAM. With the new system, Mr. Martin projected an increase in Polymold's market share from 5.1 percent in 1983 to 7.3 percent in 1988, although he believed that by 1988 the division's market share could be as little as 6.3 percent or as much as 7.7 percent.

Mr. Martin estimated that, once CAD/CAM was in full operation, overall cost of goods sold would remain at about 72 percent of sales even though materials costs would increase from 11 to 13.5 percent of sales. Cost of goods sold would be affected by the same forces with or without CAD/CAM, with overhead providing a compensating decline. However, overhead and labor were hard to forecast for a new process; the overhead forecast could be off by as much as 10 percent, and labor could be 5 percentage points higher than forecasted.

In dollars, plant administration would be the same with or without CAD/ CAM, but the savings from the new cost-efficiency program were expected to increase to $445,000 in 1984 and $802,000 by 1988. However, Polymold's accountants were less certain in making these savings forecasts than those for savings without CAD/CAM. They had given Mr. Martin a range, as shown in Exhibit 13, and had suggested that an outbreak of inflation like that recently experienced could wipe out about half of any savings.

Mr. Martin expected research and development costs with CAD/ CAM to be double what they would have been without CAD/CAM; the system, when in place, would simply require more development and engineering time. While selling this new process would initially require considerable new effort, selling, general, and administrative expenses (SG&A) were expected to decline relative to sales, by 1988 declining to as much as 2 percentage points below the level expected without CAD/CAM. Mr. Martin had been reminded by the accountants that, if sales were lower than forecasted, SG&A would not decline as much. For example, if sales were 25 percent below forecast, SG&A could be as high as 13.5 percent in 1988.

The forecast predicted that working capital would certainly decrease as a percentage of sales with the acquisition of CAD/CAM. By 1984, if things went as expected, working capital would be no higher than 12.8 percent of sales. The precise figure would depend on sales: if sales were lower than forecasted, Mr. Martin believed that both inventory and accounts receivable would be higher, and working capital would probably be at a level equal to the current level. If sales were better than expected, however, inventory would move faster and accounts receivable would be lower, because Polymold could concentrate on the faster-paying accounts.

The purchase of the new system would require further capital expenditures as old processes and machines were updated to complement it. Forecasts for capital expenditures (including CAD/CAM), interest, and depreciation are shown in Exhibit 12.

Interest expenses were computed on the basis of the long-term debt necessary to support capital expenditures. Depreciation expenses reflected the ACRS schedule that Congeries Corporation used for tax purposes (at 15 percent the first year, 22 percent the second, and 21 percent each of the following three years). In addition to full depreciation, an 8-percent investment tax credit was available for this investment. No salvage value was expected for the CAD/CAM equipment, because changes in technology could rapidly make the equipment obsolete.

Mr. Martin planned to calculate the division's cost of capital by basing his estimate of the company's systematic risk, beta, on that of similar companies, which, along with industry financial information, are given in Exhibit 14. He believed that Polymold's capital structure would have reflected the industry average if the division had been a public company.

Polymold Division

EXHIBIT 1 • Congeries Corporation Consolidated
Financial Statements (in thousands, except per-share data)

Balance Sheet	1982
Assets	
Cash	$ 3,945
Securities	2,649
Receivables	46,808
Inventories	39,706
Other current assets	10,649
Total current assets	103,757
Property, plant, and equipment	59,805
Other assets	18,546
Total assets	$182,108
Liabilities and Shareholders' Equity	
Current portion of long-term debt	$ 2,960
Accounts payable	23,533
Other current liabilities	1,298
Total current liabilities	27,791
Long-term debt	42,574
Other liabilities	6,418
Total liabilities	76,783
Preferred stock	8,169
Common stock	13,430
Additional paid-in capital	18,249
Retained earnings	88,461
Translation adjustment	(4,689)
Less treasury stock	(18,295)
Stockholders' equity	105,325
Liabilities and shareholders' equity	$182,108

Income Statements	1979	1980	1981	1982
Net sales	$280,148	$274,737	$281,886	$247,502
Operating income	34,268	28,753	29,814	12,880
Corporate expense	8,850	5,711	6,472	7,489
Interest expense	3,097	3,323	779	2,237
Earnings before taxes	22,321	19,719	22,563	3,154
Earnings of foreign affiliates	739	896	1,043	897
Provision for income taxes	(9,995)	(8,642)	(9,811)	(913)
After-tax earnings	13,065	11,973	13,795	3,138
After-tax loss, discontinued operations	(658)	(1,876)	(5,457)	(4,196)
Net after-tax earnings	$ 12,407	$ 10,097	$ 8,338	$ (1,058)
Earnings per share, common	$4.55	$3.51	$2.77	($0.89)

Polymold Division

EXHIBIT 2 • Polymold Division Financial Statements (in thousands)

	For the Years Ended December 31			
	1979	1980	1981	1982
Income Statement				
Net sales	$11,697	$13,280	$11,494	$10,763
Cost of products sold	7,838 .67	9,064 .6825	7,805 .679	7,713 .7166
Selling, general, and administrative	837	990	1,214	1,287
Depreciation	264	311	365	415
Other expense	0	0	0	37
Total costs and expenses	8,939	10,365	9,384	9,452
Pretax earnings	2,758	2,915	2,110	1,311
Taxes	1,379	1,457	1,038	632
Net earnings	$ 1,379	$ 1,458	$ 1,072	$ 679
Proceeds to parent	$ 1,252	$ 2,539	$ 655	$ 790
Balance Sheet				
Receivables, net	$ 3,630	$ 2,660	$ 2,804	$ 2,306
Inventories, net	235	97	130	110
Prepaid expenses	95	89	64	53
Total current assets	3,960	2,846	2,998	2,469
Fixed assets*	4,206	4,225	4,918	5,433
Less accumulated depreciation*	(2,058)	(2,189)	(2,379)	(2,750)
Fixed assets, net	2,148	2,036	2,539	2,683
Total assets	6,108	4,882	5,537	5,152
Accounts payable	219	194	186	64
Other current liabilities	635	515	761	609
Total current liabilities	854	709	947	673
Net worth**	5,254	4,173	4,590	4,479
Total liabilities and net worth	$ 6,108	$ 4,882	$ 5,537	$ 5,152

*Net of asset sales.

**Net worth is reduced by payments to parent each year.

Polymold Division
EXHIBIT 3 • Economic Trends and Polymold Sales Projections with CAD/CAM

	1980	1981	1982	1983	1984	Forecast			Average Growth Rate 1984–1987
						1985	1986	1987	
U.S. gross national product (GNP) (billions of nominal dollars)	$2,633	$2,937	$3,059	$3,283	$3,605	$3,992	$4,430	$4,889	10.5%
U.S. GNP (billions of 1980 dollars)	$2,633	$2,691	$2,645	$2,713	$2,813	$2,948	$3,080	$3,187	4.1
Inflation rate	13.5%	10.4%	6.1%	3.2%	6.1%	5.9%	6.5%	6.9%	N.Ap.
Correction factor for inflation	1.0	0.906	0.854	0.813	0.775	0.737	0.699	0.664	N.Ap.
Index for rubber and plastic products (1980=100)	100.0	107.0	99.5	106.6	114.8	123.8	168.0	141.8	8.9
Index for fabricated metal products (1980=100)	100.0	101.7	85.6	93.2	102.9	114.1	122.3	129.8	8.6
Injection mold market (millions of dollars)	N.Av.	N.Av.	N.Av.	$210.0	$229.0	$253.9	$267.0	$278.0	7.3
Polymold actual and forecasted sales with CAD/CAM (millions of dollars)	$13.3	$11.5	$10.8	$10.8	$12.8	$15.8	$17.4	$19.1	15.5
Polymold actual and forecasted sales with CAD/CAM (millions of 1980 dollars)	$13.3	$10.4	$9.2	$8.8	$9.9	$11.7	$12.2	$12.6	9.6%

N.Av. = not available; N.Ap. = not applicable.

Polymold Division
EXHIBIT 4 • Forecasted End-User Injection Mold Market (in millions)

	1983	1984	1985	1986	1987	1988
Consumer	$ 20	$ 25	$ 28	$ 30	$ 31	$ 30
Medical/pharmaceutical	23	26	28	29	29	29
Commercial	25	28	32	35	37	37
Home entertainment	26	26	28	30	33	34
Packaging	44	46	50	52	54	55
Miscellaneous	23	25	29	31	32	32
Subtotal	161	176	195	207	216	217
All single/simple mold products	49	53	58	60	62	63
Total	$210	$229	$253	$267	$278	$280

Polymold Division
EXHIBIT 5 • Involvement in Polymold's Markets by Competitors A–D

	Heavy	Medium	Light	No Involvement
Consumer products	Polymold C	A	D B	
Medical/pharmaceutical products		D	Polymold C A B	
Commercial products		Polymold	A B C	D
Home-entertainment products	Polymold A C		B	D
Packaging	B A	Polymold	D C	
Interdivisional sales	B A		Polymold	D C
Miscellaneous	D	Polymold C	B	A

Polymold Division
EXHIBIT 6 • Polymold Sales Have Turned Downward

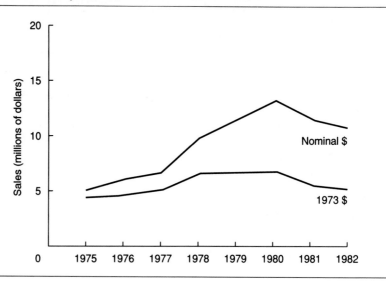

Polymold Division
**EXHIBIT 7 • Yet Two Aggressive Competitors
            (A and B) Have Increased Market Share**

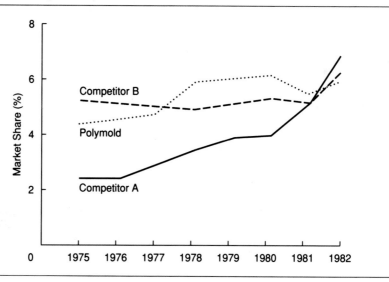

Polymold Division

EXHIBIT 8 • Productivity Has Been Consistently Better Than Expected

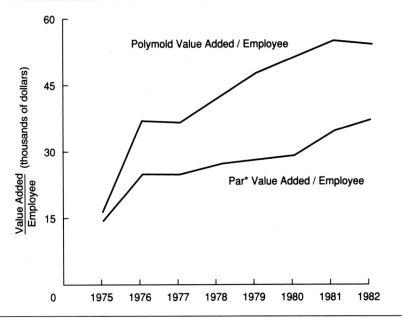

*Par indicates universe of competitors.

Polymold Division
EXHIBIT 9 • Capital Has Begun to Replace Labor

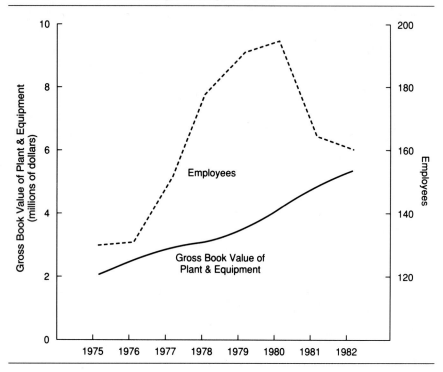

Polymold Division
EXHIBIT 10 • Yet Real Productivity Has Not Increased

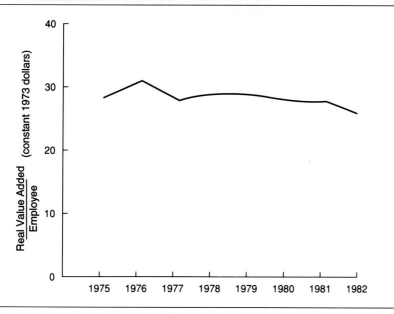

Polymold Division

**EXHIBIT 11 • Polymold Return on Investment,
Relative Product Quality, and Productivity**

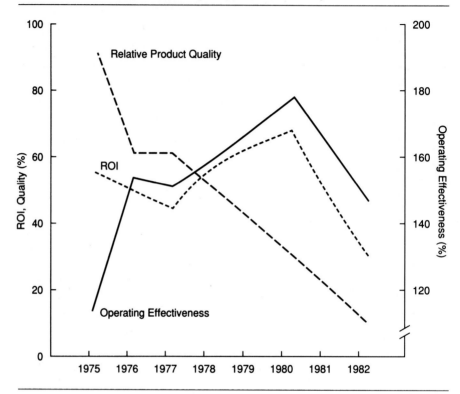

Polymold Division

**EXHIBIT 12 • Depreciation, Interest, and Capital Expenditure
Forecasts without and with CAD/CAM (in thousands)**

	1983	*1984*	*1985*	*1986*	*1987*	*1988*
Without CAD/CAM						
Depreciation	$420	$416	$436	$449	$446	$465
Interest expense	144	136	129	112	112	101
Capital expenditures	287	458	534	362	381	541
Tax credits	23	37	43	29	30	43
With CAD/CAM						
Depreciation	420	513	623	694	782	894
Interest expense	144	136	129	112	112	101
Capital expenditures	287	1,106	831	652	870	954
Tax credits	23	88	66	52	70	76

Polymold Division
EXHIBIT 13 • Efficiency-Program Savings Estimates with CAD/CAM

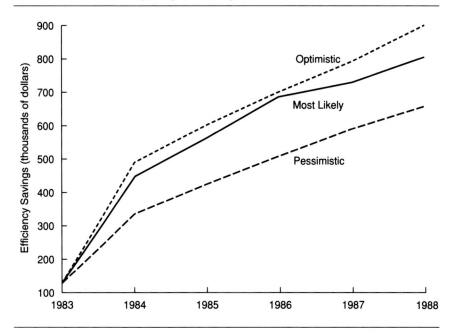

Polymold Division
EXHIBIT 14 • Tooling Industry Financial Information (dollars in millions)

	Sales		Net Income/Sales		Return on Assets		Return on Equity	
	1981	*1982*	*1981*	*1982*	*1981*	*1982*	*1981*	*1982*
Company								
Acme–Cleveland	$ 400.7	$ 327.0	2.7%	3.6%	4.8%	4.6%	9.0%	9.3%
Brown & Sharpe	205.4	143.8	2.9	−0.1	0.3	−7.0	6.8	−18.0
Cincinnati Milacron	934.4	759.7	6.5	1.6	8.7	3.5	17.4	6.7
Ex-Cell-O	1,124.6	1,027.1	5.1	4.7	8.1	7.6	13.8	13.3
Gleason Works	239.9	179.7	3.7	−0.1	4.9	5.2	8.0	−9.6
Monarch Machine	140.1	95.2	13.6	7.3	21.3	7.6	27.1	9.5
Norton	1,334.6	1,264.1	7.1	1.5	9.4	3.6	17.5	6.7
Snap-on Tools	441.5	430.5	9.1	8.7	11.8	11.9	18.8	16.0
Stanley Works	1,009.5	962.8	5.5	3.9	8.3	5.9	14.4	9.6
Starrett	122.5	112.7	11.3	10.0	14.1	11.9	19.1	14.6
Vermont American	203.9	181.9	6.2	3.6	8.6	4.5	15.8	7.8

[a]As of September 1983.

N.Av. = not available.

N.Ap. = not applicable.

Sources: *Value Line Investment Survey* and Standard & Poor's *Bond Guide*.

continued

Polymold Division
EXHIBIT 14 *continued*

Debt/Total Assets		Working Capital/Sales		Market/Book Value		Price/Earnings Ratio		S&P Debt Rating[a]	Beta[a]
1981	1982	1981	1982	1981	1982	1981	1982		
23.4%	14.3%	24.4%	22.8%	0.78×	0.66×	10.5×	7.8×	N.Av.	0.90
25.0	23.5	36.4	38.5	0.65	0.54	12.1	N.Ap.	N.Av.	0.95
15.0	13.6	28.6	30.1	1.70	1.75	12.3	24.6	N.Av.	1.10
8.6	6.8	21.8	24.5	0.82	0.89	7.4	6.2	N.Av.	1.10
10.7	17.8	18.3	23.6	0.55	0.58	9.3	N.Ap.	N.Av.	1.05
0.0	0.0	38.4	54.4	1.01	0.96	4.1	9.1	N.Av.	1.05
17.7	18.2	26.1	23.6	1.31	0.99	8.5	14.9	A	0.95
8.1	8.0	37.2	43.1	2.00	2.35	11.2	12.1	N.Av.	1.00
12.8	14.1	24.6	25.0	1.21	1.69	8.6	12.4	A+	0.95
0.0	0.0	45.0	52.0	1.38	1.34	6.7	8.3	N.Av.	0.70
23.2	21.7	26.7	32.4	1.46	1.08	7.1	11.0	N.Av.	0.80

Massalin Particulares

In early 1981, Massalin Particulares' overcrowded manufacturing facilities in Buenos Aires definitely contributed to the company's position as the high-cost producer in the competitive Argentine cigarette market. Massalin Particulares (M.P.) managers believed a potential solution might be found in their yet-to-be-developed Merlo plant, but changes to the Merlo property would be required if they were to proceed. Those changes would require investments well beyond those already approved for the initial purchase of the plant. To begin the process of adapting the Merlo plant, Massalin Particulares President Juan Munro and his staff would need to convince the board of directors to invest an additional US$59 million in the cigarette business in Argentina.

History of Massalin Particulares[1]

Massalin Particulares, S.A., (M.P.) was born of the October 1979 merger of three separate cigarette companies: Massalin y Celasco, Particulares, and Imparciales. Massalin y Celasco had been an affiliate of Philip Morris (effectively a wholly owned subsidiary) and produced a number of international (Philip Morris) brands as well as a local cigarette named Colorado. Imparciales and Particulares produced, in addition to Kent, domestic brands of blond, black, and mixed tobacco cigarettes. Both firms had been owned, in the main, by the West German firm Reemstma prior to the merger that made M.P. one of the ten largest companies in Argentina. Massalin Particulares' board of directors consisted of those representing both Philip Morris and Reemstma, although Philip Morris had equity control (51 percent) and a 62.5-percent share in the earnings.

At the time of the merger, each of the firms purchased and processed tobacco and produced and packaged cigarettes. Manufacturing consisted

---

[1] Background on the socioeconomic and political history of Argentina is in the appendix to this case.

of three steps. The purchased tobacco was sorted and graded, and the stems separated from the leaf in a stemmery. The tobacco was then processed. The leaf portions were cut to size and mixed with the stems, tobacco types, and flavorings to the brand specifications in an operation housed in the primary. The processed tobacco was then used in the manufacture of cigarettes. This process was known as a *make-pack* or *secondary operation.*

The firm's purchasing and stemming operations were conducted in one of the two main tobacco-growing regions of Argentina. Massalin and Imparciales had operations in and around Salta and Jujuy, two provinces in the foothills of the Andes near the Chilean and Bolivian borders in the northwestern part of Argentina. This area was known for its fine Virginia tobaccos grown on large farms by sophisticated producers. Burley was purchased in the province of Tucuman. Particulares' primary purchasing and processing operations were concentrated in Goya in the northeastern province of Corrientes, a large area situated between two broad rivers, the Parana and Uruguay. This area typically had small farms and sharecropper farmers who were more dependent on the success of their tobacco crop than farmers running large operations.

The cigarette-manufacturing operations of Particulares and Massalin in Buenos Aires were within ten blocks of each other. Massalin also produced cigarettes in Salta, and Imparciales in Goya. (See Exhibit 1 for a map of the locations of the three firms' operations.) The plants, while clean, were old, and at least half the equipment was antiquated. These old facilities were clearly not designed to accommodate the higher speed equipment needed to produce the quantity or quality of cigarettes M.P. management believed the consumer of international brands demanded. Exhibit 2 further describes the facilities.

Cigarette Market

Cigarettes, generally a slow-growth product, had sales growth of 6 percent per year from 1972 to 1976 in Argentina because of government-imposed price controls: price controls, in an economy experiencing high inflation, effectively decreased the real price. The combination of price controls and inflation had caused many companies, including Massalin, to experience losses on the sale of cigarettes in recent years. Once price controls were lifted, prices rose, in some cases more than 100 percent overnight, and demand dropped. Demand from 1978 to 1981 grew about 3 percent, and management expected growth in demand to dwindle to near zero over the next decade, although the infant antismoking movement had not yet had a significant impact on consumption in Argentina. Actual and forecast growth in the Argentine population and in the cigarette market and market share by cigarette type are shown in Exhibit 3.

In 1976 five companies were producing cigarettes for the Argentine market. By early 1980, mergers and acquisitions had reduced the number to two: Nobleza-Piccardo, a British–American Tobacco affiliate, and Massalin Particulares. The market was dominated by Jockey Club, a blond, filtered, Nobleza product. The many versions of Jockey Club accounted for 60 percent of Nobleza's sales and 25 percent of the total Argentine cigarette market, excepting the hard-to-define roll-your-own segment. Nobleza had other brands but none with the stunning and enduring success of Jockey Club. Currently Nobleza had 59 percent of the market volume but, because M.P.'s brands commanded a higher price, only 55 percent of market sales. In early 1981, M.P.'s market position by segment was:

Massalin Particulares Estimated Market Position by Segment, Early 1981

Cigarette Type	Market Share
Blond	45.3%
Light	20.5
Black	46.1
Imports	69.0
Total market share	41.0

M.P. had a total of 52 brands, none of which held more than a 6-percent market share. Marlboro, one of M.P.'s leading brands, had gained 3.4 share points in 1981.

M.P. management did not intend to remain number two in a two-competitor market. With the larger resource of brands from Philip Morris, and the strong position in the black cigarette market it had acquired in the recent merger, management believed it could own 52 percent of the market volume by 1984. The M.P. plan for achieving that target is outlined in the following table.

Massalin Particulares Market Position by Segment, 1981–1984 Forecast

Current Types	1981	1984 (est.)	Market Growth 1981–1984
Blond filters	45.3%	53.9%	0.2%
Light filters	20.5	40.3	14.3
Black cigarettes	46.1	53.0	0.4
New brands as percentage of total M.P. volume	10.0	24.0	N.Ap.
Total market share	41.0	52.0	N.Ap.

N.Ap. = not applicable.

This plan could be achieved only if M.P. could upgrade the quality of its cigarettes to maintain and expand the sales of international brands, increase its capacity to meet the current and projected peak-season demand, and continue mounting successful marketing campaigns. The Merlo plant might be the answer.

In part, the interest in the Merlo plant had been sparked by Nobleza's purchase of a large General Motors plant. Nobleza bought the plant just outside the Buenos Aires Federal District for several reasons. First, in 1978 the government required that all manufacturing be moved outside the capital of Buenos Aires. The move had to be made before a firm's license to manufacture expired (the mid-1980s for M.P.). While a firm could seek a variance in order to continue manufacturing within the capital,[2] M.P. management believed other, more compelling, reasons lay behind Nobleza's intended move. M.P. expected Nobleza to concentrate on improving both the quality of its product and the efficiency of its operation. Being a low-cost producer was critical in the highly competitive environment, and high quality was critical to the success of international brands.

The General Motors plant purchase by Nobleza portended increasing difficulties for M.P. Capacity had been desperately needed even before the merger; in fact, in December, the peak of the summer selling season, M.P. could not meet demand for its most popular brands and had to institute an unpopular quota system. As for quality, there were obvious and continuing problems. Thus M.P. needed to improve both quantity and quality, even without a new, aggressive marketing plan. A revision to the plan for Merlo gave M.P. management the opportunity to do both.

History of the Merlo Plant

The Olivetti plant in the Merlo barrio of Buenos Aires had originally been bought by Massalin y Celasco in early 1979 for US$20.6 million. The building, although considered modern, was actually more than ten years old. Fully air conditioned, it had been used by Olivetti to produce mechanical typewriters and calculators until 1976. By 1976 the military government, which had replaced the Peronists, had begun reducing the tariff barriers that had protected local industry, and the overvalued peso made imported goods more attractive to the Argentine consumer. The dated Olivetti line expired in a market filled with electronic alternatives. For a plant of 40,000 sq. meters (461,000 sq. ft.) on 15 hectares (38 acres), including a nearby park for employees, management believed the

---

[2] Greater Buenos Aires surrounded the Federal District of Buenos Aires. The system of government and the delivery of services resembled that of many U.S. states where independent cities operated surrounded by a county, both delivering services to their residents.

US$20.6-million price was very reasonable. Only because local industry was experiencing some slowing of business from competition with foreign-made goods, and because the size of the plant was larger than average, was the price so attractive.

The original plan had been to consolidate all Massalin y Celasco operations, except tobacco purchasing, at Merlo. Now, with the merger, another plan had been developed: to continue operations at the Goya and Salta plants, moving all other primary and cigarette-manufacturing opera-tions to Merlo. The Salta plant would continue operations and be reevalu-ated after the move to Merlo.[3] Another change in the original plan for Merlo had been made: the equipment that was to have been moved from the discontinued operations in Buenos Aires was reevaluated and found unlikely to survive the move. Management thus believed it was better to invest in new equipment for the Merlo operation.

While some intermediate adjustments would be made, by 1985 the following would constitute M.P.'s operations:

Projected Cigarette Production Facilities, 1985

	Goya/Corrientes	Perico/Jujuy	Merlo	Rosario/Salta	Total
Stemmery	Black	Blond[b]	—	Blond	3
Primary	Black/Mixed[a]	—	Blond	—	2
Secondary	Black/Mixed	—	Blond	Blond	3

[a]Black and mixed cigarette manufacture would be centralized at Goya, with blond tobacco coming from the Perico and Rosario Stemmeries, and black from the Goya Stemmery.

[b]Blond-tobacco cigarette manufacture would be centralized primarily at Merlo, with tobacco coming from the Perico and/or the Rosario de Lerma Stemmeries.

The changes that would be made to the original plans for Merlo were expected to raise the investment from US$20.6 million to a total of almost US$80 million. The majority of the funds would go into new primary and make-pack equipment—equipment designed to replace the outmoded and unmovable equipment currently being used at the two old Buenos Aires plants. While the original plan had no investment for moving old equip-ment or purchasing new equipment, the additional US$59 million would be used as follows:[4]

---

[3] By law the company paid excise taxes on cigarettes manufactured in tobacco-growing regions like Salta and Goya 36 days after shipment from the factory. From all other plants, taxes were due within 15 days after shipment. Excise taxes constituted 70 percent of the average retail price of cigarettes in 1981.

[4] All figures are expressed in constant US$. As of the exhibit date, the exchange rate used 3,953 pesos to US$ 1.00. Because of the rate of inflation, and the fact that the majority of

Stemmery improvements	$ 1.4
Merlo primary	11.1
Merlo building improvements	11.7
Make-pack equipment	20.5
Other and contingency	14.3
Total	$59.0

The cost of the Merlo plant, the equipment, and ancillary costs are detailed in Exhibit 4. With the primary operating for one shift and make-pack for two, the volume would be 15.2 billion cigarettes in 1982 and would reach 18.5 by 1985. Included were some modifications to other plants that were necessary to keep them running and to increase the quality of the tobacco that would be used at Merlo.

While the Merlo plant would add appreciably to M.P.'s fixed expenses, by using Merlo, the firm could solve its quantity and quality problems. The projected cash flows without and with Merlo are found in Exhibit 5.

While any number of items could change as the plan progressed, two variables seemed to be most important to the success of this project:

1.   The willingness of the employees at Donato Alvarez and Belaustegui to move to the Merlo plant. Manufacturing personnel and office and support staff (all unionized), many of whom lived in the residential neighborhoods surrounding the plants, might choose to avoid the additional hour of commuting across the busy back streets of Buenos Aires. The contingency funds included some temporary transportation assistance to encourage employees to make the move, but the final cost was not known.[5]
2.   Much of the equipment would be imported from the United States, Great Britain, and Germany. Thus, as the value of the peso changed, so would the cost of equipment.

Conclusion

The merger had been more successful than management had expected. While the financial results had been good, market share was up, operating

---

M.P.'s directors represented a U.S.-based corporation's interest in Massalin, all financial transactions were kept or projected in both Argentine pesos and US$s.

[5] Moving a manufacturing operation had costs peculiar to Argentina. Employees could claim, by virtue of the new commuting distance, that the move essentially eliminated their jobs. In the case of such claimed terminations, the employee was entitled to a form of severance pay equal to 1 to 2 months' pay for every year of employment by the firm. This was true for all employees in all industries in Argentina.

losses continued but were smaller, and profits from investing the excise tax float were significant, more than covering operating losses, it had been in merging the two diverse organizations that Juan Munro believed they had been most successful. Much of the management of Imparciales and Particulares had left, but what remained was a young, strong, aggressive management team.

Furthermore, Argentina itself was increasingly attractive for business investment. With the country politically stable, the military government had taken steps to increase imports (forcing local business efficiency), to control the money supply (bringing inflation down to 60 percent in early 1981 from a 1976 high of 500 percent), and to continue energy self-sufficiency. All profits that were less than 12 percent of capital could be repatriated without added taxes. While the peso was 30 to 50 percent overvalued, management believed there were no government policies that would deter foreign investment.

To convince the members of the parent company's board of directors, Mr. Munro and his staff would have to put together a persuasive case for Merlo, substantiating the return they expected and detailing the risks of this new, more capital-intensive plant producing cigarettes in the rapidly changing world of Argentina.

Massalin Particulares
EXHIBIT 1 • Map of Massalin's Operations in Argentina

Note: Distances in kilometers; plants denoted by bold dots.

Massalin Particulares
EXHIBIT 2 • Present Facilities of the Merged Companies

Buenos Aires

- Donato Alvarez: A Massalin y Celasco (M & C) plant that produced blond cigarettes. The plant was old and operated well beyond its designed capacity. Most of the international brands were produced here.

- Belaustegui: An underutilized tobacco-preparation and -manufacturing plant producing black cigarettes and supplying black tobacco to the Goya cigarette-manufacturing plant. Originally owned by Particulares, this black-tobacco operation could not be used for blond-tobacco production but could be used with limited success for the production of mixed tobacco.

Interior

- Goya, Corrientes: An Imparciales plant that produced black, blond, and mixed cigarettes. The layout was poor and the plant small, forcing some operations into adjacent buildings. An underutilized primary was also located there.

- Rosario de Lerma, Salta: A blond-tobacco primary and cigarette-manufacturing facility. The operations were inefficient, and the primary produced tobacco that could not be used in the higher quality international brands. A Massalin y Celasco plant.

- Perico, Jujuy: An Imparciales stemmery.

Merco: → New Plant

Stemmeries

	Contributed to Merger by	Capacity in Tons (Green Weight) per Season		Total Leaf Processed 1979–1980 Season (tons)	Kg/Hr.
		Virginia/Burley	Black		
Rosario de Lerma	M&C	8,750	—	8,584	5,000
Perico	Imparciales	8,750	—	6,943	5,000
Goya	Particulares	—	5,400	4,513	2,500

Cigarette-Production Facilities

	Contributed to Merger by	Production Type		Yearly Primary Capacity[a] (millions of cigarettes)
		Primary	Make-Pack	
Donato Alvarez	M&C	Blond	Blond	8,800
Belaustegui	Particulares	Black	Black	4,200
			Blond	
Goya	Imparciales	Blond	Black	7,000
			Blond	
			Mixed	
Rosario de Lerma	M&C	Blond	Blond	1,900

[a]Operated with two shifts.

Massalin Particulares

EXHIBIT 3 • Cigarette Market Profile

	1976	1977	1978	1979	1980	1981	1982	1983 Projected	1984	1985	Growth from 1981
			Actual								
1. Total population (millions)	25.2	25.6	26.2	25.6	26.5	27.3	27.7	28.1	28.5	28.9	1.4%
2. Total industry unit sales (billions)	37.0	36.9	36.9	38.2	38.7	39.3	40.2	41.0	41.5	41.8	1.6
3. Year per-capita consumption	1,470	1,440	1,410	1,440	1,440	1,440	1,451	1,459	1,456	1,446	0.1
Annual growth-rate percentage	—	—	—	—	—	—	0.8	0.6	(0.2)	(0.7)	—
4. Filter segment (percentage share of market)	98.7	98.6	98.6	98.6	99.5	99.7	100.0	100.0	100.0	100.0	—
5. Market segmentation (percentage share of market)											
a. Black filters	21.7	22.2	24.0	24.8	24.0	23.5	23.5	23.2	22.8	22.5	—
b. Blond/light filters	75.7	75.0	73.2	72.4	74.1	74.9	75.1	75.4	75.8	76.1	—
Blond	—	—	—	—	—	67.1	67.2	65.0	64.4	63.6	—
Light	—	—	—	—	—	7.8	7.9	10.4	11.4	12.5	—
c. Nonfilters	1.3	1.4	1.4	1.4	0.5	0.3	—	—	—	—	—
d. Imported brands	1.3	1.4	1.4	1.4	1.4	1.4	1.4	1.4	1.4	1.4	—

Massalin Particulares

EXHIBIT 4 • Projected Costs and Benefits of Merlo Renovation Capital-Expenditure Program (US$ in thousands)

	Previously Authorized 1980	This Request					
		1981	1982	1983	1984	1985	Total
Stemmeries	—	$ 1,413	—	—	—	—	$ 1,413
Merlo plant purchase	$20,621	—	—	—	—	—	—
Make-pack equipment	—	9,631	$4,037	$4,860	$1,476	$ 514	20,518
Other machinery and equipment	—	3,170	2,320	1,320	1,190	930	8,930
Merlo building improvement	—	10,220	1,500	—	—	—	11,720
Merlo primary	—	10,560	500	—	—	—	11,060
Subtotal	—	34,994	8,357	6,180	2,666	1,444	53,641
10 percent contingency	—	3,499	836	618	267	144	5,364
Grand total	$20,621	$38,493	$9,193	$6,798	$2,933	$1,588	$59,005

Philip Morris International Appropriation Request
Supplemental Information Detail of Cost Estimate (US$ in thousands)

Description	Previous Authorization	This Request	Total
Merlo plant purchase	$20,621	—	$20,621
Merlo plant building improvement	—	$11,720	11,720
Merlo primary	—	11,060	11,060
Stemmeries modifications	—	1,413	1,413
Make-pack equipment	—	20,518	20,518
Other production and misc. equipment	—	8,930	8,930
10 percent contingency	—	5,364	5,364
	$20,621	$59,005	$79,626
Ultimate Distribution of Expenditure			
Land	696	—	696
Land improvements	—	—	—
Buildings	14,882	5,703	20,585
Building equipment	5,043	8,512	13,555
Machinery and equipment		39,406	39,406
Data-processing equipment	—	—	—
Furniture and fixtures	—	20	20
Transportation equipment	—	—	—
Leasehold improvements	—	—	—
Other: 10-percent contingency	—	5,364	5,364
Total	20,621	59,005	79,626
Other expense	1,300	295	1,595
Total estimated expenditure	$21,921	$59,300	$81,221

continued

EXHIBIT 4 *continued*

Description	Previous Authorization	This Request	Total
Merlo Facility			
Plant purchase	$20,621	—	$20,621
Building improvement	—	$11,720	11,720
Primary	—	11,060	11,060
Total	$20,621	$22,780	$43,401
Ultimate Distribution of Expenditure			
Land	696		696
Land improvements			
Buildings	14,882	4,058	18,940
Building equipment	5,043	7,662	12,705
Machinery and equipment			
Data-processing equipment			
Furniture and fixtures			
Transportation equipment			
Leasehold improvements	1,300[a]		1,300[a]
Other: Primary		11,060	11,060
Total	$20,621	$22,780	$43,401

[a]Moving-expense item not included in capital-appropriation total.

65million → 80million

Massalin Particulares

EXHIBIT 5 • Net Earnings Projections without
　　　　　　Proposed Investments (in thousands of constant US$)

	1981	1982	1983	1984	1985
Volume (millions of units)	16,307.7	15,530.3	17,144.5	17,854.5	17,985.2
Net sales	$1,170,090	$1,260,263	$1,242,573	$1,240,984	$1,192,141
Standard variable cost of sales	72,628	93,180	96,590	97,487	98,143
Federal and federal excise taxes	948,303	1,021,384	1,007,147	1,005,759	966,174
Shipping	5,776	5,063	4,976	4,940	4,728
Marginal contribution	143,383	140,636	133,860	132,798	123,096
Leaf usage	26,123	22,074	16,757	11,395	6,710
Fixed manufacturing expenses	33,671	40,199	36,138	35,655	35,218
Depreciation	8,463	6,576	6,721	7,174	7,672
Total cost of sales	68,257	68,849	59,616	54,224	49,600
Available profit	75,126	71,787	74,244	78,574	73,496
Advertising	19,944	20,553	22,103	23,096	23,273
Sales expenses	6,929	7,122	6,797	6,948	6,555
Promotion	3,017	3,117	3,645	3,252	3,158
Affiliate royalties	3,693	3,452	3,622	3,831	3,892
Total marketing	33,583	34,244	36,167	37,127	36,878
General and administrative	28,207	26,735	25,213	23,938	22,549
Total expenses	61,790	60,979	61,380	61,065	59,427
Operating profit	13,336	10,808	12,864	17,509	14,069
Interest expenses	8,842	9,841	9,076	6,227	3,117
Currency translation gain	12,878	10,484	8,853	7,330	6,034
Earnings before income taxes	17,372	11,451	12,641	18,612	16,986
Federal income taxes	3,596	3,778	4,172	6,142	5,605
Net earnings	$ 13,776	$ 7,673	$ 8,469	$ 12,470	$ 11,381

EXHIBIT 5 *continued*

	1981	1982	1983	1984	1985
Volume (millions of units)	17,310.7	18,232.3	19,781.5	21,152.6	21,843.2
Net sales	$1,242,056	$1,381,665	$1,433,694	$1,470,212	$1,447,862
Standard variable cost of sales	76,030	99,762	108,836	112,788	116,402
Federal and federal excise taxes	1,006,628	1,119,775	1,161,941	1,191,538	1,171,280
Shipping	6,131	5,551	5,741	5,853	5,763
Marginal contribution	153,267	156,577	157,176	160,033	154,417
Leaf usage, current to historical	27,346	23,830	18,790	13,183	7,976
Fixed manufacturing expenses	33,085	39,454	35,353	34,519	33,776
Depreciation	12,734	11,602	12,284	12,517	12,677
Total cost of sales	73,165	74,886	66,427	60,219	54,429
Available profit	80,102	81,691	90,749	99,814	99,988
Advertising	21,476	23,043	26,268	28,148	29,075
Sales expenses	6,929	7,122	6,797	6,948	6,555
Promotion	3,017	3,117	3,645	3,252	3,158
Affiliate royalties	3,920	3,758	4,179	4,539	4,727
Total marketing	35,342	37,040	40,889	42,887	43,515
General and administrative	28,208	28,385	27,460	24,978	23,548
Total expenses	63,550	65,425	68,349	67,865	67,063
Operating profit	16,552	16,266	22,400	31,949	32,925
Interest expenses	8,857	10,274	9,346	6,199	2,282
Currency translation gain	13,662	11,494	10,215	8,684	6,843
Federal income taxes	5,074	4,702	7,756	11,478	12,370
Net earnings	$ 16,283	$ 12,784	$ 15,513	$ 22,956	$ 25,116

continued

EXHIBIT 5 *continued*

Cash Flows Proposed with and without Investment (in thousands of constant US$)

	1981	1982	1983	1984	1985
With Proposed Investment					
(A) Net earnings	$16,283	$12,784	$15,513	$22,956	$25,116
(B) Depreciation	12,734	11,602	12,284	12,517	12,677
(C) Interest due investment plan	6,694	8,306	8,580	8,154	7,527
(D) Income tax due to (C) (33%)	(2,231)	(2,768)	(2,860)	(2,718)	(2,509)
(E) Operating cash flow	33,480	29,924	33,517	40,909	42,811
(F) Fixed assets investment	(59,914)	(9,193)	(6,798)	(2,933)	(1,588)
(G) Expenses net of tax	(1,069)	—	—	—	—
(H) Working-capital increase	(13,452)	(21,729)	(16,922)	(16,225)	(6,047)
(I) Net cash flow	(40,955)	(998)	9,797	21,751	35,176
Without Proposed Investment					
(J) Net earnings	13,776	7,673	8,469	12,470	11,381
(K) Depreciation	8,463	6,576	6,721	7,174	7,672
(L) Interest due investment plan	852	1,145	1,624	1,800	2,021
(M) Income tax due to (L) (33%)	(281)	(378)	(536)	(594)	(667)
(N) Operating cash flow	22,810	15,016	16,278	20,850	20,407
(O) Fixed-assets investment	(4,867)	(1,681)	(3,504)	(2,080)	(2,490)
(P) Working-capital increase	(7,405)	(5,288)	(8,109)	(10,693)	(1,790)
(Q) Net cash flow	10,538	8,047	4,665	8,077	16,127
(R) Differential cash flow (I − Q)	(51,493)	(9,045)	5,132	13,674	19,049

ROI 20.01%, payback 5.1 years

EXHIBIT 5 *continued*

1986	1987	1988	1989	1990	1991	1992	1993	1994	1995
$25,116	$25,116	$25,116	$25,116	$25,116	$25,116	$25,116	$25,116	$25,116	$25,116
—	—	—	—	—	—	—	—	—	—
7,527	7,527	7,527	7,527	7,527	7,527	7,527	7,527	7,527	7,527
(2,509)	(2,509)	(2,509)	(2,509)	(2,509)	(2,509)	(2,509)	(2,509)	(2,509)	(2,509)
30,134	30,134	30,134	30,134	30,134	30,134	30,134	30,134	30,134	30,134
—	—	—	—	—	—	—	—	—	—
—	—	—	—	—	—	—	—	—	—
—	—	—	—	—	—	—	—	—	74,375
30,134	30,134	30,134	30,134	30,134	30,134	30,134	30,134	30,134	104,509
11,381	11,381	11,381	11,381	11,381	11,381	11,381	11,381	11,381	11,381
—	—	—	—	—	—	—	—	—	—
2,021	2,021	2,021	2,021	2,021	2,021	2,021	2,021	2,021	2,021
(667)	(667)	(667)	(667)	(667)	(667)	(667)	(667)	(667)	(667)
12,735	12,735	12,735	12,735	12,735	12,735	12,735	12,735	12,735	12,735
—	—	—	—	—	—	—	—	—	—
—	—	—	—	—	—	—	—	—	33,285
12,735	12,735	12,735	12,735	12,735	12,735	12,735	12,735	12,735	46,020
17,399	17,399	17,399	17,399	17,399	17,399	17,399	17,399	17,399	58,489

NPV=65million

continued

i=17.5

NPV: 65 million

EXHIBIT 5 *continued*

Detail of Financial Assumptions, 1981–1985

	1981	*1982*	*1983*	*1984*	*1985*
Inflation rate (wholesalers' prices, annual percent)	82%	65%	53%	43%	34%
Inflation rate US$ (annual percent)	10	10	10	10	10
Devaluation rate (annual percent)	79	73	61	51	40
US$ interest rate (annual percent)	17.5	17.5	17.5	17.5	17.5
Total market increase (over previous year, percent)	—	2.2	2.2	1.1	0.8
Salaries total increase (annual percent)	106	82	55	45	36
Selling-price increase (annual percent)	82	65	53	43	34
Raw-material purchasing price increase (annual percent)	73%	59%	49%	40%	33%
Dividends (US$ 000)	US$ 7,000	US$ 4,000	US$ 4,000	US$ 4,000	US$ 4,000
Royalties (US$ 000)					
With proposed investments	3,920	3,785	4,179	4,539	4,727
Philip Morris International	3,402	3,662	4,053	4,410	4,589
Others	518	123	126	129	138
Without proposed investments	3,693	3,452	3,662	3,831	3,892
Philip Morris International	3,175	3,329	3,496	3,702	3,754
Others	US$ 518	US$ 123	US$ 126	US$ 129	US$ 138

Other assumptions

Nominal excise tax rate: 70.0%

Tobacco fund rate: 5.85%

Leaf inventory duration (months at the beginning of each crop):

Virginia	12
Burley	12
Criollo Correntino	14

New office building not included.

Disposal of Belaustegui and Donato buildings not considered.

Income tax, corporate rate: 33%

Project Financial Review

Cash-Flow Analysis   The return on investment was calculated on the incremental cash flow derived from an aggressive "invest and grow" business plan. This planned investment is projected to provide an after-tax return of 20 percent with a payback period of 5.3 years. This return is attributable to increased volume, more favorable product mix, and cost-efficient machinery.

In examining the analysis, the following should be noted:

■ The Merlo Project was previously approved.

■ Expenditure request of US$20.6 million is included in the cash flow in order to reflect a total project approach.

■ Interest expense related to the investments is added back so as to not confuse the investment and financing decisions.

The cash-flow analysis includes the following assumptions:

1. All new investment is depreciated over a 10-year life.
2. The project is analyzed over a 15-year period.
3. All results after 1985 except for depreciation and investment are assumed to remain at the 1985 level.
4. Additional investment requirements after 1985 are assumed to be equal to depreciation.
5. A peso devaluation rate is used that would equal the U.S.–Argentina inflation differential by 1985.
6. Financing is assumed for the full investment at the US$ interest rate of 17.5 percent.
7. Payroll costs are increased faster than inflation. It is assumed that the government will advocate an economic policy with an objective to increase wage earners' living standards.
8. Cigarette selling prices and tobacco costs are increased in line with inflation.
9. Annual royalty payments are projected.
10. No funds for a new central office building are included. This project is being reviewed and will be submitted separately.
11. Increased volume and operating efficiencies will provide cost savings on a per-thousand basis in direct cost of sales, fixed manufacturing expense, sales expense, and administrative expense.
12. In the net earnings projections, the leaf usage, current to historical, and currency translation gain numbers are included in the cash flows to approximate further the economic reality of a hyperinflationary economy within the constraints of U.S. accounting principles. If they were excluded, the return would be higher.

▼

Massalin Particulares

Appendix
Argentina, 1979

Argentines are making their money work in an economy that defies all conventional definition. A recent visitor described the general population as
being savvy about financial matters. He told of middle-class homemakers
moving their money from one source to another as often as necessary (sometimes daily) to get the best return. Long-term investments? One month.
Other visitors believe Argentine businessmen may actually thrive on the
gamesmanship of managing money under such adverse circumstances.

To the outsider doing business in Argentina, the country has the
atmosphere of a busy casino because of the volatile economy and trading
environment. Without money, one does not play, but if one has money,
then it is solely a matter of using it in the most lucrative way.

And what is the outstanding feature of this economy? Inflation. Inflation is at such high levels that, to the outsider, coping seems impossible. In
fact, many believe the years of hyperinflation should have, by now,
brought all economic activity to a complete standstill. So difficult is the
situation to comprehend that foreign companies and investors have in the
recent past written off their Argentine interests as losses, only to be tanta-
lized, once again, by apparent opportunities for financial gain.

Referring to Argentina as a model developing country is unfair in
both political and social terms. Nevertheless, the economy has become an
interesting study for world organizations attempting to balance the needs
of have and have- not countries. The effects of various economic policies
on different sectors of the economy, and ultimately on investors, consumers, and businessmen, could prove to be instructive to other young countries attempting to stabilize in a tumultuous world.

Argentina is endowed with rich natural resources. Most of the country lies in the southern hemisphere's temperate zone. The country boasts a
90-percent literacy rate, a skilled labor force, and a relatively low birth
rate. With these things in mind, it is hard for the outsider, and perhaps
even the Argentine, to find logic and reason in the current state of affairs.

At the turn of this century, between 1880 and 1920, Argentina was
considered one of the ten strongest economic powers in the world. Politically, the people supported fair elections and a democratic process. Cultur-

ally, the sophisticated Argentines invited and received renowned world artists as visitors and performers in their country.

To understand what has happened since then, as well as to consider Argentina's possibilities for the future, one must be familiar with the country's traditions. Many have concluded that Argentina's future rests solely on the shoulders of her population. The Argentine people's ability to demonstrate discipline, patience, and perseverance is as important as their demonstrated financial savvy in their unique economy.

Argentina is a country of immigrants: 40 percent are Italian and 30 percent are Spanish; the rest are English, Irish, and German, with a smattering of Syrians, Greeks, Turks, Poles, and Russian Jews. Most groups have immigrated within the last 120 years. The native Indian population and the blacks brought as slaves have almost disappeared because of miscegenation and extermination during the Indian wars.

Since the 1500s, Argentina has been a land of promise. The vast expanses of resources awaiting exploitation have provided people with grand dreams, if not grandeur, for generations. The early settlers came primarily from the western part of South America, with a small part of the population coming directly from Europe to the Argentine coast. This dichotomy between the coast and interior established the roots for several Argentine traditions.

For three centuries, the country developed unevenly, with the interior gaining economic predominance over the coast. The interior maintained a strict loyalty to Spain; its settlers retained Spanish attitudes and lifestyles and remained closely allied with the Catholic Church. They provided the mother country with the raw materials she needed. Cottage industries for the development of basic goods developed under the protection of Spain.

In the meantime, the coastal settlers developed trading as their leading industry, even though most of it was conducted against the wishes of Spain. The region's location, combined with the type of business conducted, gave the coastal population a bolder character than that of the interior.

With independence from Spain in 1816, the coastal interests assumed leadership, leaving the interior to stagnate. Protection of cottage industries was lost and their products were no match for lower priced, higher quality imported goods. On the coast, free trade (in a sense, a free-market economy) was in vogue. When the two interests attempted to form a national government, the result was division and even opposition in political goals. Although the first national constitution was written in 1853, it wasn't until 1880 that the entire country accepted the new governmental structure.

Throughout the 19th century, the interests of the wealthy guided the development of the country. The wealthy landowners ruled their territories and assumed positions of leadership as their capabilities were demonstrated. The *caudillo,* or local strongman, usually a wealthy landowner with a cavalry of men in his employ, emerged to create the common form of leadership and local government. He provided a sense of security to those in his territory, allowing the people to pursue their own interests. The *caudillos* did not necessarily trust each other, but they shared one goal— financial gain.

During this time, the central region of the country, known as the *Pampas,* developed its potential as fertile land for livestock and agriculture. Europe, and particularly Britain, were ready markets for Argentine livestock products, and in turn viewed Argentina as an opportunity for profitable investment.

In many respects, Britain was a prime force in building Argentina. British capital helped to finance the struggle for independence, and British capital and technical skill built the railroads. At one time, Britain owned Argentina's public utilities. Trade agreements between the two countries heavily favored Britain and kept Argentina in the position of an unofficial colony.

As the economy rapidly developed through trade, immigrants from Europe poured into the country. Argentina, a country of 1,800,000 inhabitants in 1869, received 2,500,000 immigrants in less than 50 years. By 1910 three out of every four adults in the city of Buenos Aires had been born in Europe. Upon arrival in Buenos Aires, some would make their way to the interior to work the land, but the great majority gravitated to the city's neighborhoods. There they found others from their homelands, surrounded themselves with what was familiar, and effectively separated themselves from the "New World."

Most of these people were not forced into making the transatlantic voyage for religious or political reasons. Word had traveled that there was money to be made, land to own, and opportunities to be had in this New World. For a great many, the promises of Argentina were realized.

But for how long and for how many people could the Argentine economy support this rapid and profitable growth? When the world economy took a downturn in the 1920s, Argentina's ties with Great Britain weakened, and new markets had to be sought.

The constitution formulated in 1853 provided for a political system much like that in the United States. In keeping with the strong-leadership tradition, it permitted broad intervening powers for the president. While the concepts of democracy were appealing, in practice democracy in Argentina lacked the support of the total population. So long as opportunity for financial gain and social mobility existed, the majority supported the government in power. When these opportunities diminished, the seeds of discontent took root; the first publicly sanctioned coup occurred early in the 20th century. Since 1930 Argentina has been ruled by a series of military juntas, provisional governments, and dictators.

In 1949 Juan Peron came to power, and under the Peronist Constitution, the president's powers were enlarged at the expense of the provisional governments, legislature, and judiciary. Peron's support came from the labor unions, because his economic policy promoted the redistribution of wealth to the working class. Economic difficulties eventually led to a military coup in 1956, but leaders from 1955 to 1973 were unsuccessful in dealing with the political and economic problems. After 17 years of exile in Spain, Peron regained power in 1973. After his death, his widow Isabel, who succeeded him, was ousted in a military coup in 1976 following months of political and economic turmoil. The political terrorism that started in the early 1970s became pervasive throughout the country by the mid-1970s. The fear was so widespread that the general population was willing to support almost any measures that would return a sense of stability and security to the country. A junta of army, navy, and air force commanders took control, and General Jorge Videla was sworn in as president. The presidency was to be rotated every five years to establish a government as the collective responsibility of the armed forces rather than as an office for personal power. The new regime had the responsibility of ending what appeared to be terrorism on the verge of civil war and of stimulating an economy headed for ruin.

Peron's regime had advocated state participation in many areas of the economy, particularly in the oil, natural gas, coal, steel, railway, electric, and banking industries. The government also influenced economic activity through export and industrial incentives, import controls, tariffs, price controls, subsidies, support prices, and minimum-wage legislation. The government's excessive size led to deficits financed by printing money. Business cycles usually consisted of economic spurts followed by recession, inflation, balance-of-payments problems, budget deficits, and substantial foreign debt.

Early in 1976, after Videla assumed the presidency, the economy was facing three major interrelated problems: impending hyperinflation, severe domestic recession, and possible external-payments default. General Videla's first step was to select a new minister of the economy, Jose Martinez de Hoz. Sr. de Hoz was a member of one of the richest families in Argentina and was former chairman of Acindar, the country's largest private steel company. His strategy was to keep the state out of everything that private enterprise could do. He developed a massive economic reorganization program that advocated increased grain and beef exports to generate foreign exchange and new foreign investment to finance industry. Interest-rate ceilings and price controls were lifted.

By 1977 inflation had been brought from a 1976 level of over 300 percent to just over 150 percent, and the exchange rate went from 140 pesos per U.S. dollar to 408 pesos per U.S. dollar. Throughout 1978 improvements continued, creating a favorable environment for business, attracting foreign investment, and satisfying the immediate needs of the general public.

In 1979 the military had been in power for about three years, and the worst of the antiguerrilla war seemed to be over. Because the economic

situation was showing signs of improvement and the gross domestic product (GDP) was predicted to increase by fully 8.5 percent, the politicians
were fairly quiescent. There had been an improvement in the real level of
wages and salaries, inflation was at last showing signs of flagging, and
unemployment was also on the decline. The strong peso–dollar relationship had Argentines traveling extensively and made imported goods very
attractive. The balance of payments, as measured by the variation in gross
revenues, was positive by about US$4.5 billion, with the total reserves
position reaching almost US$11 billion by year's end. All told, the situa-
tion and the prospects looked distinctly rosy, and both President Videla
and Sr. de Hoz basked in the glow of national and international approval.

Argentina, 1979

• **30-Day Borrowing Interest Rates**
  (Domestic Deposit Interest Rates) (percentage per month)

	January		*February*		*March*		*April*		*May*		*June*	
1977	N.Av.	N.Av.	N.Av.	N.Av.	N.Av.	N.Av.	4.49%	N.Av.	4.49%	N.Av.	7.43%	(6.14)%
1978	13.42	(10.24)	11.14	(8.19)	9.30	(7.03)	8.34	(6.73)	8.17	(6.89)	8.30	(7.17)
1979	7.59	(6.68)	7.06	(6.36)	7.03	(6.36)	7.06	(6.42)	7.14	(6.52)	7.26	(6.68)

30-Day Borrowing Interest Rates
(Domestic Deposit Interest Rates) (percentage per month)

	July		*August*		*September*		*October*		*November*		*December*	
1977	7.17%	(6.63)%	8.20%	(7.34)%	9.17%	(8.01)%	12.23%	(9.45)%	13.66%	(10.28)%	13.58%	(10.52)%
1978	8.02	(6.52)	7.79	(6.70)	7.35	(6.16)	7.38	(6.40)	7.58	(6.74)	7.87	(7.00)
1979	7.60	(6.99)	8.10	(7.31)	8.10	(7.35)	8.00	(7.21)	7.00	(6.18)	6.90	(5.93)

N.Av. = not available.

Source: Roque B. Fernandez, "Argentina: Macroanalytic Description (1976–1981)," Preliminary Draft, World Bank, Washington, D.C., January 1983, Tables 21 and 22.

Argentina, 1979

• Economic Data on Argentina

	1974	1975	1976	1977	1978	1979
Resources and Expenditures at Current Market Prices (billions of US$)						
Gross national product at market prices	$101.5	$100.7	$99.9	$108.2	$102.2	$109.6
Net foreign investment from abroad	−0.7	−0.8	−0.9	−1.0	−1.0	−1.2
GDP at market prices	102.2	101.5	100.8	107.2	103.2	110.8
Imports of goods and NFS[a]	8.5	9.1	6.7	8.7	7.8	11.9
Exports of goods and NFS	8.3	7.4	9.7	12.3	13.2	12.9
Total resources	102.4	103.2	97.8	103.6	97.8	109.8
Private consumption	69.3	69.0	64.9	67.0	62.9	72.6
General government consumption	13.0	13.8	11.5	11.0	12.7	12.8
Gross domestic investment	20.1	20.4	21.4	25.6	22.2	24.4
Domestic Price Indexes						
Retail/consumer price index	426.5	1,204.8	6,542.2	18,072.2	49,771.0	129,168.7
Percentage change from previous year	123.3%	282.5%	543.0%	276.2%	275.4%	259.5%
Wholesale price index	444.2	1,298.7	7,779.2	19,415.6	47,766.2	119,077.9
Percentage change from previous year	120.0%	292.4%	599.0%	249.6%	246.0%	249.3%
Implicit GDP deflator	477.9	1,430.2	7,485.9	19,440.1	50,191.8	125,547.1
Export price index	544.6	1,525.7	9,677.3	22,183.7	46,207.6	97,514.7
Import price index	481.2	1,276.9	9,049.9	23,865.5	51,960.3	102,900.0
Terms of trade	113.2	119.5	106.9	93.0	88.9	94.8
Marginal domestic savings	16.8	28.4	32.9	29.9	27.6	21.7

[a]NFS = Nonfactor services.

Source: World Bank, *EPD Data Bank Country Report,* Washington, D.C., January 25, 1983.

Argentina, 1979

• Argentina Balance of Payments (millions of U.S. dollars)[a]

	1974	1975	1976	1977	1978	1979
Current Account						
Merchandise exports FOB (free on board)	$3,985	$2,961	$3,918	$5,651	$6,401	$7,810
Merchandise imports FOB	−3,216	−3,510	−2,765	−3,798	−3,488	−6,028
Other goods and services and income credit[b]	784	625	773	1,807	1,435	2,106
Other goods and services and income debt	−1,381	−1,368	−1,293	−1,844	−2,560	−4,458
Balance of trade	172	−1,292	633	1,816	1,788	−570
Private unrequited transfers	N.Av.	6	24	32	48	35
Official unrequited transfers	N.Av.	−1	−6	−1	20	22
Current-account balance	172	−1,287	651	1,847	1,856	−513
Capital Account[c]						
Net direct investments	10	N.Av.	N.Av.	145	273	265
Portfolio investment, net	−119	−56	−66	−1	101	222
Other long-term capital, net	107	−114	912	330	1,144	2,667
Other short-term capital, net	−66	373	−359	109	−1,251	1,276
Capital-account balance	−68	203	487	583	267	4,430
Errors and Omissions, Net	26	4	−219	136	12	243

N. Av. = Not available.

[a]Minus sign indicates debit.

[b]Other goods and services and income include: transportation; investment earnings, abroad and domestic; other direct-investment income; labor income; property income; other goods and services and income.

[c]Capital account:

Direct investment accounts for investment abroad and in the reporting economy and includes equity capital; reinvestment of earnings; other long-term capital; and short-term capital.

Portfolio investment accounts for public-sector bonds; other bonds, and corporate equities; and includes assets; liabilities constituting foreign authorities reserves; and other liabilities.

Other long-term capital accounts for the residential official sector; deposit money banks, and other sectors, all of which include drawings on loans extended; repayments on loans extended; other assets; liabilities constituting foreign authorities reserves; drawings on other loans received; repayments on other loans received; other liabilities.

Other short-term capital accounts for (a) residential official sector, including loans extended, other assets, liabilities constituting foreign authorities reserves, other loans received, and other liabilities; (b) the deposit money banks, including assets, liabilities constituting foreign authorities reserves, and other liabilities; and (c) the other short-term capital of other sectors, including loans extended, other assets, liabilities constituting foreign authorities reserves, other loans received, and other liabilities.

Source: Foreign Exchange Rate 1974–1979, World Bank, *EPD Data Bank Country Report*, Washington, D.C.

All other data, International Monetary Fund, *International Financial Statistics,* February 1976: October 1979, March 1983, Washington, D.C.

	1974	1975	1976	1977	1978	1979
Official Reserves Account						
Counterpart to monetization/ demonetization of gold	N.Av.	N.Av.	N.Av.	N.Av.	N.Av.	N.Av.
Counterpart to Special Drawing Rights allocation	−20	N.Av.	N.Av.	N.Av.	N.Av.	72
Counterpart to valuation change	90	N.Av.	2	−18	96	128
Liabilities constituting foreign authorities reserves	N.Av.	N.Av.	N.Av.	N.Av.	4	65
Total Changes in Reserves	−76	1,081	−921	−1,828	−2,235	−4,425
Foreign Exchange Rate— Annual Average Peso/Dollar	36.57	139.57	139.98	407.63	795.75	1,317.0

N. Av. = not available.

The Jacobs Division

Richard Soderberg, financial analyst for the Jacobs Division of MacFadden Chemical Company, was reviewing several complex issues relating to possible investment in a new product for the following year, 1984. The product, a specialty coating material, qualified for investment according to company guidelines. Mr. Reynolds, however, the Jacobs Division manager, was fearful that it might be too risky. While regarding the project as an attractive opportunity, Mr. Soderberg believed that the only practical way to sell the product in the short run would place it in a weak competitive position over the long run. He was also concerned that the estimates used in the probability analysis were little better than educated guesses.

Company Background

MacFadden, with sales in excess of $1 billion, was one of the ten largest chemical companies in the world. Its volume had grown steadily at the rate of 10 percent per year throughout the 1960s and until 1973; its sales and earnings had grown even more rapidly. Beginning in 1973, the chemical industry began to experience overcapacity, however, particularly in basic materials, which led to price cutting. Also, more funds had to be spent in marketing and research for firms to remain competitive. As a consequence of the industry problems, MacFadden achieved only a modest growth of 4 percent in sales in the 1970s and experienced an overall decline in profits. Certain shortages began developing in the economy in 1982, however, and by 1983, sales had risen 60 percent and profits over 100 percent as the result of price increases and near-capacity operations. Nevertheless, most observers believed that the "shortage boom" would be only a short respite from the intensely competitive conditions of the last decade.

The 11 operating divisions of MacFadden were organized into three groups. Most divisions had a number of products centered around one chemical, such as fluoride, sulphur, or petroleum. The Jacobs Division was an exception. It was the newest and, with sales of $30 million, the smallest division. Its products were specialty industrial products with various chemical bases, such as dyes, adhesives, and finishes, which were sold in relatively small lots to diverse industrial customers. No single product had sales over $5 million, and many had sales of only $100,000. There were 150 basic products in the division, each with several minor variations. Jacobs was one of MacFadden's more rapidly growing divisions—12 percent per year prior to 1983—with a 13 percent return on total net assets.

Capital Budgeting for New Projects

Corporatewide guidelines were used for analyzing new investment opportunities: return criteria were 8 percent for cost-reduction projects, 12 percent for expansion of facilities, and 16 percent for new products or processes. Returns were measured in terms of discounted cash flows after taxes. Mr. Soderberg believed that these rates and methods were typical of those used throughout the chemical industry.

Mr. Reynolds tended to demand higher returns for projects in his division, however, even though its earnings-growth stability in the past marked it as one of MacFadden's more reliable operations. Mr. Reynolds had three reasons for wanting better returns than corporate requirements. First, one of the key variables used in appraising management performance at MacFadden was the growth of residual income, although such aspects as market share and profit margins were also considered.[1] Mr. Reynolds did not like the idea of investing in projects that were close to the target rate of earnings imbedded in the residual-income calculation.

Second, many new projects had high start-up costs. Even though they might achieve attractive returns over the long run, such projects hurt earnings performance in the short run. "Don't tell me what a project's discount rate of return is; tell me whether we're going to improve our return on total net assets within three years," Mr. Reynolds would say. Third, Mr. Reynolds was skeptical of estimates. "I don't know what's going to happen here on this project, but I'll bet we overstate returns by 2 to 5 percent on average," was a typical comment. He thus tended to look for at least 4 percent more than the company standard before becoming enthusiastic about a project. "You've got to be hard-nosed about taking risk," he said. "By demanding a decent return for riskier opportunities, we have a better chance to grow and prosper."

---

[1] Residual income was the division's profit after allocated taxes minus a 10-percent capital charge on total assets after depreciation.

Mr. Soderberg knew that Mr. Reynolds views were reflected in decisions throughout the division. Projects that did not have promising returns according to Mr. Reynolds' standards were often dropped or shelved early in the decision process. Mr. Soderberg guessed that at Jacobs almost as many projects with returns meeting the company hurdle rates were abandoned as were ultimately approved. In fact, the projects that were finally submitted to Mr. Reynolds were usually so promising that he rarely rejected them. Capital projects from his division were accepted virtually unchanged, unless top management happened to be unusually pessimistic about prospects for business and financing in general.

The Silicone-X Project

A new product was often under study for several years after research had developed a "test tube" idea. The product had to be evaluated relative to market needs and competition. The large number of possible applications of any product complicated this analysis. At the same time, technological studies were undertaken to examine such factors as material sources, plant location, manufacturing-process alternatives, and economies of scale. While a myriad of feasible alternatives existed, only a few could be actively explored, and they often required outlays of several hundred thousand dollars before the potential of the project could be ascertained. "For every dollar of new capital approved, I bet we spend $0.30 on the analysis of opportunities," observed Mr. Soderberg, "and that doesn't count the money we spend on research."

The project that concerned Mr. Soderberg at the moment was called Silicone-X, a special-purpose coating that added slipperiness to a surface. The coating could be used on a variety of products to reduce friction, particularly where other lubricants might imperfectly eliminate friction between moving parts. Its uniqueness lay in its hardness, adhesiveness to the applied surface, and durability. The product was likely to have a large number of buyers, but most of them could use only small quantities: only a few firms were likely to buy amounts greater than 5,000 pounds per year.

Test-tube batches of Silicone-X had been tested both inside and outside the Jacobs Division. Comments were universally favorable, although $2.00 per pound seemed to be the maximum price that would be acceptable. Lower prices were considered unlikely to produce larger volume. For planning purposes, a price of $1.90 per pound had been used.

Demand was difficult to estimate because of the variety of possible applications. The division's market-research group had estimated a first-year demand of 1 to 2 million pounds with 1.2 million cited as most likely. Mr. Soderberg commented, "They could spend another year studying it and be more confident, but we wouldn't find them more believable. The estimates are educated guesses by smart people. However, they are also pretty wild stabs in the dark. They won't rule out the possibility of demand as low as 500,000 pounds, and 2 million pounds is not the ceiling." Mr. Soderberg empathized with the problem facing the market-research group. They tried to do a systematic job of looking at the most probable applications, but the data were not good.

The market researchers believed that, once the product became established, average demand would probably grow at a healthy rate, perhaps 10 percent per year. However, the industries served were likely to be cyclical, and depending on market conditions, total volume required could be 20 percent higher or lower than average. The market researchers concluded, "We think demand should level off after 8 to 10 years, but the odds are very much against someone developing a cheaper or markedly superior substitute."

On the other hand, there was no patent protection on Silicone-X, and the technological know-how involved in the manufacturing process could be duplicated by others in perhaps as few as 12 months. "This product is essentially a commodity, and someone is certainly going to get interested in it when sales volume reaches $3 million," observed Mr. Soderberg.

The cost estimates looked solid. Mr. Soderberg continued, "Basic chemicals, of course, fluctuate in purchase price, but we have a captive source with stable manufacturing costs. We can probably negotiate a long-term transfer price with Wilson [another MacFadden division], although this is not the time to do so."

Project Analysis

In his preliminary analysis, Mr. Soderberg used a discount rate of 20 percent and a project life of 15 years, because most equipment for the project was likely to wear out and need replacement during that time frame.

"We also work with most likely estimates. Until we get down to the bitter end, there are too many alternatives to consider, and we can't afford probabilistic measures or fancy simulations. A conservative definition of most likely values is good enough for most of the subsidiary analyses. We've probably made over 200 present-value calculations using our computer programs just to get to this decision point, and heaven knows how many quick-and-dirty paybacks," observed Mr. Soderberg. "We've made a raft of important decisions that affect the attractiveness of this project. Some of them are bound to be wrong—I hope not critically so. In any case, these decisions are behind us. They're buried so deep in the assumptions, no one can find them, and top management wouldn't have time to look at them anyway."

With Silicone-X, Mr. Soderberg was down to a labor-intensive, limited-capacity approach and a capital-intensive method. "The analyses all point in one direction," he said, "but I have the feeling it's going to be the worst one for the long run."

The labor-intensive method involved an initial plant and equipment outlay of $900,000. It could produce 1.5 million pounds per year. "Even if the project bombs out, we won't lose much. The equipment is very adaptable. We could find uses for about half of it. We could probably sell the balance for $200,000, and let our tax write-offs cover most of the rest. We should salvage the working-capital part without any trouble. The start-up costs and losses are our real risks," summarized Mr. Soderberg. "We'll spend $50,000 debugging the process, and we'll be lucky to satisfy half the possible demand. However, I believe we can get this project on stream in one year's time."

Exhibit 1 shows Mr. Soderberg's analysis of the labor-intensive alternative. His calculations showed a small net present value when discounted at 20 percent and a sizable net present value at 8 percent. When the positive present values were compared with the negative present values, the project looked particularly attractive.

The capital-intensive method involved a much larger outlay for plant and equipment: $3.3 million. Manufacturing costs would, however, be reduced by $0.35 per unit and fixed costs by $100,000, excluding depreciation. The capital-intensive plant was designed to handle 2.0 million pounds, the lowest volume for which appropriate equipment could be acquired. Because the equipment was specialized, only $400,000 of this machinery could be used in other company activities. The balance probably had a salvage value of $800,000. It would take 2 years to get the plant on stream, and the first year's operating volume was likely to be low— perhaps 700,000 pounds at the most. Debugging costs were estimated to be $100,000.

Exhibit 2 presents Mr. Soderberg's analysis of the capital-intensive method. At a 20-percent discount rate, the capital-intensive project had a large negative present value and thus appeared much worse than the labor-intensive alternative. However, at an 8-percent discount rate, it looked significantly better than the labor-intensive alternative.

Problems in the Analysis

Several things concerned Mr. Soderberg about the analysis. Mr. Reynolds would only look at the total return. Thus the capital-intensive project would not be acceptable. Yet, on the basis of the breakeven analysis, the capital-intensive alternative seemed the safest way to start. It needed sales of just 325,900 pounds to break even, while the labor-intensive method required 540,000 pounds (see Exhibit 3).

Mr. Soderberg was concerned that future competition might result in price cutting. If the price per pound fell by $0.20, the labor-intensive method would not break even unless 900,000 pounds were sold. Competitors could, once the market was established, build a capital-intensive plant that would put them in a good position to cut prices by $0.20 or more. In short, there was a risk, given the labor-intensive solution, that Silicone-X might not remain competitive. The better the demand proved to be, the more serious this risk would become. Of course, once the market was established, Jacobs could build a capital-intensive facility, but almost none of the labor-intensive equipment would be useful in such a new plant. The new plant would still cost $3.3 million, and Jacobs would have to write off losses on the labor-intensive facility.

The labor-intensive facility would be difficult to expand economically. It would cost $50,000 for each 100,000 pounds of additional capacity (only practical in 250,000-pound increments). In contrast, an additional 100,000 pounds of capacity in the capital-intensive unit could be added for $25,000.

The need to expand, however, would depend on sales. If demand remained low, the project would probably return a higher rate under the labor-intensive method. If demand developed, the capital-intensive method would clearly be superior. This analysis led Mr. Soderberg to believe that his breakeven calculations were somehow wrong.

Pricing strategy was another important element in the analysis. At $1.90 per pound, Jacobs could be inviting competition. Competitors would be satisfied with a low rate of return, perhaps 12 percent, in an established market. At a price lower than $1.90, Jacobs might discourage competition. Even the labor-intensive alternative would not provide a rate of return of 20 percent at any lower price. Mr. Soderberg began to think that using a high discount rate was forcing the company to make a riskier decision than would a lower rate and was increasing the chance of realizing a lower rate of return than had been forecast.

Mr. Soderberg was not sure how to incorporate pricing into his analysis. He knew he could determine what level of demand would be necessary to encourage a competitor, expecting a 50-percent share and needing a 12-percent return on a capital-intensive investment, to enter the market at a price of $1.70, or $1.90, but this analysis did not seem to be enough.

Finally, Mr. Soderberg was concerned about the demand estimates on which he had based the analysis. Even though he could not justify his estimates on the basis of demand analysis, as could the market-research department, he prepared a second set of estimates that he thought were a little less optimistic. Exhibit 4 shows his estimates for achieving various levels of demand in the first year.

Mr. Soderberg's job was to analyze the alternatives fully and recommend one of them to Mr. Reynolds. On the most simple analysis, the labor-intensive approach seemed best. Even at 20 percent, its present value was positive. That analysis, however, did not take other factors into consideration.

The Jacobs Division
EXHIBIT 1 • Analysis of Labor-Intensive Alternative for
Silicone-X (dollars in thousands, except per-unit data)

			Year			
	0	*1*	*2*	*3*	*4*	*5–15*
Investments						
Plant and equipment	$ 900					
Working capital		$ 140	$ 14	$ 15	$ 17	$ 20
Demand (thousands of pounds)		1,200	1,320	1,452	1,597	N.Av.
Capacity (thousands of pounds)		600	1,500	1,500	1,500	1,500
Sales (thousands of pounds)		600	1,320	1,452	1,500	1,500
Sales price/unit		$1.90	$1.90	$1.90	$1.90	$1.90
Variable costs/unit						
Manufacturing		1.30	1.30	1.30	1.30	1.30
Marketing		0.10	0.10	0.10	0.10	0.10
Total variable costs/unit		1.40	1.40	1.40	1.40	1.40
Contribution/unit		0.50	0.50	0.50	0.50	0.50
Contribution in dollars		300	660	726	750	750
Fixed costs						
Overhead		210	210	210	210	210
Depreciation		60	60	60	60	60
Start-up costs (DEBUGGING)		50	0	0	0	0
Total fixed costs		320	270	270	270	270
Profit before taxes		(20)	390	456	480	480
Profit after taxes (taxes @ 50%)		(10)	195	228	240	240
Cash flow from operations (Profit after taxes + depreciation)		50	255	288	300	300
Total cash flow	$(900)	$ (90)	$ 241	$ 273	$ 283	280
Terminal value (year 15)						$ 381

N.Av. = not available.

ROA

NPV 20% = 82.61
*   8%   1,158.72*

280

The Jacobs Division

EXHIBIT 2 • Analysis of Capital-Intensive Alternative for
Silicone-X (dollars in thousands, except per-unit data)

					Year			
	0	*1*	*2*	*3*	*4*	*5*	*6*	*7–15*
Investments								
Plant and equipment	$ 1,900	$ 1,400						
Working capital			$ 160	$ 11	$ 17	$ 20	$ 24	$ 30
Demand (thousands of pounds)			1,320	1,452	1,597	1,757	1,933	2,125
Capacity (thousands of pounds)			700	2,000	2,000	2,000	2,000	2,000
Sales (thousands of pounds)			700	1,452	1,597	1,757	1,933	2,000
Sales price/unit			$1.90	$1.90	$1.90	$1.90	$1.90	$1.90
Variable costs/unit								
Manufacturing			0.95	0.95	0.95	0.95	0.95	0.95
Selling			0.10	0.10	0.10	0.10	0.10	0.10
Total variable costs/unit			1.05	1.05	1.05	1.05	1.05	1.05
Contribution/unit			0.85	0.85	0.85	0.85	0.85	0.85
Contribution in dollars			595	1,234	1,357	1,493	1,643	1,700
Fixed costs								
Overhead			110	110	110	110	110	110
Depreciation			167	167	167	167	167	167
Start-up costs *(DEBUGGING)*			100	0	0	0	0	0
Total fixed costs			377	277	277	277	277	277
Profit before taxes			218	957	1,081	1,217	1,366	1,423
Profit after taxes (taxes @ 50%)			109	479	540	608	683	712
Cash flow from operations								
(Profit after taxes + depreciation)			276	646	707	775	850	879
Total cash flow	$(1,900)	$(1,400)	$ 116	$ 635	$ 690	755	$ 826	849
Terminal value (year 15)								$1,384

NPV = 202 = -507
8% - 2494

The Jacobs Division
EXHIBIT 3 • Breakeven Analysis for Silicone-X

	Labor Intensive	Capital Intensive
Normal ($1.90 price)		
Fixed costs		
Operations	$210,000	$110,000
Depreciation	60,000	167,000
Total	$270,000	$277,000
Contribution per unit	$0.50	$0.85
Units to break even	540,000	325,882
Price Competitive ($1.70 price)		
Contribution per unit	$0.30	$0.65
Units to break even	900,000	426,154

The Jacobs Division
EXHIBIT 4 • Probability Estimates of 1985 Demand for Silicone-X

Demand Range (thousands of pounds)	Market-Research Department Probabilities	Market-Research Department Expected Value (thousands of pounds)	Mr. Soderberg's Probabilities	Mr. Soderberg's Expected Value (thousands of pounds)
400– 600	2%	10	3%	15
600– 800	3	21	6	42
800–1,000	12	100	15	135
1,000–1,200	32	352	40	440
1,200–1,400	31	403	22	286
1,400–1,600	12	180	8	120
1,600–1,800	3	51	2	34
1,800–2,000	2	38	1	19
2,000–2,200	1	21	1	21
2,200–2,400	1	23	1	23
2,400–2,600	1	25	1	25
Expected value		1,224		1,160

(handwritten annotations: "PROBAB BY Midrange", "1200", "NPV for Both", "2 PRICE SCENARIOS", "3 DEMAND", "NPV FOR COMBO")

Chausson Body and Assembly

In late June 1984, Alan Foster, chairman of the consulting firm Applied Resources, Inc., was looking for companies with the potential to supply vehicle bodies to the U.S. automobile industry. A shift in customer demand from small cars to status cars and utility vehicles had taken U.S. automakers by surprise and now had them exploring their options for meeting the demand the market change created.

Mr. Foster had identified one company he believed would be a suitable supplier, Chausson Trading Corporation, a French automobile manufacturing and engineering company. It was interested in supplying the major U.S. automakers but only in a joint venture with an American company already in the vehicle-body business. Mr. Foster would have to find an equity partner for Chausson and convince the candidate of the merits of the joint venture in order to get Chausson management to enter the U.S. market.

In preparing an analysis to show a U.S. partner just how attractive this innovative production arrangement could be, Mr. Foster decided to use a time-value-of-money approach for the U.S. partner. Although an after-tax internal rate of return (IRR) was easy to compute, Mr. Foster was uncertain what rate of return to use in comparison. The key was to determine the business risk of the project. If the fundamental risks of the investment were the same as investing in a U.S. auto company, for example, the relevant rate of return would be the auto company's cost of capital. On the other hand, because the joint-venture arrangement would be unique in the industry and would certainly change the risks of the cash flows, a rate of return consistent with the new risks would have to be estimated. Mr. Foster knew he would have to carefully consider this problem before he could accurately estimate the true value of the joint venture.

The Economy and the Auto Industry

The summer of 1984 marked the second year of sustained recovery following several years of production decreases and record losses for the auto industry. The industry had undergone a difficult period of plant closings, layoffs, bitter labor concessions, and tough competition from foreign auto manufacturers, especially the Japanese. As a result, managers had become very cost and quality conscious. Their cost-control programs included self-imposed limits on both engineering expenditures and capital investments. The recent upturn in the economy, however, had resulted in a shift in consumer demand from subcompact, fuel-efficient cars to large "status" cars and utility vehicles. Because the car companies could not quickly adapt their current production lines to different body styles, the larger, more profitable automobiles could not be produced without substantial capital investments and increases in both engineering and labor forces.

The consensus among the auto companies was that an outside contractor should be used to meet the new demand. In addition to circumventing the engineering and capital-investment constraints, this so-called outsourcing had the added advantage of increasing production without substantially increasing the overall production labor force. The latest labor contract with the United Auto Workers made the use of an outside contractor that particularly appealed to management, because outside work could be done with cheaper, nonunion labor. The labor contract permitted outsourcing as long as displaced workers were reassigned within the company; thus, since an expansion program would not displace any current employees, outsourcing would not violate the union contract.

One potential drawback of using an outside contractor lay with quality control. Chausson, however, was an experienced firm that was willing to assume beginning-to-end responsibility for the production of "bodies-in-white" (the unpainted auto body with no other parts added) for the many models likely to be needed. The plan was to sell the bodies-in-white to the auto companies, which would add the other components at their own production facilities to produce the final product. By outsourcing the engineering and production of the 40,000 to 50,000 bodies-in-white per year, the auto companies could meet demand without incurring additional investment, and the vehicles could be produced at a lower than in-house cost because of the labor-cost savings.

The Chausson Trading Company

Founded in France in 1907, Chausson had developed into a leader of designing and manufacturing automotive bodies. By 1983, the firm, with sales of approximately $600 million, was the largest producer of commercial vehicles in Europe. The principal shareholders in Chausson were two French auto manufacturers, Peugeot and Renault, both of which were encouraging Chausson to expand its expertise and find new markets.

Chausson's competitive edge over the years had been its dedication to technological innovations in production. The company was known in Europe as a high-quality and efficient operation that could take complete responsibility for a project starting with the initial design through the delivery of bodies-in-white. The particular technology proposed by Chausson for the joint venture was a flexible assembly design that offered several advantages over the conventional hard automation approach. Flexible body assembly meant that major modifications in body design would not necessitate major production changes. Thus the joint-venture plant would be capable of assembling several different models simultaneously on the same production line and would be able to change the mix of models without sacrificing output. The flexibility would allow each auto company to alter its body-style orders to meet its demand without raising Chausson's production costs.

The Joint-Venture Opportunity

Alan Foster had been an executive at American Motors for many years prior to forming Applied Resources in Ann Arbor, Michigan, in 1980, and his contacts within the industry had led to his current search for a joint-venture partner for Chausson. The auto companies were interested in an outsourcing project if the cost savings were significant and they could be assured of high-quality production.

Having identified Chausson, Mr. Foster had targeted the machine-tool industry from which to find the U.S. partner. Possible candidates included Acme-Cleveland, Brown & Sharpe, Cincinnati Milacron, and Cross & Trecker. All were suppliers of auto-manufacturing equipment and therefore had extensive experience working with the Big Three automakers (GM, Ford, and Chrysler).

The U.S. partner would share equally in the equity investment with Chausson. Chausson would provide the technical expertise in the operation, and the U.S. partner would assume the responsibility of establishing and managing the joint-venture company (see Exhibit 1). Legally, Chausson Trading Company would act as a subcontractor to the joint-venture company. It would carry out all operations related to defining the product and the specific manufacturing processes and be responsible for the on-site launch and debugging of the equipment. The U.S. partner's primary operational responsibilities would include:

1. Hiring and staffing the joint venture;
2. Selecting an existing building or a suitable building site;

3. Site preparation, building, and/or building modifications;

4. Design, procurement, and installation of all building equipment, and

5. Overall project control, including financial management and manufacturing management.

Regardless of who became the investment partner, the joint venture could eventually end up producing bodies for all three of the major U.S. auto companies. The most likely specialty vehicles that were potential projects of the joint venture were

- Ford Bronco II 4-door,
- Ford Aerostar stretch body,
- General Motors Blazer and minivan (body modifications), and
- Chrysler minivan (body modifications).

In addition, the production facility could serve other markets in the future, including

- Special bodies for post office or military vehicles,
- Commercial-vehicle cab bodies for such manufacturers as Mack Truck, and
- After-market customizing of utility vehicles (for example, providing sunroofs or exterior body striping).

Mr. Foster had spoken with most of the New York money-center banks about providing the working-capital loans for the project. Several banks had expressed an interest in participating but not unless a production contract had been signed in advance with Ford, GM, or Chrysler. Moreover, Mr. Foster knew that the banks would not go along unless all the orders through the joint venture were on a take-or-pay basis. Such a contract obligates the buyer to compensate the supplier for a certain number of units over a set period of time whether the units were purchased or not. For example, if GM ordered 50,000 bodies per year for five years but decided in the last year to use only 30,000 units, GM would still be obligated to compensate the supplier for the production of 50,000 units. Compensation would include paying for the 30,000 units ordered, the contribution margin Chausson lost on the 20,000 undelivered units, and any cancellation costs incurred by Chausson as a result of the order change.

Although a purchase price for the bodies-in-white had not yet been agreed upon, Mr. Foster estimated that $1,750 per unit would probably be acceptable to all the parties, at least through 1987. His preliminary negotiations with the auto companies suggested that this unit price was attractive enough to interest them in the project. He estimated that after 1987 the price would rise approximately 4 percent per year, just enough to keep pace with the projected rate of inflation. The price had been determined by estimating the fixed costs of the project over 10 years plus an attractive before-tax return. ←

Mr. Foster's forecasted income statements and balance sheets for the first three years of the project are included as Exhibits 2 and 3. For planning purposes, he had assumed that start-up inefficiencies would push the cost of goods sold above the projected long-term level of 75 percent of sales to 85 percent in 1987 and 78 percent in 1988. Start-up inefficiencies would also prevent selling, general, and administrative expense from settling into its long-term level of 3.7 percent of sales until 1987. The calculation of the interest expense is shown in Exhibit 2 and detailed in Exhibit 4. The land and building were assumed to be financed with an Industrial Revenue Bond (IRB) at 8 precent. IRBs were a cheap source of funds for corporations because the interest payments were tax free for individual investors, yet were fully deductible by the issuing corporation. Because of these tax benefits, investors were willing to accept a much lower interest rate on an IRB than on a comparable corporate bond. In fact, the 8 percent rate for the IRB was cheaper than the current rates on both the 10-year Treasury bonds (13.7 percent) and the current average long-term borrowing costs of the auto companies (14.0 percent).

The equipment was to be leased at an imputed rate of interest equal to 4 percent.[1] The decision had been made to lease rather than buy because the joint venture would have no taxable income for the first years and therefore could not immediately realize the tax benefits of borrowing or the tax savings from the depreciation on the machinery.[2] Leasing allowed a fully taxable lessor to pass along some of the tax benefits of borrowing and depreciation to the lessee in the form of a reduced lease payment.

To answer the question of how profitable the investment would be to a U.S. equity investor, Mr. Foster decided to compute both an IRR and a net present value for the project. To simplify the analysis, he assumed that the first operating cash flows would begin at the end of 1987, when the company should have sold 35,000 units. For the following nine years, he assumed sales of 50,000 units per year. Exhibit 5 details his estimates of working-capital requirements, which also presented in Exhibit 6 as part of the schedule of investments. Mr. Foster had not yet decided what to assume about the value of the joint venture at the end of 10 years, but he did not want whatever value was assumed to represent a significant portion of the total return for the venture.

---

[1] The imputed interest rate for a leasing contract was the discount rate that equated the present value of the pre-tax lease payments with the value of the asset. The lease for the equipment would be a 10-year operating lease that would not have to be reported on the balance sheet.

[2] Because operating losses could be carried forward, the tax benefits to the joint venture would be postponed rather than permanently lost. Having to delay the tax benefits, however, substantially reduced their present value.

Estimating the relevant cash flows was only part of the problem because a discount rate was also needed to complete the analysis. Normally, Mr. Foster would rely upon the cost of capital of comparable investments to use as the discount rate. Since no other joint ventures of this type existed, however, he had decided to use the cost of capital for the auto companies, the financial data for which are presented in Exhibit 7.

Chausson Body and Assembly
EXHIBIT 1 • Chausson Joint Venture Organization

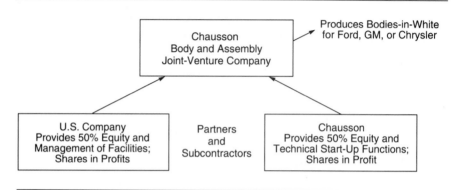

Chausson Body and Assembly
EXHIBIT 2 • Pro-Forma Income Statements (years ended December 31)

	1985	1986	1987
Sales	0	0	$61,250,000
Cost of goods sold	0	0	52,062,500
Gross margin	0	0	9,187,500
Expenses:			
General & administrative	$2,300,000	$4,500,000	$2,275,000
Depreciation[1]	0	400,000	400,000
Lease payment	0	1,479,491	1,479,491
Total expenses	2,300,000	6,379,491	4,154,491
Income (loss) from operations	(2,300,000)	(6,379,491)	5,033,009
Interest expense[2]	2,366,667	4,361,180	7,488,943
Profit (loss) before tax	(4,666,667)	(10,740,671)	(2,455,934)
Provision for income taxes[3]	0	0	0
Net income[4]	($4,666,667)	($10,740,671)	($2,455,934)

[1] 30 years, straight line.

[2] Includes interest portions of IRB payment plus 14% of notes-payable average balance. The prime rate in June 1984 was 13%.

[3] The tax shield from operating losses could be carried forward to offset future taxable income. In 1984, the maximum carry-forward period was 15 years and the tax rate was 50%.

[4] No dividends are expected from 1985 to 1987.

Chausson Body and Assembly
EXHIBIT 3 • Balance Sheet Forecasts (years ended December 31)

Assets	1985	1986	1987
Current assets			
Cash	$ 1,000,000	$ 2,000,000	$ 2,000,000
Accounts receivable	0	0	15,700,000
Inventory	0	2,200,000	17,300,000
Total current assets	1,000,000	4,200,000	35,000,000
Property, plant, equipment			
Land	3,000,000	3,000,000	3,000,000
Buildings, less accumulated depreciation	12,000,000	11,600,000	11,200,000
Total assets	$16,000,000	$18,800,000	$49,200,000
Liabilities & Net Worth			
Current liabilities			
Accounts payable	0	0	9,700,000
Notes payable	16,666,667	30,207,338	63,063,272
Total current liabilities	16,666,667	30,207,338	72,763,272
Total liabilities	16,666,667	30,207,338	72,763,272
Common stock	4,000,000	4,000,000	4,000,000
Retained earnings	(4,666,667)	(15,407,338)	(17,863,272)
Total liabilities and net worth	$16,000,000	$18,800,000	$49,200,000

Chausson Body and Assembly
EXHIBIT 4 • Payment Schedule for $15 Million Industrial Revenue Bond
Outstanding to 1994 with 8% Coupon

Year	Beginning Principal	Payment	Interest Portion	Principal Reduction	Ending Principal
1985	$15,000,000	$2,700,000	$1,200,000	$1,500,000	$13,500,000
1986	13,500,000	2,580,000	1,080,000	1,500,000	12,000,000
1987	12,000,000	2,460,000	960,000	1,500,000	10,500,000
1988	10,500,000	2,340,000	840,000	1,500,000	9,000,000
1989	9,000,000	2,220,000	720,000	1,500,000	7,500,000
1990	7,500,000	2,100,000	600,000	1,500,000	6,000,000
1991	6,000,000	1,980,000	480,000	1,500,000	4,500,000
1992	4,500,000	1,860,000	360,000	1,500,000	3,000,000
1993	3,000,000	1,740,000	240,000	1,500,000	1,500,000
1994	1,500,000	1,620,000	120,000	1,500,000	0

Chausson Body and Assembly
EXHIBIT 5 • Working-Capital Needs, 1987 (in millions)

Current Assets		*Current Liabilities*	
Cash	$2.0	Accounts payable (45 days)	$9.7
Accounts receivable (45 days)	15.7		
Inventories:			
Raw material (30 days)	4.3		
Work in process (30 days)	6.0		
Finished goods (30 days)	7.0		
Total	$35.0	Total current liabilities	$9.7
Net working capital	$25.3		

Assumptions:

Production of 240 units/day.

Sales of 240 units/day.

Net accounts receivable of $1,450 per unit ($1,750 cost less $300 consigned material).

Accounts receivables and accounts payables outstanding for 45 days.

Net raw material costs of $600 per unit ($900 cost less $300 consigned material).

Net work-in-process inventories of $769 per unit ($600 net raw materials plus 50 percent of cost of goods of $169).

Finished goods inventory per unit of $950.

All inventories expected to be outstanding for 30 days.

All working capital needs to fund passthrough costs for such things as design and prototype costs are ignored.

Chausson Body and Assembly
EXHIBIT 6 • Scheduling and Timing of Investments (in millions)

Type of Investment	1985	1986	1987 (in production)	Total
Land	$ 3.0			$ 3.0
Building	12.0			12.0
Plant equipment		12.0		12.0
Change in working capital	1.0	3.2	21.1	25.3
Total investment	$16.0	$15.2	$21.1	$52.3

Chausson Body and Assembly
EXHIBIT 7 • Financial Data for Major Auto Companies

FORD MOTOR CO.

Annotated Balance Sheets (in millions)	1982	1983
Current assets	$ 8,799	$10,819
Fixed assets	13,163	13,050
Total assets	21,962	23,869
Current liabilities	10,424	10,316
Long-term debt	2,353	2,713
Other noncurrent	3,107	3,295
Common stock	764	831
Retained earnings	5,314	6,714
Total liabilities and owners' equity	$21,962	$23,869

Common-Equity Data	1982	1983	6/1984
Beta (Value Line)	0.95	1.05	1.35
End-of-year stock price	$38	$41⅞	$35¾
Shares outstanding (000)	78,315	181,166	183,500

Bond Data

Rating	Annual Coupon	Maturity Date	1982 Price	1983 Price	6/1984 Price
A3	9¼%	1994	$ 74⅜	$ 78½	$ 74⅛
A3	14¾	1985	103½	104	101⅝
A3	14¼	1990	102⅝	105⅛	100⅞

GENERAL MOTORS

Annotated Balance Sheets (in millions)	1982	1983
Current assets	$14,043	$20,800
Fixed assets	27,355	24,895
Total assets	$41,398	$45,695
Current liabilities	$12,385	$14,909
Long-term debt	4,745	3,522
Other noncurrent	5,980	6,497
Preferred stock	284	284
Common stock	2,451	2,663
Retained earnings	15,553	17,820
Total liabilities and owners' equity	$41,398	$45,695

continued

EXHIBIT 7 • *continued*

Common-Equity Data	1982	1983	6/1984
Beta	0.95	1.00	1.05
End-of-year stock price	$57⅞	$73½	$65¼
Shares outstanding (000)	307,463	314,825	315,602

Bond Data

Rating	Annual Coupon	Maturity Date	1982 Price	1983 Price	6/1984 Price
Aa2	8⅝%	2005	$75½	$72	$64¾

CHRYSLER

Annotated Balance Sheets (in millions)	1982	1983
Current assets	$2,369	$2,754
Fixed assets, etc.	3,895	4,019
Total assets	$6,264	$6,773
Current liabilities	$2,113	$3,454
Long-term debt	2,189	1,104
Other noncurrent	971	850
Preferred stock	1,321	222
Common stock	1,194	2,398
Retained earnings	(1,524)	(1,255)
Total liabilities and owners' equity	$6,264	$6,773

Common-Equity Data	1982	1983	6/1984
Beta	1.00	1.10	1.10
End-of-year stock price	$15⅜	$27⅞	$24⅞
Shares outstanding (000)	79,457	122,090	121,877

Bond Data

Rating	Annual Coupon	Maturity Date	1982 Price	1983 Price	6/1984 Price
Ba2	8⅞%	1995	$62½	$74½	$72¾
Ba2	8%	1998	$55	$64½	$62¼

Sources: *The Wall Street Journal, Moody's Industrial Manual,* and *Value Line Investment Survey.*

The Becker Corporation

In May 1992, Dave Zalinsky of Becker Corporation's project-appraisal group was trying to decide what course of action to recommend on a capital-expenditure proposal submitted by the company's Rubber Division. The proposal called for the construction of a barge dock and storage facility, estimated to cost $810,000, at the division's New Orleans plant.

The Rubber Division managers agreed with Mr. Zalinsky that the estimated annual savings did not meet the Becker Corporation's minimum return requirements, but they argued that the proposed project should not be judged by the normal criteria. In their presentation, the Rubber Division managers had raised two issues concerning the projected return on the dock investment—"committed" savings and Becker's absolute standard for judging projects.

The first issue was the company's requirement for "commitment of savings." Savings were said to be committed when those responsible for managing the proposed project and achieving the projected savings were willing to put themselves on the line by having their future performance measured against those savings. For the dock project, although the Rubber Division managers thought that additional savings were possible, even probable, they had committed to only the portion of the potential savings of which they were certain. The result was that the projected return on investment was below Becker's minimum.

The second issue concerned the nature of the dock project itself, in comparison with other projects. If the company did not build its own dock, the division would have to continue using the public terminal. The projected savings if the dock were built would be the commercial loading and unloading rates for the raw materials and finished goods expected to be handled. The actual volume of goods and the rates charged were unlikely to fluctuate much from the projections. Because the savings were almost certain, the division management dubbed the project a "banker's risk."

Unlike the dock project, many of Becker's capital-budgeting projects were for manufacturing facilities to produce new products or expand the production of existing ones. For such projects, the return on investment depended to a great extent on prices of the products. In the rubber business, product prices had fluctuated considerably and had been generally on a downward trend for many years. Thus, managers of the Rubber Division argued, returns for production projects were much less certain that those for the dock project, and the dock project should meet different, lower standards that were commensurate with its risk.

Company Background

The Becker Corporation was a diversified company with headquarters in Houston, Texas. It was organized into operating divisions responsible for manufacturing and marketing chemicals and related products as assigned by headquarters. The company had grown, both internally and by acquisition, to sales of $376 million in 1991.

Becker's capital budgeting was controlled by a group at corporate headquarters but administered by the operating divisions. Each division requested funds annually for specific projects. Financing acceptable projects had not been a serious problem for Becker, because although the total amount of funds available for capital expenditures was something of a limiting factor, the company had been able to supplement internally generated cash with public offerings of its securities. For instance, the company's favorable credit standing had helped it recently secure long-term debt at 10 percent.

Each division's capital-spending forecasts were presented in two reports prepared annually:

1. Two-year forecasts of capital expenditures gave detailed lists of proposed projects, their returns on investment, and the capital required for each. Although the projects listed had not been formally reviewed by the corporate project-appraisal group, the total of the funds was taken as the division's estimated need for the next year.
2. Longer term forecasts of divisional activity described the types of activity that each division's management planned for the future. The report was general and listed specific projects only when major expenditures would be required.

Division management could use its own approach in evaluating capital investments unless the gross fixed investment exceeded $100,000. For those investments, the approval of the company's Administrative Committee was needed. Any project over $1 million required approval by the board of directors.

When Administrative Committee approval was required, the project appraisal group reviewed the division's request on the basis of such criteria as its financial acceptability and its fit with the company's long-range plans. Because the group was also responsible for making recommendations on changing financial requirements, it had to consider the Rubber Division's request for different standards for projects of different risk.

For a project requiring review by the project-appraisal group and approval by the Administrative Committee, the division prepared a lengthy, formal report, the Capital Spending Request. The purposes of the request were:

1. to explain and justify the project as a good investment
2. to establish a basis for later performance review

The request had four sections:

1. a summary of the project highlights,
2. data showing return on investment, payout, and the effect of the project on corporate income,
3. a description of the assumptions underlying calculations of return on investment and payout, and
4. information about the project and any effect it might have on the division and the company.

The report went to the project-appraisal group, which made a recommendation to the Administrative Committee. Although this recommendation did not represent approval or rejection, it was usually a major factor in the committee's decision.

The two financial standards used at Becker Corporation were as follows:

1. Return on investment. Annual profit, after straight-line depreciation based on the useful life of the facilities, operating expenses, and federal income taxes, had to exceed 10.5 percent of the gross investment.
2. Payback. The time required to return the cash investment to the company could not exceed 5 years.

In 1991 these standards were used for all divisions of the company and for all types of projects.

Review of the Dock Project

The project-appraisal group's review of the New Orleans dock project began on April 27, 1992. After this first review, the group did not recommend acceptance to the Administrative Committee, because the return did not meet the company's minimum guidelines. One of the members of the review group commented about the request,

> We felt that the project had some potential. The main problem was that the Rubber Division would not commit itself to an acceptable return and payout. What we suggested was that they redraft the request and include the other potential savings they mentioned. But, as written, the return was not acceptable in my mind.

After the initial comments about the project, the division revised its request. This time it described, but did not commit to, savings from other products being shipped through the new dock. The request said,

> We appreciate your comments on the initial draft, and several changes have been made based on them. We have, however, left the project as a "banker's risk."

During the period in which the members of the project-appraisal group discussed the project, conflicting opinions were expressed:

1.   "I'm not sure Becker should be in this business. There are a lot of places where we could use our staff and money to better advantage. We're not a shipping firm."
2.   "I know the dock seems like a good project. The savings committed still don't meet our standards, though. I know the division says the facility will pay for itself in time and yield a good return. But if they won't commit to the additional savings, I wonder just how sure they are of getting them. I don't go for this low-risk-business stuff. If the profit isn't there, we shouldn't go into it."
3.   "I think that the low-risk aspect should be considered. After all, these savings are a sure thing. I think we should use a different standard to judge a low-risk project like this. There aren't any prices involved except the loading and unloading rates. They have been very steady. The savings really only depend on our projected volumes, and the division seems very sure of them."

At the request of the other members of the project-appraisal group, Mr. Zalinsky met with William Sams from the Rubber Division. Mr. Sams had been deeply involved in the dock project from the beginning. "The history of this project goes back a long way," he said. "Years ago, management began to realize the economic advantage of water transportation. We have known for some time that one of the major advantages of the New Orleans Plant was its location near water deep enough for barge traffic."

"I understand that the master plant site showed a dock, Bill. Why wasn't it built before now?" asked Mr. Zalinsky.

"We haven't needed it. We were buying our main raw materials from Billingsley's plant just down the river and using trucks for the short haul involved. Now that situation has changed. We are now shipping by barge to the New Orleans Plant from another plant of ours. We have been unloading at a terminal near there. We're also shipping one of our products produced in that plant by barge from the terminal."

"But, Bill, what prompted the capital-spending request at this time? Was it the savings?"

"That was a major factor," said Mr. Sams. "We pay that terminal a lot of money every year."

"Now about the savings?"

"They are outlined here on this paper along with the other data." Mr. Sams referred Mr. Zalinsky to the information shown in Exhibit 1. "It's really a problem, though. These are only the committed savings—the ones we are sure of. A few years ago, the division asked me to justify a dock at another plant. I talked with all kinds of people in the plant. All of them felt it was a good idea—the purchasing agent, in particular. She said she could save money on raw materials and shipping costs when she bought in barge-load quantities. But when I asked how much she could save, she said that it was impossible to tell. The prices for materials varied considerably and she could not commit herself for any savings. I talked to the shipping personnel and got the same answer—no commitment. It was really difficult to firm up the savings that the dock would give us.

"To make a long story short, a request was submitted, and finally approved by the Administrative Committee. We paid for that dock in less than a year. We got savings from buying in bulk and from freight costs. This is why we are not sure just how much the dock will save. In this case, for example, there are a few other products that we might be able to ship into New Orleans, but we're just not sure."

"Just what do committed savings mean to you?" asked Mr. Zalinsky.

"Well, as you know, these projects are reviewed periodically to determine management performance. When a manager commits savings to a project, he or she is held responsible for them on that performance appraisal. I've always thought it was sort of a control procedure to ensure reasonable estimates."

"Now, Bill, how about explaining these figures for the new dock," asked Mr. Zalinsky.

"Well, the savings shown, $170,000, is our forecast of billings from the terminal if we do not install the dock. Raw materials account for $86,000, and finished goods for $84,000. The $65,000 is our cost of operating the facility. Maintenance was estimated on a fixed percentage of the investment."

"How much risk is there that these savings will not be realized?" Mr. Zalinsky asked.

"Assuming normal conditions in the economy, there is very little risk. If anything, the savings may be low. That plant has been doing very well, and some of our costs, maintenance for example, may not be that high," replied Mr. Sams.

"You know that the project-appraisal group rejected the proposal as written the first time?"

"Yes. I guess you felt it was a good project, but you wanted more savings committed to the return and payout. Our revised request did give more potential savings, $200,000 worth, but these were not committed. We sent it on without including them," said Mr. Sams.

"Bill, what about joint use with another company?" asked Mr. Zalinsky. "I noticed it was mentioned as a possibility in the request."

"Yes, but we haven't done anything about that. One company that expressed interest was a customer. But we really cannot commit ourselves to another company until after the dock is installed."

"How long will a dock like this last?" asked Mr. Zalinsky.

"It's difficult to say, Dave. We used 20 years in the depreciation schedules and income-tax calculations, but we feel sure it will last much longer than that."

"Thanks, Bill, I appreciate your coming to talk about the dock project. Let me pull my thoughts together. I really need to take your dock request back to the capital-spending group along with my thoughts about our committed-savings requirement and our two absolute standards."

While Mr. Zalinsky was preparing to take the project back to the project-appraisal group, he collected the information found in Exhibits 2 through 8.

The Becker Corporation
EXHIBIT 1 • New Orleans Dock Project (in thousands)

Initial Costs	
Dredging	$230
Dock	270
Machinery	310
Investment	810
Initial start-up costs (to be expensed for tax purposes)	6
Total costs	816
Annual Operating Expenses	
Steam	$ 10
Electricity	2
Labor	10
Maintenance	43
Total annual expenses	$ 65
Annual Savings	
Raw materials	$ 86
Finished goods	84
Total annual savings	$170

Supplementary Data

1. Straight-line depreciation over 20 years with no salvage value for income-reporting purposes.
2. Sum-of-the-years'-digits depreciation over 20 years for tax reporting.
3. Marginal tax rate of 34 percent.

The Becker Corporation
EXHIBIT 2 • Sum-of-the-Years'-Digits Depreciation Schedule (in thousands)

Year	Annual Depreciation	Cumulative Depreciation
1	$77,142.9	$77,142.9
2	73,285.7	150,428.6
3	69,428.6	219,857.1
4	65,571.4	285,428.6
5	61,714.3	347,142.9
6	57,857.1	405,000.0
7	54,000.0	459,000.0
8	50,142.9	509,142.9
9	46,285.7	555,428.6
10	42,428.6	597,857.1
11	38,571.4	636,428.6
12	34,714.3	671,142.9
13	30,857.1	702,000.0
14	27,000.0	729,000.0
15	23,142.9	752,142.9
16	19,285.7	771,428.6
17	15,428.6	786,857.1
18	11,571.4	798,428.6
19	7,714.3	806,142.9
20	3,857.1	810,000.0

The Becker Corporation
EXHIBIT 3 • Yearly Profits and Cash Flows—
              Committed Savings Only (in thousands)

Year	Terminal Billing Savings	Operating Expenses	Depreciation	Before-Tax Profits	After-Tax Profits	Net Cash Flow
1	$170	$65	$77	$28	$18.4	$95.5
2	170	65	73	32	20.9	94.2
3	170	65	69	36	23.5	92.9
4	170	65	66	39	26.0	91.6
5	170	65	62	43	28.6	90.3
6	170	65	58	47	31.1	89.0
7	170	65	54	51	33.7	87.7
8	170	65	50	55	36.2	86.3
9	170	65	46	59	38.8	85.0
10	170	65	42	63	41.3	83.7
11	170	65	39	66	43.8	82.4
12	170	65	35	70	46.4	81.1
13	170	65	31	74	48.9	79.8
14	170	65	27	78	51.5	78.5
15	170	65	23	82	54.0	77.2
16	170	65	19	86	56.6	75.9
17	170	65	15	90	59.1	74.5
18	170	65	12	93	61.7	73.2
19	170	65	8	97	64.2	71.9
20	170	65	4	101	66.8	70.6

The Becker Corporation
EXHIBIT 4 • Financial Results from the
Project's Committed Savings (in thousands)

Standard 1: Annual Profit/Gross Investment

Average yearly savings	$170.0
Costs	
Operating expenses	(65.0)
Depreciation (straight line)	(40.5)
Total costs	(105.5)
Profit before taxes	64.5
Taxes (34 percent)	(21.9)
Profit after taxes	$42.6

Yearly profit/gross investment = 5.26% ($42.6/$810)

Standard 2: Payback Calculation

Year	Annual Cash Flow	Cumultive Cash Flow
0	$(810.0)	$(810.0)
1	95.5	(714.5)
2	94.2	(620.3)
3	92.9	(527.3)
4	91.6	(435.8)
5	90.3	(345.5)
6	89.0	(256.5)
7	87.7	(168.8)
8	86.3	(82.5)
9	85.0	2.5
10	83.7	86.3

Payback = 8.97 years

The Becker Corporation
EXHIBIT 5 • Increment of Uncommitted Savings Realized

	0%	10%	20%	30%	40%	50%	60%	70%	80%	90%	100%
Average yearly income	$42.6	$55.8	$69.0	$82.2	$95.4	$108.6	$121.8	$135.0	$148.2	$161.4	$174.6
Percentage of investment[a]	5.3%	6.9%	8.5%	10.1%	11.8%	13.4%	15.0%	16.7%	18.3%	19.9%	21.6%
Payout (years)[b]	9.0	7.8	6.8	6.1	5.5	5.1	4.6	4.3	4.0	3.7	3.5
Discounted-cash-flow return[c]	8.7%	10.8%	12.9%	14.8%	16.7%	18.5%	20.3%	22.1%	23.9%	25.6%	27.3%
Net present value @ 10.5 percent[d]	($93)	$16	$125	$233	$342	$451	$559	$668	$777	$885	$994

[a]A 10-percent increment of uncommitted savings is $20,000 before taxes or $13,200 after taxes (assuming 34 percent tax rate). Each increment thus adds $113,200 to the average yearly income and 1.63 percent to the percentage return.

[b]The increment of $13,200 after taxes can be added to the net cash flow for each year for each increment. Payout is then found in the same way as for Exhibit 4.

[c]The same cash flows used to find payout are used to calculate a discounted cash flow return.

[d]The yearly 10-percent savings increment of $13,200 for 20 years has a net present value of $108,650 at a discount rate of 10.5 percent (see Exhibit 8). Each 10-percent increment thus adds $108,650 to the net present value of the project.

The Becker Corporation
EXHIBIT 6 • Financial Data 1987–1991 (millions, except per-share data)

	1987	1988	1989	1990	1991
Balance Sheets					
Assets					
Cash	$ 10	$ 21	$ 26	$ 17	$ 18
Receivables	31	36	41	49	55
Inventories	32	35	39	44	53
Net property, plant, and equipment[a]	140	158	160	180	213
Other	21	22	24	25	27
Total assets	$ 234	$ 272	$ 290	$ 315	$ 366
Liabilities and Equity					
Payables and accruals	$ 22	$ 26	$ 25	$ 32	$ 40
Income taxes payable	10	8	14	15	12
Long-term debt[b]	57	76	74	73	98
Deferred income taxes	6	7	9	10	11
Other liabilities	5	8	7	6	8
Total liabilities	100	125	129	136	169
Common stock	78	81	85	87	89
Retained earnings	56	66	76	92	108
Total liabilities and equity	$ 234	$ 272	$ 290	$ 315	$ 366
Income Statements and Retained Earnings					
Sales		$ 293	$ 320	$ 354	$ 379
Cost of goods sold		181	199	218	238
Selling, general, and administrative		83	88	92	97
Federal income tax		10	11	15	15
Total expenses		$ 274	$ 298	$ 325	$ 350
Net income		19	22	29	29
Dividends		9	12	13	13
Changes in retained earnings		$ 10	$ 10	$ 16	$ 16
Stock Market Data					
Earnings per share		$ 1.59	$ 1.18	$ 2.21	$ 2.06
Dividends per share		0.60	0.65	0.70	0.75
Stock market price high/low		$23/25	$25/30	$26/30	$28/32

[a]Depreciation is $24 million for 1991, $21 million for 1990, $20 million for 1989, and $18 million for 1988.
[b]Cost is between 9 and 10 percent.

The Becker Corporation
EXHIBIT 7 • Capitalization (in millions)

	Balance-Sheet Date[a]				
	12/31/87	*12/31/88*	*12/31/89*	*12/31/90*	*12/31/91*
Total long-term debt	$ 57	$ 76	$ 74	$ 73	$ 98
Total equity	134	147	161	179	197
Total capitalization	$191	$223	$235	$252	$295
Debt proportion	29.8%	34.1%	31.5%	29.0%	33.2%
Equity proportion	70.2%	65.9%	68.5%	71.0%	66.8%

[a]Because major debt issues occurred in 1989 and 1990, the debt proportion was determined as an average of 3 years data.

The Becker Corporation
EXHIBIT 8 • Weighted-Average Cost of Capital

	1988	*1989*	*1990*	*1991*
Dividend Yield				
Average market price/Share*	24.00	27.50	28.00	30.00
Dividend per share	0.60	0.65	0.70	0.75
Dividend yield (percent)	2.50%	2.36%	2.50%	2.54%

Average yield = 2.48 percent $\left(\dfrac{(2.50 + 2.50 + 2.54)}{4}\right)$

After-Tax Cost of Capital

	After-Tax Cost	Proportion	Weighted Value
Debt	6.60%	31.5%	2.08%
Equity	12.31%	68.5%	8.43%
Weighted-average cost of capital			10.51%

*Market-price appreciation for ten years at 9.83 percent (1982 price of $11.75, 1991 price of $30.00)

PART
4

Required Return on Investment—Cost of Capital

Star Appliance Company (A)

Case
▼

Arthur Foster, the financial vice president of Star Appliance Company, thought that the opportunity had finally presented itself. Since joining the company in early 1978, he had been concerned about the discount rate (also called the hurdle rate) used in the capital-allocation process. He had not wanted to create a controversy immediately after accepting his position, but now in early October 1979, with the company considering a move into new products, he thought that the time had come for discussing the company's required rate of return on investment (frequently referred to as the cost of capital).

History of Star Appliance Company

Star Appliance had been founded in 1922 by Ken McDonald to manufacture electric stoves and ovens. During the prosperous 1920s, the demand for electric stoves and ovens as replacements for wood- and coal-burning stoves increased, and Star became a respected brand name and the market leader. Capitalizing on this success and the burgeoning equity market during the 1920s, Mr. McDonald financed the rapid growth of the company through the sale of common stock. This move proved to be farsighted. The company was able to enter the Depression with a debt-free balance sheet. Many firms, plagued with dwindling sales and poor or nonexistent profits, had defaulted on their debts and were forced into bankruptcy and eventually out of business. Star suffered severely during the Depression, but was able to survive by significantly reducing its operations and concentrating its sales efforts on the least affected part of the market, the premium end. As a result, Star remained alive and viable, emerging at the end of World War II with a smaller base of operations, a strong balance sheet, and a well-established reputation in the marketplace.

In the ensuing three decades, the company grew and prospered. Star continued to concentrate on the premium market and over the years expanded its product line. Continuing its focus on kitchen appliances, Star first added gas ranges to its products, followed by a line of refrigerators. Microwave ovens were the company's newest product. The company's marketing program emphasized the sale of new appliances as replacements for older models, rather than targeting the market for installations in newly constructed dwellings. This strategy provided some protection from the vicissitudes of the highly cyclical housing industry.

As for financing, Mr. McDonald believed he had learned a valuable lesson from the Depression and had continued to keep debt financing to a minimum. Although he retired from active management in 1963, his philosophy concerning the capital structure had become well ingrained. Through its period of growth, the company had relied solely on equity to finance itself. In fact, Star's premium image had allowed it to price its products to command a higher margin than could its competition; as a result, all of Star's equity financing had come from its profits—additions to retained earnings.

Furthermore, Star maintained a liquidity reserve of cash and marketable securities. During seasonal and cyclical slumps, the company had been able to draw on this reserve, eliminating the need to borrow. In part because of this solvency, Star had been able to maintain a stable work force, which management believed contributed to its superior labor productivity. On the few occasions when the growth of the company had been limited by the lack of internal funds, Star had temporarily reduced its liquid reserve to provide the necessary financing. Only three times since the end of World War II had this reserve not been large enough, and Star had sold new equity. These marketing and financial strategies had created a strong company whose stock in 1978 was widely held by the investing public. The most recent financial statements for Star are shown in Exhibits 1 and 2.

Despite Star's previous growth, management believed that growth in the current product lines had slowed. Exhibit 3 provides 5-year forecasts for Star's earnings, assuming no significant changes in the current product lines. However, Star's president, Chris Weeks, who had originally joined the company in 1955 as a sales representative, believed real growth would come only with the addition of new products. Mr. Weeks believed that, in order for Star to capitalize on its market reputation and brand-name recognition, any new products should be kitchen oriented.

Evaluating Product Expansion

The desire to expand the product line was also a response to a general industry slump. Despite Star's continued growth in sales and profits during a period when its competitors' sales and margins declined, Star's stock price had fallen. Management believed the company's stock price had been adversely affected by the industry's problems. It was thought that the introduction of new products might provide an impetus to the stock market, thus increasing the company's price/earnings (P/E) ratio back to its normal levels.

Three new product lines had been proposed—a dishwasher, a food disposer to be installed in kitchen sinks, and a trash compactor. The marketing department believed that each of these products had good sales potential and would fit with the company image of high-quality, premium-priced kitchen products.

Each of the three projects had been analyzed following the requirements of Star's capital-allocation process. Like most projects at Star, these had originated in either the marketing or manufacturing departments. For each, the costs, benefits, expected lives, and terminal values had been determined. The results of the analysis for each project are shown in Exhibit 4. Using Star's marginal tax rate, the after-tax cash flows were used to calculate the internal rate of return (IRR) for each project. Following Star's usual procedures, the IRR would then be compared with the company's 10-percent discount rate. Star's management would accept projects whose IRR exceeded the discount rate as long as funds were available. In years when capital was short, projects with the highest IRRs were implemented, and lower return projects were postponed until funds became available.

Several parts of this process troubled Mr. Foster. First, he was concerned about the appropriateness of the 10-percent required rate of return. When he joined the company, he had asked about the source of the rate, but no one seemed to be able to give a precise reason for it. The best he could determine was that the return on equity seemed to have been about 10 percent during the period when the capital-budgeting system was being established, and since that time, the 10-percent rate had been used.

Mr. Foster was convinced that the discount rate was too low. The interest rate on various U.S. Treasury securities is shown in Exhibit 5. Treasury bills had recently exceeded 13 percent, and one study[1] showed that common stock historically had a return of about 8.5 percent above the average return on Treasury bills and 6 percent above longer term Treasury securities. He was certain that Star's projects were more risky than Treasury bills, and thus the projects should have a higher expected return if they were to be accepted. On the other hand, Mr. Foster did not believe that Star's stock was as risky as the average common stock. This suggested to him that the full market risk premium would not be expected by investors in Star's common stock.

At the manufacturing company where Mr. Foster had worked before joining Star, a dividend-growth model had been used in calculating the

---

[1] Roger G. Ibbotson and Rex A. Sinquefield, *Stocks, Bonds, Bills and Inflation: Historical Returns (1926–1978)* (Charlottesville, Va.: The Financial Analysts Research Foundation, 1979).

cost of equity. This model ($D_1/P_0 + g = K_e$) described the return expected by the shareholders (K_e) from investing in the company's common stock as a combination of the next dividend (D_1), current market price (P_0) [the dividend yield (D_1/P_0)], and the forecasted long-term growth in dividends (g). Star's current stock price was $22.50, and the company's management and board of directors intended to continue its policy of maintaining or slightly increasing dividends. Information about Star's historic dividends, along with other information about Star's stock and the stock market, can be found in Exhibit 6.

Because Star had only short-term debt, Mr. Foster did not believe he should consider the cost of debt in calculating the return required by Star's capital providers. However, there was one thing that perplexed him. If an all-equity-financed firm was less risky in economic downturns, why would its required cost of capital be higher? It was obvious that debt cost less than equity (especially after taking taxes into account) and that the use of debt would reduce a company's overall average required rate of return.

In his review of the discount rate and capital providers' required rate of return, several other questions occurred to Mr. Foster. First, was inflation adequately accounted for in Star's present system? Mr. Foster believed that the rates on U.S. Treasury securities (Exhibits 5 and 6) included a return to offset expected inflation, but was that enough?

Second, Mr. Foster wondered whether Star management should accept projects that just met the required rate of return, or only those that exceeded it by a margin of safety. Some of the forecasts had, in the past, exceeded the results. Perhaps the required rate should be raised to compensate for poor forecasts. Furthermore, Star, like other U.S. companies, had increased its investment in safety and environmental projects to satisfy the U.S. government's increased requirements. Like most companies, Star categorized these as nonproductive investments, investments with no return. The discount rate, Mr. Foster believed, should certainly be increased to cover those investments, for failing to do so would guarantee that Star would earn less than its required rate, and shareholders would be hurt.

Finally, the staff making the forecasts for the three projects believed that two of the projects were riskier than the other one, because they required new plant and equipment that would add appreciably to fixed costs. In downturns, or if the projects proved unsuccessful, they could cost Star more. Some of the staff thought that the rate required should be increased to compensate for risk. Others argued that the more risky projects should be evaluated on the basis of their strategic importance and that the rate used was irrelevant: the company should accept the sound strategy. One young analyst contended that, if different rates were used for different projects, the company would be mixing the financing and investment decisions—something that should not be done.

Conclusion

As Mr. Foster began to investigate Star's capital providers' required rate of return in developing a new discount rate, one contingency troubled him. Although Star had recently built up its liquid reserves in the expectation of launching some new products, whether all three of the products could be financed internally was questionable. He expected that depreciation would need to be reinvested to maintain Star's current production facilities. According to the marketing department's sales projections, he would have about $12 million from operations in 1979. In addition, he thought he could get from $15 to $20 million by reducing cash and marketable securities. If all three projects were approved, he could need as much as $40 million in external financing. Even if management decided to approve only the new dishwasher project, Star would require $3 million in new funds. Because of the strong financial position of the company, Mr. Foster was certain that he would be able to sell a reasonable amount of new equity, to net, after issue costs, about 95 percent of the current market price. He was not certain how or whether the issue costs should be included in his evaluation of the company's required rate of return.

Star Appliance Company (A)
EXHIBIT 1 • Statements of Consolidated Income
     (thousands of dollars, except per-share data)

	Year Ended December 31,1977	Year Ended December 31, 1978
Net sales	$248,505	$269,787
Interest	2,065	3,126
Miscellaneous	242	265
Total income	250,812	273,178
Cost of products sold	(160,021)	(173,338)
Selling, administrative, and general expenses	(36,533)	(41,079)
Total costs and expenses	(196,554)	(214,417)
Income before income taxes	54,258	58,761
Federal and state income taxes	(25,655)	(28,303)
Net income	$28,603	$30,458
Net income per share of common stock	$2.13	$2.27
Dividends per share of common stock	$1.45	$1.52

Star Appliance Company (A)

EXHIBIT 2 • Statements of Consolidated
Financial Condition (in thousands)

	December 31, 1977	December 31, 1978
Assets		
Cash	$ 2,122	$ 2,430
Marketable securities, including certificates of deposit—at cost (approximately market)	27,209	37,759
Trade accounts receivable, less allowance ($100,000)	15,577	17,333
Inventories		
Finished appliances	11,323	11,302
Work in process	13,527	13,100
Materials and supplies	8,309	6,930
Total inventories	33,159	31,332
Deferred federal taxes on income	1,536	1,747
Total current assets	79,603	90,601
Other assets	495	818
Property, plant, and equipment		
Land	713	713
Buildings and improvements	36,024	36,185
Machinery and equipment	76,879	79,411
Construction in progress	1,372	5,430
Less allowances for depreciation	(58,699)	(62,610)
Net property, plant, and equipment	56,289	59,129
Total assets	$136,387	$150,548
Liabilities and Shareowners' Equity		
Trade accounts payable	$ 2,860	$ 3,287
Compensation to employees	4,040	4,473
Miscellaneous accounts payable	2,122	1,778
Accrued local taxes	1,515	1,699
Accrued liabilities	2,742	2,961
Federal and state taxes on income	5,634	7,117
Total current liabilities	18,913	21,315
Deferred federal taxes on income	4,349	5,666
Shareowners' equity		
Common stock (13,414,268 shares issued, including shares in treasury)	27,835	27,835
Retained earnings	86,343	96,298
Less cost of shares of common stock in treasury	(1,053)	(566)
Total equity	113,125	123,567
Total liabilities and shareowners' equity	$136,387	$150,548

Star Appliance Company (A)
EXHIBIT 3 • Forecast of Earnings, Sales, and Dividends from Continuing Operations (in thousands, except per share)

	Sales	Profit after Tax	Dividends per Share
1979	$297,734	$34,375	$1.64
1980	307,000	35,500	1.70
1981	317,000	36,500	1.75
1982	326,000	37,300	1.80
1983	334,000	38,000	1.85

Star Appliance Company (A)
EXHIBIT 4 • Projected Cash Flows (in thousands)

Costs	Dishwasher	Food Waste Disposal	Trash Compactor
Addition to plant	$ 7,000	$ 0	$ 3,000
Production equipment	21,500	13,600	10,000
Installation of equipment	1,500	400	1,000
Initial promotion expenditures	5,000	1,000	8,000
Total costs	$ 35,000	$ 15,000	$ 22,000
Expected project life[a]	15 years	15 years	15 years
Expected net cash flow after taxes			
Year 1	$ 1,000	$ 100	$ 400
Year 2	4,000	500	1,300
Year 3	8,000	1,000	3,000
Year 4	11,000	1,650	4,500
Year 5 and subsequent years	11,000	3,000	5,500
Terminal value[a]	$ 0	$ 0	$ 0
Internal rate of return	20.8%	10.6%	15.2%

[a]Actually, the marketing department projected sales beyond 15 years; however, the engineering staff predicted that, at best, the equipment would last 15 years before it would need to be completely replaced. Thus, to be conservative, the projections had included no terminal value.

Star Appliance Company (A)

EXHIBIT 5 • U.S. Treasury Security Yields, October 25, 1979

Term	Yield
3 months	13.04%
6 months	13.54
1 year	13.35
2 years	12.53
3 years	11.97
5 years	11.31
7 years	11.15
10 years	10.97
20 years	10.43
30 years	10.28

Star Appliance Company (A)
EXHIBIT 6 • Historical Company and Stock Market Data

Year	Stock Market Price Index[a] 1943=10	Stock Market Return[b] (percent)	Annualized Treasury Bill Yield[a] (percent)	Annualized AA Corporate Industrial Bond Yield[a] (percent)	Annual Consumer Price Inflation Rate[b] (percent)	Star Appliance Company				
						Earnings per Share	P/E Ratio	Dividends per Share	Dividend Yield (percent)	Stock Return (percent)
1964	83.96	16.48%	3.856%	4.31%	1.19%	$1.01	16.1×	$0.79	4.9%	17.7%
1965	91.73	12.45	4.362	4.72	1.92	0.95	17.3	0.79	4.8	5.9
1966	81.33	(10.06)	5.007	5.38	3.35	1.00	13.3	0.81	6.1	(13.0)
1967	95.30	23.98	5.012	6.23	3.04	1.06	14.0	0.83	5.6	17.2
1968	106.50	11.06	5.916	6.56	4.72	1.30	14.8	0.94	4.9	34.5
1969	91.11	(8.50)	7.720	7.62	6.11	1.34	16.6	1.04	4.7	20.3
1970	90.05	4.01	4.860	7.36	5.49	1.41	16.0	1.08	4.8	6.2
1971	99.17	14.31	4.023	7.14	3.36	0.75	41.1	1.08	3.5	40.1
1972	117.50	18.98	5.061	7.08	3.41	1.73	19.3	1.12	3.4	11.7
1973	94.78	(14.66)	7.364	7.64	8.80	1.83	14.0	1.25	4.9	(18.4)
1974	67.07	(26.47)	7.179	8.63	12.20	1.35	14.0	1.16	6.1	(20.1)
1975	88.70	37.20	5.504	8.68	7.01	1.61	14.5	1.16	5.0	28.5
1976	98.20	23.84	4.354	8.24	4.81	2.05	13.9	1.37	4.8	26.9
1977	95.10	(7.18)	6.152	8.92	6.77	2.13	11.9	1.45	5.7	(5.3)
1978	96.11	6.56	9.336	9.28	9.03	2.27	9.5	1.52	7.0	(7.9)

[a]As of last business day in the year.

[b]Annual return of the Standard & Poor's Composite Index based on capital appreciation and dividend income. Source: Roger G. Ibbotson and Rex A. Sinquefield, *Stocks, Bonds, Bills, and Inflation: Historical Returns (1926–1978)* (Charlottesville, Va.: The Financial Analysts Research Foundation, 1979).

Star Appliance Company (B): January 1985

In 1982 Star Appliance expanded its business by purchasing a company that made machines to clean fruits, grains, and vegetables for market.[1] The firm, Rhinescour Company, was located near Star's headquarters in Nebraska and had been managed into mediocrity. The quality of its management, along with the state of the U.S. farming economy, made the price very low. Star management considered its purchase a good investment and, because Rhinescour's continuation ensured jobs in the area, a local community service. To make the purchase, Star contracted long-term debt—for the first time in the company's history— $17.8 million.

In January 1985, Arthur Foster, Star's treasurer, realized that he had not reevaluated Star's cost of capital since taking on the debt. He wondered what changes the debt had caused. Mr. Foster found that the company was considered more risky since he had begun to deal with lenders, a new experience for him.

The more he worked to develop a new corporate discount rate, the more concerned Mr. Foster became about Star Appliance's required rate of return. When he had been in business school 25 years earlier, there had been only two methods for estimating the required return on equity: the price/earnings ratio (the implicit cost of capital) and the dividend-discount model. Many of Star's recently hired MBAs said the best method to use was a capital-market equilibrium approach called the capital asset pricing model (CAPM). Mr. Foster was determined to explore all the alternatives before settling on one method to use in future discount-rate revisions.

Two issues were being discussed among the staff and needed to be resolved. Some of the younger staff members, along with Mr. Foster, questioned whether the company's present discount rate, given the debt picture, accurately reflected capital costs. Some also wondered whether one discount rate should apply to all projects. Several suggested that different discount rates should be used with different kinds of investments. The

[1] Background about Star Appliance Company is found in "Star Appliance Company (A)."

point had come up in connection with a discussion of whether to develop a market for new crop dryers or increase plant space for the production of refrigerators.

Cost of Equity

Debbie Schofield, assistant to the corporate treasurer, was one of the more vocal advocates of multiple discount rates and using the CAPM for determining the required return on equity for various projects. "The projected return of the project," she said, "should be set off against its risk to determine value, and the CAPM does that and does it well. We've had lots of experience calculating betas and the risk-free and market rates of return. That makes the CAPM easy; anyone can use it."

As its measure of risk, the CAPM used beta (β), the relative volatility of a security's return in relation to all other assets. A security's beta represented expected risk, but was often estimated by fitting a least-squares regression, also called the market model, to a series of returns for the total market and for an individual stock over the most recent 5 years. If a security's returns moved less than those of the market as a whole, its risk would be deemed lower than average and its beta would be less than 1.0; if its movement was greater, its beta would be greater than 1.0. Using a beta, the return expected for the market, and that expected for a risk-free asset, one could estimate a security's expected return on equity from the CAPM equation:

$$R_j = R_f + \beta_j (R_m - R_f)$$

where:

R_j = the expected total rate of return for a security (j)

R_f = the risk-free rate of return, for which analysts often used a U.S. Treasury security rate

β_j = the variability of total returns for a security (j) relative to those of the market, called the security's beta

R_m = the expected total rate of return for the market. Analysts often used a broad market index, such as Standard & Poor's 500 Index, as a proxy

Exhibit 1 provides the betas, profitability ratios, and other pertinent data for firms in the home-appliance and agricultural-machinery industries. Exhibit 2 provides information on Star's stock performance and that of the S&P 500 Index.

To use this model, Mr. Foster would need estimates of expected market returns. He sought help from Star's bankers. Sam Ralfson, his primary contact at Kennelworth Bank and Trust, sent the letter shown in Appendix A in response to Mr. Foster's inquiry. This letter provided some direction in determining what rate to use for the market's expected return (R_m). As for the risk-free rate (R_f), the consensus among Mr. Foster's staff seemed to be that they would use the yield on a Treasury security (see Exhibit 3), but there was little agreement on which security offered the best proxy. Mr. Foster believed that the decision boiled down to choosing the security with the least risk (very short-term) but one that incorporated the inflation expected over the investment's life.

Mr. Foster wanted to compare the CAPM estimate with those made from the implicit and dividend-discount models. He also wanted to understand how increased debt affected the required return on equity using each of the models.

Once he had determined Star's capital providers' required return, Mr. Foster knew he would need to deal with the issue of multiple discount rates that Ms. Schofield had originated. Her initial arguments for multiple rates seemed overwhelming. She said, "It is obvious that different degrees of risk should be reflected in the expected returns of the projects, just as riskier stocks and bonds typically yield higher returns." She questioned whether it was rational for Star to expect the same 10-percent rate of return from both a relatively risk-free project and a riskier one. By applying the same discount rate to both types of projects, the riskier one, which typically would have the higher expected rate of return, would appear disproportionately attractive.

The arguments against the use of multiple discount rates, however, presented by Jude Weathers, another member of the finance staff, were also compelling. Mr. Weathers said, "To me it is obvious that, given the fungibility of capital, the company should seek to invest where the expected returns are best. Less profitable projects should receive less funding. That was the reason behind establishing a single discount rate in the first place. The corporation is financed as a whole, not by product lines, divisions, or projects."

Ms. Schofield had disagreed, stating her belief that a properly applied multiple-discount-rate system would help ensure that Star remained conservative by "scientifically allocating funds to projects with various degrees of risk." As a result of this conservatism, if the company were to decide at some point to contract more long-term debt, lenders would be willing to supply funds at better rates. Similarly, she said, stockholders would be more willing to pay more for shares. The price/earnings (P/E) ratio might fall farther than at present, she warned, if riskier projects were accepted with too little consideration for their relative rates of return.

Mr. Foster was concerned about how risk and discount rates were related. He believed his staff had already accounted for risk, in an intuitive sense, by adjusting the cash flows on the returns of riskier projects, but he appreciated Ms. Schofield's approach, which he believed made the analysis systematic.

Ms. Schofield suggested that the same conclusion could be reached from a different angle. The company was historically conservative, in that it had until recently been entirely equity financed. Even now, the ratio of debt to total capital of 9.5 percent was below the industry average. "Maybe Star was too conservative in using costly equity on relatively risk-free, low-return projects," she said. A multiple-discount-rate system that used modern portfolio theory techniques such as the CAPM to determine the capital providers' required return for various divisions or projects might allocate those costlier funds more scientifically. "Perhaps," she suggested, "we could use a method like the one used by Kennelworth Bank. They combine the CAPM, or at least the beta, and the dividend-discount model to determine whether a stock is fairly valued. Maybe we could do something similar in ranking our projects."

In discussing Ms. Schofield's proposal, the staff had raised several questions. If Star were to use different discount rates for each division or project, how would the required rates of return be estimated? How would the required return on equity be estimated for divisions of companies and projects that are not publicly traded? If beta were used to determine the equity cost or in a method similar to Kennelworth Bank's, how could a beta be determined for a division or project? What was to be done about weighting debt and equity? The debt question was especially important at Star, because all financing was done at the corporate level; divisions had no long-term debt.

Mr. Weathers strongly disagreed with Ms. Schofield's total approach. He said, "Risk should be accounted for by presenting best-and worst-case scenarios for all projects and, as we already do, by making conservative cash-flow forecasts. The use of divisional or project discount rates would be redundant at best, and at worst, could prematurely discourage consideration of riskier projects." While several staff members supported his approach, one said, "In my opinion, we should forecast a number of different scenarios and discount each at an appropriate hurdle rate. Use a different rate for each scenario."

The Decision

As Mr. Foster thought about the diverse opinions expressed by his staff, he knew he had to deal with three issues. First, what effect did debt have on Star's required rate of return on capital and how should that effect be determined? Second, should the CAPM be used to evaluate Star's required return on equity? Third, should Star use multiple discount rates for future capital-budgeting decisions, and if so, how should the rates be determined and used?

Mr. Foster analyzed Star's position and the arguments for and against the CAPM and multiple discount rates in light of two strategic moves Star management was contemplating: increasing plant capacity to produce more refrigerators in an attempt to increase market share, and expanding the operations of Star's 1982 acquisition into a new product, grain dryers. A net present value of zero was expected at 14.5 percent for the refrigerator project, and Rhinescour Division's vice president said he expected a zero net present value at 17.2 percent on the dryer project. To Mr. Foster, however, the returns on this latter project would clearly be highly influenced by the state of the economy and farm prices. Intuitively, he believed that the first option was less risky than the second, but the potential rewards of the second were enticing.

Mr. Foster weighed the advantages and disadvantages of the CAPM and then, using the company's financial data provided in Exhibits 4 and 5, studied the effects of the company's long-term debt on its required return on capital. (The current long-term debt consisted of a promissory note with a variable interest rate, on which the company was currently paying 12.20 percent. Rates on various forms of public debt are shown in Exhibit 6.) Mr. Foster wanted to determine Star's required return on capital at its current ratio of debt to capital and if the company were to borrow up to the industry average of 19 percent.

Mr. Foster then attempted to apply his findings to the issue of multiple discount rates. As he did so, several questions arose:

1. Once a base rate was calculated for the least risky projects, could higher rates be scientifically determined for consistent use on other projects, or should rates be varied for strategic reasons?

2. Considering the controls already in place, would the use of multiple rates overcompensate for risk? Should multiple rates replace those controls?

3. Would multiple discount rates lend a greater sense of conservatism to the company?

4. Would the use of multiple discount rates mix the investment decision with the financing decision?

Star Appliance Company (B)

EXHIBIT 1 • Selected Data for the Home-Appliance and Agricultural-Machinery Industries

	Debt/Equity	Debt/Capital	Return on Equity	Return on Assets	Return on Sales	Beta[a]	Average Market Price	Book Value	Average Price/Earnings	Payout Ratio	Dividend Yield
Home Appliances											
Magic Chef	35%	26%	22.2%	10.6%	5.2%	1.35	$34	$25.2	6.2X	16%	2.6%
Maytag	11	10	27.6	20.7	9.8	0.90	43	16.9	10.0	60	6.1
National Presto	4	4	10.1	8.7	17.6	0.90	28	13.3	11.9	45	3.8
Ranco	39	28	14.6	7.3	4.5	0.80	19	15.1	9.4	44	4.7
Robertshaw	19	16	17.5	11.0	5.8	0.95	30	25.3	7.5	26	3.4
Toro	49	33	11.1	5.1	3.0	0.65	16	9.0	8.1	18	2.2
Whirlpool	5	5	17.2	12.4	6.0	1.00	46	29.9	9.7	42	4.3
White Consolidated	40	29	9.5	5.1	2.5	1.05	30	30.8	13.5	68	5.0
Unweighted averages	25%	19%	16.2%	10.1%	6.8%	0.95	$31	20.7	9.5	40%	4.0%
Agricultural Machinery											
Deere & Co.	43%	30%	3.1%	1.3%	1.6%	1.05	$29	$33.8	6.4X	220%	3.4%
Hesston Corp.	73	42	(10.5)	(3.5)	(2.4)	0.90	8	29.8	NMF	NMF	NMF
Massey-Ferguson	205	67	2.3	0.5	0.5	0.75	4	NMF	NMF	NMF	NMF
Steiger Tractor	20	16	4.2	2.4	1.6	0.80	9	NMF	NMF	NMF	NMF
Selected unweighted averages	85%	39%	(0.2)%	(0.2)%	0.3%	0.88	$13	NMF	NMF	NMF	NMF

NMF = no meaningful figure.

[a]Calculated using 2.5 years of weekly total returns, adjusted for known problems.

Source: Value Line *Investment Survey.*

Star Appliance Company (B)
EXHIBIT 2 • Historical Company and Stock Market Data

Year/Month		Stock Market Price Index[a] 1943=10	Star Appliance Co. Market Price Changes[b]	Year/Month		Stock Market Price Index[a] 1943=10	Star Appliance Co. Market Price Changes[b]
1979	1	99.93	2.1%	1982	1	120.40	(4.7)%
	2	96.28	1.4		2	113.11	(2.2)
	3	101.59	1.1		3	111.96	7.3
	4	101.76	8.4		4	116.44	4.3
	5	99.08	(8.2)		5	111.88	5.4
	6	102.91	9.2		6	109.61	9.7
	7	103.81	(1.0)		7	107.09	3.6
	8	109.32	2.8		8	119.51	19.1
	9	109.32	6.5		9	120.42	(2.0)
	10	101.82	(7.3)		10	133.71	10.3
	11	106.16	(5.0)		11	138.54	3.7
	12	107.94	(9.2)		12	140.64	1.6
1980	1	114.16	2.9	1983	1	145.30	8.3
	2	113.66	(4.6)		2	148.06	16.0
	3	102.09	(4.8)		3	152.96	1.3
	4	106.29	2.6		4	164.42	18.1
	5	111.24	7.8		5	162.39	(3.1)
	6	114.24	8.3		6	168.11	(7.0)
	7	121.67	0.6		7	162.56	9.7
	8	122.38	(5.7)		8	164.40	(17.5)
	9	125.46	2.3		9	166.07	3.0
	10	127.47	2.3		10	163.55	(44.8)
	11	140.52	(5.8)		11	166.40	5.8
	12	135.76	(1.7)		12	164.93	(3.3)
1981	1	129.55	(0.2)	1984	1	163.41	81.6
	2	131.27	4.5		2	157.06	(6.7)
	3	136.00	13.5		3	159.18	1.4
	4	132.81	(1.1)		4	160.05	(4.3)
	5	132.59	(3.3)		5	150.55	(11.6)
	6	131.21	4.0		6	153.18	3.0
	7	130.92	(2.9)		7	150.66	2.0
	8	122.79	(1.9)		8	166.68	11.3
	9	116.18	(6.3)		9	166.10	9.6
	10	121.89	1.4		10	167.42	(1.6)
	11	126.35	14.4		11	163.58	1.6
	12	122.55	(10.2)		12	167.24	(4.0)

[a]Standard & Poor's 500 Index as of last trading day of each month.

[b]Stock price at end of 1984 was $63.29.

Star Appliance Company (B)

EXHIBIT 3 • U.S. Treasury Security Yields (end of quarter)

	Year/ Quarter	3-Month Bill	6-Month Bill	5-Year Note	7-Year Note	10-Year Bond
1982	1	13.04%	14.12%	14.11%	14.07%	13.99%
	2	11.97	12.52	13.78	13.81	13.69
	3	8.66	10.20	12.72	12.86	12.77
	4	8.51	9.00	10.47	10.77	10.69
Monthly average		11.09	12.00	13.11	13.22	13.18
1983	1	8.15	8.38	9.92	10.14	10.24
	2	8.91	9.23	10.49	10.77	10.79
	3	9.56	10.10	11.71	11.88	11.92
	4	9.17	9.56	11.40	11.51	11.58
Monthly average		8.83	9.18	10.79	10.94	11.01
1984	1	9.47	9.89	11.80	11.99	12.04
	2	10.08	11.25	13.65	13.73	13.78
	3	11.01	11.44	12.74	12.82	12.76
	4	8.68	9.14	11.25	11.53	11.50
Monthly average		9.89	10.44	12.28	12.45	12.45

Source: *Analytical Record of Yields and Yield Spreads* (New York: Salomon Brothers, 1985).

Star Appliance Company (B)
EXHIBIT 4 • Statements of Consolidated Income (dollars in thousands, except per-share data)

	1979	1980	1981	1982	1983	1984
Income						
Net sales	$302,670	$286,346	$339,169	$352,647	$477,590	$514,048
Interest	5,516	6,549	10,153	7,603	6,505	6,207
Miscellaneous	140	457	737	755	1,039	1,167
Total income	308,326	293,352	350,059	361,005	485,134	521,422
Cost of products sold	(195,207)	(189,704)	(233,854)	(237,053)	(309,002)	(337,413)
Operating profit	113,119	103,648	116,205	123,952	176,132	184,009
Selling and administrative	(44,744)	(50,415)	(59,383)	(66,988)	(81,802)	(87,598)
Interest expense	0	0	0	1,682	3,538	3,136
Income before taxes	68,375	53,233	56,822	55,282	90,792	93,275
Federal and state taxes	(31,250)	(24,108)	(25,481)	(25,600)	(42,240)	(42,800)
Net income	$37,125	$29,125	$31,341	$29,682	$48,552	$50,175
Net income per average share	$2.58	$2.02	$2.18	$2.06	$3.38	$3.51
Dividends	$23,002	$22,926	$25,110	$23,802	$29,991	$32,697
Average dividend yield	6.7%	7.1%	7.1%	5.4%	4.4%	4.6%
Average P/E ratio	9.2×	11.0×	11.2×	14.9×	14.1×	14.0×

Star Appliance Company (B)

EXHIBIT 5 • Consolidated Statements of Financial Condition (dollars in thousands)

	1979	1980	1981	1982	1983	1984
Assets						
Current assets						
Cash	$ 2,653	$ 3,303	$ 3,259	$ 3,413	$ 5,262	$ 4,870
Short-term investments	47,036	47,625	45,587	37,191	47,315	35,482
Prepaid pension	2,460	6,150	9,180	9,600	6,800	2,000
Accounts receivable, net	18,967	20,977	16,754	30,892	38,313	37,630
Inventories	31,941	41,397	40,819	50,504	60,518	62,147
Deferred taxes	1,620	0	0	0	0	1,913
Total current assets	104,677	119,452	115,599	131,600	158,208	144,042
Other assets						
Marketable securities	0	0	0	0	0	9,758
Prepaid pension	0	0	1,079	4,000	12,000	16,800
Miscellaneous	728	1,685	1,113	1,770	2,200	3,854
Total other assets	728	1,685	2,192	5,770	14,200	30,412
Property, plant, and equipment						
Land	708	1,241	1,018	1,686	2,078	2,224
Buildings and improvements	41,511	44,782	43,462	46,631	48,794	51,398
Machinery and equipment	83,737	93,678	101,860	113,048	122,674	133,772
	125,956	139,701	146,340	161,365	173,546	187,394
Less depreciation	(65,242)	(67,899)	(74,709)	(79,344)	(88,274)	(98,120)
Total property, plant, and equipment	60,714	71,802	71,631	82,021	85,272	89,274
Total assets	$166,119	$192,939	$189,422	$219,391	$257,680	$263,728
Liabilities and Shareholders' Equity						
Current liabilities						
Accounts payable	$ 7,173	$ 9,193	$ 6,553	$ 10,076	$ 16,106	$ 13,066
Compensation to employees	5,600	6,171	6,871	8,301	9,238	10,077
Accrued liabilities	5,127	6,188	6,078	8,155	11,243	12,765
Federal and state taxes	7,523	3,954	1,315	2,609	6,317	5,539
Deferred taxes	0	0	2,322	2,079	1,418	0
Total current liabilities	25,423	25,506	23,139	31,220	44,322	41,447
Deferred taxes	6,784	8,029	10,867	8,385	13,011	16,493
Long-term debt	0	0	0	17,797	19,351	19,417
Shareholders' equity						
Common stock						
Authorized—20,000,000 shares						
Issued—14,382,518 shares	26,840	28,765	28,765	28,765	28,765	28,765
Additional paid-in capital	0	17,368	17,579	17,078	17,084	17,070
Retained earnings	109,154	115,353	121,584	127,464	146,025	163,823
Total shareholders' equity	135,994	161,486	167,928	173,307	191,874	209,658
Less treasury stock	(2,082)	(2,082)	(12,512)	(11,318)	(10,878)	(23,287)
Net shareholders' equity	133,912	159,404	155,416	161,989	$180,996	$186,371
Total liabilities and shareholders' equity	$166,119	$192,939	$189,422	$219,391	$257,680	$263,728

Star Appliance Company (B)
EXHIBIT 6 • Interest Rates on Debt of Different Qualities

Year/Quarter		Corporate Bonds		Prime Lending Rate	90-Day Treasury Bills	7-Year Treasury Notes
		Aaa	Baa			
1982	1	14.58%	16.82%	16.50%	13.04%	14.07%
	2	14.81	16.92	16.50	11.97	13.81
	3	12.94	15.63	13.50	8.66	12.86
	4	11.83	14.14	11.50	8.51	10.77
1983	1	11.73	13.61	10.50	8.15	10.14
	2	11.74	13.37	10.50	8.91	10.77
	3	12.37	13.55	11.00	9.55	11.88
	4	12.57	13.75	11.00	9.17	11.51
1984	1	12.57	13.99	11.21	9.47	11.99
	2	13.55	12.66	12.60	10.08	13.73
	3	12.66	14.35	12.97	11.01	12.82
	4	12.13	13.40	11.06	8.68	11.53

Source: *Federal Reserve Bulletin,* 1985.

Star Appliance Company (B)

Appendix

To: Mr. Arthur Foster
           Financial Vice President, Star Appliance Company

From: Sam Ralfson
           Kennelworth Bank and Trust

Date: January 3, 1985

You asked us to provide you with an estimate of the return expected for the market. Unfortunately there is no single estimate (or even definition of the market), but rather, various estimates made by various groups. On *Wall Street Week*'s year-end program, one analyst was predicting that the Dow Industrial would go from its level of about 1,200 at the end of 1984 to 1,500. Another believed the U.S. deficit would take it 100 points below its current level by year's end.

Over history, the market has yielded from −26.5 percent to 54.0 percent, but the geometric average was 9.5 percent from 1926 to 1984. As shown in Exhibit A-1, the realized market returns have been quite variable. However, some of our analysts find the long-term average a reasonable estimate since, they believe, time averages out the extremes.

The analysts in our Investment Analysis and Advisory Group prefer another method. They use a combination of the dividend discount model and a measure of risk called beta to forecast and evaluate expected returns from almost 500 common stocks.

Their first step is to forecast the dividends they anticipate from each company for at least 15 years. I have attached a chart (Exhibit A-2) they used to explain their method to me. They go about forecasting dividends by looking first at the basic sources of the company's earnings—its markets, products, and competitors—as well as its costs. Using their earnings forecasts and estimates of dividend payout ratios, they determine each company's dividend payments over three periods: for the next few years (usually 5) in detail; for a time of earnings and dividend growth (the analyst determines how long this period will be); and when the company is mature, with a final, low rate of growth in earnings and a higher payout ratio.

As you can see, this is just a more detailed version of the dividend discount model you told me Star has used to estimate its cost of equity. The model assumes that as companies mature they have more cash available than they need and can thus increase dividends.

Once the dividends have been forecast, they are compared to the stocks' current market prices, and rates of return (sometimes called internal rates of return) are calculated. The analysts then compare the expected return (the internal rate of return) with the beta for each stock.

By the way, the analysts tell me they buy their beta estimates from what they call a "beta service." These betas, they say, are calculated over 5 years of history and are adjusted for some statistical problems, but are quite similar to a simple regression historic beta. The expected returns and betas for each stock are plotted on a graph like that shown in Exhibit A-3. A line of best fit is drawn, or calculated using a regression package like that provided with most computer spreadsheet models such as *Lotus 1-2-3,* and the market's expected return is derived by looking at the return expected for a stock or portfolio with a beta of 1.0.

Star Appliance Company (B)

EXHIBIT A-1 • Basic Series: Total Annual Returns, 1926–1984

Series	Geometric Mean	Arithmetic Mean	Standard Deviation	Distribution
Common Stocks	9.5%	11.7%	21.2%	
Small Stocks	12.4	18.2	36.3	
Long-Term Corporate Bonds	4.4	4.6	7.6	
Long-Term Government Bonds	3.7	3.9	7.5	
U. S. Treasury Bills	3.3	3.4	3.3	
Inflation	3.0	3.2	4.9	

-90x   0x   +90x

Source: *Stocks, Bonds, Bills, & Inflation 1985 Yearbook* (Chicago: Ibbotson Associates, 1985).

Star Appliance Company (B)
EXHIBIT A-2 • Data for Present Value Calculation

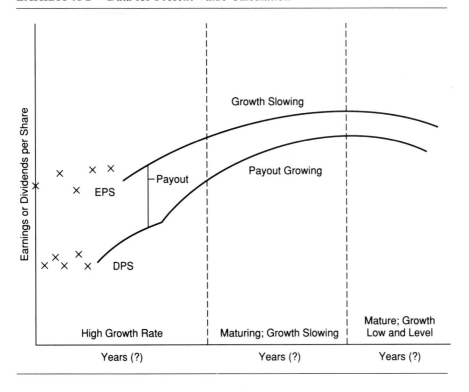

Star Appliance Company (B)
EXHIBIT A-3 • Expected Value

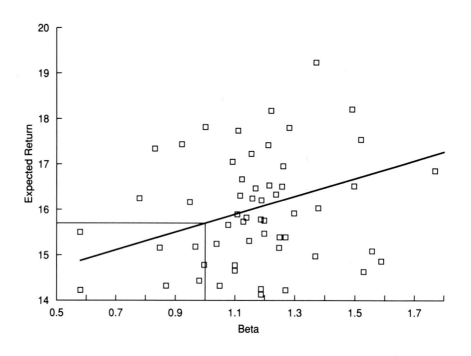

Federal Reserve Bank of Richmond (B)

▼

"I'd rather try skydiving than put this savings bond automation proposal together," Roy Fauber thought. He glanced once again at the reports his staff at the Federal Reserve Bank of Richmond (FRBR) had put together. Since up to 3 months might be required just to get the project approved, he knew he could not delay much longer. Also, depending on the system chosen, the layout of the savings bond processing area might need modification. Since the FRBR was in the process of building new offices, any necessary changes would be much easier, and cheaper, if made soon.

Each of the three options before him proposed greater computerization of the FRBR savings bond processing system. Analyzing them had been difficult because the questions they raised were complex: allocated costs versus cash outlays, decentralized versus centralized computer hardware, and differences in start-up dates. Even so, his staff had prepared estimates, and their cost/benefit analyses lay before him now (Exhibit 1). What had not been done was to choose a discount rate for use in the present value analysis. That Mr. Fauber had to do, and the choice was troublesome.

The discount rate question had been a problem in the federal government for years. By 1965 many agencies and departments had adopted cost/benefit analysis, but the discount rates they used varied both between and within the agencies. For instance, the Department of Defense evaluated weapons systems using rates ranging from 5 percent to 10 percent. The rate depended on the type of system being evaluated.

The problem had become especially vexing at the FRBR since the implementation of a new planning system that required the use of present value analysis, and thus a discount rate, for the evaluation of larger projects. Even though the concept of present value analysis had been introduced to the Federal Reserve districts, the discount rate issue had not been resolved. In order to gain approval for any one of the proposals before him, however, Mr. Fauber had to choose a discount rate.

The new planning system posed another problem: FRBR approval for the project was not enough by itself; investments in excess of $100,000 required approval by the Board of Governors of the Federal Reserve System. The three proposals Mr. Fauber was considering each exceeded $100,000. Since this would be the first proposal using present value analysis that the FRBR would send to the Board of Governors, it could set a precedent for later projects.

The FRBR Discount Rate

The methodology for the Federal Reserve System present value analysis was widely used in business. For a corporation competing for funds in the capital markets, the discount rate or standard would be the firm's cost of capital (the market-determined trade-off between present and future consumption). Any investment in which benefits would equal or exceed the total cost, including costs of capital for implementing the project, would be beneficial for the shareholders of that firm and should be accepted. Because it was difficult to estimate the cost of capital, the concept was not quite as easy for corporations to put into practice as it appeared. When it was used in a government agency, the problems multiplied.

Since the Federal Reserve did not compete for its funds in the traditional capital markets, the notion of a required rate of return or cost of capital was complicated for the FRBR. The Federal Reserve System created money when it drew a check on itself; thus, under no circumstances would it ever be short of credit. As an example, when the FRBR wrote a $70-million check for its office building under construction on the banks of the James River, the contractor took the check to his commercial bank, the bank presented the check to the Federal Reserve for payment, and the FRBR credited the member bank's reserve account—money was created. Thus it was unclear whether the FRBR even had a capital cost.

The capital budgeting system at the FRBR clearly required that the discount rate satisfy one of the following objectives, whose terms are explained in the appendix to this case:

a. Equal the FRBR's explicit cost of capital stock;

b. Allow the FRBR to operate at minimum cost to the Treasury;

c. Satisfy the FRBR's own opportunity costs; or

d. Allow the FRBR to invest at an optimal social rate.

Often several rates would satisfy an objective, and supportable arguments for each of the rates surfaced every time the question was raised. The staff had summarized the cost of capital arguments for Mr. Fauber to consider in making his decision. Those arguments are presented in the appendix to this case.

Conclusion

One statement that Mr. Fauber could make with certainty about the decision confronting him was that there was no shortage of possibilities. The fate of an investment could hinge on the discount rate chosen, and the range of discount rates being considered was very wide. What rate should be used and which, if any, of the alternatives should be recommended was now up to him.

Federal Reserve Bank of Richmond (B)
EXHIBIT 1 • Analysis of Options

I. Cost/Benefits of Four-Phase System

	Year 1	Year 2	Year 3	Year 4	Year 5
Development					
Hardware	$(285,245)				
Software					
Development	(28,000)				
Modification	(35,000)				
Conversion	(15,000)				
In-bank coordinator	(7,500)				
Operations					
Hardware maintenance	(11,556)	$(15,408)	$(15,408)	$(15,408)	$(15,408)
Software maintenance	(18,000)	(18,000)	(18,000)	(18,000)	(18,000)
Net costs	(400,301)	33,408	33,408	33,408	33,408
Personnel savings	71,634	73,932	80,488	85,317	90,435
Computer charge savings	41,000	41,000	41,000	41,000	41,000
Net benefits	$(287,667)	$ 81,524	$ 88,080	$ 92,909	$ 98,027

II. Cost/Benefits of IBM 370 In-House Software

	Year 1	Year 2	Year 3	Year 4	Year 5
Development					
Software	$(151,756)	$(134,140)			
Operations					
Software maintenance	(3,000)	(3,000)	$ (3,000)	$ (3,000)	$ (3,000)
Personnel benefits		43,191	91,564	97,058	102,882
Net benefits	$(154,756)	$ (93,949)	$ 88,564	$ 94,058	$ 99,882

III. Cost/Benefits of IBM 370 Outside Consultant Software

	Year 1	Year 2	Year 3	Year 4	Year 5
Development					
Software	$(250,000)				
Software conversion	(15,000)				
In-bank coordinator	(7,500)				
Operations					
Software maintenance		$(13,000)	$(18,000)	$(18,000)	$(18,000)
Personnel benefits		60,286	91,564	97,058	102,882
Net benefits	$(272,500)	$(47,786)	$ 73,564	$ 79,058	$ 84,882

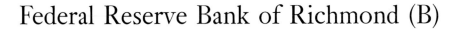

Federal Reserve Bank of Richmond (B)

Appendix
Office Correspondence

TO: R. Fauber

FROM: Computer Services and Planning Department

RE: Discount Rates and Federal Government Agencies

There has been a continuing discussion regarding the proper discount rate to use for public sector investment analysis. The following summarizes the main arguments and provides recent data for estimating each rate.

Explicit Cost of Capital Stock

The only external capital used by the Federal Reserve Bank of Richmond with an explicit cost is the stock held by Fifth District member banks. The return paid by the FRBR on that stock is 6 percent.

Minimum Cost to the Treasury

Any investment made by the Federal Reserve Bank of Richmond represents funds taken from the Treasury to be returned at some point in the future. Since one of the objectives of FRBR is to return the maximum profit to the Treasury, the discount rate should, it is argued, represent the time value of money to the Treasury. That rate could be the Treasury's marginal borrowing cost. (See Exhibit A–1.)

FRBR Opportunity Costs

Federal Reserve Banks invest funds in a variety of assets. Many believe that the rate on one of these earning assets, or an average of the rate on all of them, represents an opportunity cost. Whatever discount rate is chosen should reflect the cost of forgone opportunities. Several choices for an opportunity cost have been suggested:

1. Rediscount Rate. The rate at which member banks borrow from the FRB (Exhibit A–2).

2. The Rate on Agency Securities. These are rates on obligations of federal agencies (e.g., Federal Land Bank, Federal National Mortgage Association) owned by the FRB (Exhibit A–3).

3. Treasury Securities. The opportunity cost of investing in government securities; the rate on Treasury securities (Exhibit A–4).

All these rates have the advantage of being observable, market-determined rates. However, that does not mean that any one is the best choice for evaluating the economic potential of FRBR investments. Some suggest other, less observable choices are preferable.

Optimal Social Rate

Many argue that the discount rate should be based on circumstances beyond the Federal Reserve System alone. Since the system operates in the public sector, drawing resources away from the private sector, a rate should be used that will result in socially beneficial investment decisions. Yet very little agreement is found on the subject of what the optimal social rate actually should be. However, the discussion centers between two extremes.

The first group suggests there is a rate at which the public, in aggregate, would be willing to forgo income today for certain income at some time in the future. This rate, the *public's time preference of money,* is the optimal social discount rate. Since the public is willing to purchase long-term government bonds, and the return is default-risk free, this rate would be an adequate proxy.

The other extreme holds that public expenditures take resources from the private sector. Thus investments must earn a rate of return equivalent to what would be earned in the private sector—the *opportunity cost in the corporate sector* (Exhibit A–5).

In a society where there are no taxes and in which all investment returns are certain, corporations would be required to earn the investors' rate of time preference. However, in the real world, risk and taxes cloud the issue. If, for example, the rate of time preference is 6 percent, investors in the securities of a private corporation would demand a premium for risk. If the corporate income tax rate is 50 percent and the risk premium is 2 percent, the firm would earn 16 percent before tax on its capital expenditures if it provided an 8 percent required after-tax rate of return. All this assumes the firm had issued no debt. The proponents of this view argue that if the average corporation is required to earn 16 percent on its investments, the public sector should use this rate to ensure socially beneficial decisions. (Tax information is summarized in Exhibit A–6.)

These rates represent very different estimates of the social rate. Disagreement over these and other possible choices hinges on one's view of the riskiness of government versus corporate investments, the source of funds used for such investments, and how unestimated social benefits should be treated.

1. Risk.   The rate of individual or corporate time preference suggests there is no risk to government expenditures. Although returns from individual projects could vary, the public investment portfolio is so large that aggregate returns would vary only slightly from what is expected. In essence, there is no risk.

The use of the cost of corporate investments, on the other hand, suggests public investments of the same risk as corporate investments be discounted at the same rate. From the point of view of society, no single public or private investment carries any risk. However, the public sector is still responsible for meeting the opportunity cost established when an individual investor requires a risk premium from an individual firm.

2. Fund Source.   The use of either the rate of time preference or the corporate opportunity cost suggests resources are drawn from either the corporate sector or forgone individual consumption. However, noncorporate businesses (e.g., partnerships) also exist. Tax rates among these sectors vary significantly, and thus the pretax required return varies, as well. Whether one rate or a combination of effective rates from these sectors is appropriate is the source of some debate (Exhibit A-6).

3. Social Benefits.   Finally, many argue that the use of a market rate of interest would result in general underinvestment. Investments have nonquantified social benefits that are ignored in their economic evaluation. A new plant, for instance, may appear to break even, but the analysis ignores the benefits from the 200 new jobs the plant provides. The firm may have no economic return, yet society benefits. Thus a lower discount rate is justified when there are such benefits.

Federal Reserve Bank of Richmond (B)

EXHIBIT A–1 • Yields on New Treasury Issues in 1978[a]

	Bills		Notes						Bonds	
	3-Mo.	6-Mo.	1-Yr.	2-Yr.	3-Yr.	4-Yr.	5-Yr.	7-Yr.	10-Yr.	15-Yr.+
January (35)[b]	6.64%	7.01%	7.03%	7.55%						
February (36)	6.65	7.07	7.29	7.69	7.53	7.89		7.88		8.23
March (35)	6.51	6.98	7.34	7.56						
April (36)	6.50	7.01	7.55	7.80			7.94			
May (37)	6.64	7.37	7.95	8.09		8.27			8.29	8.47
June (37)	6.92	7.56	8.24	8.32						8.63
July (37)	7.30	7.91	8.39	8.61						
August (39)	7.28	7.72	8.48	8.38	8.46	8.41		8.36		8.43
September (39)	8.11	8.37	8.57	8.65						8.64

[a]Three- and six-month T-bill rates are the average for all issues in the month.

[b]Numbers in parentheses under each month represent the average maturity of all Treasury debt in months.

Federal Reserve Bank of Richmond (B)

EXHIBIT A–2 • Federal Reserve Bank of New York Rediscount Rate[a]

	Rate (percent)		Rate (percent)
1961	3%	1973	4.5–7.5%
1962	3	1974	7.5–8
1963	3–3.5	1975	6–7.75
1964	3.5–4	1976	5.25–6
1965	4–4.5	1977	5.25–6
1966	4.5	1/1/78	6
1967	4–4.5	1/9/78	6.5
1968	4.5–5.5	5/11/78	7
1969	5.5–6	7/3/78	7.25
1970	5.5–6	8/21/78	7.75
1971	4.5–5.5	9/22/78	8
1972	4.5		

[a]The rediscount rate at the FRBR and all other district banks followed the New York rate very closely.

Federal Reserve Bank of Richmond (B)

EXHIBIT A–3 • Average Yields on Agency Issues during 1978

	6-Mo.	1-Yr.	2-Yr.	5-Yr.	15-Yr.
3/7/78	6.99%	7.25%	7.55%	7.96%	8.15%
6/1/78	7.65	7.98	8.15	8.30	8.53
9/6/78	8.20	8.34	8.40	8.36	8.51

Federal Reserve Bank of Richmond (B)
EXHIBIT A–4 • Average Yields of Long-Term Bonds

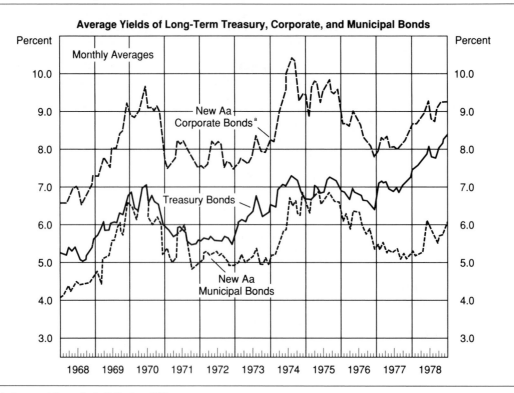

Average Yields of Long-Term Treasury, Corporate, and Municipal Bonds

[a]Change in Aa computation method effective June 1973.

Source: *Treasury Bulletin,* January 1979.

Federal Reserve Bank of Richmond (B)

EXHIBIT A–5 • Estimating Cost of Equity in the Corporate Sector

	Data for Dividend Yield Plus Growth and Earnings Price Models			
	1974	1975	1976	1977
Dividend/Price ratios[a]	4.47%	4.31%	3.77%	4.62%
Earnings/Price ratios[b]	11.59%	9.04%	8.90%	10.30%

	Five-Year Compounded Growth Rates[c] for the Period Ending				
	1974	1975	1976	1977	1978
Sales	10.9%	11.6%	11.8%	12.4%	12.9%
EPS	5.2	6.5	9.4	10.1	12.6
Stock price	−10.0%	−3.3%	−2.3%	−2.2%	4.2%

[a]Average of Standard & Poor's 500.

[b]From *Economic Report of the President,* 1978.

[c]Taken from *Forbes Annual Reports on American Industry.* Survey includes approximately 1,000 corporations.

Annual Compounded Returns Actually Realized from Common Stock Investments[a]	
1926–1964	10.4%
1965–1969	5.0
1970–1974	−2.4
1975	37.2
1976	23.8
1977	−7.2

[a]Standard & Poor's 500 (returns include dividends).

Source: Roger G. Ibbotson and Rex A. Sinquefield, *Stocks, Bonds, Bills and Inflation: Historical Returns (1926–1978),* (Charlottesville, Va.: The Financial Analysts Research Foundation, 1978).

Federal Reserve Bank of Richmond (B)
EXHIBIT A–6 • Federal, State, and Local Tax Information (in billions)

	1975	*1976*	*1977[a]*
Federal Government Receipts			
Individual income tax	$ 125.6	$ 147.3	$ 170.7
Corporate income tax	43.1	55.9	59.5
Social insurance revenue	94.2	105.7	118.9
Other	24	23.4	24.8
Total	$ 286.9	$ 332.3	$ 373.9
State and Local Government Receipts			
Personal income tax	$ 43.4	$ 49.6	$ 56.8
Corporate taxes	7.1	8.9	9.7
Indirect business taxes and nontax accruals	114.7	127.1	140.3
Social insurance receipts	15.9	18.1	20.1
Other	54.6	61.0	67.6
Total	$ 235.7	$ 264.7	$ 294.5
Gross national product	$1,528.8	$1,706.5	$1,890.4
Personal consumption	980.4	1,094.0	1,210.1
Corporate profits (pretax)	99.3	128.1	140.3

[a]Preliminary.

Source: *Economic Report of the President,* January 1978.

Procter & Gamble

Since February 19, 1990, three days previously, Mary Shiller had been looking forward to receiving a reaction from her boss regarding her estimate of Procter & Gamble's (P&G) cost of capital i.e., the required return on investment. Ms. Shiller reported directly to Ron Emory, the president of CORPSTRAT, a consulting firm located in Washington, D.C. CORPSTRAT had been successful since its founding in 1980 by providing high-quality analysis for a few large corporate clients. Recently, one of its largest clients had revealed that it was considering entering the household-products market and competing directly with P&G, the detergent and soap giant. The client's chief financial officer (CFO) had stated that the company had become "a highly diversified conglomerate with subsidiaries spanning a host of unrelated businesses" and that "our company's overall cost of capital is neither useful as a benchmark for any of the existing subsidiaries, nor as a hurdle rate for entering new markets like consumer products." Although the CFO's staff had computed its own estimate of the household-products industry's cost of capital, the CFO wanted an independent estimate before taking the plan to the board of directors in March. If the estimated cost of capital was "significantly lower than the expected return" of entering the new market, he fully expected the company to introduce its own brand of detergents, soaps, cleansers, and personal-care products by the end of 1990.

CORPSTRAT had never before been asked to compute a client's cost of capital. The company's real expertise was defining and evaluating the strategic goals of a corporation. Therefore, upon receiving the client's request, Ron Emory quickly assigned the task to Ms. Shiller in order to take advantage of her recent exposure to financial theory in her MBA curriculum. Ms. Shiller decided that she would compute P&G's cost of capital because P&G was the dominant player in the household-products and consumer-goods markets. Since this was her first project after joining CORPSTRAT, she had spent many hours preparing the first draft of her analysis as a memo to Mr. Emory (Appendix A). Unfortunately, Emory's memo in response to her work (Appendix B) indicated that much remained to be done.

▼
Procter & Gamble

Appendix A
Mary Shiller's Analysis

TO: Ron Emory

DATE: February 19, 1990

SUBJECT: Analysis of Procter & Gamble's Cost of Capital

I. Assumptions

This analysis is based upon the following set of assumptions:

A1. The cost of capital is a market-value concept. Whenever possible, market values rather than book values are used in the calculations, and only current market rates of return relevant to the estimation process.

A2. Management makes investment decisions with the goal of increasing the wealth of the company's investors. The objective of computing a cost of capital is to determine the minimum rate of return that adequately compensates the company's investors for the risk of investing in the company. Thus, only those projects that are expected to return profits in excess of the cost of capital are acceptable.

A3. The bond and stock markets are reasonably efficient and, therefore, provide an ideal vehicle for extracting the markets's assessment of the company's cost of debt and cost of equity.

A4. P&G's employee stock ownership plan (ESOP) and the capital-structure changes associated with it are not relevant to the calculation of the company's cost of capital. P&G management states in the 1989 Annual Report that ESOP debt should not be considered part of permanent capital because "the Company's total cash outflows related to the employee profit sharing plan, with or without the ESOP, are not materially different." The 1989 balance sheet has been reproduced in Exhibit 1 with the effects of the ESOP removed to make it more easily compared to 1988.

II. Procter & Gamble's Business Risk

Procter & Gamble is the leading soap and detergent producer, with annual revenues expected to be approximately $23.5 billion in 1990. Some of P&G's most recognizable detergent and soap brands are Tide, Cheer, Bold, Ivory, Zest, and Coast. The company also produces well-known toiletries such as Head & Shoulders shampoo and Scope mouthwash; paper products, including Bounty paper towels and Luvs disposable diapers; foods such as Crisco shortening, Pringles potato chips, and Folgers coffee; pharmaceuticals, including Dramamine for motion sickness and Vicks cough drops; and a few industrial products such as wood pulp and animal-feed ingredients. For 1989, laundry and cleaning products accounted for 32.5 percent of corporate sales; personal-care products contributed 45.7 percent; food and beverages, 13.8 percent; and pulp and chemicals, 8.1 percent.

The personal-care and food-and-beverage segments have risks that are similar to those of the laundry-and-cleaning products segment. Like its competitors, P&G distributes all of its consumer products through grocery stores and other retail outlets such as Krogers, Kmart, and Wal-Mart. Soaps, detergents, toothpaste, peanut butter, etc., are small-ticket items on the average homemaker's shopping list and are, therefore, relatively insensitive to swings in the economy. By contrast, pulp and chemicals are either sold directly or through jobbers and have had profit margins about double that of the personal-care and laundry-and-cleaning products groups (the food-and-beverage segment had approximately broken even over the past three years). Thus, the industrial-products segment seems to be the only business segment that is of sufficiently different risk to merit having a different cost of capital. On the other hand, since pulp and chemicals made up only 8.1 percent of 1989 sales, the small influence of the industrial-products segment can safely be ignored in the calculations.

III. The Cost of Debt

The cost of debt should represent the cost of refunding the debt on the company's books. The relevant debt is all interest-bearing debt on the books as of the end of fiscal 1989, which according to the 1989 balance sheets (Exhibit A-1) is $3,331 MM.[1] Most of P&G's debt is privately placed and therefore has no public price information available. The 8¼ percent coupon issue, however, is traded on the New York Stock Exchange and has a recent market price of $92.50 (Exhibit A-2). The yield to maturity (YTM) of 9.18 percent is very close to February's average yield for Aaa

---

[1] Computed by adding the debt due within one year to the long-term debt (i.e., $633 + $2,698 = $3,331 MM).

bonds of 9.22 percent (see Exhibit A-3). In addition, the 9.18 percent is very close to the average coupon rate of the dollar denominated debt on P&G's books.

IV. The Cost of Equity and the Capital Asset Pricing Model (CAPM)

The CAPM assumes that beta is the relevant measure of risk for a company. The most recent beta estimate published by *Value Line Investment Survey* is 0.95. This suggests that P&G stock is slightly less risky than the average stock, which has a beta of 1.0. The CAPM is usually written as

$$K_e = R_f + \beta_j (R_m - R_f)$$

where K_e is the cost of equity, R_f is the risk-free rate of interest, β is beta, which measures the firm's systematic risk, and $(R_m - R_f)$ is the expected premium of a market portfolio of stocks over the risk-free return. The interpretation of the model is that the cost of equity is composed of the risk-free rate plus a risk premium equal to the company's beta times the market-risk premium.

Most analysts use the prevailing U.S. Treasury rate for R_f and some sort of historic average for the market premium over R_f. However, there is some debate among academicians as to which risk-free rate and risk premium should be used The debate centers upon whether it makes more sense to use a short-term or long-term Treasury rate for R_f. If you believe that the current 90-day Treasury rate is appropriate, then most would argue that the average annual premium of a market index over T-bills should be used for $(R_m - R_f)$. If you like to use a 10- or 30-year Treasury bond rate, then $(R_m - R_f)$ should be the average of the market over long-term Treasuries. The table below summarizes the historic market premiums realized over the period 1926–1988 as published by Ibbotson Associates[2]:

Equity Risk Premium	Geometric Mean	Arithmetic Mean
Common Stocks − Bonds	5.4%	7.6%
Common Stocks − Bills	6.2%	8.4%

The two market premiums most frequently chosen are 8.4 percent, which is an arithmetic or simple average of annual market returns over the Treasury-bill rate, and 5.4 percent, which is a geometric or compound average of the market over Treasury bonds. Since the cost of debt is mea-

---

[2] *Stocks, Bonds, Bills and Inflation: 1989 Yearbook* (Chicago: Ibbotson Associates, Inc., 1989).

sured with YTM, which is a long-term, compound rate of return, I have chosen to use the average geometric market premium over long Treasuries to maintain consistency. Using 8.47 percent for R_f (Exhibit A-3), the long-term geometric average of 5.4 percent for $(R_m - R_f)$, and P&G's beta of 0.95 (Exhibit A-2), we get the following estimate of the cost of equity:

$$K_e = .0847 + .95 \,(.054)$$
$$= 13.6\%$$

V. The Weighted Average Cost of Capital

The overall cost of capital is the weighted average of the costs of debt and equity, where the weights are the relative proportions each source represents of the firm's total capital. The formula is

$$\text{WACC} = \frac{D}{V} \, K_d \,(1 - t) \,+\, \frac{E}{V} \, K_e$$

where V is total firm value, equal to the sum of the market value of debt (D) and equity (E), K_d is the cost of debt, K_e is the cost of equity, and t is the corporate tax rate (equal to 34 percent).

Assuming, as stated in P&G's 1989 Annual Report, that the company's target debt-to-total capital ratio (on a book value basis) is 35 percent, and substituting this into the weighted average cost of capital formula, we get

$$\text{WACC} = .35 \,(9.2\%) \,(1 - .34) + .65 \,(13.6\%)$$
$$= 11.0\%$$

VI. Recommendation

The WACC represents the minimum acceptable rate of return for investing in the consumer-products markets. In a discounted cash flow analysis, the expected after-tax cash flows should be present-valued using 11 percent and compared to the initial investment required to enter the market. If the net present value is positive, the company should proceed with the expansion plans.

Procter & Gamble

EXHIBIT A-1 • Balance Sheets for Years Ended June 30
(in millions, except per-share amounts)

	1988	1989[a]
Assets		
Current assets		
Cash and cash equivalent	$ 1,065	$ 1,448
Accounts receivable	1,759	2,090
Inventories	2,292	2,337
Prepaid expenses and other	477	564
Total current assets	5,593	6,439
Net property, plant, and equipment	6,778	6,793
Goodwill and other intangibles	1,944	2,305
Other assets	505	675
Total assets	$14,820	$16,212
Liabilities and Shareholders' Equity		
Current liabilities		
Accounts payable, trade	$ 1,494	$ 1,669
Accounts payable, other	341	466
Accrued liabilities	1,116	1,365
Taxes payable	371	523
Debt due within one year	902	633
Total current liabilities	4,224	4,656
Long-term debt	2,462	2,698
Other liabilities	475	447
Deferred income taxes	1,322	1,335
Shareholders' Equity		
Common stock par $1	169	170
Additional paid-in capital	463	595
Currency translation adjustment	17	(63)
Retained earnings	5,688	6,374
Total equity	6,337	7,076
Total liabilities and equity	$14,820	$16,212

[a]The effects of a leveraged employee stock ownership plan established in 1989 have been removed to allow comparison of 1988 and 1989.

Procter & Gamble
Exhibit A-2 • Financial Data

Income Statements for Years Ended June 30
(in millions, except per-share amounts)

	1987	*1988*	*1989*
Income			
Net sales	$17,000	$19,336	$21,398
Interest and other income	163	155	291
Total revenues	17,163	19,491	21,689
Costs and expenses			
Cost of products sold	(10,411)	(11,880)	(13,371)
Marketing, administration, other expenses	(4,977)	(5,660)	(5,988)
Interest expense	(353)	(321)	(391)
Provision for restructuring	(805)	0	0
Total costs and expenses	(16,546)	(17,861)	(19,750)
Earnings before income taxes	617	1,630	1,939
Income taxes	(290)	(610)	(733)
Net earnings	$ 327	$ 1,020	$ 1,207
Per common share			
Net earnings	$ 1.87	$ 5.96	$ 7.12
Dividends	$ 2.70	$ 2.75	$ 3.00

Historical and Expected Growth Information

	Past 10 Years	*Past 5 Years*	*Estimated Next 5 Years*[a]
Sales	7.6%	10.2%	8.0%
Earnings	7.0	5.9	15.5
Dividends	6.5%	4.6%	11.0%

Procter & Gamble
Exhibit A-2 • *continued*

Summary Financial Review, 1980–1989
(years ended June 30)

	1980	*1981*	*1982*	*1983*	*1984*	*1985*	*1986*	*1987*	*1988*	*1989*
Net sales (thousands)	$10,772	$11,416	$11,994	$12,452	$12,946	$13,552	$15,439	$17,000	$19,336	$21,397
Net earnings (thousands)	$640	$668	$777	$866	$890	$635	$709	$327	$1,020	$1,206
Earnings/Net sales (%)	5.9%	5.9%	6.5%	7.0%	6.9%	4.7%	4.6%	1.9%	5.3%	5.6%
Earnings/Common share	$3.87	$4.04	$4.69	$5.22	$5.35	$3.80	$4.20	$1.87	$5.96	$7.12
Dividends/Common share	1.70	1.90	2.05	2.25	2.40	2.60	2.63	2.70	2.75	3.00
End-of-year stock price	$73.75	$75.75	$83.00	$55.13	$52.63	$57.13	$80.13	$98.00	$77.50	$108.38
Beta[b]	0.57	0.63	0.60	0.84	0.88	0.72	1.15	1.23	0.96	0.95

Recent Stock and Bond Price Information[c]

Security	Price
8¼% bonds due in 2005, rated Aaa by Moody's	92½
P&G common stock	126¼

[a]Source: *Value Line Investment Survey,* January 26, 1990.

[b]Betas for 1980–1988 are case writer's estimates using daily stock returns with an equally weighted market-return index. The 1989 beta is taken from *Value Line Investment Survey.*

[c]Source: *The Wall Street Journal,* February 23, 1990.

Procter & Gamble
EXHIBIT A-3 • Current Market Conditions

	1989 December	1990 January	1990 February
Money Market Rates			
Commercial paper (3 month)	8.32%	8.16%	8.22%
Eurodollar deposits (3 month)	8.39	8.22	8.24
U.S. Treasury bills:			
3-month	7.63	7.64	7.74
1-year	7.21	7.38	7.55
Prime rate charged by banks	10.50	10.11	10.00
Capital Market Rates			
U.S. Treasury bonds:			
5-year	7.75	8.12	8.42
10-year	7.84	8.21	8.47
30-year	7.90	8.26	8.50
Corporate bonds by Moody's ratings:			
Aaa	8.86	8.99	9.22
Aa	9.11	9.27	9.45
A	9.39	9.54	9.75
Baa	9.82	9.94	10.14

Source: *Federal Reserve Bulletin,* May 1990.

Procter & Gamble

Appendix B
Ron Emory's Memo

Date: February 23, 1990

Subject: Cost-of-Capital Analysis

I'm on my way out to catch a plane to New York, so I'll outline my comments to save time. I'll take a look at the revised analysis when I get back in town Monday morning.

1.   P&G is only one company in the consumer-products business. However, they have such a dominant market share I question whether their cost of capital is what a new entrant like our client should expect. I think we should compute the cost of capital for many of the relevant competitors, including Clorox, Colgate-Palmolive, and Church & Dwight. I want you to compute Clorox's cost of capital as a comparison for your P&G estimate. Clorox is much smaller than P&G and should more accurately capture the risks of a new entrant. I've asked Larry Atkins to work on Colgate-Palmolive and Church & Dwight. If your Clorox number ends up being much different from the P&G number, Larry's work may help us resolve which is more reasonable.

2.   I get a cost of debt that is slightly lower than what you report. Investors look for yield plus appreciation in their investments. For a bond, the yield is the coupon payment and the appreciation is the difference between current price and par value. If the bond is selling at a discount, the appreciation is positive, and if the bond is selling at a premium, the expected price appreciation is negative (i.e., price depreciation). My estimate of the expected return on P&G's $8\frac{1}{4}$s currently selling or $92.50 is:

$$\text{Average yield} = \text{Coupon/Average price}$$
$$= \$8.25/[(\$92.5 + \$100)/2]$$
$$= 8.57\%$$

$$\text{Average gain} = (\text{Par Value} - \text{Price})/\text{Years to maturity}$$
$$= (\$100 - \$92.5)/15$$
$$= \$0.50$$

$$\text{Average percentage gain} = \text{Average gain/Average price}$$
$$= \$0.50/[(\$92.5 + \$100)/2]$$
$$= 0.52\%$$

$$\text{Total return} = \text{Yield} + \text{Gain}$$
$$= 8.57\% + 0.52\%$$
$$= 9.09\%$$

Why are our numbers different?

3.   I don't think we can sell the capital asset pricing model to the client. The model's credibility hinges upon the concept that investors value common stocks based upon betas. I'm certain that few, if any, individual investors think in terms of betas. Although stocks are riskier than bonds, investors look for the same two components of return: yield plus capital gains. Leave the CAPM estimates in your report, but add one or two additional estimates for cost of equity that are based on more intuitive techniques like the dividend growth and earnings capitalization models.

4.   Your numbers suggest that the cost of a debt-financed expansion is 9.2 percent, whereas if the company has to sell stock to finance the expansion, the cost rises to 13.6 percent. The client's last equity issue was over 30 years ago, and they just recently closed a large private placement of sinking-fund bonds, so we can safely assume that neither stock nor long-term debt will be issued to finance this project. My guess is that they will use retained earnings and short-term bank loans. The bank funds would be borrowed at prime, but I'm not sure how we should estimate the cost of retained earnings. Since retained earnings represent the amount of net income not paid out as a dividend, it would seem logical that the cost would be the capital gains portion of what equity investors demand. Be sure to say how these sources should be factored into the estimation procedure.

5.   The CFO has mentioned to me on several occasions that he never uses net-present-value numbers in presentations to the board of directors. The board has some appreciation for a discounted-cash-flow technique, but they prefer to focus on rates of return rather than absolute dollar amounts. Substitute a discussion of internal rate of return for the NPV section in the report.

6.   Clorox has a higher proportion of equity than P&G. Given this difference, will the resulting WACCs for the two firms be comparable? I am having the necessary information on Clorox sent to you separately today [Exhibits B-1 to B-5]. Clorox has no publicly traded bonds, but I would think that P&G's cost of debt would serve as a reasonable proxy for Clorox's cost of debt.

Procter & Gamble
EXHIBIT B-1 • Clorox: Business Risk

Clorox specializes in detergents and cleansers such as Clorox bleach, Liquid-plumer, Soft Scrub, and Formula 409. Like P&G, Clorox produces other product lines to take advantage of the distribution channels used for its main products. Examples include Kingsford and Match Light charcoal, Hidden Valley Ranch salad dressings, and Fresh Step cat litter. A small percentage of Clorox's sales come from Olympic and Lucite paint brands. Since Clorox's markets are mature, most of the growth has been through acquisitions. For example, since 1986, Clorox has been entering the bottled-water market by acquiring companies such as Aspen Water, Deep Rock Water, and Aqua Pure Water.

Procter & Gamble
EXHIBIT B-2 • Clorox: Balance Sheets Years Ended June 30
(in thousands except per-share)

	1988	1989
Assets		
Current assets		
Cash and short-term investments	$ 259,278	$ 23,334
Accounts receivable, less allowances	114,697	143,354
Inventories	85,458	110,633
Prepaid expenses	6,353	10,816
Net assets held for sale	0	116,704
Total current assets	465,786	614,841
Net property, plant, and equipment	357,683	410,921
Brands, trademarks, patents, and other intangibles	92,003	99,654
Other assets including investments in affiliates	76,182	87,673
Net assets of discontinued operations	147,665	0
Total assets	$1,139,319	$1,213,089
Liabilities and Stockholders' Equity		
Current liabilities		
Accounts payable	$ 86,133	$ 85,798
Accrued liabilities	118,218	142,429
Income taxes payable	12,776	8,303
Commercial paper	78,811	79,580
Current maturities of long-term debt	1,838	14,658
Total current liabilities	297,776	330,768
Long-term debt and other obligations	29,190	7,051
Deferred income taxes	99,499	89,094
Stockholders' equity		
Common stock: authorized, 17,000,000 shares, $1 par	54,044	55,398
Additional paid-in capital	93,240	103,879
Retained earnings	570,163	634,275
Cumulative translation adjustments	(4,593)	(7,376)
Total stockholders' equity	712,854	786,176
Total liabilities and equity	$1,139,319	$1,213,089

Procter & Gamble
EXHIBIT B-3 • Clorox: Income Statements Years Ended June 30
(in thousands except per-share)

	1987	1988	1989
Net sales	$1,022,339	$1,153,103	$1,356,294
Cost and Expenses			
Costs of products sold	(479,214)	(524,572)	(642,141)
Selling, delivery, and administration	(204,453)	(235,629)	(269,586)
Advertising	(139,041)	(161,722)	(200,696)
Research and development	(31,049)	(30,735)	(37,161)
Interest expense	(5,377)	(4,085)	(7,187)
Other	22,176	12,450	30,158
Total costs and expenses	836,958	944,293	1,126,608
Earnings from continuing operations before taxes	185,381	208,810	229,686
Provision for income taxes	80,599	77,884	84,126
Earnings from continuing operations	104,782	130,926	145,560
Earnings (loss) from discontinued operations	117	1,644	(21,416)
Net earnings	$ 104,899	$ 132,570	$ 124,144
Earnings per common share			
Continuing operations	$1.92	$2.37	$2.63
Discontinued operations	0.00	0.03	(0.39)
Total earnings purchase	$1.92	$2.40	$2.24
Weighted-average number of shares outstanding	54,652	55,127	55,333

Procter & Gamble
EXHIBIT B-4 • Clorox: Financial Summary Data

Summary Financial Review for Years Ended June 30, 1980–1989

	1980	*1981*	*1982*	*1983*	*1984*	*1985*	*1986*	*1987*	*1988*	*1989*
Net sales (thousands)	$ 637	714	804	825	848	932	972	1,022	1,153	1,356
Net earnings (thousands)	$ 33	38	45	66	80	86	96	105	133	124
Earnings/Net sales	5.2%	5.3	5.6	7.9	9.4	9.2	9.8	10.3	11.5	9.2
Earnings/Common share	$ 0.72	0.83	0.94	1.34	1.52	1.61	1.77	1.93	2.42	2.24
Dividends/Common share	0.39	0.41	0.43	0.48	0.54	0.62	0.70	0.79	0.92	1.09
End-of-year stock price	$10.13	11.63	13.50	33.25	27.25	38.38	55.88	32.88	28.88	40.00
Beta[a]	0.78	0.94	0.96	1.32	1.30	1.36	1.23	1.14	0.91	0.90

Recent Stock-Price Information[b]

Security	*Price*
Clorox common stock	38¼

[a]Source: Betas for 1980–1988 are case writer's estimates using daily stock returns with an equally weighted market-return index. The 1989 beta is taken from *Value Line Investment Survey.*
[b]Source: *The Wall Street Journal,* February 23, 1990.

Procter & Gamble
EXHIBIT B-5 • Clorox: Historical and Expected Growth Information

	Past 10 years	*Past 5 years*	*Estimated Next 5 years[a]*
Sales	6.6%	8.6%	13.5%
Earnings	13.4	8.1	15.5
Dividends	12.1%	15.1%	13.5%

[a]Source: *Value Line Investment Survey,* January 26, 1990.

Mead Corporation

On February 14, 1991, Cheryl Harris, business analyst at Mead Corporation, had just begun the process of estimating Mead's required rate of return, its cost of capital, for the fourth quarter of 1990. Like most other major corporations, Mead used its weighted-average cost of capital (WACC) to evaluate new investment proposals as well as to measure corporate and divisional performance. Mead was unique, however, in its practice of updating the hurdle rate every quarter and analyzing the factors responsible for its change. Looking back at the company's history of WACC estimates, Ms. Harris observed that Mead's cost of equity had been increasing relative to its cost of debt over the past few years. Hence, as part of her analysis, she hoped to explain why the cost of equity had increased and to recommend whether the company should consider the increase a problem. Her more immediate concern, however, was the presentation she was to give the next morning to William Enouen, Mead's chief financial officer, who had asked to see Ms. Harris's WACC estimate.

Mead Corporation

Mead Corporation was founded in 1846 by Daniel E. Mead and incorporated in 1930. In the ensuing years, Mead, Inc., grew to become a leading producer of paper and forest products. Included in the company's product line of forest derivatives were printing paper, writing paper, specialty paper, lumber, wood pulp, corrugated containers, and packaging products. The company also owned and operated a national distribution network for paper packaging and supplies. For beverage packages and packaging systems as well as for paper-based school and office supplies, Mead was the leading manufacturer in the United States.

In addition to its forest and paper-based products, Mead had been involved in electronic publishing and the development of color imaging.

This case was written by Associate Professor Kenneth Eades for the purposes of classroom discussion. Some figures have been changed at the request of the company. Copyright © 1991 by the University of Virginia Darden School Foundation, Charlottesville, Virginia. All rights reserved.

Mead Data Central (MDC), a wholly owned subsidiary of Mead, Inc., owned several publishing companies—for example, The Michie Company in Charlottesville, Virginia, which published and distributed the legal statutes of 23 states. MDC also marketed the LEXIS® and NEXIS® information services. LEXIS was a computer-based data-retrieval system designed for legal research that had been expanded to include financial information from leading investment banks, brokerage firms, and research companies. NEXIS was an on-line general-information-retrieval service frequently available in libraries and news departments of the print and broadcast media.

After investing approximately $200 million over five years in the development of its color-imaging process called Cycolor®, Mead had announced in December 1990 that the demand for color copying was growing too slowly to justify remaining in the business. The write-offs associated with the discontinuance had resulted in Mead's fourth-quarter earnings per share falling from the third-quarter figure of $0.63 to $0.17. The company projected that the write-offs would be completed before the second quarter of 1991, at which time profits were expected to return to normal. The announcement regarding discontinuation of its color-imaging business did not appear to have adversely affected Mead's common stock price, which had risen to $25.75 on December 31, 1990, from $24.25 on October 1, 1990.

Mead's Cost of Capital

Mead had conducted an internal study in 1984 of the company's cost-of-capital calculation method. Subsequently, top management implemented a strategy to estimate the cost of capital each quarter and decompose it into its components for comparison with historical estimates. The cost of capital had become an important benchmark for measuring both corporate and divisional performance. Although several other factors were used in the evaluation of Mead's divisions, earning a return on investment greater than the cost of capital was considered the single most important performance measure. One of the recommendations of the study was that the MDC division, because of its higher risk, should be held to a higher required rate-of-return standard than the rest of the company's divisions. Thus, while the other divisions were evaluated against the company's WACC, MDC's performance was compared with Mead's WACC plus an additional 4 percent.[1] The same 4 percent risk premium had been used for MDC's cost of capital since 1984.

In addition to measuring internal performance, the cost of capital also served as a barometer of the external market's perception of the com-

---

[1] Casewriter's estimate.

pany. For example, the cost of equity reflected the market's assessment of the company's risk. If senior management's assessment of Mead's risk was substantially less than the market's, the company could take advantage of the market's pricing by executing a share-repurchase program. Following the stock market crash in 1987, Mead repurchased approximately 282,000 shares on the open market. In 1990, the company repurchased 5 million shares at an average price of $26.69, which approximated the company's 1990 book value of $26.28 per share.

Studying the components of the WACC allowed management to discriminate between changes in capital costs caused by macroeconomic variables such as interest rates and changes caused by firm-specific variables such as the company's beta or its capital structure. Changes in firm-specific variables were considered to be somewhat under management's control, whereas a change in, for example, the general level of interest rates was viewed as an exogenous factor that could not be managed.

Exhibit 1 reports a 10-year history of Mead's cost of capital. The exhibit shows that Mead used the capital asset pricing model (CAPM) to compute its cost of equity and that the before-tax cost of debt was estimated using the yield to maturity of the company's publicly traded long-term debt. The equity risk premium of 6.0 percent in column 2 was based on the long-run average premium of the return on Standard and Poor's 500 composite index less the return on long-term government bonds. In a 1991 study, Ibbotson Associates, Inc.[2] reported (Exhibit 2) that the S&P 500 premium over long-term governments averaged 5.6 percent over the period 1926–1990, but to be conservative, Mead had been estimating its cost of equity using a 6.0 percent premium that had been reported in an earlier study by Ibbotson and Sinquefield[3] as the average for the 1926–1980 period.

Equity and debt costs were averaged according to the proportion each financing source represented of the total capital structure. The WACC formula used by Mead is

$$\text{WACC} = K_e \times E/(D + E) + K_d \times (1 - \tau) \times D/(D + E)$$

where D is the amount of Mead's long-term debt, E is Mead's equity, τ is the company's tax rate, K_e is the cost of equity, and K_d is the cost of debt. D represented the permanent sources of debt capital, which were considered to include current and noncurrent long-term debt, notes payable, and con-

---

[2] *Stocks, Bonds, Bills, and Inflation: 1991 Yearbook.* (Abottson Associates, Inc., 1991).

[3] R. Ibbotson and R. Sinquefield, *Stocks, Bonds, Bills, and Inflation: The Past and the Future,* (The Financial Analysis Research Foundation, 1982).

vertible bonds.[4] The equity component, E, included all equity accounts on the balance sheet: that is, common stock, paid-in capital, foreign-currency adjustments, and retained earnings. (See Exhibits 3 and 4 for corporate financial data.)

Ms. Harris noticed that the WACC had varied considerably over the past few years, from a low of 10.4 percent in 1986 to a high of 14.5 percent in 1981 and 1984. The cost of equity, however, had varied from 14.6 percent in 1986 to 19.5 percent in 1981 and had tended to increase relative to the cost of debt. Part of the increase in the cost of equity came from an increase in Mead's beta to 1.4 in 1988 from 1.1 in 1985. Mr. Enouen had commented during an earlier conversation with Ms. Harris that the initial increase in beta appeared to have been prompted by the high activity and price variations that accompanied the junk-bond-financed takeover period. The fact that the beta had remained at the high level and continued to increase suggested, however, a more permanent shift in the market's perception of the risk of Mead's common stock. Although she was not certain, Ms. Harris believed that the beta had remained at its high level because Mead had received increased scrutiny by financial analysts, who determined that the paper industry had become more sensitive to the state of the economy than it had been in the early 1980s. (See Exhibit 5 for historical corporate financial data and Exhibit 6 for financial data by industry segment.)

To illustrate where the changes in Mead's WACC had occurred, Ms. Harris decided to compare her estimate of the cost of capital for the fourth quarter of 1990 with the 1985 estimate, the year prior to the first increase in Mead's beta. Using 1985 as the base year, she could compute the influence that each variable in the WACC formula had on the change in Mead's WACC. For example, the increase in beta from 1.1 to 1.4 was responsible for a 1.8-percentage-point increase in the company's cost of equity (the difference between the two betas multiplied by the 6 percent equity risk premium) and a 1.07-percentage-point increase in Mead's WACC (the 1.8 percent number multiplied by Mead's proportion of equity to total capital, 59.5 percent). For the fourth-quarter estimate, she had decided to use the beta of 1.4 published by *Value Line Investment Survey* and 8.25 percent as the risk-free rate (yield to maturity on 30-year Treasury bonds as reported in the January 2, 1991, edition of *The Wall Street Journal*). Exhibit 7 presents fourth-quarter market data for a sample of Mead's publicly traded securities.

---

[4] Convertible bonds were included as part of the debt because Mead's current stock price was well below the exercise prices of the convertible bonds. With little chance of being converted into common stock, the convertible debt was essentially identical to a regular, nonconvertible debt instrument.

Mead Corporation
EXHIBIT 1 • Weighted-Average Cost of Capital: 10-year History

	(1)	(2)	(3)	(4)	(5)	(6)	(7)	(8)	(9)	(10)	(11)
	Beta	Risk Premium	Equity Risk Premium (1) × (2)	Risk-Free Rate	Cost of Equity (3) + (4)	Equity/Total Capital	Debt Rate	1−Tax Rate	After-Tax Cost of Debt (7) × (8)	Debt/Total Capital	WACC (5) × (6) + (9) × (10)
1981	1.1	6.0%	6.6%	12.9%	19.5%	55.0%	16.0%	52.0%	8.3%	45.0%	14.5%
1982	1.1	6.0	6.6	12.2	18.8	47.0	15.5	52.0	8.1	53.0	13.1
1983	1.1	6.0	6.6	10.8	17.4	59.0	12.7	52.0	6.6	41.0	13.0
1984	1.1	6.0	6.6	12.0	18.6	65.0	13.5	52.0	7.0	35.0	14.5
1985	1.1	6.0	6.6	9.3	15.9	67.0	11.5	52.0	6.0	33.0	12.6
1986	1.2	6.0	7.2	7.4	14.6	57.0	9.3	52.0	4.8	43.0	10.4
1987	1.2	6.0	7.2	9.0	16.2	62.0	10.3	56.0	5.8	38.0	12.2
1988	1.4	6.0	8.4	9.0	17.4	61.9	10.2	62.0	6.3	38.1	13.2
1989	1.4	6.0	8.4	8.0	16.4	63.6	9.4	62.0	5.8	36.3	12.6
03/31/90	1.4	6.0	8.4	8.6	17.0	63.1	9.8	62.0	6.1	36.9	13.0
06/30/90	1.4	6.0	8.4	8.4	16.8	61.2	9.7	62.0	6.0	38.8	12.6
09/30/90	1.4	6.0	8.4	9.0	17.4	59.5	10.2	62.0	6.3	40.5	12.9
Optimal[a]	1.4	6.0%	8.4%	9.0%	17.4%	65.0%	10.2%	62.0%	6.3%	35.0%	13.5%

Assumptions:

Beta as reported by *Value Line Investment Survey.*

Equity risk premium is an average return differential between S&P 500 and long-term government securities.

Risk-free rate is the yield to maturity of 30-year Treasury bond.

Debt rate is the yield to maturity of 20-year corporate bonds rated A by Moody's.

Tax rate is the effective marginal tax rate after considering both state and federal taxes.

[a]Third-quarter WACC computed at optimal debt/equity mix of 35 percent debt and 65 percent equity.

Mead Corporation

**EXHIBIT 2 • Ibbotson Associates, Inc. Report of
             Average Annual Returns for 1926–1990**

	Arithmetic Mean[a]	Geometric Mean[b]	Standard Deviation
S&P 500	12.1%	10.1%	20.8%
Small-company stocks	17.1	11.6	35.4
Long-term corporate bonds	5.5	5.2	8.4
Long-term government bonds	4.9	4.5	8.5
U.S. Treasury bills	3.7%	3.7%	3.4%

[a]The arithmetic mean is computed as the sum of the single-year returns from 1926 through 1990 divided by 65, the number of returns.

[b]The geometric mean accounts for the compound growth and equals the return earned each year from 1926 through 1990 that would generate the same final wealth as did the 65 individual annual returns. For example, if an investor earned −20 percent and +40 percent over 2 years, the arithmetic average return would be +10%, whereas his geometric average return (ρ) would be 5.83 percent.

Source: *Stocks, Bonds, Bills and Inflation: 1991 Yearbook* (Ibbotson Associates, Inc., 1991).

Mead Corporation

EXHIBIT 3 • Mead Corporate 1989 and 1990 Income Statements—Years Ended December 31 (in millions, except per-share amounts)

	1989	1990
Net sales	$4,608.2	$4,772.4
Cost of products sold	(3,675.8)	(3,850.4)
Gross profit	932.4	922.0
Selling, administrative, and research expenses	(586.3)	(617.6)
Nonrecurring operating expenses	0	(88.5)
Earnings from operations	346.1	215.9
Other revenues, net	57.4	23.7
Interest and debt expense	(81.8)	(92.6)
Earnings from continuing operations before income taxes	321.7	147.0
Income taxes	(118.5)	(52.3)
Earnings from continuing operations before equity in net earnings of jointly owned companies	203.2	94.7
Equity in net earnings of jointly owned companies	44.1	11.7
Earnings from continuing operations	247.3	106.4
Loss from discontinued operation	(31.5)	(74.8)
Earnings before extraordinary item	215.8	31.6
Extraordinary item	0	6.9
Net earnings	$ 215.8	$ 38.5
Per common and common equivalent share:		
Earnings from continuing operations	$ 3.80	$ 1.71
Loss from discontinued operations	(0.47)	(1.20)
Earnings before extraordinary item	3.33	0.51
Extraordinary item	0	0.11
Net earnings	$ 3.33	$ 0.62

Mead Corporation

**EXHIBIT 4 • Mead Corporate 1989 and 1990 Balance Sheet Statements—
Years Ended December 31 (in millions, except per-share amounts)**

	1989	1990
Current assets		
Cash and cash equivalents	$ 21.1	$ 21.1
Accounts receivable, net	536.1	528.9
Inventories	381.0	394.6
Prepaid expenses	42.4	37.4
Total current assets	980.6	982.0
Investments and other assets		
Investments in jointly owned companies	103.7	91.0
Other assets	526.2	457.2
Total investments and other assets	629.9	548.2
Property, plant, and equipment, at cost		
Land	101.0	121.5
Timber and timberlands, net of depletion	213.9	217.0
Buildings, machinery, and equipment	3,053.6	3,451.3
Total property, plant, and equipment	3,368.5	3,789.8
Less accumulated depreciation	(1,288.8)	(1,431.0)
Net property, plant, and equipment	2,079.7	2,358.8
Total assets	$3,690.2	$3,889.0
Current liabilities		
Accounts payable	$ 412.5	$ 392.1
Accruals	266.9	288.4
Current maturities of long-term debt	12.6	12.7
Total current liabilities	692.0	693.2
Long-term debt	949.8	1,256.6
Deferred income taxes	330.2	294.5
Other deferred items (see Note)	37.4	113.4
	367.6	407.9
Shareowners' equity		
Common shares	188.8	173.8
Additional paid-in capital	119.8	0.2
Foreign-currency translation adjustment	3.3	10.2
Retained earnings	1,368.9	1,347.1
Total shareholders' equity	1,680.8	1,531.3
Total liabilities and shareowners' equity	$3,690.2	$3,889.0

Note: In December 1990, the board of directors approved a plan to curtail further development of the company's imaging products. As a result, the company established a provision for the valuation of assets and future operating losses expected to be incurred in fulfilling its contractual obligations ($26.1 million, included in the $113.4 million figure).

Mead Corporation
EXHIBIT 5 • *continued*

	1981	1982	1983	1984	1985	1986	1987	1988	1989	1990
Financial Position										
Current assets	$458.4	$486.3	$602.1	$649.6	$529.3	$820.9	$958.5	$959.4	$980.6	$982.0
Investments and other assets	442.9	519.5	500.6	504.3	492.4	518.9	371.5	869.6	629.9	548.2
Land, timber, and timberlands, net	84.1	87.9	88.7	92.4	156.9	183.4	290.0	265.4	314.9	338.5
Plant and equipment, net	931.0	930.0	895.8	958.6	1,066.4	1,198.0	1,278.6	1,407.8	1,764.8	2,020.3
Net assets of discontinued operations	186.2	141.8								
Total assets	$2,102.6	$2,165.5	$2,087.2	$2,204.9	$2,245.0	$2,721.2	$2,898.6	$3,502.2	$3,690.2	$3,889.0
Current liabilities	$336.2	$393.7	$461.9	$499.5	$480.1	$635.1	$620.6	$667.2	$692.0	$693.2
Long-term debt	722.7	839.3	598.1	531.2	505.2	803.7	764.6	924.3	949.8	1,256.6
Deferred items	154.9	184.0	164.2	211.2	250.6	278.5	322.4	398.2	367.6	407.9
Shareowners' equity	888.8	748.5	863.0	963.0	1,009.1	1,003.9	1,191.0	1,512.5	1,680.8	1,531.3
Total liabilities and shareholders equity	$2,102.6	$2,165.5	$2,087.2	$2,204.9	$2,245.0	$2,721.2	$2,898.6	$3,502.2	$3,690.2	$3,889.0
Additional Data										
Capital expenditures	$298.4	$126.3	$82.6	$176.1	$298.8	$177.0	$162.5	$330.0	$595.4	$489.6
Depreciation, depletion, and amortization	$71.2	$102.5	$113.3	$121.5	$129.8	$142.5	$168.2	$198.9	$218.0	$247.5
Average shares outstanding (in millions)	54.6	54.0	58.2	61.4	62.0	62.4	62.8	67.3	67.4	62.2

Mead Corporation
EXHIBIT 5 • *continued*

	1981	1982	1983	1984	1985	1986	1987	1988	1989	1990
Financial Position										
Current assets	$458.4	$486.3	$602.1	$649.6	$529.3	$820.9	$958.5	$959.4	$980.6	$982.0
Investments and other assets	442.9	519.5	500.6	504.3	492.4	518.9	371.5	869.6	629.9	548.2
Land, timber, and timberlands, net	84.1	87.9	88.7	92.4	156.9	183.4	290.0	265.4	314.9	338.5
Plant and equipment, net	931.0	930.0	895.8	958.6	1,066.4	1,198.0	1,278.6	1,407.8	1,764.8	2,020.3
Net assets of discontinued operations	186.2	141.8								
Total assets	$2,102.6	$2,165.5	$2,087.2	$2,204.9	$2,245.0	$2,721.2	$2,898.6	$3,502.2	$3,690.2	$3,889.0
Current liabilities	$336.2	$393.7	$461.9	$499.5	$480.1	$635.1	$620.6	$667.2	$692.0	$693.2
Long-term debt	722.7	839.3	598.1	531.2	505.2	803.7	764.6	924.3	949.8	1,256.6
Deferred items	154.9	184.0	164.2	211.2	250.6	278.5	322.4	398.2	367.6	407.9
Shareowners' equity	888.8	748.5	863.0	963.0	1,009.1	1,003.9	1,191.0	1,512.5	1,680.8	1,531.3
Total liabilities and Shareholders equity	$2,102.6	$2,165.5	$2,087.2	$2,204.9	$2,245.0	$2,721.2	$2,898.6	$3,502.2	$3,690.2	$3,889.0
Additional Data										
Capital expenditures	$298.4	$126.3	$82.6	$176.1	$298.8	$177.0	$162.5	$330.0	$595.4	$489.6
Depreciation, depletion, and amortization	$71.2	$102.5	$113.3	$121.5	$129.8	$142.5	$168.2	$198.9	$218.0	$247.5
Average shares outstanding (in millions)	54.6	54.0	58.2	61.4	62.0	62.4	62.8	67.3	67.4	62.2

Mead Corporation
EXHIBIT 6 • Selected Six-Year Financial Data by Mead Industry Segment—Years Ended December 31 (in millions)

	1985	1986	1987	1988	1989	1990
Sales						
Industry Segment						
Paper	$1,083.1	$1,160.8	$1,258.3	$1,354.2	$1,346.7	$1,341.8
Packaging and paperboard	844.2	924.9	1,010.1	884.2	856.5	977.5
Distribution and school and office products	774.6	1,076.3	1,868.3	2,069.8	2,163.0	2,188.6
Electric publishing	153.7	187.5	231.2	307.8	401.5	440.3
Corporate and other	0	0	0	0	0	0
Gross sales	2,855.6	3,349.5	4,367.9	4,616.0	4,767.7	4,948.2
Intersegment elimination	(115.2)	(131.8)	(159.1)	(162.1)	(159.5)	(175.8)
Total sales	$2,740.4	$3,217.7	$4,208.8	$4,453.9	$4,608.2	$4,772.4
Earnings: Continuing Operations						
Industry Segment						
Paper	155.0	180.7	210.6	247.3	240.8	184.7
Packaging and paperboard	54.1	86.0	151.5	159.5	94.1	97.4
Distribution and school and office products	34.7	36.1	56.4	59.9	67.1	(1.7)
Electronic publishing	15.6	19.4	25.5	34.2	36.9	27.8
Corporate and other	(111.2)	(120.8)	(149.8)	84.1	(117.2)	(161.2)
Total earnings	$148.2	$201.4	$294.2	$585.0	$321.7	$147.0

continued

Mead Corporation
EXHIBIT 6 • *continued*

	1985	1986	1987	1988	1989	1990
Assets						
Industry segment						
Paper	$1,070.1	$1,128.5	$1,183.3	$1,158.9	$1,213.3	$1,213.5
Packaging and paperboard	347.6	372.8	654.6	710.7	1,078.2	1,311.3
Distribution and school and office products	204.4	676.3	638.3	678.1	632.1	574.4
Electronic publishing	100.9	137.8	164.9	418.1	428.1	441.5
Corporate and other	539.4	421.6	275.1	556.3	354.8	366.7
Gross assets	2,262.4	2,737.0	2,916.2	3,522.1	3,706.5	3,907.4
Intersegment elimination	(17.4)	(15.8)	(17.6)	(19.9)	(16.3)	(18.4)
Total assets	$2,245.0	$2,721.2	$2,898.6	$3,502.2	$3,690.2	$3,889.0
Capital Expenditures						
Industry segment						
Paper	$191.3	$72.5	$76.6	$73.4	$136.7	$102.0
Packaging and paperboard	40.1	28.9	27.4	201.6	383.3	291.0
Distribution and school and office products	9.7	8.5	10.5	12.9	22.3	13.9
Electronic publishing	40.5	46.2	30.0	24.1	44.0	66.5
Corporate and other	17.2	20.9	18.0	18.0	9.1	16.2
Total capital expenditures	$298.8	$177.0	$162.5	$330.0	$595.4	$489.6

Mead Corporation
EXHIBIT 7 • Fourth-Quarter History of Mead Stock and Bond Prices

Stocks

Month	High Price	Low Price	Close Price	Daily Volume
October	$25.375	$19.500	$21.000	155,300
November	25.125	21.250	24.500	113,600
December	$28.250	$24.625	$25.750	244,900

Bonds

October 1990	Rating	Month-End Price	Current Yield	Yield to Maturity
SF Deb 8½s 1995	A−	$94.91	8.96%	9.79%
SF Deb 9⅞s 2000	A−	99.82	9.89	9.91
SF Deb 9s 2017	A−	87.03	10.34	10.45
CV 6¾s 2012[a]	BBB+	$74.00	9.12%	9.61%

November 1990	Rating	Month-End Price	Current Yield	Yield to Maturity
SF Deb 8½s 1995	A−	$94.16	9.03%	9.22%
SF Deb 9⅞s 2000	A−	103.07	9.58	9.39
SF Deb 9s 2017	A−	90.37	9.96	10.04
CV 6¾s 2012	BBB+	$71.00	9.51%	10.05%

December 1990	Rating	Month-End Price	Current Yield	Yield to Maturity
SF Deb 8½s 1995	A−	$97.81	8.69%	9.06%
SF Deb 9⅞s 2000	A−	102.44	9.64	9.48
SF Deb 9s 2017	A−	91.37	9.85	9.93
CV 6¾s 2012	BBB+	$76.00	8.88%	9.35%

[a]Convertible bond issue (CV) is subordinate to sinking fund (SF) debentures.

Source: *Bloomberg Financial Market Service* and *Standard and Poor's Bond Guide.*

PepsiCo, Inc.

"At PepsiCo Inc. cola was king, but it is quietly being dethroned."

It was this lead sentence of a front-page article in *The Wall Street Journal* that had caught Michael McCartt's eye on June 13, 1991, exactly one week ago. The timing of the article could not have been more appropriate, because Mr. McCartt had just received a call from PepsiCo on the morning of June 13 to schedule an interview for a position on the company's treasury staff. As Mr. McCartt read the article, he had decided that, because of PepsiCo's diversification, he would focus during the interview on the concept of PepsiCo's cost of capital as a means of displaying the analytical abilities and knowledge of financial concepts he had just honed in business school. The past week had been spent reading PepsiCo's annual reports and gathering information on its competitors in preparation for the interview tomorrow afternoon in New York.

Michael McCartt's research had revealed some interesting facts about PepsiCo. For example, he had been surprised to learn that PepsiCo had invested more than 40 percent of its capital spending over the last two years in fast-food restaurants, opening them at the rate of three per day, and that during the 1991 fiscal year, the restaurant group was expected to surpass beverages as the company's biggest revenue producer among its three business segments (see Exhibit 1 for financial summary by business segment). Snack foods, PepsiCo's third line of business, was the biggest profit generator of the three business segments. These findings had raised a central question that Mr. McCartt wanted to be prepared to answer for the interview: How should PepsiCo's investment dollars be allocated among the three divisions; that is, what criteria should be used in a diversified company like PepsiCo to evaluate potential investments?

PepsiCo History

In its 1990 annual report, PepsiCo described itself as

> first and foremost a grown company. Our primary corporate objective
> is to maximize the value of our shareholders' investments through a
> strategy of rapid sales growth, close control of costs, and astute
> investment of our financial resources.

The company was originally incorporated in 1919 under the name of
Loft, Inc. The company name was changed to the Pepsi-Cola Co. in 1941
after Loft merged with its Pepsi-Cola subsidiary, which it had acquired
some three years earlier. The current name, PepsiCo, was adopted in 1965
after Pepsi-Cola merged with Frito-Lay. Under the name of PepsiCo, the
company had made several significant acquisitions. In November 1977,
the Pizza Hut chain was acquired as a PepsiCo subsidiary, as was Taco Bell
some seven months later. In July 1986, PepsiCo purchased Seven-Up
International for $246 million in cash, and three months and $841 million
later, Kentucky Fried Chicken joined the corporate fold. In 1988 and
1989, the cash outlays continued as two bottling operations, Grand Metropolitan and General Cinema, were bought for $705 million and $1.77 billion, respectively. PepsiCo expanded internationally in 1989 with the
purchase of Smiths Crisps Ltd. and Walkers Crisps Holding Ltd., the leading snack-food companies in the United Kingdom, and in 1990 with the
acquisition of Mexico's number one cookie manufacturer, Gamesa.

The resulting conglomerate was a leader in all three of its business
segments. As noted by Wayne Calloway, chairman and chief executive
officer of PepsiCo, the soft-drink division generated more revenue than
General Mills, Inc., the restaurant group was bigger than Campbell Soup
Co., and the snack-food business approximated Kellogg Co. "PepsiCo
doesn't have one flagship; it has three flagships," stated Mr. Calloway,
"and people would kill to have *one* of our flagships." Indeed, PepsiCo
could boast of having eight different brands—Doritos, Ruffles, Kentucky
Fried Chicken Original Recipe, Pizza Hut Pan Pizza, Pepsi, Diet Pepsi,
Mountain Dew, and Seven Up—that achieved over $1 billion in retail
sales each year. Of the other brands, 25 achieved at least $100 million in
annual retail sales.

The financial success of PepsiCo is detailed in Exhibits 2, 3, and 4.
Between 1985 and 1990, company sales increased at a compound rate of
19 percent, and income from continuing operations at a compound rate of
21 percent. In the beverage segment, PepsiCo had Pepsi Cola, the largest
selling food product of any type in U.S. supermarkets and a $13 billion
brand worldwide. In the global market, Pepsi Cola was joined on the list of
the top 10 selling brands by Diet Pepsi, Caffeine Free Diet Pepsi, and

Mountain Dew. With its latest bottling acquisitions, PepsiCo was running the nation's largest network of soft-drink bottling plants. As for the snack-food division, Frito-Lay had the largest share of the U.S. chip market and was more than four times the size of its nearest competitor. With the purchase of Smiths Crisps and Walker Crisps, PepsiCo Foods International became the leading chip company in Europe. It was in the restaurant segment, however, that the size and scope of PepsiCo's accomplishments may have been the most impressive.

PepsiCo was running the largest restaurant system in the world, with close to 18,500 units, and the three categories of food served by PepsiCo restaurants (pizza, chicken, and Mexican food) were among the fastest growing segments of the quick-service market. PepsiCo's worldwide sales were greater than $11 billion, and the number of its U.S. restaurants was growing at more than twice the industry average. Pizza Hut not only had a 24 percent share of the U.S. market of 1990, but it was also represented in 54 countries internationally and was the leading pizza chain in 46 of those markets. Taco Bell was the leading Mexican-food chain domestically and was just beginning to expand internationally. KFC opened its 3,000th restaurant outside the United States in 1989, making it the largest restaurant chain overseas and the number one quick-service chicken restaurant in the world.

Financial Strategy

Some industry analysts believed that Pepsi had obtained Frito-Lay in 1965 partly because chips go well with cola, and had obtained the restaurant franchises as a means of getting new fountain outlets. Over the years, however, the company's focus had clearly shifted. *The Wall Street Journal* article asserted that CEO Calloway was not on any sort of "global beverage quest," but was more interested in building a consumer-products company with the best possible return on equity. PepsiCo's emphasis on performance was clearly stated in the 1990 annual report: "PepsiCo's principal objective is to increase the value of its shareholders' investments through integrated operating, investing and financing strategies that maximize cash returns on investments and optimize the cost of capital."

Although PepsiCo's stock price had increased substantially over the past several years, the aggressive investment strategy had also resulted in an increased amount of debt on the books. Regarding the debt financing, PepsiCo management said,

> We support these investments with financial policies that strive to fund our businesses at the lowest possible cost, while giving us the flexibility to pursue growth. Every company faces the question of how much debt is appropriate. PepsiCo's philosophy hasn't changed much over the

years, despite leveraged buyouts and the ups and downs of the bond market. We carefully set a corporate leverage target, or a ratio of our net debt[1] plus market value of equity. Over time, we strive to achieve a ratio of 20 percent to 25 percent. We use market value as a yardstick, rather than the traditional book value, because the market standard reflects the tremendous value of our intangible assets—especially our brands' reputations—while also taking into account our strong potential for growth. Our leveraged target is set with an eye toward maintaining flexibility, which means we can exceed our target occasionally to take advantage of attractive investment opportunities.

The Cost of Capital

According to PepsiCo management, "The cost of capital is a weighting of the cost of debt and equity, with the latter representing a measure of expected returns to investors in PepsiCo's stock. PepsiCo estimates its current cost of capital to be approximately 11 percent." It was this statement that Michael McCartt had decided to use as the centerpiece of his interview strategy. He had learned in business school that the true cost of capital depended on how the capital was put to use. For instance, *The Wall Street Journal* article stated that PepsiCo's restaurants were a lot "trickier" to manage than soft drinks. They commanded lower margins, were more fragmented, more capital intensive, and more vulnerable to shifts in consumer spending. Mr. McCartt concluded that investments in the restaurant division should not be evaluated by using the corporate weighted-average cost of capital (WACC), but by a higher cost of capital.

He recalled reading an article by Russell Fuller and Halbert Kerr[2] that outlined how to estimate the cost of capital of a division in a multidivision firm. Essentially, each division was matched with a publicly traded company having a single line of business that was as similar as possible to the division's. The cost of capital of such a so-called "pure-play" company served as the best guess of the division's cost of capital. Mr. McCartt knew finding perfect pure-plays would be impossible, but he had succeeded in putting together a list of companies with publicly traded stocks that competed in the same business segments with PepsiCo (Exhibit 5).

Michael McCartt assumed that PepsiCo was calculating its cost of equity by using the capital asset pricing model, the formula for which is

$$K_e = R_f + \beta(R_m - R_f).$$

---

[1] PepsiCo measured financial leverage net of its large offshore short-term investment portfolios. Because these investments were not required to support the day-to-day operations of the company, PepsiCo considered the funds available to retire debt.

[2] Russell J. Fuller and Halbert S. Kerr, "Estimating the Divisional Cost of Capital: An Analysis of the Pure-Play Technique," *The Journal of Finance,* December 1981.

To choose the appropriate risk-free rate (R_f), he looked up the Treasury bond yields in the December 31, 1990, issue of *The Wall Street Journal,* the date of the latest financial information he had for PepsiCo (Exhibit 6). The market risk premium ($R_m - R_f$) was more difficult to determine, but once he gathered the information in Exhibit 7, he believed he could decide the appropriate risk premium. The betas (β) of the pure-play comparable companies are reported in Exhibit 8. Although the pure-plays exhibited a wide range of financial leverage, Fuller and Kerr had reported that unadjusted pure-play betas were better approximations of the division betas than were adjusted betas. McCartt therefore decided not to worry about adjusting betas for financial leverage.

Once he had determined the costs of equity for PepsiCo's three divisions, Michael McCartt intended to calculate their respective hurdle rates using the WACC formula,

$$\text{WACC} = K_d^*(1 - \tau)^* \, D/(D + E) + K_e^* E/(D + E),$$

where K_d is the firm's cost of debt, τ is the corporate tax rate, D is the amount of debt, and E is the amount of equity. His research had revealed that PepsiCo's effective marginal tax rate was 38 percent, which reflected the combined effects of federal, state, and local taxes, and that its cost of publicly traded debt on December 31, 1990, was 9.6 percent. After computing each business segment's WACC, Mr. McCartt wanted to weight the three costs of capital to see if they summed to the 11 percent number given in the annual report. If the individual costs of capital did not prove to be consistent with the corporate cost of capital, Mr. McCartt would have difficulty presenting his findings convincingly to his interviewers.

McCartt could not remember reading any other company's annual report that touched on as many financial concepts as PepsiCo's: shareholder value creation, the cost of capital, market valuation of equity, target debt ratios, and so on. The more he read, the more he could understand why PepsiCo had recently been named one of *Fortune* magazine's most admired corporations in America and the more he was determined to make the best of his job interview.

PepsiCo Inc.
EXHIBIT 1 • Financial Summary by Business Segment (in millions)

	1987	1988	1989	1990
Snack Foods				
Net sales	$ 3,202.0	$ 3,514.3	$ 4,215.0	$ 5,054.0
Operating profit	547.6	632.2	805.2	934.4
Identifiable assets	1,632.5	1,608.0	3,310.0	3,892.4
Depreciation	154.1	156.8	189.3	232.5
Capital expenditures	195.6	172.6	257.9	381.6
Soft Drinks				
Net sales	3,975.6	4,638.2	5,776.7	6,523.0
Operating profit	409.6	455.3	676.2	767.6
Identifiable assets	2,779.8	3,994.1	6,198.1	6,465.2
Depreciation	166.5	195.7	306.3	338.1
Capital expenditures	202.0	198.4	267.8	334.1
Restaurants				
Net sales	3,840.5	4,380.7	5,250.7	6,225.7
Operating profit	319.4	340.3	414.3	522.4
Identifiable assets	2,782.9	3,061.0	3,070.6	3,448.9
Depreciation	237.1	271.3	269.9	306.5
Capital expenditures	370.8	344.2	424.6	460.6
Corporate				
Corporate expenses	(331.0)	(300.6)	(545.2)	(557.0)
Identifiable assets	1,827.5	2,472.2	2,548.0	3,336.9
Depreciation	5.3	5.5	6.5	6.9
Capital expenditures	6.6	14.9	9.2	21.9
Totals				
Net sales	11,018.1	12,533.2	15,242.4	17,802.7
Operating profit	945.6	1,127.2	1,350.5	1,667.4
Identifiable assets	9,022.7	11,135.3	15,126.7	17,143.4
Depreciation	563.0	629.3	772.0	884.0
Capital expenditures	$ 775.0	$ 730.1	$ 959.5	$ 1,198.2

PepsiCo, Inc.
EXHIBIT 2 • Consolidated Statements of Income
(in millions, except per-share)

	1989	1990
Net sales	$15,242.4	$17,802.7
Costs and expenses		
Cost of sales	(7,467.7)	(8,609.9)
Selling, administrative, and other	(5,841.4)	(6,829.9)
Amortization of goodwill	(150.4)	(189.1)
Interest expense	(609.6)	(688.5)
Interest income	177.2	182.1
Total expenses	(13,891.9)	(16,135.3)
Income from continuing operations before income taxes	1,350.5	1,667.4
Provision for income taxes	(449.1)	(576.8)
Income from continuing operations	901.4	1,090.6
Discontinued operation charge	0	(13.7)
Net income	$ 901.4	$ 1,076.9
Income (charge) per share		
Continuing operations	$ 1.13	$ 1.37
Discontinued operation	0	(0.02)
Net income per share	$ 1.13	$ 1.35
Average shares outstanding	796.0	798.7

PepsiCo, Inc.
Exhibit 3 • Consolidated Balance Sheets
(in millions, except per-share)

	1989	1990
Assets		
Current assets		
Cash and cash equivalents	$ 76.2	$ 170.8
Short-term investments	1,457.7	1,644.9
Accounts receivable	1,239.7	1,414.7
Inventories	546.1	585.8
Prepaid expenses and other current	231.1	265.2
Total current assets	3,550.8	4,081.4
Investments in affiliates	970.8	1,505.9
Property, plant, and equipment, net	5,130.2	5,710.9
Goodwill and other intangibles	5,474.9	5,845.2
Total assets	$15,126.7	$17,143.4
Liabilities and shareholders' equity		
Current liabilities		
Short-term borrowings	$ 866.3	$ 1,626.5
Accounts payable	1,054.5	1,116.3
Income taxes payable	313.7	443.7
Other current liabilities	1,457.3	1,584.0
Total current liabilities	3,691.8	4,770.5
Long-term debt	6,686.9	6,525.9
Deferred income taxes	856.9	942.8
Shareholders' equity		
Capital stock at par	14.4	14.4
Capital in excess of par	323.9	365.0
Retained earnings	3,978.4	4,753.0
Currency translation adjustment	66.2	383.2
Gross shareholders' equity	4,382.9	5,515.6
Treasury stock	(491.8)	(611.4)
Total shareholders' equity	3,891.1	4,904.2
Total liabilities and shareholders' equity	$15,126.7	$17,143.4

PepsiCo, Inc.
EXHIBIT 4 • Selected Financial Data (in millions, except per-share)

	1981	1982	1983	1984	1985	1986	1987	1988	1989	1990
Summary of Operations										
Net sales	$5,873.3	$6,232.4	$6,568.6	$7,058.6	$7,584.5	$9,017.1	$11,018.1	$12,533.2	$15,242.4	$17,802.7
Cost of sales and operating expenses	(5,278.8)	(5,684.7)	(5,995.7)	(6,479.3)	(6,802.4)	(8,187.9)	(9,890.5)	(11,184.0)	(13,459.5)	(15,628.9)
Gross profit	594.5	547.7	572.9	579.3	782.1	829.2	1,127.6	1,349.2	1,782.9	2,173.8
Interest expense	(147.7)	(163.5)	(175.0)	(204.9)	(195.2)	(261.4)	(294.6)	(344.2)	(609.6)	(688.5)
Interest income	35.8	49.1	53.6	86.1	96.4	122.7	112.6	122.2	177.2	182.5
Earnings from continuing operations before taxes	482.6	433.3	451.5	460.5	683.3	690.5	945.6	1,127.2	1,350.5	1,667.8
Provision for income taxes	(213.7)	(229.7)	(169.5)	(180.5)	(256.7)	(226.7)	(340.5)	(365.0)	(449.1)	(576.8)
Income from continuing operations	268.9	203.6	282.0	280.0	426.6	463.8	605.1	762.2	901.4	1,091.0
Net income	$297.5	$224.3	$284.1	$212.5	$543.7	$457.8	$594.8	$762.2	$901.4	$1,076.9
Data Per common Share										
Income per share from continuing operations	$0.32	$0.24	$0.33	$0.32	$0.51	$0.59	$0.76	$0.96	$1.13	$1.37
Net income per share	0.36	0.26	0.33	0.25	0.65	0.58	0.75	0.96	1.13	1.35
Cash dividends declared per share	$0.16	$0.18	$0.18	$0.19	$0.20	$0.21	$0.22	$0.27	$0.32	$0.38
Average shares and equivalents outstanding	837.5	854.1	859.3	862.4	842.1	786.5	798.3	790.4	796.0	798.7

continued

PepsiCo, Inc.
EXHIBIT 4 • continued

Year-End Position

Total assets	$3,960.2	$4,052.2	$4,446.3	$4,876.9	$5,889.3	$8,027.1	$9,022.7	$11,135.3	$15,126.7	$17,143.4
Total debt	1,214.0	1,033.5	1,073.9	948.9	1,506.1	2,865.3	3,225.0	4,107.0	6,942.8	7,526.1
Shareholders' equity	1,556.3	1,650.5	1,794.2	1,853.4	1,837.7	2,059.1	2,508.6	3,161.0	3,891.1	4,904.2
Book value per share	1.89	1.96	2.13	2.19	2.33	2.64	3.21	4.01	4.92	6.22
Market price per share	$4.125	$3.75	$4.25	$4.625	$7.875	$8.75	$11.25	$13.125	$21.375	$25.75
Shares outstanding	824.4	840.4	842.0	845.2	789.4	781.0	781.2	788.4	791.1	788.4

Cash-Flow Data

Net cash generated by continuing operations	$515.0	$661.5	$670.2	$981.5	$817.3	$1,212.2	$1,334.5	$1,894.5	$1,885.9	$2,110.0
Acquisitions and investments in affiliates for cash	0	130.3	0	0	160.0	1,679.9	371.5	1,415.5	3,296.6	630.6
Purchase of property, plant and equipment for cash	414.4	447.4	503.4	555.8	770.3	858.5	770.5	725.8	943.8	1,180.1
Cash dividends paid	$126.2	$142.5	$151.3	$154.6	$161.1	$160.4	$172.0	$199.0	$241.9	$293.9

PepsiCo, Inc.
EXHIBIT 5 • Description of Snack-Food, Beverage, and Restaurant Companies

PepsiCo
The world's second largest producer of soft drinks controls more than 1,000 bottlers throughout the world. Major soft-drink products include PepsiCola, Diet Pepsi, and Mountain Dew. Operations include specialty snack foods: Frito-Lay (major product offerings include Doritos, Ruffles, and Lay's), Walker Crisps, Smiths Crisps; quick-service restaurants: Pizza Hut, Kentucky Fried Chicken, and Taco Bell.

A & W Brands
Manufactures, markets, and sells soft-drink concentrates to licensed bottlers under the A&W Root Beer, A&W Cream Soda, Squirt, Country Time Lemonade, and Vernors trademarks. The company's brands have the leading U.S. market share in the root beer, cream soda, citrus/grapefruit, and lemonade categories.

Coca-Cola
The world's largest soft-drink company. Distributes its major brands through bottlers throughout the world. Foreign operations accounted for about 55% of total sales and 75% of profits in 1989. Food division produces and markets over 100 items including citrus concentrates. 49% owner of Coca-Cola Enterprises.

Coca-Cola Bottling
One of the largest independent bottlers, with franchises covering 10–12 million people in the Southeast. Has exclusive franchises under which it produces Coca-Cola, Coca-Cola Classic, and all other Coca-Cola soft drinks as well as Dr. Pepper, Canada Dry, Schweppes, Welch's Barq's root beer, and Lipton tea in selected markets.

Coca-Cola Enterprises
The world's largest soft-drink bottling company.

Flowers, Inc.
Fifth largest producer of bakery and snack-food goods in the U.S. Brand names include Nature's Own, Cobblestone Mill, Evangeline Maid, Holsum, Dandee, and Beebo. Produces fresh and frozen breads, buns, and specialty rolls, cakes and pies, and frozen vegetables and fruits.

General Mills
Processes and markets consumer foods, including Big G cereals, Betty Crocker desserts, Gold Medal flour, Gorton's seafood, and Yoplait yogurt. Operates 785 restaurants in the United States, Canada, and Japan: Red Lobster, The Olive Garden.

Golden Enterprises, Inc.
Holding company for Golden Flake Snack Foods, Inc. (Golden Flake and Super Snack brands), Steel City Bolt and Screw, Inc. (specialized metal fasteners), Nall & Associates, Inc. (manufacturer's representatives) and The Sloan Major Agency, Inc. (advertising). Snack-food operations account for over 95% of sales and profits.

Goodmark Foods
Engaged in producing and marketing meat snack products, including Slim Jim, Beef Jerky, pickled meats, and pork skins. Also engaged in producing and marketing grain and potato products, including cheese curls, Andy Capp pretzels, and various other snack foods.

Lance, Inc.
Manufactures snack foods and bakery products and distributes them through its own sales organization and through brokers to retailers and institutional customers.

McDonald's Corp.
Licenses and operates a chain of over 11,400 fast-food restaurants throughout the United States, Canada, and overseas under the name of "McDonald's." Outlets serve standardized menu built around hamburgers.

National Pizza
Largest franchisee of PepsiCo's Pizza Hut chain. As of 3/90, operated 354 Pizza Hut restaurants and delivery kitchens. Restaurants offer full table service and feature pizza, Italian pies, pasta, sandwiches, a salad bar, and, in most units, beer. Acquired Skipper's restaurants 10/89.

Ryan's Family Steak House
Develops, operates, and franchises family-style steak house restaurants featuring cafeteria-style entry; self-service food bar (the "MegaBar"), soup bar, and ice cream bar; and table service of dinners. As of 1/91 had 126 company-owned and 33 franchised restaurants.

TCBY
"The country's Best Yogurt" is the largest franchisor of soft-serve frozen yogurt stores in the United States. TCBY also sells equipment for use in TCBY stores. As of 11/30/90, had 1,845 stores, of which 1,677 were franchised.

Wendy's International, Inc.
Licenses and operates the nation's third largest chain of quick-service hamburger restaurants. Has 3,727 units (71% franchised).

PepsiCo, Inc.

EXHIBIT 6 • Prevailing Interest Rates and Yields as of December 31, 1990

U.S. Government Interest Rates

Maturity	Rate
26 weeks	6.57%
1 year	6.88
10 years	8.16
30 years	8.30
Money Rates	
Prime rate	9.75
6-month certificate of deposit	7.47%

Moody's Corporate Bond Yield Averages by Rating Class

Moody's Rating	Rate
Aaa	9.05%
Aa	9.39
A	9.64
Baa	10.43%

PepsiCo, Inc.

EXHIBIT 7 • Average Annual Returns for 1926–1990

Series	Geometric Mean[a]	Arithmetic Mean[a]	Standard Deviation
S&P 500	10.1%	12.1%	20.8%
Small company stocks	11.6	17.1	35.4
Long-term corporate bonds	5.2	5.5	8.4
Long-term government bonds	4.5	4.9	8.5
U.S. Treasury bills	3.7%	3.7%	3.4%

[a]The arithmetic mean is computed as the sum of the single-year returns from 1926 through 1990 divided by the number of returns (65). The geometric mean accounts for the compound-interest effect such that, when the interest is compounded over 65 years, the final wealth that results is the same as if an investor had invested successively in each year to earn a sequence of 65 single-year returns. For example, if an investor earned −20 percent and +40 percent over two years, the arithmetic average return would be +10 percent. The geometric average return (ρ) would be 5.83 percent—computed as $(1-.2)*(1+.4) = (1+\rho)^2$.

Source: *Stocks, Bonds, Bills and Inflation, 1991 Yearbook* (Ibbotson Associates, Inc., 1991).

PepsiCo, Inc.
EXHIBIT 8 • Financial Information on Snack-Food, Beverage, and Restaurant Companies

Company	Sales (000s)	Beta[a]	Number of Shares (000s)	Price per Share		Long-term Debt (000s)	Current Portion (000s)	Capital Leases (000s)	Notes Payable (000s)	Total Debt (000s)	Estimated[b] Cost of Debt
				Market	Book						
A&W Brands	$119,000	1.50	9,098	$34.75	$ 7.62	0	0	0	$ 22,345	$ 22,345	10.00%
Coca-Cola	10,236,000	1.00	688,239	46.50	5.59	$ 535,861	$ 97,272	0	1,903,611	2,536,744	9.50
Coca-Cola Bottling	431,000	0.75	9,181	19.00	18.31	237,564	1,222	0	0	238,786	12.00
Coca-Cola Enterprises	4,034,000	1.00	114,835	15.50	14.16	1,960,164	576,630	0	0	2,536,794	10.00
Flowers, Inc.	835,000	0.90	33,617	14.00	6.00	52,691	4,857	0	0	57,548	10.00
General Mills	6,448,000	1.05	164,734	44.38	5.98	785,400	56,700	0	198,200	1,040,300	9.60
Golden Ent., Inc.	133,000	0.55	12,692	7.00	4.10	243	63	0	0	306	10.00
Goodmark Foods	137,000	1.49	4,302	10.25	6.95	17,054	3,759	0	0	20,813	10.00
Lance, Inc.	445,000	0.70	31,252	20.75	7.42	0	0	0	0	0	10.00
McDonald's Corp.	6,776,000	1.00	359,164	29.13	11.65	4,428,700	64,700	0	299,000	4,792,400	9.50
National Pizza	275,000	1.00	13,849	17.50	5.8	66,397	628	$ 6,851	0	73,876	10.00
PepsiCo	17,803,000	1.10	788,400	25.75	6.22	6,525,900	0	0	1,626,500	8,152,400	9.64
Ryan's Family Steak House	273,000	1.10	52,637	5.75	2.89	0	0	0	$ 26,600	26,600	10.00
TCBY	151,000	1.15	26,162	7.63	4.06	18,973	2,893	0	0	21,866	10.00
Wendy's	$1,011,000	1.10	96,821	$ 6.38	$ 4.62	$ 123,307	8,242	$44,754	0	$ 176,303	12.18%

[a]Betas as reported by *Value Line Investment Survey*, except for Coca-Cola Bottling and Goodmark Foods, which were obtained from Lotus One Source.
[b]Casewriter's estimates.

PART
5

Financing Capital Investments

New Hampshire
Savings Bank Corporation

After operating for over 150 years as a state-chartered mutual institution, the New Hampshire Savings Bank decided to convert to a stockholder-owned bank in 1982. A number of other mutual savings banks and mutual savings and loan institutions had completed or were planning conversions for similar reasons—increased flexibility with and access to capital. A mutual institution, owned by its depositors, could only increase its equity base through additions to retained earnings. Conversion offered the opportunity to raise capital through the sale of stock. Furthermore, being a stock corporation would facilitate the bank's execution of its plans for gradual expansion through acquisition of other banks, particularly commercial banks that were also organized as stock corporations. (The company had recently entered into an agreement to purchase all the outstanding common shares of Rockingham County Trust Company of Salem, N.H., at a purchase price of $80 per share for a total of $3.2 million.)

The conversion, which had occurred on March 4, 1983, with a public offering, raised a question that had previously never been an issue for New Hampshire Savings Bank's management or directors: whether to pay a cash dividend, and if so, how much? The bank's president, John Hardie, who was particularly anxious to settle the matter, had made the dividend-policy issue the first item on the agenda for the August 9 meeting of the bank's board of directors.

The Thrift Industry

Historically, the savings and loan, or "thrift," industry had been involved in attracting savings deposits from the general public and making loans secured by first-mortgage liens on residential and other real estate. A number of variables influenced the savings flows of thrifts: interest rates, personal income levels, and regulatory ceilings on interest rates payable on

Copyright Professor J. Peter Williamson, Amos Tuck Graduate School of Management, Dartmouth College, Hanover, N.H., © 1984.

Note: Names of individual directors have been disguised.

savings accounts and other government policies and regulations. Lending activities had been influenced by such factors as demand for and supply of housing, conditions in the construction industry, and availability of funds. Because of its strong correlation with potentially volatile economic measures, the industry was also considered to be quite sensitive to changes in economic conditions.

The October 1979 decision by the board of governors of the Federal Reserve System to shift its focus in controlling the rate of inflation from short-term interest rates and commercial bank reserves to the rate of growth of certain monetary aggregates had a significant impact on the performance of the thrift industry. This policy change, combined with persistently high levels of inflation and interest-rate volatility, had both increased the cost and reduced the availability of funds to thrifts. The recent drop in the inflation rate as a result of the economic recovery and more relaxed Federal Reserve Board policies had helped to reduce the levels of interest rates and, consequently, increased the amount of funds available to thrifts.

Earnings

The earnings of thrifts had largely depended on the difference, or spread, between the average yield received from loans and investments and the average costs of maintaining savings accounts and of borrowings. Because lending activities of the thrifts had been limited primarily to long-term, fixed-rate mortgage loans secured by real estate, the average rate of interest realized by a thrift on its loan portfolio could not adjust as quickly to changes in interest rates as could the cost of its savings accounts and borrowings.

The relatively large operating losses common in the thrift industry during the last decade had been attributed to several key factors. Competing investment securities offering higher yields and greater liquidity than those of thrifts reduced deposit inflows, and increased outflows. In addition, rapidly rising interest rates reduced the spread, adversely affecting the performance of the traditional areas of business within the thrift industry. While changes in regulation had broadened their lending and borrowing powers by allowing them into different types of investments and mortgage loans, thrifts' earnings and operations were still tightly linked to changes in the level of interest rates, financial-market conditions, and most thrifts' relatively large investments in long-term, low-yielding mortgage loans.

Recent Legislative Developments

The deregulation of the industry had enhanced thrifts' competitive position with other financial institutions. Several federal and state legislative actions within the past few years had eliminated many of the distinctions between commercial banks and thrifts:

1. Since December 1982, thrifts had been authorized to offer new insured money market accounts with no required minimum maturity period or interest ceiling (but with a minimum deposit of $2,500—accounts that were directly equivalent to, and competitive with, money market mutual funds.
2. Since January 1983, insured Super NOW accounts, with a minimum deposit of $2,500, no interest ceiling, and no limit on the number of transactions in any given period, had been authorized.
3. No later than January 1984, all interest-rate differentials favoring thrifts would be eliminated; all interest-rate ceilings would be eliminated by April 1986.

New Hampshire state laws regulating state-chartered thrift institutions were less restrictive than comparable federal laws for federally chartered thrifts. For example, New Hampshire state-chartered thrifts might invest a higher percentage of their assets in commercial loans and in the equity and debt securities of unrelated companies.

New Hampshire Savings Bank

Originally established in 1830, the New Hampshire Savings Bank (NHSB) was a state-chartered mutual savings bank operating with six offices and one remote service facility in central New Hampshire. With total assets of approximately $295 million, NHSB was ranked third in asset size among all thrifts and savings banks in New Hampshire. NHSB had consistently been among the most profitable thrifts in the United States in recent years, and its ratio of net worth to deposits, a popular measure of financial stability, was well above the industry average. NHSB's net interest spread, another key comparative measure, had not dropped below 1.04 percent for any quarter since the beginning of 1979. Highlights of NHSB's financial progress are shown in Exhibits 1 through 3.

NHSB's principal business consisted of investing its funds in first-mortgage loans on residential and commercial properties, on small- to medium-sized businesses, and in an unusually large number of consumer loans, including education, mobile-home, and home-improvement loans. The bank had been expanding its commercial activities for some time, and it intended to consider further expansion, subject to regulatory limitations. As a thrift institution, NHSB was subject to supervision and regulation by the Federal Deposit Insurance Corporation, the bank commissioner of the state of New Hampshire, and the Federal Home Loan Bank of Boston

(FHLB). As was typical in thrifts, the capital-to-deposit ratio was 3 percent, although it had been as high as 5 percent in the recent past.

The bank had three primary sources of funds: savings deposits from the general public; advances from the FHLB; and sales of loans in the secondary market, particularly residential and commercial first-mortgage and education loans.

In an attempt to protect itself from violent fluctuations in the cost of its funds, NHSB had chosen to limit the growth of higher cost funds, such as high-rate certificates, and had originated adjustable-rate and short-term, fixed-rate mortgages to replace long-term, fixed-rate mortgages. Furthermore, the bank consciously limited its growth during periods of high interest rates in order to manage both its liabilities and its assets better. Savings-deposit growth was reduced substantially by offering less-than-market rates on long-term deposits. In addition, the bank structured its mortgage loans to facilitate their resale in the secondary market. As a result of its emphasis on adjustable-rate and short-term, fixed-rate mortgages, only 59 percent of its year-end 1982 mortgage loan portfolio was interest-rate sensitive.

In 1981 and 1982, NHSB had operated at a loss, primarily because of the portfolio restructuring it had done late in those years. During December 1981, the bank sold low-rate mortage loans at a pretax loss of $1,183,000 (resulting in an income tax benefit of $355,000) and pass-through securities at a pretax loss of $1,487,000 (resulting in an income tax benefit of $446,000). During December 1982, the bank sold additional low-rate mortgage instruments at a pretax loss of $7,097,000 (resulting in an income tax benefit of $2,200,000). The proceeds from these sales of low-yielding assets were reinvested at higher rates and for shorter terms, primarily in commercial real-estate loans, with three principal effects on the bank's asset portfolio: the yield was increased; the composition was diversified away from residential first-mortgage loans; and the average maturity was shortened, improving the matching of asset and liability maturities. In essence, the bank exchanged assets yielding 11.9 percent with an average maturity of 17.9 years for assets yielding 13.3 percent with an average maturity of 10.4 years. In the absence of these sales, net income in 1981 would have been approximately $2,205,000, and net income in 1982 would have been approximately $996,000.

NHSB's relatively high current level of profitability was a direct result of its unusually large short-term, rate-sensitive consumer-loan portfolio, its substantial activity as originator of education loans (subsequently sold in the secondary market), its strong capital position, and its excellent management. Furthermore, the bank's commitment to computer-based forecasting enhanced its managers' ability to estimate the consequences of interest-rate changes and assisted them in using such innovative portfolio-management techniques as option writing and investing in financial futures.

Competition

In attracting deposits, NHSB faced strong competition from a number of sources. Historically, competition had come from other thrifts and commercial banks located in its primary market area of Merrimack and Belknap Counties in central New Hampshire. Recently, short-term money market funds and other corporate and government securities yielding higher interest rates than those allowed to be paid by the bank under federal regulations had significantly cut into NHSB's available funds. Although this additional competition had reduced the bank's recent deposit growth, the forthcoming elimination of federal regulatory controls on savings deposits and interest rates was expected to improve the competitive position of the thrifts.

NHSB's strategy for attracting new customers in the highly competitive thrift industry had been to offer depositors a wide variety of savings programs, convenient branch locations, a wide network of automated teller machines, and pre-authorized payment and withdrawal systems. In addition, NHSB offered its customers new personal investment products such as tax-deferred retirement plans, individual retirement accounts, and Keogh plans, as well as such traditional services as money orders, traveler's checks, and safe-deposit boxes.

Within NHSB's real-estate lending business, the bank's main competition came principally from mortgage banking companies, other thrifts, commercial banks, insurance companies, and other institutional lenders. NHSB's strategy in this segment had been to provide high-quality, efficient service while varying the interest rates and loan fees it charged borrowers, real estate brokers, and builders.

Background to the Conversion

The Federal Home Loan Bank Board (FHLBB), the government institution that regulated savings and loan banks, had established a procedure for the conversion of mutual savings banks to stockholder-owned banks. After an independent appraisal of the market value of the institution, a public offering of shares could be arranged with an underwriter who would, based on this valuation, set a maximum price on the shares to be issued. Before the shares were offered to the public, however, the bank's depositors were given an opportunity to subscribe for shares at the maximum price. The remaining shares were publicly sold at a fair price (less than or equal to the maximum price) determined by the underwriter. If the public offering price was lower than the price offered to the depositors, the depositors were entitled to purchase their shares at the lower price. In a few instances, 70 percent or more of the shares issued in a conversion had been subscribed for by the bank's depositors. More commonly, about 20 percent to 30 percent were purchased by depositors, with the balance going to the general public.

The only advantage enjoyed by a depositor of the bank over a member of the general public, therefore, was having the first opportunity to subscribe for shares. Before the FHLBB developed its rules, depositors were given shares in their banks in some cases without payment on the grounds that a mutual bank belonged to its depositors and that, when it converted to a stock corporation, the depositors should be given the entire stock ownership. However, the amended rules prohibited giving shares of stock to depositors or even offering them a discount from the public offering price.

The conversion of the NHSB involved one feature that had not been tried before. Rather than simply being converted from a state-chartered mutual institution to a state-chartered corporation, the bank itself was converted to a stock corporation with all of its stock held by a simultaneously created holding company. The holding company then offered its stock to the bank depositors and to the general public. The result was a stockholder-owned holding company, New Hampshire Savings Bank Corporation, which in turn held all the stock of the NHSB. The conversion of NHSB was completed without incident at a price of $13.75 per share for each of the 1,563,984 shares distributed in March 1983. Since then, NHSB's common stock had been traded over the counter and was included in the National Association of Security Dealers daily quotes (in *The Wall Street Journal,* for example). Exhibit 4 contains the NASD report on trading in NHSB stock for the month of July 1983, and Exhibit 5 shows the price performance and trading volume for the stock since it was first issued.

The August 9 Directors' Meeting.

Management's Perspective.   The first item on the agenda for the bank's directors was the discussion of a dividend policy. President John Hardie opened the subject by observing that he and Robert Dustin, the executive vice president (evp), held quite different opinions with respect to dividends. Mr. Hardie favored the declaration of a dividend of about 15 cents a share in the third quarter of 1983. This would represent an annual rate of 60 cents, or about 4.3 percent of the $13.75 issue price of the shares. He observed that Merchants Savings Bank, a major competitor, had just converted from a mutual savings bank to a stockholder-owned institution and had established a dividend of a little over 5 percent on the issue price of its shares. In urging the cash dividend, Mr. Hardie commented that he believed the shareholders of NHSB expected a dividend; some had withdrawn money from savings accounts that were paying them 5½ percent interest per year in order to buy their shares. He believed that these stockholder/depositors would be very disappointed if there were no dividend to replace the interest they had once earned on their savings. After stressing the importance of inspiring loyalty among the stockholders who were also bank customers, he invited the evp to state his opinion.

Mr. Dustin opposed the payment of any cash dividends. He believed that many of the stockholders were more interested in capital gains than in dividends, and he observed that a dividend of 5 percent on the original issue price would amount to over $1 million a year, an amount he believed NHSB could better use by investing in the business.

With respect to the dividends paid by the Merchants Savings Bank, Mr. Dustin said the board should not be stampeded by what Merchants had decided to do. Because the stock price of both Merchants and NHSB had dropped in the past few days (NHSB had declined from $18 to $17 per share, while Merchants lost $2 down to $23), he believed that the payment of a cash dividend would not offer any extra protection from a market decline. Mr. Dustin added that, while the initial offering prospectus had mentioned a dividend, it made no promise of a cash dividend, and there was no evidence that the shareholders were counting on such a dividend. Furthermore, once NHSB began paying cash dividends, he did not believe that it would be able to stop.

The Directors' Perspectives.   Most of the directors had ideas to express about the dividend-policy question. One director, Martin Long, expressed the opinion that many shareholders were anticipating a dividend and would be disappointed if none were paid. He suggested, however, that it was not necessary to pay as much as a 5 percent dividend; perhaps the shareholders would be satisfied with a lesser amount, which would allow NHSB to reinvest a substantial portion of its earnings in the business.

Another director, Catherine Johanson, disagreed. She believed that, although the prospectus did not explicitly promise a cash dividend, it did strongly indicate that, if there were to be a dividend, it would be 5 percent of the issue price of the shares. (See Exhibit 6 for excerpts from the prospectus.)

A third director, Jennings Wilson, observed that he thought the bank and its earnings belonged to the shareholders. It was only fair, he believed, to distribute the earnings to the shareholders in the form of dividends and let the shareholders decide whether they wanted to spend this money or to reinvest it in the stock of the bank or in that of another company. Noting that there was a substantial personal income tax burden on dividends, another director, Fred Piel, expressed the belief that any shareholder who wanted to reinvest dividends in NHSB stock would be better off if no dividends were paid. Mr. Wilson called this idea a rather sophisticated view of dividends, one that he doubted many of the shareholders would understand.

Another director, Ross Byrd, flatly stated that he would vote against the payment of cash dividends. He did not believe the shareholders had purchased stock in the bank for the sake of dividends. If they had been looking for dividends, they would have purchased stock in a utility with a proven high-dividend yield.

At this point, Mr. Dustin commented that whatever was to be done should be simple. His conclusion, based on several conversations with NHSB depositors when the stock was first offered, was that many of those depositors had only a vague idea of what it meant to become a stockholder of the bank. The president supported this point. He stressed that the depositors were enthusiastic about their bank and were interested in buying stock because of their loyalty to the bank rather than because they thought the stock would be a profitable investment.

The bank's legal counsel, Sharon Marino, also a director, observed that the investment banking firm that had underwritten the offering of stock had suggested that dividends would have little effect on the stock price. Exhibits 7 and 8 contain excerpts from two of the investment bankers' publications that had been distributed to NHSB account executives about the time of the offering.

Mr. Wilson, who had suggested a modest dividend payout, repeated his argument that many of the stockholders had probably purchased their stock in anticipation of at least some dividends. He was supported by Ms. Marino, who said she thought that many of the stockholders were probably quite unsophisticated but were loyal to the bank and deserved some dividend, although it might not be necessary to pay the entire 60 cents. Mr. Wilson underlined the importance of building loyalty to the bank, saying that shareholder/depositors would bring more business to NHSB if they were paid dividends.

In response to Mr. Wilson's question about how many of the bank shares were held by depositors, Mr. Hardie replied that most of the shares were held in street names, and it just was not possible to identify the true ownership. However, some blocks of stock were known to be held by other savings banks and by at least one mutual fund. At that point, the president tabled the discussion. He said he was glad the subject had been aired but thought that at least one more meeting would be needed before the board was ready to vote on a dividend policy. He thus proposed putting the topic on the agenda for the following month's meeting.

The Investment Committee's Meeting

A week after the August directors' meeting, the NHSB investment committee met to discuss the investment policy of the bank, its liquidity position, and the maturity structure of its assets and liabilities. As was customary at these meetings, the committee heard a brief presentation on financial planning from its consultant, B. D. Turner. Toward the end of the meeting, the question of an appropriate dividend policy came up.

Mr. Turner, who had been involved in the decision to convert the bank from a mutual institution to a stockholder-owned bank, observed that he believed the prospectus had held out a strong expectation that the bank would begin paying dividends fairly soon. Were dividends to be declared, he thought that the prospectus had provided assurance that stockholders would be paid at an annual rate of at least 5 percent of the original offering price. On the other hand, he also agreed that a stock dividend might be appropriate. He noted that more recent conversions of mutual to stock savings banks had prospectuses that specifically disclaimed any intention of paying cash dividends in the near future. This, he said, did not seem to have hurt the attractiveness of their shares.

Still opposed to cash dividends, Mr. Dustin nevertheless described a conversation he had had with a stockbroker that morning. The broker had urged NHSB to pay cash dividends becaue NHSB was a particularly strong bank with a successful earnings record and should demonstrate that strength publicly. The broker had also pointed out that a number of institutions, especially bank trust departments, would probably buy the bank's stock if cash dividends were declared (in some cases, institutions and trust departments were simply not permitted to buy stocks that did not pay cash dividends). Finally, the broker had said that, in his opinion, bank stock investors did expect cash dividends.

After a brief conversation, Mr. Turner agreed with Mr. Dustin that the stock price performance of Merchants Bank had been no better than that of NHSB despite Merchants' cash dividend policy. Furthermore, he noted that he understood a good deal of the NHSB stock issue had been purchased by other savings banks. Their interest was presumably not in dividends but in ready access to all of the information distributed to stockholders. Mr. Dustin said that he had received that same information, and he knew of a number of mutual funds that had purchased a portion of the offering. They both concluded that to analyze the dividend preferences of the stockholder group at this point was extremely difficult.

As the president closed the discussion, he commented that when he presided over the coming November's special stockholders' meeting called to authorize a stock-option program for NHSB senior executives, he would like to be able to announce the establishment of a cash dividend policy.

The September 13 Directors' Meeting

On September 13, 1983, several months after NHSB had published its second-quarter earnings report, the directors met for their final discussion of the dividend-policy question. Mr. Byrd said that he was very impressed by a letter received from Moseley, Hallgarten (Exhibit 9), an investment organization, which had strongly urged the bank to pay a cash dividend.

"That letter seems to say it all," he observed. However, Mr. Piel said that he did not see why the NHSB had to follow the pattern set by other savings banks and added that cash dividends usually involved significant income taxes to shareholders.

As the discussion continued, Mr. Wilson reiterated his earlier support for a dividend and said that instituting cash dividend payments might increase NHSB's stock price, so that the shareholder looking for capital gains would benefit from this action. Agreeing, Ms. Johanson reminded the board of the dividend statement in the prospectus and added, "I suppose we could be in some trouble with the SEC if we did not initiate the cash dividend soon."

The president reported that he had recently had a conversation with a local depositor who had subscribed for an unusually large number of shares. This shareholder said that he had no personal desire for cash dividends, but he believed that most bank shareholders did; at least this is what he had been told by stockbrokers. Mr. Hardie added that approximately 900 depositors of the bank had subscribed for shares in the original offering. As a group, they had purchased about 20 percent of the offering. (Approximately 34,000 depositors were eligible and had been invited to subscribe. Another 20,000 had account balances below $50 and were not eligible to participate.)

Finally, Mr. Wilson said that he could understand why a newly formed company might not pay dividends. "But," he said, "we're a mature institution more than 150 years old. How can we possibly justify not paying a dividend?"

The president called for a vote.

New Hampshire Savings Bank Corporation
EXHIBIT 1 • Financial Highlights
(dollars in thousands, except per-share amounts)

	June 30, 1982	June 30, 1983
For the Quarter Ended June 30		
Increase in deposits	$ 2,660	$ 7,315
Increase in loan originations	29,444	46,877
Increase in loan receivables	6,221	17,136
Total income	2,231	3,664
Net income	$ 416	$ 1,249
For the Six Months Ended June 30		
Increase in deposits	$ 5,469	$13,321
Increase in loan originations	44,569	77,647
Increase in loan receivables	(1,006)	22,132
Total income	3,585	6,570
Net income	$ 488	$ 2,487
Weighted-Average Yield and Costs at June 30		
Yield on total loans	11.68%	12.40%
Yield on investments	10.24	8.90
Combined weighted-average yields	11.28	11.47
Cost of deposit accounts	8.96	8.04
Cost of borrowings	10.76	10.21
Combined weighted-average costs	9.16%	8.27%
Per-Share Data:		
Earnings per share for quarter	N.Ap.	$ 0.80
Book value per share at end of quarter	N.Ap.	$ 28.77

N.Ap. = not applicable.

New Hampshire Savings Bank Corporation
EXHIBIT 2 • New Hampshire Savings Bank Corporation and Subsidiaries Consolidated Statements of Financial Position (thousands of dollars, unaudited)

	June 30, 1982	June 30, 1983
Assets		
Cash and due from banks	$ 4,136	$ 14,526
Federal funds sold	7,456	8,493
Investment securities		
U.S. government and federal agency securities	10,999	23,430
Mortgage-secured investments	14,697	4,763
Certificates of deposit	3,278	3,998
Other securities	32,041	38,633
Total investment securities	61,015	70,824
Loans	215,977	236,809
Less unearned discount	(5,887)	(5,827)
Less reserved for loan losses	(591)	(739)
Net loans	209,499	230,243
Accrued interest receivable on loans	1,825	1,662
Property, furniture, and equipment, net	5,089	6,025
Other real estate owned	795	385
Other assets	4,451	4,396
Total assets	$294,266	$336,554
Liabilities and Stockholders' Equity		
Deposits		
Savings	$ 92,229	$ 86,557
Money market accounts	0	43,681
Six-month money market CDs	68,884	47,078
Other term deposits	74,933	76,142
Total deposits	236,046	253,458
Liabilities under repurchase agreements	1,342	0
Other borrowed funds	25,898	33,866
Accrued expenses and other liabilities	3,581	4,236
Total liabilities	266,867	291,560
Stockholders' equity		
Common stock, $1 par value/share	0	1,564
Paid-in surplus	0	17,933
Guarantee fund	12,000	12,000
Retained earnings	15,399	13,497
Total stockholders' equity	27,399	44,994
Total liabilities and stockholders' equity	$294,266	$336,554

New Hampshire Savings Bank Corporation

EXHIBIT 3 • New Hampshire Savings Bank Corporation and
Subsidiaries Consolidated Statements of Income
(thousands of dollars, except per-share amounts, unaudited)

	Three Months Ended		Six Months Ended	
	June 30, 1982	June 30, 1983	June 30, 1982	June 30, 1983
Interest and dividend income				
Interest on loans	$5,963	$6,972	$11,548	$13,289
Interest on bonds and other investments	1,353	1,402	2,503	2,694
Dividends on stock investments	217	178	424	323
Interest on federal funds sold	304	262	483	572
Total interest and dividend income	7,837	8,814	14,958	16,878
Interest expense				
Regular savings	1,266	1,116	2,410	2,229
Time deposits	4,052	2,982	8,246	6,063
Money market accounts	—	872	—	1,569
Borrowed funds	722	766	1,405	1,602
Total interest expense	6,040	5,736	12,061	11,463
Net interest and dividend income	1,797	3,078	2,897	5,415
Provision for possible loan losses	37	81	75	42
Net interest and dividend income after provision for possible loan losses	1,760	2,997	2,822	5,373
Other income				
Income from fees and service charges	423	599	660	1,015
Other	48	69	103	182
Total other income	471	668	763	1,197
Total income	$2,231	$3,665	$ 3,585	$6,570
Operating expenses				
Salaries and benefits	$ 785	$1,028	$ 1,607	$1,961
Occupancy costs	240	208	379	387
Other operating costs	586	975	1,442	1,993
Total operating expenses	1,611	2,211	3,428	4,341
Income (loss) before provision for federal income taxes and securities transactions	620	1,454	157	2,229
Provision (benefit) for income taxes	191	574	47	799
Income (loss) before securities transactions	429	880	110	1,430
Net gain (loss) on sale of securities	(13)	369	378	1,057
Net income	$ 416	$1,249	$ 488	$2,487
Earnings per share				
Income before securities transactions	N.Ap.	$0.56	N.Ap.	$0.91
Net income	N.Ap.	$0.80	N.Ap.	$1.59
Weighted-average shares outstanding	N.Ap.	1,563,984	N.Ap.	1,563,984

N.Ap. = not applicable.

New Hampshire Savings Bank Corporation
EXHIBIT 4 • NASDAQ System Statistics

	Composite Index	Other Finance Index		
High	321.58	279.43		
Low	303.09	268.74		
Close	303.96	272.80		
Previous close	318.70	269.96		
Percentage change	+4.62	+1.05		
Total NASDAQ volume		1,294,387,100	NASDAQ symbol	NHSB
Average daily volume		64,719,355	Security description	Common stock ($1.00 par value)
Total market value		$229,384,748,000	Total shares outstanding	1,563,984

Summary for this Security

Quote range:	High bid	18⅝	Low bid	17⅝	New Hampshire Savings Bank Corp.
	High ask	18¾	Low ask	17⅞	John Hardie
Closing bid	(JUN)	18⅛			President
	(JUL)	18½	Percentage change	+2.07	27 North State Street
Volume for month	185,453				Concord, NH 03301

Daily Statistical Report

Date	High Bid	Low Bid	Close Bid	High Ask	Low Ask	Close Ask	Change (Bid)	Volume	NASDAQ Volume	Composite Close
Fri. 1	18⅛	18⅛	18⅛	18⅜	18⅜	18⅜	0	5,850	62,996,300	321.58
Week	18⅛	18⅛	18⅛	18⅜	18⅜	18⅜	0	5,850	62,996,300	321.58
Mon. 4	Holiday							0		
Tue. 5	18⅛	17⅝	17⅝	18⅜	17⅞	17⅞	−½	13,873	58,190,100	317.15
Wed. 6	17⅝	17⅝	17⅝	17⅞	17⅞	17⅞	0	2,100	63,383,400	319.14
Thu. 7	17¾	17⅝	17¾	18	17⅞	18	+⅛	2,285	72,620,100	320.30
Fri. 8	17¾	17⅝	17⅝	18	17⅞	18	−⅛	3,620	62,055,200	319.57
Week	18⅛	17⅝	17⅝	18⅜	17⅞	18	−½	21,878	256,248,800	319.57
Mon. 11	18	17⅝	18	18⅛	18	18⅛	+⅜	14,925	60,917,100	320.38
Tue. 12	18	17⅝	17⅝	18¼	17⅞	17⅞	−⅜	8,250	72,131,800	316.93
Wed. 13	17¾	17⅝	17¾	18	18	18	+⅛	2,885	65,863,200	314.59
Thu. 14	18¼	17¾	18¼	18½	18	18½	+½	9,800	65,024,700	315.49
Fri. 15	18¼	18¼	18¼	18½	18½	18½	0	2,700	57,384,700	312.87
Week	18¼	17⅝	18¼	18½	17⅞	18½	+⅝	38,560	321,321,500	312.87
Mon. 18	18¼	18	18	18½	18½	18½	−¼	3,715	54,151,900	310.29
Tue. 19	18⅛	17⅞	17⅞	18½	18¼	18¼	−⅛	10,350	69,379,200	311.17
Wed. 20	18	17⅞	18	18¼	18¼	18¼	+⅛	3,400	76,078,200	316.76
Thu. 21	18¼	18	18¼	18½	18¼	18½	+¼	27,400	77,995,900	319.29
Fri. 22	18⅜	18¼	18¼	18½	18½	18½	0	14,400	64,634,700	320.71
Week	18⅜	17⅞	18¼	18½	18¼	18½	0	59,265	342,239,900	320.71
Mon. 25	18¼	18¼	18¼	18½	18⅜	18½	0	1,300	54,044,000	320.84
Tue. 26	18¼	18¼	18¼	18½	18½	18½	0	3,000	62,549,400	320.38
Wed. 27	18½	18¼	18½	18¾	18½	18¾	+¼	18,700	71,025,000	315.04
Thu. 28	18⅝	18⅝	18⅝	18¾	18¾	18¾	+⅛	2,400	65,496,800	308.47
Fri. 29	18½	18½	18½	18¾	18¾	18¾	−⅛	34,500	58,525,400	303.96
Week	18⅝	18¼	18½	18¾	18⅜	18¾	−¼	59,900	311,640,600	303.96

NASDAQ Market Makers in this Security as of 07/15/83: Carl P. Sherr and Company; Tucker, Anthony & R. L. Day; Smith Barney/Harris Upham; E. F. Hutton & Company Inc.; Moseley Hallgarten Estabrook; Oppenheimer & Co., Inc.; and Bear, Sterns & Co.

New Hampshire Savings Bank Corporation
EXHIBIT 5 • 1983 Stock Price Performance and Trading Volume

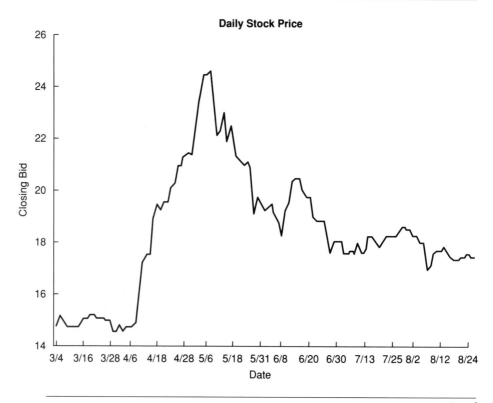

continued

EXHIBIT 5 • *continued*

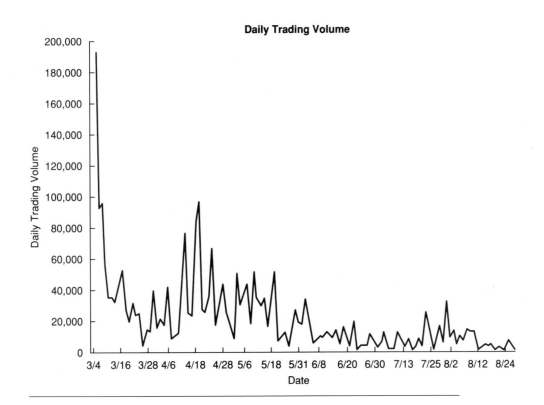

New Hampshire Savings Bank Corporation
EXHIBIT 6 • New Hampshire Savings Bank Corporation Prospectus

Prospectus

1,139,836 Shares

New Hampshire Savings Bank Corp.

Common Stock

The above shares constitute a portion of the 1,450,000 shares of the common stock ("Conversion Stock") of New Hampshire Savings Bank Corp. ("Holding Company") to be issued upon the conversion of New Hampshire Savings Bank ("Bank"). The simultaneous conversion of the Bank from mutual to stock form, issuance of all of the Bank's stock to the Holding Company, and offer and sale of the Conversion Stock by the Holding Company is herein referred to as the "Conversion." The remaining shares of Conversion Stock have been subscribed for by savings account holders of the Bank in a subscription offering by the Holding Company (the "Subscription Offering") and will be purchased at the Public Offering Price set forth below.

The Holding Company's common stock has been approved for quotation on the National Association of Securities Dealers Automated Quotation System ("NASDAQ"). Its NASDAQ symbol is "NHSB." Prior to this offering ("Public Offering") there has been no public market for the common stock of the Holding Company, and there can be no assurance that an established market for such stock will develop.

Certain limitations on the purchase of Conversion Stock are described under "The Conversion — Limitations on Conversion Stock Purchases" and "The Conversion — Restrictions on Acquisition of the Holding Company."

THESE SECURITIES HAVE NOT BEEN APPROVED OR DISAPPROVED BY THE SECURITIES AND EXCHANGE COMMISSION NOR HAS THE COMMISSION PASSED UPON THE ACCURACY OR ADEQUACY OF THIS PROSPECTUS. ANY REPRESENTATION TO THE CONTRARY IS A CRIMINAL OFFENSE.

	Public Offering Price	Underwriting Discount(1)	Proceeds to Holding Company(2)(3)
Per Share	$13.75	$ .95	$12.80
Total	$15,672,745	$1,082,844	$14,589,901
Total, as Adjusted(4)	$17,240,025	$1,191,129	$16,048,896

(1) The Holding Company has agreed to indemnify the Underwriters against certain liabilities.

(2) Before deducting expenses payable by the Holding Company which relate to the Conversion, Subscription Offering and Public Offering and which are estimated to be $754,656. Of such amount, $593,230 is allocable on a pro rata basis to the shares offered hereby. See "Use of Proceeds" for the net proceeds available to the Holding Company from the sale of all 1,450,000 shares of Conversion Stock.

(3) Of the proceeds to the Holding Company, approximately 93% will be transferred to the Bank in exchange for all of the capital stock of the Bank. It is expected that the balance of the net proceeds will be retained by the Holding Company.

(4) Assuming exercise of a 30-day over-allotment option granted to the Underwriters to purchase up to an additional 113,984 shares. See "Underwriting."

E. F. Hutton & Company Inc.

March 4, 1983   *continued*

EXHIBIT 6 · *continued*

Use of Proceeds.   Approximately 92 percent of the net proceeds from the sale of the Common Stock will be used by the Holding Company to purchase all of the stock of the Bank. These funds will be added by the Bank to its working capital and used for general business purposes. It is expected that the balance of the net proceeds will be retained by the Holding Company to be used in connection with its efforts to acquire and develop other banks and other businesses as is permitted by New Hampshire law. The Holding Company has not at this time identified any business it intends to acquire or develop, and the net proceeds to be retained by it may not be sufficient for such purposes if and when such businesses are identified. Until the net proceeds are used as indicated, they will be invested by the Holding Company and the Bank in short-term securities.

Dividend Policy.   It is intended that, following the Conversion, the Holding Company will establish a dividend policy to pay cash dividends on the Conversion Stock. The Holding Company may also consider the payment of stock dividends from time to time in addition to, or in lieu of, cash dividends. If a cash dividend policy is established, it is anticipated that dividends would initially be set by the Holding Company at an annual rate of approximately 5 percent of the initial Public Offering Price of the Conversion Stock. Payment of dividends by the Holding Company is, however, subject to determination and declaration by the board of directors of the Holding Company. Since the Holding Company currently has no significant source of income other than dividends from the Bank, Holding Company dividends will depend upon receipt of dividends from the Bank, which in turn will depend on the dividend policy of the Bank. It is intended that the Bank establish a dividend policy following Conversion to pay dividends to the Holding Company in such amounts as will permit the payment of the aforesaid dividends by the Holding Company. In each case, the determination and declaration will take into account the Holding Company's and the Bank's respective financial condition and results of operations, economic conditions, and other factors, including the regulatory restrictions discussed below. No assurances can be given that dividends will in fact be paid or that, if paid, such dividends will not be reduced or eliminated in future periods.

   The New Hampshire Business Corporation Act ("Business Corporation Act") permits the Holding Company to pay dividends on its capital stock only from the unreserved and unrestricted earned surplus of the corporation or from unreserved and unrestricted net earnings of the current fiscal year and the next preceding fiscal year taken as a single period. The Bank is not subject to the Business Corporation Act, but the BTCI rules prohibit the payment of a cash dividend if the effect thereof would cause the net worth of the Bank to be reduced below either the amount required for the liquidation account or the net worth requirements imposed by New Hampshire or federal laws or regulations.

   The BTCI rules prohibit the Bank, without the approval of the BTCI, from paying a cash dividend for a period of ten years from the effective date of the Conversion in an amount in excess of one half of the greater of (i) the Bank's Net Income for its current fiscal year, or (ii) the average of the Bank's Net Income for its current fiscal year and no more than two of the immediately preceding fiscal years. *Net Income* means all gross income less all expenses, including interest on FHLB advances and borrowed money, interest or dividends on withdrawable and nonwithdrawable accounts (but not on capital stock) and income taxes, if any, and all losses.

   Furthermore, the Federal Deposit Insurance Act prohibits the Bank from paying dividends on its capital stock if it is in default in the payment of any assessment to the FDIC.

   In addition, the Bank cannot pay dividends if such payment would impair its "guaranty fund," which New Hampshire law requires it to maintain at a level of 3 percent of all deposits.

New Hampshire Savings Bank Corporation
EXHIBIT 7 • Excerpt from Investment Bankers'
                 Publication "Regional Bank Monthly" August 1983

	Percent Change, 1981–1982	*7/29/83*	*Year-to-Date Percent Change, 1983*
NASDAQ Bank Index	+ 9.27	−190.88	+22.07
S&P 500	+14.71	−162.56	+15.54
Dow Jones Utilities	+ 9.60	−129.77	+ 8.63

In this issue of the "Regional Bank Monthly" we have expanded our traditional "New England Bank Stock Monthly" to include some interesting banks in the Middle Atlantic region from New York to Washington, D.C., and the Sunbelt.

Banks Show Strong First Half Earnings

Half of the banks on the Moseley Regional Bank Monthly achieved net earnings for the first six months of 1983 of 20 percent or more. Special note should be taken of the banks listed below, which year to date have achieved higher than 25 percent net earnings growth over the first six months of 1982.

		First Half 83/82 Net Earnings Percent Growth
Connecticut	Colonial Bancorp	+37.8
Maine	Casco–Northern Corp.	+72.2
	Maine National Corp.	+25.8
	Merrill Bancshares	+56.9
Massachusetts	Bank of Boston	+42.0
	Bank of New England	+29.9
	UST Corp.	+29.0
New Hampshire	Bankeast	+76.7
	Indian Head Banks	+49.1
New Jersey	Citizens First Bankcorp.	+25.9
New York	Key Banks	+35.1

Pennsylvania	Core States Financial	+30.3
	Dauphin Deposit	+31.5
	Fidelcor	+51.9
Vermont	First Vermont Financial	+47.7
	Howard Bank	+58.3
	Vermont Financial	+31.0

In May and June short-term interest rates rose, increasing costs and putting pressure on second quarter earnings. The recent (August 8) rise in the prime rate should help ease the pressure on margins at many of these banks. The surge in consumer spending which has been leading the national economic recovery is favorable for the consumer-oriented retail banks we follow at Moseley. The good prospects for low inflation and continuing economic recovery should help the banking industry.

Big Savings Banks Convert

In order to raise capital to strengthen their competitive positions, mutual savings banks are "going public" and converting to stockholder-owned savings banks. Two of the largest such conversions in our region, in July, were *Howard Savings Bank,* New Jersey, with 8.6 million shares, and *The Provident Institution for Savings in the Town of Boston,* Mass., with 3.3 million shares.

In August, the *Philadelphia Savings Fund Society* is planning the largest new offering in history with 32 million shares.

1983 Market Outlook

Year to date, the NASDAQ Bank Index (+22.07%) has sharply outperformed the S&P 500 (+15.54%). The regional bank stocks on this list are yielding an average of 4.95 percent and selling at 7.04 times our 1983 earnings estimate and at only 101 percent of book value. The S&P 400 stocks are yielding an average of 4.5 percent and selling at a multiple of 11.1 times 1983 estimates. These bank stocks are still selling at a substantially lower multiple than the industrial stocks. We expect the bank stocks' relative valuation to improve significantly in the next year.

Given the expected multiple expansion and the favorable economic fundamentals, the regional bank stocks should *outperform* the general market again over the next year.

continued

EXHIBIT 7 • continued

	Symbol	1982–1983 Range	7/29/83 Bid Price	Percent Price Change from 12/31/82	Percent Price Change from Prior Month	Net Income per Share**			Price/Earnings 1983E	Individual Dividend	Yield	Dividend Payout	6/30/83 Book Value	Market Value to Book Value
						1981	1982	1983						
Connecticut														
CBT Corp.[kl]	CBCT*	38–20	$31.25	19%	1%	$4.61	$5.36	$4.90	6.38X	$1.64	5.25%	33%	$32.68	96%
Citytrust Bancorp[c]	CITR*	43–21	42.00	50	0	4.08	5.20	6.05	6.94	1.48	3.52	24	34.67	121
Colonial Bancorp	CBCN*	28–12	25.50	89	(5)	3.91	(9.43)	2.50	10.20	0.80	3.14	32	22.74	112
First Bancorp	FBAN*	53–21	51.00	62	(3)	4.35	4.78	5.35	9.53	1.60	3.14	30	37.53	136
First Connecticut Bancorp[c]	FCBC*	44–25	42.50	18	1	4.64	5.12	5.60	7.59	1.60[b]	3.76	29	33.68	126
Hartford National Corp.[j]	HNAT*	41–19	36.38	(2)	(1)	4.29	4.46	5.90	6.17	2.00	5.50	34	33.10	110
Northeast Bancorp[cf]	NBIC*	45–26	40.50	16	(2)	4.73	4.72	5.00	8.10	2.29[h]	5.65	46	38.71	105
Maine														
Canal Corp.[cj]	—	26–20	26.00	0	4	1.46	2.30	3.00	11.30	0.50	1.92	22	23.15	112
Casco–Northern Corp.[cj]	CNOB	41–20	25.00	(30)	(30)	2.41	3.18	3.60	6.94	1.40	5.60	39	31.85	78
Depositors Corp.[i]	DEP	30–19	29.50	10	2	3.38	3.79	4.20	7.02	1.90	6.44	45	25.08	118
Maine National Corp.[dh]	MMAC*	24–13	23.50	45	0	1.85	2.48	2.85	8.25	1.00[b]	4.26	35	19.26	122
Merrill Bankshares[g]	MERB*	17–07	16.50	8	(4)	1.59	1.74	2.25	7.33	0.88	5.33	39	13.79	120

EXHIBIT 7 • *continued*

Massachusetts

Bank of Boston[ml]	18,122†	11,966†	10,716†	894.00†	658,625	18,280	740.34	4.93	142,203	0.78	15.91
Bank of New England[el]	5,169	3,390	2,675	251.00	200,500	4,392	226.19	4.86	38,564	0.75	15.36
Baybanks	4,067	3,546	2,129	235.00	305,250	6,318	207.70	5.78	33,660	0.83	14.32
Capitol Bancorp[c]	201†	140†	88†	14.30†	NA	1,020	24.99	7.11	4,418	2.20	30.90
Conifer/Essex Group[c]	995	866	663	57.20	26,592	1,775	63.01	5.75	9,330	0.94	16.31
Multibank Financial[cc]	1,175†	1,010†	764†	64.60†	71,083	1,984	68.45	5.50	11,015	0.94	17.05
Patriot Bancorp[c]	211	172	90	20.60	NA	997	24.93	9.76	3,658	1.73	17.76
Shawmut Corp.[c]	5,223	3,793	2,817	275.00	315,715	6,161	194.07	5.27	31,509	0.60	11.46
State Street Boston[g]	4,043	2,476	1,259	219.00	383,267	8,645	404.15	5.42	50,337	1.25	22.98
UST Corp.[cg]	631†	399†	283†	30.30†	11,018	2,755	59.23	4.80	6,602	1.05	21.79

New Hampshire

Bank of New Hampshire[g]	293†	241†	164†	17.90†	NA	981	16.68	6.11	3,763	1.28	21.02
Bankeast[c]	482	424	273	35.40	NA	1,076	27.98	7.34	3,846	0.80	10.86
First New Hampshire Banks[o]	602†	500†	381†	39.60	NA	1,533	44.46	6.58	5,845	0.97	14.76
Indian Head Banks[f]	675	579	477	38.60	NA	1,361	36.75	5.72	5,075	0.75	13.15
Merchants Savings Bank	391	303	315	32.60	NA	1,318	26.36	8.34	1,357	0.35	4.16
New Hampshire Savings Bank	326†	244†	225†	45.00†	NA	1,564	28.36	13.80	(913)	NM	NM

continued

EXHIBIT 7 • continued

	1983 2d Quarter (millions of dollars)				Average Monthly Trading Volume	Common Shares Out. (thous.)	Market Capital (millions of dollars)	6/30/83 Average Equity to Average Assets	Last 12 Months Net Earnings	6/30/83 Return on Average Assets	6/30/83 Return on Average Equity
	Average Assets	Average Deposits	Average Net Loans	Average Equity							
Connecticut											
CBT Corp.[kl]	$ 4,809	$ 3,539	$ 2,811	$278.10	267,650	8,662	$268.52	5.78%	$ 35,541	0.74%	12.78%
Citytrust Bancorp[c]	963	812	674	55.50	20,350	1,635	68.67	5.76	8,926	0.93	16.08
Colonial Bancorp	1,265	1,076	842	73.60	127,467	2,236	59.81	5.82	(18,174)	NM	NM
First Bancorp	820	456	523	55.50	24,700	1,473	77.33	6.77	7,638	0.93	13.76
First Connecticut Bancorp[c]	753	602	330	56.90	16,967	1,715	72.03	7.56	8,979	1.19	15.78
Hartford National Corp.[j]	3,943	3,162	2,252	227.00	438,558	5,871	216.49	5.76	29,138	0.74	12.84
Northeast Bancorp[cf]	1,463	1,245	848	105.70	33,492	2,747	114.00	7.22	13,171	0.90	12.46
Maine											
Canal Corp.[cl]	264†	198†	123†	15.30†	NA	691	17.28	5.80	1,791	0.68	11.71
Casco–Northern[cl]	663	577	424	37.20	4,325	1,139	40.86	5.61	4,777	0.72	12.84
Depositors Corp.[i]	659	531	321	42.70	11,942	1,777	51.53	6.48	7,314	1.11	17.13
Maine National Corp.[dh]	552†	460†	263†	38.00†	NA	2,703	63.52	6.88	5,661	1.03	14.90
Merrill Bankshares[g]	578†	446†	237†	45.00†	20,463	3,443	59.39	7.79	7,603	1.32	16.90

EXHIBIT 7 • continued

Massachusetts

Bank of Boston[ml]	18,122†	11,966†	10,716†	894.00†	658,625	18,280	740.34	4.93	142,203	0.78	15.91
Bank of New England[cl]	5,169	3,390	2,675	251.00	200,500	4,392	226.19	4.86	38,564	0.75	15.36
Baybanks	4,067	3,546	2,129	235.00	305,250	6,318	207.70	5.78	33,660	0.83	14.32
Capitol Bancorp[c]	201†	140†	88†	14.30†	NA	1,020	24.99	7.11	4,418	2.20	30.90
Conifer/Essex Group[c]	995	866	663	57.20	26,592	1,775	63.01	5.75	9,330	0.94	16.31
Multibank Financial[ce]	1,175†	1,010†	764†	64.60†	71,083	1,984	68.45	5.50	11,015	0.94	17.05
Patriot Bancorp[c]	211	172	90	20.60	NA	997	24.93	9.76	3,658	1.73	17.76
Shawmut Corp.[c]	5,223	3,793	2,817	275.00	315,715	6,161	194.07	5.27	31,509	0.60	11.46
State Street Boston[g]	4,043	2,476	1,259	219.00	383,267	8,645	404.15	5.42	50,337	1.25	22.98
UST Corp.[cg]	631†	399†	283†	30.30†	11,018	2,755	59.23	4.80	6,602	1.05	21.79

New Hampshire

Bank of New Hampshire[g]	293†	241†	164†	17.90†	NA	981	16.68	6.11	3,763	1.28	21.02
Bankeast[c]	482	424	273	35.40	NA	1,076	27.98	7.34	3,846	0.80	10.86
First New Hampshire Banks[o]	602†	500†	381†	39.60	NA	1,533	44.46	6.58	5,845	0.97	14.76
Indian Head Banks[f]	675	579	477	38.60	NA	1,361	36.75	5.72	5,075	0.75	13.15
Merchants Savings Bank	391	303	315	32.60	NA	1,318	26.36	8.34	1,357	0.35	4.16
New Hampshire Savings Bank	326†	244†	225†	45.00†	NA	1,564	28.36	13.80	(913)	NM	NM

continued

EXHIBIT 7 • continued

	Symbol	1982–1983 Range	7/29/83 Bid Price	Percent Price Change from 12/31/82	Percent Price Change from Prior Month	Net Income per Share**			Price/Earnings 1983E	Individual Dividend	Yield	Dividend Payout	6/30/83 Book Value	Market Value to Book Value
						1981	1982	1983						
Rhode Island														
Fleet Financial Group^c	FLT	51–23	$47.13	37%	3%	$5.30	$6.28	$7.00	6.73X	$2.20	4.67%	31%	$37.52	126%
Old Stone Corp.^c	OSTN*	28–17	25.25	10	(10)	(8.56)	3.69	3.50	7.21	2.08	8.24	59	29.56	85
RIHT Financial^cn	RIHT*	49–22	45.00	58	(2)	6.06	3.18	NE	14.15	2.32	5.16	73	45.82	98
Vermont														
Chittenden Corp.	CNDN*	23–11	19.25	4	(13)	2.19	2.38	2.65	7.26	1.00^b	5.19	38	20.37	95
First Vermont Financial	FIVT*	18–13	18.00	20	3	2.37	2.11	2.75	6.55	1.20	6.67	44	20.69	87
Howard Bank^c	HOBK*	23–12	21.00	25	0	2.03	2.85	3.65	5.75	1.09^b	5.19	30	21.40	98
Merchants Bank	—*	20–11	20.00	38	0	2.91	3.52	3.85	5.19	1.20^b	6.00	31	18.50	108
Vermont Financial Services^p	VFSC*	20–11	20.00	33	5	2.68	3.13	3.50	5.71	1.10^b	5.50	31	24.74	81

1983 2d Quarter (millions of dollars)

	Average Assets	Average Deposits	Average Net Loans	Average Equity	Average Monthly Trading Volume	Common Shares Out. (thous.)	Market Capital (millions of dollars)	6/30/83 Average Equity to Average Assets	Last 12 Months Net Earnings	6/30/83 Return on Average Assets	6/30/83 Return on Average Equity
Rhode Island											
Fleet Financial Group^c	$ 4,214^†	$ 2,683^†	$ 2,667^†	$255.40^†	181,892	6,189	$282.37	5.35%^b	$40,052	0.95%	17.77%
Old Stone Corp.^c	1,976^†	1,574^†	1,454^†	91.40^†	45,625	2,223	62.24	4.63	8,348	0.42	9.13
RIHT Financial^cn	1,938	1,429	1,149	97.00	111,158	2,127	97.84	5.01	5,845	0.30	6.03
Vermont											
Chittenden Corp.	535^†	480^†	386^†	29.20^†	37,308	1,488	32.74	5.46	3,678	0.69	12.60
First Vermont Financial	329^†	294^†	215^†	25.00^†	NA	1,248	21.84	7.60	3,074	0.93	12.30
Howard Bank^c	338^†	292^†	244^†	18.00^†	NA	896	18.82	5.33	3,050	0.90	16.94
Merchants Bank	248^†	217^†	179^†	14.00^†	NA	828	16.56	5.65	3,108	1.25	22.20
Vermont Financial Services^p	321^†	284^†	220^†	18.10^†	NA	789	14.99	5.64	2,756	0.86	15.23

EXHIBIT 7 • continued

Middle Atlantic Region

	Symbol	1982–1983 Range	7/29/83 Bid Price	Percent Price Change from 12/31/82	Percent Price Change from Prior Month	Net Income per Share** 1981	1982	1983	Price/Earnings 1983E	Individual Dividend	Yield	Dividend Payout	6/30/83 Book Value	Market Value to Book Value
New Jersey														
Citizens First Bancorp[g]	CFB	23–10	$23.25	47%	11%	$0.75	$2.46	$3.40	6.84X	$1.00	4.30%	29%	$17.88	130%
Commercial Bancshares[c]	CBNJ*	31–13	29.75	70	(3)	2.75	3.72	4.30	6.92	1.68	5.65	39	33.09	90
First National State Bancorp[d]	FNS	42–22	36.25	16	(8)	5.66	6.59	NE	5.50	2.40	6.62	36	43.34	84
Heritage Bancorp[c]	HRTG*	26–12	25.25	38	(1)	3.45	3.36	3.70	6.82	1.52	6.02	41	28.58	88
Horizon Bancorp	HZB	27–14	25.75	32	(1)	3.48	3.35	4.00	6.44	1.52	5.90	38	24.82	104
Midlantic Banks[d]	MIDL*	42–20	42.25	50	7	4.89	5.94	6.70	7.11	1.88	4.45	28	38.52	110
Summit Bancorp[c]	SUBN	27–17	22.50	(16)	2	4.05	4.60	NE	4.89	1.20	5.33	26	19.09	118
United Jersey Banks	UJB	30–12	28.63	56	8	2.90	3.17	NE	9.03	1.24	4.33	39	26.04	110
New York														
Bank of New York	BK	62–37	61.25	23	3	7.61	8.30	9.20	6.66	3.40	5.55	37	72.14	85
First Empire State	FEMP*	33–17	29.50	22	(6)	3.60	4.11	NE	7.18	1.00	3.39	24	44.22	67
Key Banks[d]	KEY	29–12	29.00	84	20	2.78	3.50	4.00	7.25	1.50	5.17	38	27.73	105
Lincoln First Banks[c]	LFBK*	40–24	36.00	0	(3)	4.84	6.61	NE	5.45	2.00	5.56	30	59.14	61
Norstar Bancorp[d]	NOR	38–22	36.38	21	6	3.99	4.62	4.80	7.58	2.20[b]	6.05	46	30.79	118
Security New York State[d]	SNYK*	33–12	32.75	90	(1)	3.21	3.47	NE	9.44	1.50	4.58	43	28.09	117
Pennsylvania														
Commonwealth National[c]	CMHC	34–24	28.50	(2)	20	2.06	1.40	NE	20.36	2.32	8.14	166	46.39	61
Continental Bancorp[c]	CBRP	30–22	27.75	(3)	(4)	4.07	4.65	4.00	6.94	2.04	7.35	51	26.96	103
Core States Financial[c]	CSFN	66–32	66.38	29	6	6.13	9.73	11.00	6.03	3.52	5.30	32	68.50	97
Dauphin Deposit[cg]	DAPN	34–21	33.50	29	16	3.24	3.52	NE	9.52	1.64	4.90	47	27.04	124
Fidelcor[c]	FICR	37–17	35.50	41	1	5.91	5.47	6.50	5.46	2.00	5.63	31	43.63	81
First Pennsylvania Corp.	FPA	09–02	7.13	43	(14)	0.02	(1.66)	NE	NM	0.00	0.00	NM	11.28	63
Independence Bancorp[d]	—*	30–20	29.50	28	(2)	3.77	4.21	4.80	6.15	1.72	5.83	36	26.42	112
Industrial Valley Bk. & Tr.[c]	IBKT	25–16	23.50	11	6	3.32	3.18	3.20	7.34	2.20	9.36	69	32.02	73
Mellon National[f]	MEL	57–27	51.50	36	2	5.88	6.83	8.00	6.44	2.44	4.74	31	51.35	100
Meridian Bancorp[s]	MRDN	36–24	31.75	27	(2)	4.45	4.71	4.87	6.52	2.20	6.93	45	36.00	88
PNC Financial[d]	PNCF	45–24	44.50	39	11	4.71	5.09	5.80	7.67	1.92	4.31	33	33.85	131
Washington, D.C.														
American Security Corp.[c]	ASEC*	30–18	28.25	15	3	3.62	3.93	4.60	6.14	1.40	4.96	30	28.93	98

1983 2d Quarter (millions of dollars)

	Average Assets	Average Deposits	Average Net Loans	Average Equity	Average Monthly Trading Volume	Common Shares Out. (thous.)	Market Capital (millions of dollars)	6/30/83 Average Equity to Average Assets	Last 12 Months Net Earnings	6/30/83 Return on Average Assets	6/30/83 Return on Average Equity
New Jersey											
Citizens First Bancorp[g]	$832†	$707†	$414†	$43.40†	15,808	2,559	$53.42	5.22%	$7,085	0.85%	16.32%
Commercial Bancshares[c]	569†	441†	220†	44.90†	35,967	1,402	43.11	7.89	5,389	0.95	12.00
First National State Bancorp[d]	4,295†	3,336†	2,247†	236.00†	99,508	5,794	227.41	5.49	37,223	0.87	15.77
Heritage Bancorp[c]	1,645†	1,389†	866†	114.50†	1,100,558	4,272	109.47	6.96	20,674	1.26	18.06
Horizon Bancorp	1,572†	1,247†	952†	99.80†	57,650	4,189	108.91	6.35	15,022	0.96	15.05
Midlantic Banks[d]	4,145†	3,223†	2,230†	237.00†	219,617	5,134	202.79	5.72	40,431	0.98	17.06
Summit Bancorp[c]	1,024†	875†	555†	79.60†	NA	3,225	70.95	7.77	11,394	1.11	14.31
United Jersey Banks	3,416†	2,540†	1,602†	159.60†	182,142	5,797	154.35	4.67	20,379	0.60	12.77
New York											
Bank of New York	12,822	9,062	7,796	597.70	481,592	7,247	429.38	4.66	73,256	0.57	12.26
First Empire State	1,946†	1,578†	1,211†	123.40†	71,942	2,868	89.63	6.34	9,532	0.49	7.72
Key Banks[d]	2,765	2,323	1,428	204.10	187,292	7,410	178.77	7.38	27,830	1.01	13.64
Lincoln First Banks[c]	3,909	3,047	2,176	206.90	230,200	3,402	126.72	5.29	24,531	0.63	11.86
Norstar Bancorp[d]	3,720	3,078	1,627†	327.40†	104,900	9,427	324.05	8.80	46,654	1.25	14.25
Security New York State[d]	1,633†	1,323†	863†	76.70	34,092	1,695	55.94	4.70	8,001	0.49	10.43
Pennsylvania											
Commonwealth National[c]	1,233†	935†	735†	68.50†	NA	1,490	35.39	5.56	4,348	0.35	6.35
Continental Bancorp[c]	2,907	2,477	1,898	210.90	90,800	7,908	229.33	7.25	34,234	1.18	16.23
Core States Financial[c]	6,253	4,205	3,298†	396.00†	369,717	5,824	365.46	6.33	59,133	0.95	14.93
Dauphin Deposit[eg]	1,270†	1,057†	518†	97.80	27,242	3,775	109.48	7.70	14,172	1.12	14.49
Fidelcor[c]	4,062	2,969	1,709	218.70	460,467	5,180	181.30	5.38	42,170	1.04	19.28
First Pennsylvania Corp.	5,149†	3,294†	3,011†	194.60†	1,118,867	16,218	133.80	3.78	(23,477)	NM	NM
Independence Bancorp[d]	420†	327†	179†	26.10†	NA	1,042	31.26	6.21	4,179	1.00	16.01
Industrial Valley Bank & Trust[c]	1,778†	1,416†	878†	88.80†	60,067	2,864	63.72	4.99	11,559	0.65	13.02
Mellon National[f]	24,956	14,988	14,672	1,268.00	778,150	25,316	1,275.29	5.08	160,246	0.64	12.64
Meridian Bancorp[s]	3,403†	2,768†	2,303†	234.70†	329,308	6,852	111.35	6.90	34,250	1.01	14.59
PNC Financial[d]	11,317	7,058	5,098	697.00	628,642	20,621	830.00	6.16	106,873	0.94	15.33
Washington, D.C.											
American Security Corp.[c]	3,272	2,329	1,781	211.00	68,542	7,386	203.12	6.45	29,072	0.89	13.78

Averages for All Regions

	Percent Price Change from 12/31/82	Percent Price Change from Prior Month	P/E 1983E	Yield	Dividend Payout	Market Value to Book Value	Average Equity to Average Assets	Return on Average Assets	Return on Average Equity
Averages: All regions	27%	0.02%	6.96×	4.96%	36%	101%	6.26%	0.83%	13.33%

ªEPS do not include $53 million ($1.21 per share) after-tax gain on sale of aircraft.

ᵇPlus stock.

ᶜBased on March 31, 1983, balances.

ᵈReorganized into bank holding company. Old stock exchanged for new stock on 2 for 1 basis.

ᵉAdjusted for 50 percent stock dividend 1983.

ᶠAdjusted for 5 percent stock dividend 1983.

ᵍAdjusted for 2 for 1 split 1983.

ʰAdjusted for 20 percent dividend 1983.

ⁱEPS excludes nonrecurring gain of $1.68 per share on sale of real-estate purchase options.

ʲIncludes pooling of interest with Connecticut National Bank.

ᵏIncludes merger with State National Bancorp.

ˡMerger pending.

ᵐName change from First National Boston.

ⁿName change from Hospital Trust Corp.

ºName change from First Bancorp of New Hampshire.

ᵖName change from Vermont National Bank.

ᑫPercent price change from initial offering date.

ʳName change from American Bancorp as a result of consolidation with Central Penn National.

*Moseley makes a market in this stock.

ˢSimple average.

NE No estimate.

NA Not available.

NM Not meaningful.

**All earnings have been restated to reflect an SEC ruling requiring banks to report earnings on a one-line basis.

EXHIBIT 8 • Excerpt from Investment Bankers' Publication

Valuing S&L Stocks

Investors use two basic ratios to value publicly traded thrift institution stocks:

Market price to book value per share.

Market price to total assets per share.

The chart below shows that, based on price to book value, NHSB's stock will be priced at a significant discount to industry averages, despite its extraordinary yield spread and superior profitability. NHSB's ratio of price to assets is somewhat better than industry averages, reflecting its unusually strong net worth position.

Note also the percentage increases in price from initial offering to present. Thrift stocks in today's market are consistently doing well for their investors.

Institution	Symbol	Initial Offering Price(s)	Current Market Price 2/15/83	Percentage Change in Market Price(s)	Market Price to Book Value		Market Prices to Total Assets		Most Recent Yield Spread	Total Assets (thousands)
					Initial	Current	Initial	Current		
New Hampshire										
	NHSB	$13.75	—	—	48.62%[b]	—	6.35%[c]	—	2.24%	$ 313,831
		12.00	—	—	45.06[b]	—	5.59[c]	—		311,436
		10.25	—	—	41.03[b]	—	4.81[c]	—		309,040
Recent Offerings										
Fortune Federal	FORF	14.00	$14.00	—	44.93	44.93%	2.38	2.38%	(0.51)	1,293,099
Mid-State Federal	MSSL	13.75	16.25	18.18%	59.24	70.01	3.64	4.30	0.92	472,025
Washington Federal	WFSL	11.75	23.25	97.87	39.91	83.18	4.59	9.09	0.55	695,921
Puget Sound	SBFS	12.00	20.00	66.67	48.02	82.58	7.03	11.72	0.71	467,998

FN Financial	FNFC	18.00	18.75	4.17	97.88	101.96	3.74	3.89	(2.48)	7,163,398
Westside Federal	WFHC	11.50	15.00	30.43	46.13	60.17	3.95	5.15	0.09	262,342
University Federal	UFSL	12.00	20.75	72.92	29.15	53.19	2.28	3.94	(0.58)	294,758
Fidelity Federal	FFED	10.00	12.13	21.25	36.11	46.53	1.86	2.26	(0.44)	1,705,439
Other Thrifts										
Napies Federal	NAF	11.13	26.50	106.37	63.57	118.09	5.74	7.44	NA[d]	783,718
City Federal (NJ)	CTYF	11.00	18.50	253.18	33.48	77.57	1.50	2.65	1.32	4,440,606
American Federal—Colorado	AFSL	11.00	25.00	127.27	43.93	94.63	3.08	3.88	NA	322,457
First Financial—Stevens Pt.	FFIN	11.00	14.50	31.82	57.86	92.24	3.35	3.66	0.90	277,206
Land of Lincoln	LOLS	7.50	9.00	20.00	38.54	31.19	2.99	2.26	0.46	600,149
Sooner Federal	SFOK	11.50	21.25	84.78	29.03	61.86	1.75	2.87	(0.27)	1,313,717
Texas Federal	TXSL	10.75	13.75	27.91	33.86	59.83	2.01	2.52	NA	818,287
Industry Averages										
Recent offerings						71.86		4.53		
All other publicly traded institutions										
NYSE						140.91		4.69		
ASE						159.33		2.25		
OTC						70.60		3.20		
All publicly traded institutions						96.04		3.97		

[a] Adjusted for stock splits.

[b] Based on pro forma stockholders' equity.

[c] Based on pro forma total assets.

[d] Not available.

New Hampshire Savings Bank Corporation
EXHIBIT 9 • Dividend-policy Statement from Investment Advisory Service

Moseley, Hallgarten, Eastabrook & Weeden, Inc.
Investments Since 1850
Post Office Box One
60 State Street
Boston, Massachusetts 02101
(617) 367–2400

August 19, 1983

Mr. Robert E. Dustin
Executive Vice President
New Hampshire Savings Bank
27 N. State Street
Concord, New Hampshire 03301

Dear Bob,

I have enclosed for your perusal our most recent publication of the Moseley Regional Bank Stock Monthly. For the first time, we have included the New Hampshire Savings Bank and as you can see your numbers compare rather favorably with the rest of the group, particularly your capital ratio.

It would be especially helpful to us in our work if you could provide us with some earnings projection for 1983 to assist in the computation of our data base.

As you can see, yours is the only company in this group that does not currently pay a dividend. Since this is a shortcoming, it does make marketing efforts on your behalf somewhat more difficult. If NHSBC were to initiate even a nominal dividend, the marketing potential for the stock would be opened up to a myriad of new investors.

For instance, most trust department and money managers across the country require that before any company be put on their approved list it must pay some sort of cash dividend, however nominal. Additionally, many of the state and municipal retirement systems across the United States function under a prudent-man rule which also requires a cash dividend from stock investments.

Such investors—in the long run—are the advantageous ones for us to seek out. Two illustrations that immediately come to mind are, first, when Texas Instruments declared a nominal dividend of 20¢ per year. It was immediately placed on most trust department buy lists and the price of the stock more than doubled in the ensuing year.

Closer to home, when Compugraphic Corp. initiated a small dividend, they also were placed on the recommended list of a number of trust departments and the price of the stock more than tripled in the next 12 months. Granted, a cash dividend is not the only determinant in evaluating the market price of a stock, but certainly reaching out to new investors should help your market performance over the long run.

Should your strategy be one whereby you might be considering an aggressive acquisition policy both intra and interstate, certainly a higher market evaluation for NHSBC's stock would be beneficial in this endeavor.

Another sound point regarding a quarterly dividend: it provides you with the opportunity to communicate with shareholders on a regular basis and sometimes this type of communication inspires your shareholders to consider extending their investment in your company. I would suggest a February, May, August and November 15th payment date in conjunction with your quarterly releases.

Further, should you initiate a cash dividend, I would strongly recommend a dividend reinvestment program which in all probability would be favorably received by your share-holders. This would provide a small means of acquiring new capital for your company.

To conclude, we are delighted that we can include your company on our Monthly, and feel that it will be useful to NHSBC and its shareholders. I do hope that we might have a chat soon, since there are a number of other comments I should like to offer to help explain further why your consideration of a cash dividend can be a most effective and beneficial move for NHSBC, its shareholders, and the marketability of the stock. And when you are able to decide to take such action, we will be delighted to let our followers know that you have declared a cash dividend which can only mean that the outlook for your company is a good one!

Sincerely,

James E. Moynihan, Jr.,
Senior Vice President—Investments
JEM/hh
encl.

Hop-In Food Stores, Incorporated

In early March 1977, Charles Merriman was attempting to set a price for the first public offering of stock by Hop-In Food Stores, Incorporated, a regional convenience-food store chain headquartered in Roanoke, Virginia. Mr. Merriman, who was vice president of corporate finance for Scott and Stringfellow, a small investment banking firm located in Richmond, Virginia, had agreed to underwrite 60,000 shares of Hop-In's common stock at a price bringing not less than $10 per share to the company. The underwriter's commission was to fall somewhere between 6 and 7 percent of the aggregate offering price, making $10.60 per share the minimum acceptable market price. Under this agreement, Scott and Stringfellow was required to purchase the entire issue from Hop-In, thereby assuming the risk that they would be unable to resell the issue to the public at something more than $10.60 per share. Beyond the $10 commitment, however, Scott and Stringfellow had no legal liability and was given leeway to price the issue at whatever level seemed appropriate.

Company Background

Hop-In Food Stores, incorporated on June 23, 1966, by John M. Hudgins, Jr., started in Roanoke as a single store selling a broad line of foodstuff and convenience items. Since 1966 sales had grown at a 55-percent annual rate, and by the end of 1976, the company operated 84 stores in two states. Table 1 shows the increase in the number of stores over the 5 fiscal years and 6 months ended December 31, 1976.

Hop-In had grown primarily through the acquisition of established stores rather than by internal expansion; of the 84 stores operating at the end of 1977, 58 had been acquired. The company pursued this policy of growth by acquisition because experience had proven both the costs and risks of operating a new store to be greater than those of purchasing an established one. New store sites were selected on the basis of residence

TABLE 1 • Change in Number of Stores

Period	Stores Added during Period	Stores Closed during Period	Stores Operating at End of Period
Fiscal 1972	9	0	19
Fiscal 1973	4	1	22
Fiscal 1974	5	0	27
Fiscal 1975	10	1	36
Fiscal 1976	41	1	76
Six months ended December 31, 1976	10	2	84

Source: Preliminary *Prospectus*, March 1977.

density, the extent of street and highway access, and the proximity of competing stores.

Product Line and Competition

Hop-In stores emphasized the sale of traffic-building items such as beer, soft drinks, cigarettes, wine, bread, milk, and other dairy and bakery products. Only nationally advertised brands in the grocery field and better known local or regional brands of dairy and bakery products and meats were sold. Prices on staple foodstuff and convenience items were slightly higher than at conventional supermarkets but competitive with other convenience food stores. Because of the nature of the product line, advertising was kept to a minimum except in connection with new store openings.

Gasoline was sold at 68 of Hop-In's 84 store locations. Pumping and storage facilities at 19 of the stores offering gasoline were owned by Hop-In. Facilities at the remaining 49 stores were owned by suppliers under arrangements whereby Hop-In received a rental commission from the supplier based on the amount of gasoline sold. Traditionally, gasoline prices at these stores had been lower than those charged by stations selling nationally branded gasoline and competitive with those charged by independent stations in the area. However, this pricing policy had been possible only to the extent permitted by the company's and supplier's costs of gasoline.

In the past several years, sales of grocery and other staple items had declined as a percentage of sales primarily because of increased gasoline sales. Also, the company had made an effort to emphasize the sale of faster moving and more profitable items. Table 2 shows the breakdown of sales by product category.

Another factor contributing to the decline in sales of grocery and other staple items was the increasing competition within the retail food industry. Hop-In's stores competed with local and national chain groceries, supermarkets, drugstores, and similar retail outlets, most of which had

TABLE 2 • Convenience Stores' Sales by
Product Category (fiscal year ended June 30)

	1973	1976
Beer and wine	26.2%	23.4%
Gasoline	1.9	18.3
Grocery	15.2	12.3
Soft drinks	11.5	8.7
Tobacco	11.3	8.3
Health, beauty, household	7.1	7.1
Milk and dairy	11.0	7.1
Chips and snacks	4.6	3.6
Sandwiches and salads	3.9	3.8
Publications	1.5	3.8
Bakery	5.1	3.4
Miscellaneous	0.7	0.2
Total	100.0%	100.0%

Source: Preliminary *Prospectus*, March 1977.

extended operating hours and expanded product lines in response to competition provided by convenience stores. Hop-In's most direct competition, however, came from other convenience-food stores. The three major convenience-food store chains with which Hop-In competed in Virginia and North Carolina were Seven-Eleven, Munford, and L'il General. Several of these competitors, because of their greater size, had developed competitive advantages that included greater financial resources, economies of scale in purchasing, and national advertising. Exhibit 1 presents financial data on two of these competitors. Exhibit 2 provides information on six publicly held convenience-food store companies.

Financial History

Mr. Hudgins operated the company as a closed corporation until November 1968 when a 60,000-share intrastate offering of common stock was made. By 1976, primarily as a result of a two-for-one split in 1972, the number of shares outstanding had grown to 124,657, of which 34 percent was owned by insiders and 13 percent was owned by the company's employee stock-ownership plan (ESOP); the remaining shares were held by outsiders. No single individual owned more than 10 percent of the outstanding shares. Hop-In stock was traded informally and only within the state of Virginia. In March 1977, it was selling at $9.50 per share.

Since the 1968 offering, Hop-In had been operating as much like a public company as possible. Financial statements had been prepared according to generally accepted accounting principles, and annual reports had been published each fiscal year. Exhibit 3 presents the statement of earnings for the fiscal years from 1972 to 1976 and the 6 months ended December 31, 1975 and 1976. Exhibit 4 shows Hop-In's financial position.

Prior to fiscal year 1976, Hop-In's cash flow from operations had provided enough working capital to support operations, while capital expenditures were supported by long-term borrowings or small injections of equity capital. This balance was threatened by the increasing number of acquisitions. During the 18 months ended December 31, 1976, the company purchased the assets (inventory and equipment) of 45 convenience-food stores for a total of $1,396,945. Although the majority of funds required for these acquisitions was provided by internal sources, an additional $539,000 was short-term debt. As of December 31, 1976, $400,000 of this balance outstanding was payable to a bank under a line of credit totaling $550,000. Because Mr. Hudgins was expecting additional working-capital needs in anticipation of the seasonal increase in sales generally experienced during the late spring and summer months, he wanted to reduce the level of short-term debt to provide some debt capacity should the need for additional funds arise.

Going Public

For some time, Mr. Hudgins had been contemplating the move to issue stock—to go public. Up until 1976, however, Hop-In's need for funds had not exceeded internal sources to the extent that the need could not be covered by small stock purchases by management. The growth that Hop-In had experienced in 1975 and 1976 suggested, however, that a new financing strategy was needed.

In addition to the need for external funds to finance growth, a number of considerations made going public attractive to Mr. Hudgins: (1) publicly traded stock would be a more effective tool for use in acquisitions; (2) it would establish a trading market for managers, directors, and employees who participated in the company's ESOP; (3) it would simplify estate settlement in the case of death of a major stockholder; and (4) it would strengthen the company's bargaining power with its lenders.

Having balanced these advantages of a public offering against the possible disadvantages, which included initial high costs and the risk of a poor aftermarket, Mr. Hudgins decided that the time to go public had come. Subsequently, contact was made with Mr. Merriman, and the offering was scheduled for late March 1977.

Current Situation

The decision facing Mr. Merriman was a delicate one; risks were associated with either an underpricing or an overpricing of the equity issue. If the new stock were overpriced, there was a chance that a market would not develop, leaving the securities "on the banker's shelf." Such a delay in the sale of stock would not only tie up Scott and Stringfellow's capital, but it would also increase the firm's exposure to potential downturns in the market, which might lower the stock's value further and force sale at reduced prices or even at a loss. If this occurred, goodwill among the selling group and investors who had purchased the stock at issue price would be damaged, which would weaken Scott and Stringfellow's distribution network for future new issues. An underpriced issue, on the other hand, might be equally damaging. Scott and Stringfellow would draw criticism for not obtaining maximum value for Hop-In, which could lead to loss of underwriting business, not only with Hop-In, but with other corporate clients.

Before preparing the offer price, Mr. Merriman reviewed the economic and equity-market conditions of March 1977. In early 1977, the general feeling about the nation's economy was one of optimism. A newly elected president had just taken office, and all indicators pointed toward recovery from the lull that followed the 1975 recession. Although the consumer price index for January rose by a seasonally adjusted annual rate of 9.6 percent, the largest increase in 18 months, most forecasters predicted an inflation rate of no more than 6 percent, and interest and bond coupon rates were falling. It was expected that the declining interest rates would draw investors' funds away from the fixed-income securities market and into the equity securities market, creating a favorable equity-market climate. Stock market observers, cautiously optimistic about 1977, were expecting market price growth of 10 to 20 percent followed by a leveling off or a partial reversal of growth by the end of the year.

As a supplement to the comparative market and financial statistics shown in Exhibits 1 and 2, Mr. Merriman collected the following data: operating ratios on the retail grocery industry shown in Exhibit 5, a listing of recent equity issues and their respective prices shown in Exhibit 6, and some stock price indexes shown in Exhibit 7. Current bond yields and interest rates are reported in Exhibit 8.

Additional considerations that concerned Mr. Merriman were (1) prospective problems with the Securities and Exchange Commission and shareholders because Hop-In's auditors were not one of the big eight firms; (2) the limited extent to which the new shares could be distributed geographically; and (3) Hop-In's lack of an established dividend policy. Finally, one other factor interested Mr. Merriman as he sought a pricing benchmark. He had heard that major petroleum companies were buying companies with gasoline sales facilities similar to Hop-In for roughly book value.

Hop-In Food Stores, Incorporated

EXHIBIT 1 • Comparative Financial Data: Industry Leaders,
         Years Ended December 31 (dollars in millions, except per-share data)

	Net Sales	Net Working Capital	Current Ratio	Operating Income	Net Income before Taxes	Net Income	Earnings/ Share	Dividends/ Share	Price Range (calendar years)	Book Value/ Share[a]
Southland Corporation (Seven-Eleven)										
1966	$ 449.80	$ 41.20	2.3×	$ 15.10	$10.91	$5.63	$0.50	$0.10	$ 8⅝–6⅝	$ 2.69
1967	527.30	41.10	2.0	21.53	14.26	7.21	0.62	0.11	12⅝–5¾	3.26
1968	621.10	56.60	2.1	29.03	19.60	9.35	0.73	0.12	22⅜–11½	5.48
1969	840.80	76.70	2.2	39.24	24.82	12.10	0.81	0.12	22–15½	6.45
1970	980.90	79.90	2.1	45.28	30.09	14.90	0.96	0.12	18¼–13	7.28
1971	1,079.80	83.60	2.1	51.32	34.56	17.30	1.09	0.15	29⅛–14½	8.39
1972	1,226.10	107.90	2.1	59.12	39.34	20.37	1.14	0.19	34½–22½	10.52
1973	1,393.60	96.00	2.0	68.05	44.15	23.33	1.26	0.22	27⅞–11	11.57
1974	1,609.30	89.80	1.8	87.03	57.84	29.74	1.60	0.31	19½–11¾	12.78
1975	1,789.70	94.70	1.8	103.63	68.18	34.32	1.80	0.37	26⅞–14⅜	14.21
Munford, Inc.										
1966	75.46	—	—	5.34	2.62	1.55	0.67	0.60	15½–8⅛	13.36
1967	90.99	8.00	1.9	6.37	3.95	2.17	0.87	0.60	25¼–9⅜	14.02
1968	99.31	12.44	2.3	6.41	3.81	2.06	0.80	0.51	35½–14⅜	4.84
1969	116.41	9.83	1.9	7.40	3.91	2.03	0.78	0.24	31⅜–11⅝	6.05
1970	127.99	11.38	1.9	7.62	4.01	1.97	0.82	0.24	14⅞–5½	6.44
1971	140.81	17.32	2.5	8.44	8.78	2.69	1.03	0.24	19¼–8⅝	6.81
1972	155.22	19.59	2.5	8.91	5.56	3.15	1.20	0.24	19⅞–13	8.78
1973	198.52	22.43	2.4	10.11	6.31	3.57	1.36	0.28	14⅛–5	10.15
1974	227.26	20.33	2.1	11.17	7.00	3.89	1.48	0.32	8½–4	11.52
1975	273.16	24.64	1.8	12.38	7.64	4.29	1.63	0.36	8¾–4¼	13.00

Source: *Standard and Poor's Industry Survey.*

[a]Two-for-one stock split in 1966.

Hop-In Food Stores, Incorporated
EXHIBIT 2 • Comparative Financial Data on Selected Companies

	Hop-In	Southland	Munford	Dillon	Sunshine Junior	National Convenience Stores	Circle K
Latest complete fiscal year	6/30/76	12/31/75	1/1/76	7/3/76	12/31/75	6/30/76	4/30/76
Sales (thousands)	$14,078	$1,789,754	$273,161	$1,148,399	$58,050	$212,606	$302,600
Net income (thousands)	$281	$34,319	$4,287	$22,433	$1,300	$2,652	$6,910
Net income/sales	1.99%	1.92%	1.56%	1.9%	2.2%	1.25%	2.3%
Net income/net worth	22.38%	12.63%	11.63%	23.73%	14.94%	15.41%	18.03%
Earnings per share (primary)							
1971	N.Ap.	$1.09	$1.03	$0.78	$0.59	N.Av.	$0.84
1972	$0.55	1.14	1.20	0.95	0.48	$0.82	0.94
1973	1.11	1.26	1.36	1.28	0.62	0.90	0.99
1974	1.61	1.60	1.48	1.53	1.04	1.24	0.99
1975	1.73	1.80	1.63	1.97	0.95	0.67	1.07
1976	2.26	2.10	1.30	2.50	0.82	1.37	1.43
Market price, 10/29/76	N.Ap.	$26⅛	$9⅜	$31⅝	$6	$9¾	$7½
Price/earnings ratio, 10/29/76	N.Ap.	14.5X	6X	13X	6X	7X	5X
Price/earnings range							
1972	N.Ap.	20–30	11–17	18–25	17–32	17–28	27–43
1973	N.Ap.	9–22	4–10	12–18	5–18	4–16	6–37
1974	N.Ap.	7–12	3–6	10–14	3–7	3–7	5–10
1975	N.Ap.	6–15X	3–5X	8–17X	4–11X	4–9X	5–8X

continued

EXHIBIT 2 • *continued*

Current cash dividend rate	N.Ap.	$0.37	$0.35	$0.96	$0.20	0	$0.51
Current cash yield	N.Ap.	1.4%	3.7%	2.3%	3.3%	0	6.8%
Where traded	N.Ap.	NYSE	NYSE	NYSE	AMEX	OTC	AMEX
Number of shares outstanding, 10/29/76	124,657	18,061,047	2,107,455	8,601,539	1,237,880	1,583,766	4,814,938
Book value/share	$10.06	$14.21	$13.00	$9.30	$7.03	$10.87	$7.95
Book value/market value	N.Ap.	54%	138%	30%	117%	111%	106%
Beta	N.Ap.	1.15	1.10	0.65	N.Av.	N.Av.	N.Av.
Capitalization (thousands)							
Short-term debt[a]	$ 551	$ 4,627	$ 2,090	$ 3,995	0	$ 363	$ 170
Long-term debt	577	119,911	26,448	13,769	0	6,085	13,846
Shareholders' equity	1,254	271,821	36,847	94,519	8,700	17,210	38,316
Total capital	$ 2,382	$ 396,359	$ 65,385	$ 112,283	$ 8,700	$ 23,658	$ 52,332
Percentage short-term debt	23%	1%	3%	4%	0	2%	1%
Percentage long-term debt	24	30	40	12	0	26	26
Percentage equity	53%	69%	57%	84%	100%	72%	73%

N.Ap. = not applicable.

N.Av. = not available.

[a]Includes bank notes due within 12 months and current maturities of long-term debt.

Sources: Company annual reports; company *10–K Reports*; *Value Line*; and *Standard & Poor's Stock Report*.

EXHIBIT 2 • *continued*

SOUTHLAND CORPORATION

The Southland Corporation, incorporated in Texas in 1961 as the successor to an ice business organized in 1927, was the country's largest operator and franchiser of convenience stores and a major processor and distributor of dairy products. On December 31, 1975, the company's operations included 5,579 convenience stores, 124 Gristede's and Charles & Co. food stores and sandwich shops, 20 Barricini and Loft's candy shops, dairy distribution under 12 regional brand names, and chemical, ice, truck-leasing, and food-processing operations in a total of 41 states, the District of Columbia, and four provinces of Canada.

MUNFORD, INC

Munford, Inc., an Atlanta-based company operating in 26 states, was primarily engaged in the retail marketing of goods through convenience-food stores, import stores, and building material stores. On January 1, 1976, the company's operations included 1,304 convenience-food stores, 42 import stores specializing in imported gift and homefurnishing items; 14 building-material stores; 19 refrigerated warehouses, and 25 ice facilities. The company had also franchised 33 fast-food operations and 38 convenience-food stores.

DILLON COMPANIES

Dillon Companies, primarily engaged in retail food distribution, operated 185 supermarkets and 186 convenience stores serving all or part of 11 states under a number of different trade names. This Kansas-based company also operated several junior department stores and a real estate company.

SUNSHINE-JR. STORES, INC.

Sunshine-Jr. Stores, Inc., was engaged in the business of operating food supermarkets and convenience-food stores in Florida, Alabama, Georgia, and Mississippi. All stores were supplied by a company-owned 112,200-square-foot distribution center in Panama City, Florida. The company also operated a bakery that supplied the supermarkets and a commissary that prepared prepackaged salads and sandwich items for the Florida stores. The company initially was in the supermarket business exclusively, but since 1961, convenience-food stores had become an increasing factor in company operations. On December 31, 1975, the company operated 7 supermarkets and 236 convenience-food stores.

NATIONAL CONVENIENCE STORES, INC.

National Convenience Stores, Inc., and its consolidated subsidiaries operated convenience-food stores under the names STOP N GO and SHOP N GO. As of June 30, 1976, 743 stores were operating in the states of Arizona, California, Colorado, Florida, Georgia, Kansas, Louisiana, Mississippi, Missouri, Nevada, Oklahoma, Tennessee, and Texas. Of this number, 729 were operated by the company directly and 14 were operated by its franchisees.

CIRCLE K FOOD STORES, INC.

Circle K Corporation, incorporated in Texas in 1951, operated 1,049 convenience-food stores in the West and Southwest. In addition to selling food and food-related items, 540 of the stores had self-service gasoline pumps.

Source: Company *10–K Reports.*

Hop-In Food Stores, Incorporated

EXHIBIT 3 • Hop-In Statement of Earnings, 1972–1976

	Year Ended June 30					Six Months Ended December 31 (Unaudited)	
	1972	*1973*	*1974*	*1975*	*1976*	*1975*	*1976*
Revenue							
Net grocery sales	$2,359,352	$4,346,235	$6,565,500	$8,565,668	$11,466,085	$5,048,806	$9,163,641
Net gasoline sales		28,737	321,596	1,445,826	2,477,427	1,149,062	1,532,188
Gasoline commissions	18,925	56,570	68,213	87,389	95,846	41,229	82,561
Net equipment sales			210,170	231,905	17,095	9,714	12,133
Money/order commissions	3,080	7,592	10,455	11,260	21,431	8,270	16,120
Total revenue	2,381,357	4,439,134	7,175,934	10,342,048	14,077,884	6,257,081	10,806,643
Costs and expenses							
Cost of sales							
Grocery	(1,742,885)	(3,205,151)	(4,752,908)	(5,936,491)	(7,685,318)	(3,429,247)	(6,148,906)
Gasoline		(25,714)	(278,955)	(1,298,581)	(2,317,334)	(1,072,408)	(1,457,866)
Equipment			(200,668)	(204,186)	(14,082)	(9,057)	(11,615)
Total cost of sales	(1,742,885)	(3,230,865)	(5,232,531)	(7,439,258)	(10,016,734)	(4,510,712)	(7,618,387)
Operating, general, and administrative	(550,724)	(1,031,452)	(1,611,855)	(2,497,104)	(3,364,258)	(1,426,799)	(2,721,043)
Depreciation	(34,667)	(60,565)	(105,732)	(148,991)	(202,761)	(80,560)	(140,201)
Total costs and expenses	(2,328,276)	(4,322,882)	(6,950,118)	(10,085,353)	(13,583,753)	(6,018,071)	(10,479,631)
Operating profit	53,081	116,252	225,816	256,695	494,131	239,010	327,012
Other expense (income)							
Interest expense	(17,435)	(32,630)	(50,252)	(78,785)	(86,433)	(32,256)	(44,347)
Other	(3,713)	(5,811)	(12,096)	(24,964)	(45,864)	(16,280)	(41,246)
Total other	(13,722)	(26,819)	(38,156)	(53,821)	(40,569)	(15,976)	(3,101)
Earnings before income taxes and extraordinary credit	39,359	89,433	187,660	202,874	453,562	223,034	323,911
Federal and state income taxes							
Current	(13,951)	(12,650)	(48,544)	(111,270)	(64,000)	(33,705)	(110,000)
Deferred	0	(5,133)	(19,581)	(44,380)	(109,000)	(57,389)	(22,318)
Total taxes	(13,951)	(17,783)	(68,125)	(66,890)	(173,000)	(91,094)	(132,318)

continued

EXHIBIT 3 • *continued*

		Year Ended June 30				Six Months Ended December 31 (Unaudited)	
	1972	*1973*	*1974*	*1975*	*1976*	*1975*	*1976*
Earnings before extraordinary credit	25,408	71,650	119,535	135,984	280,562	131,940	191,593
Extraordinary credit	11,900	6,682	0	0	0	0	0
Net earnings	$ 37,308	$ 78,332	$ 119,535	$ 135,984	$ 280,562	$ 131,940	$ 191,593
Earnings per share							
Primary							
Earnings before extraordinary credit	$0.37	$1.01	$1.61	$1.73	$2.26	$1.06	$1.54
Extraordinary credit	0.18	0.10	0	0	0	0	0
Net earnings	$0.55	$1.11	$1.61	$1.73	$2.26	$1.06	$1.54
Fully diluted							
Earnings before extraordinary credit	$0.37	$0.80	$1.19	$1.35	$1.55	$0.73	$1.06
Extraordinary credit	0.18	0.07	0	0	0	0	0
Net earnings	$0.55	$0.87	$1.19	$1.35	$1.55	$0.73	$1.06

Source: Preliminary *Prospectus,* March 1977.

Hop-In Food Stores, Incorporated
EXHIBIT 4 • **Hop-In Balance Sheet**

	June 30, 1976	December 31, 1976 (Unaudited)
Assets		
Current assets		
Cash	$209,930	$106,154
Accounts receivable		
Trade	51,942	71,279
Employees and other	11,816	19,034
Note receivable	18,516	19,269
Inventories	1,364,465	1,495,518
Prepaid expenses	109,511	152,784
Total current assets	1,766,180	1,864,038

EXHIBIT 4 • *continued*

	June 30, 1976	December 31, 1976 (Unaudited)
Property and equipment		
Equipment and fixtures	2,252,513	2,531,446
Office furniture and fixtures	66,164	69,090
Leasehold improvements	325,485	330,008
Total property, plant, and equipment	2,644,162	2,930,544
Less accumulated depreciation and amortization	(584,366)	(724,567)
Net property and equipment	2,059,796	2,205,977
Other assets		
Note receivable	77,766	67,939
Miscellaneous	37,894	49,764
Total other assets	115,660	117,703
Total assets	$3,941,636	$4,187,718
Liabilities and Stockholders' Equity		
Current liabilities		
Notes payable—unsecured		
Banks	$500,000	$400,000
Others	39,000	25,000
Current installments of long-term debt	141,010	125,977
Accounts payable	1,244,672	1,379,152
Accrued expenses		
Salaries and bonuses	188,220	111,529
Other	38,451	121,613
Federal and state income taxes	3,166	81,984
Total current liabilities	2,154,519	2,245,255
Long-term debt—less current maturities	635,590	577,027
Deferred income taxes	89,335	111,653
Stockholders' equity		
Common stock: $2.50 par value per share: Authorized 300,000 shares; issued and outstanding 124,657 shares	311,642	311,642
Additional paid-in capital	154,220	154,220
Retained earnings	596,330	787,923
Total stockholders' equity	1,062,192	1,253,785
Total liabilities and stockholders' equity	$3,941,636	$4,187,720

Source: Preliminary *Prospectus,* March 1977.

Hop-In Food Stores, Incorporated
EXHIBIT 5 • Retail Grocery Industry Comparative Financial Data

	Under $250M[a]	Between $250M and $1MM	Between $1MM and $10MM	Between $10MM and $50MM	All Sizes
		132 Statements Ended on or about June 30, 1975			
		152 Statements Ended on or about December 31, 1975			
Number of Statements	67	89	90	38	284
Assets (percentages)					
Cash	10.6%	11.6%	8.9%	8.5%	8.7%
Marketable securities	1.3	0.8	0.9	0.4	0.5
Receivables, net	6.0	5.3	5.0	4.8	4.9
Inventory, net	36.3	34.5	36.3	39.5	38.6
All other current	1.2	2.8	1.9	1.9	1.9
Total current	55.4	54.9	53.1	55.1	54.7
Fixed assets, net	33.6	33.0	37.7	38.6	38.1
All other noncurrent	11.1	12.0	9.2	6.3	7.2
Total assets	100.0%	100.0%	100.0%	100.0%	100.0%
Liabilities and Net Worth (percentages)					
Due to banks—short-term	2.3%	5.6%	3.2%	1.6%	2.1%
Due to trade	20.2	20.0	28.6	26.5	26.6
Income taxes	1.5	1.7	2.3	1.5	1.7
Current maturities long-term debt	4.9	5.1	3.6	2.2	2.7
All other current	7.3	10.5	8.2	8.4	8.4
Total current debt	36.1	42.9	45.9	40.2	41.5
Noncurrent debt, unsubordinated	21.7	18.9	19.6	18.5	18.8
Total unsubordinated debt	57.8	61.8	65.5	58.8	60.3
Subordinated debt	1.1	1.3	1.5	0.3	0.6
Tangible net worth	41.1	36.9	33.0	40.9	39.1
Total liabilities and net worth	100.0%	100.0%	100.0%	100.0%	100.0%
Income Data (percentages)					
Net sales	100.0%	100.0%	100.0%	100.0%	100.0%
Cost of sales	80.0	81.2	80.7	79.2	79.6
Gross profit	20.0	18.8	19.3	20.8	20.4
All other expense, net	18.0	17.2	18.0	19.1	18.8
Profit before taxes	2.0×	1.6×	1.3×	1.7×	1.6×
Ratios[b]					
Quick	0.8×	0.7×	0.5×	0.5×	0.6×
	0.3	0.4	0.3	0.3	0.3
	0.1	0.2	0.2	0.3	0.2

EXHIBIT 5 · *continued*

	Under $250M[a]	*Between $250M and $1MM*	*Between $1MM and $10MM*	*Between $10MM and $50MM*	*All Sizes*
	132 Statements Ended on or about June 30, 1975				
	152 Statements Ended on or about December 31, 1975				
Current	2.6	2.0	1.5	1.8	1.8
	1.4	1.4	1.1	1.4	1.3
	1.1	0.9	0.9	1.1	1.0
Fixed/worth	0.4	0.5	0.8	0.6	0.6
	0.8	0.9	1.1	0.8	1.0
	1.8	1.7	1.9	1.4	1.8
Debt/worth	0.5	0.8	1.3	0.9	0.9
	1.4	1.8	2.1	1.7	1.7
	2.9	3.3	3.9	2.1	3.2
Unsubordinated debt/capital funds	0.5	0.8	1.2	0.8	0.8
	1.3	1.5	2.0	1.6	1.7
	2.9×	3.2×	3.5×	2.1×	3.1×
Sales/receivables[c]	0　INF	0　999.8%	1　578.8%	1　326.4%	0　999.8%
	1　412.0	1　449.8	1　309.6	2　178.2	1　303.6
	3　106.9	3　115.1	3　142.5	3　106.7	3　110.5
Cost of sales/inventory[d]	16　22.8	15　23.6	16　21.9	21　17.6	16　22.0
	23　15.8	22　16.3	24　14.8	29　12.4	23　15.7
	33　10.9	29　12.4	34　10.6	34　10.5	33　10.9
Sales/working capital	56.4	45.3	78.7	80.8	59.4
	17.9	20.0	26.8	30.9	24.4
	2.0	(182.0)	(170.2)	22.2	(999.8)
Sales/worth	24.8	28.2	35.1	22.9	27.1
	11.4	16.4	19.1	15.1	16.2
	7.6	9.2	11.6	10.9	9.4
Percentage profit before taxes/worth	67.0	46.8	47.5	37.0	46.2
	31.6	30.3	27.4	25.0	28.5
	13.6	15.6	13.3	17.6	14.0
Percentage profit before taxes/total assets	24.9	19.0	16.2	15.1	18.7
	15.1	9.6	8.9	10.7	10.1
	4.6%	3.8%	4.0%	6.0%	4.3%
Net Sales	$61,747M	$339,002M	$1,843,562M	$5,701,526M	$7,945,837M
Total Assets	9,161M	47,152M	267,002M	923,519M	1,246,834M

[a]Asset size M = thousands of dollars; MM = millions of dollars.

[b]Ratios are given for upper quartile, median, and lower quartile.

[c]Boldfaced number is receivables turnover in days.

[d]Boldfaced number is inventory turnover in days.

Source: *1976 Annual Statement Studies*, Robert Morris Associates.

Hop-In Food Stores, Incorporated
EXHIBIT 6 • Recent Common Equity Issues

Offering Date	Company	Offer Price	Recent Bid
1977			
1/6	Madison Gas & Electric Co.	16⅜	16⅛
1/6	Tetra Tec, Inc.	8	8¼
1/11	Middle South Utilities, Inc.	16¾	16¾
1/11	Wacoal Corp.	22⅝	22⅜
1/12	Iowa Public Service Co.	21½	21⅝
1/13	Surgicot, Inc.	7⅛	6¾
1/18	Freemont General Corp.	14½	14⅛
1/19	Intermountain Gas Co.	16¾	17½
1/25	Omega Optical Co.	10	8¾
1/25	Grow Chemical Corp.	10¼	10⅜
1/27	Brougham Industries, Inc.	7½	7¾
1/27	Makita Electric Works, Ltd.	33⅞	33⅝
2/1	Continuous Curve Contact Lenses, Inc.	10	10¾
2/8	Kennametal, Inc.	25¼	24⅝
2/9	New York State Electric and Gas Corp.	29½	29⅛
2/9	St. Jude Medical, Inc.	3½	6½

Source: *Investment Dealer's Digest.*

Hop-In Food Stores, Incorporated
EXHIBIT 7 • Stock Price Indexes

	OTC NBQ 35 Stock Industrials[a]	*OTC NASDAQ Composite*[b]	*S&P 500 Composite*	*Dow Jones 30 Industrials*
1976[c]				
High	461.02(2/26)	92.52(7/15)	107.83(9/21)	1,014.79(9/21)
Low	374.31(11/11)	78.06(1/2)	90.90(1/2)	858.71(1/2)
November 11	374.31	88.15	99.64	931.43
18	383.75	89.81	101.89	950.13
24	386.41	90.69	102.41	950.96
December 2	394.51	91.84	102.12	946.64
9	412.28	94.10	104.51	970.74
16	411.01	94.93	104.80	981.30
23	409.68	95.22	104.84	985.62
29	417.03	96.29	106.34	994.93
1977				
January 6	418.58	97.20	105.02	979.89
13	408.90	96.84	104.20	976.15
20	414.48	97.08	102.97	959.03
27	420.79	96.04	101.79	954.54
February 3	424.28	96.33	101.85	947.14
10	420.30	96.29	100.82	937.92
17	419.57	96.56	100.92	943.73
24	411.23	94.84	99.60	932.60
March 3	402.47	95.53	100.88	948.64

[a]National Quotation Bureau.
[b]National Association of Security Dealers Automated Quotations.
[c]Numbers in brackets indicate date low or high achieved.
Source: *Investment Dealer's Digest.*

Hop-In Food Stores, Incorporated
EXHIBIT 8 • Bond Yields and Interest Rate, March 1977

3-month Treasury	4.61%
3–5 year Treasury	6.73
Aaa corporate	8.10
Baa corporate	9.12%

Source: *1978 Economic Report to the President.*

Kelly Services, Inc.

As part of his rotation training, William Murry, a new analyst with Shack, Stripes, & Roam Securities (SS&R), had been assigned a portfolio of service companies. Three of the companies provided temporary help, and of the three, he found one, Kelly Services, Inc., to be particularly interesting. Kelly's growth and profitability record, and lack of debt, were what caught Mr. Murry's attention.

In his MBA program, Mr. Murry had been taught that debt was less expensive than equity, so he wondered whether a company that shied away from borrowing could be successful compared with its competitors. Could it be maximizing value for shareholders? Because interest rates had declined considerably over the previous couple of years (as shown in Exhibit 1), reducing the cost of debt even further than previously, Mr. Murry wondered how Kelly might have been affected if the company had taken on some debt either in 1985 or early in 1986. Had Kelly's share price been penalized because the company had not taken sufficient advantage of debt financing?

In contrast to Mr. Murry's MBA teachings, many of his colleagues at SS&R believed that Kelly had been a superior performer because it had no debt, and that it needed no debt now.

The Industry

Temporary employed in the United States is booming. According to the Bureau of Labor Statistics, employment growth in the temporary help services industry has averaged 11 percent a year over the last 13 years, compared with a 2.1 percent growth rate for non-agricultural jobs throughout the economy.[1]

---

[1] The quote and statistics in this section are from Cherlyn S. Granrose and Eileen Appelbaum, "The Efficiency of Temporary Help and Part-Time Employment," *Personnel Administrator,* January 1986, 71.

The increasing use of temporary help could be attributed to at least three factors. First, such help was used as an employment buffer; it would decline early in a recession, but would rebound rapidly in an economic recovery. In 1983, the first year of recovery from a recession, the use of temporary help had increased by 17.5 percent.

Second, companies had begun to hire temporary workers under long-term contracts. According to labor economist Audrey Freedman,

> "What the companies are doing is organizing so they don't have to pay for vacation, holidays, health benefits or pensions. In addition, they don't have to allocate money for training and for promotion." The savings can be large, and some firms are now building temporary work into their employment strategies.[2]

Third, temporary workers had expanded beyond secretaries and clerical workers to include engineers, accountants, nurses, and even lawyers and doctors costing up to $150 per hour. Ms. Freedman said,

> "In the make-or-buy decision, a lot of companies are deciding to buy, rather than make, something they need." Renting a professional instead of hiring one fits in with this trend, she says. The new temps choose temporary work to get money and experience at the beginning of a career, a lighter work load at the end, or a more relaxed lifestyle along the way.[3]

By 1982, 46 percent of temporary employment and 57 percent of receipts of temporary-help services firms were earned at non-office jobs.

A 1985 survey indicated that, of temporary help hired for office jobs, 58 percent were used in clerical positions and 25 percent were used for secretarial duties; the remaining 17 percent were used for such tasks as word and data processing and accounting functions. About half were hired to alleviate work overloads, and one-third were hired to cover for absent employees.

The Company

Kelly Services, Inc., was founded in 1946 in Detroit, Michigan, and had remained under family management, with William R. Kelly as chief executive officer. The company emphasized clerical and secretarial services but

---

[2] Ibid., 72.

[3] "These 'Temps' Don't Just Answer the Phone," *Business Week*, June 2, 1986, 74.

also provided some marketing, light industrial, technical, and nursing and home health-care temporary-help services through over 650 offices in the United States, Canada, the United Kingdom, and France. Kelly opened 64 new offices in 1985 and 47 in 1984, but most of the company's growth had come from increased business from existing markets and customers.

As shown in Exhibit 2, Kelly's sales and profits had more than quintupled between 1976 and 1985 and had more than doubled since 1982. Kelly's sales had grown more rapidly than its assets and equity base and had done so with no long-term debt.

Wages and salaries (cost of goods sold) amounted to about 74 percent of Kelly's total revenues, and accounts receivable from businesses constituted about 55 percent of total assets. On the other side of the balance sheet, wages, payroll taxes, and insurance constituted 71 percent of total liabilities. In 1985 Kelly had $17.6 million in common stock and $11.5 million of treasury stock; retained earnings had increased from $102.1 million in 1984 to $123.0 million in 1985.

Kelly had split its stock ten times since 1962, when it first issued shares to the public. In June 1984, to improve the stock's marketability, each common share was split and reclassified as 1½ shares of nonvoting Class A and one-half share of voting Class B common stock. A five-for-four stock split took place in August 1985. Insiders controlled 60 percent of the Class A and 76 percent of the Class B shares. In 1985 dividends averaged 54 cents per share, representing the 14th consecutive and 23d overall annual increase in dividends since 1962. Exhibit 3 provides stock price data for Kelly Services between 1980 and 1985.

The Competition

Mr. Murry had similar information in his portfolio on two of Kelly Services' competitors, Volt Information Sciences, Inc., and Olsten Corporation. Olsten was the more successful of the two competitors. (Manpower, Inc., better known than Volt or Olsten, had been sold recently, and public data were no longer available for it.)

Olsten Corporation was the third largest temporary-help company in North America, with 119,000 personnel available through 322 offices in 39 states and Canada. About 31 percent of Olsten's offices were operated under franchise. The company had no long-term debt, and the Olsten family owned 40 percent of the stock.

Volt Information Sciences, Inc., earned about 60 percent of its revenues through its temporary-help operations and 32 percent through typesetting-equipment sales and service; the remaining 8 percent was earned through the installation of automatic directory-assistance systems and the sale of technical manuals. Volt employed 13,800 people, 70 percent of whom were temporary workers. The company had a long-term debt/equity ratio of 124 percent and a long-term debt/assets ratio of 42 percent. Insiders owned 32 percent of Volt stock.

Financial data for Volt, Olsten, and Kelly Services are compared in Exhibit 4.

Projections

Being curious about the effect that debt might have on Kelly Services, Mr. Murry created three pro forma financial statements based on the company's 1985 figures. He had worked out some rough figures for different capital structures (shown in Exhibit 5) by assuming that

1. the debt would be used to repurchase stock in January 1986 at $25 per share,
2. the interest rate on the long-term debt would be 12.5 percent,
3. the tax rate would be 50 percent, close to the average of the past 10 years, and
4. the payout ratio would be 28 percent.

From this analysis, he found earnings would decrease as leverage increased, but earnings per share would increase, with no negative impact on dividends per share, as shown below:

Proportion of Debt to Equity

	Actual	*30 Percent*	*50 Percent*	*70 Percent*
Net income (millions)	$32.6	$29.6	$27.9	$26.3
Earnings/share	2.01	2.03	2.06	2.10
Dividends/share	0.56	0.57	0.58	0.59

These results seemed in conflict to Mr. Murry. In addition, he was certain that whatever the shareholders perceived about the company would be reflected in its share price. The stock price was $25 per share at the beginning of 1986. What would it be if debt increased? Did these same results hold true for Olsten and Volt? Was his business-school lesson that leverage increased performance right or wrong? Did these data, or would further analysis, prove his professor's techniques correct?

Mr. Murry was determined to solve this enigma and show others at SS&R the exact source of the value of leverage—if he could determine whether increasing debt increased shareholder value.

Kelly Services, Inc.
EXHIBIT 1 • Interest Rates on Debt of Different Quality

Year/Month		Prime Rate	U.S. Treasury Bonds		Corporate Bonds			
			3-Year	10-Year	Aaa	Aa	A	Baa
1980		15.27%	11.55%	11.46%	11.94%	12.50%	12.89%	13.67%
1981		18.87	14.44	13.91	14.17	14.75	15.29	16.04
1982		14.86	12.92	13.00	13.79	14.41	15.43	16.11
1983		10.79	10.45	11.10	12.04	12.42	13.10	13.55
1984		12.04	11.89	12.44	12.71	13.31	13.74	14.19
1985	1	10.61	10.43	11.38	11.37	11.82	12.28	12.72
	2	10.50	10.55	11.51	12.13	12.49	12.80	13.23
	3	10.50	11.05	11.86	12.56	12.91	13.36	13.69
	4	10.50	10.49	11.43	12.23	12.69	13.14	13.51
	5	10.31	9.75	10.85	11.72	12.30	12.70	13.15
	6	9.78	9.05	10.16	10.94	11.46	11.98	12.40
	7	9.50	9.18	10.31	10.97	11.42	11.92	12.43
	8	9.50	9.31	10.33	11.05	11.47	12.00	12.50
	9	9.50	9.37	10.37	11.07	11.46	11.99	12.48
	10	9.50	9.25	10.24	11.02	11.45	11.94	12.36
	11	9.50	8.88	9.78	10.55	11.07	11.54	11.99
	12	9.50	8.40	9.26	10.16	10.63	11.19	11.58

Sources: *Federal Reserve Bulletin*, various issues; and *Economic Report of the President*, 1986.

Kelly Services, Inc.
EXHIBIT 2 • Financial Data (dollars in millions, except per-share data)

	1976	1977	1978	1979	1980	1981	1982	1983	1984	1985
Sales	$152.4	$202.6	$279.0	$369.3	$409.7	$462.6	$419.9	$524.4	$741.2	$876.4
Net income	5.7	7.3	12.6	15.0	15.2	18.2	12.0	17.5	26.7	32.6
Earnings/share	0.35	0.45	0.77	0.91	0.92	1.10	0.72	1.08	1.65	2.02
Dividends/share										
Common	0.09	0.10	0.14	0.19	0.26	0.30	0.36	0.38	N.Ap.	N.Ap.
Class A common	N.Av.	N.Av.	N.Av.	N.Av.	N.Av.	N.Av.	N.Av.	N.Av.	0.46	0.55
Class B common	N.Av.	N.Av.	N.Av.	N.Av.	N.Av.	N.Av.	N.Av.	N.Av.	0.37	0.45
Assets	$37.0	$44.5	$60.3	$75.1	$87.9	$104.2	$108.8	$124.2	$148.9	$178.6
Cash	—	—	—	9.8	22.5	37.9	47.7	35.7	39.5	48.1
Net working capital	22.0	20.1	27.5	38.0	48.3	60.9	67.0	71.5	86.0	102.4
Stockholders' equity	27.4	32.8	42.8	54.7	65.7	78.4	84.2	89.4	108.8	129.1
Average price/earnings ratio	5.5	6.9	6.8	6.1	8.6	10.6	15.1	15.0	10.9	12.8
Average dividend yield	4.5%	3.5%	3.2%	3.5%	3.4%	2.5%	3.3%	2.4%	2.5%	2.2%
Return on sales	3.7	3.6	4.5	4.1	3.7	3.9	2.9	3.3	3.6	3.7
Return on assets	15.4	16.4	20.9	20.0	17.3	17.5	11.0	14.1	17.9	18.3
Return on equity	20.8%	22.3%	29.4%	27.4%	23.1%	23.2%	14.3%	19.6%	24.5%	25.3%
Shares outstanding (000)[a]										
Common	16,266	16,303	16,365	16,489	16,563	16,553	16,539	16,174	16,192	16,147
Class A	N.Av.	N.Av.	N.Av.	N.Av.	N.Av.	N.Av.	N.Av.	N.Av.	13,875	13,946
Class B	N.Av.	N.Av.	N.Av.	N.Av.	N.Av.	N.Av.	N.Av.	N.Av.	2,317	2,201
Beta	N.Av.	N.Av.	N.Av.	N.Av.	N.Av.	N.Av.	N.Av.	N.Av.	0.75	0.75

N.Av. = not available.
N.Ap. = not applicable.
[a] Adjusted for stock splits and reclassification.

Kelly Services, Inc.
EXHIBIT 3 • Quarterly Stock Price Data[a]

Year/ Quarter		Standard & Poor's 500	Common		Class A		Class B	
			High	*Low*	*High*	*Low*	*High*	*Low*
1980	1	102.9	$8.625	$5.125				
	2	114.2	7.25	6.5				
	3	125.5	9.875	7.25				
	4	135.8	9.375	8.75				
1981	1	136.0	11.25	8.875				
	2	131.2	13.75	11.125				
	3	116.2	13.75	11.5				
	4	122.6	13.5	11.625				
1982	1	111.9	12.5	10.875				
	2	109.6	12.875	9.5				
	3	122.4	10.625	7.875				
	4	139.4	13.125	9.875				
1983	1	151.9	15	12.125				
	2	166.4	16.25	14				
	3	167.2	17.5	16.125				
	4	164.4	20	16				
1984	1	159.2	20	17.75				
	2	168.1	$18	$17.25				
	3	166.1			$20.5	$16.5	$20.125	$15.5
	4	165.0			21.25	16	20.5	13.25
1985	1	153.2			23.25	18	23	18.25
	2	166.1			28	22	30.125	23.125
	3	167.2			29.375	25.5	29.375	26.125
	4	180.7			$29	$24.875	$26.5	$24.75

[a]Kelly data adjusted for stock splits.

Kelly Services, Inc.

EXHIBIT 4 • Comparative Financial Statements,
1984–1985 (dollars in millions, except per-share data)

	Kelly (December 31)		Olsten (December 31)		Volt (October 31)	
	1984	1985	1984	1985	1984	1985
Sales	$741.2	$876.4	$218.8	$262.9	$391.7	$389.8
5-year growth	16.2%	17.6%	24.4%	25.0%	22.3%	18.6%
Net profit	$ 26.7	$ 32.6	$ 6.0	$ 7.3	$ 13.0	$ (6.0)
5-year growth	17.1%	21.2%	23.2%	31.0%	9.6%	C/C
Earnings/share	$ 1.65[a]	$ 2.02[a]	$ 0.74	$ 0.90	$ 1.77	$ (0.85)
5-year growth	17.1%	21.2%	17.5%	24.7%	4.4%	(5.5)%
Dividends/share	$ 0.46[a]	$ 0.56[a]	$ 0.12	$ 0.16	0	0
5-year growth	20.1%	16.0%	15.7%	22.4%	0	0
Average annual P/E	10.9×	12.8×	10.5×	15.9×	11.9×	N.Ap.
Dividend payout ratio	27.0%	27.0%	16.0%	17.8%	0	0
Cash	$ 39.5	$ 47.9	$ 15.6	$ 20.8	$ 37.2	$ 27.2
Total current assets	126.2	151.9	55.0	63.5	190.2	159.4
Total assets	148.9	178.6	59.8	71.8	361.0	309.0
Total current liabilities	40.2	49.5	23.6	29.4	115.0	73.9
Long-term debt	0.0	0.0	0.0	0.0	125.9	125.9
Long-term debt and capital leases	0.0	0.0	0.0	0.0	127.3	127.3
Net worth	$108.8	$129.1	$ 36.2	$ 42.3	$115.5	$102.8
5-year average tax rate	49.5%	49.4%	48.0%	47.7%	46.1%	45.7%[b]
Stock price (end of year)	$18	$25	$18	$30	$17	$20
Beta	0.75	0.75	1.25	1.25	1.40	1.40
Return on sales	3.6%	3.7%	2.7%	2.8%	3.3%	(1.5)%
Return on assets	17.9	18.3	10.0	10.2	3.6	(1.9)
Return on capital	24.6	25.3	16.6	17.3	5.4	(2.6)
Return on equity	24.6%	25.3%	16.6%	17.3%	11.3%	(5.8)%
Common shares (millions)	16.19	16.15	8.11	8.13	7.35	7.05

C/C = cannot calculate because of a loss in at least one year.

N.Ap. = not applicable.

[a]Class A common stock.

[b]Four-year average because of loss during period.

Kelly Services, Inc.
EXHIBIT 5 • Pro Forma 1986 Results for Alternative Capital
Structures (dollars in millions, except per-share data)

	Actual	Pro Forma Debt/Total Capital		
		30 Percent	50 Percent	70 Percent
Sales	$876.4	$876.4	$876.4	$876.4
Earnings before interest and taxes	64.0	64.0	64.0	64.0
Interest	0.0	4.8	8.1	11.3
Earnings before taxes	64.0	59.2	55.9	52.7
Taxes	31.4	29.6	28.0	26.4
Net earnings	$ 32.6	$ 29.6	$ 27.9	$ 26.4
Dividends	$ 8.9	$ 8.3	$ 7.8	$ 7.4
Shares outstanding (millions)	16.15	14.60	13.57	12.53
Earnings/share[a]	$ 2.02	$ 2.03	$ 2.06	$ 2.10
Price/earnings ratio	12.38×	N.Av.	N.Av.	N.Av.
Dividends/share	$ 0.55	$ 0.57	$ 0.58	$ 0.59
Dividend yield	2.20%	N.Av.	N.Av.	N.Av.
Beginning of year				
Debt	0.0	$ 38.7	$ 64.5	$ 90.4
Net worth	$129.1	90.4	64.6	38.7
Stock price/share	$ 25.0	N.Av.	N.Av.	N.Av.

N.Av. = not available.

[a]At a 50-percent tax rate, the EPS would be $1.98.

Marriott Corporation

In January 1980, the management of the Marriott Corporation found itself in an interesting dilemma: not only did the corporation have considerable excess debt capacity, but projections of future operations and cash flows indicated that this capacity would increase during the upcoming year. Management had stated that unused debt capacity was inconsistent with the goal of maximizing shareholder wealth. Excess debt capacity was viewed as comparable to unused plant capacity because the existing equity base could support additional productive assets.

Management's negative view of excess debt capacity had been strengthened by the rising inflation rates of the late 1970s, which were thought to increase the costs of unused debt capacity both directly and indirectly. As stated in Marriott's 1979 *Annual Report:*

> Both the cost of equity and the cost of debt increase with inflation. However, as inflation accelerates, tax deductibility partially offsets the rising cost of debt. On the other hand, business absorbs the full inflationary impact of equity cost increases. A firm which prudently utilizes its full debt capacity substitutes marginally cheaper debt for more expensive equity, thus optimizing the weighted cost of capital.

High inflation rates also had subtle effects on the firm's capital structure. Measured by its current value, debt previously committed at comparatively low interest rates actually declined in value. When the company's balance sheet was recast on a current-value basis, the debt-to-total capital ratio actually declined, implying an increase in debt capacity.

Management was therefore faced with two problems. First, it needed to determine the amount of funds that would be available if Marriott's full debt capacity were utilized. Second, management needed to decide whether to invest the excess funds in new or existing businesses, or to return them to the company's shareholders by paying higher cash dividends or repurchasing stock.

Marriott Corporation: Background

Operations through 1974.   The Marriott Corporation (MC) was founded by J. Willard Marriott in 1927, beginning as a root beer stand. The family first broadened its operation in 1937 when it pioneered in the field of airline catering, and again in the 1950s when it entered the hotel business and began providing food-service management to hospitals. The corporation's period of greatest diversification occurred in the late 1960s when, in addition to expanding the company's existing businesses, MC management made the following moves: (1) acquired several foreign airline catering kitchens; (2) bought the Big Boy coffee shop chain; (3) obtained the rights to use Roy Rogers's name on a chain of family restaurants; (4) entered the amusement business by initiating plans to develop up to three theme parks; and (5) purchased a cruise ship business, the Sun Line Shipping Co.

The corporation's aggressive growth proceeded unchecked until 1975. From 1968 to 1974, both sales and net income increased at an average annual rate of 22 percent, while earnings per share nearly tripled. The absolute growth in the size of the corporation was perhaps best reflected in the quadrupling of its capital base in this seven-year period, as shown in Exhibit 1. By the end of 1975, the Marriott Corporation had been organized into the five operating groups described in Exhibit 2: restaurant operations; the business and professional services group; the hotels group; Sun Line Cruises; and theme parks.

In 1975, Marriott's profits declined for the first time in 20 years. While domestic sales and profits had grown during the year, their rates of growth were slowed and profit margins were eroded by the combined effects of inflation and recession. In addition, the rapid business expansion resulting from management's targeted growth rate of 20 percent per year had generated sizable new-venture start-up costs and significant increases in interest expenses. However, the major factor that affected Marriott's 1975 performance was the $5.8 million loss incurred by Sun Line Cruises. Inflation had a devastating effect on this business, as rapidly escalating oil prices increased costs and declining consumer interest in cruise vacations reduced sales. The outbreak of the Greek–Turkish war on Cyprus, one of the company's areas of operation, further reduced the company's revenues.

The combined effect of all of these problems was a 12.6 percent decline in Marriott's 1975 net income and a 14 percent drop in earnings per share. The company's return on average equity reached a new low of 8.8 percent.[1]

---

[1] Marriott changed the end of its operating year in 1978 from July to December to accommodate the seasonality of the theme parks. The financial statements for the five preceding years,

Reappraisal, 1975–1976. In view of the company's 1975 performance, MC management reassessed its long-term goals and developed the following objective: to continue the company's growth by renewing the corporation's historic emphasis on the hotel business. However, management believed that the company was too highly leveraged and too dependent on inflexible secured debt to reach this goal easily.

Until 1975, MC had relied on the traditional mortgage markets for most of its long-term financing. By the end of 1975, 63 percent of Marriott's long-term obligations (about 81 percent of the company's net worth) was in the form of secured debt. Roughly 54 percent of Marriott's net property, plant, and equipment was pledged against this debt, making any significant modification to or disposition of these assets extremely difficult. This situation was regarded by Marriott management as a constraint on the company's maneuverability.

Furthermore, the corporation's continued expansion into the restaurant, catering, and amusement businesses had changed the composition of its assets. The assets associated with these new businesses could not be readily mortgaged. For instance, lenders were unwilling to grant mortgages on the assets associated with Marriott's theme parks. Originally estimated to cost $80 million, these assets had a final cost of $160 million. Lastly, the mortgage markets had shown wide swings in both interest rates and availability of funds. These variations raised additional questions about the future costs and availability of long-term mortgage debt financing.

In short, MC management viewed its continued reliance on the mortgage markets as a constraint on the company's growth and its ability to capitalize rapidly on high-return investments. Consequently, management decided to diversify the company's source of debt by making MC an A-rated unsecured borrower and by developing a wider market for the debt associated with its hotels. Before it could take these steps, however, MC had to improve its returns and restructure its liabilities.

To increase the rate of growth in revenues, MC management accelerated the corporation's marketing efforts. Concurrently, cost-control programs were initiated to improve margins. Moreover, about $100 million of marginally productive assets were disposed of. Reflecting management's renewed commitment to the hotel business, the dispositions included several foreign airline catering kitchens, the majority interest in an idle cruise ship, a security company, excess land around the existing theme parks, and land originally purchased in anticipation of a third

---

1974–1977, when restated to the new operating year, showed the following results for 1974–1975: net income increased 0.2 percent; earnings per share declined 1.4 percent; and return on average equity reached a low of 9.5 percent.

theme park. Exhibit 2 details the changes in Marriott's operating units between 1975 and 1979.

MC management also reduced planned capital expenditures and increased its hurdle rates for new investments. Some existing hotels were sold to counteract the capital intensity of the hotel business, although MC retained management contracts for these hotels, thereby keeping operational control of the units. MC also increased its reliance on off-balance-sheet financing as a further means of reducing the company's capital intensity.[2] Finally, the company issued 1.25 million shares of common stock, the first equity issue since 1972.

Results through December 1978.   The results of management's actions were almost immediately apparent. All key performance ratios had shown improvement as early as 1976, and the corporation's cash flow had increased strongly, up 25 percent over the 1975 level. In addition, both the proportion of mortgage notes payable to total capital and the ratio of assets pledged to net property, plant, and equipment had declined, while the corporation's debt maturities had been lengthened. Management had decided that the corporation's annual cash flow should, at a minimum, equal the sum of the next 5 years' debt maturities. It was able to meet this self-imposed debt limit as early as 1976, when Marriott's cash flow exceeded its 5-year debt maturities by 6 percent. Continued strong returns through 1977 allowed the corporation to place $40 million of 20-year unsecured debt.

Several further steps were taken during 1978. First, MC initiated the payment of cash dividends. In addition, management redefined its debt criterion: long-term debt was, at a minimum, to equal 45 percent of total capital.[3] And last, management adjusted the corporation's target debt rating from A to BBB. An A rating, management believed, was not all that desirable for growth-oriented companies that required financial flexibility. Furthermore, in the case of companies such as Marriott that used borrowed funds to meet restrictive loan covenants relative to working capital requirements, the higher credit rating could also be more expensive. MC management had decided that the interest payments saved by less restrictive loan covenants relative to working-capital balances would more than offset the increased interest rates resulting from the lower credit rating.

By the end of 1978, management believed that Marriott Corporation was in a financially liquid and flexible position. Sales had increased 15

---

[2] By keeping its investments in ventures to less than 50 percent, management could, for accounting purposes, record its investments using the equity method, thereby increasing the rates of return earned.

[3] Long-term debt was defined as senior debt plus capital-lease obligations. Total capital was defined as total assets less current liabilities.

percent, but earnings were up 39 percent, more than double management's goal of 15 percent per year earnings' growth. Marriott's cash flows had increased 22 percent, boosted both by the increased earnings as well as by the receipt of $35 million in after-tax proceeds from the sale of assets. The return on average equity had increased from the 1975 low of 9.5 to 14 percent. The return on total capital had risen from 13 to 16 percent.

For the most part, each of the corporation's business segments had done well during the period. While operating margins in the contract food service and restaurant groups had eroded slightly, those of the hotel group had increased, resulting in an overall 2 percent improvement in the corporate operating margin from 9 percent in 1975 to 11 percent in 1978. The major profit gains came from the theme parks, which began operations in 1976, and from a turnaround in the cruise ship business. Exhibit 3 provides operating results for Marriott's five business groups.

Long-term debt was at an all-time low of 37.5 percent of total capital, and the 1978 cash flow exceeded the sum of the next 5 years' debt maturities by 11 percent. These improvements led management to believe that it had $150 million in excess debt capacity.

Operating Year 1979. On the basis of Marriott's 1978 returns and those projected for 1979, management increased the company's capital budget for the year by 14 percent and repurchased 5 million shares of common stock at a cost of $74 million. This purchase was intended to offset the dilutive effects of the company's stock option plan.

Despite these major investments, Marriott's 1979 performance exceeded that of 1978, as shown in Exhibits 4 and 5. As a result, management continued to believe that the corporation was significantly underleveraged despite the increase in debt to 41 percent of total capital.

In 1979, the Financial Accounting Standards Board required firms of Marriott's size to report the effects of inflation on their financial statements for the first time. The results of recasting Marriott's financial statements into constant dollar and current value bases are shown in Exhibit 6. MC management favored the current value approach over the constant-dollar method for several reasons: (1) the company's assets were largely real-estate based and tended to appreciate rather than depreciate in value; (2) the assets were not subject to any major technological or competitive obsolescence that might necessitate their replacement; and (3) the company's annual repair and replacement costs traditionally averaged only 50 percent of the yearly depreciation charge. Management concluded that its reliance on the company's historical financial statements had caused it to undervalue MC's assets and to overstate its liabilities. Once again, management believed that the company's debt capacity had been underestimated.

At the same time, management concluded that the debt-to-total capital ratio was not the best measure of debt capacity. This ratio ignored the market value of assets and liabilities, the reliability and size of cash flows, and the structural differences among competitors within an industry. Instead, management chose to measure debt capacity in terms of earnings' coverage of net interest. Specifically, they concluded that earnings before interest and taxes, adjusted for actual repair and replacement expenses rather than by the income statement's depreciation charge, should cover net interest five times. (Exhibit 7 displays the results of applying this and other debt criteria to the company's historical financial data.)

The uncertainty about the best measure of the company's debt capacity spilled over into MC management's investment and capital-budgeting processes. Originally very project-oriented in its investment and financing decisions, management had taken a broader perspective when it diversified away from the mortgage markets. The use of unsecured debt had allowed management to separate the investment and financing decisions. However, it was still faced with determining the relationship between the corporation's debt capacity and the earning power of a given project. Management thought that MC's debt capacity was directly related to a project's ability to generate a reliable stream of cash to cover the interest charges associated with its financing. This view implied that the corporation's prevailing debt criterion should be applied project by project in the capital-budgeting procedure.

Marriott's 1979 Investment Alternatives

While management did have considerable discretion in determining the best investments for the corporation,[4] each of the preceding decisions and factors, as well as the prevailing capital market conditions detailed in Exhibit 8, contributed to the complexity of the 1979 investment decision. Management had identified two general categories of investments: (1) promoting growth by expanding existing operations or diversifying into new businesses; or (2) returning capital to the shareholders by increasing the company's dividends or by buying back some of the outstanding stock.

I. Promote Growth

Alternative 1. Accelerate Expansion of Existing Businesses.   MC management could increase its rate of investment in existing operations. The most

---

[4] Management's decision-making abilities were constrained only by the corporation's articles of incorporation, which required the approval of two-thirds of the outstanding shares for any merger, sale, or exchange of substantially all of the assets or businesses of the company.

promising area for investment was the hotel business. Although a mild recession was anticipated for early 1980, its effects on the lodging industry in general and on Marriott in particular were expected to be mild. Marriott hotels catered to business people and convention-goers whose travel plans were less subject to change than those of vacationers. MC hotels had come through the 1970 recession and the even more severe one in 1974 to 1975 with healthy earnings increases. Prevailing trends in the lodging industry also appeared to favor rapid room expansion. Industrywide construction had been somewhat constrained recently because of high interest rates, rising construction costs, and selective institutional lending.

An increase in the rate of hotel-room expansion also made sense from a competitive viewpoint. During the latter half of the 1970s, both Hilton and Holiday Inn, two of Marriott's major competitors, had diversified their investments away from the pure lodging business into gambling and casino ventures. MC management had decided to avoid the gambling business for ethical reasons and was in a good position to expand in the more traditional markets.

At the end of 1979, Marriott had 50 hotels in various stages of development. Completion of these units would result in about a 20 to 25 percent annual rate of growth in hotel rooms. More than half of these planned hotels were to be managed rather than wholly owned by the Marriott Corp. The large proportion of managed hotels among the planned units reflected management's emphasis on higher returns on invested capital rather than increased margins. The operating margin on a managed hotel was lower than that of an owned property—8 to 10 percent versus 15 percent, on average.[5]

If Marriott management chose to invest additional funds in the hotel business, it could do so in one of the following ways:[6]

1. Limited capital investment: MC could take up to a 50-percent equity position, thus minimizing its capital investment while maximizing the probability of being awarded the management contract on the property.

2. Full capital investment in a property with high and reasonably well-assured returns: MC could expand existing MC hotels where occupancy rates were high and the local market's demand was known and readily forecast.

[5] Joseph J. Doyle, "Marriott Corporation–Lodging and Restaurants–1/3/79." Research Report for Smith Barney Harris Upham & Co., Inc., New York.

[6] Ibid.

3.   Full capital investment, but low entry cost: MC could acquire an existing hotel where the Marriott name, management expertise, and referral systems were expected to improve the property's results.

4.   Capital put fully at risk in a new hotel at a new location.

Details regarding hotel life cycles and average construction costs for hotel properties are shown in Exhibit 9. In 1979, the average annual occupancy rate in the U.S. lodging industry was about 73 percent, slightly higher than the 1978 level of 72 percent. Marriott hotels, however, had an average occupancy rate of over 80 percent in 1979, well above the industry average.

Alternative 2. Diversify through Acquisition.   Marriott management could also use the company's funds to acquire another company. Management had every reason to believe that it could identify a company and a situation that would benefit from Marriott's principal asset: the operating expertise that cut across a broad range of food-service, lodging, and entertainment businesses.

Exhibit 10 displays recent data on merger and acquisition activity in the market.

II. Return Shareholders' Capital

Alternative 3. Increase Dividends.   MC management could also increase the company's cash dividends. Although a single lump-sum payment could be paid to the shareholders, this tactic would offer only a short-term solution to the company's problem of excess debt capacity and steadily increasing cash flows. A permanent increase in the company's payout ratio seemed a more reasonable alternative.

A major increase in cash dividends had significant ramifications for existing shareholders as well as for potential investors.

Per share data and other financial data for Marriott and its principal competitors are shown in Exhibits 11 and 12.

Alternative 4. Repurchase Shares of Common Stock.   A repurchase of common stock carried with it many of the same advantages and disadvantages as the previous alternative. Most serious, potentially, was the possible market interpretation of the move: the idea that Marriott had fully utilized its growth opportunities. The fact that management had only recently repurchased about five million shares on the open market was also of some significance. By shrinking the company in this manner, however, management had expected that the company's earnings per share and return on equity would increase enough to offset any negative interpretation of the strategy. Trends in Marriott's stock price relative to those of its major competitors are shown in Exhibit 12.

If management selected this alternative, it would need to make several decisions: (1) how many shares to tender, (2) at what price, and (3) whether or not to retire the shares repurchased.

At the end of 1979, the Marriott family owned about 6.5 million shares of the company's common stock. Nonfamily members of management owned an additional 1.5 million shares through the company's stock option and profit-sharing plans. Ownership of the remaining shares was largely dispersed among about 50,000 shareholders.

Marriott Corporation
EXHIBIT 1 • Marriott Corporation: Historical Performance[a]

	Sales— Percentage Change/Yr.	Net Income— Percentage Change/Yr.	PAT/Avg. Equity/Yr.	Pre-Debt Cash Flow[b] Percentage Change/Yr.	Average Capital[c] Percentage Change/Yr.	Pre-Debt Cash Flow/ Avg. Capital	Debt/ Total Capital[d]
1968	35.0%	23.1%	N.Av.[e]	N.Av.	N.Av.	N.Av.	49.0%
1969	31.0	20.6	12.9%	28.0%	N.Av.	13.1%	43.4
1970[e]	23.0	23.9	12.9	36.2	32.6%	13.4	49.4
1971	10.6	24.3	12.4	27.4	25.9	13.6	48.0
1972	20.2	28.7	11.6	22.3	23.9	13.4	49.7
1973	27.3	18.3	11.2	20.0	21.6	13.2	53.4
1974	19.0	15.8	11.4	25.3	20.1	13.8	50.4
1975	14.4	(12.6)	8.8	10.0	18.9	12.8	54.1
1976[e]	21.6	41.7	10.7	23.0	15.9	13.5	50.5
1977	22.5	26.3	10.7	11.2	6.9	14.1	45.3
1978	14.6	39.1	12.3	15.1	0.4	16.1	38.2

[a]Marriott changed its year end in 1978 from the last Friday in July to the Friday closest to December 31, to accommodate the seasonality of the theme park business better. At that time, the corporation restated its financial statements for the four preceding years (1974–1978) to reflect the change in its operating year. However, the data shown above have not been restated to reflect more accurately the corporation's historical performance and the results management was faced with in 1975 when it changed its business and financial strategies. All data were taken from the *1978 Annual Report* (7/28/78) but reflect the effects of changes in accounting policies instituted subsequent to 1975 (e.g., accounting for leases).

[b]Pre-debt cash flows = PAT + Depreciation and other non-cash charges + After-tax interest payments.

[c]Average capital = Two-year average of total assets − Current liabilities.

[d]Debt = End-of-year senior debt + Capital leases. Total capital = End-of-year total assets − Current liabilities.

[e]The year is 53 weeks long.

N.Av. = not available.

Marriott Corporation
EXHIBIT 2 • Marriott Activities, 1975 and 1979

	Number of Units	
Operating Group	7/25/75	12/28/79
A. Restaurant Operations Group		
1. Company-owned restaurants	407	476
a. Dinner houses and restaurants	18	9
b. Ice cream parlour restaurants (Farrells)	83	77
c. Cafeterias (principally Hot Shoppes)	40	16
d. Coffee shops (principally Bob's Big Boy)	132	180
e. Fast foods (principally Roy Rogers)	124	194

Marriott Corporation
EXHIBIT 2 • *continued*

	Number of Units	
Operating Group	7/25/75	12/28/79
2. Franchised restaurants	846	1,013
a. Coffee shops (Big Boys)	746	901
b. Ice cream parlour restaurants (Farrells)	22	32
c. Fast foods (Roy Rogers)	78	80
3. Production facilities		
a. Kitchens providing food research and production for Marriott restaurants, hotels, and flight kitchens as well as for sale to the food-service industry and retail food chains.	2	0
B. *Business and Professional Services Group* (subsequently named Contract Food Services)		
1. Domestic flight kitchens (airline catering)	40	39
2. International flight kitchens (airline catering)	20	23
3. Management contracts: Provision of food service to business and industry, health care and educational institutions, highway restaurants, etc.	168	217
4. Airline terminal contracts	10	12
5. Special services (including institutional catering from in-flight kitchens and food service to auto-train passengers)	19	0
6. Security systems	12	0
C. *Hotels Group*		
1. Company-owned properties		
a. Hotels	19[a]	20
b. Rooms	8,371[a]	8,348
2. Company-managed properties		
a. Hotels	11[a]	27
b. Rooms	4,616[a]	12,608
3. Franchised Marriott Inns		
a. Inns	12	18
b. Rooms	2,841	5,328
4. Resort/hotel condominiums		
a. Properties with condominiums held for retail sale	2	1
5. Full-service travel bureau	1	0
D. *Sun Line Cruises*		
a. Number of ships	3	3
E. *Theme Parks* (parks completed in 1976)	0	2

[a]Hotel data have been revised to a calendar-year basis and show units in operation at end of December 1975.

Source: Marriott Corporation, 1975 and 1979 *Annual Reports.*

Marriott Corporation
EXHIBIT 3 • Segment Data (dollars in millions)

	Fiscal Years									
	Unaudited									
	1975		1976		1977		1978		1979[a]	
	Dollars	Percent	Dollars	Percent	Dollars	Percent	Dollars	Percent	Dollars	Percent
Sales										
Hotel group	$238.3	31%	$281.3	30%	$ 334.7	31%	$ 408.3	33%	$ 535.0	35%
Contract food services	256.3	33	289.4	30	342.6	31	388.0	31	479.8	32
Restaurant group	267.3	34	295.4	31	316.9	29	347.2	28	377.3	25
Theme parks	0	0	64.1	7	71.9	7	75.5	6	83.9	6
Cruise ships and other	14.0	2	16.5	2	24.2	2	30.6	2	34.0	2
Total sales	$775.9	100%	$946.7	100%	$1,090.3	100%	$1,249.6	100%	$1,510.0	100%
Operating profit[a]										
Hotel group	$ 33.3	47%	$ 38.1	41%	$ 54.1	47%	$ 66.5	49%	$ 86.6	51%
Contract food services	18.7	26	19.2	20	21.2	18	23.5	17	31.6	18
Restaurant group	21.7	31	20.2	22	26.1	23	27.6	21	28.5	17
Theme parks[b]	0.0	0	14.7	16	10.0	9	11.8	9	17.5	10
Cruise ships and other	(2.6)	(4)	0.9	1	4.0	3	4.8	4	6.4	4
Total operating profit	$ 71.1	100%	$ 93.1	100%	$ 115.4	100%	$ 134.2	100%	$ 170.6	100%
Gross Margin: Operating Profit/Sales										
Hotel group	14.0%		13.5%		16.2%		16.3%		16.2%	
Contract food services	7.3		6.6		6.2		6.1		6.6	
Restaurant group	8.1		6.8		8.2		8.0		7.6	
Theme parks[b]	—		22.9		13.9		15.6		20.9	
Cruise ships and other	(18.6)		5.5		16.5		15.7		18.8	
Total Marriott	9.2%		9.8%		10.6%		10.7%		11.3%	

Identifiable Assets

Segment	1977	1978	1979
Hotel group	$379.1	$ 351.2	$ 434.3
Contract food services	127.9	138.6	163.2
Restaurant group	162.0	184.9	198.8
Theme parks[b]	169.0	167.5	162.9
Cruise ships and other	45.1	43.9	45.3
Corporate	66.4	114.2	75.9
Total	$949.5	$1,000.3	$1,080.4

Net Assets Employed [c]

Segment	1977	1978	1979
Hotel group	$353.7	$303.6	$371.9
Contract food services	99.3	99.3	124.0
Restaurant group	143.8	161.7	175.4
Theme parks[b]	164.0	161.4	158.0
Cruise ships and other	36.0	32.0	32.0
Corporate	32.9	68.9	30.6
Total	$829.7	$826.9	$891.9

Capital Expenditures and Acquisitions

Segment	1977	1978	1979
Hotel group	$43.1	$ 62.9	$ 80.6
Contract food services	9.9	10.8	20.3
Restaurant group	23.7	34.1	45.0
Theme parks[b]	9.7	9.2	6.3
Cruise ships and other	0.8	0.4	1.2
Corporate	11.2	21.7	5.1
Total	$98.4	$139.1	$158.5

Depreciation and Amortization

Segment	1977	1978	1979
Hotel group	$17.7	$16.0	$16.0
Contract food services	7.4	7.9	7.6
Restaurant group	11.8	12.5	14.7
Theme parks[b]	7.9	8.0	9.2
Cruise ships and other	1.7	1.8	1.4
Corporate	0.8	0.9	1.7
Total	$47.3	$47.1	$50.6

Sales/Total Capital [a,c]

Segment	1977	1978	1979
Hotel group	0.95X	1.34X	1.44X
Contract food services	3.67	3.91	3.87
Restaurant group	2.20	2.15	2.15
Theme parks[b]	0.44	0.47	0.53
Cruise ships and other	0.67	0.96	1.06
Total Marriott	1.32	1.51	1.69

Return on Capital (Operating Profit/total Capital) [a,c]

Segment	1977	1978	1979
Hotel group	15.4%	21.8%	23.3%
Contract food services	22.7	23.7	25.5
Restaurant group	18.1	17.1	16.3
Theme parks[b]	6.1	7.3	11.1
Cruise ships and other	11.1	15.1	20.0
Total Marriott	14.0	16.2	19.1

Source: Marriott Corporation, 12/28/79 and 12/29/78 *Annual Reports*. The company changed its year end in 1978 to the Friday closest to December 31. The segment results are presented on the new fiscal-year basis. The unaudited data for 1975 and 1976 as restated were prepared using the same procedures employed to obtain the audited 1977 and 1978 results.

[a]Operating profit represents total operating results before interest, corporate administrative expense, unallocated corporate charges, and dispositions of business and idle property.

[b]Theme park operating results for 1976 are not comparable with subsequent years because the initial year did not bear the full burden of off-season costs and included charges for depreciation and real estate taxes only from the opening of the parks.

[c]Net identifiable assets = Total identifiable assets − Identifiable current liabilities = Total capital.

Marriott Corporation

EXHIBIT 4 • Consolidated Income Statements
(thousands of dollars, except per-share data)

	Year Ending				
	7/25/75[a]	7/30/76[a]	12/30/77	12/29/78	12/28/79
Sales	$732,396	$890,403	$1,090,313	$1,249,595	$1,509,957
Costs and Expenses					
Cost of sales and operating expenses	(533,222)	(647,044)	(815,510)	(935,504)	(1,135,855)
General and administrative expenses	(31,469)	(35,023)	(43,935)	(50,182)	(53,616)
Rent	(30,427)	(34,146)	0	0	0
Taxes—payroll, etc.	(28,455)	(35,929)	(45,246)	(50,300)	(56,495)
Depreciation and amortization[b]	(30,637)	(36,119)	(47,279)	(47,144)	(50,623)
Advertising and promotion	(12,289)	(18,858)	(28,518)	(34,901)	(46,535)
Gross interest	(28,328)	(31,187)	(32,565)	(28,454)	(32,545)
Interest capitalized	10,353	10,432	2,359	4,766	4,705
Net interest	(17,975)	(20,755)	(30,206)	(23,688)	(27,840)
Profit-sharing contributions	(3,604)	(4,582)	(5,730)	(7,792)	(10,337)
Pre-opening and development expenses	(5,911)	(6,183)	(4,766)	(4,785)	(5,511)
Total costs and expenses	(693,989)	(838,639)	(1,021,190)	(1,154,296)	(1,386,812)
Profit before taxes	38,407	51,764	69,123	95,299	123,145
Gross taxes	(19,564)	(26,819)	(34,638)	(46,334)	(58,879)
Investment tax credit (flow-through)[c]	2,975	5,900	4,565	5,335	6,734
Net taxes	(16,589)	(20,919)	(30,073)	(40,999)	(52,145)
Profit after taxes	$21,818	$30,845	$39,050	$54,300	$71,000
Primary EPS	$0.66	$0.87	$1.06	$1.48	$2.21
Fully diluted EPS	N.Av.	N.Av.	1.04	1.43	1.95
Cash dividends/share[d]	N.Av.	N.Av.	0.30	0.13	0.17
Funds from operations[e]	70,320	87,543	99,834	121,588	140,934
Capital expenditures	$159,178	$143,235	$81,887	$134,738	$149,000

Footnotes for Exhibit 4:

*a*Data for 1975 to 1976, if restated to an operating year ending in December, would show the following summarized results, unaudited (in millions of dollars).

	12/75	12/76
Sales	$775.9	$946.7
Operating expenses	(704.8)	(853.6)
Gross interest	(33.5)	(33.2)
Interest capitalized	10.5	6.4
Net interest	(23.0)	(26.8)
Corporate expenses + Income + Dispositions	(8.0)	(13.4)
Profit before taxes	40.1	52.9
Gross taxes	(20.3)	(26.0)
Investment tax credit	4.4	5.1
Net taxes	(15.9)	(20.9)
Profit after taxes	$ 24.2	$ 32.0
Fully diluted earnings per share	$ 0.69	$ 0.86
Funds provided from operations	$ 77.6	$ 92.2
Capital expenditures	$154.6	$113.4

*b*Depreciation and amortization are accounted for on a straight-line basis.

*c*Investment tax credits are accounted for using the flow-through method.

*d*Marriott used 2.5 percent stock dividends annually from 1970 to 1977, except in 1972 when the stock split two for one.

*e*Funds provided from operation = Net income + Depreciation, Deferred taxes, and Other items not requiring current outlay of working capital.

Source: Marriott Corporation, 1976 *Annual Report.*

Marriott Corporation
EXHIBIT 5 • Consolidated Balance Sheets[a] (thousands of dollars)

		Year Ending			
	7/25/75[a]	7/30/76[a]	12/30/77	12/29/78	12/28/79
Assets					
Current Assets					
Cash and equivalent	$ 18,318	$ 17,760	$ 16,990	$ 14,747	$ 12,445
Marketable securities at cost	6,490	2,993	0	38,510	8,825
Accounts receivable	43,588	50,293	61,484	76,774	99,955
Inventories (FIFO)	27,667	35,504	41,498	41,108	46,629
Prepaid expenses	4,492	7,580	9,444	9,571	9,868
Total current assets	100,555	114,130	129,416	180,710	177,722
Lincolnshire Hotel (net assets under sale/leaseback)	7,282	0	0	0	0
Property and Equipment					
Land	58,932	73,784	106,919	100,053	103,009
Buildings and improvements	174,053	270,686	293,679	264,038	323,059
Leasehold improvements	165,742	198,280	213,118	213,791	251,409
Furniture/equipment	164,967	228,401	248,066	250,265	284,733
Capital leases	0	0	53,408	29,243	29,724
Cruise ships	11,219	11,367	11,441	11,814	11,903
Idle land and ship	33,262	37,610	0	0	0
Construction in progress	98,044	16,483	29,441	88,270	62,501
Total property and equipment	706,219	836,611	956,072	957,474	1,066,338
Depreciation and amortization	(128,169)	(155,218)	(204,152)	(212,430)	(241,160)
Net property and equipment	578,050	681,393	751,920	745,044	825,178
Other Assets					
Investment in/advances to affiliates[b]	11,557	10,467	26,548	25,506	27,160
Goodwill	18,960	18,656	17,549	19,257	19,106
Notes receivable	0	0	11,670	17,805	16,284
Deferred pre-opening costs	5,636	5,388	0	0	0
Other	14,470	14,192	12,407	11,933	14,915
Total other assets	50,623	48,703	68,174	74,501	77,465
Total assets	$736,510	$844,226	$949,510	$1,000,255	$1,080,365

[a]Data for 1975 to 1976 do not reflect changes in accounting requirements relative to capital leases which were adopted in subsequent years. When instituted in the July 1978 financial statements, the change had the cumulative effect of a $2.4-million decline in the 1976 retained earnings balance of $63.6 million.

[b]The aggregated numbers (dollars in millions) and balance sheet characteristics of Marriott's affiliates in 1975 and 1979 are summarized below:

	Nos. of Investments	Total Assets	Total Liabilities	Total Equity
July 1975	2	$ 53	$ 46	$ 9
Dec. 1979 (5 of 11 investments)	11	211	155	56

Source: Marriott Corporation, *Annual Reports.*

Marriott Corporation
EXHIBIT 5 • *continued*

	7/25/75[a]	7/30/76[a]	12/30/77	12/29/78	12/28/79
			Year Ending		
Liabilities and Shareholders' Equity					
Current Liabilities					
Short-term loans	$ 2,752	$ 2,989	$ 3,976	$ 3,473	$ 4,054
Accounts payable	33,111	41,503	46,666	66,960	71,528
Accrued liabilities	37,843	43,653	51,376	72,509	79,909
Income taxes payable	0	0	13,034	18,672	22,511
Current portion of debt and capitalized leases	11,424	10,119	10,813	11,758	10,497
Total current liabilities	85,130	98,264	125,865	173,372	188,499
Senior Debt					
Interim construction financing	4,948	16,000	0	0	0
Mortgage notes payable[c]	207,135	219,906	214,090	175,565	163,520
Unsecured notes payable	117,941	115,022	107,332	110,457	178,075
Total senior debt	330,024	350,928	321,422	286,022	341,595
Capital lease obligations	0	0	48,092	23,877	23,684
Deferred income taxes	34,514	47,343	56,385	59,903	65,597
Deferred income and other liabilities	866	1,007	2,435	10,260	20,569
Convertible subordinated debentures	32,240	31,340	29,515	28,165	26,918
Shareholders' Equity					
Common stock ($1 par)[d]	32,507	35,567	36,674	36,891	36,900
Capital surplus	169,974	212,250	222,785	224,915	224,533
Net deferred compensation payable in stock	3,256	3,952	4,967	6,350	7,670
Retained earnings	47,999	63,575	103,037	152,555	217,779
Treasury stock at cost	N.Av.	N.Av.	(1,667)	(2,055)	(73,379)
Total equity	253,736	315,344	365,796	418,656	413,503
Total liabilities and shareholders' equity	$736,510	$844,226	$949,510	$1,000,255	$1,080,365

N.Av. = not available.

[c]The value of the net assets pledged against this debt was estimated at $243 million in 1975 and $293 million in 1979.

[d]Changes in Marriott's common stock accounts are summarized below (figures in thousands):

	7/26/74–7/25/75	7/25/75–7/30/76	7/30/76–7/29/77	12/30/77–12/29/78	12/29/78–12/28/79
Opening number of shares	31,183	32,507	35,567	36,507	36,715
Shares issued	1,324	3,060	1,101	385	235
Shares repurchased	0	0	0	177	4,851
Closing number of shares	32,507	35,567	36,668	36,715	32,098
Estimated number of shareholders, end of period	43,200	47,000	52,800	50,700	N.Av.

Marriott Corporation

EXHIBIT 6 • Inflation-Adjusted Financial Statements (thousands of dollars)

A. *Current Value Accounting*
   Changes in Shareholders' Equity[a]

Current value, December 29, 1978	$ 767,719
Discretionary cash flow	99,123
Reduction in current value of debt	25,287
Increase in current value of assets	77,227
Purchase of treasury stock	(74,187)
Cash dividends	(5,776)
Common stock issued and other	3,810
Current value, December 28, 1979	$ 893,203[b]

Shareholders' Equity—12/28/79	*Historical Cost*	*Current Value*
Non-monetary assets (primarily property and equipment)	$927,287	$1,356,244
Less net monetary liabilities		
Senior debt and capital leases	365,279	320,736
Convertible debt	26,918	20,718
Other monetary liabilities, net	121,587	121,587
Total net monetary liabilities	513,784	463,011
Shareholders' equity	$413,503	$ 893,203
Senior debt and capital leases to total capital	41%	24%
Gain from Decline in Purchasing Power of Net Monetary Liabilities		
Negative working capital		$ 6,322
Debt and other monetary liabilities		48,787
Total gain		$ 55,109

B. *Total Constant-Dollar Accounting (average 1979 dollars)*

	12/28/79
Net income as reported	$ 71,000
Constant-dollar adjustments	
Cost of sales	(5,203)
Depreciation and amortization of property and equipment	(18,427)
Total constant-dollar adjustments	(23,630)
Constant-dollar net income	$ 47,370
Constant-dollar gain from decline in purchasing power of net amounts owed	$ 55,109
Constant-dollar net income per share (excluding gain from decline in purchasing power of net amounts owed)	$ 1.31
Shareholders' equity (constant 1979 dollars)	$ 703,598
Effective 1979 income tax rate	52.4%

Marriott Corporation
EXHIBIT 6 • *continued*

C. *Five-Year Comparison of Selected Supplementary Financial Data*
   Adjusted for the Effects of Chainging Prices (average 1979 dollars)

Fiscal Years Ended	Net Sales and Other Operating Revenue	Cash Dividends Declared per Common Share	Market Price per Common Share at Year End	Average Consumer Price Index
1975	$1,045,878	$0	$20.17	161.2
1976	1,206,576	0	16.88	170.5
1977	1,305,371	0.04	13.73	181.5
1978	1,389,647	0.14	12.99	195.4
1979	$1,509,957	$0.17	$16.53	217.4

*a*Property and equipment and investments in affiliates are valued on a discounted cash flow basis. Projections of future cash flows are adjusted to reflect anticipated asset-maintenance requirements. Goodwill is assigned no value. The interest rates used to discount the cash flows reflect current market rates.

*b*If the current value of existing hotel management agreements were included in the data, this figure would increase by about $275.8 million to $1,169 million.

Source: Marriott Corporation, 1979 *Annual Report.*

Marriott Corporation
EXHIBIT 7 • Alternative Measurements of Debt and Marriott Results

	1974	1975	1976	1977	1978	1979
1. Cash flow/Year/5-year debt maturities*a*	0.63×	0.84×	1.06×	1.11×	1.15×	N.Av.
2. (Senior debt + Capital leases)/(Total assets − Current liabilities)*b*	53%	55%	48%	45%	38%	41%
3. EBIT/Net interest*b*	3.06×	2.74×	2.98×	3.29×	5.02×	5.42×
4. EBIT adjusted/Net interest*bc*	3.74×(est.)	3.51×	3.80×	4.27×	6.43×	6.64×
5. EBIT adjusted/Gross interest*b*	2.65×(est.)	2.40×	3.07×	3.95×	5.35×	5.66×

N.Av. = not available.

*a*Data reflect July fiscal year. Figure for 1978, if restated to December calendar year, would be 1.19.

*b*Data reflect December calendar year.

*c*EBIT adjusted = EBIT + Depreciation − Actual repairs/replacements.

Marriott Corporation
EXHIBIT 8 • Market Data, 1975–1979

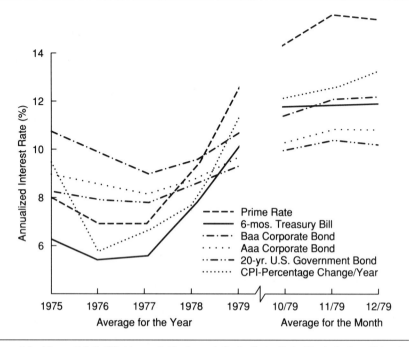

Source: *Federal Reserve Bulletin.* CPI data compiled by Economic Studies Center, Tayloe Murphy Institute, University of Virginia.

Marriott Corporation
EXHIBIT 9 • Typical Life Cycle, 150-Room Motel

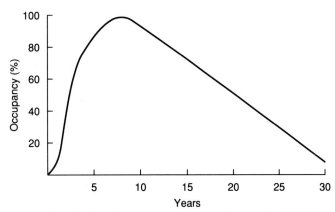

Typical Hotel–Motel Costs per Room 1978 (thousands of dollars)

	Improvements	Furniture, Fixtures, and Equipment	Land	Pre-Opening	Operating Capital	Total
Luxury	$32–55	$5–10	$4.0–12.0	$1.0 –2.0	$1.0 –1.50	$43.0–80.5
Standard	20–32	3–6	2.5– 7.0	0.75–1.5	0.75–1.00	27.0–47.5
Economy	$ 8–15	$2–4	$1.0– 3.5	$0.5 –1.0	$0.5 –0.75	$12.0–24.23

Source: "The Appraisal of Lodging Facilities," by Stephen Rushmore, *The Cornell Hotel and Restaurant Administration Quarterly*, August 1978. Life-cycle data have been adjusted to show occupancy rather than operating-income data.

Marriott Corporation
EXHIBIT 10 • Data on the Merger and Acquisition Market, 1975–1978

Year and Market Value of Companies Receiving Tender Offers (millions of dollars)	Number of Tender Offers Received	Average 5-Year Sales Growth per Year[a]	Average 5-Year Earnings Growth per Year[a]	Market Price/Book Value[b] (average)	Market Price/Earnings Ratio[b] (average)	Market Price/Cash Flow[b] (average)	Average Return on Equity[b]	Average Total Debt/Equity[b]	Average Tender Price/Market Value = Premium[b]
1975									
$20	6	5.5%	11.3%	0.52X	7.72X	4.06X	7.5%	0.94X	43.97%
$20–250	6	19.8	29.2	1.03	6.60	4.87	15.6	0.75	44.65
$250	—	—	—	—	—	—	—	—	—
1976									
$20	2	8.9	N.Av.	0.45	7.60	4.39	6.0	0.46	29.56
$20–250	11	17.3	20.7	1.45	11.81	6.83	16.6	1.43	28.98
$250	3	13.8	13.2	1.37	10.77	7.30	12.8	0.99	43.25
1977									
$20	1	4.2	N.Av.	0.72	10.69	3.55	7.0	1.76	36.50
$20–250	12	12.7	12.8	1.52	9.43	5.46	16.7	1.19	39.64
$250	6	12.9	19.9	1.56	9.29	7.99	14.9	0.71	62.55
1978									
$20	—	—	—	—	—	—	—	—	—
$20–250	10	11.5	3.7	1.15	7.37	4.17	18.6	1.70	60.05
$250	3	10.9	17.9	1.32	6.38	4.58	19.7	1.13	35.30
Control Group 1978[c]									
$20	—	18.8	6.3	1.05	9.0	4.30	6.0	1.32	N.Ap.
$20–250	—	14.1	13.5	1.74	8.9	6.46	19.2	0.54	N.Ap.
$250	—	18.3%	10.2%	1.49X	8.8X	5.80X	17.3%	1.07X	N.Ap.

N.Av. = not available.

N.Ap. = not applicable.

[a]Five years prior to tender offer.

[b]All numbers reflect actual data two weeks prior to receipt of tender offer.

[c]Control group is random sample of companies in operation in 1978.

Marriott Corporation
EXHIBIT 11 • Travel Services Industry Competitors:
Historical Data (millions of dollars, except per-share or as noted)

Company and Year	Annual Revenues	Annual Profit after Tax	Return on Average Equity	Debt/ Total Capital	Primary Earnings per Share	Cash Flow per Share	Dividends per Share	Average Equity/ Average Shares	Average Market Price	Beta
Holiday Inns										
1975	$ 912	$41.0	9.4%	36.9%	$1.36	$3.43	$0.35	$14.73	$11.65	1.50
1978	1,188	63.0	11.9	33.3	2.04	4.17	0.56	17.74	18.77	1.55
1979	1,092	71.0	12.0	31.1	2.25	3.47	0.66	19.03	18.48	1.60
Hilton Hotels										
1975	351	42.0	20.5	34.7	1.43	2.35	0.28	7.26	6.05	1.40
1978	444	68.0	26.6	36.0	2.62	3.72	0.74	10.88	20.70	1.45
1979	484	99.0	29.1	23.4	3.76	4.77	1.09	13.51	29.33	1.40
Ramada Inns										
1975	212	1.0	0.8	67.0	0.04	0.59	0.06	4.88	4.00[a]	1.70
1978	308	10.2	7.1	63.7	0.40	1.09	0.12	5.54	7.56	1.55
1979	348	15.5	10.2	63.3	0.57	1.39	0.12	5.66	10.43	1.50
Marriott										
1975	732	21.8	9.0	55.5	0.65	1.54	N.Ap.	7.12	10.99	1.55
1978	1,250	54.3	14.0	40.9	1.43	2.57	0.13	10.22	11.34	1.55
1979	1,510	71.0	17.1	44.0	1.96	3.79	0.17	11.75	14.90	1.50
S&P 500										
1975	999.7 bil.	50.9 bil.	12.4	31.0	2.31	4.22	1.01	19.14	22.80	1.00
1978	1,454.0 bil.	82.7 bil.	15.1	29.0	3.52	6.00	1.44	23.97	27.43	1.00
1979	$1,725.6bil.	$101.2 bil.	16.7%	29.0%	$4.25	$7.04	$1.61	$26.19	$29.29	1.00

N.Ap. = not applicable.

[a]Estimated.

Sources include *Value Line; Standard & Poor's Computer Services, Inc.;* and *S&P Standard NYSE Stock Reports.*

Marriott Corporation

**EXHIBIT 12 • Comparative Common Stock
Data, 1978–1979 (monthly closing price)**

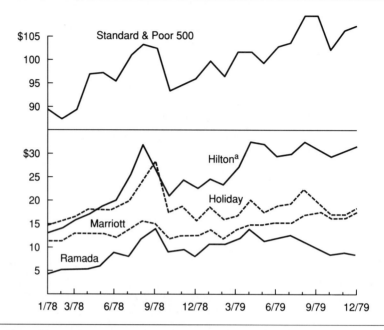

Source: New York Stock Exchange Daily Stock Index.

[a]Market price per share for Hilton has been adjusted for a two-for-one stock split in December 1978.

Philip Morris, Incorporated: Swiss Franc Financing

On October 24, 1980, Hans Storr, vice president and chief financial officer of Philip Morris, Inc., knew that he had a difficult selling job ahead of him. After much analysis and discussion with investment bankers and other Philip Morris financial officers, he still believed that the company should undertake a major financing in the Swiss franc (SFr) Eurobond market. He knew that not everyone in the company shared his enthusiasm for the opportunities in the Euromarkets, and should he decide to issue SFr bonds, he would need to convince other members of senior management that this was the best course of action.

In any event, the company would require significant external funding over the next few years. Although the company was more leveraged than some outside analysts thought appropriate, management was comfortable with the current debt/equity ratio and intended to continue the current financing mix. Given the projected profitability of the company, management believed that additional funding should be raised in the debt markets. Thus the decision facing Mr. Storr was where to issue debt at the most favorable terms.

Company Background

Philip Morris was founded in the 19th century and was incorporated in Virginia in 1919. Originally a cigarette manufacturer, the company began a series of diversification moves in the late 1960s. In 1970 Philip Morris acquired the Miller Brewing Company, and in 1978 it purchased the Seven-Up Company. In addition, the company diversified into specialty chemicals and papers, tissue papers, packaging materials, and real-estate and community development.

By 1980 Philip Morris was one of the largest industrial companies in the United States. The company had achieved the enviable record of 26 consecutive years of growth in revenues, net profits, and earnings per share. The financial statements for 1978 and 1979 are shown in Exhibits 1 and 2.

As a result of the diversification and growth of the company, Philip Morris had six operating divisions:

- Philip Morris U.S.A. (tobacco products)
- Philip Morris International (tobacco products and Seven-Up)
- Miller Brewing Company (beer)
- The Seven-Up Company (Seven-Up, North America only)
- Philip Morris Industrial (specialty papers and chemicals)
- Mission Viejo Company (community development)

A breakdown of the operating companies' performance, along with other financial highlights, is shown in Exhibit 3.

The company's growth had not been limited to the domestic U.S. market. Philip Morris marketed cigarettes in over 160 countries and, in addition to being the largest cigarette exporter in the United States, had offshore manufacturing facilities as well as joint venture and licensing arrangements. Seven-Up, a significant international product, was marketed in approximately 90 countries. In these international markets, the distribution was primarily through franchised bottlers and distributors.

International operations had sales-and-profits growth records matching their domestic counterparts: operating revenues for 1979 increased 42.5 percent over 1978 results, and operating income, 38.2 percent. This growth was expected to continue. Financial results for 1978 and 1979 by region are shown in Exhibit 4. Foreign operations accounted for about 25 percent of the operating revenues but only about 9 percent of operating income in 1979. About 18 percent of the identifiable assets of the consolidated subsidiaries were held offshore. Further financial data for the consolidated and unconsolidated subsidiaries are shown in Exhibit 5.

Although the international operations had contributed to the growth of the company, they had also created a financial-reporting problem. This resulted from the company's adoption on January 1, 1976, of the Financial Accounting Standard (FAS) #8.

Translating Foreign Subsidiary Statements

FAS #8 required all U.S. companies to use the temporal method of translating the financial statements of foreign subsidiaries for consolidated reporting purposes. The temporal method prescribed which exchange rate to use for translating assets and liabilities denominated in foreign curren-

cies. Historical exchange rates (i.e., those in existence at the time of acquisition) were to be used for all fixed assets. Inventories were to be valued at
the lower of (1) cost translated at historical rates or (2) market value translated at current rates (i.e., those in existence at the date of the balance
sheet). In almost all cases, inventories were translated at historical
exchange rates. All other accounts were to be translated at the current
exchange rates. This being the case, the temporal method produced results
virtually equivalent to the monetary/nonmonetary translation method that
translated monetary items at current rates and nonmonetary items at historical rates.

Whether the company experienced a gain or loss depended on the
difference between the assets and the liabilities that were translated at the
current exchange rate. For companies with a net monetary asset position
(i.e., with assets exceeding the liabilities translated at current rates), a
strengthening foreign currency resulted in a foreign-exchange translation
gain. The gain occurred because the value of the assets stated in U.S.
dollars had increased by an amount greater than the increased value of the
foreign liabilities stated in U.S. dollars. Conversely, a net monetary liability position in the same situation yielded a translation loss. The impact of
the translation process was reversed if the foreign currency weakened
(devalued) against the U.S. dollar.

FAS #8 directed that these translation gains or losses be included in
the income statement for the reporting period, even though they were only
paper gains or losses and had not actually been realized in the cash flows of
the multinational company. This requirement for immediately including
the translation results in the income statement, along with other concerns
about the appropriateness of the exchange rate assigned to various balance-
sheet accounts, had caused much discussion in the accounting and financial
community. Most of the discussion had suggested that FAS #8 was unacceptable and should be changed.

FAS #8 at Philip Morris

Philip Morris had concurred with the arguments that FAS #8 distorted the
company's financial reporting. In an effort to eliminate the impact of the
translation gains and losses, Mr. Storr had undertaken regular balance-
sheet hedging in the forward currency markets. This policy was pursued
with some reluctance because it involved taking economic positions to
hedge noneconomic positions. Nevertheless, management was justifiably
proud of the earnings record of Philip Morris and believed that the FAS #8
requirements were a potential threat to the continuation of annual and
quarterly income gains.

Philip Morris was particularly vulnerable to translation gains
and losses. Foreign-currency debt incurred to finance its large tobacco

inventories held offshore and its plant and equipment investments in foreign subsidiaries resulted in an exposed liability position for the company.

Although the FAS #8 reporting requirements had caused considerable earnings fluctuations in the ensuing years, Mr. Storr had been reasonably successful in mitigating these fluctuations through the hedging operations. Operating primarily on the foreign-exchange market with currency futures, the company had attempted to forecast the future exchange rates for the major currencies. When Mr. Storr's forecasts differed from the markets' forward exchange rates, he would enter into open contracts to buy or sell currencies in the future. In essence, the company was speculating against the market. Mr. Storr believed that he and his staff were successful in forecasting the results of normal economic factors, but political and other shocks were difficult, if not impossible, to predict.

Potential FAS Changes

Because of the controversy surrounding FAS #8, the FASB had announced in January 1979 that it would evaluate proposed changes to the standard. Although FAS #8 had not yet been officially superseded, Mr. Storr had received in late August an exposure draft of some proposed changes. If the exposure draft were accepted, the revisions to FAS #8 would be significant.

The exposure draft proposed replacing the temporal translation method of FAS #8 with an all-current method. All balance-sheet accounts would be translated at the current or most recent exchange rate. This change would eliminate the need to translate any accounts at historical rates, even though the accounts reflected on the subsidiaries' balance sheets might still be recorded at historical costs.

A further change would be to eliminate the inclusion of translation gains and losses in the income statement for the parent. Instead, they would be recorded as a separate component of stockholders' equity. Any transaction gains or losses would continue to be included in the income statement just as they were under FAS #8.

Although these changes would eliminate the provisions of FAS #8 that had received the most opposition, the proposed standard was not without its critics. The FASB had approved the exposure draft by only a four-to-three vote. In the short time since the exposure draft had been issued, many accountants and financial managers had voiced their displeasure with various aspects of the proposed standards. First, some managers were content with FAS #8 and believed that it was consistent with long-time accounting methods and theories. Second, the exposure draft proposed a departure from the tradition of having all changes in the owners' equity accounts flow through the income statement. Third, because of the use of current exchange rates, some argued that the proposed standard would result in an unacceptable mix of historical and inflation accounting.

The FASB had scheduled a public meeting for December 1980 to discuss the proposed accounting standard. Although the exposure draft specified that the new standard would become effective in December 1981, the growing opposition to the proposed standard made its adoption uncertain.

Previous Foreign Financing

In 1972 Philip Morris had been attracted by the lower borrowing rates in Switzerland and other European countries. With US$ long-term bond rates at about 7½ percent, corporations could benefit from a 75-basis-point spread by financing in Swiss francs at 6¾ percent. Philip Morris decided to take advantage of this interest-rate differential and had floated and sold some Swiss franc bonds in 1972. Taking advantage of similar spreads, the company also issued Deutsche mark and Dutch guilder bonds.

This decision proved to be disastrous for Philip Morris and the other U.S. corporations that had undertaken similar financings. After the change to floating exchange rates in 1973, the Swiss franc strengthened appreciably from the SFr 3.20/US$ exchange rate that had existed in 1972. The effective cost of the SFr bonds was thus very high. Exhibit 6 shows historic SFr/US$ exchange rates. Exhibit 7 provides information on Swiss and U.S. inflation and interest rates.

Even though this initial foray into the foreign debt markets had proven to be less than satisfactory and the SFr bonds had been called in 1978, the earliest date possible, Mr. Storr was convinced that the current SFr situation was an excellent opportunity to obtain low-cost financing.

Current Situation

Because of the need to raise debt funds, Mr. Storr had investigated the available rates in several markets. US$ rates for a US$60 million, 7-year, A-rated bond were about 14½ percent. A comparable issue in the Swiss franc market would be priced at about 6½ percent. Because both rates were quoted on the basis of annual coupon payments, the standard for Eurobonds, the yields were directly comparable. The 8-percent interest-rate differential between the two rates appeared to be reflected in the forward exchange rates, where the SFr was selling at a substantial premium over the spot rate of SFr 1.6755/US$. The 30-, 60-, and 180-day forward rates were SFr 1.6608, SFr 1.6405, and SFr 1.6088, respectively.

The foreign-exchange markets had recently entered a period of hectic trading that resulted in significant volatility in exchange rates. This volatility was at least partially fueled by the uncertain political environment caused by continued speculation about the fate of the U.S. hostages in

Iran. Mr. Storr believed that the markets' volatility overshadowed the underlying economic situation. Based on his analysis, he believed that the high forward premium for the Swiss franc was unwarranted, and the strength of the franc was, therefore, overstated.

Although he believed that the franc would probably strengthen against the dollar, he believed that the 8-percent interest-rate differential was a sufficient cushion. The SFr would need to appreciate by more than 8 percent before the SFr debt would become more expensive than the alternative US$ financing. His view of the economic factors led him to think that an 8-percent devaluation of the dollar against the Swiss franc was unlikely. Information about the Swiss and U.S. balance of payments and currencies are contained in Exhibits 8, 9, and 10.

Some uncertainties were connected with the sale of the SFr debt, however. The European debt markets evaluated issuers differently from U.S. markets. Rather than relying on rating agencies to grade the quality of the borrower, the European markets relied primarily on the reputation of the borrower. For this reason, most of the borrowers in the Euromarkets were governments or governmental agencies. The corporations that tapped the Euromarkets were large, well-known companies.

Because Philip Morris had not been a regular participant in the Euromarkets, Mr. Storr did not know how an issue would be accepted. He thought that being a major multinational company would work in his favor, however.

Given the uncertainties associated with the SFr Eurobond, Mr. Storr wondered if he shouldn't just resign himself to the more conservative approach and issue U.S.-dollar debt. If he were right about the Swiss franc, the company would benefit from substantial interest savings. If wrong, however, he would be opening himself to a repeat of the last SFr financing fiasco.

Philip Morris, Incorporated: Swiss Franc Financing
EXHIBIT 1 • Consolidated Statements of Earnings for the Years Ending
December 31 (thousands of dollars, except per-share amounts)

	1978	1979
Operating revenues	$6,632,463	$8,302,892
Cost of sales		
Cost of products sold	(3,072,134)	(3,778,737)
Federal and foreign excise taxes on products sold	(1,663,600)	(2,158,801)
Gross profit	1,896,729	2,365,354
Marketing, administration, and research costs	(931,978)	(1,195,667)
	964,751	1,169,687
Equity in net earnings of unconsolidated foreign subsidiaries and affiliates	3,331	20,947
Operating income of operating companies	968,082	1,190,634
Corporate expense	(54,106)	(70,207)
Interest expense (excluding capitalized interest of $13,425,000 in 1978 and $23,680,000 in 1979)	(149,794)	(205,476)
Other deductions, net	(18,685)	(9,515)
Earnings before income taxes	745,497	905,436
Provision for income taxes	(336,916)	(397,555)
Net earnings	$ 408,581	$ 507,881
Earnings per common share	$3.38	$4.08

Philip Morris, Incorporated: Swiss Franc Financing
EXHIBIT 2 • Consolidated Balance Sheets for the
Years Ending December 31 (thousands of dollars)

	1978	1979
Assets		
Cash and cash equivalents	$ 72,930	$ 59,060
Receivables	473,586	576,858
Inventories		
Leaf tobacco	1,459,048	1,548,422
Other raw materials	198,541	253,767
Work in process and finished goods	419,551	432,614
Housing programs under construction	111,413	136,497
Total inventories	2,188,553	2,371,300
Prepaid expenses	21,688	21,097
Total current assets	2,756,757	3,028,315
Investments in and advances to unconsolidated foreign subsidiaries and affiliates	243,271	260,172

continued

Philip Morris, Incorporated: Swiss Franc Financing
**EXHIBIT 2 • ** *continued*

	1978	1979
Land and off-tract improvements	72,836	114,445
Property, plant, and equipment, at cost		
Land and land improvements	101,256	133,980
Buildings and building equipment	476,152	562,489
Machinery and equipment	1,231,438	1,547,558
Construction in progress	408,485	581,069
Total property, plant, and equipment, at cost	2,217,331	2,825,096
Less accumulated depreciation	(479,726)	(595,594)
Net property, plant, and equipment	1,737,605	2,229,502
Brands, trademarks, patents, and goodwill	652,368	645,586
Long-term receivables	66,258	51,534
Other assets	79,070	49,298
Total assets	$5,608,165	$6,378,852
Liabilities and Stockholders' Equity		
Notes payable	$ 211,345	$ 59,909
Current portion of long-term debt	13,866	8,699
Accounts payable and accrued liabilities	785,201	897,415
Federal and other income taxes	129,388	190,186
Dividends payable	31,867	38,920
Total current liabilities	1,171,667	1,195,129
Long-term debt	2,146,968	2,447,761
Deferred income taxes	149,952	233,604
Other liabilities	24,918	31,403
Total liabilities	3,493,505	3,907,897
Cumulative preferred stock, par value $100 per share	7,693	0
Common stock, par value $1 per share	62,136	124,544
Additional paid-in capital	439,443	385,085
Earnings reinvested in the business	1,608,954	1,961,326
Total stockholders' equity	2,118,226	2,470,955
Less cost of treasury stock	3,566	0
Net stockholders' equity	2,114,660	2,470,955
Total liabilities and stockholders' equity	$5,608,165	$6,378,852

Philip Morris, Incorporated: Swiss Franc Financing
EXHIBIT 3 • Financial Highlights (thousands of dollars, except per-share amounts)

	1975	*1976*	*1977*	*1978*	*1979*
Operating revenues	$3,642,414	$4,293,782	$5,201,977	$6,632,463	$8,302,892
Net earnings	211,638	265,675	334,926	408,581	507,881
Earnings per common share	1.810	2.240	2.800	3.380	4.08
Dividends declared per common share	$0.463	$0.575	$0.781	$1.025	$1.25
Percentage Increase over Prior Year					
Operating revenues	21.0%	17.9%	21.2%	27.5%	25.2%
Net earnings	20.6	25.5	26.1	22.0	24.3
Earnings per common share	14.9	23.8	25.0	20.7	20.7
Dividends declared per common share	19.4%	24.2%	35.8%	31.2%	22.0%
Operating Companies' Revenues					
Philip Morris U.S.A.	$1,721,549	$1,963,144	$2,160,362	$2,437,465	$2,767,035
Philip Morris International	1,040,002	1,083,970	1,349,280	1,810,861	2,581,270
Miller Brewing Company	658,268	982,810	1,327,619	1,834,526	2,236,481
The Seven-Up Company	0	0	0	186,494	295,480
Philip Morris Industrial	151,960	169,096	216,699	237,165	268,847
Mission Viejo Company	70,635	94,762	148,017	125,952	153,779
Consolidated operating revenues	$3,642,414	$4,293,782	$5,201,977	$6,632,463	$8,302,892
Operating Companies' Income					
Philip Morris U.S.A.	$ 337,314	$ 401,426	$ 474,400	$ 568,145	$ 701,340
Philip Morris International	112,975	130,104	153,791	188,561	260,620
Miller Brewing Company	28,628	76,056	106,456	150,300	180,894
The Seven-Up Company	0	0	0	26,291	6,985
Philip Morris Industrial	8,052	10,620	14,860	15,024	18,268
Mission Viejo Company	5,875	16,333	33,225	19,761	22,437
Consolidated operating income	$ 492,844	$ 634,539	$ 782,732	$ 968,082	$1,190,634

Compounded Average Annual Growth Rate

	1954–1979	*1964–1979*	*1969–1979*	*1974–1979*
Operating revenues	13.5%	18.6%	21.9%	22.5%
Net earnings	15.8	23.1	24.2	23.7
Primary earnings per share	14.4%	20.5%	20.4%	20.9%

Philip Morris, Incorporated: Swiss Franc Financing
EXHIBIT 4 • Consolidated Financial Data by
Geographical Region (thousands of dollars)

	1978	1979
Operating revenues		
United States	$5,230,535	$6,228,752
Europe	1,268,127	1,736,002
Other foreign	133,801	338,138
	$6,632,463	$8,302,892
Operating profit		
United States	$ 877,947	$1,067,265
Europe	67,991	102,911
Other foreign	11,129	(12,754)
	$ 957,067	$1,157,422
Reconciliation		
Equity in net earnings of unconsolidated foreign subsidiaries and affiliates	$ 3,331	$ 20,947
Amortization of goodwill and trademarks	7,684	12,265
Operating income of operating companies	$ 968,082	$1,190,634
Identifiable assets		
United States	$4,394,028	$4,984,037
Europe	765,760	927,350
Other foreign	129,671	140,956
	5,289,459	6,052,343
Investments in and advances to unconsolidated foreign subsidiaries and affiliates	243,271	260,172
Corporate assets	75,435	66,337
Total assets	$5,608,165	$6,378,852

Philip Morris, Incorporated: Swiss Franc Financing

EXHIBIT 5 • Principal Financial Data of Foreign
Subsidiaries and Affiliates (thousands of dollars)

	Consolidated (wholly owned)	Unconsolidated (partially owned)
1978		
Assets	$ 944,956	$ 667,850
Liabilities	552,052	346,099
Net assets	392,904	321,751
Equity and advances	392,904	226,871
Operating revenues	1,401,928	1,099,767
Net earnings	58,398	13,561
Equity	$ 58,398	$ 3,331
1979		
Assets	$1,087,005	$ 776,255
Liabilities	588,811	421,391
Net assets	498,194	354,864
Equity and advances	498,194	242,808
Operating revenues	2,074,140	1,269,794
Net earnings	56,638	34,433
Equity	$ 56,638	$ 20,947

Philip Morris, Incorporated: Swiss Franc Financing

EXHIBIT 6 • Swiss Franc Exchange Rates

	SFr/US$
1973[a]	3.2440SFr
1974	2.5400
1975	2.6200
1976	2.4505
1977	2.0000
1978	1.6200
1979	1.5800
1980–July 31	1.6500
1980–October 24	1.6755SFr

[a]Annual exchange rates are those existing at the end of the year.

Source: *The Wall Street Journal* and IMF, *International Financial Statistics.*

Philip Morris, Incorporated: Swiss Franc Financing

EXHIBIT 7 • Interest and Inflation Rates for Switzerland and the United States

	Switzerland		United States	
	Consumer Price Index[a]	Government Bond Yield[b]	Consumer Price Index[a]	Government Bond Yield[b]
1973	85.4	5.60%	82.6	6.95%
1974	93.7	7.15	91.6	7.82
1975	100.0	6.44	100.0	7.49
1976	101.7	4.99	105.8	6.77
1977	103.3	4.05	112.7	6.69
1978	104.1	3.33	121.2	8.29
1979	107.9	3.45	134.9	9.71
1980–July	112.5	4.60%	153.6	9.27%

[a]CPI is for the end of the period.

[b]Yields are averages for the period.

Source: IMF, *International Financial Statistics*, September 1980.

Philip Morris, Incorporated: Swiss Franc Financing

EXHIBIT 8 • Balance of Payments, Switzerland (millions of US$)

	1973	1974	1975	1976	1977	1978	1979
Exports	$ 9,626	$ 12,056	$ 13,109	$ 14,907	$ 17,695	$ 23,618	N.Av.
Imports	(11,404)	(14,256)	(13,118)	(14,597)	(17,690)	(23,623)	N.Av.
Other goods and services	2,727	3,078	3,292	3,788	4,435	5,363	N.Av.
Unrequited transfers	(670)	(705)	(693)	(598)	(665)	(923)	$(1,020)
Direct investment	0	0	0	0	0	0	0
Portfolio investment	(1,755)	(954)	(3,503)	(5,172)	(4,760)	(6,210)	N.Av.
Other long-term capital	(1,001)	(630)	(962)	(2,067)	(2,190)	(4,734)	(7,150)
Other short-term capital	508	(489)	(2,897)	2,632	598	4,674	924
Errors and omissions	2,346	2,331	6,293	4,089	3,610	8,619	N.Av.
Foreign government holdings	6	(61)	23	3	14	538	755
Other official	190	107	0	(1)	20	36	(8)
Change in reserves	$ (574)	$ (476)	$ (1,543)	$ (2,986)	$ (1,066)	$ (7,354)	$(1,859)

Note: Parentheses indicate a debit.

N.Av. = not available.

Source: IMF, *International Financial Statistics*, September 1980.

Philip Morris, Incorporated: Swiss Franc Financing
EXHIBIT 9 • Balance of Payments, United States (billions of US$)

	1973	1974	1975	1976	1977	1978	1979
Exports	$ 71.42	$ 98.31	$107.13	$ 114.76	$ 120.82	$ 142.05	$ 182.05
Imports	(70.47)	(103.64)	(98.06)	(124.04)	(151.71)	(175.83)	(211.50)
Other goods and services	10.20	14.87	14.10	18.96	21.76	25.02	34.93
Unrequited transfers	(4.15)	(7.40)	(4.88)	(5.33)	(4.99)	(5.52)	(6.13)
Direct investment	(8.53)	(4.27)	(11.59)	(7.62)	(9.23)	(8.47)	(14.62)
Portfolio investment	3.20	(1.38)	(3.32)	(4.62)	(0.32)	0.40	(0.69)
Other long-term capital	(1.59)	(1.84)	(4.74)	(2.95)	(4.15)	(3.45)	(2.92)
Other short-term capital	(2.78)	(1.76)	(8.99)	(10.08)	(6.57)	(18.98)	5.06
Errors and omissions	(2.54)	(1.66)	5.68	10.43	(0.69)	11.44	23.66
Foreign government holdings	5.10	10.24	5.51	13.05	35.43	31.06	(13.56)
Other official	0.21	0.02	(0.50)	(0.04)	0.22	0.89	1.23
Change in reserves	$ (0.07)	$ (1.49)	$ (0.35)	$ (2.52)	$ (0.58)	$ 1.39	$ 2.47

Note: Parentheses indicate a debit.

Source: IMF, *International Financial Statistics*, September 1980.

Philip Morris, Incorporated: Swiss Franc Financing
EXHIBIT 10 • Excerpts from Articles Discussing Economic Conditions in Switzerland and the United States in Late 1980

International Currency Review 12, No. 5

U.S. Dollar. A brief pre-election period of improving morale during the third quarter, fostered by wishful thinking on the part of certain senior U.S. officials, punctuated the pervasive pessimism which has gripped the business community in the United States this year. The euphoria was quickly smothered, however, by rising interest rates and friction between the discredited Carter regime and the Federal Reserve Board following accusations from the White House that the central bank had been interfering with "the recovery." In practice, despite the speed with which the U.S. economy responds to monetary initiatives, the Federal Reserve system is in no better position to stabilise this inflationary economy than the man in the moon. But at least its preoccupation with domestic economic matters has been relatively unhampered by serious dollar crises in recent months, despite the grave turn of events in the Middle East—a point which officials have been anxious to stress. Indeed the dollar's "stability" has been just about the only positive development they have been able to report.

As severe inflationary distortions have multiplied, it has become increasingly difficult for officials, let alone outside observers, to monitor accurately what has been happening in the U.S. economy. Spokesmen sometimes employ misleading short-hand methods of making economic and political scoring points which merely confuse matters further. Use is also typically made of unreliable statistics as a basis for doubtful conclusions.

It is our considered view that, with economies so distorted, the international financial system swamped with capital flows and abruptly transferable liquidity, and political instability mounting, it has become impossible to anticipate how the dollar is likely to perform other than on a bilateral basis. All we know for sure is that the Federal Government has embarked on an unprecedented orgy of deficit spending which reached a peak in election year—a fact which, when considered in the context of the continued proliferation of external dollar-denominated liquidity, cannot fail to undermine the eventual purchasing power of the dollar both at home and abroad.

Yet in response to pressures resulting from the clash between the Federal sector's borrowing needs and those of private borrowers, market rates have risen and any early correction seems unlikely in the absence of drastic public spending reductions. Perversely, therefore, the medium-term outlook for the dollar is for continued artificial "strength," as the worldwide transactions' demand for dollars persists at inflated levels to pay for sky-high oil bills. With spot oil prices under upward pressure and another oil price explosion perhaps only months away, this artificial "strength" looks like [it is] becoming a semipermanent feature of the international economic environment.

Swiss Franc.   Although the current account of the Swiss balance-of-payments will be in deficit this year for the first time since 1965, the Swiss franc will not be unsettled. Indeed with inflation falling to a negligible level, the franc has fully recovered from the weakness it demonstrated during the first quarter of 1980; and it may again be facing a period of appreciation, especially as it is no longer protected by a battery of controls warding off foreign money.

Economic growth in Switzerland was fairly brisk during the first half of 1980. Although signs of a slowdown are now becoming more apparent (stocks are rising, and foreign orders are less buoyant), private consumption has recovered from last year's fall, while fixed investment seems likely to be the most vigorous sector of domestic demand. Business expenditure on plant and equipment is expected to rise by 5% in real terms this year. . . . .

Certainly, the 1981 budget announced in early October gave no indication of any stresses and strains in the allocation of resources. Even the budget deficit, the most intractable of all aggregates in the affairs of practically every other developed country, is diminishing in line with a medium-term programme—which specifies that it will be no greater than SFr 1500 million in 1983. Next year's budget deficit is estimated SFr 1.17 billion against SFr 1.29 billion in the current year and SFr 1.17 billion in 1979.

During the first quarter of 1980, the Swiss franc was seriously weakened by the combined impact of mounting inflation and a widening trade deficit. The elimination of most of the remaining controls on capital inflows had little immediate impact—although, at the time, the Swiss authorities made no attempt to match the higher interest rates that were on offer in all other financial centres. Only at the end of February was the discount rate raised by 1%, to 3%; now that rates in other financial centres are generally lower than they were 6 months ago, the differential against Switzerland is obviously less marked. Even so, Swiss rates are still much lower than elsewhere

The attraction appears to be that 3% earned on a deposit in Switzerland is very close to providing a real rate of return (as well as the renewed prospect of a capital gain through the currency's appreciation), while 15–20% earned in certain other European centres is still less than the current rate of reported or presumed inflation.

However, there would not appear to be any serious chance that the old problem of unwanted appreciation will return. Next year, when the current account may be in balance and inflation negligible, the attraction of the Swiss franc, no longer surrounded by a barricade of controls, may well prove irresistible. . . . There seems little doubt that many treasurers, either in national Treasuries or within multinational corporations, would welcome the opportunity to diversify at least a proportion of their dollar portfolios into Swiss francs, should appropriate opportunities become available.

Nigel Bance, "The World Economy in 1981," *Euromoney,* October 1980

There will be a sharp increase in world unemployment next year, matched by a sharp fall in world inflation. Economic growth rates will decline, but on the whole will be positive.

That is the summary of the average of more than 300 forecasts for 33 major economies that *Euromoney* has collected for our annual survey of the world economy.

As it turns out, the average of these forecasts—or if you like, the forecast of forecasts—has been a remarkably accurate guide to world growth, inflation, and unemployment. In the August issue of its *Monitor,* Dillon, Read analyzed the forecasts in our annual surveys on the world economy for 1977, 1978, and 1979. The analysis showed that average forecasts are a much better indicator of actual performance than individual forecasts. On economic growth, for example, the average error of the forecasts of forecasts for all countries in the survey was only 0.5%, that for inflation 1.1%.

The forecasters' expectations for this year and next are set out in the tables in this survey. But here's a brief summary of the major economies:

United States. All 32 forecasters expect an absolute decline in GNP this year. The average forecast is a negative 1.4%, coinciding exactly with the official forecast from the Council of Economic Advisors. But a modest recovery is expected in the first half of 1981 and the average forecast for next year is a positive 1%, although the Council of Economic Advisors expects only 0.3%. Inflation is expected to decline to below 10% in 1981, from 13% this year. And *all* forecasters expect U.S. unemployment to rise next year from an average of 7.6%, in 1980, to 8.6%.

	Real GNP		Consumer Prices		Unemployment Rate	
	1980	1981	1980	1981	1980	1981
United States						
Highest forecast	−0.5%	4.0%	14.0%	11.7%	7.9%	9.3%
Average forecast	−1.4	1.0	13.0	9.5	7.6	8.6
Lowest forecast	−3.0	−1.0	11.0	7.5	7.0	7.6
Switzerland						
Highest forecast	2.5	2.0	7.1	5.7	0.9	1.2
Average forecast	1.5	1.1	4.4	3.6	0.4	0.6
Lowest forecast	0.4%	0.5%	3.5%	2.5%	0.2%	0.2%

Burlington Northern Railroad Company

On July 9, 1990, Paul Weyandt, Director, Equipment Finance at Burlington Northern Railroad Company (BNRR), was leafing through the bids he had received for the lease financing deal being proposed by his office. Included in the $150 million of equipment to be leased were new and remanufactured diesel electric locomotives, bi-level and tri-level auto racks, box cars, coal gondola cars, and covered hopper cars (see Exhibit 1 for equipment descriptions). Mr. Weyandt had decided that the bid submitted by Phyllis Grossman, Vice President, Norwest Equipment Finance, had the most attractive attributes for the auto racks. In addition to a reasonable annual lease payment, Ms. Grossman's proposal also granted BNRR an option to purchase the auto racks at the end of the 15-year period.

Because of BNRR's good working relationship with Norwest over the years, Mr. Weyandt was confident that Rob McKenney, Vice President and Treasurer BNRR, would support the choice of Norwest. Before accepting the bid, however, Mr. Weyandt needed to demonstrate to Mr. McKenney that leasing through Norwest would be better for BNRR than borrowing $22 million to purchase the auto racks directly. Mr. Weyandt had already demonstrated to Mr. McKenney that the equipment was a good investment by showing that the discounted expected cash flows exceeded BNRR's 20 percent investment hurdle rate; now he had to determine the best way to finance the investment.

Burlington Northern Railroad Company

In 1990, Burlington Northern Railroad Company was the primary subsidiary of Burlington Northern Inc. (BNI), a holding company. With over 25,000 miles of track in the system, BNRR operated one of the largest railroads in the United States. When the railroad industry was essentially dereg-

This case was written by Associate Professor Kenneth Eades for the purposes of classroom discussion with the support of the Foundation for Leasing Education, the education foundation of the Equipment Leasing Association of America. Some figures have been altered at the request of the participating companies. Copyright © 1991 by the University of Virginia Darden School Foundation, Charlottesville, Virginia. All rights reserved.

ulated in 1980, BNRR's revenues became subject to the competition of the marketplace. Revenues were generated by transporting bulk freight across the country. Coal, the most important, accounted for approximately one-third of the company's total revenues. Other major products transported included those from the agricultural, forest, and automotive industries.

In May 1988, Burlington Resources, another subsidiary of BNI, was spun off as an independent corporation, and certain aspects of this spin-off were still having an effect on BNRR's financing decisions in 1990. Burlington Resources had contained the natural-resource operations of BNI, including the exploration, development, and production of oil, gas, coal, and other minerals. It also included the transportation and sale of natural gas, the sale of timber and logs, the manufacture and sale of forest products, and the management and development of real estate.

In the Burlington Resources spin-off, BNI stockholders were distributed shares of Burlington Resources Inc. proportionate to their ownership of BNI.[1] After the spin-off, BNI stockholders held both their old BNI shares plus new Burlington Resources shares. Because the BNI shares no longer represented a claim on the assets of Burlington Resources, the price of BNI shares dropped in value as soon as the Burlington Resources shares were distributed. The total wealth of BNI shareholders increased, however, because the loss in value of the BNI shares was more than offset by the market value of the new Burlington Resources shares distributed.

The spin-off had a significant effect on BNI's capital structure, because virtually no long-term debt was transferred along with Burlington Resources' assets. The act of removing Burlington Resources' assets and yet retaining the debt associated with those assets left BNI in the position of being a highly levered company with long-term debt representing 76 percent of its total capital in 1988. The company had publicly stated its intent of reducing the debt by $1 billion during 1989–1994 to keep its financial leverage within manageable limits. The combination of heavy capital needs and a recent fall in BNRR's revenue (see Exhibits 2 and 3 for financial data on BNI) made the reduction of debt an ambitious undertaking.

Capital expenditures were projected at $550 million in 1990 and had been $465 million in 1989. For 1990, $325 million was being invested in roadwork (railway track, track bedding, and track equipment), and the remaining $225 million was being spent on equipment (locomotives, rail cars, auto racks, etc.). Despite these heavy investments, BNRR had managed to fund most of its needs internally. The choices of external financing, however, were limited by the philosophy of BNI management that the interest of BNI shareholders should be the overriding consideration with every decision. Issuing new equity, for example, had been ruled out

---

[1] A spin-off is a form of corporate divestiture in which a holding company distributes shares of one of its subsidiaries to the holding company's shareholders. Thus, a spin-off creates a new company by slicing off part of the holding company.

because railroads rarely went to the equity markets and doing so might be interpreted negatively by the marketplace. Rather than risk a fall in the stock price, management had decided that if new investments could not be funded internally, they would either have to be funded with debt or be in the form of leases.

Norwest Equipment Finance

On December 31, 1989, Norwest Corporation, with $24.3 billion in assets, was one of the largest regional bank holding companies in the United States. Despite the difficult times facing many members of the banking industry, Norwest maintained a strong return on common equity of 19.6 percent and, on December 1, 1990, had increased its quarterly dividend to $0.205 from $0.185, the second increase for the year. The strong return on equity and increased dividends resulted in a record-high stock price of $24.13 on a book value of $13.67/share. The premium over book value reflected Norwest's relatively low number of highly levered transactions and its avoidance of the depressing effect that real estate loans were having on the market values of many other banks. The proportion of nonperforming assets in Norwest was less than half that of the average regional bank holding company.

Norwest Equipment Finance, which specialized in leasing to corporations, was a wholly owned subsidiary of Norwest Corporation. For over 20 years, Norwest Equipment Finance had leased equipment ranging from trucks to machine tools, computers, and railroad equipment to some of the largest companies in the United States. BNRR had been leasing equipment through Norwest for over 15 years.

Leasing at BNRR

Leasing played an important role at BNRR because of the company's tax status in 1990. The 1986 Tax Reform Act required that corporations not only compute their taxes as they had in the past, but also compute an alternative minimum tax (AMT). The AMT amount had to be paid if it exceeded the tax liability computed by the regular method. The 20 percent tax rate for AMT was much lower than the normal rate of 34 percent, but taxable income for AMT was computed much differently and could be much higher than the regular taxable income.[2]

A likely candidate for AMT was a company that reported large amounts of "tax-preference items," which included depletion allowances,

---

[2] For a more complete discussion of the AMT for corporations, see *Handbook of Equipment Leasing* by Richard Contino, New York, AMACOM, 1989.

intangible drilling costs, and accelerated depreciation of assets placed in service after 1986. Tax-preference items were deductible under the regular tax method but were not allowable deductions when taxable income was computed for AMT. The heavy demands for capital equipment in a railroad meant that BNRR carried a great deal of equipment on its books, and as a result, the company incurred large accelerated-depreciation expenses. The accelerated-depreciation expenses combined with other tax preference items had been sufficient to make BNI subject to the AMT in the past and into the foreseeable future.

As long as BNI was subject to the AMT, the value of owning an asset would be reduced because assets would have to be depreciated on a straight-line basis rather than on an accelerated basis. As a lessee, however, the lease payments made by BNRR were deductible regardless of whether the company was subject to AMT or not. Regarding BNRR's use of leases, Mr. Weyandt had recently stated:

> For the most part, leasing is either credit motivated or tax motivated. Sometimes a company will lease because it's a relatively weak credit and wants to use the lessor's ability to borrow money at a lower rate. Burlington, however, is a good credit. Our equipment-backed securities are rated Aa3 by Moody's and A+ by Standard and Poor's, so even a AAA-rated lessor could not realize enough advantage in the markets to make it worthwhile for us to lease through them. Because of our current tax situation, on the other hand, we are in a position of benefiting by leasing from a company that is not subject to AMT like we are. If a company is paying the 34 percent tax rate, it can fully utilize the depreciation expenses of an asset and then pass the depreciation benefits along to Burlington by leasing us the asset. So right now, leasing is basically a tax play for Burlington Northern.[3]

The leasing terms proposed by Norwest for the auto racks had the added advantage for BNRR of being an off-balance-sheet item. According to accounting principles, a lease had to be classified as either an operating or a capital lease (see Exhibit 4). If a lease were capitalized, the lessee had to report the value of the leased equipment as an asset and the value of the lease as a liability. Assuming that the asset value and lease value were identical, capitalizing a lease was equivalent to adding a 100 percent debt-financed asset to the books, which would increase BNRR's debt-to-equity ratio. Operating leases, on the other hand, were reported in the footnotes of the company's annual reports but were not required to be reported on the company's balance sheets. To achieve the objective of decreasing its financial leverage, therefore, BNRR was careful to make sure that all its new leases were classified as operating leases.

---

[3] Casewriter interview, March 25, 1991.

Two of the four criteria necessary to qualify as an operating lease were critical—the economic-life test and the value test. The estimated life of the auto racks was approximately 22 years; thus, the 15-year lease was shorter than required by the economic-life-test—75 percent of the asset's life. For purposes of the value test, Mr. Weyandt had computed the present value of the lease payments by discounting them at BNRR's cost of equipment-secured debt. His preliminary calculations indicated that the value test was also satisfied as the present value of the lease payments was less than 90 percent of the auto racks' current value.

Leasing the Auto Racks

Exhibit 5 illustrates the various methods of structuring a lease. In a *direct lease,* the manufacturer either leased directly to the lessee or sold the asset to an intermediary who acted as the lessor. In a *sale-and-lease-back* arrangement, the owner of an asset sold the asset to a lessor and then leased it back. Like most large leasing deals, however, BNRR's equipment lease would be structured as a *leveraged lease.*

Typical of most leveraged leases, the auto rack deal involved three parties: a lessee, an equity participant-lessor, and a debt participant. The auto racks would be purchased from the manufacturer by Norwest, who would act as the lessor and realize all the tax benefits of ownership. The leverage aspect of the lease arose because Norwest would contribute only 20 percent of the purchase price, with the remaining 80 percent being borrowed with either a public or private debt offering. Because of the large amount of debt required and the relatively attractive rates in the public market, it had been decided to issue public debt. To limit Norwest's exposure in the deal, however, the debt would be structured as a nonrecourse loan. Under such a loan, the debtholders had a first lien on the auto racks and, in the event of default, could repossess the auto racks directly from BNRR. The debtholders would not, however, have recourse to any other assets held by either BNRR or Norwest. The debt would provide leverage for Norwest, therefore, without being a general liability to the firm. From the debtholders' perspective, the nonrecourse debt would be virtually identical to an equipment-secured loan issued directly by BNRR.

The bankruptcy laws treated default on equipment-secured loans for railroads and airlines differently from the way it treated default on identical loans in other industries. If a railroad was forced into bankruptcy, the equipment-secured creditors had the right to repossess the pledged asset directly without waiting more than 60 days for a judgment from the bankruptcy court. In the case of a company in another industry, bankruptcy meant that the secured creditors would receive the proceeds of the sale of their collateral, but only if the courts deemed liquidation to be the appropriate action and only after protracted and costly legal proceedings. Thus, the special treatment by the bankruptcy laws made equipment-secured loans less risky for railroads than for other companies and allowed railroads to pay much lower interest rates for secured borrowing than for general credit. The nonrecourse loan arranged by BNRR for the auto racks gave the lenders virtually the same rights they would have had if the bonds had been issued by BNRR as a loan secured directly by the auto racks.

Morgan Stanley, an investment-banking firm retained by BNRR, had advised that the $17.6 million, 15-year bond issue would be rated by the rating agencies as Aa3/A+ and carry a rate of 9.81 percent with annual coupon payments and principal due at maturity. The notes would be serviced by BNRR's lease payments made to a trustee who would be obligated to make the interest and principal payments on the debt before any excess rent, renewal, or purchase option payments could be distributed to Norwest. In the event that BNRR missed a lease payment, Norwest could take one of several actions: keep the lease alive by making the missed payment for BNRR, pay off the debtholders and keep the auto racks, or cut its losses by allowing the debtholders to repossess the racks.

As part of the bidding process, Paul Weyandt had informed the bidders what the terms of each lease should be for each class of equipment. For example, the new locomotives were to be bid as a 23-year lease and the auto racks were to be bid as a 15-year lease. The leases were to have annual payments and allow BNRR to purchase the assets at a predefined price at the end of each lease. According to FASB 13, an operating lease could not give the lessee the right to purchase the asset at a bargain price—that is, at substantially below its residual value, the fair market value of the asset at the end of the lease (see the alternative-ownership test in Exhibit 4). Typically, industry practice was for the lessor to hire an independent appraiser and offer a purchase price to the lessee of no less than the inflation-adjusted appraised residual value. Currently, the industry was using a rate of 3.5 percent per annum to inflate the purchase price to future dollars. Thus, if an asset worth $1 million were to be leased for 15 years and the appraised residual value equaled 25 percent of its current value, the lowest purchase price Norwest would offer was $0.42 million [$0.25 \times \$1$ million $\times (1+.035)^{15}$].

The estimate of the auto racks' residual value played a significant role in how Norwest and BNRR valued the lease. The lease gave BNRR the right to buy the auto racks at a predefined purchase price, but neither Ms. Grossman nor Mr. Weyandt knew with any certainty what the market for used auto racks would be in 15 years. The major determinants of the residual value would be inflation and supply-and-demand forces. If inflation turned out to be higher than anticipated during the term of the lease, the value of the auto racks would also be high (and vice versa). If another railroad happened to go out of business close to the termination of the lease, a glut of used auto racks on the market would keep the market price of auto racks low. New auto racks being produced at significantly reduced prices or significantly higher quality would also exert downward pressure on the price of used auto racks.

Ms. Grossman realized that the purchase price was a critical part of the lease. If the purchase price ended up being higher than the market value of the auto racks at the end of the lease, BNRR would simply decline to buy from Norwest unless the auto racks were offered at the prevailing market price. On the other hand, if Ms. Grossman offered BNRR a purchase-option price that was too low, BNRR would almost certainly end up buying the racks and Norwest's yield on the lease would suffer. The trick was to offer Mr. Weyandt an attractive purchase price that satisfied the IRS's interpretation of the alternative-ownership test and also kept enough of the upside value of the asset to give Norwest a reasonable return on the lease.

For the auto racks, Norwest had bid a two-tier lease payment of $2.3 million for the first 7 years and $2.8 million for the last 8 years. The 15 lease payments were to be made annually beginning at the end of the first year. At the end of the lease, BNRR had the right to purchase the auto racks for $9.2 million, 25 percent of $22.1 million inflated at 3.5 percent per year for 15 years.

Analyzing the Lease

The lease-versus-buy analysis required several assumptions. In particular, BNRR's tax status was critical to how it assessed the value of the lease. BNRR's tax department had told Mr. Weyandt that the company would, assuming that the tax laws were not changed in the interim, be subject to AMT for at least the next 15 years. The auto racks would be depreciated on a straight-line basis over 14 years (to a 0 salvage value) rather than an accelerated basis [Modified Accelerated Cost Recovery System (MACRS) for 7-year property[4]]. Leasing meant, of course, that BNRR would forfeit the right to depreciate the asset altogether.

Another assumption critical to the analysis was the residual value of the auto racks. Because of the fixed purchase price, a high residual value in 2005 increased the value of the lease significantly. A low residual value in 2005 meant that the fixed purchase price would have no value to BNRR. Because of the uncertainty associated with its estimation and its potential impact on the overall decision, Mr. Weyandt had decided to compute the present value of the residual value separately. If the overall value of the lease depended too much on his estimate of residual value, he would have to reconsider whether he should recommend that BNRR lease the auto racks.

---

[4] See Exhibit 6 for MACRS depreciation schedule.

Burlington Northern Railroad Company
EXHIBIT 1 • Equipment Description

Equipment Type	Market Value	Description
New locomotives	$19,600,000	Built by Electro-Motive Division, General Motors Corporation—3800 HP diesel electric locomotive.
Remanufactured locomotives	47,740,000	Remanufactured by Morrison-Knudsen Company, Inc., Electro-Motive Division, General Motors Corporation, and VMV Enterprises, Inc. Remanufactured locomotives met or exceeded the performance standards and requirements for new locomotives.
Auto racks	22,067,600	Bi-level and tri-level auto racks built by Trinity Industries, Inc., and Thrall Car Manufacturing Company. Completely enclosed structures used to haul automobiles.
Box cars	7,680,000	Built by Gunderson Inc. 50.5-ft. hi-cube box cars with 8-ft. double plug doors.
Gondolas	12,288,000	Built by Bethlehem Steel Corp. Aluminum-bodied rotary coal gondolas, 4,400-cu.-ft. capacity with a maximum load of 120 tons of coal.
Covered hoppers	43,500,000	Built by Trinity Industries, Inc. Trough hatch-covered hoppers designed for 4,750 cu. ft. of grain up to a maximum of 110 tons.
	$152,875,600	

Burlington Northern Railroad Company
EXHIBIT 2 • BNI Income Statements, Bond, and Equity Data

Consolidated Income Statements, as of December 31
(in thousands of dollars)

	1989	1988
Revenue	$4,606,286	$4,699,517
Costs and expenses	(3,949,750)	(4,020,617)
Operating income	656,536	678,900
Interest expense on long-term debt	(270,272)	(292,050)
Other income (expense), net	4,397	(207,655)[a]
Income from continuing operations before taxes	390,661	179,195
Provision for income taxes	(147,670)	(80,493)
Income from continuing operations	242,991	98,702
Income from discontinued operations net of income taxes	0	57,048
Net income	$ 242,991	$ 155,750

[a]Includes litigation settlement of $175,000.

Bond Data as of July 9, 1990

Rating	Annual Coupon	Maturity Date	52-Week Price		Current Price
			High	Low	
Baa1	9⅝%	1996	102	97¾	100½
Baa1	9	2016	95	88	90¼
Baa1	8½%	1996	98⅞	95¾	97½

Equity Data

Shares common stock outstanding: 75,678,974 (3/31/90)

Share price: $37 (7/9/90)

Beta: Not a meaningful figure because of recent spin-off; 0.9 prior to spin-off.

Burlington Northern Railroad Company
EXHIBIT 3 • Consolidated Balance Sheets,
                as of December 31 (in thousands of dollars)

	1989	1988
Assets		
Cash and equivalents	$ 82,627	$ 83,620
Accounts receivable, net	430,355	685,018
Materials and supplies	133,286	157,954
Current portion of deferred income taxes	119,589	98,339
Other current assets	31,137	39,740
Total current assets	796,994	1,064,671
Property and equipment		
Road, roadway, and real estate	6,566,015	6,362,153
Equipment	1,777,927	1,766,458
Total PP&E	8,343,942	8,128,611
Accumulated depreciation and amortization	3,189,410	3,050,349
Property and equipment, net	5,154,532	5,078,262
Other assets	196,254	187,401
Total assets	$6,147,780	$6,330,334
Liabilities		
Accounts payable	$ 645,077	$ 628,008
Compensation and benefits payable	222,218	178,957
Accrued interest on long-term debt	77,375	96,972
Taxes payable	135,564	117,684
Other current liabilities	94,242	85,053
Current portion of long-term debt	113,490	112,083
Total current liabilities	1,287,966	1,218,757
Long-term debt	2,219,619	2,722,625
Other liabilities	268,721	270,702
Deferred income taxes	1,277,715	1,186,124
Total liabilities	5,054,021	5,398,208
Preferred stock	13,512	14,101
Common stock	967,528	992,405
Retained earnings (deficit)	131,544	(20,624)
Cost of treasury stock	(18,825)	(53,756)
Net worth	1,093,759	932,126
Total liabilities and net worth	$6,147,780	$6,330,334

Burlington Northern Railroad Company
EXHIBIT 4 • Rules for Determining Operating versus Capital Lease

According to the Financial Accounting Standards Board in Financial Accounting Standard No. 13, a lease must be capitalized if it meets any one of the following criteria:

1. *Ownership test:* The lessee automatically is transferred ownership of the asset by the end of the lease.

2. *Alternative-ownership test:* The lessee has the right to buy the asset at a price substantially below the fair market price.

3. *Economic-life test:* The lease term is greater than or equal to 75 percent of the estimated economic life of the asset.

4. *Value test:* The present value of the minimum lease payments is greater than or equal to 90 percent of the fair market value of the asset at the time of the lease.

Burlington Northern Railroad Company
EXHIBIT 5 • Lease Structures

Lease Structures

1. Direct Lease

2. Sale and Lease Back

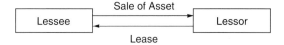

3. Leveraged Lease

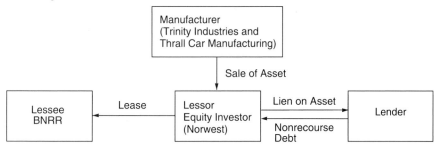

Burlington Northern Railroad Company
EXHIBIT 6 • MACRS 7-Year Property-Depreciation Schedule[a]

Tax Year	MACRS Schedule	Beginning Tax Basis
1	0.1429	1.0000
2	0.2449	0.8571
3	0.1749	0.6122
4	0.1249	0.4373
5	0.0893	0.3124
6	0.0892	0.2231
7	0.0893	0.1339
8	0.0446	0.0446

[a]Because of the half-year convention, 7-year MACRS involves 8 years of depreciation expenses.

Bearings, Inc.

In late November 1983, Raymond Smiley, vice president of finance for Bearings, Inc., was focusing his thoughts on the upcoming Finance Committee meeting. Since joining Bearings 2 years earlier, Mr. Smiley had become convinced that the company's capital structure needed to be altered to facilitate funding of the growth planned for the company by John R. Cunin, chairman of the board. While Mr. Smiley's most immediate concern was to determine the best method of funding the company's $45-million need, he had two general questions on his mind: (1) what funding alternatives were open to him, given the company's historically conservative management philosophy, and (2) what funding options needed to be available to fund future growth requirements.

He wanted to begin discussion of these topics at the meeting. Before recommending a significant change in the financial structure, Mr. Smiley knew he should carefully think through his ideas.

Products and Customers

Bearings was the leading national distributor of ball, roller, linear, and thrust bearings, power-transmission equipment, and other industrial supplies. The company did not manufacture any of the products it sold; it bought bearings and bearing accessories from over one hundred manufacturers, such as Timken, SKF, Fafnir, Torrington, and MRC/TRW. Bearings stocked over 145,000 types and sizes of bearings. Sales were made through an extensive network of 262 service centers located across the United States.

In the fiscal year ended June 30, 1983, Bearings reported $5.4 million in net income on $351.2 million of sales—its first sales decline in 25 years. (Exhibit 1 presents recent financial statements.) A breakdown of 1983 sales showed that ball, roller, thrust, and linear bearings amounted to 55 percent

---

of sales, power-transmission equipment to 32 percent, and specialty products such as seals, lubricants, and bearing-related devices to 13 percent. The fiscal year 1976 breakdown had been 67 percent, 20 percent, and 13 percent, respectively.

Bearings had more than 175,000 customers, and its average order was $180. About 10 percent of the company's sales came from the forest-products industry, followed by primary metals, food processing, mining, and textiles. These top five industry groups accounted for just under 30 percent of Bearings' 1983 revenues.

In keeping with its founder's original strategy, 85 percent of the company's business was from the replacement and maintenance markets. Only 15 percent was from the original equipment market (OEM), which bearing manufacturers dominated.

History

Bearings, Inc., was founded in 1923 by Joseph M. Bruening when he was 27. He borrowed $5,000 and started selling replacement parts for cars and trucks. Over the next 6 decades, the company grew through product-line expansion and acquisition of regional distribution companies. By 1983 Bearings had total assets of nearly $200 million and an equity base of $120 million. Management owned 14 percent of the common stock; institutions held about 50 percent.

Bearings' business philosophy clearly reflected Mr. Bruening's spartan management style; the company prided itself on its lean profile. It had only two vice presidents when its revenues reached $275 million in 1978. As one observer noted, "Bruening ran a metal-desk, linoleum-floor kind of company." This conservative attitude could also be seen in the company's balance sheet, where long-term debt was seldom greater than 7 percent of equity. The strength of the company's balance sheet made it a very attractive takeover candidate, however, and several times in the 1970s, Mr. Bruening had been approached by conglomerates seeking to acquire Bearings. Mr. Bruening always responded that his most important goal was to maintain Bearings as an independent company.

In 1980 Mr. Bruening, then 84 years old, decided that the time had come for him to step down from the day-to-day management of Bearings. While retaining the position of chairman of the board, he transferred the responsibility of president and chief executive officer to Mr. Cunin, a 35-year company veteran. In 1983 Mr. Cunin assumed the position of chairman and chief executive officer. Although trained in the Bruening school of management, he and the new president brought more aggressive leadership to the company. First, they increased the number of corporate officers, hiring Mr. Smiley among others. Second, they expanded the number of sales offices. Third, and perhaps most important, Mr. Cunin established a corporate goal of $1 billion in sales by 1988. Exhibit 2 provides projected income statements reflecting Mr. Cunin's sales goal.

The Industrial Distribution Industry

Bearings, Inc., competed in the very fragmented industrial distribution industry. This $40-to-$45 billion market included sales of machinery, tools, pulleys, chains, power-transmission equipment, and bearings. Highly cyclical, sales for the industry declined by 10 percent during the 1982 recession. As of November 1983, sales were down an additional 2 percent. Prior to the 1982 recession, however, the industry had shown solid growth of 12.7 percent per year from 1975 through 1981 (see Exhibit 3).

The sale of bearings and other antifriction components totaled $2.9 billion in 1982. This figure represented a 20-percent drop from the $3.6 billion of bearing sales in 1981. Sales data for 1958 to 1983 are shown in Exhibit 4. Power-transmission items accounted for another $4.5 billion in sales in 1982. Over 3,400 independent distributors handled nearly 80 percent of all bearings sold.

Although the industrial distribution industry was highly fragmented, and competition tended to be regional, Bearings management viewed two companies as its primary national rivals: Motion Industries and Kaman Bearing and Supply.

Motion Industries, a division of Genuine Parts Company, sold a product line comparable to Bearings' to 100,000 customers in 20 states through 160 branches and distribution centers. Genuine Parts had entered the industrial-parts replacement business in 1976 with the acquisition of Motion Industries. By 1982 Genuine Parts had acquired three more industrial distribution concerns and was second in the industry behind Bearings. In 1982 Genuine Parts' Industrial Parts Group had sales of $374 million, an operating profit of $22 million, and assets of $156 million.

Kaman Corporation was a diversified, technology-oriented company with strengths in precision measurement, aerospace manufacturing, and military software and systems. In addition, Kaman had a major presence in industrial distribution as both a bearing manufacturer and distributor. Kaman Bearing and Supply was formed in the early 1970s in order to expand the corporation's bearing-manufacturing capability and to balance its exposure to the aerospace market. In 1982 Kaman's industrial distribution division recorded $199 million in revenues and operating profits of $9.2 million on an asset base of $65 million. That division accounted for roughly 40 percent of Kaman Corporation's total sales and operating profits. Data for both Kaman and Genuine Parts are presented in Exhibit 5.

Bearings' current strategy was to compete as the highest priced, highest value-added player. Genuine's strategy was similar to Bearings', but it offered a slightly lower price with noticeably less service. Kaman, on the other hand, aimed at offering the lowest cost product with little value-added service. Kaman's low-cost products were imported from Japan, a source that Bearings and Genuine had avoided.

Recent Developments

The fiscal year that ended on June 30, 1983, had been Bearings' most difficult in recent memory. As a result of the overall economic downturn of 1982 and 1983, Bearings posted quarterly income results below those of the previous year for 6 consecutive quarters. (Exhibit 6 presents quarterly earnings and market price information.) While most of the company's situation could be attributed to the business cycle, some internal decisions had also adversely affected results during this period.

On June 30, 1982, Bearings made its first acquisition in more than 15 years when it purchased Advance Bearing and Supply Company of Worcester, Massachusetts. This move provided Bearings with an immediate position in the New England market, which the company previously had not tapped. In November 1982, the company purchased the Cottingham Bearing Corporation of Dallas for $12 million cash. As it had in New England, Bearings penetrated the southwestern regional market more quickly than would have been possible through internal growth. However, the startup costs associated with the acquisitions had an adverse impact on the financial statements: inventory buildups increased interest expenses.

Bearings' stock price had remained remarkably strong during the recessionary period and as it made its acquisitions. Mr. Smiley attributed the strength partly to the market's approval of the new management and partly to the market's implicit endorsement of the company's new momentum. He wondered, however, whether the two acquisitions had caused Bearings to be identified as a possible takeover candidate. Its strong balance sheet and solid cash flows could attract a raider. Although Mr. Smiley knew of no effort to accumulate a position in Bearings' shares, any institutional holder might be prepared to sell if an attractive takeover offer were made.

Funding Options

Because of the capital market's lack of familiarity with Bearings, Mr. Smiley wished to raise enough external funds to last the company for the next several years. Previous external financing raised by Bearings had been in the form of a term loan through a local bank. Mr. Smiley wanted to repay the $7-million long-term note (due in 1986); to cover refinancing the two recent acquisitions, which had been funded through short-term debt totaling $15.5 million; and to provide the company with another $22 million to finance the next several years' working-capital and capital-expenditure needs. By raising $45 million in this first trip into the capital markets, Mr. Smiley believed Bearings would be in a strong position to move toward Mr. Cunin's $1-billion sales goal.

As Mr. Smiley pondered the upcoming Finance Committee meeting where he would make a recommendation to Mr. Cunin, he reviewed the list of funding alternatives presented by the company's investment banker. Management's initial inclination had been to make an equity issue. Although Bearings' common stock was currently trading just below its recent all-time high of almost $41 a share, Mr. Smiley was confident the company could net $36 a share after discounts and issuing costs. The strong market price and the belief that an equity issue would best maintain Bearings' reputation as a conservatively financed company were the major arguments in favor of the stock issue. Mr. Smiley believed that the company would maintain its $0.25 quarterly dividend policy except under the most dire circumstances.

He had one other funding option to consider. The company could contract a 20-year debenture for $45 million. Mr. Smiley believed that Bearings could line up funding at 13.00 percent. Annual sinking-fund payments of $3 million would begin in 1989. Exhibit 7 provides data on historical interest rates.

With this information in hand, Mr. Smiley set out to draft his recommendation for the Finance Committee.

Bearings, Inc.
EXHIBIT 1 • Financial Information, Fiscal Years Ending June 30, 1980–1983
    (millions of dollars, except per-share data)

	1980	1981	1982	1983
Income Statements				
Sales	$332.9	$358.2	$370.2	$351.2
Cost of goods sold	234.4	252.8	262.6	247.2
Gross profit	98.5	105.4	107.6	104.0
Selling, general, and administrative	68.8	73.9	80.4	89.8
Depreciation	1.6	1.7	1.8	2.6
Earnings before interest and taxes	28.1	29.8	25.4	11.6

Bearings, Inc.
EXHIBIT 1 • *continued*

	1980	1981	1982	1983
Interest	2.5	2.3	2.6	2.1
Profit before taxes	25.6	27.5	22.8	9.5
Taxes	12.4	13.3	10.8	4.1
Net income	$ 13.2	$ 14.2	$ 12.0	$ 5.4
Balance Sheets				
Assets				
Cash	$ 2.3	$ 2.2	$ 1.5	$ 3.4
Accounts receivable	40.0	47.0	41.4	44.1
Inventories	84.4	81.7	90.2	107.2
Other current assets	2.2	1.6	4.2	4.5
Total current assets	128.9	132.5	137.3	159.2
Property, plant, and equipment	27.8	30.7	37.3	46.7
Less depreciation	(8.8)	(10.3)	(11.8)	(14.1)
	19.0	20.4	25.5	32.6
Other assets	0.3	0.3	0.3	0.7
Total assets	$148.2	$153.2	$163.1	$192.5
Liabilities and Equity				
Notes payable	$ 9.6	$ 5.2	$ 5.5	$ 23.0
Accounts payable	23.8	20.4	22.6	30.8
Other current liabilities	6.7	9.3	8.4	10.0
Total current liabilities	40.1	34.9	36.5	63.8
Long-term debt	7.0	7.0	7.0	7.0
Deferred taxes	0.0	0.0	0.3	0.9
Total liabilities	47.1	41.9	43.8	71.7
Common stock	10.0	10.0	10.0	10.0
Retained earnings	91.2	101.4	109.4	110.9
Treasury stock	(0.1)	(0.1)	(0.1)	(0.1)
Total equity	101.1	111.3	119.3	120.8
Total liabilities and equity	$148.2	$153.2	$163.1	$192.5
Other Relevant Data				
Common shares (millions)	3.99	3.99	3.99	3.99
Earnings per share	$ 3.30	$ 3.55	$ 3.01	$ 1.36
Dividends per share	0.96	1.00	1.00	1.00
Average market price	28.50	26.50	29.25	32.88
Price/earnings ratio	8.6×	7.5×	9.7×	24.3×
Dividend yield	3.4%	3.8%	3.4%	3.0%

Bearings, Inc.

EXHIBIT 2 • Summary Projected Income Statements, 1984–1988 (millions of dollars)

	1984	1985	1986	1987	1988
Sales	$431	$530	$652	$802	$1,000
Gross profit	121	148	183	225	280
Selling, general, and administrative (includes depreciation)	95	117	143	176	220
Earnings before interest and taxes	$ 26	$ 32	$ 39	$ 48	$ 60

Assumptions:

Sales growth of 23 percent per year.

Gross profit margin of 28 percent.

Selling, general, and administrative at 22 percent of sales includes depreciation of $2.9, $3.2, $3.8, $4.2, and $4.5 (millions) for 1984–1988.

Bearings, Inc.

EXHIBIT 3 • Industrial Distributor Sales

Year	Distributor Sales (billions)	Percentage Change from Previous Year
1972	$16.4	N.Ap.
1973	20.8	26.8%
1974	23.5	13.9
1975	23.3	(0.9)
1976	24.9	6.9
1977	29.4	18.1
1978	33.2	12.9
1979	37.8	13.9
1980	41.6	10.1
1981	47.8	14.9
1982	43.3	(9.4)

N.Ap. = not applicable.

Source: *Industrial Distribution,* July 1983.

Bearings, Inc.
EXHIBIT 4 • Total Value of U.S. Sales of Antifriction
Bearings and Components (dollars in millions)

Year	Total Value	Annual Change	Value in 1967 Dollars	Annual Change
1958	$ 636.8	N.Ap.	N.Ap.	N.Ap.
1963	961.0	N.Ap.	N.Ap.	N.Ap.
1967	1,292.2	N.Ap.	$1,292.2	N.Ap.
1968	1,293.7	0.1%	1,274.6	(1.4)%
1969	1,396.0	7.9	1,350.1	5.9
1970	1,295.3	(7.2)	1,186.2	(12.1)
1971	1,258.2	(2.9)	1,101.8	(7.1)
1972	1,418.7	12.8	1,212.6	10.1
1973	1,695.7	19.5	1,403.7	15.8
1974	1,960.7	15.6	1,395.5	(0.6)
1975	2,046.3	4.4	1,246.2	(10.7)
1976	2,195.2	7.3	1,243.0	(0.3)
1977	2,444.5	11.4	1,277.2	2.8
1978	2,799.3	14.5	1,356.9	6.2
1979	3,260.5	16.5	1,438.9	6.0
1980	3,284.5	0.7	1,239.0	(13.9)
1981	3,607.7	9.8	1,183.6	(4.5)
1982	2,888.7	(19.9)	871.4	(26.4)
1983 (est.)	$2,746.3	(4.9)%	$ 826.9	(5.1)%

N.Ap. = not applicable.
Source: *Industrial Distribution,* October 1983.

Bearings, Inc.
EXHIBIT 5 • Selected Data on Competitors (millions of dollars)

	1981	*1982*
Sales		
Genuine Parts Company	$1,875.7	$1,936.5
Industrial Parts Group	413.7	374.1
Kaman Corporation	416.5	475.4
Industrial Distribution Division	162.4	198.5
Operating Profit		
Genuine Parts Company	200.1	200.8
Industrial Parts Group	30.7	22.1
Kaman Corporation	26.5	33.9
Industrial Distribution Division	9.2	8.6
Identifiable Assets		
Genuine Parts Company	705.8	754.4
Industrial Parts Group	159.6	155.6
Kaman Corporation	160.3	170.5
Industrial Distribution Division	$ 63.8	$ 65.0

Bearings, Inc.
EXHIBIT 6 • Quarterly Summary Income Data and Stock Prices

Year/ Quarter	Sales (millions)	Earnings per Share	Stock Price Range		S&P 500 Index Closing Price
			High	Low	
1980					
3	$76.4	$0.79	$35½	$29	102.9
4	80.6	0.81	32⅛	28½	114.2
1981					
1	89.3	0.92	33⅜	22¾	125.5
2	86.6	0.78	25⅛	21½	135.8
3	79.6	0.65	29¾	23¾	136.0
4	85.3	0.75	27⅞	23¾	131.2
1982					
1	94.4	1.01	29½	22½	116.2
2	98.8	1.14	29⅝	25¾	122.6
3	95.6	0.94	27	25⅛	111.9
4	91.8	0.79	36	26⅝	109.6
1983					
1	92.9	0.75	35⅛	27¾	122.4
2	90.0	0.53	29⅝	26¾	139.5
3	81.3	0.37	30	26	151.9
4	82.0	0.17	36	28¼	166.4
1984					
1	90.6	0.34	39	32	164.4
2	97.2	0.48	40⅜	31¼	167.4
3	$98.9	$0.50	$41	$33	159.2

Note: Bearings' beta was 0.75 at the end of 1984.

Source: New York Stock Exchange, *Stock Price Guides—1980–1984.*

Bearings, Inc.
EXHIBIT 7 • Interest Rates[a]

Year		Prime Bank Rate	Corporate Bonds	
			Aaa	Baa
1978		9.06%	8.43%	9.36%
1979		12.67	9.55	10.65
1980		14.88	11.75	13.48
1981		19.10	14.23	16.23
1982		15.00	13.68	15.76
1983	Jan.	11.50	11.00	12.38
	Feb.	11.00	11.13	12.25
	March	10.50	10.50	11.88
	April	10.50	11.00	11.75
	May	10.50	10.60	11.25
	June	10.50	11.25	12.13
	July	10.50	11.38	12.13
	Aug.	10.50	12.20	13.00
	Sept.	11.00	12.38	13.25
	Oct.	11.00	11.85	12.50
	Nov.	11.00%	12.00%	12.88%

[a]Average for the period.

Sources: *Economic Report of the President,* 1985; and *Federal Reserve Bulletin,* various issues.

Van Dusen Air, Inc.

In June 1985, Gordon Foster, the chief financial officer at Van Dusen Air, Inc., studied the alternatives for financing the company's most recent acquisition. Acquisitions were normal for Van Dusen, because its historical strategy had been to grow through friendly purchases of smaller firms. The $14.5-million purchase of Burlington Northern Airmotive, however, was by far the largest the company had ever made. Its size and Van Dusen management's desire to maintain financial flexibility in order to grow would require careful financing; Van Dusen had already begun analyzing its next potential acquisition.

The Industry

Van Dusen provided repair service, fuel, and replacement parts to both the general and commercial aviation markets. The U.S. general aviation market consisted of over 200,000 aircraft, all of which required maintenance, periodic engine overhauls, and replacement parts. The commercial aviation market consisted of approximately 2,700 aircraft; service to commercial carriers was restricted almost entirely to refueling at major airports, because the airlines generally performed the other services themselves.

The industry served everyone from the private pilot needing a new tire for a plane through companies in need of engine overhauls for corporate aircraft to major commercial airlines in need of fuel. Thus the aviation services industry was highly fragmented, with small aircraft-maintenance shops scattered throughout the United States.

The demand for services in the industry depended on airport activity. In 1984 the Federal Aviation Administration (FAA) reported that control-tower activity was up 5 percent for general aviation and 12 percent for commercial aviation from the prior year. The FAA projected that the activity level of general aviation aircraft would increase at low-to-

This case was prepared as a basis for class discussion rather than to illustrate either effective or ineffective handling of an administrative situation. Copyright © 1986 by the University of Virginia Darden School Foundation, Charlottesville, Virginia. All rights reserved.

moderate rates through the early 1990s but that the use of the more sophisticated aircraft (generally those with turbine engines) would more than double by the mid-1990s.

Van Dusen had a broad customer base. In fiscal year 1985, the company's top 10 customers accounted for 6.4 percent of total revenue, and the top 40 provided only 12.1 percent of the total. Van Dusen was thought to have a 10-percent share of the market, which was enough to dominate it because the nearest competitor had only a 2-percent share of part of the market (the piston-overhaul business). Van Dusen's share of the turbine-overhaul market was small, because it had only recently entered this segment of the industry. The wholesale price of an overhaul on a piston engine was $8,000, while that for a turbine engine was $65,000.

Given Van Dusen's broad range of services in the general aviation industry, few companies were in full competition with Van Dusen. As Exhibit 1 shows, however, some competitors did have considerable resources. Van Dusen occasionally had to compete with parts manufacturers, many with superior financial resources, that sold their goods directly to the end user. Thus, while Van Dusen was thought to be an overall leader in the industry, it did face substantial competition in nearly all phases of its operations.

Although many manufacturers of parts-and-supplies for general aviation aircraft sold directly to end users, the majority sold through independent distributors like Van Dusen. The parts manufacturers relied on these distributors to provide much of the advertising and servicing for their products. These parts were sold both as original equipment and as replacement parts.

The wholesale side of the general aviation parts-and-supplies industry was also fragmented. Van Dusen purchased roughly 10 percent of its parts from its largest supplier and thought that other distributors purchased from an equally diverse range of suppliers.

The Company

Van Dusen Air, Inc., was a multinational company serving the worldwide aviation market. The company had been incorporated in 1942 when G. B. Van Dusen started selling parts at the Minneapolis–St. Paul International Airport. The company currently had operations in over 30 domestic locations and in 20 international branches and had roughly 1,100 employees.

The three operating divisions at Van Dusen were Domestic Parts, International Parts, and Aviation Services. Both parts divisions distributed parts and supplies, primarily to corporate and general aviation customers, in their respective regions. The Aviation Services Division provided maintenance, engine overhaul, and fueling services to the general aviation market throughout the United States.

Van Dusen had recently begun to shift some emphasis from its parts-distribution business to its Aviation Services Division's fixed-base operations (FBO) locations. In 1980, parts and supplies represented nearly 80 percent of Van Dusen's total revenue; in 1985, the company projected 70 percent of total revenue would come from parts and supplies. Management expected this trend to continue. The repair market was growing faster than the parts market, and management thought that the FBOs were a way to tap into the growing market for repairs. The company wanted to maintain its parts business but integrate it into the FBOs.

As it suffered through the recession and the air traffic controllers' strike of 1982, the company's net income fell from $4.6 million in 1981 to $361,000 in 1983. Van Dusen had not been hit as hard by previous recessions, and it was largely because of this drop in earnings that it had begun to emphasize the faster-growing FBO side of the business.

At the same time, the company's strategy had included growth through the friendly acquisition of smaller companies in the general aviation industry, many of which consisted of FBOs. Recent acquisitions included Burlington Northern Airmotive (FBO) in April 1985, Mattituck Airbase, Inc. (FBO) in June 1984, and Universal Export Corporation (parts manufacturer) and Hughes Aviation Services Aircraft Products Division (FBO), both in fiscal year 1983.

This strategy had been very successful for Van Dusen. Revenue had grown from $52 million in 1976 to an estimated $126 million in 1985. The company's net income over that same time period had grown from $1.7 million to an estimated $4.3 million. Exhibits 2 and 3 show the company's financial statements for the years 1976 to 1984. To continue strong growth, management had concluded that both geographical expansion and expansion into the FBO market (both by aggressive acquisition) were necessary.

In addition to this expansionary strategy, Van Dusen also planned to emphasize further the maintenance and overhaul of turbine-type engines of general aviation aircraft. The company was in a good position in the piston market because, except for piston and engine manufacturers, it had the largest piston-overhaul facilities in the industry. The number of turbine engines in use was significantly lower than that of piston engines, but as noted, the use of turbine engines, with their more advanced technology, was expected to increase at a higher rate. Exhibit 4 contains forecasts of piston and turbine engine use. Management believed that a strong presence in the turbine market, coupled with the company's advanced capabilities, would increase maintenance revenues and parts sales.

Van Dusen had a goal of reaching over half a billion dollars in total revenues by 1990 through its expansionary strategy. Exhibits 5 and 6 contain the company's financial-statement projections through 1990. As Exhibit 6 shows, management expected the parts business to grow at a steady rate, but expectations were much higher for the Aviation Services Division.

Burlington Northern Airmotive

In April 1985, Van Dusen agreed to acquire Burlington Northern Airmotive (BNA), which had been a subsidiary of Burlington Northern, Inc., for $14.5 million in cash. BNA was strategically attractive to Van Dusen for several reasons. First, its broad range of services and excellent reputation would definitely increase Van Dusen's presence in the FBO industry. Its location at Minneapolis–St. Paul International Airport gave Van Dusen an FBO to serve the upper Midwest. One of the top 20 FBO locations in the United States, the area was thought to account for 5 percent of the total U.S. general aviation market. Van Dusen currently had a parts distribution outlet in Minneapolis but no FBO. In addition to the FBO operation for fueling and storage of general aviation aircraft, BNA specialized in the maintenance and overhaul of turbine engines. Furthermore, BNA's long profit history fit with Van Dusen's strategy to purchase only companies that required no extensive turnaround efforts.

Mr. Foster had secured short-term funds to pay for the purchase in April, but those notes were fast coming due. He was uncertain how to achieve the flexible long-term financing Van Dusen wanted.

Financing Alternatives

Van Dusen Air already had a 9.4 percent, $6.5-million term loan due in 1992, capitalized leases with a principal value of $1.2 million due in varying amounts through 1988, and a $10-million revolving credit arrangement with an insurance company,[1] of which $7.5 million had been drawn down. Van Dusen was in compliance with all covenants, including one from the revolver that prohibited Van Dusen from incurring any unsubordinated debt in excess of 75 percent of its consolidated tangible net worth.[2]

The acquisition of BNA had looked good not only to Van Dusen, but also to many bankers and investment bankers. Mr. Foster had been approached by several different companies that wanted to provide Van Dusen with the long-term financing needed. He had narrowed the choices down to four alternatives he found most attractive:

---

[1] The interest rate on the revolver was 1⅞ percent over the 30-day certificate of deposit rate and 0.5 percent on the undrawn portion. In 1980 the 30-day certificate of deposit rate averaged 12.91 percent; in 1981 it averaged 15.91 percent. The rate dropped back to 12.04 percent in 1982 and to an average of 8.96 percent in 1983. In 1984 it rose to 10.17 percent, but by late June 1985, it had fallen to 7.10 percent

[2] Consolidated tangible net worth = Stockholders' equity − Intangible (other) assets.

1.   The first alternative was a straight equity issue for a total of $15 million. Although Mr. Foster was not sure what price per share would be placed on the offering, he had been told by the investment banker proposing the issue that (after fees) the proceeds to the company would most likely be $13 per share, which could be compared with a high stock price of $15 in the prior year and a current price of $14. The company would have to issue 1,153,846 new shares to obtain the funds needed. Exhibit 7 provides Van Dusen's recent stock-price history.

2.   Mr. Foster had also received a proposal that offered a new seven-year term loan for $22.5 million at an interest rate of 13.3 percent per year. Payments would be made semiannually. A covenant of the current revolver loan restricted Van Dusen to an additional $8.6 million of long-term debt unless the revolver was fully repaid. At the time, ten-year Treasuries were yielding 10.2 percent and three-month Treasuries were yielding 7.0 percent.

3.   The third proposal Mr. Foster evaluated was a private placement of subordinated convertible debentures for $15 million. Mr. Foster expected the coupon rate to be 12 percent and the fees 1 percent of the total offering. A sinking fund would begin after the fifth year, with equal payments (at par value) made until the bonds matured in 15 years (if they had not been converted). Each bond was convertible into 57 shares of common stock. The conversion price of $17.50 was 25 percent over the current $14 stock price. After the third year, Van Dusen could call the bonds for $24.50 in cash.

4.   The fourth option was similar to the third, except that it would be a publicly placed subordinated convertible debenture. The coupon for this offering would be 11 percent, and the fee paid would be 4 percent of the total issue. The public placement would have the same sinking fund, maturity, and conversion provisions that the private issue would have.

Van Dusen Air, Inc.

EXHIBIT 1 • Selected Data for Competitors in the General Aviation Parts-and-Supplies Industry (in thousands, except per-share amounts)

	Van Dusen	AAR	Aviall	Butler
Revenues				
1982	$143,097	$175,924	$221,754	$343,808
1983	137,460	155,006	299,933	342,587
1984	144,902	177,762	400,520	313,745[a]
Net Income				
1982	3,086	1,225	2,960[b]	6,311
1983	361	2,795	1,891	5,112
1984	1,792	4,487	8,140	6,266
Long-term Debt				
1983	9,384	23,504	154,000	15,764
1984	15,391	13,040	150,000	11,100
Stockholders' Equity				
1982				
1983	33,056	43,225	5,773	67,683
1984	33,302	81,085	13,794	64,600
Dividends per Share				
1984	0.40	0.44	0.0	0.52
Earnings per Share				
1982	1.01	0.33	0.79	1.13
1983	0.12	0.71	(0.06)	0.82
1984	0.59[c]	0.97	1.59	0.96
Recent Stock Prices[d]				
1982 High	20.50	14.75	N.Av.	17.38
Low	9.50	6.13	N.Av.	7.88
1983 High	12.50	9.88	N.Av.	24.50
Low	8.25	5.75	N.Av.	14.88
1984 High	15.00	17.75	15.00	20.75
Low	$10.25	$8.63	$10.00	$12.13

N.Av. = not available (because Aviall was privately held before 1984).

[a]Total before extraordinary items.

[b]Butler 1984 totals exclude discontinued operations.

[c]Van Dusen was not extremely closely held. G. B. Van Dusen and his family controlled roughly 16 percent of the company's stock, the largest block of shares outstanding.

[d]A comparable index, Standard & Poor's 500, was 119.71 in 1982, 160.41 in 1983, and 160.39 in 1984.

Van Dusen Air, Inc.
EXHIBIT 2 • Balance Sheets for Years Ended December 31 (thousands of dollars)

	1976	1977	1978	1979	1980	1981	1982	1983	1984
Assets									
Cash	$ 3,418	$ 1,323	$ 1,492	$ 1,836	$ 1,775	$ 5,602	$ 671	$ 2,748	$ 2,312
Accounts receivable	9,657	10,970	13,414	17,384	21,719	23,633	24,549	17,469	22,233
Inventories	14,853	16,522	15,397	18,811	24,259	23,486	25,743	20,519	27,865
Prepaid expenses	185	330	438	301	581	799	909	900	923
Federal tax refunds	0	0	0	0	0	0	0	1,236	447
Total current assets	28,113	29,145	30,741	38,332	48,334	53,520	51,872	42,872	53,780
Buildings	1,430	1,501	1,588	1,508	2,740	2,750	3,534	3,987	4,413
Leasehold improvements	3,126	2,706	2,911	3,044	3,887	4,575	5,236	5,553	4,992
Airplanes and equipment	2,201	2,364	3,049	3,372	4,370	5,074	7,814	9,988	9,794
Accumulated depreciation	(2,144)	(2,297)	(2,517)	(2,756)	(3,239)	(4,206)	(5,446)	(7,091)	(7,953)
Net property, plant, equipment	4,613	4,274	5,031	5,168	7,758	8,193	11,138	12,437	11,246
Other assets	697	234	316	310	224	390	736	1,571	2,066
Total assets	$33,423	$33,653	$36,088	$43,810	$56,316	$62,103	$63,746	$56,880	$67,092
Liabilities and Stockholders' Equity									
Notes payable	$ 0	$ 76	$ 0	$ 0	$ 8,201	$ 341	$ 2,808	$ 34	$ 4
Current maturities	597	820	670	674	781	1,989	1,374	1,734	1,679
Accounts payable	6,689	6,278	5,563	8,665	8,739	9,352	6,937	6,410	8,810
Accrued salaries	1,170	1,231	1,457	2,313	2,560	3,349	2,133	2,124	2,514
Other accrued liabilities	0	0	0	0	0	0	1,482	1,018	1,705
Accrued taxes	1,782	911	1,512	1,291	1,202	2,033	820	595	935
Total current liabilities	10,238	9,316	9,202	12,943	21,483	17,064	15,554	11,915	15,647
Deferred taxes	804	948	1,389	1,872	2,263	2,366	2,580	2,298	2,304
Long-term debt	12,563	11,953	12,321	11,559	11,919	10,377	10,949	9,384	15,391
Accrued pensions	0	0	0	0	0	0	13	227	448
Long-term liabilities	$13,367	$12,901	$13,710	$13,431	$14,182	$12,743	$13,542	$11,909	$18,143
Common stock	1,161	1,161	1,328	1,725	2,453	3,014	3,069	3,149	3,149
Paid-in capital	1,835	2,192	3,327	8,049	8,095	15,441	15,772	15,702	15,702
Retained earnings	6,822	8,083	8,521	7,662	10,103	13,841	15,809	15,026	15,596
Treasury stock	0	0	0	0	0	0	0	(821)	(1,145)
Stockholders' equity	9,818	11,436	13,176	17,436	20,651	32,296	34,650	33,056	33,302
Total liabilities and stockholders' equity	$33,423	$33,653	$36,088	$43,810	$56,316	$62,103	$63,746	$56,880	$67,092

Van Dusen Air, Inc.
EXHIBIT 3 • Income Statements (in thousands)

	1976	1977	1978	1979	1980	1981	1982	1983	1984
Revenues									
Parts and supplies	$52,709	$61,369	$72,915	$86,059	$104,157	$114,701	$119,041	$116,261	$123,438
Fuel and airplanes	4,238	4,965	6,137	7,313	11,364	14,770	16,540	13,751	12,396
Airport services	5,249	4,887	5,459	5,886	6,138	7,080	7,516	7,448	9,068
Total revenues	62,196	71,221	84,511	99,258	121,659	136,551	143,097	137,460	144,902
Operating expenses									
Cost of parts and supplies	38,494	44,999	54,079	64,056	77,218	82,275	85,407	84,658	91,356
Cost of fuel and airplanes	8,765	8,905	10,472	11,892	15,402	19,631	22,205	19,804	19,549
Selling and warehousing	8,813	10,077	11,675	12,585	16,047	20,174	23,206	23,607	22,586
Total operating expenses	56,072	63,981	76,226	88,533	108,667	122,080	130,818	128,069	133,491
Operating income	6,124	7,240	8,285	10,725	12,992	14,471	12,279	9,391	11,411
Corporate expenses and other income									
Administrative expenses	1,544	1,719	1,886	3,198	3,755	4,081	5,875	6,879	7,025
Interest expense	1,305	1,967	1,551	1,132	1,831	1,937	1,087	2,229	1,271
Interest income	246	842	504	167	28	122	88	40	258
Total corporate expenses	2,603	2,844	2,933	4,163	5,558	5,896	6,874	9,068	8,038
Income before taxes	3,521	4,396	5,352	6,562	7,434	8,575	5,405	323	3,373
Taxes	1,759	2,313	2,826	3,353	3,518	4,001	2,319	-38	1,581
Net income	$ 1,762	$ 2,083	$ 2,526	$ 3,209	$ 3,916	$ 4,574	$ 3,086	$ 361	$ 1,792
Dividends	$ 324	$ 373	$ 449	$ 584	$ 788	$ 836	$ 1,118	$ 1,251	$ 1,222
Common shares outstanding	2,101	2,121	2,151	2,301	2,493	2,598	3,069	3,108	3,045

Van Dusen Air, Inc.
EXHIBIT 4 • Forecasted General Aviation Aircraft
by Type of Aircraft (in thousands)

	Piston		Turbine	
	Single Engine	Multi-Engine	Turboprop	Turbojet
1985	162.9	25.0	6.0	4.5
1986	166.7	25.6	6.6	4.9
1987	172.0	26.5	7.1	5.2
1988	178.7	27.5	7.6	5.5
1989	187.1	28.8	8.1	5.7
1990	192.2	29.6	8.6	5.9
1991	197.0	30.5	9.1	6.2
1992	202.4	31.4	9.6	6.5
1993	207.7	32.2	10.1	6.7
1994	212.6	33.0	10.5	6.9
1995	216.8	33.7	10.9	7.1

Source: Van Dusen Air management estimate.

Van Dusen Air, Inc.
EXHIBIT 5 • Balance Sheet Projections (in thousands)

	1985	1986	1987	1988	1989	1990
Assets						
Current assets	$65,159	$73,284	$ 82,482	$ 98,845	$115,656	$125,922
Net property and other assets	14,654	20,233	24,097	27,015	32,717	39,176
Total assets	$79,813	$93,517	$106,579	$125,860	$148,373	$165,098
Liabilities and stockholders' equity						
Current liabilities	$26,659	$41,108	$ 47,659	$ 58,125	$ 68,891	$ 73,405
Long-term liabilities	16,746	13,049	14,862	16,806	18,467	21,598
Stockholders' equity	36,408	39,360	44,058	50,929	61,015	70,095
Total liabilities and stockholders' equity	$79,813	$93,517	$106,579	$125,860	$148,373	$165,098

Assumptions

1. As a result of programs in place to reduce receivables and inventories and extend payables, current assets will grow at an average annual rate of 14 percent and current liabilities at 22 percent.

2. Property and other assets will increase at an average rate of 21 percent per year as a result of acquisitions.

3. Long-term liabilities were used as the plug for the balance sheet.

Van Dusen Air, Inc.
EXHIBIT 6 • Income-Statement Projections (in thousands)

	1985	1986	1987	1988	1989	1990
Revenues						
Parts and supplies	$126,312	$141,126	$158,176	$175,047	$191,211	$209,380
Aviation services	45,897	101,874	142,462	190,436	247,652	315,454
Total revenues	172,209	243,000	300,638	365,483	438,863	524,834
Operating income	14,971	23,072	28,464	37,197	44,756	55,774
Administrative expense	7,061	10,807	12,928	16,246	16,508	18,818
Earnings before interest and taxes	7,910	12,265	15,536	20,951	28,248	36,956
Interest expense	2,523	4,180	4,060	4,667	5,135	4,153
Earnings before taxes	5,387	8,085	11,476	16,284	23,113	32,803
Taxes	1,069	3,921	5,566	7,898	11,210	15,910
Net income	$ 4,318	$ 4,164	$ 5,910	$ 8,386	$ 11,903	$ 16,893
Dividends	$ 1,212	$ 1,212	$ 1,212	$ 1,515	$ 1,818	$ 1,818

Assumptions

1. Total revenue will grow at an average rate of 25 percent per year. The majority of that growth will come from the Aviation Services Division's future acquisitions.

2. Cost of goods sold and administrative expense/revenue will gradually decrease because of the synergy experienced with future acquisitions.

3. Interest expense will remain fairly stable as new debt used to make acquisitions replaces existing long-term debt.

4. Dividends will be $0.40/share through 1987, $0.50/share in 1988, and $0.60/share for 1989 to 1990.

5. Shares outstanding will remain constant at 3.03 million shares.

Van Dusen Air, Inc.
EXHIBIT 7 • 1985 Weekly Stock-Price History

Date	High	Low	Close
1/4	$13.50	$13.00	$13.50
1/11	14.25	13.50	14.25
1/18	14.00	13.50	13.50
1/25	13.75	13.00	13.00
2/1	13.25	13.00	13.00
2/8	13.25	13.00	13.00
2/15	13.25	13.00	13.00
2/22	13.25	13.00	13.25
3/1	13.25	13.00	13.25
3/8	13.25	13.00	13.25
3/15	13.50	13.00	13.50
3/22	13.50	13.25	13.38
3/29	13.50	13.13	13.25
4/5	13.00	12.88	12.88
4/12	12.75	12.50	12.63
4/19	12.50	12.13	12.50
4/26	12.38	12.25	12.25
5/3	12.25	11.75	12.00
5/10	12.50	11.75	12.50
5/17	13.00	12.50	13.00
5/24	13.00	13.00	13.00
5/31	$13.75	$13.00	$13.50

Dozier Industries (A)

▼

Richard Rothschild, the chief financial officer of Dozier Industries, returned to his office after a meeting with two officers of Southeastern National Bank. He had requested the meeting to discuss financial issues related to Dozier's first major international sales contract, which had been confirmed the previous day, January 13, 1986. Initially, Rothschild had contacted Robert Leigh, a vice president at the bank who had primary responsibilities for Dozier's business with Southeastern National. Leigh had in turn suggested that John Gunn of the bank's International Division be included in the meeting since Leigh felt that he, himself, lacked the international expertise to answer all the questions Rothschild might raise.

The meeting had focused on the exchange risk related to the new sales contract. Dozier's bid of £1,175,000 for the installation of an internal security system for a large manufacturing firm in the United Kingdom had been accepted. In accordance with the contract, the British firm had transferred by cable £117,500 (i.e., 10 percent of the contract amount) as deposit on the contract, with the balance due at the time the system was completed. Dozier's production vice president, Mike Miles, had assured Rothschild that there would be no difficulty in completing the project within the 90-day period stipulated in the bid. As a result, Rothschild was planning on receiving £1,057,500 on April 14, 1986.

History of the Company

Dozier Industries was a relatively young firm specializing in electronic security systems. It had been established in 1973 by Charles L. Dozier, who was still president and the owner of 78 percent of the stock. The remaining 22 percent of the stock was held by other members of management. Dozier had formerly been a design engineer for a large electronics firm. In 1973 he began his own company to market security systems and began by concentrating on military sales. The company experienced rapid growth for almost a decade. However in 1982, as Dozier faced increased competition in this market, management attempted to branch out to design systems for the private sector, namely small firms and households. Dozier's inexperience in this market, combined with poor planning efforts, slowed sales growth and led to a severe reduction in profits (see Exhibit 1). The company shifted its focus to larger corporations and met with better success. In 1985 the company showed a profit for the first time in three years, and management was confident that the company had turned the corner. Exhibit 2 contains the balance sheet at the end of 1985.

The company's management believed that sales to foreign corporations represented good prospects for future growth. Consequently, in the spring of 1985, Dozier had launched a marketing effort overseas. The selling effort had not met with much success until the confirmation of the contract discussed previously. The new sales contract, although large in itself, had the potential of being expanded in the future since the company involved was a large multinational firm with manufacturing facilities in many countries.

Foreign Exchange Risk and Hedging

On January 13, the day the bid was accepted, the value of the pound was $1.4480. However, the pound had weakened over the past six weeks (see Exhibit 5). Rothschild was concerned that the value of the pound might depreciate even further during the next 90 days, and it was this worry that prompted his discussion at the bank. He wanted to find out what techniques were available to Dozier to reduce the exchange risk created by the outstanding pound receivable.

Gunn, the international specialist, had explained that Rothschild had several alternatives. First, of course, he could do nothing. This would leave Dozier vulnerable to pound fluctuations that would entail losses if the pound depreciated, or gains if it appreciated versus the dollar. On the other hand, Rothschild could choose to hedge his exchange risk.

Gunn explained that a hedge involved taking a position opposite to the one that was creating the foreign exchange exposure. This could be accomplished either by engaging in a forward contract or via a spot transaction. Since Dozier had an outstanding receivable in pounds, the appropriate hedging transactions would be to sell pounds forward 90 days or to secure a 90-day pound loan. By selling pounds forward, Dozier would incur an obligation to deliver pounds 90 days from now at the rate established today. This would insure that Dozier would receive a set dollar value for its pound receivable, regardless of the spot rate that existed in the future.

The spot hedge worked similarly in that it also created a pound obligation 90 days hence. Dozier would borrow pounds and exchange the proceeds into dollars at the spot rate. On April 13, Dozier would use its pound receipts to repay the loan. Any gains or losses on the receivable due to a change in the value of the pound would be offset by equivalent losses or gains on the loan payment.

Leigh assured Rothschild that Southeastern National would be able to assist Dozier in implementing whatever decision Rothschild made. Dozier had a $3 million line of credit with Southeastern National. John Gunn indicated that there would be no difficulty for Southeastern to arrange the pound loan for Dozier through its correspondent bank in London. He believed that such a loan would be priced 1½ percent above the U.K. prime rate. In order to assist Rothschild in making his decision, Gunn provided him with information on interest rates and spot and forward exchange rates (see Exhibits 4 and 5).

Rothschild was aware that in preparing the bid Dozier had allowed for a profit margin of only 6 percent in order to increase the likelihood of winning the bid and, hence, developing an important foreign contact. The bid was submitted on December 3, 1985. In arriving at the bid, the company had estimated the cost of the project, added an amount as profit, but kept in mind the highest bid that could conceivably win the contract. The calculations were made in dollars and then converted to pounds at the spot rate existing on December 3 (see Exhibit 3), since the U.K. company had stipulated payment in pounds.

Rothschild realized that the amount involved in the contract was such that an adverse move in the pound exchange rate could put Dozier in a loss position for 1986 if the transactions were left unhedged. On the other hand, he also became aware of the fact that hedging had its own costs. Still, a decision had to be made. He knew that no action implied that an unhedged position was the best alternative for the company.

Dozier Industries (A)

EXHIBIT 1 • Sales and Income Summary (in thousands)

Year Ended December 31	Sales	Net Income
1973	$ 456	$ 41
1974	631	54
1975	890	73
1976	1,610	151
1977	3,860	324
1978	7,242	760
1979	11,338	1,162
1980	15,138	1,488
1981	20,371	1,925
1982	21,455	712
1983	22,501	(242)
1984	23,986	(36)
1985	$25,462	$ 309

Dozier Industries (A)
EXHIBIT 2 • Balance Sheet as of December 31, 1985

Assets

Current assets

Cash and securities		$ 294,572
Accounts receivable		1,719,494
Inventories		2,227,066
Total current assets		$ 4,241,132

Property, plant, and equipment:

At cost	8,429,812	
Less accumulated depreciation	2,633,404	
Net plant		5,796,408

Other assets

Investments and loans		450,000
Total assets		$10,487,540

Liabilities and Equity

Current liabilities

Accounts payable		$ 934,582
Notes payable—bank		652,800
Total current liabilities		1,587,382

Long-term liabilities

Notes payable		550,000

Common equity

Common stock		2,253,410
Reserves		627,244
Retained earnings		5,469,504
Total equity		8,350,158
Total liabilities and equity		$10,487,540

Dozier Industries (A)
EXHIBIT 3 • Bid Preparation

Materials	$ 847,061
Direct Labor	416,820
Shipping	70,000
Direct overhead[a]	208,410
Allocation of indirect overhead	100,492
Total cost	1,642,783
Profit factor	98,567
Total	$1,741,350

Spot pound rate on December 3: 1.4820

Pound value of the bid: £1,175,000

[a]Based on 50% of direct labor.

Dozier Industries (A)
EXHIBIT 4 • Interest and Exchange Rate
Comparisons—January 14, 1986

	United States	United Kingdom
Three-month money[a]	7.65%	13.41%
Prime lending rate	9.50	13.50
Three-month deposits (large amounts)	8.00	12.90
Euro $ 3 month (LIBOR)	N.Ap.	8.3
Euro £ 3 month (Paris)	13.2	N.Ap.
Three-month treasury bills in London		12.2
The spot rate for the pound:	1.4370	N.Ap.
Three-month forward pound:	1.4198	N.Ap.

N.Ap. = not applicable.

[a]Prime commercial paper in the United States; interbank rates in the United Kingdom.

Source: *The Economist*

Dozier Industries (A)
EXHIBIT 5 • Historical Spot and Forward Pound Rates in U.S. Dollars

Date	Spot	Three-month Forward Rate
7/9/85	$1.3640	$1.3490
7/16	1.3880	1.3744
7/23	1.4090	1.3963
7/30	1.4170	1.4067
8/6	1.3405	1.3296
8/13	1.3940	1.3828
8/20	1.3900	1.3784
8/27	1.3940	1.3817
9/4	1.3665	1.3553
9/10	1.3065	1.2960
9/17	1.3330	1.3226
9/24	1.4200	1.4089
10/1	1.4120	1.4005
10/8	1.4155	1.4039
10/15	1.4120	1.4007
10/22	1.4290	1.4171
10/29	1.4390	1.4270
11/5	1.4315	1.4194
11/12	1.4158	1.4037
11/19	1.4320	1.4200
11/26	1.4750	1.4628
12/3	1.4820	1.4704
12/10	1.4338	1.4214
12/17	1.4380	1.4249
12/23	1.4245	1.4114
12/30	1.4390	1.4260
1/7/86	1.4420	1.4284
1/14/86	$1.4370	$1.4198

Source: *Chicago Mercantile Exchange Statistical Yearbook.*

Dozier Industries (B)

Richard Rothschild, the chief financial officer of Dozier Industries, was still contemplating how best to manage the exchange risk related to the company's new sales contract. The £1,057,500 balance of the contract was due in three months on April 14, 1986, creating a long position in British pounds. Rothschild had spoken previously to John Gunn, an officer in the International Division of Southeastern National Bank, about hedging his long pound exposure. Gunn had explained two alternatives available to Dozier to reduce the exchange risk: a forward contract or a spot transaction. Either transaction would ensure that Dozier would receive a set dollar value for its pound receivable, regardless of any change in the value of the pound. Given his previous analysis of the foreign exchange market, Rothschild was concerned that both of these hedging alternatives would "lock in" a profit margin below the 6 percent he had originally anticipated for the contract. He wondered if there were some way to get the upside potential without all the risk.

The pound had weakened since his bid submission date on December 3 (See Exhibit 1), but he was not entirely convinced it would continue to fall, or at least not as much as the forward rate indicated. If the future spot rate were greater than the current forward rate, an unhedged position could lead to a gain, whereas a hedged position would create an opportunity lost. Rothschild wondered if other alternatives were available, and he again called John Gunn at the bank for advice.

Gunn explained that Rothschild could also use currency options to hedge against his uncertain foreign exchange exposure. Options provide a means of hedging against volatility without taking a position on expected future rates. Gunn explained that there are two basic varieties of options contracts: puts and calls. A put gives the holder the right, but not the obligation, to sell foreign currency at a set exercise or "strike" price within a specified time period. A call gives the holder the right to buy foreign currency at a set price. In comparison with a forward or futures contract, the holder of an option does not have to transact at the agreed-on price, but has the choice or option to do so. Gunn told Rothschild that options are complicated and increase the front-end cost of hedging in comparison with a forward hedge. He said Rothschild could find the prevailing option contract prices in *The Wall Street Journal* (See Exhibit 2).

It appeared to Rothschild that options contracts might provide some benefit. He wondered if options contracts were the best alternative for Dozier right now. He also wondered whether he could have used options contracts when preparing his bid.

Dozier Industries (B)
EXHIBIT 1 • Historical Spot and Forward Pound Rates in U.S. Dollars

Date	Spot	Three-month Forward Rate
7/9/85	$1.3640	$1.3490
7/16	1.3880	1.3744
7/23	1.4090	1.3963
7/30	1.4170	1.4067
8/6	1.3405	1.3296
8/13	1.3940	1.3828
8/30	1.3900	1.3784
8/27	1.3940	1.3817
9/4	1.3665	1.3553
9/10	1.3065	1.2960
9/17	1.3330	1.3226
9/24	1.4200	1.4089
10/1	1.4120	1.4005
10/8	1.4155	1.4039
10/15	1.4120	1.4007
10/22	1.4290	1.4171
10/29	1.4390	1.4270
11/5	1.4315	1.4194
11/12	1.4158	1.4037
11/19	1.4320	1.4200
11/26	1.4750	1.4628
12/3	1.4820	1.4704
12/10	1.4338	1.4214
12/17	1.4380	1.4249
12/23	1.4245	1.4114
12/30	1.4390	1.4260
1/7/86	1.4420	1.4284
1/14/86	$1.4370	$1.4198

Source: *Chicago Mercantile Exchange Statistical Yearbook.*

Dozier Industries (B)
EXHIBIT 2 • Foreign Currency Options on January 14, 1986

Options and Underlying	Strike Price	Calls-Last			Puts-Last		
		Jan.	Feb.	Mar.	Jan.	Feb.	Mar.
12,500 British Pounds—cents per unit							
British Pound	.130	s	r	13.50	s	r	r
144.41	.135	s	r	9.20	s	0.20	0.50
144.41	.140	s	4.50	4.75	s	0.80	1.55
144.41	.145	s	1.55	2.50	s	3.10	4.40
144.41	.150	s	0.40	0.90	s	r	r

r—not traded; s—no option offered
Last is premium (purchase price).

Source: *The Wall Street Journal.* Foreign Currency Options listed on the Philadelphia Exchange.

Dozier Industries (B)
EXHIBIT 3 • Foreign Currency Options on December 3, 1985

Options and Underlying	Strike Price	Calls-Last			Puts-Last		
		Dec.	Jan.	Mar.	Dec.	Jan.	Mar.
12,500 British Pounds—cents per unit							
British Pound	.120	29.00	s	28.95	r	s	r
148.86	.130	19.10	r	r	r	r	r
148.86	.135	13.80	r	14.60	0.05	r	r
148.86	.140	8.80	r	10.00	0.05	r	s
148.86	.145	4.00	4.50	5.70	0.20	1.05	3.20
148.86	.150	0.65	1.65	3.35	r	r	5.60
148.86	.155	r	0.50	1.70	r	r	r

r—not traded; s—no option offered
Last is premium (purchase price).

Source: *The Wall Street Journal.* Foreign Currency Options listed on the Philadelphia Exchange.

General Motors:
Valuation of Class E Contingent Notes

On July 3, 1989, the treasury staff at General Motors was busy projecting the company's cash flows for the next three years. GM's board of directors used the projections to make quarterly dividend and capital spending decisions as well as to identify borrowing needs. Projecting the revenues and production costs for the various production divisions was relatively easy compared to the task of estimating the impact of certain contingent liabilities facing the company. In particular, GM had issued contingent notes as part of the compensation package for the purchase of Electronic Data Systems (EDS) in 1984, and these notes were due to mature within the three-year planning period. Therefore, the treasurer's staff was faced with two tasks: estimating a fair value of the notes, which were not publicly traded, and assigning a reasonable value to the expected impact of the notes on GM's cash flows.

General Motors and Electronic Data Systems

With revenues of $59.63 billion in the first six months of 1989, General Motors boasted the largest total sales figure of any U.S. company. More importantly, GM's profits had improved over the past few years despite significant changes in the auto business. (Exhibits 1 and 2 provide GM's financial highlights and consolidated balance sheets through the year ended December 31, 1988.)

At the beginning of the decade, the company faced many challenges, as reflected in the following passage taken from the 1989 General Motors Public Interest Report:

> Imports from off-shore manufacturers were on the increase, customer expectations were rising, and technology was changing the way in which cars and trucks were being built. In addition, the economy of scale efficiencies that had historically contributed to the success of GM

The case was adapted from a study by Anne L. Hinckley, under the supervision of Associate Professor Kenneth M. Eades as a basis for classroom discussion. Copyright © 1991 by the University of Virginia Darden School Foundation, Charlottesville, Virginia. All rights reserved.

were beginning to shrink and change in light of a worldwide market that was fragmenting into smaller, more specialized, and more numerous product niches.

In response to these challenges, GM had undertaken a massive reindustrialization program that focused on improving quality and profitability. The program enabled GM to offset a shrinking domestic market share with increased productivity and profits: GM's market share in the United States had declined to 35 percent from more than 40 percent, whereas overseas sales had increased. The net effect was that GM was using 26 percent fewer workers to produce 15 percent fewer cars in 1989 than it had ten years earlier.

As part of its strategy, GM had employed EDS to design large-scale data-processing systems and communications networks for GM's worldwide administration, distribution, and manufacturing processes. EDS's expertise was instrumental in the application of advanced computer-aided design (CAD), engineering (CAE), and manufacturing (CAM) systems and computer-integrated manufacturing (CIM) technologies. These methods allowed GM to build the same quality motor vehicles with shorter production lead times, thus reducing overall production costs. EDS also assisted GM on a variety of other automation projects, including benefits administration, dealer network communication, and comprehensive business information systems.

Class E Contingent Notes

According to a Wall Street rumor, when GM analysts valued potential EDS billings to GM at more than EDS's market value, GM opted to purchase the company for $2 billion. When the merger was consummated on October 18, 1984, the EDS shareholders were given the choice of exchanging each of their EDS shares for either $22 in cash or $17.60 in cash plus $2/10$ of a unit which included one share of Class E common stock (GME) and one contingent promissory note.[1] The new Class E shares were issued to reduce the amount of cash required for the merger without diluting the interest of GM shareholders. The main differences between the Class E shares and the regular GM common shares (referred to as $1-2/3$ shares) were voting rights and dividends. Because Class E shareholders had received cash as part of their compensation packages, each E share was entitled to only 0.25 votes, compared with one vote for each $1-2/3$ share. The E shares also received a lower dividend than the $1-2/3$ shares. The dividend was structured to

---

[1] All the per-share amounts in the case have been adjusted to reflect a 2-for-1 stock split of the GME shares, which occurred in 1985. Thus the original offer of $44/share is reported as $22/share to be consistent with the post-split GME share prices.

depend directly on the performance of EDS, not GM, and therefore served as an effective incentive compensation for key EDS employees.

Following the merger, the chairman and majority shareholder of EDS, Ross Perot, frequently voiced his public displeasure with GM management. This conflict was resolved in 1986 when GM bought all of Perot's E shares and contingent notes leaving 10,475,164 notes outstanding in 1989.

Although the contingent notes paid no interest, noteholders were entitled to receive a principal payment that depended on the price of the Class E shares. The payoffs to the contingent notes were such that if investors held E shares and contingent notes, the value of their combined holdings would be worth at least $62.50/share when the notes matured seven years after issuance. For example, if at maturity (October 18, 1991) E shares were selling for $60.00, GM would have to pay $2.50 for each note to meet the promised value of $62.50/share. On the other hand, GM would have no liability if the E shares were selling for $62.50 or higher at maturity.

The notes could be offered for prepayment at discounted amounts on certain dates prior to maturity. As illustrated in the following table, October 28, 1989, was the first date on which a contingent noteholder could demand a prepayment from GM:

Class E Contingent Note Prepayment Schedule		Contingent Note Price
Optional prepayment dates:	October 28, 1989	$46.38
	April 28, 1990	49.97
	October 28, 1990	53.84
	April 28, 1991	58.01
Final maturity date:	October 18, 1991	$62.50

The treasury staff expected few investors to take advantage of the optional prepayment opportunities, however, because the contingent note price increased to $62.50 from $46.38 over two years, which equaled a 16.1 percent annual increase. Thus, a reasonable assumption was that payments would occur only on the final maturity date. How large that payout was likely to be and the value of that option to the noteholders needed to be assessed for cash planning purposes in light of the current stock price.

Valuing the Contingent Notes

The staff had concluded that the contingent notes should be valued using an option pricing framework such as the model derived by Professors Black and Scholes in 1973. Black and Scholes had approached valuing a

call option by determining the option price that eliminated arbitrage
opportunities in the market. The model was derived under the assumption that an investor could create a riskless hedge by holding a portfolio
containing the option and its underlying stock in the precise proportions
that guaranteed a riskless return regardless of the stock price at the end
of the holding period. Other assumptions of the model are that the stock-
price volatility and riskfree rate are constant and known over the life of
the option, stock returns are normally distributed, the option can be
exercised only at maturity (a European option), and transaction costs are
zero. The dividend-adjusted Black-Scholes equation for the value of a
call option is

$$C = (S - De^{-rt})N(d_1) - Ee^{-rt}N(d_2)$$

where:

$$
\begin{aligned}
C &= \text{value of call option,} \\
S &= \text{current stock price,} \\
D &= \text{stock dividends received over the life of the option,} \\
N(d) &= \text{normal distribution evaluated at d,} \\
d_1 &= \frac{\ln(S/E) + (r + (\sigma^2/2)t}{\sigma\sqrt{t}} \\
d_2 &= \frac{\ln(S/E) + (r - (\sigma^2/2)t}{\sigma\sqrt{t}} \\
E &= \text{exercise price of the option (also called the strike price),} \\
r &= \text{continuously compounded riskfree interest rate (annual basis),} \\
t &= \text{time (in years) to option exercise date,} \\
\sigma &= \text{annual volatility (standard deviation of stock returns), and} \\
e &= 2.7183.
\end{aligned}
$$

To compute the value of a put option (P) on the same underlying stock (S)
at the same exercise price (E), the put–call parity formula is invoked,

$$P = C + Ee^{-rt} - (S - De^{-rt})$$

Although mathematically complex, the option pricing model had
become a standard tool for estimating the value of many types of options
and other contingent claims. Most of the inputs to the model were fairly
straightforward. For example, the current stock price, exercise price, time
to maturity and riskfree rate were directly observable. Estimating the present value of future dividends (De^{-rt}), however, frequently required some

judgment. Like most option contracts, the GM contingent noteholders did not have the rights to dividend distributions made on the underlying stock. Therefore, subtracting the value of future dividends made sense, because as earnings were paid out as dividends,the expected future common stock price was reduced, which in turn reduced the call option value and increased the put option value.[2] GM's policy was to pay a dividend for the E shares equal to 25 percent of EDS's earnings in the prior year. For 1989 management had announced that the payout ratio would be raised to 30 percent. (See Exhibit 3 for a summary of dividends and earnings for GM and GME stocks.) Thus, in this instance, an accurate prediction of future dividends did not appear difficult.

Computing the appropriate volatility would be much more demanding. Volatility was supposed to capture the market's expectation of how future stock prices would fluctuate as measured by the annual variance of stock returns (σ^2). Whether future expectations could accurately be measured using past stock price data, however, was unclear. In any case, historical prices for Class E shares, GM shares, and the Standard & Poor's 500 were available to estimate weekly volatility, which could then be converted into an annual estimate (see Exhibit 4).

An alternative method of estimating volatility was to determine the volatility implicit in the price of a traded option. As indicated in Exhibit 5, both GM and GME shares had options outstanding that were traded on exchanges. The problem was to find the volatility measure that, combined with all the other model inputs, produced the observed market price of the option. Assuming that the option pricing model was correct, the volatility implied by the market price should reflect the market's expectation of *future* volatility—at least over the life of the option being analyzed.

Before deciding how best to estimate volatility, a more fundamental issue was whether the notes should be modeled as a put or call option. In addition, some thought had to be given to how reasonable it was to ignore the prepayment opportunities. The basic Black-Scholes model assumed that options were European; i.e., they could be exercised only at maturity. An American option was one that was exercisable any time up to and including the maturity date. Since the contingent notes had specific prepayment opportunities, they might be best considered American options. If so, the European version of the model would give a downward biased estimate of the true value, because American options are always worth at least as much as their European counterparts. On the other hand, the prepayment schedule could make investors view the notes as European options. Because the prepayment prices increased over time, a noteholder

---

[2] The valuation of the future dividends in this formulation of the model is only an approximation for a couple of reasons. First, the dividend stream is valued as if the dividends were received as a lump sum on the maturity date. Secondly, the dividends are assumed to be known with certainty and are therefore discounted at the riskfree rate.

would sacrifice some guaranteed price appreciation by accepting an early prepayment. If the increase in prepayment were large enough, most noteholders would choose to hold their notes to October 18, 1991, the final maturity, to capture the full guaranteed price appreciation.

After estimating a value for the contingent notes, the impact of the notes on GM's cash flows had to be estimated. Calculating a single expected cash flow did not make sense, because there was a good chance that GM would pay nothing. At the current price of $50.50, GME stock would have to increase at a rate of only 9.7 percent per year to reach $62.50 by October 1991. Of course, anything could happen when it came to the movements of stock prices, but 9.7 percent annual appreciation seemed a good possibility for a stock with a beta of 1.10 in a market where two-year Treasury notes were yielding 8.2 percent.[3]

---

[3] GME's beta is taken from *Value Line Investment Survey,* and the Treasury yield is from the July 3, 1990, issue of *The Wall Street Journal.*

General Motors
EXHIBIT 1 • Financial Highlights (dollars in millions except per-share amounts)

	1986	1987	1988
Sales and revenues			
GM, excluding GMAC[a]	$102,813.7	$101,781.9	$110,228.5
GMAC and other financing and insurance operations	11,335.5	10,932.4	10,667.9
Other income	2,863.0	3,912.3	4,913.9
Intersegment transactions	(1,402.3)	(1,756.2)	(2,168.7)
Total sales and revenues	115,609.9	114,870.4	123,641.6
Worldwide factory sales of cars and trucks (units in thousands)	8,576	7,765	8,108
Net income	$2,944.7	$3,550.9	$4,856.3
As a percentage of sales and revenues, excluding GMAC	2.9%	3.5%	4.4%
As a percentage of average common stockholders' equity	9.8%	11.3%	14.6%
Earnings attributable to:			
$1-⅔ par value common stock[b]	$2,607.7	$3,178.9	$4,413.1
Class E common stock	136.2	139.1	160.3
Class H common stock[c]	190.0	219.2	256.9
Earnings per share attributable to:			
$1-⅔ par value common stock	4.11	5.03	7.17
Class E common stock	2.13	2.65	3.15
Class H common stock	1.48	1.67	2.01
Taxes			
United States, foreign, and other income taxes	611.1	857.6	2,102.8
Other taxes (principally payroll and property taxes)	3,431.6	2,904.8	3,594.8
Total	$4,042.7	$3,762.4	$5,697.6
Average number of shares outstanding (in millions)			
$1-⅔ par value common stock	635.3	631.5	615.7
Class E common stock	63.8	52.6	50.9
Class H common stock	127.8	130.8	127.9
Number of stockholders as of December 31 (in thousands)			
$1-⅔ par value common stock	868	830	812
Class E common stock	456	438	423
Class H common stock	540	506	489
Average number of employees (in thousands)	877	813	766

[a]General Motors Acceptance Corporation provided financing to GM franchised dealers and to their customers in the form of new auto loans. In addition, GMAC provided insurance to dealers and leased vehicles directly.

[b]All GM $1-⅔ data adjusted to reflect two-for-one stock split in the form of a 100 percent stock dividend declared February 6, 1989, payable March 31, 1989.

[c]H shares were issued in connection with the purchase of Hughes Aircraft Company on December 31, 1985.

General Motors

EXHIBIT 2 • Consolidated Balance Sheets as of December 31
(dollars in millions except per-share amounts)

	1987	*1988*
Assets		
Cash and cash equivalents	$ 3,723.0	$ 5,800.3
Other marketable securities and time deposits	4,096.3	4,381.1
Total cash and marketable securities	7,819.3	10,191.4
Finance receivables	85,994.5	87,476.9
Accounts and notes receivable	7,859.5	4,540.6
Inventories (less allowances)	7,939.7	7,984.3
Contracts in progress (less advances and progress payments of $2,174.4 and $1,981.2)	1,756.0	2,035.4
Net equipment on operating leases	5,558.2	5,005.1
Prepaid expenses and deferred charges	4,615.6	5,156.6
Other investments and miscellaneous assets (less allowances)	3,204.6	4,360.3
Property		
Real estate, plants, and equipment (at cost)	59,963.5	60,810.6
Less accumulated depreciation	(31,033.1)	(32,798.8)
Net real estate, plants, and equipment	28,930.4	28,011.8
Special tools (at cost, less amortization)	3,207.0	3,918.9
Total property	32,137.4	31,930.7
Intangible assets (at cost, less amortization)	5,458.4	5,391.8
Total assets	$162,343.2	$164,063.1
Liabilities and Stockholders' Equity		
Liabilities		
Accounts payable (principally trade)	$ 7,261.0	$ 7,896.9
Notes and loans payable	88,693.4	88,130.1
United States, foreign, and other income taxes	5,169.2	4,930.3
Capitalized leases	346.4	294.8
Other liabilities	25,565.7	25,520.6
Deferred credits (including investment tax credits of $1,604.4 and $1,438.7)	2,082.4	1,618.7
Total liabilities	129,118.1	128,391.4
Stockholders' Equity		
Preferred stocks	234.4	234.4
Preference stocks	2.0	2.0
Common stocks		
$1-⅔ par value common stock	521.1	510.7
Class E common stock	5.2	5.1
Class H common stock	6.5	12.8
Capital surplus (principally unadjusted paid-in capital)	6,764.6	6,235.2
Net income retained for use in the business	25,771.7	28,970.5
Subtotal	33,305.5	35,970.7
Accumulated foreign currency translation and other adjustments	(80.4)	(299.0)
Total stockholders' equity	33,225.1	35,671.7
Total liabilities and stockholders' equity	$162,343.2	$164,063.1

Source: General Motors 1988 Annual Report and General Motors Form 10-K for the year ended December 31, 1988.

General Motors

EXHIBIT 3 • Quarterly Earnings and Dividends
for GM and GME (estimates in italic)

GME

Earnings per Share

	Mar. 31	Jun. 30	Sep. 30	Dec. 31	Annual
1986	$0.46	$0.52	$0.58	$0.58	$2.14
1987	0.54	0.60	0.68	0.84	2.66
1988	0.74	0.78	0.80	0.84	3.16
1989	$0.82	$0.88	*$0.92*	*$1.00*	*$3.62*

Dividends per Share

	Mar. 31	Jun. 30	Sep. 30	Dec. 31	Annual
1986	$0.10	$0.10	$0.10	$0.10	$0.40
1987	0.13	0.13	0.13	0.13	0.52
1988	0.17	0.17	0.17	0.17	0.68
1989	$0.24	$0.24	*$0.24*	*$0.24*	*$0.96*

GM ($1-²/₃)

Earnings per Share

	Mar. 31	Jun. 30	Sep. 30	Dec. 31	Annual
1986	$1.76	$1.46	$0.80	$0.97	$4.11
1987	1.31	1.40	1.14	1.18	5.03
1988	1.21	2.26	1.23	2.12	6.82
1989	$2.37	$2.23	*$0.72*	*$1.01*	*$6.33*

Dividends per Share

	Mar. 31	Jun. 30	Sep. 30	Dec. 31	Annual
1986	$0.625	$0.625	$0.625	$0.625	$2.50
1987	0.625	0.625	0.625	0.625	2.50
1988	0.625	0.625	0.625	0.625	2.50
1989	$0.750	$0.750	*$0.750*	*$0.750*	*$3.00*

Source: *Value Line Investment Survey.*

General Motors

EXHIBIT 4 • Weekly Closing Prices and Returns for
GM, GME, and S&P 500 in Second Quarter 1989[a]

		Closing Prices ($)		Weekly Returns (%)		
	GM	GME	S&P 500	GM	GME	S&P 500
March 31	$41.500	$44.750	$294.870	NA	NA	NA
April 7	40.250	44.500	297.160	−3.01%	−0.56%	0.78%
14	40.875	46.750	301.360	1.55	5.06	1.41
21	42.875	47.250	309.610	4.89	1.07	2.74
28	41.500	48.000	309.640	−3.21	1.59	0.01
May 5	39.625	48.625	307.610	−4.52	1.30	−0.66
12	39.875	49.375	313.840	0.63	1.54	2.03
19	42.125	51.500	321.240	5.64	4.30	2.36
26	40.500	52.250	321.590	−3.86	1.46	0.11
June 2	41.125	53.250	325.520	1.54	1.91	1.22
9	41.250	52.875	326.690	0.30	−0.70	0.36
16	41.875	52.500	321.350	1.52	−0.71	−1.63
23	41.250	52.250	328.000	−1.49	−0.48	2.07
30	$41.750	$50.500	$317.980	1.21	−3.35	−3.05
Estimated weekly return sigma =				3.06%	2.12%	1.61%
Annualized standard deviation of returns = weekly sigma × $\sqrt{52}$ =				22.05%	15.29%	11.58%

[a]Closing prices taken from *Standard and Poor's Daily Stock Price Record,* April–June 1989. Weekly returns computed by dividing the price change over the week by the closing price of the previous week. For example, GME's return for the week ending April 14 is [(46.75 − 44.50)/44.50] = 5.06%.

General Motors

EXHIBIT 5 • Premiums for GM and GME Options Chicago
Board Options Exchange Closing Prices as of June 30, 1989

Option & NY Close	Strike Price	Calls: Last			Puts: Last		
		Jul.	Aug.	Sep.	Jul.	Aug.	Sep.
GM	40	$2^{1}/_{16}$	$2^{1}/_{2}$	$2^{5}/_{8}$	$^{3}/_{8}$	$^{7}/_{8}$	$1^{1}/_{8}$
$41^{5}/_{8}$	$42^{1}/_{2}$	s	s	$1^{1}/_{16}$	s	s	$2^{3}/_{8}$
$41^{5}/_{8}$	45	$^{1}/_{8}$	$^{1}/_{4}$	$3^{7}/_{16}$	$3^{1}/_{4}$	4	$4^{7}/_{8}$
Days to maturity		18	46	81	18	46	81
Treasury rate		8.27%	8.28%	8.22%	8.27%	8.28%	8.22%

Philadelphia Options Exchange Closing Prices as of June 28, 1989

Option & NY Close	Strike Price	Calls: Last			Puts: Last		
		Jul.	Aug.	Sep.	Jul.	Aug.	Sep.
GME							
$51^{5}/_{8}$	50	r	r	$3^{1}/_{4}$	r	r	r
Days to maturity		20	48	83			
Treasury rate		8.25%	8.27%	8.22%			

r = not traded; s = no option.

Source: *The Wall Street Journal.*

PART

6

*Strategic Investment
and Financing Decisions*

Superior Industries International

Teresa Blackman, a recent MBA, worked in the corporate finance department of a large commercial bank. She had been in the department only six months and had spent the last month, May 1989, preparing an analysis of a potential acquisition. The report on it would be her first presentation, and she felt herself to be under greater than usual pressure to make sure all the loose ends were tied up. At present, her concerns were in two areas: the interpretation of her results and a technical valuation issue.

Background

Ms. Blackman had been assigned the job of finding a suitable acquisition candidate in the original equipment manufacturer (OEM) automobile supplier industry that could help a large diversified company expand into this industry. An important part of her job was to determine whether the shares of the acquisition candidate were underpriced in the stock market. The OEM automotive supply industry was interesting because since 1982 it had been undergoing a consolidation process. Essential for success in this highly competitive industry were a variety of factors such as market base, plant proximity to auto manufacturers, quality ratings, access to Japanese business, technology, and low cost base. Since the major auto manufacturers negotiated stringent cost-reduction formulas into contracts, industry margins had been reduced and the weaker players were exiting the market. Only the low-cost producers with the high-quality ratings were able to survive. After an analysis of the OEM automotive supplier industry, Ms. Blackman concluded that Superior Industries International was as an ideal acquisition candidate.

Superior Industries

Superior manufactured cast-aluminum road wheels and automotive accessories (see Exhibit 1). Sales of wheels were to the OEM market and com-

---

posed 79 percent of Superior's total sales. Suspension products and miscellaneous accessories for the aftermarket (products sold by retailers to vehicle owners to improve the appearance or performance of a vehicle) were 21 percent of sales. Although the majority of its manufacturing was done domestically, Superior had facilities in Canada, Mexico, and Puerto Rico.

The market for aluminum wheels had been steadily growing. From 1981 to 1985, the use of aluminum wheels in domestic automobiles had increased from 4 to 12 percent. During model year 1988, 28.2 percent of General Motors cars sold and 27.9 percent of Ford cars were equipped with aluminum wheels, compared with 20.1 percent and 20.6 percent, respectively, in model year 1987. Over the next five to seven years, analysts believed the market share could increase to 35 percent. In large part, this growth was attributable to the superior performance characteristics of aluminum wheels as compared with conventional wheels. Aluminum wheels were stronger and lighter than steel wheels which resulted in increased fuel efficiency and allowed auto makers to meet federally mandated Corporate Average Fuel Economy targets. Handling performance of aluminum wheels was also superior, because of the lighter weight of aluminum and the precision with which the wheels could be manufactured. In addition, aluminum wheels came in a wider and more attractive variety of styles. Finally, significant impact on growth had come from dealers, because aluminum wheels were high-margin items and were usually offered as optional features with markups of over 100 percent.

The huge increase in the market for aluminum wheels had been reflected in Superior's stock price shown in Exhibits 2 and 3. The company had shown dramatic earnings growth during the last six years, and had a strong balance sheet (see Exhibits 4 and 5). A favorite of Wall Street, Superior appeared to be poised for more growth over the next five years.

Sales to the OEM manufacturers depended greatly on the quality ratings a manufacturing plant received. Superior had the distinction of having been awarded Ford's highest rating, known as "Q-1 Preferred Quality." The firm was one of only two aluminum-wheel manufacturers given this award and was the only one in the continental United States. General Motors had given Superior its "Mark of Excellence" award. Superior's quality and its experience as a low-cost producer made it a very attractive supplier. Certification of production facilities generally took between 15 to 18 months. The company was currently operating at full capacity.

Superior had devised aggressive expansion plans to position itself for the anticipated sales growth. Currently, it had three plants in the United States, two in Canada, and one in Puerto Rico. A fourth U.S. plant was nearing completion and would be operational by the end of 1989. This plant had already been approved for quality by both Ford and GM. A fifth plant, in the design phase, was planned for completion by the end of 1990.

These fourth and fifth plants would double production from 3.5 to 7 million wheels per year.

Superior held a 35 percent share of the aluminum-wheel market. The company's only significant competitor in this fragmented market was Kelsey Hayes, a division of Fruehauf Corporation. Barriers to entry were high, and cost-reduction-sharing formulas of the large auto manufacturers mandated that one be a low-cost producer. More experienced low-cost producers such as Superior had a distinct advantage over newer companies. Superior was working to that advantage.

Since technological superiority was essential to maintaining a competitive edge and achieving cost reductions, Superior had an active R&D department and was teamed with AMAX, Inc., in developing a proprietary semi-solid metal-forging process, a very promising technology that could radically change the economics of aluminum-wheel production and could significantly reduce production time. In addition, the company had recently upgraded its computer system to allow for sophisticated design techniques such as three-dimensional modeling.

The outlook for Superior's aftermarket sales, which represented 21 percent of total sales, was different. They had intense competition, and industry consolidation of the accessories market caused margins to decline 7.2 percent in 1988. Sales growth was expected to remain flat, and the company was considering a restructuring of this division.

Financial Analysis

Since the information on Superior Industries indicated to Ms. Blackman that it had great potential, she set about the valuation with real optimism. Her basic approach was to estimate free cash flows and discount them at the weighted-average cost of capital.

Cash Flows

To estimate the free cash flow shown in Exhibit 6, Ms. Blackman assumed:

1. Growth in sales would be high through 1991 after which growth was expected to taper off.
2. Gross margins, selling, general, and administrative, were expected to continue their historical relationship to sales.
3. Depreciation would reflect past experience.
4. The marginal tax rate would be 34 percent.
5. Management expected the efficiency of the new plants would bring working capital down to approximately 18 percent of sales. The estimate was based on the forecasted efficiency of the new plants.

Weighted-Average Cost of Capital

The estimate of the weighted-average cost of capital (WACC) was based on the following assumptions:

6.   Debt to capital would not change from its present 15 percent (see Exhibit 7).

7.   After discussions with investment bankers, Ms. Blackman estimated Superior could secure financing using 30-year debentures with a yield to maturity of 11 percent.

8.   A cost of equity of 14.75 percent based on the CAPM: This was based on a beta estimate of 1.07 (see Exhibit 7), a long-term, risk-free rate of 8.65 percent and a market-risk premium of 5.7 percent, the capital-asset-pricing model (CAPM) yielded an estimate of Superior's cost of equity of 14.75 percent. The dividend-growth model, assuming a 5 percent long-term growth rate, yielded an estimate of approximately 12 percent. Considering the relative merits of the two models, Ms. Blackman decided to give more weight to the CAPM estimate of 14.75 percent.

Based on these assumptions, Ms. Blackman estimated the WACC at 13.6 percent.

Terminal Value

A simple constant-growth model was used with a long-run growth rate of 5 percent.

Firm Value

Based on the free cash flows and the WACC (see Exhibit 8), the value of Superior Industries International equity was estimated at $22.83 per share. This figure was lower than the latest closing price.

The Issues

Ms. Blackman was concerned about some of the key elements of her presentation. The first was making sure she could explain her results. The second was getting some idea about how much in the way of synergies would be required in order to generate a value that was consistent with a 20 percent premium over the current stock price. Ms. Blackman believed that her initial approach was quite conservative, that with some synergies a value of $30 per share was not unrealistic. The final item was something that was always part of presentations at her firm: a direct valuation of the equity with the focus on the residual cash flows to shareholders (after debt service). She remembered from school that the result would be the same as the free cash flow approach, but she needed to make sure this was true in case this issue was raised during her presentation.

Superior Industries International
EXHIBIT 1 • Product Lines

Car Lines That Offered Superior Industries' Cast-Aluminum Road Wheels

GMC S-10 Blazer 4 × 4[b]	Lincoln Towncar[b]	Ford Taurus LX[b]
GMC S-10 Pickup 4 × 4	Lincoln Mark VII	Ford Taurus LX Wagon[b]
Chevy S-10 Blazer 4 × 4[b]	Mercury Sable Sedan[b]	Ford Mustang GT[a]
Chevy Camaro Sport Coupe[a]	Mercury Sable Wagon[b]	Ford Mustang LX[b]
Chevy Camaro IROC-Z[a]	Mercury Grand Marquis	Ford LTD Wagon[b]
Cadillac Eldorado[b]	Mercury Topaz	Ford LTD Sedan[b]
Cadillac Seville	Mercury Topaz LTS[a]	Ford T-Bird LX[b]
Cadillac Deville	Mercury Topaz XR5[b]	Ford Ranger STX 4WD[b]
Buick Le Sabre	Mercury Cougar LS[b]	Ford Bronco II 4WD[b]
Buick Le Sabre Wagon[b]	Mercury Cougar XR7[a]	Ford Bronco II XLT[b]
Buick Electra Wagon[b]		Ford Tempo
Buick Regal		Ford Tempo 4WD[a]
Buick Century		
Buick Park Avenue		
Oldsmobile Cutlass Supreme[b]		
Oldsmobile '98 Touring Sedan		

Aftermarket Products

General Automotive Accessories	**Truck and Recreational-Vehicle Accessories**
Steering-wheel covers	Running boards
Steering wheels	Running-board lights
Curb feelers	Chrome tailgate protectors
Locking gas cap	External spare-tire carriers
Safety belts	External steps
License-plate frames	Side rails
Exhaust extensions	Grab bars and hooks
Custom road wheels	E-Z slider pass-thru windows
Wheel lug nuts	Towing equipment
Splash guards	Tie-downs
High-level rear-window brake lights	

Suspension Products

Kits designed to increase vehicles' load capacity and improve handling

Lifters

Products to rejuvenate worn-out suspension systems

[a]Indicates standard equipment.

[b]Indicates high usage of Superior cast-aluminum wheels.

Superior Industries International
EXHIBIT 2 • Closing Price History

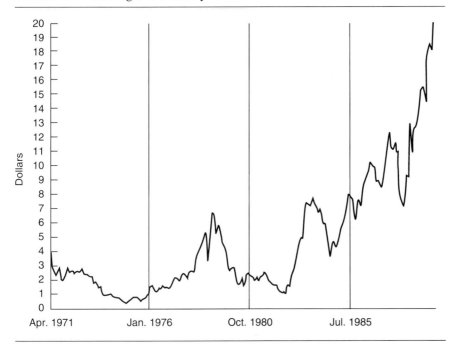

Superior Industries International
EXHIBIT 3 • Daily Stock Prices and Other Market Data

Week Ending	Stock Price Closing Price
1/03/89	$20.87
1/10/89	22.00
1/23/89	22.25
1/30/89	22.37
2/08/89	23.00
2/13/89	23.75
2/21/89	22.00
2/27/89	23.25
3/06/89	23.00
3/13/89	22.75
3/20/89	23.50
3/27/89	23.12
4/03/89	23.87
4/10/89	24.00
4/17/89	23.87
4/24/89	23.00
5/01/89	23.12
5/08/89	24.25
5/15/89	25.50
5/22/89	25.12
5/30/89	$25.25

Treasury Rates as of 5/31/89[a]	
Term	Rate
3 mos.	8.95%
1 year	8.98
10 year	8.65
30 year	8.65%

[a]Source: *The Wall Street Journal.*

Superior Industries International
EXHIBIT 4 • Income Statements, 1983–1988 (in millions of dollars except per-share data)

	12/83	12/84	12/85	12/86	12/87	12/88
Net sales	$85.22	$111.62	$130.84	$148.55	$169.50	$200.15
Cost of sales	(70.91)	(93.98)	(106.79)	(120.92)	(136.51)	(159.46)
Gross profit	14.31	17.64	24.05	27.63	32.99	41.69
Selling, general, and administrative expenses	(6.41)	(8.10)	(10.11)	(10.62)	(12.30)	(14.83)
Depreciation and amortization	(1.76)	(2.21)	(2.61)	(3.44)	(4.66)	(5.55)
Operating income	6.15	7.33	11.33	13.57	16.03	21.31
Other income (net)	0.91	0.73	0.84	2.66	2.15	2.70
Earnings before interest and taxes	7.06	8.06	12.17	16.23	18.18	24.01
Interest expense	(0.80)	(1.47)	(1.21)	(1.81)	(3.14)	(3.48)
Pretax income	6.26	6.59	10.96	14.43	15.04	20.53
Income taxes	(1.97)	(2.18)	(3.71)	(5.92)	(5.57)	(7.39)
Net income before extraordinary items	4.29	4.42	7.25	8.51	9.48	13.14
Extraordinary items discontinued operations	1.12	0.00	0.00	0.00	0.00	0.00
Net income	$5.40	$4.42	$7.25	$8.51	$9.48	$13.14
Common dividends	$0.01	$0.19	$1.19	$1.36	$1.48	$1.67
Earnings per share						
Primary	0.67	0.72	1.20	1.30	1.46	2.07
Fully diluted	$0.67	$0.72	$1.20	$1.30	$1.46	$2.07

Superior Industries International
EXHIBIT 5 • Balance Sheets, 1983–1988 (in millions of dollars)

	12/83	12/84	12/85	12/86	12/87	12/88
Assets						
Cash and equivalents	$4.27	$13.56	$15.61	$38.91	$20.90	$35.16
Receivables	16.83	22.47	20.83	20.93	29.51	35.33
Inventories	9.86	15.99	17.04	21.51	30.18	35.28
Other current assets	0.96	0.70	0.69	1.46	2.14	4.85
Total current assets	31.91	52.72	54.17	82.81	82.73	110.62
Net property, plant, and equipment	15.62	17.16	20.59	31.83	40.25	50.43
Other assets	1.09	0.68	0.30	0.67	0.68	0.58
Total Assets	$48.62	$70.56	$75.06	$115.31	$123.66	$161.63
Liabilities and Net Worth						
Short-term debt	$3.02	$10.53	$4.85	$7.14	$0.88	$3.15
Accounts payable	7.57	11.38	13.03	17.23	24.27	28.15
Taxes payable	0.32	0.56	0.00	1.35	0.38	1.22
Other current liabilities	4.31	5.23	6.17	7.78	9.19	14.93
Total current liabilities	15.22	27.70	24.05	33.49	34.72	47.45
Long-term debt (LTD)	8.34	9.53	5.88	28.51	27.91	41.59
Deferred taxes and investment tax credit	0.64	4.41	5.14	5.68	7.11	7.69
Other liabilities	0.00	0.00	0.00	0.00	0.00	0.50
Minority interest	0.00	0.00	0.00	0.42	0.30	NA
Total liabilities	24.19	41.64	35.07	68.09	70.04	97.22
Common equity	24.43	28.92	39.99	47.22	53.62	64.41
Total liabilities and net worth	$48.62	$70.56	$75.06	$115.31	$123.66	$161.63

Superior Industries International
EXHIBIT 6 • Free Cash Flow Projections (in millions of dollars)

	1989	1990	1991	1992	1993	1994	1995	1996
Growth rate in sales	23.00%	19.00%	18.00%	11.00%	10.00%	10.00%	10.00%	5.00%
Sales[a]	$246.0	$292.7	$345.4	$383.4	$421.8	$464.0	$510.3	$535.9
Cost of goods sold	(191.9)	(228.3)	(269.4)	(299.1)	(329.0)	(361.9)	(398.1)	(418.0)
Gross margin	54.1	64.4	76.0	84.4	92.8	102.1	112.3	117.9
Selling, general, and administrative expenses	(18.0)	(21.5)	(25.3)	(28.1)	(30.9)	(34.0)	(37.4)	(39.3)
Depreciation	(8.3)	(14.0)	(14.0)	(15.4)	(15.6)	(16.0)	(16.4)	(16.1)
Operating profit	27.8	28.9	36.7	40.8	46.3	52.1	58.5	62.5
Taxes	(9.4)	(9.8)	(12.5)	(13.9)	(15.7)	(17.7)	(19.9)	(21.3)
Earnings before interest, after taxes	18.3	19.1	24.2	27.0	30.5	34.4	38.6	41.3
+Depreciation	8.3	14.0	14.0	15.4	15.6	16.0	16.4	16.1
Capital expenditures[b]	(18.0)	(22.0)	(10.0)	(11.0)	(13.0)	(15.0)	(16.0)	(20.0)
Changes in working capital	(8.3)	(8.4)	(9.5)	(6.8)	(6.9)	(7.6)	(8.4)	(4.6)
Free cash flow	$0.3	$2.7	$18.7	$24.6	$26.2	$27.8	$30.6	$32.8
Terminal value (5% growth in perpetuity)								$399.9

[a] 1988 sales of $200.
[b] Analysts' estimates.

Superior Industries International
EXHIBIT 7 • Automotive-Component Manufacturers[a]

	Historical Beta	Book Debt/ Equity	Market Debt/ Equity	Market Debt/ Capital
Arvin Industries Inc.	1.16	0.96	50.28%	33.46%
Bailey Corp.	1.45	1.57	36.53	26.76
Champion Parts Inc.	1.13	0.98	208.87	67.62
Clarcor Inc.	1.00	0.45	0.54	0.54
Dana Corp.	0.85	1.14	119.26	54.39
Durakon Inds Inc.	0.78	0.92	85.07	45.97
Eaton Corp.	0.93	0.56	35.74	26.33
Echlin Inc.	0.99	0.17	13.31	11.75
Excel Industries Inc.	1.09	1.15	31.97	24.23
Federal-Mogul Corp.	1.09	0.34	35.25	26.07
Filtertek Inc.	1.17	0.57	18.49	15.61
Gentex Corp.	1.63	0.04	0.49	0.49
Hastings Mfg. Co.	0.68	0.49	121.71	54.90
J. P. Industries Inc.	1.22	2.20	115.03	53.50
Larizza Industries Inc.	0.65	5.70	28.81	22.37
Magna International	1.43	1.48	229.98	69.69
Masco Industries Inc.	1.24	3.66	128.14	56.17
Modine Mfg. Co.	0.76	0.19	16.15	13.91
Mr. Gasket Co.	0.68	2.29	249.89	71.42
Simpson Industries	0.72	0.43	20.42	16.96
Smith (A.O.) Corp.	1.00	0.57	89.80	47.31
Sparton Corp.	0.86	0.02	24.38	19.60
Standard Products Co.	0.80	0.48	8.38	7.73
Sudbury Inc.	0.94	2.99	280.84	73.74
Superior Industries Intl.	1.07	0.65	18.10	15.33
Talley Industries Inc.	1.09	1.91	197.29	66.36
Teleflex Inc.	1.25	0.42	18.70	15.75
Trico Products Corp.	0.70	0.11	51.59	34.03
Voplex Corp.	0.61	0.23	20.72	17.16
Walbro Corp.	0.65	1.70	36.30	26.63
Industry Average	0.99	1.15	76.40%	33.86%

[a]All firms were engaged in automotive-component manufacturing for both the OEM and aftermarket. The companies were similar to Superior in that they all had 3714 listed as their primary SIC code.

Source: LOTUS ONESOURCE.

Superior Industries International

EXHIBIT 8 • Estimated of Firm Value

(in millions of dollars, except share price)

	1989	1990	1991	1992	1993	1994	1995	1996
Yearly free cash flow	$0.3	$2.7	$18.7	$24.6	$26.2	$27.8	$30.6	$432.7
Present value @ 13.6%	$0.3	$2.1	$12.8	$14.7	$13.8	$12.9	$12.5	$156.0

Firm value = $225.2 million

Debt value   = −44.7

Equity value   = $180.5 million

Equity value per share = $22.83

"Based on 7.9 million shares outstanding.

Omni Services, Incorporated

what are the shares worth?

This was not the first time someone had shown an interest in buying Omni Services, Inc., a linen-rental service headquartered in Culpeper, Virginia. In 1975 a Minnesota firm offered to buy the Omni stock and to pay for it with notes, but Omni's major shareholders objected to holding notes of the other company. Since then, other offers had been rejected. Each time, the major shareholders had expressed concern over the strength of the potential purchaser or the terms of the offer: those making the offers were either too small, had too much debt, or were in a different line of business. But now, the interest of Jean Leducq, the owner of the Société Générale de Location et Services Textiles (Textiles), a large, strong French firm that was also in the linen-rental business, seemed more promising. Mr. Leducq was considering buying a majority interest in Omni, with his eventual ownership position to reach two-thirds or better.

Although there had been considerable correspondence and many visits by Textiles employees, Mr. Leducq himself had never visited Omni's headquarters until mid-April. Now he was in the midst of meeting the Omni management and visiting the Culpeper plant. Knowing that Mr. Leducq had engaged a New York firm to value Omni's closely held stock, N. B. Martin, Omni's founder and president, was sure the Frenchman was serious about his proposal. In preparation for the visit, Mr. Martin had asked Omni's comptroller, Larry Thomson, to determine a fair price for a majority of Omni's stock and to consider a method that could be used now to place a price on the remaining shares for sale in 1985.

Omni Services, Inc.

Omni Services, Inc., was a holding company for the 12 companies listed in Exhibit 1. Each of the subsidiaries was called Rental Uniform Service and was located in the eastern United States. Firms like Omni were traditionally considered to be part of the industrial laundry business, but the industry had recently become known as textile lessors.

The industrial laundry business was fragmented. Multidivisional firms that manufactured, rented, and laundered garments were in direct competition with local businesses that bought their uniforms and serviced their customers in a limited geographical area. Many of Omni's major competitors were closely held, and little financial information was available about those operations. Of the firms that were public, the five described in Exhibits 2 and 3 were most similar to Omni.

Mr. Martin had learned about the business while working for an industrial laundry in Cincinnati, Ohio. In 1954 he went into partnership with his father-in-law to operate a small ($2,000-per-week volume) uniform-rental business in Roanoke, Virginia. In partnership with his father-in-law, he opened the Culpeper plant in 1959, and Mr. Martin moved to Culpeper to operate it. It was quickly successful, and sales had grown at a rate of 20 percent almost every year since its founding. The only thing that seemed to stem growth of that operation had been a plant fire in 1974.

By 1968 Mr. Martin had started new operations in Hanover, Pennsylvania, and Morgantown, West Virginia. The three plants, each called Rental Uniform Service (RUS), were separately incorporated. Even though the shareholders and board members were virtually identical, the Internal Revenue Service had treated them as separate entities, and the combined taxes were thus somewhat lower. By 1972 nine RUSs had been added, the separate incorporation tax advantages had disappeared, and the 11 separate operations had become subsidiaries of the newly formed Omni Services, Inc.

Omni supplied industrial uniforms to 75,000 people. Four days a week, a total of 150 trucks left the plants operated by Omni's 12 Rental Uniform Services. Each day, every truck had an established route in a nearby metropolitan area. The driver stopped at such places as service stations, garages, and automobile dealerships to deliver six prepackaged shirts and trousers for each employee. Because employees needed specific sizes, the shirts and trousers delivered were the same as those that the driver had picked up the previous week. The employees' names, and often the names of the companies, were stitched on the shirts. The soiled uniforms were returned to the plant for washing or dry cleaning and mending. In addition, Omni provided executive garments for office and management personnel, shop towels, walk mats, fender covers, and linen roll towels.

Most of Omni's business was in large metropolitan areas, and 11 of its 12 subsidiaries were located on the fringes of those areas. For example, the largest and oldest operation, the plant in Culpeper, served the Washington, D.C., area, as well as several less populated areas—Culpeper, Charlottesville, and Lynchburg, Virginia. While these nonmetropolitan processing plants tended to increase transportation time and costs, Mr. Martin had always believed their locations allowed them to attract employees that were more dependable and productive than the more transient and higher paid city worker. Mr. Martin thought much of Omni's success came from the edge loyal employees gave the firm.

Over the years, Omni had been innovative in managing these employees. By 1971 a four-day work week had been instituted. In 1975 Omni was the first firm of any size in Virginia to offer an employee stock-ownership plan (ESOP), a kind of profit-sharing plan in which Omni stock was purchased and held in trust for each employee. None of Omni's 600 employees belonged to a union.

Omni had a total of 48 investors, although three were of primary importance: N. B. Martin, the founder, president, and chairman of the board, with 56 percent of the stock; T. Y. Martin, N. B.'s brother, Omni's secretary–treasurer, and president of the Culpeper RUS, who held 23 percent; and the Omni ESOP with 12.5 percent.

Mr. Martin was quite pleased with Omni's present position. Except for the time of the 1974 Culpeper plant fire, when destroyed uniforms had to be replaced and Washington, D.C., laundry and dry cleaning had to be trucked to Hanover, Pennsylvania, and back, the firm had prospered and grown. Exhibits 4 and 5 summarize Omni's operations over the previous 7 years. Compared with the other uniform-rental services shown in Exhibits 2 and 3, Omni had reason to be proud. The industry average profit before taxes was about 5.5 percent, but Omni's was almost double that figure. Even with this past success, however, Mr. Martin had begun to plan changes for Omni's future.

Mr. Martin wanted to be less involved in the daily operations and concentrate more on the future of the firm. As a first step, he had in 1978 appointed two regional managers to oversee the 12 individual RUS managers.

In the fall of 1979, Mr. Martin had put together a 5-year plan for Omni with the following goals:

1. double profits by 1984;
2. double sales by 1984;
3. reduce the debt-to-equity ratio substantially.

Capital would be reinvested in new services, except for the following planned dividend payments and annual contributions to the ESOP of 7 to 10 percent of the payroll:

	1980	1981	1982	1983	1984
Total dividends	$216,000	$240,000	$264,000	$288,000	$336,000
Dividends per share	0.36	0.40	0.44	0.48	0.56
Payout ratio (estimated)	14.8%	14.3%	13.5%	12.7%	12.8%

Two other goals, subject to yearly revision, had been spelled out by Omni management:

1. the formation of two or three new RUSs by 1984;
2. the potential acquisition of one or two industrial laundries with annual sales of $500,000 to $2 million by 1984.

If the possibility of selling or merging the firm developed, Mr. Martin stated, "We will examine any serious offer made to us during the next 5 years. . . . [But] at this time, we do not plan to seek out buyers."

Before the 5-year plan could be formally reviewed and approved by Omni's board in January 1980, the contact with Textiles had been established.

The Textiles Offer

In September 1979, Mr. Martin had received a letter from an old friend, the president of Workwear, Inc., which manufactured uniforms and until 1976 had been in the rental business. The two men had known each other through the Textile Rental Services Association, a trade group. The letter to Mr. Martin had introduced Jean Leducq, the owner of Textiles, the largest linen-supply company in France. One-third of Textiles' $120 million in sales came from the rental of linen roll towels. Mr. Leducq, the letter said, would like to talk to Mr. Martin about the possibility of a merger.

By mid-October, Mr. Leducq's nephew and heir apparent, Christian Colas, a 40-year-old ex-test pilot and Stanford MBA, had visited several of Omni's plants with two other Textiles employees. While in the United States, the trio had also visited other industrial-laundry firms. Textiles was obviously serious about investing in a U.S. firm in the uniform-rental or industrial-laundry business.

When Mr. Martin visited several of Textiles' operations in France in November, he was treated royally. He and Mr. Leducq had talked at length about the differences between the U.S. and French industrial-laundry businesses. Mr. Leducq believed that the uniform-rental market in France was about where the U.S. market had been in the early 1950s—quite a different business from what it was today.

Up to the late 1940s, U.S. launderers would wait outside the gates of manufacturing plants so they could collect the heavily soiled garments of the workers. These garments were laundered, often in crude processing facilities, and returned several days later. Family laundries and linen supply companies were uninterested in processing heavily soiled garments, and because there were few home washers, housewives were happy to rid themselves of this task. In the late 1940s, the firms found that they could purchase work garments at wholesale prices, add a laundering charge, and still compete with the nonrental laundries handling these garments. In addition, the rental-laundry operations could schedule production more efficiently, adding a further cost advantage.

By 1980, 95 percent of the industry's U.S. sales volume was in the rental business. In contrast, about 50 percent of the French market sales were in uniform rentals. Textiles predominantly supplied linens to hotels, hospitals, and restaurants—a very competitive, low-profit business. Mr. Leducq considered uniform rental to hold great promise in France. Furthermore, he believed Textiles' skill in the roll-towel business might be useful to Omni, which had little expertise in linen-towel sales.

Mr. Martin had carefully explained Omni's relationships with its employees to Mr. Leducq and Mr. Colas. He had taken care to explain exactly what the ESOP was and why the firm had started it. He emphasized that he thought the ESOP was very important to the employees and served to make them involved and committed to Omni. Mr. Leducq had stated that, if Textiles did buy a majority of Omni's stock, the company would want to set the maximum ESOP ownership at 25 percent of the stock. Although Mr. Martin had briefly mentioned a per-share price "in the thirties," the discussion of price had gone little further.

Mr. Leducq said he would want assurances from Mr. Martin that he and the rest of Omni management would stay. Because Mr. Martin would continue to operate Omni as he had in the past, Mr. Martin could offer management contracts to current Omni managers if he wished; it was up to him. Mr. Leducq also wanted assurances that Mr. Martin would continue to operate the business as had been planned: seeking new businesses and making the capital-investment outlays and dividend payments detailed in the 5-year plan.

After Mr. Martin's return from France, he had talked with the other shareholders, Omni management, and the board of directors. One board member recalled that, when his firm had been sold 10 years earlier, the buyer had moved right in and taken over. Several years later, after the firm had deteriorated, he had managed to repurchase it and recover the lost business. He then sold it once again 3 years previously, but the circumstances were different. He kept his job; the new owners were investors and not interested in managing the firm. In fact, they seldom even came to Culpeper; he ran the business and also had the cash from the sale. He noted that the same sort of thing had happened to a uniform-rental business in Roanoke, Virginia. The ex-owner said the new owner moved right in and "made monkeys of us." The key to success, they all agreed, would be very little operating interference by Textiles' management. Mr. Martin told them that he felt sure that Mr. Leducq had no intention of actively managing Omni.

By mid-March, Mr. Martin believed that most of the details could be worked out. Mr. Leducq wanted him to sign a 5-year management contract.

Mr. Martin had toyed with the idea of looking for a new challenge, but he wasn't ready to leave the company entirely. He liked the idea of being the CEO of a $20-million business, having the company airplane at his disposal, and being needed by the business. On the other hand, selling some of his stock would provide enough cash to allow him to pay off all his debts, including the mortgage on the new house he was building. Taking Textiles' offer seemed ideal, but the price of the stock had yet to be resolved.

Mr. Leducq had proposed that Textiles purchase 51 percent of Omni's shares in 1980. In 1985 Textiles would make an additional purchase of 90,000 shares, bringing its total ownership position to 66 percent. Of the remaining shares, up to 170,000 more could be sold to Textiles in 1985 at the previously agreed price, if any shareholder wished to sell.

Because this agreement would spread the purchase over 5 years, the French government required that Textiles show the ability to honor the contract by pledging stock or having a line of credit for the full amount of the contractual obligation. Thus Textiles would have to secure the current price plus whatever it agreed to pay for additional shares in 1985 before the initial purchase.

The 1985 price would be determined by a formula worked out during the current negotiations. Mr. Leducq's objective was to limit his obligation, hence the amount of security required by the French government, until 1985. Thus he wanted a maximum 1985 price established, regardless of the formula outcome. Because the initial understanding was that the shares necessary to make up the purchase would be solicited from all other shareholders first, with Mr. Martin selling only enough shares to reach the 306,000-share, 51-percent total, Mr. Martin wanted a floor price set, below which the 1985 price would not drop.

Mr. Leducq had engaged Hudson Securities, a New York firm, to value Omni's shares and devise the formula for pricing the remaining shares in 1985. Their report had been expected in time for the April 11 visit to Culpeper. That visit, Mr. Martin had expected, would resolve all remaining questions—except price. The price was to be negotiated later by Mr. Martin, Omni Comptroller Mr. Thomson, and a team composed of people from Hudson Securities and Textiles. In preparation for the pricing meeting, Mr. Thomson asked a consultant who had valued Omni's ESOP shares in the past for a valuation of the Omni stock. That report was to be completed on April 14.

Mr. Leducq's April 11 Visit

On April 11, Mr. Martin, Mr. Leducq, and Mr. Thomson spent the afternoon visiting the Culpeper plant. Mr. Martin wanted to return the courtesy he had been shown during his visit to France, and it looked like they had succeeded.

The talk, for the most part, centered around how Omni's Culpeper operation differed from the uniform-rental business in France. As the day wore on, Mr. Leducq had gotten more and more excited about the prospects of Textiles aggressively expanding into uniform rental, which was Omni's strength.

As the men returned to Omni's headquarters, the tone of the conversation changed. Before, it had been process, market, and growth. Now, it was merger. Hudson Securities, however, had been dragging its heels. Already it had broken two appointments. Mr. Martin and Mr. Thomson knew that the valuation would drag on for some time when Mr. Leducq blurted out: "N. B., what's your lowest price? We want this merger to be amicable; we want the company to continue just like it is with you at the head. We don't want you or your employees dissatisfied. But we don't want to feel we've paid too much for the company, either. Give me your lowest price and the 1985 range. We will either agree right now, or we will drop our talks of merger and I'll leave this afternoon."

Omni Services, Incorporated
EXHIBIT 1 • Location of Omni Subsidiaries

Omni Services, Incorporated
EXHIBIT 2 • Similar Uniform-Rental Service Firms

Unitog manufactured, rented, and sold heavy-duty, soil-resistant uniforms for service-station employees, route drivers, and sales people. The rental business operated out of nine locations and contributed 38 percent of revenues. Headquarters in Kansas City, Missouri. Approximately 420 stockholders and 2,189 employees.

Rentex provided laundry and rental services, linen-supply services, and dust-control services through nine facilities. Rentals composed 100 percent of revenues. There were 640 stockholders and 950 employees. Headquarters in Philadelphia, Pennsylvania.

Means Services provided textile maintenance services by rental to businesses in midwestern states, with a concentration on providing work garments, industrial wiping cloths, dust-control textiles, bed and table linens, towels, aprons, uniforms, and continuous-towel cabinets. The rental business was 100 percent of its revenue. It had 25 processing plants, 2,718 stockholders, and 3,900 employees. Headquarters in Chicago, Illinois.

Servisco manufactured, rented, and laundered work clothes and uniforms, machine-wiping towels, fender covers, and linens. It also provided contract building maintenance, housekeeping consultant services, and guard (security) services. Its main office was in Hillside, New Jersey, and it operated through 27 full-service rental plants. There were 1,501 stockholders and 6,300 employees.

National Service Industries obtained 26 percent of revenues from renting table linen, bed linen, operating-room packs, towels, uniforms, and dust-control materials, but lighting equipment and chemical products were also manufactured. NSI was further diversified into insulation service, men's apparel, envelopes, furniture marketing services, safety products, furniture leasing, and amusement parks. Headquarters in Atlanta, Georgia; 10,994 stockholders and 19,200 employees.

Omni Services, Incorporated

EXHIBIT 3 • Financial Data—Similar Rental Uniform Service Firms

	5-Year Growth in After-Tax Net Profit	5-Year Growth in Revenues	Current Ratio	1978–1979 Growth in Net Worth	Net Profit on Sales	Debt to Common Equity	EPS[a]	Dividend-Payout Ratio	Average Yield	Book Value per Share	Return on Common Equity	Sales (in millions)	P/E Ratio[b]	Percent of Sales in Laundry
Omni	27.2%	19.2%	1.5×	17.8%	6.1%	35.6%	$2.05	15.6%	N.Av.	$11.48	17.9%	$ 20.0	N.Av.	99%
Rentex	6.6	8.6	1.7	3.9	2.0	60.0	0.60	32.9	5.5%	10.90	5.5	30.7	6.0×	100
Servisco	20.4	8.4	3.7	9.3	3.7	29.5	1.60	24.0	6.0	11.84	13.5	92.4	4.0	57
Means Services	10.2	7.0	2.0	5.6	4.4	2.6	2.95	41.0	6.3	25.22	11.7	113.6	6.5	100
NSI	11.8	8.4	2.4	14.4	5.6	5.4	3.12	33.0	5.5	16.48	18.9	708.1	6.0	26
Unitog	(2.8)%	10.2%	2.9×	9.6%	3.0%	37.6%	$3.12	26.0%	5.2	$29.80	10.5%	$ 56.4	5.0×	38%

[a]Earnings per share.
[b]Price/earnings ratio.
N.Av. = not available.

Omni Services, Incorporated

EXHIBIT 4 • Statements of Consolidated Income and Retained Earnings,
Years Ending December 31 (thousands of dollars, except per-share data)

	1973	1974	1975	1976	1977	1978	1979	First Quarter 1980
Operating revenues	$7,048	$8,383	$10,247	$12,467	$15,008	$16,785	$20,178	$5,493
Costs and expenses								
Cost of products and plant operations	(3,609)	(4,587)	(5,231)	(6,677)	(7,799)	(8,738)	(10,898)	(2,866)
Selling and delivery	(1,291)	(1,610)	(2,040)	(2,450)	(3,092)	(3,350)	(3,930)	(1,051)
General and administrative	(947)	(1,243)	(1,483)	(1,804)	(2,129)	(2,476)	(3,038)	(859)
Total costs and expenses	5,847	7,440	8,754	10,931	13,020	14,564	17,866	4,776
Income from operations	1,201	943	1,493	1,536	1,988	2,221	2,312	717
Other income (expense)	(102)	(317)	(89)	(117)	(224)	(215)	(242)	0
Income before taxes	1,099	626	1,404	1,419	1,764	2,006	2,070	717
Provision for income taxes	(543)	(293)	(669)	(653)	(784)	(956)	(840)	(315)
Income before extraordinary item	556	333	735	766	980	1,050	1,230	402
Extraordinary item	27	37	19	0	0	0	0	0
Net income	$ 583	$ 370	$ 754	$ 766	$ 980	$ 1,050	$ 1,230	$ 402
Less: Dividends paid	$ 96	$ 96	$ 132	$ 144	$ 150	$ 168	$ 192	$ 48
Plus: Retained earnings, beginning of year	1,530	2,017	1,291	2,913	3,535	4,365	5,247	6,285
Retained earnings, end of year[a]	$2,017	$2,291	$ 2,913	$ 3,535	$ 4,365	$ 5,247	$ 6,285	$6,639
Per-Share Data								
Income before extraordinary item	$ 0.93	$ 0.56	$ 1.23	$ 1.28	$ 1.63	$ 1.75	$ 2.05	$ 0.67
Extraordinary item	0.04	0.06	0.03	0	0	0	0	0
Net income	0.97	0.62	1.26	1.28	1.63	1.75	2.05	0.67
Dividends	$ 0.16	$ 0.16	$ 0.22	$ 0.24	$ 0.25	$ 0.28	$ 0.32	$ 0.08

[a]Does not include common stock account, but does include the $6,930 paid-in surplus.

Omni Services, Incorporated

EXHIBIT 5 • Consolidated Balance Sheets, Years Ending December 31 (thousands of dollars)

	1973	1974	1975	1976	1977	1978	1979
Assets							
Cash	$ 222	$ 859	$ 968	$ 686	$ 781	$ 619	$ 824
Accounts receivable	478	604	729	819	978	1,152	1,464
Due from employees	9	22	21	18	4	6	4
Income taxes refundable	23	69	0	54	0	0	0
Inventory	456	485	468	719	531	804	646
Prepaid expenses	22	39	40	53	66	104	101
Total current assets	1,210	2,078	2,226	2,349	2,360	2,685	3,039
Land	154	154	154	334	387	524	581
Buildings	1,604	1,262	1,857	2,727	3,470	3,760	4,396
Equipment	2,717	2,472	3,134	3,969	4,913	5,842	7,688
Aircraft	104	104	104	416	434	544	544
Total plant, property, and equipment	4,579	3,992	5,249	7,446	9,204	10,670	13,209
Accumulated depreciation	(1,507)	(1,368)	(1,801)	(2,330)	(3,042)	(3,903)	(4,897)
Net plant, property, and equipment	3,072	2,624	3,448	5,116	6,162	6,767	8,312
Goodwill	346	310	274	246	207	168	130
Noncompetition agreements	424	330	236	172	59	0	0
Other assets	10	16	7	10	17	22	31
Total other	780	656	517	428	283	190	161
Total assets	$5,062	$5,358	$6,191	$7,893	$8,805	$ 9,642	$11,512
Liabilities and Stockholders' Equity							
Accounts payable	$ 330	$ 468	$ 251	$ 410	$ 317	$ 518	$ 617
Current portion of long-term debt	235	248	270	516	542	567	623
Accrued salaries and wages	75	102	179	129	154	174	231
Other accrued expenses	50	59	315	356	348	398	481
Income taxes payable	13	12	357	33	109	201	108
Total current liabilities	703	889	1,372	1,444	1,470	1,858	2,060
Long-term debt	1,742	1,482	1,215	2,212	2,244	1,813	2,452
Deferred income taxes	0	96	91	102	126	124	115
Stockholders' equity (3,000,000 shares authorized of $1 par value; 600,000 shares outstanding)	600	600	600	600	600	600	600
Retained earnings	2,017	2,291	2,913	3,535	4,365	5,247	6,285
Total stockholders' equity	2,617	2,891	3,513	4,135	4,965	5,847	6,885
Total liabilities and stockholders' equity	$5,062	$5,358	$6,191	$7,893	$8,805	$ 9,642	$11,512

Diamond Shamrock Corporation

During early 1981, the management of Diamond Shamrock faced a critical set of decisions regarding the very nature of the company. Historically, Diamond Shamrock had been a major chemicals firm with a moderately sized, regional oil and gas unit. However, increased emphasis on oil and gas coupled with rising energy prices and stagnant growth in the industrial economy had made oil and gas the company's greatest source of revenues. An in-depth strategic analysis indicated that the 1980s would be a time of intense competition in chemicals, and many of Diamond's chemical businesses would face continued low growth and reduced return on investment. The company's energy businesses would be its primary source of growth.

It appeared to management that the company's changing business mix had depressed the price of Diamond Shamrock's shares in the market-place. Chemical analysts continued to follow the company and, as a result, investors seeking shares in companies with good prospects in energy were unlikely to know about Diamond Shamrock. To understand the company, traditional chemicals-oriented investors now had to become much more knowledgeable about oil and gas in order to evaluate their investment.

Two primary courses of action had been proposed. First, management could continue to oversee an evolutionary change in the company, emphasizing oil and gas. This approach would be coupled with an effort to inform Wall Street about their oil and gas business, but management knew it might take some time, and some believed it might not be successful: one of Diamond's staff had suggested that the company might be viewed as a conglomerate, a type of corporation that recent academic research indicated had a history of undervalued stock prices.

The second course was much more dramatic: they could selectively divest the chemical businesses (which were underperforming or were not significant) and become an oil and gas company. While management thought this course would focus Diamond Shamrock's resources on its

TABLE 1 • Business Segment Results, 1976

Segment	Percentage of Sales	Percentage of Profits
Chemicals	45%	56%
Plastics	13	5
Oil and gas	38%	33%

strengths, the company's stock had no following among oil investors or analysts. Thus this move would mean changing from a well-known, leading chemicals firm to an unknown, middle-sized oil company.

The two alternatives were quite different, and the latter would change the very nature of the company. Management was determined to examine the choices carefully before taking action.

Background

Diamond Shamrock was formed in December 1967 through a merger between Diamond Alkali Company, a Cleveland-based producer of inorganic commodity chemicals, and Shamrock Oil and Gas Corporation of Amarillo, Texas, an independent oil and gas producer with regional downstream operations, refining plants, and retail distribution networks. By emphasizing the chemical portion of the company, Diamond Shamrock was able to participate in the growth of the chemical industry during the first half of the 1970s. By 1976, sales had grown to $1,374 million with, as shown in Table 1, 45 percent of sales and 56 percent of profits coming from chemicals.

During the mid-1970s, however, the world and domestic economic environments changed, affecting all of Diamond's businesses. First, the oil embargo in late 1973 created an energy crisis and caused worldwide oil prices to skyrocket. The U.S. response was not only to conserve energy, but also to pass legislation that encouraged production of domestic crude oil. While Diamond was positioned to participate in the increased production of domestic oil, the oil business had not been the company's primary emphasis, and thus participation was limited.

Also during the mid-1970s the United States increased regulation governing proprietary chemicals. This legislation required additional testing for new chemicals, thus increasing the initial development costs and reducing the profitability of Diamond's specialty and proprietary chemical division. While Diamond also manufactured commodity chemicals, patents had historically protected the profitability of proprietary chemicals.

Although Diamond's managers had previously emphasized the chemical business, top management believed the company should be in businesses that had high earnings potentials. Management had a history of using acquisitions and divestitures as one way of changing corporate focus. The Falcon Seaboard acquisition in 1979 began to move the company toward the energy industry. Recent acquisitions and divestitures of assets toward this end are listed in Exhibit 1. These changes were accompanied by a 23-percent compound growth rate in sales and a 10.5-percent compound growth rate in operating profit over the period 1976 to 1980. Exhibit 2 contains financial statements for the 5-year period.

Current Situation

By 1980 Diamond Shamrock had four separate businesses—oil and gas, industrial chemicals and plastics, proprietary and specialty chemicals, and coal. The oil and gas unit was predominantly committed to the exploration and production of crude oil and natural gas. However, the unit also refined crude oil into motor fuels, which were sold through branded service stations operated by jobbers and independent dealers in the Southwest and Rocky Mountain areas.

The industrial chemicals and plastics unit produced commodity chemicals and continued to be supported by efficient production processes and a strong marketing staff. The plastics division, a part of this unit, produced products for ultimate use primarily in the construction and automotive industries. The proprietary chemicals and technology unit included agricultural chemicals, electrolytic systems, and specialty chemicals. These segments each produced proprietary products requiring research and development. Finally, a coal unit had been initiated with the purchase of Falcon Seaboard Inc. in 1979. This unit was not expected to be a major part of the business until the mid-1980s.

The oil and gas unit dominated the company, contributing 52 percent of the company's sales and 63 percent of the operating profits in 1980. Exhibit 3 contains data for each of the business segments. The focus of the company had clearly shifted from chemicals to oil and gas, but security analysts still included Diamond Shamrock in the financially diverse chemical industry. Selected financial data for Diamond Shamrock, similar chemical companies, and domestic oil companies are presented in Exhibit 4.

Confusion regarding Diamond Shamrock was also reflected in the company's stock price. A comparison of Diamond's stock price to indexes of chemical and domestic oil companies, found in Exhibit 5, illustrated that Diamond Shamrock was frequently priced between the two indexes. Exhibit 6 contains monthly returns on Diamond Shamrock's common stock and Standard & Poor's 500 Index. Whether the current market price of $32 per share accurately reflected the company's business mix was of concern to management. They believed that being followed by the wrong analysts contributed to the stock's undervaluation; only 2 of the 19 security research firms following Diamond categorized it as an oil company.

Corporate Financial Goals

Management continued to believe that Diamond Shamrock should invest in those businesses that had a high earnings potential and, if necessary, divest assets that had not and were not expected to earn a fair return for the shareholders. In order to make these decisions, management established a financial strategy for the 1980s. They required a corporate return on shareholders' equity (ROSE) of 20 percent. The 20-percent return was based on an assumed 7-percent inflation rate, a 3-percent real rate of return, a 5-percent premium for equity, and a 5-percent premium for Diamond Shamrock stock. Management also selected a target range for the total debt/capitalization of 35 to 37 percent. A return on capital employed (ROCE[1]) of 10.6 to 11.0 percent was computed by management from these measures. Assuming 30 percent of capital spending was noneconomic, management established hurdle rates for new projects of 15.1 to 15.7 percent.[2] A goal for growth in net income was set at a minimum of 13 percent (ROSE of 20 percent and a target dividend payout ratio of 25 to 35 percent). Finally, knowing they wanted a ROCE of 10.6 percent, management targeted a divisional pre-tax operating profit return on capital employed of 25.8 percent.

Forecasts for Each Division

As part of the 1980 business plan, management reviewed each of the divisions in light of corporate objectives, each division's ability to generate or use cash, its sales growth versus operating profit, and its competitive position in relation to its industry's maturity. Results of the analysis, presented in Exhibit 7, indicated that the energy divisions would maintain high sales growth and high operating returns, while the chemical divisions' returns would be low.

Forecasted income statements for each of the individual units through 1988 were also provided by unit managers. As shown in Exhibit 8, the oil and gas and the coal units were expected to meet the required ROCE measure but chemicals were not.

---

[1] ROCE = ROSE × Percentage of equity in total capital structure.
Percentage equity = [1 − (Percentage of debt + Percentage of deferred taxes)]
Deferred taxes assuming 10 percent of capital.

[2] Hurdle rate = ROCE/Percentage of economic projects.

In a Standard & Poor's debt rating seminar on March 17, 1980, Roy Taub, vice president of corporate ratings for Standard & Poor's, commented on the future of the chemical industry.

> The chemical industry has had a lot of downgradings. We are concerned about two things: There have been declining margins in commodity chemicals and the forecast for the energy costs indicates this pressure will continue. Many companies have the bulk of their assets in below average return products and if the company has chosen not to spend money to maintain its plant, returns will get even worse eventually. However, with some price relief and a good 1979, ratings in chemicals are not under the extreme pressure that they were recently.

Gerald Unterman, also from Standard & Poor's, commented on the oil industry.

> We see only modest volume growth in oil in the 1980s, but price will continue to go up fast. The key rating issues are that domestic reserves are steadily declining and it is extremely costly and difficult to replenish spent reserves. In our opinion, ownership of domestic oil reserves is most important in determining quality of the firm's earnings.
>
> We are not interested in oil companies' attempts to diversify since a recent analysis showed that they were only able to earn 2.2% on businesses other than oil.
>
> We are very positive about the short-term prospects of domestic oil producers.

Alternative Solutions

Diamond Shamrock's management believed the company's changing business mix had caused its stock to be undervalued. Strategically, they were considering two most likely courses of action. The conservative approach involved maintaining the status quo as revenues continued to shift toward energy and mounting an educational campaign designed to tell existing security analysts and investors about the "new" Diamond Shamrock. The dramatic strategy involved the divestiture of some or all of Diamond's chemical segments, an increased investment in oil and gas, and building an entirely new investor and analyst following from scratch. Both strategies had risks.

Diamond Shamrock Corporation

EXHIBIT 1 • Acquisitions and Divestitures, 1976–1980

1976

Acquired Julian Laboratories, a producer of Vitamin D-3 intermediate. Became part of Animal Nutrition Division.

1977

Acquired Federal Yeast Company. Became part of Foods Division.

Acquired Lankro Chemicals Group, Ltd. Name changed to Diamond Shamrock Europe, Ltd.

Acquired remaining 50 percent in Dia Prosim S.A.

Sold polypropylene plastics business.

1978

Acquired 21 percent interest in Sigmor Corporation.

Sold Chemetals Division.

Sold 320 service stations.

1979

Acquired Falcon Seaboard, Inc.

Acquired Shell's animal health business.

Sold Harte and Co.

Sold Mexia Tank Co. (a subsidiary of Falcon Seaboard).

1980

Acquired Fallek Chemical Co. (Assets were primarily cash and cash equivalents.)

Sold Ardco (a subsidiary of Falcon Seaboard).

Diamond Shamrock Corporation

EXHIBIT 2 • Financial Statements, 1976–1980 (thousands of dollars)

	1976	1977	1978	1979	1980
Revenues	$1,374,644	$1,553,336	$1,851,851	$2,393,935	$3,181,878
Cost of products sold	(965,177)	(1,112,829)	(1,419,472)	(1,811,787)	(2,517,904)
Selling and administrative	(111,092)	(122,964)	(156,950)	(192,782)	(220,107)
Research and development	(24,046)	(29,266)	(36,131)	(41,842)	(49,964)
Interest	(33,300)	(44,089)	(59,154)	(71,301)	(64,374)
Facility sales and shutdowns	(5,000)	(9,300)	(13,323)	0	0
Income before taxes	236,029	253,488	193,467	276,223	329,529
Taxes	(97,305)	(91,365)	(54,335)	(98,100)	(128,315)
Net income	$ 138,724	$ 162,123	$ 139,132	$ 178,123	$ 201,214
Assets					
Current assets					
Cash	$ 30,465	$ 33,523	$ 45,758	$ 31,347	$ 28,368
Receivables	206,181	267,102	318,614	443,051	484,600
Inventories	195,850	201,487	239,474	316,168	387,730
Prepaid insurance, etc.	3,582	5,248	5,694	7,150	10,855
Total current assets	436,078	507,360	609,540	797,716	911,553
Property, plant, and equipment	935,307	1,140,768	1,318,299	1,382,931	1,600,250
Investments	32,908	58,918	85,614	134,534	177,142
Intangible assets	91,496	91,700	89,187	87,673	85,764
Deferred charges	8,449	11,722	18,541	14,711	18,339
Total assets	$1,504,238	$1,810,468	$2,121,181	$2,417,565	$2,793,048

continued

Diamond Shamrock Corporation
EXHIBIT 2 • *continued*

	1976	1977	1978	1979	1980
Liabilities and shareholders' equity					
Current liabilities					
Notes payable	$ 19,419	$ 10,258	$ 38,821	$ 28,192	$ 13,464
Accounts payable	95,356	131,776	158,645	232,225	263,644
Long-term debt due within 1 year	6,897	6,366	13,149	7,495	7,464
Accrued interest, taxes, etc.	103,649	106,739	98,720	145,775	138,451
Total current liabilities	225,321	255,139	309,335	413,687	423,023
Long-term debt	428,730	540,497	672,628	712,544	809,847
Long-term capital lease obligations	39,226	41,629	40,783	38,372	35,128
Deferred taxes	126,993	167,895	183,435	224,949	275,989
Other	13,632	12,429	11,434	9,073	7,347
Stockholders' equity					
Preferred stock	7,115	0	0	0	0
Common stock	183,926	200,322	222,950	237,039	348,267
Retained earnings	479,420	592,668	680,715	781,981	893,515
Less: common treasury shares	125	111	99	80	68
Total shareholders' equity	670,336	792,879	903,566	1,018,940	1,241,714
Total liabilities and shareholders' equity	$1,504,238	$1,810,468	$2,121,181	$2,417,565	$2,793,048

Diamond Shamrock Corporation
EXHIBIT 3 • Business Segment Data, 1976–1980 (millions of dollars)[a]

	Energy		Chemicals			Technology	
	Oil and Gas	Coal	Industrial Chemicals	Plastics	Electrolytic Systems	Specialty Chemicals	Ag Chemicals and Health Products
1976							
Revenue	$ 515.5	$ 0	$403.2	$180.3	$ 39.9	$121.1	$122.2
Operating profit	96.2	0	138.0	14.3	16.0	14.9	13.2
Assets	561.7	0	354.5	176.0	100.0	119.5	87.3
Expenditures for plant and equipment	138.7	0	53.1	64.9	5.8	7.5	16.2
Depreciation, depletion, and amortization	32.8	0	20.6	5.5	6.8	3.9	2.3
1977							
Revenue	630.9	0	411.8	183.1	46.9	150.3	140.2
Operating proft	131.4	0	115.8	8.5	13.5	17.0	16.8
Assets	639.7	0	380.4	233.6	93.8	174.7	131.6
Expenditures for plant and equipment	110.1	0	53.8	126.3	2.4	38.8	27.8
Depreciation, depletion, and amortization	42.2	0	17.6	4.3	9.4	4.9	3.5
1978							
Revenue	669.1	110.9	407.1	184.2	48.1	261.1	191.1
Operating profit	99.0	14.6	80.5	11.5	14.0	17.8	12.7
Assets	659.9	92.2	419.0	283.2	87.9	202.1	189.9
Expenditures for plant and equipment	128.9	20.9	50.9	50.5	2.5	14.2	40.4
Depreciation, depletion, and amortization	65.2	8.4	21.7	12.8	8.6	9.1	5.8
1979							
Revenue	969.2	155.9	498.4	264.4	52.9	289.2	231.4
Operating profit	163.0	32.6	89.4	27.0	16.7	19.4	17.8
Assets	794.3	94.8	452.7	268.9	107.0	218.8	274.0
Expenditures for plant and equipment	135.6	11.8	35.1	11.8	5.5	8.6	42.3
Depreciation, depletion, and amortization	67.2	11.9	24.8	15.6	8.2	10.7	11.2
1980							
Revenue	1,691.4	158.3	553.2	184.6	63.1	329.1	286.7
Operating profit	275.5	33.4	86.6	(9.9)	21.3	15.6	8.6
Assets	1,027.9	116.9	512.3	276.0	114.9	237.8	322.6
Expenditures for plant and equipment	219.3	7.9	77.3	9.4	10.9	13.6	25.9
Depreciation, depletion, and amortization	$ 74.9	$ 9.0	$ 26.0	$ 15.2	$ 6.0	$ 9.1	$ 13.9

[a]Totals do not include corporate and other.

Diamond Shamrock Corporation
EXHIBIT 4 • Comparison with Chemical and Oil Companies' 5–Year Averages, 1975–1979

	Sales Growth Rate	Net Income Growth Rate	Net Profit Margin	Earnings per Share Growth Rate	Dividend Payout	ROSE	ROCE	Debt/Capital[a]	P/E High	P/E Low
Chemicals										
Diamond Shamrock	18.4%	13.6%	9.3%	22.8%	34.0%	23.5%	13.5%	37%	9.2×	5.6×
Allied	13.6	3.1	4.5	2.8	40.2	8.8	6.4	36	9.8	6.6
Dow	17.6	6.0	9.8	18.8	32.5	23.1	14.2	39	12.8	8.2
Hercules	11.3	12.9	5.0	4.3	56.4	12.3	9.4	27	19.2	11.6
Monsanto	13.6	0.5	6.9	13.0	34.5	15.1	11.2	28	9.0	6.0
Rohm & Hass	12.1	5.1	4.3	-3.7	32.8	7.5	6.3	33	20.0	11.2
Stauffer	15.2	12.9	9.7	20.8	30.2	20.3	14.3	32	9.0	4.8
Oils										
Cities Service	16.5	11.3	4.5	6.2	43.8	10.0	7.7	29	9.2	6.6
Getty Oil	15.0	16.6	9.8	17.4	21.2	14.2	12.1	6	12.6	8.4
Phillips Petroleum	16.6	15.7	8.3	21.6	29.4	19.5	14.7	20	10.4	7.2
Shell Oil	16.5	12.7	7.3	15.5	31.4	15.8	12.3	22	7.8	5.0
Standard Oil of Indiana	18.1	9.2	7.7	14.4	36.0	16.7	12.7	23	9.0	6.4
Standard Oil of Ohio	22.0	9.2	7.7	26.9	29.8	19.5	8.7	62	17.8	11.4
Sun Company	22.7	13.1	5.7	12.2	28.6	16.1	10.6	19	7.0	4.8
Union Oil of California	16.3%	11.7%	5.7%	11.4%	27.2%	15.8%	10.9%	27%	7.8×	5.4×

[a]Total capital is defined as total assets less current liabilities.

Source: *Standard & Poor's Industry Surveys,* 1980.

continued

Diamond Shamrock Corporation

EXHIBIT 4 continued • Comparison with Chemical and Oil Companies'—1980

	Sales Growth Rate	Net Income Growth Rate	Net Profit Margin	Earnings per Share Growth Rate	Dividend Payout	ROSE	ROCE	Debt/Capital[a]	P/E High	P/E Low	Book Value	Debt Rating	Beta
Chemicals													
Diamond Shamrock	33.3%	12.9%	6.4%	$3.66	45%	17.4%	7.5%	36%	11X	6X	$20.56	A−	1.15
Allied	27.4	64.2	5.2	8.15	27	17.2	6.1	28	8	5	47.81	A	1.20
Dow	14.9	2.7	7.6	4.42	37	19.2	7.4	40	9	6	23.71	A+	1.25
Hercules	6.1	(34.1)	4.6	2.60	45	11.7	6.2	23	10	6	23.79	A	1.30
Monsanto	6.1	(55.0)	2.3	4.10	87	5.3	2.6	30	17	10	77.52	A	1.00
Rohm & Hass	8.7	(1.9)	5.4	7.26	30	14.0	7.7	25	8	5	54.49	A	1.10
Stauffer	11.1	0.7	8.1	3.11	28	15.3	6.8	25	8	5	20.70	A	0.90
Oils													
Cities Service	32.1	26.5	5.7	8.82	23	41.4	11.1	26	4	2	24.28	AA	1.15
Getty Oil	10.1	44.4	8.6	10.60	18	23.1	12.2	11	10	6	50.44	AAA	1.10
Phillips Petroleum	40.9	20.1	8.0	7.01	26	23.4	11.7	12	9	5	32.44	AA+	1.15
Shell Oil	37.4	36.9	7.8	4.99	29	20.4	9.0	33	13	5	26.21	AA+	1.05
Standard Oil of Indiana	40.4	27.1	7.3	6.54	31	21.8	10.4	19	5	6	32.10	AAA	1.00
Standard Oil of Ohio	39.3	52.7	16.4	7.37	19	47.3	17.0	40	12	5	18.57	AA	1.15
Sun Company	21.5	3.3	5.6	5.92	29	18.1	7.8	35	10	5	34.38	AA	1.00
Union Oil of California	31.9%	29.1%	6.5%	$3.73	19%	20.1%	10.1%	22%	15X	6X	20.04	AA	1.10

aTotal capital is defined as total assets less current liabilities.

Source: *Standard & Poor's Industry Surveys*, 1980.

Diamond Shamrock Corporation
EXHIBIT 5 • Stock Price Comparisons

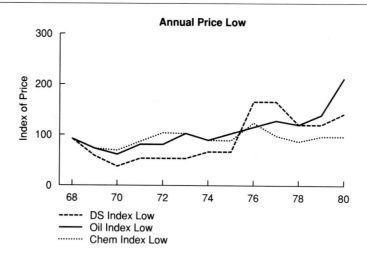

Annual Price Low

DS Index Low
Oil Index Low
Chem Index Low

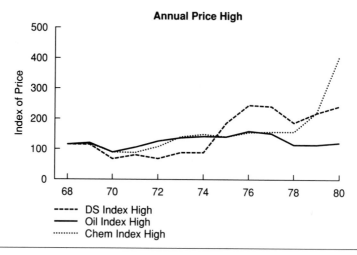

Annual Price High

DS Index High
Oil Index High
Chem Index High

Diamond Shamrock Corporation

EXHIBIT 5 • *continued*

Year	Annual High/Share	Annual Low/Share		Year	Annual High/Share	Annual Low/Share
1968	$18.7	$14.2		1975	$29.0	$10.9
1969	17.9	9.0		1976	40.0	26.6
1970	11.6	5.9		1977	38.6	26.4
1971	12.6	8.3		1978	29.8	19.0
1972	11.0	8.5		1979	35.1	19.1
1973	14.4	8.4		1980	$38.9	$23.2
1974	$14.7	$10.3				

Diamond Shamrock Corporation

EXHIBIT 6 • Monthly Returns on Diamond Shamrock Stock and Standard & Poor's 500

Date	Diamond Shamrock	S&P 500	Date	Diamond Shamrock	S&P 500
1976			*1978*		
Jan.	−28.34%	11.99%	July	1.46	5.60
Feb.	8.32	−0.58	Aug.	8.56	3.40
March	−7.29	3.26	Sept.	−9.87	−0.48
April	0.18	−0.99	Oct.	−17.91	−8.91
May	2.48	−0.73	Nov.	−4.27	2.60
June	12.90	4.27	Dec.	−0.65	1.72
July	−0.79	−0.68	*1979*		
Aug.	−9.02	0.14	Jan.	3.90%	4.21%
Sept.	−4.60	2.47	Feb.	−0.65	−2.84
Oct.	−0.37	−2.06	March	15.39	5.75
Nov.	−2.53	−0.09	April	−1.11	0.36
Dec.	5.59	5.40	May	−0.02	−1.68
1977			June	14.29	4.10
Jan.	6.57	−4.89	July	−0.50	1.09
Feb.	−0.96	−1.51	Aug.	6.01	6.11
March	−2.79	−1.19	Sept.	1.44	0.25
April	1.43	0.14	Oct.	−6.16	−6.56
May	−0.28	−1.50	Nov.	8.18	5.14
June	−8.57	4.75	Dec.	19.43	1.92
July	−6.25	−1.51	*1980*		
Aug.	−1.17	−1.33	Jan.	5.95	6.10
Sept.	3.40	0	Feb.	4.94	0.31
Oct.	−8.23	−4.15	March	−24.55	−9.87
Nov.	3.95	3.70	April	8.13	4.29
Dec.	3.49	0.48	May	4.51	5.62
1978			June	0.86	2.96
Jan.	−8.02	−5.96	July	7.66	6.76
Feb.	−6.51	−1.61	Aug.	−1.11	1.31
March	−7.46	2.76	Sept.	6.48	2.81
April	14.52	8.70	Oct.	−2.66	1.86
May	12.11	1.36	Nov.	14.59	10.95
June	−13.14	−1.52	Dec.	−2.41%	−3.15%

Diamond Shamrock Corporation

EXHIBIT 7 • Comparison of Divisions
Divisional Pre-Tax Operating Profit Returns

	Historic Period	Average Historic Return	1979	1980	Average, 1980–1982
Energy					
Oil and gas unit					
Exploration and Production (E&P)	70–78	10%	21%	24%	25%
Refining and Marketing (R&M)	70–78	34	57	61	72
Natural Gas Processing	70–78	43	25	73	68
Ammonia	70–78	50	38	13	14
Coal division	76–78	33	36	33	—
Chemicals					
Industrial chemicals					
Electro chemicals	70–78	35	19	19	23
Soda products	70–78	32	61	62	60
Plastics division	70–78	14	13	15	19
Technology					
Electrolytic systems	76–78	28	28	30	36
Specialty chemicals					
Process chemicals	76–78	32	36	37	43
Functional polymers	76–78	12	0	5	7
Metal coatings	76–78	96	51	74	85
Agricultural chemicals and health products					
Agricultural chemicals	71–78	23	17	15	18
Nutrition and Animal Health (NAH)	76–78	13	12	14	21
Health group	76–78	(30)	(71)	(67)	—
Foods	76–78	32%	23%	31%	36%

continued

Diamond Shamrock Corporation
EXHIBIT 7 • *continued*

Segments
Energy
Oil and Gas Unit
 9 = Exploration and Production (E&P)
11 = Refining and Marketing (R&M)
10 = Natural Gas Processing (NGP)
12 = Ammonia
15 = Coal Unit
Chemicals
Industrial Chemicals
 1 = Electro Chemicals
 2 = Soda Products
 3 = Plastics Division
Technology
 5 = Electrolytic Systems
      Speciality Chemicals
 4 = Process Chemicals
14 = Functional Polymers
13 = Metal Coatings
Agricultural Chemicals and Health Products
 6 = Agricultural Chemicals (Ag Chem)
 7 = Nutrition and Animal Health (NAH)
16 = Health Group
 8 = Foods

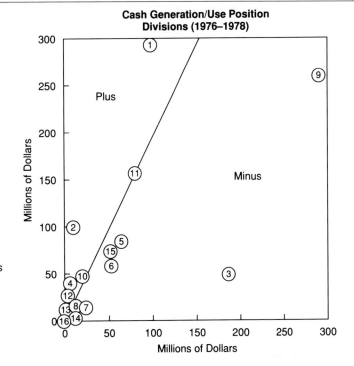

Cash Generation/Use Position Divisions (1976–1978)

O = 1976—1979
◊ = 1976—1982
1 = E&P
2 = NGP
3 = R&M
4 = Ammonia
5 = Coal

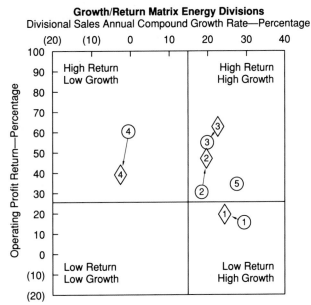

Growth/Return Matrix Energy Divisions
Divisional Sales Annual Compound Growth Rate—Percentage

continued

Diamond Shamrock Corporation
EXHIBIT 7 • *continued*

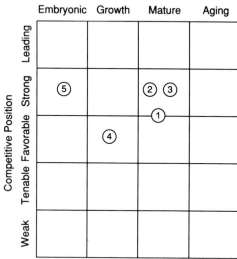

Competitive Position/Industry Maturity Matrix
Energy Segments Industry Maturity

Segments
Oil and Gas
1 = R&M
2 = E&P
3 = NGP
Coal
4 = Eastern Steam
    Coal
5 = Lignite

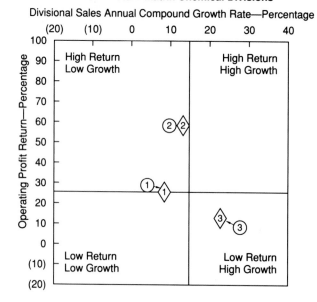

Growth/Return Matrix Chemical Divisions

Divisional Sales Annual Compound Growth Rate—Percentage

○ = 1976–1979
◇ = 1976–1982
1 = Electro Chem
2 = Soda Products
3 = Plastics

Diamond Shamrock Corporation
EXHIBIT 7 • *continued*

Competitive Position/Industry Maturity Matrix
Chemical Segments Industry Maturity

Segments
Electro Chemicals
1 = CL_2/H_2
2 = Liq. Caustic
3 = Dry Caustic
4 = Pot. Chem.
5 = Solvents–PCE
6 = Solvents–EDC
7 = Solvents–MEC
8 = Solvents–CFM
9 = Chlorowax
10 = TCI
Plastics
11 = PVC
12 = VCM
Soda Products
13 = Chrome
14 = Det. Silicates
15 = Liq. Silicates

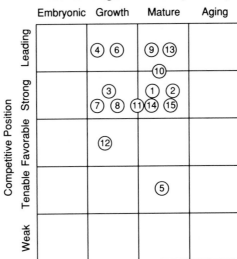

Growth/Return Matrix Technology Divisions

Divisional Sales Annual Compound Growth Rate—Percentage

O = 1976—1979
◊ = 1976—1982
1 = Process Chem (DOM)
2 = Electrolytic Sys.
3 = Ag Chem
4 = NAH
5 = Foods
6 = Metal Coatings
7 = Func. Polymers (DOM)
8 = Health Group

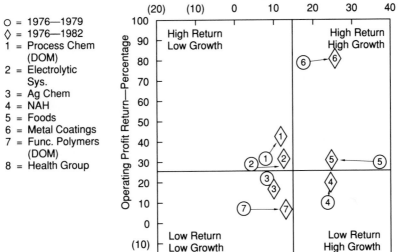

continued

Diamond Shamrock Corporation
EXHIBIT 7 • *continued*

Competitive Position/Industry Maturity Matrix
Technology Segments Industry Maturity

Segments
Functional Polymers
 1 = Functional Polymers
Metal Castings
 2 = Dacromet 320
 3 = Dacromet 220
Process Chem
 4 = Process Chem–Specialty
 5 = Process Chem–Textile
 6 = Process Chem–Paper
Ag Chem
 7 = Ag Chem–Arsonates
 8 = Ag Chem–Daconil
 9 = Ag Chem–Dacthal
 10 = Ag Chem–Phenoxies
NAH
 11 = Feed Supplements
 12 = Animal Health
Health
 13 = DSHS
 14 = DSMP
Foods
 15 = Foods–Bakery
 16 = Foods–Dairy

Diamond Shamrock Corporation

EXHIBIT 8 • Forecasts for Divisions, 1980

Industrial Chemicals and Plastics

Unit ROCE Report from Unit's Plans (dollars in millions)

	1979	1980	1981	1982	1983	1984	1985	1986	1987	1988
Net sales	$609.9	$652.1	$794.6	$889.0	$989.6	$1,100.0	$1,224.0	$1,362.0	$1,517.0	$1,689.0
Gross profit	150.0	160.4	189.3	229.0	237.5	262.9	291.6	321.9	358.5	396.4
Gross margin	24.6%	24.6%	23.8%	25.8%	24.0%	23.9%	23.8%	23.6%	23.6%	23.5%
Operating profit	$124.2	$130.6	$159.2	$206.9	$190.0	$210.1	$232.8	$256.5	$285.7	$315.1
Corporate allocations	35.5	27.7	31.1	34.5	38.4	46.2	55.8	64.6	73.1	82.7
Profit before tax	88.7	102.9	128.1	172.4	151.6	163.9	177.0	191.9	212.6	232.4
Taxes	29.8	42.2	52.5	70.7	62.2	67.2	72.6	78.7	87.2	95.3
Net income	$ 58.9	$ 60.7	$ 75.6	$ 101.7	$ 89.4	$ 96.7	$ 104.4	$ 113.2	$ 125.4	$ 137.1
Average capital employed	$672.3	$683.1	$725.7	$818.4	$946.5	$1,109.1	$1,287.4	$1,474.0	$1,675.4	$1,900.2
ROCE	8.76%	8.89%	10.42%	12.43%	9.45%	8.72%	8.11%	7.68%	7.48%	7.22%

Technology Unit ROCE Report from Unit's Plans (dollars in millions)

	1979	1980	1981	1982	1983	1984	1985	1986	1987	1988
Net sales	$500.0	$604.5	$719.0	$826.4	$911.0	$1,002.0	$1,103.0	$1,213.0	$1,334.0	$1,468.0
Gross profit	133.9	159.1	207.7	241.4	244.0	269.0	296.0	325.0	358.0	393.0
Gross margin	26.8%	26.3%	28.9%	29.2%	26.8%	26.8%	26.8%	26.8%	26.8%	26.8%
Operating profit	$ 30.0	$ 36.5	$ 45.6	$ 54.5	$ 63.8	$ 70.1	$ 77.2	$ 84.9	$ 93.4	$ 103.0
Corporate allocations	13.8	12.2	14.2	15.9	17.8	21.4	25.7	29.7	33.5	37.8
Profit before tax	16.2	24.3	31.4	38.6	46.0	48.7	51.5	55.2	59.9	65.2
Taxes	5.7	10.2	13.2	16.2	18.8	20.0	21.1	22.5	24.6	26.7
Net income	$ 10.5	$ 14.1	$ 18.2	$ 22.4	$ 27.2	$ 28.7	$ 30.4	$ 32.7	$ 35.3	$ 38.5
Average capital employed	$245.0	$283.4	$326.0	$375.3	$436.9	$513.4	$595.0	$678.8	$768.4	$868.1
ROCE	4.29%	4.98%	5.58%	5.97%	6.23%	5.59%	5.11%	4.82%	4.59%	4.43%

Oil and Gas Unit ROCE Report from Unit's Plans (dollars in millions)

Net sales	$969.1	$1,443.7	$1,595.9	$1,838.2	$2,024.0	$2,231.0	$2,460.0	$2,720.0	$2,997.0	$3,311.0
Gross profit	169.4	257.4	308.2	354.7	390.8	434.3	487.3	543.8	609.0	675.4
Gross margin	17.5%	17.8%	19.3%	19.3%	19.3%	19.5%	19.8%	20.0%	20.3%	20.4%
Operating profit	$173.0	$225.1	$289.1	$333.0	$340.2	$380.5	$425.8	$475.9	$534.1	$598.7
Corporate allocations	37.2	34.5	40.3	49.2	56.5	69.7	85.8	100.7	114.4	130.1
Profit before tax	135.8	190.6	248.8	283.8	283.7	310.8	340.0	375.2	419.7	468.6
Taxes	51.3	81.4	106.3	121.4	122.0	133.7	146.2	161.3	180.5	201.5
Net income	$84.5	$109.2	$142.6	$162.4	$161.7	$177.1	$193.8	$213.9	$239.2	$267.1
Average capital employed	$668.5	$783.1	$922.2	$1,147.4	$1,373.0	$1,665.4	$1,963.9	$2,284.2	$2,617.7	$2,997.3
ROCE	12.64%	13.94%	15.45%	14.15%	11.78%	10.63%	9.87%	9.36%	9.14%	8.91%

Coal Unit ROCE Report from Unit's Plans (dollars in millions)

Net Sales	$155.9	$150.0	$158.0	$198.0	$220.0	$249.0	$279.0	$313.0	$351.0	$393.0
Gross profit	37.0	35.0	38.5	47.0	52.2	58.5	65.6	73.6	82.5	92.4
Gross margin	23.7%	23.3%	24.4%	23.7%	23.7%	23.5%	23.5%	23.5%	23.5%	23.5%
Operating profit	$33.1	$31.0	$34.0	$42.0	$46.7	$52.5	$59.1	$66.6	$75.0	$84.4
Corporate allocations	5.1	3.9	4.1	5.7	5.0	8.6	10.6	12.4	14.2	16.3
Profit before tax	28.0	27.1	29.9	36.3	41.7	43.9	48.5	54.2	60.8	68.1
Taxes	8.6	6.7	7.3	9.0	10.3	10.8	11.9	13.3	15.0	16.7
Net income	$19.4	$20.4	$22.6	$27.3	$31.4	$33.1	$36.6	$40.9	$45.8	$51.4
Average capital employed	$92.9	$97.7	$99.3	$123.4	$139.3	$178.2	$242.2	$281.5	$324.1	$371.1
ROCE	20.88%	20.88%	22.76%	22.12%	22.54%	18.57%	15.11%	14.53%	14.13%	13.85%

Philip Morris, Incorporated: Seven-Up Acquisition (A)

The decision had been made. Philip Morris, Inc., (PM) was going to make a takeover bid for the Seven-Up Company. The difficulties and intricacies of that decision paled, however, in the face of the next one: at what price should PM management make its tender offer?

It was the latter half of April 1978, and in the face of an increasingly active merger/acquisition market, PM management recognized the need for the utmost speed and secrecy in developing its bidding strategy.

Background

Philip Morris, Inc., was one of the 50 largest companies in the United States in 1977 with revenues of $5.2 billion and an asset base of $4 billion. The company had achieved record increases in sales and earnings over the 5 years ending 1977, as shown in Exhibit 1, and its stock was extremely highly rated. However, while market analysts predicted that PM's annual sales growth would continue at 13 to 14 percent between 1977 and 1982, earnings were expected to increase by only 12 to 13 percent per year.

Philip Morris, originally founded in the 19th century, had primarily manufactured and sold cigarettes until the late 1960s. What diversification the company had undertaken was largely vertical and included manufacturing paper, packaging, and chemical products used in making cigarettes.

In the late 1960s, the first reports regarding the potential dangers of smoking began to emerge, and by the early 1970s, cigarette advertising was banned from television. These events led PM management to modify its corporate strategy by diversifying into new businesses. PM's experience with its early acquisitions eventually led the company's managers to the following conclusion: future acquisition targets should be significant players within large industries, i.e., relatively large companies whose performance could make a significant contribution to that of the corporation as a whole. Because of the healthy cash flows of the cigarette business, management was willing to forgo strong early returns from an acquired company if its long-term potential appeared attractive. Management decided, however, to limit its diversification to companies that produced consumer goods, hoping for synergies from the broader use of PM's existing marketing expertise.

The first major step in this strategy was the acquisition of Miller Brewing Co. in 1970. PM management used essentially the same consumer-driven strategy with its beer products as it had with its cigarette products. Sophisticated marketing programs were undertaken that included (1) detailed market studies identifying target consumer groups and their salient characteristics, (2) the identification of existing, or the development of new, products for the groups so identified, and (3) the creation of a product packaging, distribution, and advertising program suitable for the product and the specific consumer group. Concurrently, management committed itself to constructing modern, efficient production facilities adequate for the volume that PM's marketing programs were expected to generate.

While PM management's strategies for beer and tobacco products were procedurally similar, they differed in terms of their practical applications. Specific cigarette brands were being marketed to increasingly well-defined (and, therefore, smaller) consumer groups, but PM management redefined Miller beer's target market in a dramatic move that greatly increased the number of the product's potential consumers. When PM acquired the Miller Brewing Co., that company marketed one major product, Miller Beer, which, with a 4-percent share of market, was the seventh largest-selling beer in the country. The company had annual sales of 5 million barrels, making it the fifth largest brewer in the United States.

PM management refocused Miller's marketing program away from the female, upper-income consumer implicitly targeted by the "Champagne of Bottled Beer" theme. Management believed that the use of *champagne* isolated the beverage from the mainstream of the beer market and implied that the beer should be offered only on special occasions. Instead, the beer was now targeted toward the male, blue-collar, heavy beer-drinking segment of the market.

By 1977 Miller's share of market exceeded 15 percent, the second largest share in the industry. In addition, PM management had increased the company's production capacity to 30 million barrels per year, making Miller the second largest U.S. brewer. Plans to increase this capacity to 50 million barrels per year by 1982 had already been approved.

In addition, PM management developed and introduced two new products: Miller Lite and domestically brewed Lowenbrau. The latter product was targeted at the super premium-priced segment historically dominated by Michelob. Miller Lite, however, was a relatively new concept in the beer industry. Although most other national brewers subsequently introduced competitive products of their own, Miller Lite retained its position as the leading low-calorie beer in the United States through 1977. The financial and share-of-market results of PM management's strategy are shown in Exhibit 2.

The success of PM management's marketing strategy in both the beer and the cigarette industries was reflected in its financial statements. In 1977 alone, Philip Morris's net earnings increased 26 percent on a sales increase of 21 percent, and the return on average equity reached a 10-year high of 22 percent. Total debt to equity was at a 10-year low of 0.93, and the company's net cash flow (after-tax cash flow less common and preferred dividends) exceeded planned capital expenditures by 19 percent. PM's most recent financial statements are shown in Exhibits 3 and 4.

At the end of 1977, Philip Morris's operations were divided into five groups:

1. Philip Morris U.S.A. (cigarettes),
2. Philip Morris International (cigarettes),
3. Miller Brewing Company (beer),
4. Philip Morris Industrial (specialty papers, chemicals, etc.),
5. The Mission Viejo Company (real estate and community development).

Each group's contribution to Philip Morris's revenues and operating income is shown in Exhibit 1.

On the basis of the increasing share-of-market success and the returns of its existing products and operations, PM management decided to make another acquisition. Management settled on the soft-drink industry, focusing on the Seven-Up Company as the most likely target.

Soft-Drink Industry

The soft-drink industry was large and growing. Soft-drink sales of the top five competitors alone were about $4.7 billion in 1977, up 16 percent from the 1976 figure of $4.0 billion. In the 5-year period from 1973 to 1977, these companies generally outperformed the S&P 500 composite average, as shown in Exhibits 5 and 6. Detailed financial statements for the Seven-Up Company appear in Exhibits 7 through 9.

Soft-Drink Product

Soft drinks were the quintessential consumer product. They were a low-cost, multipurchase consumer item, the sales of which were highly influenced by sophisticated marketing programs. The industry's successful combination of advertising, promotional efforts, packaging, and distribution had, by the end of 1977, made the drinks the most popular beverage in the United States. There was every indication that the drinks were well on their way to acquiring the same status worldwide.

Soft drinks traced their origin to two different sources, both medicinal. On the one hand, research into the therapeutic properties of naturally effervescent spring waters had begun as early as the 1600s in Europe. By the beginning of the 19th century, artificially carbonated soda water was being bottled and sold commercially in both the United States and Europe. Concurrently, various syrups were being developed to cure a wide range of ills. Among these was Coca-Cola, invented in May 1886. Coke was originally marketed as a medicinal syrup, whose chief components, cocaine and opium, would cure a wide range of nervous afflictions, such as neuralgia and hysteria. By chance, the product was mixed with soda water by the end of 1886, giving rise to the soft-drink product known in 1977. (The major intervening modifications to the product were the deletions of the cocaine and opium.)

Similarly, Seven-Up, introduced in 1929 as "Bib-Label Lithiated Lemon-Lime Soda," was advertised as a hangover cure for home and hospital use. The fact that Seven-Up was also widely perceived as an excellent mixer for alcoholic drinks provided an added boost to sales. In fact, Seven-Up management did not consciously redefine and market Seven-Up as a soft drink until 1968.

Soft drinks were deceptively simple in their composition, which included only four basic categories of ingredients: a base-flavor concentrate or extract, such as cola, a sweetener, water, and carbonation. However, the base concentrates contained numerous flavorings, the specific names and proportions of which were secrets closely guarded by the concentrate manufacturers. The type of sweetener used in the soft drink was also variable. At the end of 1977, saccharin was the major sugar substitute used in diet drinks, while either sugar or high-fructose corn syrup (HFCS)[1] might be used in the production of regular soft drinks.

Soft drinks came in numerous flavors: cola, orange, root beer, lemon-lime, etc. Cola-flavored drinks were the most popular in the United States, enjoying a 62-percent share of the total domestic soft-drink market (regular and diet drinks). Coca-Cola and Pepsi-Cola were the two top-selling cola products, with 39 percent and 28 percent of this segment's volume. Lemon-lime drinks constituted the next largest flavor category with a 12-percent share of the total market. Seven-Up and Sprite (a Coca-Cola Co. product) were the leading competitors within the segment, holding 49 percent and 23 percent of the segment, respectively. The distance between the

---

[1] HFCS was sold at a 20-percent discount to sugar for an equivalent sweetening power. At the end of 1977, most concentrate manufacturers (except Coca-Cola and PepsiCo) had authorized its use in whole or in part in the production of soft drinks. Seven-Up, which required less sweetener than the colas, derived a special economic advantage from the substitution of HFCS for sugar.

cola and lemon-lime segments was slightly less in the international market, where lemon-lime drinks had a 15 percent share of the total market.

Since their introduction, diet drinks had enjoyed increasing popularity. By 1977, sales of diet drinks had grown to roughly 11 percent of the total market. Each of the top soft-drink companies had introduced one or more diet products. The success of the different flavor categories within the diet-drink market paralleled the patterns in the total market. Cola-flavored products of the Coca-Cola Co. and PepsiCo., Inc., Tab and Diet Pepsi, dominated the market with 23-percent and 19-percent shares of the diet-drink market. Diet Seven-Up was the only major lemon-lime product in the diet market and, with an 11-percent share, was the third largest-selling diet drink in the country.

Market data for the soft-drink industry and its leading competitors are shown in Exhibits 10 and 11.

Market-Growth Analysis

By 1977 soft drinks had surpassed coffee as the most popular beverage in the United States. In the period between 1963 and 1977, soft-drink consumption grew from 3.4 billion gallons per year to 7.9 billion gallons, representing an increase in consumption of from 191 to 389 12-oz. cans per person per year, roughly comparable to 20 percent of the average daily liquid intake.

Numerous factors contributed to the phenomenal growth in soft-drink sales. In the early years, the United States' rapid rate of population growth provided a steadily increasing number of consumers. Per-capita consumption was spurred by the product's relatively low price, by intensive marketing efforts, and by the spread of distribution networks across the country.

By the 1960s, the wide availability of soft drinks was forcing competition to proceed along other dimensions:

> The frontiers of the American market had been conquered, and henceforth domestic growth would come by priming the market with new products and using new ways to market the old ones. The need for a complete soft-drink line was underscored by the widespread acceptance of the multiple-flavor vending machine and the triple-drink fountain dispenser. To avoid being outflanked by competitors, each manufacturer introduced a spate of new containers intended to make soft-drink consumption as convenient as possible. The most noticeable trend was nonreturnable bottles and cans, the latter particularly after the introduction of the easy opening flip-top in 1962.[2]

---

[2] J. C. Louis and Harvey Z. Yazijian, *The Cola Wars* (New York: Everest House, 1980), pp. 107–108.

Further constraints on the industry's growth appeared in the latter half of the 1970s as America's population growth rate gradually declined. Down to about 1 percent per year by 1977, the decline implied a major demographic shift toward an older population. Whether or not America's teenagers, historically the industry's primary target market, would carry their soft-drink consumption patterns with them into their twenties and thirties was a question of major concern to both concentrate manufacturers and other industry participants.

The increasing saturation of the market, together with the country's changing demographics, led to greatly increased competition among the soft-drink companies, as each strove to maintain and improve its historical growth record. Media advertising budgets were sharply increased (as shown in Exhibit 12), and price discounting became commonplace.

Internationally, soft drinks were meeting the same acceptance that they had received in the United States. Although per-capita consumption was considerably less than that in the United States, this phenomenon resulted largely from the products' later entry into the international market. Furthermore, the growth rates in certain countries were roughly comparable to patterns experienced earlier in the United States.

Industry Structure

There were four major groups of participants in the soft-drink industry: concentrate or extract manufacturers, raw-material and packaging suppliers, bottling and distribution companies, and retailers. The general relationships between these groups are outlined below.

Concentrate Manufacturers. More than 30 companies manufactured branded products and marketed them regionally or nationally, while numerous food chains produced private-label soft drinks. Sales within the industry were, however, highly concentrated. Five companies (Coca-Cola Co.; PepsiCo, Inc.; Seven-Up Co.; Dr. Pepper Co.; and Royal Crown Cos.) accounted for 75 percent of the 1977 sales volume, as shown in Exhibit 10. The leading brands of each of these companies (Coca-Cola, Pepsi-Cola, Seven-Up, etc.) accounted for 56 percent of the total industry volume.

Each of the top five competitors could trace its origin to the turn of the century. By the end of World War II, each had begun to market its product internationally. In fact, Coca-Cola was being distributed through 64 bottlers in 28 countries as early as 1930. By the end of 1977, Coke was available in more than 135 countries, Pepsi-Cola in 140 countries, Seven-Up in 86 countries, and Royal Crown products in 51 countries.

The industry leaders had also grown by expanding their product lines (as highlighted in Exhibit 10) and by diversifying into other products. As shown in Exhibit 13, by 1977 only the Dr. Pepper Co. derived 100 percent of its revenues from the sale of soft drinks.

Soft-Drink Industry: General Structure

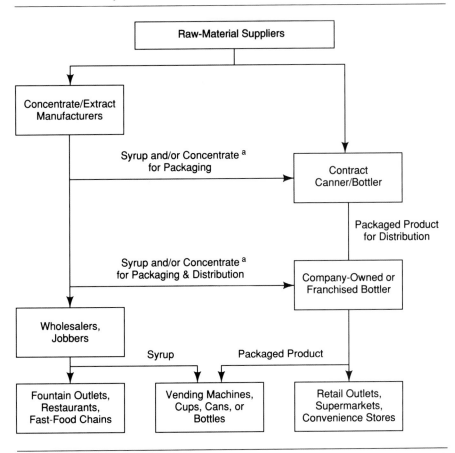

[a]Concentrate, when combined with the sweetener, was referred to as *syrup*. Only Coca-Cola and PepsiCo sold syrup to their bottlers.

Soft-Drink Bottlers and Distributors. The distribution system in the soft-drink industry was almost as old as the products themselves. The system had been established by the Coca-Cola Co. in 1899 and subsequently adopted by other soft-drink companies. Briefly, Coca-Cola's owner, Asa Candler, had signed a contract with Benjamin Franklin Thomas and Joseph Brown Whitehead, giving them the right to set up bottling plants throughout the nation at no expense or liability to the Coca-Cola Co. In addition, Mr. Candler agreed to sell the syrup exclusively to the two men, to furnish labels and advertising materials, and to grant them the sole rights to use the Coca-Cola trademark. Mr. Thomas and Mr. Whitehead promptly set out to find enterprising individuals with adequate capital for their own bottling operations. In exchange for its investment, each franchisee was granted the exclusive right to bottle and market a given product within a certain geographical market.[3] Typically, in the early years, family members would use the earnings from one franchise territory to set up a relative in an adjacent area. Because the franchises were granted in perpetuity, the arrangement fostered a closed system within which franchises were passed from parent to child through the years.

The franchised bottlers operated under certain contractual constraints. Bottlers had to maintain quality standards, provide adequate bottling and distributing facilities, and participate in marketing programs. Furthermore, they were not allowed to sell in other franchised territories (or to sell to second parties who were likely to sell the product in another territory), nor could they sell directly competing products. However, a bottler was under no legal obligation to handle the full product line of any single concentrate manufacturer and could select which product to distribute within a given flavor category. Thus, for example, an independent Pepsi franchisee could distribute Seven-Up within the lemon-lime segment, rather than Teem, PepsiCo's competitive entry.

The franchise bottling system had originally evolved because of economic necessity. The concentrate manufacturers needed to maximize their products' distribution and availability, while the bottlers needed some guarantee of territorial exclusivity to make it worth their while to invest in the necessary capital equipment. The result, early in the industry's history, was a multiplicity of small bottlers. As time passed, a plethora of container sizes and shapes put many small bottlers at an economic disadvantage: they could not invest in all of the production lines necessary to ensure a complete line of any given product. Many bottlers therefore entered into joint ventures with one another to share production facilities. Alternatively, several concentrate manufacturers, such as the Seven-Up Company, made separate contracts with independent canners which guaranteed the provision of the full line of products to the company's franchised bottlers.

Regardless of the production system used, all products were still distributed through the territorially franchised bottlers. The numbers of bottlers were declining, however, while their territories were expanding. Of the estimated 5,200 domestic bottlers in operation in 1947, only 2,300 were thought to remain in business in 1970.[4] This change derived in part from mergers among the individual bottlers as one means of providing the

---

[3] The bottlers' specific production responsibilities included (1) purchasing raw materials, principally sweeteners and packaging materials; (2) mixing the concentrate, sweetener, water, and carbonation; and (3) packaging the finished product.

[4] J. C. Louis and Harvey Z. Yazijian, *The Cola Wars* (New York: Everest House, 1980), p. 334.

Breakdown of 1977 Domestic Sales by Type of Bottler

Company	Company-Owned Bottlers		Franchised Bottlers	
	Nos.	Percent Sales	Nos.	Percent Sales
Coca-Cola Co.	11	10	555	90
PepsiCo, Inc.	13	22	404	78
Seven-Up Co.	1[a]	3	473[b]	97
Dr. Pepper Co.	5	12	494	88
Royal Crown Cos.	13	25	272	75

[a]The Seven-Up Bottling Co. of Phoenix, Ariz., was acquired in 1972. The company also owned a second bottling operation in Ontario, Canada.

[b]It was estimated that only three bottlers handled the Seven-Up line exclusively; all others marketed one or more competitive products. Industry analysts also estimated that about 330 of Seven-Up's bottlers (70 percent of the total) handled Coca-Cola or Pepsi-Cola.

Source: Company annual reports and 10–K's, *Value Line,* and industry reports.

necessary production equipment. However, the trend was also caused by the acquisition of certain bottlers by larger corporate entities, which included newcomers to the soft-drink industry as well as certain concentrate manufacturers themselves. In the former case, the trend toward acquisitions by outsiders started in the late 1960s when certain medium-sized conglomerates such as RKO General and General Cinema, started buying bottlers. By the late 1970s, however, larger conglomerates were making the acquisitions, the size of the purchasers reflecting the attractive cash flows of many bottlers. In the case of the concentrate manufacturers, the primary goal was to maintain or increase their control over marketing and distribution. The results of the increased concentration among the bottlers and concentrate manufacturers are shown in the table of domestic sales by bottler.

The increasing concentration among soft-drink bottlers and concentrate manufacturers did not go unnoticed. In the mid-1970s, the Federal Trade Commission brought an antitrust action against the industry in general and against the territorial franchise system in particular. Although a decision on the case was not imminent at the end of 1977, the industry was lobbying strongly against the action. Dissolution of the franchise system, the industry argued, would cause irreparable economic damage to the independent bottlers by opening the door for a warehouse distribution system along the lines of that used in the beer industry.

Competitive Environment

The soft-drink industry had long been dominated by its two leading competitors, the Coca-Cola Co. and PepsiCo, Inc. These two companies, through their competition with each other, determined the industry's pricing schedules and marketing programs.

For instance, until 1975 the Coca-Cola Co. was the industry price leader in both the fountain and take-home segments of the market. Coke's pricing schedule was based on the terms originally negotiated with its bottlers at the turn of the century. As a result, the price of the company's base concentrate had remained at 88 cents per gallon for many years.[5] In 1974, however, PepsiCo initiated an aggressive campaign against Coca-Cola. The company's theme, "the Pepsi Challenge," asked customers to taste test the two beverages. The campaign was supported by heavy consumer discounts as well as increased advertising expenditures. With this campaign, PepsiCo seized the position of industry price leader within the take-home segment.

This escalation of the competition between Coke and Pepsi affected the rest of the industry in two ways. The widespread use of consumer discounts reflected the growing emphasis on volume and share-of-market data rather than earnings. Those concentrate manufacturers electing not to discount their products, such as the Seven-Up Company, ran the risk of weakening their relations with their bottlers. The budgets allocated to marketing were also increasing.

These trends were not expected to abate in the near future. In fact, early in 1978, the Coca-Cola Co. began negotiations with its bottlers to change their fixed-price contracts. Coke's aim was to revise its pricing schedule such that the syrup's price could be raised commensurate with increases in the consumer price index. In return for this concession, Coke promised its bottlers that the company would use a large portion of the anticipated increase in earnings to augment its marketing budget in the Coke–Pepsi dispute. Negotiations on this matter were ongoing in March 1978.

These negotiations had several implications for Coke's competitors. Because most companies strove to approximate Coke's pricing schedule, the negotiations appeared to offer some relief from inflation's negative effect on margins. However, this benefit was largely offset by the specter of the increased marketing budgets Coke had promised its bottlers.

In addition, Coca-Cola Co.'s and PepsiCo's marketing programs were becoming more successful, as reflected in the increases in their individual shares of market as well as in the continued preference for cola-flavored products. Both the Seven-Up Company and the Dr. Pepper Co. responded with campaigns highlighting the differences between their products and the colas. Seven-Up management introduced the "Uncola" theme in 1968,

---

[5] Coca-Cola charged its bottlers for sugar on the basis of the average price of sugar at the ten largest Northeast refiners during the first 10 days of each quarter. Coca-Cola was one of the world's leading purchasers of sugar and procured its needs under futures contracts.

while Dr. Pepper relied on "the most misunderstood soft drink" theme. Although Seven-Up introduced modest variations on its Uncola message in the intervening years, the basic theme had not changed substantially by 1977: "7-Up is a drink with a style all its own, and the people who drink it have a style all their own." This theme was re-emphasized and repackaged in 1977 and presented by management as its vehicle to regain its former share of the market. Specifically, management announced its goal of growing at a rate of 1 to 2 percent higher than the industry as a whole.

Early in 1978, however, Seven-Up's president made the following statement to *Advertising Age* (4/17/78): "Research has found that the 'Seven-Up image is confused and cloudy.'" The company subsequently terminated its relationship with its advertising agency of 36 years and announced its intent to test market a new graphics program in late 1978 and to increase the product's advertising budget. Market analysts generally approved of this move, thinking that the Uncola campaign had succeeded too well: consumers had come to see Seven-Up as a specialty product.

Competition in the industry was also proceeding along two other major fronts: international expansion and new-product development. The Middle East was the major arena of expansion during 1977. The Coca-Cola Co., previously well-established in Israel, was finally granted permission to enter the Egyptian market. Less than 12 months later, Seven-Up management announced its intent to introduce Seven-Up into the Cairo market in May 1978 and to open 11 other bottling operations abroad during the year.

With respect to new product entries, the last major spurt of activity had been in the early 1960s. PepsiCo acquired and introduced Mountain Dew nationally. PepsiCo and Coca-Cola introduced Teem and Sprite into the lemon-lime segment, and all companies developed and started marketing diet drinks. In early 1978, the Coca-Cola Co. was test marketing Mello Yello, and the Seven-Up Company introduced Quirst, a new entry into the lemonade market. Quirst, which had been developed by Seven-Up's recently acquired subsidiaries, was to be test marketed in about one-fifth of the U.S. market starting in early May. The product's introductory campaign was to be backed by an annual advertising budget of $5 million.[6]

Industry Outlook

The outlook for the soft-drink industry in the latter half of the 1970s was mixed. While domestic demographic trends and a tight competitive environment implied reductions in the rates of soft-drink sales growth, the

---

[6] Shortly after Seven-Up management introduced Quirst, the company was sued by the Squirt Co. for trademark infringement. The outcome of the case had not been determined by April 1978.

international market appeared to be wide open. According to certain security analysts, "Foreign markets continue to hold great potential for the major producers. Per-capita soft-drink consumption in most overseas nations is only a small fraction of the U.S. rate. Although it is highly unlikely that consumption in Third World nations will ever match the U.S. level, there remains great room for growth." Taking the domestic and international markets together, industry analysts predicted a 5- to 6-percent growth rate in the industry over the next 5 years.

There was, however, the possibility that certain other forces might affect future sales levels. The soft-drink industry was under attack on several fronts at the end of 1977. Nutrition experts, alarmed at increasing per-capita soft-drink consumption, were vocal in their criticism of the product. Their concerns were reinforced by research into the possible toxic effects of heavy sugar ingestion. Saccharin, the sugar substitute used in diet soft drinks, was also a source of controversy. Saccharin's safety was under continuing study by the federal Food and Drug Administration. Caffeine, a component of most soft drinks but not of Seven-Up, had recently re-emerged as a potential problem. The FDA had initiated a study on the safety of heavy caffeine consumption, particularly as it pertained to children and teenagers, the industry's primary market. Although the caffeine content of soft drinks was considerably less than that of comparable amounts of tea or coffee, the study represented an additional source of uncertainty for the industry.

Conclusion

Despite their uncertain futures, little about either the soft-drink industry or the Seven-Up Company reduced their attractiveness to PM management. On the contrary, Seven-Up appeared particularly attractive from both financial and operational points of view. Although the product was new to PM management, the problems of its merchandising were very familiar.

Unfortunately, however, the current status of the merger and acquisition market implied that the Seven-Up Company might well evoke interest among other acquisitive corporations. This realization put additional pressure on PM management to act quickly and provided an additional consideration in its initial tender offer. On its part, Seven-Up's management recognized that the company was not only attractive, but also potentially vulnerable to a takeover. Seven-Up management proposed and received approval of two actions at the company's April 1978 shareholders' meeting. First, dividends were increased, presumably to strengthen investor interest in and support of the stock. Second, and more telling, the shareholders approved amendments to the company's articles of incorporation providing for the establishment of three classes of directors, each of which would serve a staggered three-year term.

Thus, it appeared that the conditions in the market, as well as the position of Seven-Up's management and shareholders, demanded a very careful, competitive tender offer.

Philip Morris, Inc.: Seven-Up Acquisition (A)
EXHIBIT 1 • Philip Morris: 5-Year Performance
(dollars in millions, except per-share amounts)

	1973	1974	1975	1976	1977
Operating Companies' Revenues (percent)					
Philip Morris U.S.A.	50.1%	49.9%	47.3%	45.7%	41.5%
Philip Morris International	31.6	29.5	28.6	25.2	25.9
Miller Brewing Co.	10.6	13.4	18.1	22.9	25.5
Philip Morris Industrial	5.1	5.2	4.2	3.9	4.2
Mission Viejo	2.6	2.1	1.9	2.2	2.8
Total percentage[a]	100.0%	100.0%	100.0%	100.0%	100.0%
Total dollars	$2,602.5	$3,011.0	$3,642.4	$4,293.8	$5,202.0
Operating Companies' Income (percent)					
Philip Morris U.S.A.	69.0%	70.9%	68.4%	63.3%	60.6%
Philip Morris International	28.0	23.3	22.9	20.5	19.6
Miller Brewing Co.	(1.0)	1.6	5.8	12.0	13.6
Philip Morris Industrial	2.5	3.0	1.6	1.7	1.9
Mission Viejo	1.3	1.2	1.2	2.6	4.2
Total percentage[a]	100.0%	100.0%	100.0%	100.0%	100.0%
Total dollars	$ 329.5	$ 403.6	$ 492.8	$ 634.5	$ 782.7
Other Expenses					
Interest expense	$ 51.0	$ 82.7	$ 99.0	$ 102.8	$ 101.6
Provision for income taxes	107.0	122.0	149.2	206.3	290.6
Net Earnings	$ 148.6	$ 175.5	$ 211.6	$ 265.7	$ 334.9
Per-Share Data					
Primary earnings	$ 2.71	$ 3.15	$ 3.62	$ 4.47	$ 5.60
Dividends declared	0.67	0.78	0.93	1.15	1.56
Book value	14.66	16.97	20.63	23.99	28.16
Market price of common: High	68.38	61.38	59.25	63.25	64.88
Low	48.75	34.13	40.88	49.75	51.50
Market price of common: End of year	$ 57.38	$ 48.00	$ 53.00	$ 61.75	$ 61.88
Operating Performance					
Pre-tax profit margin	9.80%	9.90%	9.90%	11.00%	12.00%
Return on average equity	19.70%	19.60%	19.20%	20.00%	21.50%
Total debt/equity[b]	1.16	1.27	1.18	1.07	0.93
Net cash flow/capital expenditures[c]	0.81%	0.79%	0.85%	1.19%	1.19%
Beta	1.11	1.15	1.15	1.15	1.10
Date of beta estimate	11/30/73	11/1/74	10/31/75	10/29/76	10/28/77

[a] Numbers may not add up to 100 percent due to rounding.

[b] Total debt = Long-term debt + Notes payable + Current portion of long-term debt.

[c] Net cash flow = Profit after tax + Depreciation − Dividends on common and preferred stock.

Source: Philip Morris, Inc., 1977 *Annual Report; Value Line.*

Philip Morris, Inc.: Seven-Up Acquisition (A)

EXHIBIT 2 • Miller Brewing Company, 1968–1977 (all data in millions)

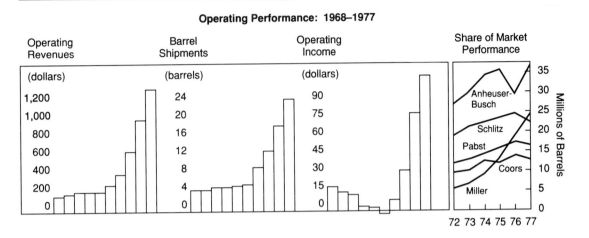

Source: Philip Morris, Inc., *Annual Reports.*

Source: Robert J. Flaherty, "Philip Morris' Year of Decision," *Forbes,* July 10, 1978, p. 30.

Philip Morris, Inc.: Seven-Up Acquisition (A)
EXHIBIT 3 • Philip Morris Income Statements
(thousands of dollars, except per-share amounts)

	Results for Year Ending December 31		Results for Three Months Ending March 31	
	1976	*1977*	*1977*	*1978*
Operating revenues	$4,293,782	$5,201,977	$1,142,617	$1,390,709
Cost of sales				
Cost of products sold	(1,966,871)	(2,401,680)	(527,077)	(638,882)
U.S. federal and foreign taxes on goods sold	(1,159,286)	(1,352,487)	(296,160)	(371,838)
Gross profit	1,167,625	1,447,810	319,380	379,989
Marketing, administrative, and research	(547,287)	(676,772)	(150,475)	(178,478)
Equity in net earnings of unconsolidated foreign subsidiaries and affiliates	14,201	11,694	2,911	2,303
Operating income of operating companies	634,539	782,732	171,816	203,814
Corporate expense	(35,229)	(38,523)	(11,089)	(12,491)
Gross interest	(109,258)	(108,747)	(27,007)	(32,159)
Capitalized interest	6,424	7,163	1,273	2,599
Net interest expense	(102,834)	(101,584)	(25,734)	(29,560)
Net currency translation hedging costs	(15,520)	(11,633)	2,047	(2,645)
Other deductions, net	(9,028)	(5,476)	(4,258)	1,944
Earnings before income tax	471,928	625,516	132,782	161,062
Provision for federal and other income tax	(206,253)	(290,590)	(61,365)	(73,541)
Net earnings	265,675	334,926	71,417	87,521
Earnings per common share	$ 4.47	$ 5.59	$ 1.19	$ 1.46

Source: Philip Morris, Inc., *Annual Reports.*

Philip Morris, Inc.: Seven-Up Acquisition (A)
EXHIBIT 4 • Philip Morris Balance Sheets (thousands of dollars)

	Results for Year Ending December 31		Results for Three Months Ending March 31	
	1976	*1977*	*1977*	*1978*
Assets				
Cash and cash equivalents	$ 64,353	$ 72,231	$ 47,070	$ 75,026
Net receivables	267,943	316,723	310,260	332,138
Inventories				
Leaf tobacco	1,089,301	1,271,235	1,083,092	1,256,118
Other raw materials	125,620	142,231	125,855	143,436
Work in process and finished goods	379,446	314,519	393,322	385,699

Philip Morris, Inc.: Seven-Up Acquisition (A)
EXHIBIT 4 • *continued*

	Results for Year Ending December 31		Results for Three Months Ending March 31	
	1976	*1977*	*1977*	*1978*
Housing programs under construction	63,137	89,576	74,821	94,317
Total inventories	1,657,504	1,817,561	1,677,090	1,879,570
Prepaid expenses	15,945	14,505	21,582	22,585
Total current assets	2,005,745	2,221,020	2,056,002	2,309,319
Investments in and advances to unconsolidated foreign subsidiaries and affiliates	220,147	229,508	219,158	227,920
Land and offtrack improvements	58,766	69,576	59,648	70,464
Property, plant, and equipment, at cost	1,323,923	1,594,910	1,355,123	1,693,442
Less accumulated depreciation	330,044	392,478	340,157	409,696
Net property, plant, and equipment	993,879	1,202,432	1,014,966	1,283,746
Brands, trademarks, patents, and goodwill	211,570	222,492	211,594	222,183
Long-term receivables	66,463	64,762	65,047	67,073
Other assets	25,639	38,249	42,434	41,435
Total assets	$3,582,209	$4,048,039	$3,668,849	$4,222,140
Liabilities and Shareholders' Equity				
Notes payable	$ 260,131	$ 121,139	N.Av.	N.Av.
Accounts and notes payable	N.Av.	N.Av.	$ 396,581	$ 309,407
Accounts payable and accrued liabilities	402,775	503,767	N.Av.	N.Av.
Accrued liabilities	N.Av.	N.Av.	272,355	390,825
Current portion long-term debt	17,729	15,740	N.Av.	N.Av.
Federal and other income taxes	103,527	139,766	119,917	157,971
Dividends payable	19,359	24,741	19,463	30,737
Total current liabilities	803,521	805,153	808,316	888,940
Long-term debt	1,247,778	1,426,619	1,249,596	1,443,229
Deferred income taxes	77,714	104,429	87,449	119,519
Other liabilities	23,214	21,772	28,878	23,284
Total liabilities	2,152,227	2,357,973	2,174,239	2,474,972
Cumulative preferred stock ($100 par)	8,812	8,262	8,812	7,787
Common stock ($1 par)	59,490	59,922	59,806	59,928
Additional paid-in capital	294,225	300,538	292,947	301,055
Earnings reinvested in business	1,071,488	1,325,149	1,137,148	1,381,934
Less treasury stock, at cost	(4,033)	(3,805)	(4,103)	(3,536)
Total shareholders' equity	1,429,982	1,690,066	1,494,610	1,747,168
Total liabilities and shareholders' equity	$3,582,209	$4,048,039	$3,668,849	$4,222,140

Source: Philip Morris. Inc., *Annual Reports.*

Philip Morris, Inc.: Seven-Up Acquisition (A)

EXHIBIT 5 • Top Four Soft-Drink Companies: Performance, 1973–1977

Company and Year	Primary EPS	Cash Flow per Share	Dividends per Share	Book Value per Share	Return on Equity	Market Price High–Low[a]	Average Annual P/E	Long-Term Debt/ Equity
Coca-Cola[b] Beta @ 3/10/78: 1.20								
1973	$1.80	$2.29	$0.90	$ 7.44	22.7%	$75.0–57.8	38.9×	0.9%
1974	1.64	2.13	1.04	8.01	19.2	63.9–22.3	26.8	1.1
1975	2.00	2.55	1.15	9.45	19.5	46.8–26.6	19.9	0.7
1976	2.38	2.95	1.33	10.53	21.0	47.6–36.7	17.7	0.6
1977	$2.67	$3.33	$1.54	$11.92	21.0%	$40.9–35.5	14.3×	0.9%
PepsiCo, Inc.[b] Beta @ 3/10/78: 1.15								
1973	$1.12	$1.71	$0.38	$ 5.32	16.0%	$29.9–21.3	24.3×	44.7%
1974	1.23	1.90	0.43	6.12	15.7	23.9–9.8	13.9	62.7
1975	1.47	2.20	0.50	7.11	16.7	24.8–13.6	14.2	45.0
1976	1.85	2.68	0.63	8.44	18.1	29.2–23.2	14.0	37.0
1977	$2.15	$3.19	$0.83	$ 9.57	19.3%	$28.6–22.3	11.5×	44.0%
Seven-Up Co.[b] Beta @ 3/10/78: 1.25								
1973	$1.30	$1.47	$0.43	$ 5.08	21.4%	$37.3–21.8	23.6×	4.7%
1974	1.54	1.76	0.61	6.04	21.9	30.8–10.5	14.3	3.6
1975	1.88	2.14	0.75	7.54	23.0	36.0–15.5	16.0	2.4
1976	2.28	2.59	1.13	8.75	24.4	41.0–29.8	15.6	0.9
1977	$2.38	$2.70 est.	$1.25	$ 9.90 est.	23.0% est.	$32.8–23.8	11.7× est.	0.6% est.
Dr. Pepper[b] Beta @ 3/10/78: 1.50								
1973	$0.51	$0.60	$0.23	$ 1.99	25.5%	$30.0–18.8	49.2×	0.0%
1974	0.52	0.62	0.28	2.27	22.7	22.9–6.5	26.1	0.0
1975	0.62	0.74	0.32	2.58	24.0	15.1–7.0	18.1	0.0
1976	0.81	0.95	0.40	2.80	27.0	17.8–11.0	18.6	0.0
1977	$1.01	$1.23	$0.53	$ 3.42	26.5%	$17.3–11.0	13.3×	0.9%
S&P 500: Industry Composite[c]								
1973	$2.27[d]	$3.78[e]	$0.91	$17.26	13.5%	$ 38–24	13.7×[f]	48%
1974	2.46[d]	4.11[e]	0.98	18.55	13.7	31–16	9.7[f]	50
1975	2.29[d]	4.10[e]	1.01	19.71	12.0	30–18	10.0[f]	52
1976	2.85[d]	4.76[e]	1.14	21.37	13.7	34–24	10.0[f]	49
1977	$3.11[d]	$5.20[e]	$1.31	$23.07	13.8%	$ 32–24	9.4×[f]	48%

[a] All stocks traded on NYSE except Seven-Up, which trades in the OTC market.

[b] Source: *Value Line.*

[c] Source: *Standard & Poor's Compustat Services, Inc.*

[d] Primary EPS includes extraordinary items and discontinued operations.

[e] Estimated by casewriter: [PAT + Depr. + Depl. + Amort.] ÷ Primary nos. of shares.

[f] Computed by casewriter.

Philip Morris, Inc.: Seven-Up Acquisition (A)

EXHIBIT 6 • Common Stock Movement, January 1977–April 1978
(closing price at end of month or at date shown)

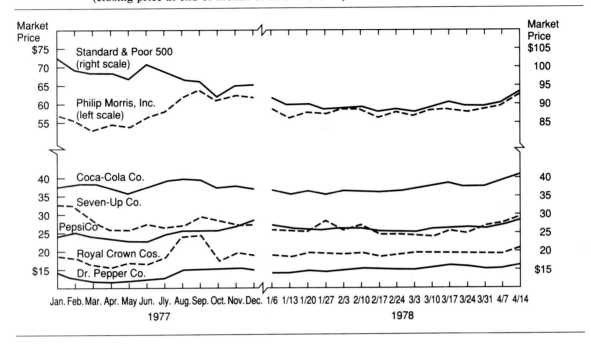

Philip Morris, Inc.: Seven-Up Acquisition (A)

EXHIBIT 7 • Seven-Up Company Income Statements
(thousands of dollars, except per-share amounts)

	Results for Year Ending December 31		Results for Three Months Ending March 31[a]	
	1976	*1977*	*1977*	*1978[b]*
Net sales	$233,283	$250,998	$50,416	$60,271
Cost of products sold	(117,166)	(129,040)	(24,863)	(29,878)
Gross profit	116,117	121,958	25,553	30,393
Selling, administrative, and general expense	(71,482)	(76,815)	(17,184)	(20,004)
Interest expense	289	335	37	139
Other expenses, net of other income	2,800	2,401	579	799
Earnings before income tax	47,146	47,209	8,911	11,049
Income taxes	(22,394)	(21,420)	(4,047)	(5,278)
Net earnings	$ 24,752	$ 25,789	$ 4,864	$ 5,771
Earnings per common share	$ 2.28	$ 2.38	$ 0.45	$ 0.53
Dividends per common share	$ 1.13	$ 1.25	$ 0.30	$ 0.35

[a]Quarterly data are unaudited.

[b]Results for 1978 exclude operations of Oregon Freeze Dried Foods, acquired in February 1978. Had the company been included for the entire three-month period, sales at 3/31/78 would have been $62,015,000, net earnings, $5,830,000, and earnings per share, $0.54.

Source: Seven-Up Company, *Annual Reports.*

Philip Morris, Inc.: Seven-Up Acquisition (A)
EXHIBIT 8 • Seven-Up Company Balance Sheets (thousands of dollars)

	Results for Year Ending December 31		Results for Three Months Ending March 31[a]	
	1976	*1977*	*1977*	*1978[a]*
Assets				
Cash	$ 5,462	$ 4,517	$ 9,707	$ 13,723
Short-term investments	34,589	42,616	29,704	22,534
Accounts and notes receivable	18,469	20,487	19,991	23,398
Allowance for doubtful accounts	(275)	(220)	(289)	(220)
Net receivables	18,194	20,267	19,702	23,178
Inventories				
Finished products (FIFO)	12,029	13,067	12,606	16,880
Extract and raw materials (sugar carried at LIFO)	14,025	14,088	16,454	17,515
Total inventories	26,054	27,155	29,060	34,395
Prepaid expenses and other current assets	2,547	2,635	2,861	2,679
Total current assets	86,846	97,190	91,034	96,509
Other assets	2,671	2,330	2,628	2,498
Property, plant, and equipment, at cost				
Land	6,527	6,407	6,464	6,537
Orchards	1,989	2,113	2,146	2,113
Buildings and improvements	15,739	18,866	15,626	19,254
Machinery and equipment	23,942	29,290	24,512	31,044
Orchards under development	1,535	1,706	1,446	1,752
Construction in progress	3,782	2,450	4,639	3,498
Depreciation (straight line)	(15,932)	(18,632)	(16,459)	(19,557)
Net property, plant, and equipment	37,582	42,200	38,374	44,641
Net intangible assets: trademarks, formulas, and goodwill	4,144	4,009	4,081	9,726
Total assets	$131,243	$145,729	$136,117	$153,374

continued

Philip Morris, Inc.: Seven-Up Acquisition (A)
EXHIBIT 8 • *continued*

	Results for Year Ending December 31		Results for Three Months Ending March 31[a]	
	1976	*1977*	*1977*	*1978[a]*
Liabilities and Shareholders' Equity				
Current liabilities				
Notes payable to foreign banks	$ 489	$ 2,189	$ 2,302	$ 1,998
Accounts payable	7,933	8,653	9,366	9,874
Employee compensation	1,981	2,261	1,785	2,264
Accrued advertising	8,774	9,949	7,761	10,513
Other accrued liabilities	2,317	2,932	2,101	3,425
Income taxes	4,396	3,385	6,308	6,333
Current portion of long-term debt	354	259	352	419
Total current liabilities	26,244	29,628	29,975	34,826
Other liabilities				
Long-term debt (excluding current portion)	943	689	842	703
Deferred income taxes	2,504	1,979	2,539	2,390
Total liabilities	29,691	32,296	33,356	37,919
Shareholders' equity				
6-percent cumulative preferred stock	3,588	3,076	3,076	3,076
Common stock ($1 par value)[b]	10,720	10,722	10,720	10,725
Additional capital	11,150	11,345	11,277	11,389
Retained earnings	76,094	88,290	77,688	90,265
Total shareholders' equity	101,552	113,433	102,761	115,455
Total liabilities and shareholders' equity	$131,243	$145,729	$136,117	$153,374

[a]Quarterly data are unaudited.

[b]The descendants of the Seven-Up Company's three original founders owned 45 percent of Seven-Up's common stock, roughly half of which was held in beneficiary trusts for future generations. Common stock held by unrelated members of management increased the total controlled by the company to about 51 percent. Twenty-one percent of the stock was held by a group of 53 institutional investors, and the remainder was owned by unrelated parties. Although members of the founding families had not taken a particularly active role in the management of the company in recent years, two grandsons of the original founders were elected directors of the company at the April 1978 shareholders' meeting. This brought the total number of family representatives on the board to three and was interpreted as an apparent attempt to strengthen the families' hands in the business.

Source: Seven-Up Company, *Annual Reports.*

Philip Morris, Inc.: Seven-Up Acquisition (A)
EXHIBIT 9 • Seven-Up Company Historical Data (millions of dollars, except per-share amounts)

	1969	1970	1971	1972	1973	1974	1975
Earnings Data							
Net sales	$103.0	$111.6	$124.4	$132.5	$146.7	$190.9	$213.6
Gross profit	48.0	51.6	58.1	62.8	71.0	80.8	101.2
Selling, general, and administrative	(30.0)	(32.5)	(36.6)	(40.2)	(45.2)	(51.2)	(61.3)
Operating profit	18.0	19.1	21.5	22.6	25.8	29.6	39.9
Net miscellaneous income	0.2	0.5	0.7	0.6	1.3	2.5	(0.1)
Profit before tax	18.2	19.6	22.2	23.2	27.1	32.1	39.8
Income taxes	(9.6)	(9.8)	(10.9)	(11.2)	(13.0)	(15.5)	(19.5)
Profit after taxes and extraordinary items	8.6[d]	9.8	11.3	12.0	14.1	16.6	20.3
Depreciation and amortization	1.1	1.2	1.1	1.3	1.8	2.3	2.9
Capital expenditures	2.9	1.9	2.6	3.1	7.5	6.8	6.8
Per-Share Data							
Earnings[a]	0.75	0.89	1.03	1.10	1.30	1.54	1.88
Dividends[b]	0.24	0.33	0.40	0.42	0.43	0.61	0.75
Book value[b]	2.50	3.08	3.72	4.62	5.50	6.45	7.93

continued

	$22¾–14¼	$30¾–17¾	$36⅛–26¾	$50⅛–33⅜	$37¼–21¾	$30¾–10½	$36–14¾
Market-price range[b,c]							
Average number of shares[a]	10,326,961	10,335,038	10,345,034	10,378,538	10,457,812	10,467,739	10,636,841
Balance-Sheet Data							
Current assets	$ 35.4	$ 40.7	$ 45.8	$ 52.3	$ 58.8	$ 67.3	$ 86.6
Plant, property, and equipment	14.8	16.0	17.2	19.3	24.6	29.1	32.7
Other	5.2	4.5	4.4	5.8	6.2	7.3	6.7
Total assets	55.4	61.2	67.4	77.4	89.6	103.7	126.0
Current liabilities	14.7	15.2	15.9	17.7	20.1	24.9	34.8
Long-term debt	3.2	2.8	1.7	2.4	3.1	2.7	2.1
Other	0.7	0.4	0.4	0.4	0.4	0.4	0.6
6-percent cumulative preferred stock	3.6	3.6	3.6	3.6	3.6	3.6	3.6
$5.71 convertible Class A preferred stock	7.4	7.4	7.3	5.1	4.9	4.6	—
Owners' equity	25.8	31.8	38.5	48.2	57.5	67.5	84.9
Total liabilities and owners' equity	$ 55.4	$ 61.2	$ 67.4	$ 77.4	$ 89.6	$103.7	$126.0

[a]Based on the weighted-average number of shares outstanding during the year. Data have been adjusted to reflect stock splits in 1969 and 1972 and to reflect those shares issuable upon the exercise of stock options.

[b]Adjusted retroactively for two-for-one stock splits in 1969 and 1972.

[c]High-low bid prices, OTC.

[d]Extraordinary loss of $0.2.

Source: Seven-Up Company. *Annual Reports.* All data have been restated on pooling-of-interest basis to reflect the operations of the Warner Jenkinson Co. and Ventura Coastal Corp., acquired in 1970 and 1973, respectively. Numbers may not add up due to rounding.

Philip Morris, Inc.: Seven-Up Acquisition (A)

EXHIBIT 10 • Volume Sales and Share-of-
Market Data: Top Five Soft-Drink Companies

	1975	1976	1977
Coca-Cola Co.			
Coca-Cola	24.2%	24.3%	24.5%
Sprite	2.5	2.7	2.8
Tab	2.5	2.6	2.6
Fanta	2.1	2.3	2.3
Mr. Pibb	0.8	0.7	0.9
Fresca	0.6	0.6	0.5
Others	0.1	0.2	0.3
Total	32.7%	33.4%	33.9%
PepsiCo, Inc.			
Pepsi-Cola	17.4%	17.0%	17.2%
Mountain Dew	1.1	1.5	1.9
Diet Pepsi	1.6	1.9	2.1
Pepsi Light	0.1	0.5	0.5
Teem	0.3	0.2	0.2
Others	0.3	0.3	0.4
Total	20.8%	21.4%	22.3%
Seven-Up Company[a]			
7-Up	6.6%	6.3%	6.0%
Diet 7-Up	1.0	1.2	1.2
Total	7.6%	7.5%	7.2%
Royal Crown Cos.			
Royal Crown	3.4%	3.3%	3.2%
Diet Rite Cola and RC 100	0.8	0.8	0.8
Nehi and others	1.2	1.2	1.0
Total	5.4%	5.3%	5.0%
Dr. Pepper Co.			
Dr. Pepper	4.9%	5.0%	5.3%
Sugar Free Dr. Pepper	0.6	0.8	1.0
Total	5.5%	5.8%	6.3%
Total share of market, top 5	72.0%	73.4%	74.7%
Millions of cases sold, top 5[b]	3,208.5	3,587.9	3,925.5

[a]Sales of Seven-Up's Howdy Flavors were a negligible proportion of total soft-drink sales in the years shown, case sales are included in the total of the cases sold by the top five companies.

[b]1 case = 24 8-oz. containers or 16 12-oz. cans.

Source: Lehman Brothers Kuhn Loeb Research, as printed in *Beverage Industry*, April 24, 1981. Copyright: John C. Maxwell and *Beverage Industry*. Reprinted by special permission of John C. Maxwell.

Philip Morris, Inc.: Seven-Up Acquisition (A)
EXHIBIT 11 • Trends in the Soft-Drink Industry

A. Estimated Share of Soft-Drink Market by Flavor Category[a]

	Cola	Lemon-Lime	Pepper Type	Orange	Root Beer	Other
1970	63.0%	12.0%	3.9%	8.3%	4.5%	8.4%
1971	63.0	12.0	3.9	8.4	5.0	7.7
1972	63.0	12.0	4.6	8.4	5.0	7.0
1973	62.5	12.5	5.0	8.2	5.0	6.8
1974	61.7	12.8	5.2	8.0	5.2	7.1
1975	62.1	12.9	5.3	7.9	5.2	6.6
1976	62.2	12.7	6.7	7.8	5.2	5.4
1977	62.4%	12.4%	7.3%	7.4%	5.3%	5.2%

B. Composition of U.S. per-Capita Annual Liquid Consumption[b]

	Soft Drinks	Beer	Wine and Dis-tilled Spirits	Coffee[c] and Tea	Milk[d]	Other[d]
1970	14.8%	10.1%	1.7%	22.6%	12.7%	38.1%
1971	15.8	10.6	1.9	22.5	12.6	36.7
1972	16.6	10.8	1.9	22.5	12.7	35.4
1973	17.4	11.3	2.0	22.7	12.5	34.1
1974	17.4	11.8	2.0	21.9	12.2	34.7
1975	17.1	12.0	2.0	21.5	12.4	35.0
1976	18.7	12.1	2.1	19.9	12.3	34.9
1977	20.0%	12.5%	2.1%	19.2%	12.2%	34.0%

[a]Source: *Beverage Industry,* April 24, 1981; Copyright: John C. Maxwell and *Beverage Industry.* Based on data from Lehman Brothers Kuhn Loeb Research. Figures include diet drinks in the appropriate flavor category.

[b]Source: *Beverage Industry,* May 22, 1981, p. 19. Data are based on USDA, DSI, USBA, American Bottled Water Assoc., and Lehman Brothers Kuhn Loeb Research estimates.

[c]Coffee data are based on three-year moving average to counterbalance inventory savings.

[d]Data for milk and juice (the latter is included in *Other* category) reflect USDA revisions as of 7/1/80.

Philip Morris, Inc.: Seven-Up Acquisition (A)
EXHIBIT 12 • Major Media Spending by Top Five
Soft-Drink Competitors (thousands of dollars)

	1973	1974	1975	1977
Coca-Cola Co.				
Coca-Cola	$24,013.4	$22,122.1	$20,261.3	$24,227.1
Tab	5,315.8	5,099.3	6,369.5	4,195.5
Fresca	2,589.9	2,544.5	2,381.3	1,273.0
Sprite	1,738.0	2,463.1	2,542.3	4,188.3
Diet Sprite	N.Av.	N.Av.	10.2	293.4
Fanta beverages	391.8	147.2	74.5	117.6
Mr. Pibb	264.3	911.1	1,297.4	1,208.2
Mr. Pibb Diet	N.Av.	N.Av.	13.0	11.2
Other, general[a]	412.7	817.8	407.4	790.9
Total	34,725.9	34,105.1	33,356.9	36,305.2
Company total[b]	$40,980.9	$41,605.6	$41,931.8	$52,385.8
PepsiCo, Inc.				
Pepsi-Cola	$13,383.2	$14,795.4	$14,557.1	$24,410.0
Diet Pepsi	4,097.5	4,138.8	3,673.1	6,387.5
Mountain Dew	349.5	634.6	2,577.3	4,457.5
Pepsi-Light	N.Av.	N.Av.	918.2	6,565.0
Teem	0.8	N.Av.	61.2	248.8
Other[a]	466.7	60.8	366.8	1,225.6
Total	18,297.7	19,629.6	22,153.7	43,294.4
Company total[b]	$36,040.1	$37,607.0	$42,447.6	$77,851.8
Seven-Up				
7-Up	$10,430.6	$10,185.0	$ 9,230.5	$12,897.9
Diet 7-Up	2,068.4	1,967.1	743.3	N.Av.
Sugar Free 7-Up	N.Av.	N.Av.	2,482.6	1,489.1
Other[a]	218.4	252.6	949.4	327.2
Total	12,717.4	12,404.7	13,405.8	14,714.2
Company total[b]	$13,048.8	$12,911.6	$14,013.9	$14,714.2

Philip Morris, Inc.: Seven-Up Acquisition (A)
EXHIBIT 12 • *continued*

	1973	*1974*	*1975*	*1977*
Dr. Pepper Co.				
Dr. Pepper	$5,245.8	$5,401.9	$ 4,574.5	$ 6,871.0
Sugar Free Dr. Pepper	95.7	1,739.1	1,547.6	1,771.5
Diet Dr. Pepper	1,113.4	N.Av.	N.Av.	N.Av.
Other[a]	30.8	20.1	297.3	155.4
Total	6,485.7	7,161.1	6,419.4	8,797.9
Company total[b]	$6,604.2	$7,279.5	$ 6,506.1	$ 8,881.5
Royal Crown Cos.				
Royal Crown Cola	$1,279.9	$ 579.9	$ 486.1	$ 7,418.8
Diet Rite Cola	626.4	2,130.6	3,388.6	2,289.3
Diet Rite beverages	2,351.2	133.5	108.8	4.8
Other[a]	3,605.7	5,116.8	10,088.3	245.5
Total	7,863.2	7,960.8	14,071.8	9,958.4
Company total[b]	$8,064.3	$8,094.2	$14,784.8	$17,589.2

[a]Figures in this category are an aggregate of all nonproduct-specific expenditures, e.g., general company promotions, promotional tie-ins between products (Tab and Fresca or Diet and Regular Dr. Pepper), sweepstakes, youth sports programs, etc. The numbers are included inasmuch as the expenditures are likely generally to support specific products. Expenditures for lower volume products, such as the Dr. Pepper Co.'s Big Red Soft Drink or PepsiCo's Rebel beverage, are not included in the *Other* category.

[b]Represents total media spending by the company for all products.

Source: Leading National Advertisers, New York, January–December 1973–1975 and 1977. Figures represent total expenditures in 6 media areas: magazines, newspaper supplements, network television, spot television, network radio, and outdoor advertising. All numbers are estimates.

Philip Morris, Inc.: Seven-Up Acquisition (A)

EXHIBIT 13 • Five Leading Concentrate Manufacturers:
Analysis of Sales, 1976–1977 (millions of dollars)

Company and Product Line	1976		1977	
	Sales	*Earnings*	*Sales*	*Earnings*
Coca-Cola Co.	$3,033	$586	$3,560	$678
Soft drinks	77%	87%	75%	87%
Other (juices, tea, coffee, wine, etc.)	23	13	25	13
Total	100%	100%	100%	100%
PepsiCo,Inc.	$3,109	$360	$3,649	$412
Beverages	37%	40%	38%	44%
Food products	30	30	29	28
Food service	12	17	14	18
Transportation	13	6	12	6
Sporting goods	8	7	7	5
Total	100%	100%	100%	100%
Seven-Up Company[a]	$ 233	$ 44	$ 251	$ 45
Soft drinks	79%	90%	78%	90%
Lemon products	13	2	14	5
Flavors/colors	8	8	8	4
Total	100%	100%	100%	100%
Dr. Pepper Co.	$ 187	$ 32	$ 227	$ 37
Beverages (total)	100%	100%	100%	100%
Royal Crown Cos.	$ 287	$ 38	$ 350	$ 39
Soft drinks	61%	61%	58%	56%
Citrus	16	17	15	21
Home decorating	21	20	16	12
Fast food	2	2	11	12
Total	100%	100%	100%	100%

[a]Diversification within the Seven-Up Company had occurred fairly steadily in the period from 1970 to 1978, as shown below:

1970 Acquired Warner-Jenkinson Co., the dominant source of Seven-Up extract for over 50 years and a highly respected technical leader in the manufacture of flavors, colors, and fragrances.

1972 Acquired the first company-owned bottling company, subsequently named the Seven-Up Bottling Co. of Phoenix, Ariz.

1973 Acquired Ventura Coastal Corp., which grew, processed, and sold fresh lemons and lemon products, including frozen concentrate for lemonade. Ventura supplied roughly one-third of the lemonade market and provided the Seven-Up Co. with one-fifth of its lemon oil needs. Warner-Jenkinson acquired a small company with operations related to its own.

1974 Ventura Coastal Corp. acquired the Golden Crown Citrus Co., a manufacturer of juices. Golden Crown's product line was subsequently expanded to handle the frozen concentrates being produced by Ventura, and a new powdered lemonade was developed and put into test marketing. Warner-Jenkinson acquired a second small company with related operations.

1978 Oregon Freeze Dried Foods was acquired in February for $9.8 million in cash. The company, which had sales of $10.5 million in the year ending 6/30/77, was touted as the world's leading processor of freeze-dried goods.

Source: Company reports and *Value Line.*

Philip Morris, Incorporated: Seven-Up Acquisition (B)

It was late April 1978, and the management of Philip Morris, Inc., (PM) expected to make its bid for the Seven-Up Company within several days. Sam Baxter, a recent Stanford MBA, was a member of the acquisition team. As a financial analyst, his job was to help develop the forecasts necessary to support the price to be offered by PM.

Mr. Baxter decided to base his analysis on a discounted cash flow (DCF) model he had used in business school.[1] He believed that this method would be useful in the valuation of the Seven-Up Company for several reasons. First, he regarded the expected cash flows of an investment to be a more realistic indicator of its future potential than its earnings, even though many managers had traditionally based their valuations on earnings and earnings multiples. PM management did use a cash flow approach to rank its capital investment decisions, so the use of the DCF model was a logical extension of current practice.

Valuation Technique

Before starting the process of forecasting Seven-Up's expected cash flows, a critical question had to be answered: from whose point of view should the analysis be done? That of Philip Morris management, Seven-Up management, or the capital markets? Clearly, the current market price of Seven-Up's stock represented one set of expectations for the company's future—expectations that theoretically incorporated estimates of the future performance of the Seven-Up Company, the soft-drink industry, and the market as a whole. However, early in 1978, Seven-Up manage-

---

[1] The model was very similar to one described by Alfred Rappaport in an article published in the *Harvard Business Review* ("Strategic Analysis for More Profitable Acquisitions," July–August, 1979, pp. 99–110.) Quotations subsequently appearing in this case are taken from that article and publication.

ment had taken certain actions that indicated its dissatisfaction with the company's performance and the value ascribed to it by the market. For instance, management had fired the company's advertising agency of 36 years and had announced a goal of 7- to 8-percent growth in sales for 1978, as compared with the 5 to 6 percent expected for the industry as a whole. Seven-Up management's actions clearly reflected its belief in a bright future for the company, perhaps brighter than that envisioned by the stock market. The analysis could also be made from the viewpoint of PM management. The company had a history of introducing innovative changes to newly acquired companies, each of which implied certain costs and benefits that should, perhaps, be reflected in the analysis.

Mr. Baxter recognized that the viewpoint taken in the analysis affected not only the cash flows, but also the discount rate that would be used. Hoping to resolve his uncertainties, he decided to review his notes from business school on the DCF model.

The model defined the cash flows in the following way:

Yearly cash flows = (Earnings before interest and taxes, EBIT) ×
$\qquad$ (1 − Income tax rate) +
$\qquad$ Depreciation and other noncash charges −
$\qquad$ Capital expenditures −
$\qquad$ Cash required for increases in net working capital

Certain comments were offered on how to estimate some of the cash-flow variables. First, the income tax rate used in the analysis should be "the effective cash rate rather than a rate based on the accountant's income tax expense, which often includes a portion that is deferred." Second, the model suggested that both the estimates of future capital expenditures and investments in working capital could, for simplicity's sake, be based on their historical relationship to past increases in sales. With respect to capital expenditures, the analyst could "simply take the sum of all capital investments less depreciation over the past 5 or 10 years and divide this total by the sales increase from the beginning to the end of the period. With this approach, the resulting coefficient not only represents the capital investment historically required per dollar of sales increase but also impounds any cost increases for replacement of existing capacity."

While working capital could be estimated in a similar fashion to capital expenditures, two caveats to the procedure were offered: "1) the year-end balance sheet figures may not reflect the average or normal needs of the business during the year, and 2) both the accounts receivable and inventory accounts may overstate the magnitude of the funds committed by the company." While no specific action other than being careful was recommended with respect to the first problem, the following recommendation was made with respect to the second. "To estimate the additional cash requirements, the increased inventory investment should be measured by the variable costs for any additional units of inventory required and by the receivable investments in terms of the variable costs of the product delivered to generate the receivable rather than the absolute dollar amount of the receivable.'

In using a DCF approach, the analyst must select an appropriate horizon and determine the target's residual value at the horizon. Although it was possible to rely simply on gut feel (e.g., "I don't feel comfortable making projections beyond 10 years out"), a more pragmatic approach to the problem had been suggested:

> A better approach suggests that the forecast duration for cash flows should continue only as long as the expected rate of return on incremental investment required to support forecasted sales growth exceeds the cost-of-capital rate.
>
> If for subsequent periods one assumes that the company's return on incremental investment equals the cost-of-capital rate, then the market would be indifferent whether management invests earnings in expansion projects or pays cash dividends that shareholders can in turn invest in identically risky opportunities yielding an identical rate of return. In other words, the value of the company is unaffected by growth when the company is investing in projects earning at the cost of capital or at the minimum acceptable risk-adjusted rate of return required by the market.
>
> Thus, for purposes of simplification, we can assume a 100 percent payout of earnings after the horizon date or, equivalently, a zero growth rate without affecting the valuation of the company. (An implied assumption of this model is that the depreciation tax shield can be invested to maintain the company's productive capacity.)[2]

A "simple yet analytical, nonarbitrary" method of determining that period for which the expected rate of return on any incremental investments would exceed the cost-of-capital rate was to:

> compute the minimum pretax return on sales *(P min)* needed to earn the minimum acceptable rate of return on the acquisition *(k)* given the investment requirements for working capital *(w)* and fixed assets *(f)* for each additional dollar of sales and given a projected tax rate *(T)*. The formula for *P min* is:[3]

$$P\ min = \frac{(f + w)k}{(1 - T)(1 + k)}$$

[2] Ibid.

[3] Ibid.

For example, assume one company's management is considering the acquisition of another company with the following characteristics: (1) working capital and fixed-asset requirements per incremental sales dollar are 17 percent and 18 percent, respectively; (2) the tax rate is 48 percent; and (3) the appropriate cost of capital is 15 percent.

$$P\ min = \frac{(.17 + .18)(.15)}{(1 - .48)(1 + .15)} = .088 \text{ or } 8.8\%$$

Thus the management of the acquisitor should develop projections only for those years it believes the target can earn a pretax return on sales of 8.8 percent or greater.

Having thus established the horizon date to use in the analysis, the determination of the target's residual value became simple: "The residual value is then the present value of the resulting cash flow perpetuity beginning one year after the horizon date."

Conclusion

After refreshing his memory as to the mechanics of the discounted cash flow model, Mr. Baxter considered how best to apply it to the Seven-Up Company. Gathering all of the information he had available on the company and the soft- drink industry,[4] he settled down to a long day's and a longer night's work.

---

[4] "Philip Morris Incorporated: Seven-Up Acquisition (A)" provides all requisite data for the Seven-Up and Philip Morris companies.

Koppers Co.

Charles Pullin was planning to retire as chief executive officer of Koppers Co. in December 1988. He had successfully moved the Pittsburgh-based conglomerate from steel-mill construction into two major business lines: construction materials and services (including products used in highway and bridge construction) and chemical and allied products (including commodity and specialty chemicals and treated wood products). These businesses were well positioned to profit from the renewed emphasis on repairing the aging infrastructure in the United States.

The improved operating performance and tremendous potential of Koppers Co. had not, however, gone unnoticed. Brian Beazer had built Beazer PLC, the home-building firm his father had founded in England in 1933, into a diversified company with approximately $2 billion in worldwide revenues. When Mr. Beazer visited the United States in June 1987 looking for acquisition candidates in the building industry, his investment banker, Shearson Lehman Hutton, gave him a list of 20 companies, including Koppers. Mr. Beazer and Shearson pared the list down to six, and after more than 50 days of discreetly examining Koppers and its properties (often driving out to see plants firsthand), Mr. Beazer made his move.

Charles Pullin and other Koppers executives noticed several large blocks of Koppers stock trading hands in early 1988, and the stock price had climbed substantially after the market crash in October 1987. (Exhibit 1 provides trading-volume and closing price history for Koppers common stock.) Executives traced a cache of stock to a confidential custodial account belonging to Shearson Lehman Hutton.[1] Shearson had amassed more than 1.2 million shares of Koppers stock by late January 1988 (slightly less than the 4.9 percent ownership threshold that required a report to the Securities and Exchange Commission). When Shearson suddenly sold off Koppers' 290,000 shares, however, First Boston Corp. (Koppers' investment banker), convinced Mr. Pullin that no bona fide bidder

---

This case was adapted from a study by Larry J. Puglia under the supervision of Robert S. Harris, Professor of Business Administration, as a basis for classroom discussion. Copyright © 1990 by the University of Virginia Darden School Foundation, Charlottesville, Virginia. All rights reserved.

[1] Information in this paragraph is from Mark Maremont and Michael Schroeder, "Why Koppers Fell before Beazer's Bulldozer," *Business Week* (June 20, 1988), p. 83.

was behind Shearson's accumulation. Satisfied that Koppers was not subject to a takeover threat, Mr. Pullin focused on communicating the company's turnaround to the investment community.

Then, on March 3, 1988, a reporter called Mr. Pullin with shocking news: Brian Beazer had taken out a full-page advertisement in *The Wall Street Journal* announcing that a bidding group whose investors included Mr. Beazer and Shearson had launched a $45-per-share tender offer. Mr. Pullin was now faced with several pressing questions:

1. What strategy was driving the unsolicited tender offer made by Beazer PLC; what particular characteristics of Koppers or the current operating and financial environment had triggered the bid?

2. How could Mr. Pullin use his knowledge of forces motivating Brian Beazer to negotiate with him and either improve the bid price or defeat the tender offer?

3. What was the extent of Shearson's involvement? Did Beazer PLC have the necessary financing to complete the $1.3 billion tender offer by paying $45 in cash for the 28,090,141 outstanding shares of Koppers common stock?

4. Was $45 per share an adequate offer? If Mr. Pullin believed it was inadequate or that a higher bid was equally unacceptable, how could he counter Mr. Beazer's offers? Could he attempt either to discredit the tender offer or to provide more value for shareholders?

Beazer PLC

Beazer PLC was the holding company for a group of companies involved in home construction, property development, contracting, engineering, and the production and sale of cement and construction materials or aggregates (including crushed stone, sand and gravel, ready-mixed concrete pipe, fly ash, and construction chemicals). The company was founded in 1933 as a home-building company, but Brian Beazer had crafted the company into a diversified group with operations around the globe. The company had grown steadily in the past 10 years—in particular, through acquisitions in the housing and construction industries. Beazer PLC had assets of approximately $1.5 billion at June 30, 1988, and revenues of over $2 billion for that fiscal year. Fully diluted earnings per share had grown at a compound rate of over 23 percent per year for the 10-year period ending June 30, 1988.[2]

Beazer PLC already had a position in the construction market in the United States through its Gifford-Hill & Company subsidiary. The United States construction market could be segregated into three sectors: residen-

---

[2] Information on Beazer PLC and U.S. Infrastructure needs is from Brian Beazer, "Chairman's Statement," *Beazer Report and Accounts 1988.*

tial, commercial, and the nonbuilding market (highway and road construction and other public works). Although these sectors were somewhat related, each was affected by its own economic forces. For example, regional economies greatly influenced the level of demand, particularly for aggregates and other construction materials with relatively high transportation costs. The demand for Gifford-Hill's products and services had been mixed by region during 1987. The company had noted rapidly increasing demand in the U.S. East, Southeast, and West, but Gifford-Hill did not have a particularly strong presence in these regions.

Koppers Co.

Headquartered in Pittsburgh, Pennsylvania, Koppers Co. ranked as the second largest supplier of construction aggregates and the second largest producer of bituminous concrete (the primary material for resurfacing roadways in the United States). With its operations located primarily in the densely populated states in the East, Southeast, and on the West Coast, Koppers was well positioned to take advantage of the projected increase in funding by federal, state, and municipal governments for new construction and repair of infrastructure (particularly roads, bridges, and water and sewer systems).

In addition, Koppers served all types of privately financed construction, including residential, commercial, and industrial development in dozens of metropolitan areas throughout the United States. The company operated approximately 200 facilities that served markets in 24 states in the northeastern, central, southeastern, and western regions of the country. Approximately 40 percent of sales were in the West, 30 percent in the Southeast, and 30 percent in the Northeast and Midwest.

Charles Pullin had masterminded the company's transition from pursuing steel-mill construction to serving the growing markets for repairing the nation's infrastructure. Koppers' effective positioning of business units in construction markets had resulted in a strong financial turnaround at the company. Net profit from operations jumped to $70.2 million in 1987. (See Exhibit 2 for recent Koppers' income statements and Exhibit 3 for Koppers' balance sheets.)

Strategic Issues

Charles Pullin decided that Mr. Beazer's strategy was motivated by some powerful trends.

Improving America's Infrastructure

The U.S. Department of Transportation had told Congressional committees that $70 billion in annual spending until the year 2000 would be required simply to control the deterioration in the nation's highway system. Annual expenditures in 1987 amounted to $40 billion.

Congress had signalled its concern for infrastructure, particularly nonbuilding construction, with the passage of major legislation:

1. The Highway Transportation Act would provide $88 billion through 1991 for building, upgrading, and maintenance.

2. The Water Resources Development Act would add $12 billion for improvement of ports and waterways in the 1990s.

3. The Airport and Airway Act allocated $9 billion through 1992 for airport and runway improvements.

Koppers had a strong presence in 15 of the 20 most active markets for aggregates in the United States.

Globalization

While Beazer PLC already served many national markets, many forces such as improved communication, industry structure, and increasingly homogenized consumer needs were facilitating globalization. Tremendous advantages might be achieved through a global competitive strategy:

1. Economics of scope stemming from a broader product line and increased volume, which would allow costs and product and process improvements to be shared across national markets.

2. The ability to cross-subsidize operations among product lines or national markets. This process (sometimes called "global chess") involved using cash from dominant markets for fast penetration of growing foreign markets.

3. The information access and learning potential available to global companies (sometimes called the global "scanning advantage").

4. The ability to identify and use favorable labor or raw-material pricing, obtain scarce skills (i.e., finance or engineering expertise), or tap government subsidies in national markets.[3]

---

[3] For discussion of industry globalization and corporate responses, see Theodore Levitt, "The Globalization of Markets," *Harvard Business Review* (May/June 1983), pp. 92–102; Michael Porter, "Changing Patterns of International Competition," *California Management Review,* 28/2 (Winter 1986): pp. 9–40; Gary Hamel and C. K. Prahalad, "Do You Really Have a Global Strategy," *Harvard Business Review* (July/August 1985); pp. 139–148; and C. A. Bartlett and S. Ghoshal *Managing Across Borders: The Transnational Solution,* Boston, Mass.: Harvard Business School Press, 1989.

Foreign-Exchange Rates

The British pound had appreciated steadily against the dollar from 1985 through 1987, and each increase in the pound's relative valuation made the acquisition of U.S. companies or dollar-denominated assets that much more affordable. Exchange rates had continued to move in Mr. Beazer's favor through the date of his initial bid in March 1988. (See Exhibit 4 for a history of relevant exchange rates.)

Differences Between U.K. and U.S. Accounting Practices

As an acquiror reporting financial results under U.K. accounting standards, Beazer PLC could take advantage of certain accounting treatments not available at competing acquirors in the United States. (Exhibit 5 lists differences between U.K. and U.S. accounting practices.)

One of the primary differences was the treatment of goodwill arising in an acquisition accounted for under the purchase method (versus the pooling method). Goodwill represented the excess of the consideration paid over the fair value of net assets acquired.

Because of U.K. accounting treatment of goodwill, British companies could pay premiums over book value for companies without creating an asset that had to be amortized. They also received favorable tax treatment on the goodwill through a process called merger relief. Competing U.S. bidders, on the other hand, had to amortize goodwill as an expense for reporting purposes but received no tax deduction for amortization of goodwill (it was a permanent difference between book income and taxable income).

Financing and the Role of Shearson Lehman

First Boston, Koppers' investment banker, worked to assess Shearson Lehman Hutton's role and the ability of Mr. Beazer to finance the hostile bid. They learned that Shearson stood ready to provide over $500 million in temporary financing, or bridge loans, to facilitate Mr. Beazer's bid. They were shocked to find that Shearson held a 46 percent stake in BNS Inc., the investment company set up by Brian Beazer to finance the takeover.[4] Essentially, Shearson was willing to commit $23 million of its own money as an equity partner.

First Boston and Mr. Pullin knew that, with Shearson's strong backing, Brian Beazer was definitely a credible threat. They also knew that by taking a large equity stake, Shearson had crossed a line that most investment bankers were reluctant to cross. Participating in a hostile take-

---

[4] Maremont and Schroeder, p. 83.

over was a dangerous game for an investment bank, because it could alienate corporate clients. First Boston and Charles Pullin wondered how they might use this factor to their advantage.

Koppers' Reaction

After considering all the strategic issues behind the hostile bid, Shearson's role in the takeover attempt, and the feasibility of financing the bid, Mr. Pullin concluded that Mr. Beazer had a sound strategy for assembling a global construction-materials business and capitalizing on the infrastructure rebuilding in the United States. Mr. Pullin was keenly aware that Koppers fit into the strategy well and that Mr. Beazer and Shearson would be determined in their bid to acquire Koppers.

Mr. Pullin had worked in Koppers' construction-materials businesses since 1949. He decided to fight the takeover attempt aggressively. He publicly complained of "a sneak attack in the night" and dug in his heels. He later said, "Koppers was doing well and didn't need outside help."[5] Mr. Pullin realized, however, that Koppers needed a substantive alternative to the $45 bid.

First Boston hastened to put together a recapitalization plan. Under it, shareholders would receive a large cash dividend and new shares of preferred stock. First Boston set about determining the appropriate value for the preferred shares.

Public-Relations Campaign

Koppers was advised by First Boston and the Hill & Knowlton public-relations firm to exploit certain vulnerabilities in the Beazer and Shearson position.[6] Shearson's CEO, Peter Cohen, had said that his firm had "no interest in owning or running Koppers" but had put up the equity stake so that Beazer PLC would not exceed acceptable levels of corporate debt in the United Kingdom.[7] Koppers argued every chance it got, however, that an American investment bank was helping an overleveraged foreign firm continue the buyout of American manufacturing capacity. Koppers' executives publicly cut up their American Express cards to hit back at Shearson's parent company.

The state of Pennsylvania, which did $7 billion of financing with Shearson in 1987, dropped it as an underwriter and adviser. The deal also attracted the attention of Congressman John Dingell, who was examining whether Shearson or other Wall Street firms were improperly putting the targets of

---

[5] Ibid.
[6] Monci Jo Williams, "Brash New Mogul on Wall Street," *Fortune* (May 23, 1988), p. 95.
[7] Ibid.

hostile takeovers into play.[8] Public officials, including Pennsylvania Governor Robert P. Casey (a Democrat) and U.S. Senator John Heinz (a Republican), criticized Shearson for its unusual involvement in the hostile bid.

White Knights or Equity Partners

Mr. Pullin engaged in preliminary discussions with several other possible friendly suitors, or "white knights." In early April 1988, Koppers also sent a team to Japan to seek an equity partner from among the chemical and construction companies. Such talks ceased after Mr. Beazer sweetened the bid to $60, however, and it became apparent that the company had the financing needed to complete the takeover at that price.[9]

Litigation

Koppers also attempted to stall Brian Beazer in court. Both companies filed suit in Pennsylvania, Delaware, and California (Beazer PLC had a presence in California through its Gifford-Hill subsidiary). On April 4, 1984, a U.S. district court in California blocked the takeover on antitrust grounds. A Pittsburgh court also delayed the takeover until it could study the financing arrangements to determine if there were violations of U.S. banking laws. As the courts began to resolve these issues, however, it became clear that Koppers' hopes of independence from Beazer PLC rested on either negotiating the sale of key assets to Beazer PLC or on the success of its recapitalization offer to shareholders.

Negotiation of Asset Sale

Brian Beazer and Charles Pullin met only once during the battle—in a Pittsburgh hotel on April 5 for less than five minutes. Mr. Pullin inquired whether Mr. Beazer would be interested in buying assets. Mr. Beazer would only discuss buying the whole company.

Talks between the companies' lawyers, who met three or four times in Pittsburgh and New York, were equally fruitless. The talks centered around selling a portion of the company or key assets but Beazer PLC clearly wanted all of the choice assets, those in the high-growth construction-materials markets.

Recapitalization

By late May 1988, Koppers' recapitalization plan was almost final. The company planned to sell its construction-materials businesses to raise

---

[8] Ibid., p. 92.

[9] Maremont and Schroeder, pp. 82–84.

funds for a special dividend to shareholders (the size of the dividend had not been determined). A key component of the deal was a $450 million sale of assets to Tilcon Holdings, Inc., the U.S. subsidiary of Britain's BTR PLC. On May 20, BTR notified Koppers that the deal was off, however, because it "didn't want to get involved in the prospect of litigation." Earlier, Mr. Beazer had threatened to sue companies, such as Vulcan Materials Co., that were interested in buying Koppers' assets.

Charles Pullin's Dilemma

As Mr. Beazer came close to satisfying the conditions set by the courts for the last injunctions to be lifted, Mr. Pullin faced a serious crossroads: Since all of his takeover defenses were apparently failing, should he or should he not continue to fight Mr. Beazer to the bitter end? If he fought on, would he perhaps be in a weakened negotiating position should Mr. Beazer prevail? Mr. Pullin and the Koppers board of directors also needed to consider their fiduciary duty to shareholders. The board had rejected the initial $45 per share offer as inadequate. A revised offer of $56 per share was also rejected, but now a third offer of $60 in cash per share had evoked no formal board response. Would board members be subject to litigation if they did not accept this offer? If they decided to negotiate now, was $60 per share a fair price for Koppers, or should they fight vigorously for a better offer?

Mr. Pullin knew that the valuation of comparable companies in the construction-materials industry (see Exhibit 6) and the interest-rate environment (see Exhibit 7) would influence the determination of an appropriate stock price. Mr. Pullin believed his company's free cash flow would grow substantially in the next few years (see Exhibit 8 for projected cash flows).

Mr. Pullin marshalled the talents of First Boston and his internal finance staff. He wanted the best information available before deciding his next move. Most of all, he did not want to be surprised by Brian Beazer again.

Koppers Co.
EXHIBIT 1 • Volume and Closing Prices for Koppers Common Stock, 1988

Date	Volume (100s)	Closing Price	Date	Volume (100s)	Closing Price
2/1	580	$32.000	4/1	Holiday	
2	980	31.750	4	9,930	$57.250
3	440	31.750	5	17,517	56.125
4	821	31.750	6	13,364	55.375
5	1,008	31.500	7	4,235	56.125
8	1,029	30.500	8	3,484	56.750
9	1,107	31.125	11	2,792	55.875
10	874	32.125	12	5,417	54.375
11	686	32.375	13	2,609	54.500
12	1,037	32.125	14	6,379	53.875
15	Holiday		15	3,262	53.625
16	1,405	32.250	18	3,760	53.250
17	384	33.000	19	1,762	54.000
18	381	32.625	20	1,004	54.375
19	550	33.875	21	2,901	53.750
22	713	36.500	22	1,688	53.750
23	831	36.625	25	821	53.625
24	4,614	37.750	26	3,258	53.875
25	5,216	38.750	27	942	54.500
26	3,956	39.500	28	3,860	55.375
29	2,155	40.250	29	2,084	55.875
3/1	5,637	42.750	5/2	1,412	56.125
2	9,847	45.125	3	1,999	56.000
3	31,013	51.750	4	5,367	56.250
4	15,057	53.125	5	1,131	56.500
7	9,099	53.625	6	1,648	55.625
8	7,141	53.000	9	1,015	55.125
9	4,542	52.500	10	1,608	55.000
10	7,433	51.250	11	2,355	54.625
11	5,450	51.625	12	1,490	54.125
14	5,177	51.750	13	2,536	54.125
15	10,303	54.500	16	2,854	55.125
16	7,864	53.625	17	1,840	54.625
17	9,396	53.625	18	1,792	54.375
18	4,936	53.750	19	691	55.125
21	14,444	57.500	20	7,266	53.500
22	9,477	57.000	23	2,671	55.000
23	6,940	57.375	24	4,740	55.875
24	7,817	58.750	25	1,153	56.000
25	12,825	58.625	26	1,497	56.000
28	5,670	57.375	27	2,358	56.500
29	746	58.500	30	Holiday	
30	5,949	57.625	31	9,374	$59.000
31	6,366	$57.750			

Source: Standard & Poor's *Daily Stock Price Record.*

Koppers Co.

EXHIBIT 2 • Income Statements for Years Ended December 31 (in millions of dollars)

	1985	*1986*	*1987*
Net sales	$1,400.1	$1,396.4	$1,515.7
Cost of sales	(1,125.0)	(1,029.0)	(1,109.6)
Gross profit	275.1	367.4	406.1
Selling, general, and administrative expenses	(149.8)	(152.8)	(150.3)
Depreciation and amortization	(66.4)	(70.5)	(76.3)
Taxes other than income taxes	(39.6)	(40.2)	(43.9)
Operations disposed	(32.6)	4.8	3.2
Operating profit	(13.3)	108.7	138.8
Other income (expense)	(10.7)	15.0	(13.9)
Interest expense	(23.7)	(21.4)	(11.2)
Profit before tax	(47.7)	102.3	113.7
Provision (benefit) for income taxes	17.7	(39.1)	(43.5)
Income from continuing operations	(30.0)	63.2	70.2
Income (loss) on discontinued operations	(71.1)	0	(59.4)
Extraordinary item	0	14.2	0
Net income	$ (101.1)	$ 77.4	$ 10.8
Earnings per share, continuing operations	($1.23)	$2.09	$2.44
Earnings per share	($3.72)	$2.59	$0.36

Source: *Moody's Industrial Manual, Value Line,* and casewriter's estimates.

Koppers Co.

EXHIBIT 3 • Balance Sheets at December 31 (in millions of dollars)

	1986	1987
Assets		
Cash	$ 72.5	$ 20.2
Accounts receivable	183.9	189.3
Inventories	116.6	120.5
Other	133.3	143.4
Current assets	506.3	473.4
Investments	67.8	76.5
Fixed assets	1,081.5	1,130.2
Accumulated depreciation	(626.8)	(653.7)
Net property, plant, and equipment	454.7	476.5
Other assets	38.3	48.5
Total assets	$1,067.1	$1,074.9
Liabilities		
Accounts payable	$ 70.6	$ 76.2
Short-term debt	14.6	13.4
Other	197.3	171.4
Current liabilities	282.5	261.0
Long-term debt	117.7	172.4
Deferred compensation	17.6	20.0
Deferred income taxes	41.8	30.8
Long-term environmental and benefit reserves	84.1	104.3
Other long-term liabilities	29.4	40.5
Total liabilities	573.1	629.0
Cumulative preferred stock	15.0	15.0
Common stock, $1.25 par, 60,000,000 shares authorized, 28,090,141 outstanding in 1987	37.3	37.3
Less: cost of treasury stock	(24.7)	(56.4)
Capital in excess of par value	176.6	176.5
Retained earnings	289.8	273.5
Total shareholders' equity	494.0	445.9
Total liabilities and shareholders' equity	$1,067.1	$1,074.9

Source: 1987 Annual Report, *Value Line,* and casewriter's estimates.

Koppers Co.
EXHIBIT 4 • Foreign-Exchange Rates,
1985 Through 1988 (dollars per pound sterling)

Year	Month	Dollars per Pound
1985	March	$1.1253
	April	1.2377
	May	1.2483
	June	1.2808
	July	1.3807
	August	1.3840
	September	1.3642
	October	1.4215
	November	1.4396
	December	1.4447
1986	January	1.4244
	February	1.4297
	March	1.4674
	April	1.4985
	May	1.5211
	June	1.5085
	July	1.5071
	August	1.4861
	September	1.4698
	October	1.4264
	November	1.4238
	December	1.4393
1987	January	1.5054
	February	1.5280
	March	1.5923
	April	1.6299
	May	1.6666
	June	1.6288
	July	1.6090
	August	1.5996
	September	1.6446
	October	1.6620
	November	1.7754
	December	1.8288
1988	January	1.8009
	February	1.7582
	March	$1.8330

Source: *Federal Reserve Bulletin.*

Koppers Co.
EXHIBIT 5 • Differences Between U.K. and U.S. Accounting Practices

Goodwill
Under U.K. generally accepted accounting practices (GAAP), goodwill arising on acquisition of subsidiaries was written off against consolidated reserves (stockholders' equity) in the year of acquisition. Under U.S. GAAP, such goodwill was amortized through charges against income over the estimated useful life of the assets acquired. This amortization was *not* tax deductible under the U.S. tax code.

Revaluation of properties and depreciation
Under U.K. GAAP, the book value of properties could be restated on the basis of appraised values for presentation in financial statements that had been prepared, in all other respects, in accordance with the historical-cost convention. Increases in value were credited directly to revaluation reserves. Reductions in value below original cost (less accumulated depreciation) were charged against the income statement. Depreciation was based on the restated amount. Under U.S. GAAP, such adjustments were generally not permitted.

Extraordinary items
Under U.K. GAAP, costs or credits associated with major restructuring programs or the disposal of businesses could be classified as extraordinary items. Under U.S. GAAP, extraordinary items were strictly defined as items that were unusual in nature and nonrecurring. Restructuring or disposals of businesses were not considered extraordinary.

Discontinued operations
Under U.K. GAAP, income or loss from discontinued businesses was not disclosed separately. Under U.S. GAAP, such income or loss was disclosed separately.

Koppers Co.

EXHIBIT 6 • Comparables for Year Ended December 31, 1987

	Sales (in Millions)	Net Profit Margin	Stock Price		Book Value per Share	Earnings per Share	Average Price/ Earnings Ratio	Beta	Percent Debt[a]
			High	Low					
Ameron, Inc.	$ 308.2	1.50%	$ 37.3	$24.8	$32.2	$ 2.42	13.5×	0.85	25%
Centex Corp.	1,450.0	1.70	35.6	15.1	40.8	2.35	15.7	1.20	36
Dravo Corp.	248.1	4.40	21.9	8.8	6.1	0.75	15.0	1.30	31
Koppers Co.	1,515.7	4.60	50.4	29.6	15.5	2.44	15.6	1.25	28
Morrison Knudsen	1,856.6	NMF	55.6	29.5	42.1	(1.64)	NMF	1.00	18
Vulcan Materials	$ 923.3	13.40%	$164.0	$95.0	$71.7	$11.32	12.3×	0.85	11%

NMF = not a meaningful number.

[a]Interest bearing debt as percent of total book value capital.

Source: *Value Line* and casewriter's estimates.

Koppers Co.
EXHIBIT 7 • Interest Rates for Year Ended December 31, 1987

Security	Rate
U.S. Treasury bills	
3 month	5.82%
6 month	6.05
U.S. Treasury notes and bonds	
3 year	7.68
10 year	8.39
30 year	8.59
Corporate bond (Moody's)	
Aaa	9.38
Baa	10.58
Municipal bonds	7.73
Commercial paper, 6 months	6.85
Prime lending rate	8.21
Federal Reserve discount rate	5.66%

Source: *Federal Reserve Bulletin.*

Koppers Co.
EXHIBIT 8 • Projected Cash Flow, Fiscal 1988–1992 (in millions of dollars)

	1988	1989	1990	1991	1992
Net sales	$1,630.0	$1,776.7	$1,936.6	$2,110.9	$2,300.9
Net income	81.0	100.4	124.5	154.4	191.5
Deferred taxes	2.0	4.0	6.0	8.0	10.0
Depreciation and amortization	76.3	82.0	90.0	95.0	100.0
Additions to working capital	(18.0)	(20.0)	(20.0)	(20.0)	(20.0)
Capital expenditures	(112.0)	(110.0)	(120.0)	(130.0)	(140.0)
Free cash flow	$ 29.3	$ 56.4	$ 80.5	$ 107.4	$ 141.5
Growth assumptions:					

Growth assumptions:	
Sales	9%
Earnings	24%

Source: *Value Line* and casewriter's estimates.

Colt Industries

"God made man, and Colonel Samuel Colt made them equal."
Anonymous

On Sunday afternoon, July 20, 1986, at 4:00, Fred Graham, an analyst with Goldman Sachs, was enjoying a cookout with his family when a phone interrupted his meal. Mr. Graham's boss, Jack Roberts, informed him that one of his companies, Colt Industries, had just declared a startling major recapitalization.

The basics of the plan called for shareholders to exchange each of their Colt shares for $85 in cash plus one new share of stock in the recapitalized company. Shares held in the employee pension fund, 7 percent of the outstanding shares, would receive new shares in lieu of the $85 cash. The number of additional shares exchanged for each pension share would equal $85 divided by the average trading price of the new shares for the 15 days following the exchange. Thus, if the new shares traded for an average price of $17 following the recapitalization, each pension would receive a total of 6 new shares: one share in exchange for the old Colt share plus 5 new shares at $17 in lieu of the $85 cash payment.

Colt was going to finance the cash payout by issuing $1.5 billion in new debt. Management announced that it expected $900 million to be provided by a group of banks led by Bankers Trust Co., which had agreed to provide $400 million itself, and an additional $525 million was expected to be raised through the sale of debt securities.

Mr. Roberts advised Mr. Graham to get to the office as soon as possible to assess what impact this announcement would have on Colt's stock price the next morning when the market opened. Colt's common stock had closed on the previous Friday at $66.75 per share. A staff meeting was scheduled for Monday, and he would be expected to answer questions and present some Goldman Sachs' recommendations before the market opening.

This case was written by Robert M. Conroy, Associate Professor of Business Administration, as a basis for classroom discussion. Copyright © 1989 by the University of Virginia Darden School Foundation, Charlottesville, Virginia. All rights reserved.

Colt Industries

Colt Industries was best known for its firearms division, founded in 1836 by Colonel Samuel Colt. The division manufactured the M16 military rifle and manufactured and marketed a line of single- and double-action revolvers, pistols, and sporting rifles for the commercial and law-enforcement markets. The division was only a small part of a large diversified company, however. In fact, the original Colt Firearms was acquired in 1954 by the Penn-Texas Corp., a diversified company whose primary subsidiary was the Pratt & Whitney Co. and which, until that year, had operated under the name of Pennsylvania Coal & Coke Corp. Not until 1964 was the company name officially changed to Colt Industries.

Colt had sales of almost $1.5 billion in 1985. Its diversified operations could be separated into three business segments: aerospace/government, automotive, and industrial. Exhibit 1 lists the divisions and their products. Most of the growth in the company since the 1950s had come from acquisitions, although the company had actively divested over the same period. As recently as 1985, Colt had sold two subsidiaries (Crucible Materials Corp. and Crusteel Ltd.) to management and employees in a leveraged buyout. During the same period, Colt acquired Lewis Engineering and Walbar, Inc., for cash. Management viewed this process of acquisition and divestiture as a way of constantly updating Colt's product lines.

The last few years had been good for Colt, as shown in Exhibit 2. Sales were level at about $1.5 billion, but in 1985 earnings increased by about 8 percent. Earnings per share increased from $3.95 in 1981 to $6.91 in 1985. Return on equity increased to about 34 percent in 1985. Dividends had increased every year since 1981. Much of the improvement in equity performance, however, came from Colt's aggressive share-repurchase plan. Colt had reduced its share base by about 30 percent over the preceding four years. Colt Industries' stock price nonetheless rose consistently over that period, as shown in Exhibit 3.

During 1985, Standard and Poor's and Moody's raised its ratings of Colt senior debt from A to A+ and from A3 to A2, respectively. As of the end of that year, cash and marketable securities had increased to $215 million, while at the same time, because of the acquisitions in 1985, long-term debt increased to $342 million (see Exhibit 4.) Most of the long-term debt was added in December 1985 when Colt had two new bond issues of $150 million each. The bond issues were 10⅛ percent notes due 1995 and 11¼ percent debentures due 2015. Most of the other long-term debt was the capitalized value of long-term leases.

Colt also had a $270 million revolving-credit agreement with various banks. Under this agreement, the company could borrow, and repay and reborrow at any time until June 30, 1988, amounts aggregating up to the committed amount of $270 million. Upon the agreement's maturity, Colt could convert the outstanding balance to a four-year term loan payable in equal semiannual principal installments commencing December 30, 1988. At the option of the company, interest on the unpaid principal balances was calculated based upon either the prime rate, the certificate-of-deposit rate, or the London interbank rate. A commitment fee of ¼ of 1 percent per annum was payable quarterly on the average daily unused portion.

Although, as the data in Exhibit 5 show, Colt had performed well during the past several years, the financial community had some concerns about its potential for growth over the next few years. Some of its business segments were experiencing increased competition and technical obsolescence. Exhibit 6 presents financial performance by business segment, and the following comments from the 1985 annual report summarize the company's assessment of prospects in each segment:

> Aerospace/Government segment operating income in 1985 was level with that of a year ago on an eight percent gain in sales. The segment accounted for 34 percent of total company sales in 1985 and 36 percent of operating income.
>
> Both sales and operating income from the company's Automotive industry segment were down in 1985 from the previous year, reflecting primarily the continuing trend away from carburetion and toward fuel injection as the industry's major fuel management system. The segment accounted for 34 percent of total company sales and 39 percent of operating income.

This general assessment was reflected in the latest Paine Webber report on Colt, dated July 15, 1986:

> We expect a moderate recovery in earnings in 1987 to approximately $6.60 per share, primarily because of the absence on the effect of the 1986 strike at Firearms. We believe that Colt's automotive segment will again trail the prior year reflecting further customer switching from carburetion to fuel injection and probably reduction in U.S. manufacturer new car assemblies. Colt Aerospace/Defense should be up again. In fact, the longer term outlook for this segment is very good and should be an ongoing source of earnings growth for Colt. Industrial segment operations are likely to be about flat at a relatively high level.

One other thing could affect the value of the recapitalization, the tax rate.

The Tax Environment

A vigorous discussion of tax reform had been going on in Washington. The House of Representatives passed a tax reform bill in December 1985, and the Senate passed its version of the bill in June 1986. On Friday, July 18, 1986, a committee was formed to reconcile the differences in the two bills. An important provision expected to emerge as part of the final tax bill was the lowering of the statutory corporate tax rate of 46 percent to approximately 34 percent.

The Problem

After reviewing his material, Fred Graham decided he must address three major issues by the opening of the financial markets on Monday. The first was the price per share at which he thought Colt stock would sell when the market opened. An important element in this price was the characteristics of the new equity shares that would remain after the restructuring. The second scale related to the impact of the announced restructuring on the outstanding debt. His boss had not explicitly asked for such an analysis, but Mr. Graham believed it was an important question that was sure to be raised in any discussion with clients. Finally, he needed to consider the likely impact of the restructuring on Colt's strategy. Specifically, would the restructuring affect the operational aspects of Colt fundamentally and thus the stock price, or was it just a financial restructuring?

Colt Industries
EXHIBIT 1 • Colt Industries Divisions by Business Segment

Business Segment (date of acquisition)	*Products*
Aerospace/Government	
Chandler Evans Control Systems	Jet engine fuel controls
Colt Firearms (1954)	Military and commemorative arms
Delvan Gas Turbine Products (1983)	Gas turbine products
Fairbanks Morse Engine (1955)	Diesel engines
Lewis Engineering (1985)	Aircraft instrumentation
Menasco Aerospace (1977)	Aircraft landing gear
Walbar (1985)	Jet engine turbine blades
Automotive	
Colt Automotive Products	Automotive products
Fairbanks Morse	Ignition systems
Holley Special Products (1968)	Carburetors and replacement parts
Farnum Sealing Systems (1979)	Gaskets
Stemco Truck Products	Truck and bus products and instrumentation
Industrial	
Central Moloney Transformer (1968)	Distribution transformers
Woodville Polymer Engineering	Molded rubber products
Pratt & Whitney Machine Tools	Machine and cutting tools
Garlock (1975)	Mechanical packaging
Elox (1967)	Electrical discharge machining
France Compressor	Compressor components
Quincy Compressor (1966)	Air compressors

Colt Industries

EXHIBIT 2 • Colt Industries Income Statements
1983–1985 (as of December 31, in thousands)

	1983	*1984*	*1985*
Net sales	$ 1,343,130	$ 1,581,750	$ 1,579,325
Cost and sales	(1,003,130)	(1,170,770)	(1,159,264)
Selling and administrative	(172,099)	(192,607)	(187,614)
Interest expense	(17,228)	(14,275)	(14,331)
Interest income	24,556	15,705	8,724
Total costs and expenses	1,167,901	1,361,947	1,352,485
Earnings from continuing operations before taxes	175,229	219,803	226,840
Provision for taxes	77,834	99,834	97,540
Earnings from continuing operations after taxes	97,395	119,969	129,300
Discontinued operations	1,860	12,260	8,733
Net earnings	$ 99,255	$ 132,229	$ 138,033
Per-share Data			
Earnings per share			
Continuing operations	$3.93	$5.43	$6.47
Discontinued operations	.08	.56	.44
Net earnings per share	$ 4.01	$ 5.99	$ 6.91
Average number of common shares (000s)	24,778	22,093	19,979
Cash dividend per share	$2.00	$2.27½	$2.50

Market closing price per share (7/18/86): $66.75
Common Shares outstanding (7/18/86): 19,404

Colt Industries
EXHIBIT 3 • End of Quarter Closing Stock Prices, 1982–1986

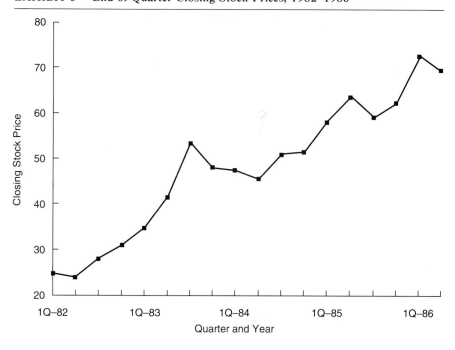

Colt Industries
EXHIBIT 4 • Balance Sheets as of December 31 (in thousands)

	1984	*1985*
Assets		
Cash	$ 3,858	$ 14,082
Marketable securities	2,529	201,499
Accounts receivable	180,587	179,867
Inventory	266,107	277,230
Deferred taxes	18,493	17,339
Other current assets	4,941	5,520
Current assets of discontinued operations	77,667	0
Total current assets	554,182	695,537
Property, plant, and equipment (net)	251,775	301,932
Other assets	154,156	253,075
Total assets	$960,113	$1,250,544
Liabilities and Net Worth		
Notes payable (bank)	$ 12,120	$ 4,091
Current maturities of debt	3,889	4,489
Accounts payable	89,639	85,803
Accrued expenses	158,280	184,568
Current liabilities of discontinued operations	17,350	7,008
Total current liabilities	281,278	285,959
Long-term debt	108,859	342,414
Deferred income taxes	(8,919)	5,612
Other liabilities	231,332	202,255
Common stock ($1 par)	20,584	19,374
Retained earnings	335,133	405,664
Foreign-currency translation	(11,998)	(10,734)
Total stockholders' equity	343,719	414,304
Total liabilities and net worth	$960,113	$1,250,544

Colt Industries
EXHIBIT 5 • Colt Selected Financial Data,
1981–1985 in thousands, except per share and employee data

	1981	1982	1983	1984	1985
Sales	$1,451,611	$1,277,736	$1,343,130	$1,581,750	$1,579,325
Earnings from continuing operations	122,709	81,865	97,395	119,969	129,300
Earnings (loss) of discontinued operations					
Crucible Materials Corp. and Crusteel, Ltd.	17,141	677	1,860	12,260	(1,067)
Discontinued steelmaking facility	(30,000)	(243,000)	0	0	9,800
Net earnings (loss)	$ 109,850	$ (160,458)	$ 99,255	$ 132,229	$ 138,033
Earnings (loss) per share					
Continued operations	$4.43	$3.21	$3.93	$5.43	$6.47
Crucible Materials Corp. and Crusteel Ltd.	0.62	0.03	0.08	0.56	(0.05)
Discontinued steelmaking facility	(1.1)	(9.57)	0	0	0.49
Net earnings per share	$3.95	$(6.33)	$4.01	$5.99	$6.91
Common share dividends					
Total paid	$ 41,470	$ 44,834	$ 48,484	$ 48,766	$ 49,262
Per share	$1.54	$1.80	$2.00	$2.28	$2.50
Common share dividends:					
Total paid	$ 41,470	$ 44,834	$ 48,484	$ 48,766	$ 49,262
Per share	1.54	1.80	2.00	2.28	2.50
Cash and marketable securities	181,494	143,919	163,038	6,387	215,581
Working capital	$ 594,411	$ 513,131	$ 409,974	$ 272,904	$ 409,578
Current ratio	3.16×	3.16×	2.43×	1.97×	2.43×
Quick ratio	1.31	1.56	1.15	0.66	1.38
Interest-coverage ratio	8.00×	5.90×	8.40×	11.50×	11.20×
Total assets	$1,312,773	$1,128,006	$1,113,748	$ 960,113	$1,250,544
Long-term debt	$ 221,398	$ 175,223	$ 129,255	$ 108,589	$ 342,414
Long-term debt to capitalization	23.10%	28.30%	21.70%	24.00%	45.20%
Return on average shareholders' equity:					
Continued operations	17.40	17.50	21.40	29.60	34.10
Return on sales:					
Continued operations	8.50%	6.40%	7.00%	7.60%	8.20%
Book value per common share	$27.06	$18.51	$19.65	$17.58	$21.39
Capital expenditures	$ 40,391	$ 27,482	$ 27,473	$ 40,960	$ 41,278
Depreciation and amortization	24,653	27,347	29,408	33,208	31,626
Order backlog	$ 647,116	$ 595,342	$ 756,491	$ 800,971	$ 962,743
Number of employees	21,900	18,400	19,400	19,600	19,700

Colt Industries

EXHIBIT 6 • Industrial-Segment Information (in millions of dollars)

	1981	1982	1983	1984	1985
Sales					
Aerospace/Government	$ 461	$ 424	$ 441	$ 497	$539
Automotive	441	405	478	580	542
Industrial	560	458	427	506	501
Intersegment elimination	(10)	(9)	(3)	(1)	(3)
Total sales	$1,452	$1,278	$1,343	$1,582	$1,579
Operating Income					
Aerospace/Government	$81.8	$74.4	$78.3	$91.8	$91.8
Automotive	59.0	45.3	81.6	106.4	97.8
Industrial	65.2	31.7	40.3	57.6	61.9
Total operating income	206.0	151.4	200.2	255.8	251.3
Interest expense	(23.8)	(21.1)	(17.2)	(14.3)	(14.3)
Interest income	28.1	19.2	24.6	15.7	8.7
Corporate unallocated expenses	(21.2)	(16.9)	(32.4)	(37.4)	(19.1)
Gain on sale of leasehold	19.3	0	0	0	0
Earnings from continued operations before income taxes	$208.4	$132.6	$175.2	$219.8	$226.8
Operating Margin					
Aerospace/Government	17.7%	17.5%	17.8%	18.5%	17.0%
Automotive	13.4	11.2	17.1	18.3	18.0
Industrial	11.6	6.9	9.4	11.4	12.4
Total operating margin	14.2%	11.8%	14.9%	16.2%	15.9%
Total Assets					
Aerospace/Government	$254	$246	$311	$303	$535
Automotive	188	186	214	198	189
Industrial	324	279	272	275	244
Corporate unallocated	211	234	189	46	283
Discontinued operations	336	183	128	135	0
Total assets	$1,313	$1,128	$1,114	$960	$1,251
Depreciation and Amortization					
Aerospace/Government	$6.3	$7.7	$10.1	$11.9	$13.4
Automotive	7.4	8.4	8.3	11.4	13.4
Industrial	10.8	11.2	10.9	10.2	10.9
Corporate unallocated	0.2	0	0.1	0	0
Total depreciation and amortization	$24.7	$27.3	$29.4	$33.5	$37.7
Capital Expenditures					
Aerospace/Government	$13.8	$12.8	$10.6	$17.3	$18.9
Automotive	12.6	6.6	6.9	8.1	10.0
Industrial	13.9	8.1	9.9	15.5	12.2
Corporate unallocated	0.1	0	0.1	0.1	0.1
Total capital expenditures	$40.4	$27.5	$27.5	$41.0	$41.2

Norris Industries

In mid-August 1981, Sam Mencoff, an investment manager at First Chicago Investment Corporation (FCIC), reclined pensively in his chair after his first thorough reading of the prospectus before him. FCIC had been invited to make a major investment in the leveraged buyout of Norris Industries, a large California-based firm engaged in the design and manufacture of industrial, construction, and defense products using metalworking technology. Mr. Mencoff was struck by the purchase price, which at $43.05 per share represented nearly a 50-percent premium over Norris's market price ($29) the day before the announcement and nearly a 90-percent premium over what it had been selling for in 1979 before negotiations began. Norris was listed on the New York Stock Exchange, and its $420-million purchase price would make the buyout one of the largest in history. Much had been written about the supposed "restructuring" of industrial America that Norris exemplified. Would the housing and auto industries, and hence Norris, ever return to their former viability, Mr. Mencoff wondered, or was this the "final" down cycle that spelled the beginning of the end?

The proposed buyout had been arranged and structured by Kohlberg, Kravis, Roberts & Co. (KKR), a leading New York investment firm that specialized in leveraged buyouts. FCIC had worked with KKR in the past, and Mr. Mencoff considered them one of the top performers in the industry. He was far from confident, however, about this particular deal. Because the total purchase price was so large, FCIC would be expected to invest a major sum, close to $9 million, for a "strip" of investment instruments. This investment would be one of the largest in a single company that FCIC had ever made. Furthermore, Norris's business was tied to the housing and auto industries, which had been devastated by the current recession. The timing and extent of those industries' recoveries would in large part determine the safety of FCIC's investment.

Company Background

Norris Industries was founded by Kenneth T. Norris in 1930 as Norris Stamping and Manufacturing Company for the purpose of making fabricated metal products. The company was operated as an individual proprietorship until 1940, when it was incorporated. In 1938 Norris won its first military contract, to build practice bombs, which was followed by another contract for the manufacture of aluminum cartridge containers. During World War II, the company's defense business dominated what little commercial business remained. Following the war, Norris expanded into automobile wheels, stainless-steel cookware, and plumbing fixtures.

In 1950 Norris became a publicly held corporation when the Norris family sold 30 percent of its stock. Thermador Electrical Manufacturing Company, a maker of consumer appliances, and Compressed Gas Cylinders Company were acquired in 1951, and Norris changed its name to Norris–Thermador Corporation to capitalize on the public acceptance of Thermador products. The company's growth in commercial products was halted during the Korean War, when once again the defense business grew sharply and became dominant.

Norris's shares were listed on the New York Stock Exchange in 1960, and during the 1960s, a more active acquisition program expanded the company's commercial product lines at the same time the Vietnam War caused rapid expansion of its defense business. Among the acquisitions made during the 1960s that formed a major part of the current commercial business were: Bowers Manufacturing Company (electrical hardware) in 1963, Trade-Wind Motor Fans (currently part of Thermador–Waste King) in 1965, and Price Pfister Brass Manufacturing Company (household plumbing) in 1969. The company changed its name again in 1966 to Norris Industries to reflect its growing diversification.

The 1970s began with the acquisitions of Artistic Brass and Pressed Steel Tank Company in 1970 and the Automotive Trim Division in 1973. In 1977 Norris acquired the McIntosh Corporation, which significantly added to its automotive product lines. Despite acquisitions during the 1970s, the major emphasis of Norris's strategy (more than a quarter of a billion dollars) was on providing modern equipment and adequate capacity to existing businesses to capitalize on future opportunities. During 1980 the company concentrated more on market and product development and metal-working technology and less on capital expansion.

In 1981 the company operated 38 factories, which were organized into 12 divisions. Norris was a market leader or one of the leaders for most of its product lines. For instance, it held 30 percent of the U.S. residential lock market and 42 percent of the decorative brass market, and was the largest producer of wheel covers in the United States. In defense products, it held a dominant share in cartridge cases and projectile bodies.

Norris's revenues were derived from building and remodeling products (43 percent), from automotive and industrial products (42 percent), and from defense products (15 percent). The company had $599 million in sales in 1980 on $365 million in assets. Because of the company's heavy reliance on cyclical industries, net income was down to $23.8 million in 1980, compared with $35.4 in 1979 and $41.7 in 1978. Capital expenditures had consistently exceeded depreciation in recent years, and the company had little debt. Exhibits 1 to 4 present details of Norris's financial performance. Exhibits 5 and 6 show the impact on the results if Norris had used the proposed financing structure over that same period.

First Chicago Investment Corporation

FCIC was founded in 1972 under the Bank Holding Company Act and was a wholly owned subsidiary of First Chicago Corporation (the parent of the First National Bank of Chicago). FCIC and the First Chicago Corporation composed the Equity Group at First Chicago, which was the leading institutional investor in the U.S. private-equity capital markets. In 1980 the firm's portfolio was roughly $180 million (at cost) invested in 90 companies. These companies generally fell into one of two categories: start-up ventures requiring equity to finance additional growth or management buyouts where equity was required for the acquisition of operating assets by a management team through the use of significant debt leverage. In analyzing an investment opportunity, the Equity Group at First Chicago emphasized the strength of the management team, the value of a unique market opportunity or competitive advantage, and attractive economics and returns commensurate with the risks.

Terms of the Financing

KKR was forming a new company (NEWCO) to acquire all the outstanding stock of Norris. The purchase price was $420.1 million, based on $43.05 per share for approximately 9.8 million outstanding shares. The purchase price was 10.6 times 1981 estimated earnings of $39.8 million, or approximately $4.00 per share. Norris projected excess cash of approximately $60 million, which was to be used as part of this financing. After deducting the cash, the purchase price was approximately $360.1 million, or 9.9 times 1981 estimated earnings.

The funds necessary to finance the acquisition of Norris Industries were to be raised and used as shown in Table 1. The subordinated notes would be sold to institutional investors along with 4.5 million shares of stock at $5.50 per share. Upon completion of the acquisition, and after the exercise of the stock options issued to management, ownership of NEWCO on a fully diluted basis would be as follows:

	Number of Shares	Book Value	Ownership Position
Banks	430,550	$ 2,368,025	4.3%
Institutions	4,505,780	24,781,790	45.4
Management	1,300,000[a]	7,150,000[a]	13.1
KKR	3,700,000	20,350,000	37.2
Total	9,936,330	$54,649,815	100.0%

[a]Management was to purchase approximately 401,500 shares for cash at a price of $5.50 per share and be issued stock options to purchase approximately 576,900 shares at an option exercise price of $5.50 per share at the closing.

TABLE 1 • Source and Use of Funds in Buyout (millions of dollars)

Funds Available

9-year declining-balance revolving bank credit with required annual amortization in years 3 through 9[a]	$275.0
5-year bank credit at 18 percent; interest only in first 5 years; issued with warrants to purchase 430,550 shares at $5.50 per share	12.8
19.5 percent subordinated notes with required amortization in years 10 and 11[b]	39.9
Common equity from the sale of 8.6 million shares at $5.50 per share[c]	47.3
Total raised	375.0
Estimated cash on December 31, 1981	60.6
Total funds available	$435.6

Funds Used

Purchase of stock[d]	$420.1
Purchase of deferred stock plan and employee stock options[e]	1.3
Fees and expenses[f]	9.0
Excess cash and working capital	5.2
Total funds used	$435.6

[a]$25 million in years 3 through 6, $45 in years 7 and 8, and a final reduction of $85 at maturity. Mandatory reductions were also to be made with the proceeds from the sale of specific assets held for sale (Exhibit 7). Interest would be at prime plus ¾ percent, with a maximum annual interest payment of 17 percent. Any interest beyond 17 percent would be accrued and added on to the loan, up to a maximum of $40 million. The company would also have available a $30-million line of credit. (U.S. Treasury bills were yielding 15.5 percent.)

[b]Of the 19.5 percent, 16.5 would be payable on a quarterly basis with the balance payable annually and subject to a restrictive payment clause to be negotiated with the banks.

[c]Approximately 9.9 million shares were to be issuable on a fully diluted basis. Banks were to be issued 430,550 warrants at closing, management was to be issued approximately 576,900 options at closing, and approximately 321,600 shares were to be reserved but unissued for future management employees.

[d]9,758,254 shares at $43.05 per share.

[e]148,500 options exercisable at $25.50. Amount shown is net of taxes.

[f]Includes fee to Goldman, Sachs of $3.0 million and to KKR of $4.0 million.

The balance sheets would be as shown in Exhibit 8.

The Investment Decision

As Mr. Mencoff looked again at the pro formas (Exhibits 5, 6, and 8), several concerns came to mind. First and foremost, he pondered the $43.05 price per share. The purchase premium itself did not seem out of line with other leveraged buyouts shown in Exhibits 9 and 10, but he knew that Norris, through Goldman, Sachs, had been seeking a buyer for 2 years without success. He was also aware that the price had been set at $38, but that it had suddenly been raised when another corporation made an unexpected offer of $43.00 per share. All of these things made him want to look at a valuation rather carefully.

The biggest risk that Mr. Mencoff saw was the default risk. Could Norris service its huge debt obligations should the housing and auto markets not perform as projected? (A summary of the loan covenants is shown in Exhibit 11.) How much financial slack did Norris have? How long could Norris survive a prolonged recession? Were there risks that he, Norris, and KKR had overlooked?

Mr. Mencoff decided he would have to generate some estimates of return to FCIC on its investment. It had been suggested by KKR that FCIC invest a total of $8,999,996 in a "strip" of securities—$3,075,000 in the 19.5 percent subordinated notes, $1,909,875 in common stock (347,250 shares), and an additional investment of $4,015,121 in the KKR fund, which would invest directly in the common stock of NEWCO (730,022 shares)—which would bring the total fully diluted ownership to 10.8 percent of NEWCO. Would the returns on this investment vary, Mr. Mencoff wondered, depending on what happened in the economy? What were the critical factors in making this a good investment?

Norris Industries

EXHIBIT 1 • Consolidated Balance Sheets (dollars in thousands)

	December 31	
	1979	1980
Assets		
Current assets		
Cash	$ 5,411	$ 346
Short-term investments	0	28,193
Accounts receivable	89,802	86,850
Inventories	97,394	86,136
Prepaid expenses	6,926	7,474
Total current assets	199,533	208,999
Property, plant, and equipment	230,090	254,615
Less accumulated depreciation	111,588	128,302
Net property, plant, and equipment	118,502	126,313
Special tooling, net of amortization	3,317	4,916
Total net property, plant, and equipment	121,819	131,229
Other assets		
Leases and contracts receivable	12,171	13,704
Excess cost of businesses over net assets acquired	7,129	4,961
Other	8,438	5,756
Total other assets	27,738	24,421
Total assets	$349,090	$364,649
Liabilities and Shareholders' Equity		
Current liabilities		
Current portion of long-term debt	$ 245	$ 1,521
Accounts payable	27,381	29,002
Other liabilities	36,217	40,161
Total current liabilities	63,843	70,684
Deferred incentive compensation	9,145	11,126
Long-term debt	24,786	23,265
Shareholders' equity		
Common stock—par value $.50 per share (authorized 20,000,000 shares; issued 9,758,254 shares in 1980 and 1979)	5,090	5,090
Additional paid-in capital	8,528	8,528
Retained earnings	237,698	245,956
Total shareholders' equity	251,316	259,574
Total liabilities and shareholders' equity	$349,090	$364,649

Norris Industries

EXHIBIT 2 • Consolidated Statements of Income and
Retained Earnings (dollars in thousands, except per share data)

	For the Years Ending December 31		
	1978	*1979*	*1980*
Net sales	$628,273	$659,008	$599,179
Costs and expenses			
Cost of sales	487,607	530,091	488,341
Selling and advertising expense	28,775	31,324	32,361
General and administrative expense	27,752	31,255	33,527
Interest expense	2,839	2,818	1,652
Loss on disposition of products	0	0	4,520
Other, net	352	(161)	(3,489)
Total costs and expenses	547,325	595,327	556,912
Income before income taxes	80,948	63,681	42,267
Income taxes	39,256	28,287	18,396
Net income	$ 41,692	$ 35,394	$ 23,871
Retained earnings at beginning of year	$186,374	$215,966	$237,698
Cash dividends to shareholders (per share: $1.24 in 1978; $1.40 in 1979; $1.60 in 1980)	(12,100)	(13,662)	(15,613)
Retained earnings at end of year	$215,966	$237,698	$245,956
Net income per common share	$ 4.27	$ 3.63	$ 2.45

Norris Industries
EXHIBIT 3 • Revenues and Profits by Industry Segment

	1976	1977	1978	1979	1980	1981[a]
Revenues						
Building and remodeling						
Hardware products	19.8%	19.3%	18.2%	19.5%	19.3%	17.7%
Housing products	12.4	12.5	12.7	13.1	12.8	12.4
Plumbing products	15.4	15.9	15.1	14.5	14.7	13.2
Total	47.6	47.7	46.0	47.1	46.8	43.3
Industrial						
Automotive products	32.3	34.6	36.2	35.6	30.2	36.7
Cylinder products	5.0	5.3	4.5	4.5	5.3	4.8
Total	37.3	39.9	40.7	40.1	35.5	41.5
Defense	15.1	12.4	13.3	12.8	17.7	15.2
Total	100.0%	100.0%	100.0%	100.0%	100.0%	100.0%
Pre-Tax Contribution						
Building and remodeling						
Hardware products	19.4%	19.0%	17.8%	18.3%	11.9%	17.0%
Housing products	6.2	8.2	8.0	10.3	2.0	8.2
Plumbing products	10.0	12.1	11.7	6.8	(1.1)	8.7
Total	35.6	39.3	37.5	35.4	12.8	33.9
Industrial						
Automotive products	45.4	44.0	50.5	49.5	59.2	50.7
Cylinder products	5.2	5.6	3.1	5.8	10.6	2.9
Total	50.6	49.6	53.6	55.3	69.8	53.6
Defense	13.8	11.1	8.9	9.3	17.4	12.5
Total	100.0%	100.0%	100.0%	100.0%	100.0%	100.0%

[a]Estimated.

Norris Industries
EXHIBIT 4 • Depreciation and Capital Expenditures (thousands of dollars)

Industry Segments	Depreciation and Amortization			Capital Expenditures		
	1978	*1979*	*1980*	*1978*	*1979*	*1980*
Building and remodeling						
Hardware products	$ 3,723	$ 5,400	$ 5,254	$ 8,007	$ 4,884	$ 4,131
Houseware products	1,395	1,452	1,249	1,614	1,273	2,512
Plumbing products	2,715	2,920	2,968	2,929	4,490	3,294
Total	7,883	9,772	9,471	12,550	10,647	9,937
Industrial						
Automotive products	5,142	6,384	7,862	10,095	17,703	7,303
Cylinder products	464	460	496	714	1,825	9,223
Total	5,606	6,844	8,358	10,809	19,528	16,526
Defense	2,543	969	1,081	2,047	1,883	2,584
General corporate	360	401	451	265	346	252
Total	$16,342	$17,986	$19,361	$25,671	$32,404	$29,299

Norris Industries
EXHIBIT 5 • Historical and Estimated Income Statements (millions of dollars)

	1976	*1977*	*1978*	*1979*	*1980*	*1981 Estimated*
Income before taxes and interest	$75.4	$86.7	$83.8	$66.5	$43.9	$77.7
Interest expense						
Industrial revenue bonds	(1.6)	(1.6)	(1.6)	(1.6)	(1.6)	(1.6)
Senior bank debt (17%)[a]	(48.8)	(48.8)	(48.8)	(48.8)	(48.8)	(48.8)
Subordinated notes (19.5%)[b]	(8.0)	(8.0)	(8.0)	(8.0)	(8.0)	(8.0)
Total	(58.4)	(58.4)	(58.4)	(58.4)	(58.4)	(58.4)
Pre-tax income	17.0	28.3	25.4	8.1	(14.5)	19.3
Income taxes (50%)	(8.5)	(14.2)	(12.7)	(4.0)	7.3	(9.7)
Net income	$ 8.5	$14.2	$12.7	$ 4.1	$ (7.3)	$ 9.7
Interest coverage ratio						
Senior debt	1.50×	1.72×	1.66×	1.32×	0.87×	1.54×
All debt	1.29×	1.48×	1.43×	1.14×	0.75×	1.33×
Cash flow						
Net income	$ 8.5	$14.2	$12.7	$ 4.1	$ (7.3)	$ 9.7
Depreciation	12.3	13.0	16.3	18.0	19.4	22.4
Cash flow from operations	$20.8	$27.2	$29.0	$22.1	$12.1	$32.1

[a]17 percent is assumed to reflect a reasonable long-term average bank rate. The actual rate in effect would float, with a cash-flow limit of 17 percent per year.

[b]16.5 of the 19.5 percent would be payable on a quarterly basis with the balance payable annually, subject to a restrictive payment clause to be negotiated with the banks.

EXHIBIT 5 *continued* • Historical and Pro Forma Balance Sheets,[a]
June 30, 1981 (millions of dollars)

	Actual	*Adjustments*	*Pro Forma*
Assets			
Cash and equivalents	$50.3	$(55.4)[c]	$(5.1)[c]
Accounts receivable	98.4		98.4
Inventory (LIFO basis)[b]	73.3		73.3
Prepaid expenses	7.5		7.5
Total current assets	$229.5	(55.4)	$174.1
Net property, plant, and equipment	127.5		127.5
Other assets	27.0	158.5[d]	185.5
Total assets	$384.0	$103.1	$487.1
Liabilities and Shareholders' Equity			
Current liabilities	$76.9		76.9
Deferred compensation	12.0		12.0
Industrial revenue bonds	23.2		23.2
Revolving credit		286.0[e]	286.0
Subordinated debt		41.0[e]	41.0
Equity	271.9	(223.9)	48.0
Total liabilities and shareholders' equity	$384.0	$103.1[d]	$487.1

[a]This exhibit assumes that the transaction had occurred on June 30, 1981.

[b]The excess of current cost over the amount determined under LIFO (last in, first out) was $52.1 million on June 30, 1981.

[c]
Proceeds from financing	$375.0
Purchase of stock	(420.1)
Stock options and deferred stock repurchase	(1.3)
Fees and expenses	(9.0)
Net cash	$(55.4)

Norris's cash balance is projected to increase to $60.6 million by December 31, 1981.

[d]While the estimate was that NEWCO would write up the assets of Norris immediately after completion of the acquisition, thereby eliminating much of the goodwill, the excess purchase price over book value on acquisition would be:

Purchase price		$420.1
Book value	271.9	
Less stock option and deferred stock purchase not previously recorded	(1.3)	
Less fees	(9.0)	
Total	$261.6	
Adjusted book value		261.6
Excess purchase price over book value of assets acquired		$158.5

[e]Proceeds from acquisition financing.

Norris Industries

EXHIBIT 6 • Forecasted Income Statements, 1982–1990 (millions of dollars, except per share amounts)

	1982	1983	1984	1985	1986	1987	1988	1989	1990
Income before taxes and interest	$91.6	$100.7	$110.7	$121.7	$133.8	$147.1	$161.8	$177.9	$195.6
Interest expense									
Industrial revenue bonds	(1.6)	(1.6)	(1.6)	(1.6)	(1.6)	(1.5)	(1.5)	(1.4)	(1.4)
Bank debt (17%)	(48.8)	(48.8)	(48.8)	(44.5)	(40.2)	(34.0)	(29.8)	(22.1)	(14.5)
Subordinated notes (19.5%)	(8.0)	(8.0)	(8.0)	(8.0)	(8.0)	(8.0)	(8.0)	(8.0)	(8.0)
Total	(58.4)	(58.4)	(58.4)	(54.1)	(49.8)	(43.5)	(39.3)	(31.5)	(23.9)
Pre-tax income	33.2	42.3	52.3	67.6	84.0	103.6	122.5	146.4	171.7
Income taxes (50%)	(16.6)	(21.1)	(26.1)	(33.8)	(42.0)	(51.8)	(61.3)	(73.2)	(85.9)
Net income	$16.6	$21.2	$26.2	$33.8	$42.0	$51.8	$61.3	$73.2	$85.9
Earnings per share	$1.66	$2.12	$2.62	$3.38	$4.20	$5.18	$6.13	$7.32	$8.59
Book value per share[a]	$7.16	$9.28	$11.90	$15.28	$19.48	$24.66	$30.79	$38.11	$46.70
Interest-coverage ratio									
Senior debt	1.8X	2.0X	2.2X	2.6X	3.2X	4.1X	5.2X	7.6X	12.3X
All debt	1.6X	1.7X	1.9X	2.2X	2.7X	3.4X	4.1X	5.6X	8.2X

Capitalization at Year End (millions of dollars)

	1982	1983	1984	1985	1986	1987	1988	1989	1990
Bank debt	$286.0	$286.0	$261.0	$236.0	$200.0	$175.0	$130.0	$85.0	$0.0
Industrial revenue bonds	23.0	22.7	22.4	21.9	21.3	20.7	20.1	19.7	19.3
Total senior debt	309.0	308.7	283.4	257.9	221.3	195.7	150.1	104.7	19.3
Subordinated debt	41.0	41.0	41.0	41.0	41.0	41.0	41.0	41.0	41.0
Equity	64.6	85.8	112.0	145.8	187.8	239.6	300.9	374.1	460.0
Total subordinated debt and equity	$105.6	$126.8	$153.0	$186.8	$228.8	$280.6	$341.9	$415.1	$501.0

[a]Assumes 10 million shares outstanding at $5.50 per share.

Forecasted Cash Flows as of Year End, 1982–1990 (millions of dollars)

	1982	1983	1984	1985	1986	1987	1988	1989	1990
Net income	$16.6	$21.1	$26.1	$33.8	$42.0	$51.8	$61.3	$73.2	$85.9
Depreciation	23.0	23.1	23.1	22.0	21.5	21.5	21.5	21.5	21.5
Cash flow from operations	39.6	44.2	49.2	55.8	63.5	73.3	82.8	94.7	107.4
Principal payments									
Bank payments	0.0	0.0	25.0	25.0	36.0	25.0	45.4	45.0	85.0
Industrial revenue bond payments	0.3	0.3	0.3	0.5	0.6	0.6	0.6	0.4	0.4
Subordinated payments—industrial revenue bond payments	0.0	0.0	0.0	0.0	0.0	0.0	0.0	0.0	0.0
Total payments	0.3	0.3	25.3	25.5	36.6	25.6	45.6	45.4	85.4
Cash flow available for working capital and capital expenditures	39.3	43.9	23.9	30.3	26.9	47.7	37.2	49.3	22.0
Capital expenditures	15.0	16.0	17.0	18.0	19.0	25.0	25.0	25.0	25.0
Working capital	12.0	8.0	8.0	5.0	5.0	5.0	5.0	5.0	5.0
Net cash flow	12.3	19.9	(1.1)	7.3	2.9	17.7	7.2	19.3	(8.0)
Beginning cash	5.2	17.5	37.4	36.3	43.6	46.5	64.2	71.4	90.7
Ending cash	$17.5	$37.4	$36.3	$43.6	$46.5	$64.2	$71.4	$90.7	$82.7

Assumptions for Forecasted Statements for 1982–1990

1. Income before taxes and interest is based on management's estimate for net income before taxes and interest of $91.6 million for 1982 compared with the current estimate of $77.7 for 1981. Principal underlying assumptions include the following:
   a. Domestic automobile and light-truck production at 10.3 million units for 1982 versus estimate for 1981 of 9.0 million units.
   b. Residential construction at 1.65 million units for 1982 versus estimate for 1981 of 1.35 million units.
2. Income before taxes and interest beyond 1982 based on projections made by KKR assumption of a 10-percent compounded growth rate.
3. There is no interest income on excess cash.
4. No proceeds from the sale of assets. Norris currently has assets held for sale that could generate $14.1 million.
5. No charges resulting from the revaluation of assets pursuant to Accounting Principles Board #16.
6. Working capital includes net change in receivables, inventories, and accounts payable.
7. Existing industrial revenue bonds will be assumed by NEWCO.

Norris Industries
EXHIBIT 7 • Assets Held for Sale (millions of dollars)

Description	Action Contemplated	Estimated Price	Net Book Value	Net Cash after Taxes
Sponge Cushion	Sell all assets, including receivables, as going concern	$ 3.8	$ 3.6	$ 3.7
O. L. Anderson plant	Sell inventory and property, plant, and equipment as going concern	2.4	1.7	2.1
Leases and contracts currently financed by the company in-house	Sell to financial institution	14.5[a]	17.0	14.5
Ypsilanti plant currently partially leased to General Motors (205,000 square feet on 20 acres)	Sell	3.0	1.7	2.5
Other miscellaneous property (129,000 square feet of buildings)	Sell	1.7	0.5	1.3
Total		$25.4	$24.5	$24.1

[a]A 15-percent discount rate was used to estimate the value of fixed longer term low-rate leases and contracts outstanding.

Norris Industries

EXHIBIT 8 • Balance Sheets before and after Recapitalization as of December 31, 1981 (dollars in millions, except per-share amounts)

	Projected Balance Sheet 12/31/1981	Redeem Stock Options	Redeem Share-holders' Equity	Issue NEWCO Stock	Record New Debt Structure	Record Fees and Expenses	NEWCO Pro Forma Balance Sheet 12/31/1981
Assets							
Current assets							
Cash and cash equivalents	$ 60.6	$(1.3)	$(420.1)	$48.0	$327.0	$(9.0)	$ 5.2
Accounts receivable	93.6	0.0	0.0	0.0	0.0	0.0	93.6
Inventories	79.3	0.0	0.0	0.0	0.0	0.0	79.3
Prepaid expenses	7.9	0.0	0.0	0.0	0.0	0.0	7.9
Total current assets	$241.4	$(1.3)	$(420.1)	$48.0	$327.0	$(9.0)	$186.0
Property, plant, and equipment	134.0						134.0
Excess of purchase price over net worth	0.0	0.0	137.6	0.0	0.0	9.0	146.6
Other assets[a]	24.8	0.0	0.0	0.0	0.0	0.0	24.8
Total assets	$400.2	$(1.3)	$(282.5)	$48.0	$327.0	0.0	$491.4
Liabilities and Shareholders' Equity							
Current liabilities	$ 80.8	0.0	0.0	0.0	0.0	0	$ 80.8
Deferred incentive compensation	12.6	0.0	0.0	0.0	0.0	0	12.6
Long-term debt	23.0	0.0	0.0	0.0	$327.0	0	$350.0
Total liabilities	$116.4	0.0	0.0	0.0	$327.0	0	$443.4
Equity							
Common stock	4.1	$(5.1)[b]	48.0	0.0	0.0	0	$ 48.0
Additional paid-in capital	8.5	$(8.5)	0.0	0.0	0.0	0	0.0
Retained earnings	270.2	(1.3)	(268.9)	0.0	0.0	0	0.0
Total equity	$283.8	$(1.3)	$(282.5)	$48.0	0.0	0	$ 48.0
Total liabilities and shareholders' equity	$400.2	$(1.3)	$(282.5)	$48.0	$327.0	0	$491.4
Net working capital	$160.0						$105.2
Current ratio	2.99×						2.30×
Common shares outstanding	9,758,254						10,000,000[c]
Book value per common share	$29.08						$ 5.50

[a]Includes excess of investment over net assets acquired of $4.9.

[b]To adjust stock to $43.05 per share and record payout net of related income tax effects.

[c]Fully diluted.

Norris Industries
EXHIBIT 9 • Data on Leveraged Buyouts and Other Acquisitions

Company Acquired	Date	Acquisition of Stock or Assets	Premium/Price One Day Prior to Announcement	Offer as a Percentage of Net Income	Multiple of Book Value	Senior Debt/ Total Debt	Subordinated Debt/ Total Debt	Subordinated Debt/Total Capital
Houdaille Industries	10/28/78	S	93%	13.9X	2.0X	65.5%	34.5%	29.6%
Bliss & Laughlin	8/10/79	S	23	8.7	1.7	N.Av.	N.Av.	N.Av.
Carrier Corp.	9/16/78	A	39	10.2	1.6	N.Av.	N.Av.	N.Av.
Gardner-Denver	1/22/79	A	46	12.2	2.1	N.Av.	N.Av.	N.Av.
Eltra Corp.	6/29/79	A	25	11.6	1.5	N.Av.	N.Av.	N.Av.
Washington Steel	3/12/79	A	34	7.3	1.3	N.Av.	N.Av.	N.Av.
Studebaker-Northington	7/25/79	A	17	10.7	1.4	N.Av.	N.Av.	N.Av.
Marathon Manufacturing	8/13/79	A	13	11.4	2.1	N.Av.	N.Av.	N.Av.
Congoleum	1980	A/S	50%	9.4X	2.4X	68.6%	31.4%	27.6%

N.Av. = not available.

Norris Industries
EXHIBIT 10 • Average Market Prices of Norris Shares[a]

Period	High	Low
1977	$31	$19
1978		
First quarter	23¾	19¾
Second quarter	26	21½
Third quarter	27	20⅝
Fourth quarter	26¾	20
1979		
First quarter	25¼	20⅜
Second quarter	28	22¾
Third quarter	28⅞	23¼
Fourth quarter	26⅝	19
1980		
First quarter	26⅜	18¼
Second quarter	23½	19
Third quarter[b]	33½	22⅜
Fourth quarter	32½	23¾
1981		
First quarter	31½	25½
Second quarter	32½	27½
Third quarter[c]	$39¾	$29

[a]Norris shares currently traded on the New York Stock Exchange and the Pacific Stock Exchange.

[b]On August 4, 1980, the last business day prior to the public announcement of proposals for the acquisition of Norris by KKR and another firm, the closing price per Norris share was $29.

[c]On July 22, 1981, the last business day prior to the public announcement of a proposal for the acquisition of Norris at a price of $38 per share by an investor group to be formed by KKR, the closing price per share of the Norris shares was $29.13. On August 19, 1981, the last business day prior to the announcement that an agreement had been executed with KKR for an increased price of $43.05 per Norris share, the closing market price per share was $36.00.

Norris Industries

EXHIBIT 11 • Summary of Loan Covenants

1. Working capital, minimum of $75,000,000.
2. Current ratio, minimum of 1.5 to 1.
3. Tangible net worth, minimums of:

Amount	Period
$ 41,000,000	Closing to 12/31/82
52,000,000	12/31/82 to 12/31/83
64,000,000	12/31/83 to 12/31/84
84,000,000	12/31/84 to 12/31/85
109,000,000	12/31/85 to 12/31/86
144,000,000	12/31/86 to 12/31/87
179,000,000	12/31/87 to 12/31/88
$219,000,000	12/31/88 and thereafter

4. No prepayment of subordinated debt.
5. Sale of assets is unlimited, except by other financial covenants, and proceeds must be applied to the revolving credit to the extent of:

   a. 50 percent for all assets sold in a single sale or in an integrated series of sales over $1,000,000.

   b. 100 percent for all assets held for sale in excess of $4,000,000.

Gaylord Container Corporation

In March 1991, Kerry Bitetti was considering what she should recommend to the management of Gaylord Container Corporation. Ms. Bitetti had been involved with the formation of Gaylord in 1986 and was now faced with helping the management of a company that was in short-term financing difficulty. An aggressive capital-investment program, coupled with a severe economic downturn in the United States, meant that Gaylord might not be able to make the interest and principal payments on its debt. Indeed, it might need more money just to get through the current recession.

Gaylord and the Brown-Paper and Corrugated-Container Industry

Gaylord Container, created in 1985, had grown by acquisition and merger. In late 1986, Ms. Bitetti had helped Mr. Pomerantz purchase the paper packing division of Crown Zellerback, a company acquired by Sir James Goldsmith in 1985. The division, consisting of 3 containerboard (board used to make corrugated containers) and paper mills, 14 corrugated-container plants, 3 corrugated-sheet plants, a specialty-chemicals facility, and a cogeneration facility, cost $260 million.[1] At that time Ms. Bitetti believed that, because paper-industry earnings were depressed and the high-yield market was strong, the acquisition price was reasonable. The acquisition resulted in the creation of a new, privately held company, Gaylord Container Corporation. In early 1988, Gaylord acquired the paper-container operations of Louisiana-Pacific, with its

This case was prepared by Diana Harrington with assistance from Bowen Smith, Dillon Read & Co., Inc. Copyright © 1991 by the University of Virginia Darden School Foundation, Charlottesville, Virginia. All rights reserved.

[1] This acquisition was financed with senior bank borrowings of $165 million, $114 million of subordinated debt, preferred stock of $13 million, and $12 million of common stock.

attractive major containerboard production facility near Gaylord's California operation and the possible synergies that might exist.[2] In addition to the containerboard plant, 2 corrugated-container and a corrugated-sheet plant were acquired. On June 1, 1988, Gaylord merged with Mid-America Packaging, Inc.[3]

By the end of 1989, Gaylord was the 10th largest containerboard, the 9th largest corrugated-container, and one of the largest multiwall-bag (bags used in such industries as chemical and agricultural-product manufacturing) and grocery-bag producers in the United States. It manufactured and distributed all types of brown-paper bags and brown-paper packaging products, such as corrugated containers. In total, it had 3 paper mills and 26 converting plants that converted kraft paper to bags or corrugated sheet to containers.

Corrugated Containers

Containerboard, a combination of a corrugating medium and linerboard, was used to manufacture corrugated containers to customer order. The bulkiness and value-added nature of the containers made shipping costs an important component of the cost of production. Therefore, corrugated-container plants tended to be located close to customers, and one company's containerboard production was often exchanged for that produced by other manufacturers to reduce shipping costs or to maximize the production of a particular weight by a manufacturer's paper machine. In 1988 industry sales were estimated at $15.5 billion, and containerboard capacity-utilization rates were at 95 percent.

Gaylord Container produced most varieties of corrugated containers and sold to end users from 17 plants. From 1987 to 1988, sales increased by 50 percent on a volume increase of 37 percent, as seen in Exhibit 1. As with all of Gaylord's products, each converting plant had a sales force of its own to market its products to local customers. Because few barriers to entry existed in the industry, Gaylord generally competed with a number of other companies in each area it served.

Gaylord had the capacity to produce a wide variety of weights and grades of containerboard. In 1987 only 37 percent of the production of Gaylord's 52 containerboard production plants was sold outside the company. Manufacture of containerboard was capital intensive, and new facilities could take two years or more to build. In the recent past, companies

---

[2] The $156 million purchase price was financed with senior bank borrowings of $124 million and seller notes of $32 million.

[3] At the time of the merger, Gaylord issued and sold $250 million of 13½ percent subordinated notes due in 1998. The bulk of the proceeds was used to repay senior bank lenders ($211.8 million), redeem cumulative preferred stock ($15.1 million), and prepay accreted value on Mid-America's 19 percent zero-coupon, callable, subordinated promissory notes.

wanting new production facilities had often found acquiring productive capacity in the stock market cheaper and faster than building new plants or expanding old facilities.

Unbleached Kraft Paper

Gaylord was a major supplier of unbleached kraft paper. It produced and sold to independent grocery-bag and -sack manufacturers, as well as to its own bag-fabricating plants. About 50 percent of its two plants' production of kraft paper was used in the company's bag operations. Sales in this industry had been hit by the introduction of the plastic grocery bag. By 1988, however, while industrywide kraft paper production had declined, Gaylord had increased productive capacity slightly, as shown in Exhibit 1. Productive capacity of all U.S. manufacturers of kraft paper was estimated to be 31 million tons in 1989.

Multiwall and Grocery Bags and Sacks

Gaylord owned one plant producing multiwall bags and leased two to produce bags for grocery stores.[4] This segment of the bag industry was estimated at $2.2 billion in the United States in 1988. Gaylord's sales of multiwall bags had increased 41 percent from 1987 to 1988, a tonnage increase of 31 percent, but remained essentially unchanged in 1989 and 1990.

Financing at Gaylord

For the first few years of the company's life, financings were done primarily to support mergers or acquisitions. The first public issue to support Gaylord Container's operations was a common stock issue in June 1988. Both the strong market and earnings for the paper industry had made the time ripe for a public offering of the Gaylord Container common stock. Gaylord issued 2.85 million shares, and stockholders added 950,000 of their own for a total issue of 3.8 million shares. These shares were issued at $20.50 per share and netted the company almost $55 million, all of which, according to the prospectus dated June 29, 1988, was to be "used for corporate purposes."

---

[4] Since May 1989, Gaylord had owned 65 percent of the profits and losses of a joint venture operating two bag-manufacturing plants. The equity was worth $3.3 million in 1989. By September 1990, the company's cumulative net losses were $4.5 million. Equity in net losses was classified as other expenses. Voting rights were determined by the four partners, two of whom Gaylord elected.

In part, the equity issue reduced the debt-to-total capital ratio by 10 percent, as shown in Exhibit 2. At the same time, Gaylord announced a major capital-investment program designed to make Gaylord Container the low-cost producer in the industry.

By August 1989, Gaylord was back in the market to finance the continuation of its capital-investment plans. This time Gaylord Container issued $150 million of 13¾ percent subordinated debentures due in 2001. By year-end 1990, the company had $733 million in debt and assets of $1,199 million, as shown in Exhibit 3. Senior debt was largely in the hands of Bankers Trust Co.

Gaylord Container's Situation in Late 1990 and Early 1991

In the prospectus for the common stock issue in 1988, management had described the industry as follows:

> Demand for corrugated containers, containerboard and unbleached kraft paper is cyclical and has historically corresponded to changes in the rate of growth in the U.S. economy and exchange rates for the U.S. dollar. Growth in the U.S. economy generally stimulates demand for packaging products. In addition, weakness of the U.S. dollar versus the currencies of the United States' major trading partners encourages production of containerboard for export as well as domestic demand for packaging. . . . Accordingly, in the event of a weakening of the U.S. economy or a strengthening of the U.S. dollar, demand for the Company's principal products could drop, thus adversely affecting the Company's financial condition and the results of operations.

By mid-1988 kraft paper and containerboard prices were at historic highs. Prices continued to rise through mid-1989 before falling 7 percent in 1990, despite good exports.

By late 1990 and early 1991, all the worst fears of management in this industry had been realized. The U.S. economy was weak, and the recession continued. In its December 31, 1990, 10-Q report to the Securities and Exchange Commission (SEC), management reported,

> Given current market conditions, the Company believes fiscal 1991 will not show a return to profitability due to lower product prices, higher depreciation expense and higher interest expense from increased borrowings and a reduction in capitalized interest. Management also believes that, given the uncertainty in the Middle East, there can be no assurance that cash generated by operations and borrowing under the Company's bank credit agreement will be sufficient to meet the Com-

pany's financial obligations during the remainder of fiscal 1991. Therefore, the Company has begun discussions with its bank group to gain
increased financial flexibility under its bank credit agreement. Such
financial flexibility would include modifying certain covenants in the
bank agreement and increasing the size of the facility. If the company is
unable to obtain increased financial flexibility, it will be forced to
attempt to implement other measures to obtain additional liquidity,
including, but not limited to, further cost reductions, cuts in capital
spending, sales of assets, additional debt or equity financings, debt
restructurings, or a combination thereof, in order to avoid a shortfall in
the Company's ability to meet its financial obligations during the
remainder of fiscal 1991.

Gaylord's sales for the first quarter of 1991 were down 5 percent from the
year before, operating earnings were down 46 percent, and the company
lost $9.9 million for the quarter. Lower prices, changes in the product mix,
and higher costs for raw materials—all contributed to the declines. To
forestall further losses, management had idled two linerboard machines
(650 tons per day) and related equipment.

Gaylord's stock price declined from a high of over $20 per share in
mid-1988 to less than $5 in late 1990, as shown in Exhibit 4A, and the
decline was not merely part of an industrywide drop; an index of comparable companies[5] dropped by 10 percent over the same time (see Exhibit 4B).
In addition, the price of Gaylord's two bond issues were downgraded in
mid-1990 and had dropped like rocks: both were trading at only 37 percent
of face value, resulting in a yield to maturity of over 38 percent.

What did the state of the U.S. economy and the capital markets have
in store for Gaylord?

U.S. Financial Markets

By early 1991, the Dow Jones Industrial Average had declined by almost
20 percent from its July 1990 high. Market pundits were saying that the
market appeared more fairly valued than previously, but it was not cheap.
Debt markets had also been hurt by the fears of rising inflation born out of
the concern that oil prices would rise further from their already doubled
state. (The Iraqi invasion of Kuwait had greatly exacerbated these fears.)
High-yield securities had been especially hard hit, and highly leveraged
companies were out of favor.[6] These circumstances plus other problems

---

[5] Chesapeake, Georgia-Pacific, Longview Fibre, Stone Container, Temple-Inland, Union
Camp, and Willamette.

[6] From January 1989 to August 1989, $21.8 billion of high-yield bonds were issued. In the last
four months of 1989, only $6.9 billion were issued; in the first six months of 1990, the total

hanging over the U.S. economy—the S&L crisis and the budget deficit—
made the outlook for the markets negative and uncertain.

In addition to the general problems in the capital markets, banks were
under significant pressure. Third World loans, fears about the health of
highly leveraged companies in a recessionary economy, and scarce, higher
costs for new funds made banks acutely aware of a borrower's credit standing. Institutional lenders followed the lead of bankers. Many of them were
quite exposed to highly leveraged companies and to the real estate market.
In addition, the securities ratings guidelines promulgated by the National
Association of Insurance Commissioners had imposed higher capital
ratios on lenders. The effect was to limit those lenders' appetites for
noninvestment-grade securities to those that had an equity component. For
all new debt, covenants tended to be more restrictive than previously.

Ms. Bitetti's Analysis of the Situation

Ms. Bitetti had made the following list of Gaylord's strengths and weaknesses:

Strengths

- Gaylord's $300 million capital-investment program is virtually
  complete, and the company has world-class facilities.
- $400 million of debt has no amortization for eight years.
- Subordinated debt does not restrict additional senior financing.

Weaknesses

- Gaylord is not the top ranked in any industry.
- Production is geographically concentrated (see Exhibit 5 for map of
  production facilities).
- Existing bank debt constrains added senior financing.
- Operating results are worse than those of comparable companies.
- Debt and equity securities are selling at a discount to the industry.

---

was $2.6 billion; little had been issued since then. Part of the reason was the savings and loan
crisis; S&Ls were forced to divest their high-yield securities by the Financial Institutions
Reform, Recovery and Enforcement Act of 1989. Other causes were fears of possible defaults
by private and mutual-fund investors, regulations by the National Association of Insurance
Commissioners that increased standard and reserve requirements of issuers, and investors'
market-liquidity concerns.

- Start-up costs relative to the capital-investment program will continue to affect operating results negatively through 1991.

- Because of tight coverage ratios, further deterioration in industry conditions will have a very negative effect.

Ms. Bitetti had worked with company management to develop a basic set of forecasts, which were based on different prices in different regions of the country by product line. In general, the prices were expected to change in the following ways:

Year	Price Change
1992	8.5%
1993	7.8
1994	(7.2)
1995	10.4%

Volumes were expected to stay steady or decline except for linerboard. Forecasts for 1990–95 are shown in Exhibit 6. If the economy recovered slightly, the coverage ratios were sufficient for Gaylord to weather the current storm. Ms. Bitetti was quite concerned, however, about whether principal and interest could be covered for the current year. Full descriptions of debt requirements are found in Exhibit 7, and payments for leases are described in Exhibit 8.

In spite of the current situation, Ms. Bitetti concluded that Gaylord had plenty of assets to make new debt secure, especially in light of the Georgia-Pacific sale of assets to Tenneco at higher than book values.[7] Her analysis is shown in Exhibit 9.

Conclusion

Ms. Bitetti wanted to be able to go to Gaylord managers with a plan for steps they should take to confront their current situation. She did not want them to take action they did not need to take in light of the recovery she and her firm were predicting for the end of 1991. On the other hand, companies such as Gaylord that were highly leveraged and found themselves in trouble were at the mercy of their creditors.

---

[7] Exhibit 10 shows recent deals in the U.S. paper industry.

Gaylord Container Corporation

EXHIBIT 1 • Production: Four Product Lines

	Fiscal 1987				Fiscal 1988				Fiscal 1989				Fiscal 1990			
	12/86	3/87	6/87	9/87	12/87	3/88	6/88	9/88	12/88	3/89	6/89	9/89	12/89	3/90	6/90	9/90
Containerboard production (thousand tons)	75.6	181.0	175.5	189.6	180.4	195.4	254.0	244.0	242.9	225.6	253.3	243.0	228.2	195.1	222.8	289.0
Unbleached-kraft-paper production (thousand tons)	27.3	65.8	61.7	63.6	56.5	64.0	66.6	70.0	67.2	69.1	65.3	73.3	65.4	59.6	62.0	64.8
Corrugated shipments (billion square feet)	0.8	1.9	2.0	2.1	2.0	2.1	2.5	2.7	2.5	2.4	2.7	2.6	2.4	2.4	2.5	2.9
Multiwall-bag shipments (million bags)	12.2	26.6	26.3	30.9	31.1	31.8	32.4	32.5	31.5	31.9	34.5	39.5	44.5	40.7	42.0	52.2

Source: 1991 Annual Report, pp. 30–31.

Gaylord Container Corporation

EXHIBIT 2 • Selected Financial Information (dollars in millions, except per-share dollars)

	Fiscal 1987[a]				Fiscal 1988[a]				Fiscal 1989[a]				Fiscal 1990[a]			
	12/86	3/87	6/87	9/87	12/87	3/88	6/88	9/88	12/88	3/89	6/89	9/89	12/89	3/90	6/90	9/90
Net sales	$48.4	$121.2	$128.7	$139.5	$137.7	$151.1	$188.2	$194.2	$182.7	$178.0	$193.5	$191.8	$183.0	$161.5	$172.2	$201.6
Gross margin	9.1	27.3	29.0	29.4	32.4	36.7	42.7	46.6	41.5	38.2	46.3	46.7	34.8	17.3	25.1	29.9
Selling and administrative costs	3.9	10.1	10.6	11.5	13.2	13.4	13.7	13.5	12.9	14.6	15.7	16.0	15.5	16.7	16.7	16.8
Operating earnings	5.2	17.2	18.4	17.9	19.2	23.3	29.0	33.1	28.6	23.6	30.6	30.7	19.3	0.6	8.4	13.1
Interest expense, net	3.9	9.1	8.3	8.3	9.0	9.0	13.4	15.3	14.6	13.8	13.4	14.5	15.2	15.5	19.1	22.6
Earnings (loss) before income taxes	1.3	8.1	10.1	9.6	10.2	14.3	15.6	17.8	14.0	9.8	17.2	16.2	4.1	(14.9)	(10.7)	(9.5)
Net income (loss)	0.7	5.4	6.7	6.5	6.7	10.1	12.4	12.7	12.4	6.0	10.9	10.1	2.0	(12.5)	(6.9)	(5.8)
Net income (loss) per share	0.1	0.5	0.6	0.5	0.5	0.8	1.0	0.8	0.8	0.4	0.7	0.6	0.1	(0.8)	(0.4)	(0.4)
Average number of common and common-equivalent shares outstanding	11.9	11.9	12.0	12.2	12.5	12.5	12.6	15.5	15.9	15.9	15.9	15.9	15.9	15.9	16.0	15.3
Earnings before depreciation, interest, amortization, and taxes (EBDIAT)	8.1	23.8	25.1	25.2	26.5	31.2	39.1	44.3	46.2	35.0	42.0	42.8	30.9	8.3	22.0	28.6
Capital expenditures[b]	3.3	5.8	14.0	21.4	11.4	15.4	15.9	24.3	36.9	41.7	38.9	63.5	49.3	67.0	29.5	26.9
Total assets	NA	NA	NA	506.3	500.9	522.8	728.8	805.4	802.8	812.5	844.9	1010.0	992.6	1036.3	1065.4	1099.5
Property, net	NA	NA	NA	345.3	350.4	358.7	520.1	542.2	560.1	595.6	626.7	689.1	746.3	806.6	825.5	838.2
Long-term debt	NA	NA	NA	303.1	295.8	293.9	483.3	472.1	475.1	471.9	495.7	623.5	626.1	673.1	713.5	733.7
Total debt	NA	NA	NA	325.3	318.0	320.1	193.8	483.9	486.9	483.8	507.7	635.5	638.1	685.1	738.5	766.9
Common stockholders' equity	NA	NA	NA	37.9	43.6	53.3	65.9	141.1	153.5	159.1	170.0	180.3	182.0	169.3	162.4	153.3
Book value per share	NA	NA	NA	3.11	3.49	4.26	5.23	9.10	9.65	10.48	10.69	11.34	11.45	10.65	10.21	10.02
Interest coverage	1.33X	1.89X	2.22X	2.16X	2.13X	2.59X	2.16X	2.16X	1.96X	1.71X	2.28X	2.12X	1.27X	0.04X	0.44X	0.58X
EBDIAT to cash interest (times)	2.08X	2.62X	3.02X	3.04X	2.94X	3.47X	2.92X	2.90X	3.16X	2.54X	3.13X	2.95X	2.03X	0.54X	1.15X	1.27X
Long-term debt to total capital[c]	NA	NA	NA	88.9%	87.2%	84.6%	88.0%	77.0%	75.6%	74.8%	74.5%	77.6%	77.5%	79.9%	81.5%	82.7%

[a] The period November 18, 1986, through September 27, 1987 (fiscal 1987); the period September 18, 1987, through September 30, 1988 (fiscal 1988); the year ended September 30, 1989 (fiscal 1989); and the year ended September 30, 1990 (fiscal 1990). Fiscal 1990 was a 53-week period, and the fourth quarter of fiscal 1990 was a 14-week period.

[b] Excludes capitalized interest.

[c] Total capital includes long-term debt, deferred income taxes, preferred stock, and common stockholders' equity.

Source: 1991 Annual Report, pp. 30–31.

Consolidated Balance Sheet

	Sept. 30, 1987	Sept. 30, 1988	Sept. 30, 1989	Sept. 30, 1990	Dec. 30, 1990
Long-term debt	303.1	472.1	623.5	733.7	773.9
Other long-term liabilities	22.4	15.4	14.6	14.3	18.4
Deferred income taxes	21.3	37.7	53.0	40.9	34.5
Common stockholders' equity					
Class A common stock:					
par value, $0.01 per share; authorized 45,000,000 shares; issued as of Sept. 30, 1988—9,277,500; 1989—9,316,273; 1990—9,380,963 shares.	0.1	0.1	0.1	0.1	0.1
Class B Common stock:					
par value, $0.01 per share; authorized 15,000,000 shares; issued and outstanding 1988 and 1989—6,000,000; 1990—5,983,809 shares.	0.1	0.1	0.1	0.1	0.1
Capital in excess of par value	16.8	79.4	79.6	79.8	79.9
Retained earnings	20.9	61.5	100.9	77.7	67.8
Common stock in treasury, at cost	0	0	(0.4)	(0.8)	(0.8)
Recognition of minimum pension liability	0	0	0	(3.6)	(3.6)
Total common stockholders' equity	52.2	141.1	180.3	153.3	143.5
Total liabilities and shareholders' equity	$506.3	$805.4	$1,010.0	$1,099.5	$1,106.1

continued

Gaylord Container Corporation
EXHIBIT 3 • Financial Statements (in millions)

Consolidated Balance Sheet

	Sept. 30, 1987	Sept. 30, 1988	Sept. 30, 1989	Sept. 30, 1990	Dec. 30, 1990
Current assets					
Cash and equivalents	$ 23.0	$ 71.8	$ 107.5	$ 13.3	$ 0.5
Trade receivables (less allowances of $2.4 million and $3.2 million, respectively)	66.0	90.2	96.2	95.2	97.2
Inventories	35.8	46.6	43.3	50.7	63.9
Prepaid expenses	7.5	0	8.0	2.8	0
Receivables from unconsolidated subsidiaries	3.5	7.0	5.5	0.4	0
Other	3.2	4.7	7.5	16.0	21.4
Total current assets	$139.0	$220.3	$ 268.0	$ 178.4	$ 183.0
Property, net	345.3	542.2	689.1	838.2	835.8
Other assets					
Investments in and notes receivable from unconsolidated subsidiaries	0	0	8.4	24.6	87.3
Notes receivable	14.5	14.4	13.9	18.5	0
Deferred charges	7.5	28.5	30.6	39.8	0
Total assets	$506.3	$805.4	$1,010.0	$1,099.5	$1,106.1
Current liabilities					
Current maturities of long-term debt	22.2	11.8	12.0	33.2	33.2
Trade payables	46.8	49.6	61.2	53.8	48.8
Accrued and other liabilities	38.3	77.7	65.4	70.3	53.8
Total current liabilities	$107.3	$139.1	$ 138.6	$ 157.3	$ 135.8

continued

EXHIBIT 3 • Gaylord Container Corporation continued

Income Statements

	Sept. 30, 1987	Sept. 30, 1988	Sept. 30, 1989	Sept. 30, 1990	Dec. 30, 1990
Net sales	$437.8	$671.2	$746.0	$718.3	$173.0
Cost of goods	(343.0)	(512.8)	(573.3)	(611.2)	(147.4)
Gross margin	94.8	158.4	172.7	107.1	25.6
Selling and administrative costs	(37.4)	(56.3)	(59.2)	(64.5)	(15.2)
Operating earnings	57.4	102.1	108.2	41.4	10.4
Interest expense net	(28.3)	(44.2)	56.3	72.4	25.8
Other income, (expense), net	0.2	0.2	(6.3)	7.5	0.9
Earnings (loss) before income taxes	29.3	58.1	63.5	(38.5)	(16.3)
Income taxes	(10.0)	(16.2)	(24.1)	15.3	6.4
Net income	19.3	41.9	39.4	(23.2)	(9.9)
Preferred stock dividends	(1.3)	(1.3)	0	0	0
Net income (loss) available to common stockholders	$ 18.0	$ 40.6	$ 39.4	$ (23.2)	$ (9.9)
Net income (loss) per common and common-equivalent share	$ 1.50	$ 3.06	$ 2.45	$ (1.45)	$ 0.67
Average number of common and common-equivalent shares outstanding	12.0	13.3	15.9	15.8	15.4
Consolidated Statements of Cash Flows					
Net income (loss)	$ 19.3	$ 41.9	$ 39.4	$ (23.2)	$ (9.9)
Adjustment to reconcile net income to net cash provided by operations					
Depreciation and amortization	23.3	36.3	46.2	55.9	16.3
Noncash interest expense	9.8	12.4	13.4	15.5	4.2
Deferred income taxes	6.6	9.0	15.5	(5.4)	(6.4)
Deferred start-up costs	(16.3)	0	0	(6.2)	(0.8)
(Gain) loss on sale of assets	4.9	0	(5.6)	1.0	0.1

Change in current assets and liabilities, excluding acquisitions and dispositions

Receivables	(16.3)	(23.7)	(5.9)	(4.0)	0
Inventories	4.9	(0.5)	5.1	(4.0)	0
Prepaid expenses and other current assets	(0.6)	(2.3)	(1.7)	(7.6)	0
Accounts payable and other accrued liabilities	22.6	29.9	13.0	(5.3)	0
Other, net	1.6	(0.7)	1.5	4.7	1.0
Net cash provided by operations	71.2	102.3	120.9	21.4	(28.2)
Capital expenditures	(45.5)	(68.9)	(181.0)	(172.7)	(13.0)
Capitalized interest	0	0	(10.0)	(21.3)	(0.5)
Acquisitions	0	(120.0)	(9.7)	(17.0)	0
Proceeds from sale of assets	0	0	13.1	2.1	0.4
Restructuring expenditures	(5.1)	(11.1)	(15.0)	(7.2)	(1.5)
Other investments, net	0	0	(15.3)	(12.0)	(4.4)
Net cash used for investments	(50.6)	(200.0)	(217.9)	(228.2)	(19.0)
Senior bank debt, repayments	(14.3)	(214.4)	(7.1)	(8.2)	(1.1)
Senior bank debt, borrowings	20.0	92.1	0	0	37.0
Capital-expenditures facility	0	0	0	111.9	0
Export-Import Bank facility	0	0	0	17.0	0
Proceeds from issuance of Class A common stock	0	62.2	0	0	0
Redemption of preferred stock	0	(15.6)	0	0	0
Issuance of subordinated debt	0	250.0	150.0	0	0
Debt-issuance costs	0	22.4	(5.1)	(2.9)	(1.5)
Other financing, net	(20.8)	(5.4)	(5.1)	(5.3)	0
Net cash provided by financing	(15.1)	146.5	132.7	112.5	34.4
Net increase (decrease) in cash and equivalents	5.5	48.8	35.7	(94.2)	(12.8)
Cash and equivalents, beginning of period	17.5	23.0	71.8	107.5	13.3
Cash and equivalents, end of period	$ 23.0	$ 71.8	$107.5	$ 13.3	$ 0.5
Cash paid for					
Interest expense	$ 17.9	$ 25.2	$ 50.9	$ 80.5	$ 26.3
Income taxes	$ 6.3	1.2	11.5	3.2	$ 0
Supplemental schedule of noncash investing and financial activities:					
Fair value of noncash assets acquired	0	176.2	$ 9.7	16.3	0
Liabilities assumed in acquisitions	0	$ 56.2	0	$ 3.0	0

Gaylord Container Corporation
EXHIBIT 4(A) • **Gaylord Stock Price and Trading Volume, 7/01/88–10/19/90**

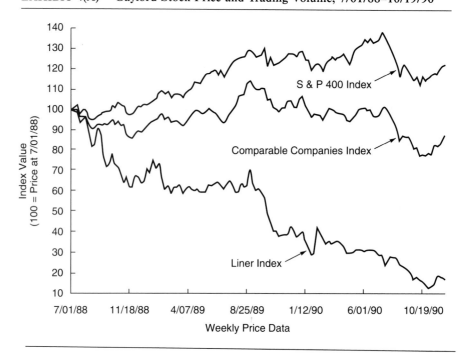

Gaylord Container Corporation
EXHIBIT 4(B) • Historical Stock Performance: Gaylord vs. Comparable Companies

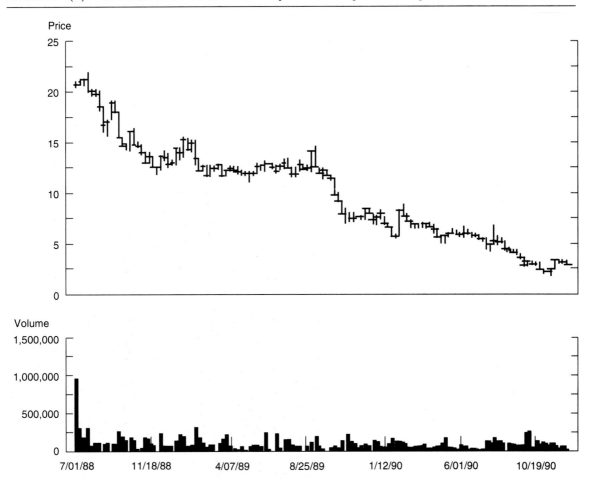

Gaylord Container Corporation
EXHIBIT 5 • Location of the Company's Manufacturing Properties

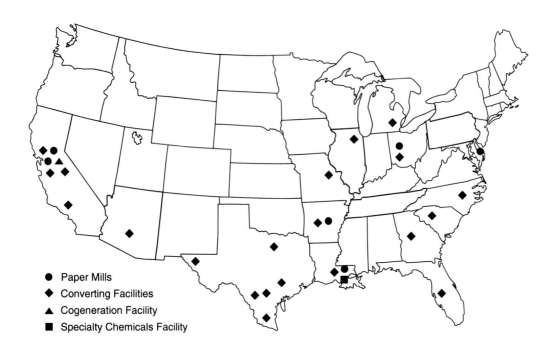

● Paper Mills
◆ Converting Facilities
▲ Cogeneration Facility
■ Specialty Chemicals Facility

Gaylord Container Corporation
EXHIBIT 6 • Financial Projections

Original Projections

	1990	1991	1992	1993	1994	1995
Net sales/Revenues	$698.9	$796.0	$886.9	$944.8	$901.5	$980.8
Operating income	0	117.1	179.1	228.5	172.4	232.5
Net income	$ (23.2)	$ 9.2	$ 47.3	$ 80.0	$ 48.7	$ 88.1

Base-Case Projections[a]

	1990	1991	1992	1993	1994	1995
Net sales/Revenues	$718.3	$777.0	$866.3	$924.0	$881.1	$960.0
Operating income	0	91.6	151.4	199.6	143.2	203.1
Net income	$ (23.2)	$ 7.9	$ 27.3	$ 59.8	$ 31.9	$ 73.6

[a]Base-case projections based on price reductions from original projections.

Gaylord Container Corporation
EXHIBIT 7 • Financial Statement Long-Term Debt Footnotes

Long-term debt consists of the following (in millions):

	September 30, 1989	September 30, 1990
Term loan, varying interest rates, due through March 1995(a)	$ 39.3	$ 32.1
Capital-expenditure facility, varying interest rates, due in semiannual installments from June 1991 through December 1994(a)	0	111.9
Export-Import Bank loan, 6.5%, due in equal semiannual installments through March 1998(b)	0	15.9
Fibreboard acquisition notes, varying interest rates, due through April 1999(c)	27.3	24.2
Note payable, 8.5%, due in annual installments of $1.0 million through December 1994	6.2	5.2
Pollution control and industrial revenue bonds, interest at 4.7% to 8.3%, due at various dates to 2008(d)	14.4	14.1
Capital lease obligations (Note 11)	1.5	1.2
Total senior debt	88.7	204.6
Subordinated notes, 13½%, due June 1998(e)	250.0	250.0
Discount subordinated notes, 16½%, due November 1998 (net of unamortized discount of $36.0 million and $20.5 million, respectively)(f)	89.8	105.3
Subordinated notes, 13½%, due November 1996(g)	57.0	57.0
Subordinated debentures, 13¾%, due August 2001(h)	150.0	150.0
Total subordinated debt	546.8	562.3
Total debt	635.5	766.9
Less current maturities	(12.0)	(33.2)
Total long-term debt	$623.5	$733.7

EXHIBIT 7 • *continued*

Aggregate annual principal payments due on long-term debt during each of the next five years are (in millions) $33.2, $44.4, $40.0, $40.0, and $22.4, respectively.

(a) In connection with the Merger and the issuance in June 1988 of $250 million of subordinated notes, the Company amended and restated its Banks Credit Agreement (the Bank Credit Agreement). At May 24, 1988, the Bank Credit Agreement provided for total credit facilities of $293 million consisting of:

  (1) An $80 million revolving-credit facility maturing September 1993, which can be extended under certain conditions through March 1995. Availability under the revolving-credit facility is reduced by certain outstanding letters of credit, which amounted to approximately $5.7 million at September 30, 1990. A fee of 1.75 percent per annum is paid on the outstanding face amount of such letters of credit. At September 30, 1990, in connection with an amendment to the Bank Credit Agreement, such fee was increased to 2.75 percent per annum. A commitment fee of 0.375 percent per year is paid on the unused portion of the revolving credit facility. The highest outstanding principal balance under the facility during fiscal 1990 was $68 million, and the weighted-average interest rate was 10.8 percent. At September 30, 1990, no amounts were outstanding under the revolving credit facility.

  (2) A $50 million term loan facility to be repaid in 14 equal semiannual installments beginning September 30, 1988. The highest outstanding principal balance under the facility during fiscal 1990 was $39.3 million, and the weighted-average interest rate was 10.6 percent. At September 30, 1990, $32.1 million was outstanding under the term loan carrying a weighted-average interest rate of 11.2 percent.

  (3) A $33 million letter-of-credit facility under which letters of credit were issued to collateralize the notes issued by the Company in connection with the Fibreboard acquisition. See (c) below. At September 30, 1990, $25.2 million of such letters of credit were outstanding against the facility. A fee of 2 percent per annum is paid on the outstanding face amount of the letters of credit. At September 30, 1990, in connection with an amendment to the Bank Credit Agreement, such fee was increased to 3 percent per annum. The facility and the outstanding letters of credit are reduced periodically as payments are made on the notes. The facility expires in March 1995.

  (4) During Fiscal 1990, the Company activated the first and the second tranche of its $130 million capital-expenditure facility. The Company's ability to borrow under the capital-expenditure facility was reduced by an $18.1 million letter of credit used to collateralize a $17 million loan from the Export-Import Bank of the United States (Export-Import Bank). The highest outstanding principal balance under the facility during fiscal 1990 was $111.9 million, and the weighted-average interest rate was 10.9 percent. At September 30, 1990, $111.9 million was outstanding under the capital-expenditure facility carrying a weighted-average interest rate of 11.25 percent. At September 30, 1990, the principal balance outstanding under the capital-expenditure facility was converted to a four-year term loan due in eight equal semiannual installments beginning in June 1991.

The Company has various interest-rate and period options for Bank Credit Agreement borrowings based on the prime rate (as defined), certificate-of-deposit rates, or Eurodollar rates for 30-, 60-, 90- or 180-day periods. Interest is payable periodically, depending on the Company's selected borrowing option. At September 30, 1990, the Company had available unused credit of $74.3 million under the Bank Credit Agreement. The Company's ability to draw amounts under the Bank Credit Agreement, however, may be limited under certain bank covenants, depending upon the Company's future financial performance and levels of capital spending. All obligations of the Company under the Bank Credit Agreement are secured by liens on substantially all of the Company's assets.

During fiscal 1990, the Company completed amendments of its Bank Credit Agreement, which provided for modification of certain bank covenants, an increase in the interest rate under the facility of ½ of a percentage point and the payment of a fee in connection with the

EXHIBIT 7 • *continued*

amendments of approximately $0.7 million. Subsequent to September 30, 1990, the Company further amended its Bank Credit Agreement. This amendment granted the Company additional flexibility under the Bank Credit Agreement by modifying certain covenants, provided for a ⅜ to ½ percentage point increase in the interest rate under the facility and the payment of a fee in connection with the amendment of approximately $1.5 million.

(b) During fiscal 1990, the Company secured $17 million of 6.5 percent financing from the Export-Import Bank to partially fund construction of a new recovery boiler at its Bogalusa, Louisiana, mill. The principal balance is to be repaid in 16 equal semiannual installments beginning September 15, 1990. The loan was collateralized by an $18.1 million letter of credit, which reduces the amount available under the Company's $130 million capital-expenditure facility by an equal amount. At September 30, 1990, $17.0 million of such letter of credit was outstanding.

A fee of 2 percent per annum is paid on the outstanding face amount of the letter of credit. At September 30, 1990, in connection with an amendment to the Bank Credit Agreement, such fee was increased to 3 percent per annum. At September 30, 1990, $15.9 million was outstanding under the Export-Import Bank loan.

(c) As part of the Fibreboard acquisition, the Company issued to Fibreboard two $5 million notes payable March 1991 and 1996. Interest is payable at 10 percent per annum in quarterly installments. The Company also issued to Fiberboard approximately $22 million in notes that contain repayment terms and interest rates substantially the same as pollution control bonds partially secured by assets that were acquired. At September 30, 1990, $9.4 million of such notes bearing interest at 6.625 percent and $4.8 million bearing interest at 85.56 percent of the prime rate (as defined) were outstanding. At September 30, 1990, and for fiscal 1990, the weighted-average interest rate on the variable-rate notes was 8.6 percent.

(d) The pollution control and industrial revenue bonds were assumed by the Company from Crown Zellerbach Corporation. The Company also acquired a note receivable from Crown Zellerbach for an identical amount and with repayment terms identical to those of the bonds.

(e) The Company issued $250 million principal amount of 13½ percent subordinated notes due 1998 concurrent with the closing of the merger. Interest on the notes is payable semiannually. Commencing June 1991, the notes may be redeemed in whole or in part at the Company's option at redemption prices commencing at 107.75 percent of par value declining to 100 percent of par value at June 1995, plus accrued interest. The Company may not redeem the notes prior to June 1992 using borrowed funds having an effective interest cost less than or equal to 13.5 percent.

(f) The discount subordinated notes, for which the Company received $57 million of proceeds upon issuance, have a face amount of $125.8 million and an effective interest rate of 16.5 percent. No interest is payable until May 1992. Interest is payable semiannually commencing May 1992 at 16.5 percent of the face amount of the notes. Beginning November 1991, the Company may redeem some or all of these notes at declining redemption prices commencing at 105 percent of face amount and declining to 100 percent of face amount at November 1994, plus accrued interest. The notes are subject to mandatory redemption of not less than one-third of the notes outstanding in November 1996 and not less than one-half the remaining notes outstanding in November 1997.

(g) The subordinated notes bearing interest at 13.5 percent, payable semiannually. The Company may redeem these notes under substantially the same terms as the discount subordinated notes. However, no mandatory redemption is required prior to maturity.

(h) In August 1989, the Company issued $150 million principal amount of 13¾ percent subordinated debentures due 2001. Under certain circumstances, in the event the Company incurs indebtedness in connection with certain acquisitions, holders of debentures will be entitled to require the Company to repurchase the debentures at 108

EXHIBIT 7 • *continued*

percent of par value commencing August 1989 and declining to 100 percent of par value at August 1997. Commencing August 1994, the debentures may be redeemed in whole or in part at the Company's option at redemption prices commencing at 105 percent of par value and declining to 100 percent of par value at August 1997, plus accrued interest. Interest on the notes is payable semiannually.

The Company neither declared nor paid dividends on its Class A common stock or Class B common stock during fiscal 1990, fiscal 1989, or fiscal 1988. The Company does not currently intend to pay cash dividends on the Class A common stock or the Class B common stock, but intends instead to retain future earnings for reinvestment in the business and for repayment of debt.

The Company has restrictions on the size of dividend payments, mergers, and sales of assets, and transactions with affiliates under the terms of the debt agreements referred to in (a), (e), (f), (g), and (h) above. Under the most restrictive agreement, the Bank Credit Agreement, as of September 30, 1990, the Company may declare or pay cash dividends or distributions, or purchase or redeem its capital stock, up to an aggregate amount of $250,000. The Company must also meet specified financial covenants under the terms of the debt agreement referred to in (a).

Such covenants include, but are not limited to, net worth, current ratio, interest coverage ratio, and indebtedness ratio.

Source: 1990 Annual Report, pp. 22–23.

Gaylord Container Corporation
EXHIBIT 8 • Financial Statement Footnotes on Leases

The Company has capital leases for certain buildings and equipment included in Property, net. The present value of future minimum lease payments relating to these leased assets are capitalized based on the lease contract provisions. Capitalized amounts are amortized over either and lives of the leases or the normal depreciable lives of the assets. All other leases are defined as operating leases. Lease expenses related to operating leases are charged to expense as incurred.

Future minimum lease payments at September 30, 1990, are as follows (in millions):

Fiscal Year	Operating Leases	Capital Leases
1991	$ 4.4	$0.4
1992	3.3	0.4
1993	2.1	0.4
1994	1.8	0.2
1995	1.7	0
1996 and thereafter	7.4	0
Total future minimum lease payments	$20.7	1.4
Less interest		0.2
Present value of future minimum lease payments		$1.2

Rent expense for fiscal 1988 and fiscal 1989 and fiscal 1990 was $2.7 million, $4.5 million, and $4.8 million, respectively.

Source: 1990 Annual Report, p. 25.

Gaylord Container Corporation
EXHIBIT 9 • Analysis of Debt Securities

Plant asset values cover the book value of the total debt.	Implied Value Range (in millions)	
	Low	High
Debt at Book Value		
Total value of assets	$825	$1000
Plus net working capital[a]	42	42
Less book value of total debt @ 100% of book value [a]	739	739
Less cash [a]	6	6
Unlevered value of assets	$122	$ 297
Value of assets/Book value of total debt	1.1×	1.4×
Debt at Estimated Market Value[b]		
Total levered value of assets	$825	$1000
Plus net working capital[a]	42	42
Less market value of total debt[b]	394	394
Less cash[a]	6	6
Unlevered value of assets	$467	$ 642
Value of assets/Adjusted value of total debt	2.1×	2.5×

[a]As estimated by management as of September 30, 1990, in projections.

[b]Estimated value for illustrative purposes only. Private debt valued at face. All public debt valued at 37 percent of face.

Gaylord Container Corporation
EXHIBIT 10 • Selected Transactions in the Paper Industry (dollars in millions)

Date Announced	Target	Acquiror	Value of Offer for Equity	Unlevered Value of Offer	Value of Offer for Equity as a Multiple of:		Unlevered Value of Offer as a Multiple of:				
					Book	Net Income	Sales	EBIT	Peak 5-Yr. EBIT	EBITD	Net Assets
01/30/91	G-P Tomahwk Mill	PCA/Tenneco	NA	$ 200	NA	NA	0.5E	5.7E	3.1E	4.7E	2.5E
01/30/91	G-P Valdosta Mill	PCA/Tenneco	NA	220	NA	NA	0.3E	9.9E	4.7E	7.3E	2.7E
10/31/89	Great Northern Nekoosa	Georgia Pacific	$3,700	$5,118	2.1X	11.5X	1.3X	7.8X	7.4X	6.0X	1.5X
08/07/89	Jefferson Smurfit Corp.	Investor Group	1,638	1,832	4.4	11.1	1.4	8.4	8.0	7.2	2.6
04/20/89	CIP Inc. (Canadian Pacific)	Great Lakes Forest Products Ltd.	1,087	1,332	1.1	7.5	0.7	4.0	4.0	3.0	0.9
01/27/89	Consolidated-Bathurst, Inc.	Stone Container Corp.	2,607	3,011	2.5	11.2	1.3	7.8	7.8	5.9	1.5
08/23/88	Brunswick Pulp & Paper Company	Georgia-Pacific Corp.	535	665	4.3	33.2	2.1	16.0	15.7	9.2	2.1
07/01/88	Fort Howard Corp.	Morgan Stanley and mgmt.	3,577	4,051	2.7	22.5	2.3	12.9	12.7	9.1	2.0
03/29/88	Container Products Division	Gaylord Container Ltd.	156	156	1.5	25.1	1.2	16.6	14.3	13.1	1.5
01/14/88	Paperboard Industries Corp.	Kinbum Corporation	157	406	1.4	27.0	0.9	10.0	N.Ap.	7.5	1.0
10/16/87	Rexham Corp.	Bowater Industries plc	235	310	2.9	23.1	1.1	15.5	14.8	10.6	1.8
07/17/87	01 Forest Products FTS (KKR)	Great Northern Nekoosa Corp.	1,150	1,187	2.7	20.9	1.8	12.2	12.2	9.4	2.5
06/01/87	Georgia Kraft Inc.	Macon Kraft Inc. (Pratt Group)	272	272	2.4	25.1	1.4	9.1	N.Ap.	6.6	N.Ap.
11/18/86	Ampad Corp.	The Mead Corporation	93	172	2.8	24.8	1.3	16.3	15.9	12.7	1.9
10/03/86	Gaylord Container Ltd.	Investor Group	260	260	0.8	N.Ap.	0.7	16.5	10.5	7.3	0.8
09/11/86	Southwest Forest Industries, Inc.	Stone Container Corp.	434	712	2.0	N.Ap.	1.1	16.9	13.1	9.5	1.3
08/08/86	Hammermill Paper Company	International Paper Co.	1,093	1,466	1.9	25.0	0.8	19.3	12.8	10.9	1.3
07/25/86	Container Corp. of America (Mobil Corp.)	Morgan Stanley and Jefferson Smurfit	968	1,143	1.2	23.6	0.6	15.3	9.0	6.9	0.8
04/30/86	Lily-Tulip, Inc.	Fort Howard Paper Co.	327	381	3.0	15.1	1.2	9.6	7.6	7.9	2.1

Date	Acquirer	Target								
02/21/86	Jefferson Smurfit Corp.	Publishers Paper Co. (Times Mirror)	$163	$167	1.1X	11.7X	0.4X	5.1X	5.1X	2.8X	0.6X
02/04/86	Temple-Inland Inc.	Assets of Owens-Illinois Inc.	220	221	1.5	N.Ap.	1.3	N.Ap.	N.Ap.	N.Ap.	1.4
10/01/85	Stone Container	Assets of Champion International	426	462	1.1	N.Ap.	0.7	N.Ap.	24.6	N.Ap.	1.1
09/26/85	Citicorp Capital Investors and mgmt.	Papercraft Corp.	234	241	2.0	15.9	1.4	8.1	6.8	7.3	2.3
07/01/85	Chesapeake Corp.	Wisconsin Tissue Mills, Inc.	210	226	1.4	18.6	1.1	10.4	10.4	6.7	1.1
04/05/85	James River Corp.	Crown Zellerbach Corp. core business	695	1,288	1.7	13.1	0.5	8.7	N.Ap.	5.7	1.1
11/12/84	Federal Paper Board Company, Inc.	Kiewit-Murdoch Paperboard	305	378	1.5	N.Ap.	1.2	21.2	21.2	10.0	1.7
08/01/84	Champion International Corp.	St. Regis Corp.	2,010	2,872	1.4	18.7	1.0	12.9	9.3	8.6	1.1
08/18/83	Stone Container	Assets of Continental Forest Industries	390	510	1.2	N.Ap.	1.0	N.Ap.	N.Ap.	N.Ap.	1.1
06/27/83	Fort Howard Paper Co.	Maryland Paper Cup Corp.	575	633	2.2	17.5	1.0	10.5	10.5	7.8	1.8
05/10/83	Assets of Diamond Int'l Corp.	James River Corp.	171	171	1.1	36.8	0.9	22.8	N.Ap.	8.8	1.2
02/18/82	Assets of American Can Co.	James River Corp.	432	441	1.2	8.5	0.4	4.6	4.5	3.7	1.3
12/02/81	Diamond International Corp.	Generale Occidentale Investment Co.	$658	$811	1.3X	N.Ap.	0.8X	21.5X	8.3X	9.8X	1.2X

E = estimate; N. Ap. = not applicable.

Gaylord Container Corporation

Appendix • Competitor Information from *Value Line*

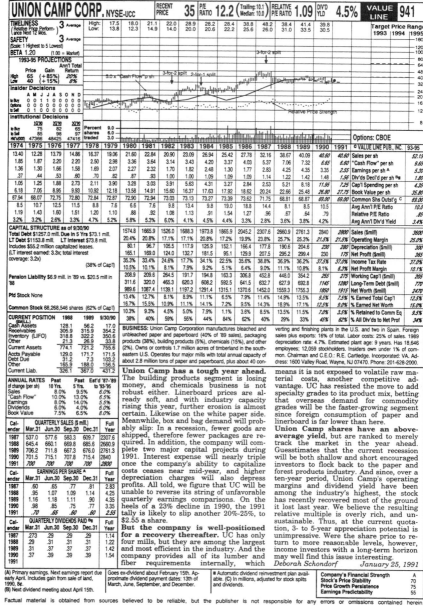

Source: *Value Line.*

Appendix • *Gaylord Container Corporation continued*

CHESAPEAKE CORP. NYSE-CSK	RECENT PRICE 13	P/E RATIO 19.4 (Trailing: 10.6 / Median: 12.0)	RELATIVE P/E RATIO 1.73	DIV'D YLD 5.5%	VALUE LINE 922

| TIMELINESS 4 Below Average | High: | 8.5 | 9.5 | 13.3 | 9.8 | 13.5 | 13.2 | 13.1 | 18.4 | 26.6 | 21.9 | 24.1 | 21.5 | | Target Price Range 1993 1994 1995 |
| (Relative Price Perform-ance Next 12 Mos.) | Low: | 5.2 | 5.5 | 8.3 | 6.3 | 9.2 | 10.4 | 10.7 | 12.7 | 14.3 | 16.4 | 17.9 | 12.6 | | |

SAFETY 3 Average
(Scale: 1 Highest to 5 Lowest)

BETA 1.15 (1.00 = Market)

1993-95 PROJECTIONS
	Price	Gain	Ann'l Total Return
High	40	(+210%)	35%
Low	25	(+90%)	21%

Insider Decisions
	A	M	J	J	A	S	O	N	D
to Buy	0	1	0	0	0	0	0	0	0
Options	0	0	0	3	1	0	0	0	
to Sell	0	1	0	0	0	0	0	0	0

Institutional Decisions
	1Q90	2Q90	3Q90
to Buy	12	11	10
to Sell	18	16	10
Hld's(000)	9458	9531	9659

| Percent shares traded | 6.0 4.0 2.0 |

5.0 x "Cash Flow"p sh
2-for-1 split
3-for-2 split
2-for-1 split
Relative Price Strength
Options: None
© VALUE LINE PUB., INC. 93-95

1974	1975	1976	1977	1978	1979	1980	1981	1982	1983	1984	1985	1986	1987	1988	1989	1990	1991		
8.50	8.03	9.08	9.19	10.12	12.70	14.01	15.04	12.65	13.85	17.65	22.64	29.58	33.07	34.80	39.54	42.70	45.10	Sales per sh	55.00
1.49	1.23	1.40	1.36	1.72	2.01	2.20	1.43	1.49	2.24	2.40	2.86	3.79	4.67	4.64	3.85	4.30	"Cash Flow" per sh	6.80
.94	.62	.70	.62	.46	1.03	1.28	1.41	.43	.44	.98	.79	.68	1.53	2.51	2.31	.90	1.00	Earnings per sh A	3.05
.22	.20	.22	.23	.24	.27	.30	.33	.36	.37	.39	.43	.43	.46	.52	.72	.72	.72	Div'ds Decl'd per sh B ■	.85
.87	1.07	1.98	1.82	1.11	.96	1.41	3.40	1.82	1.42	2.37	4.55	2.13	1.90	3.50	6.48	6.35	5.10	Cap'l Spending per sh	3.75
4.60	5.01	5.48	5.86	6.07	6.72	7.71	8.76	8.83	9.22	9.94	10.32	10.61	11.68	13.66	15.27	15.10	15.25	Book Value per sh C	21.75
16.21	16.31	16.42	16.52	17.32	18.27	18.41	18.79	18.96	19.77	19.84	20.06	20.27	20.44	20.44	20.56	20.50	20.50	Common Shs Outst'g D	20.00
3.8	6.0	6.9	7.8	12.9	6.7	6.1	7.3	18.5	24.8	11.7	15.2	21.8	13.8	7.6	9.2	19.5		Avg Ann'l P/E Ratio	11.0
.53	.80	.88	1.02	1.76	.97	.81	.89	2.04	2.10	1.09	1.23	1.48	.92	.63	.70	1.46		Relative P/E Ratio	.90
6.2%	5.5%	4.6%	4.8%	4.0%	3.9%	3.9%	3.2%	4.5%	3.4%	3.4%	3.6%	2.9%	2.2%	2.7%	3.4%	4.1%		Avg Ann'l Div'd Yield	2.5%

CAPITAL STRUCTURE as of 9/30/90

	257.8	282.6	239.9	273.8	350.2	454.1	599.8	675.7	711.3	813.1	875	925	Sales ($mill)	1100
Total Debt $381.9 mill. Due In 5 Yrs $55.2 mill.	21.4%	17.2%	12.9%	13.4%	17.4%	14.5%	14.8%	18.5%	20.7%	18.5%	13.7%	14.8%	Operating Margin	18.5%
LT Debt $378.2 mill. LT Interest $35.5 mill.	13.6	15.2	19.0	20.9	24.4	32.5	44.2	45.9	44.0	47.9	60.0	68.0	Depreciation ($mill)	75.0
Includes $50.9 million capitalized leases.	23.5	26.2	8.1	8.5	20.1	15.7	13.7	31.5	51.5	47.6	18.5	20.5	Net Profit ($mill)	61.0
(LT interest earned: 2.0x; Total interest coverage:	43.1%	23.7%	9.0%	32.5%	40.2%	8.2%	37.4%	45.2%	38.8%	39.4%	42.0%	42.0%	Income Tax Rate	39.5%
1.9x)	9.1%	9.3%	3.4%	3.1%	5.7%	3.5%	2.3%	4.7%	7.2%	5.9%	2.1%	2.2%	Net Profit Margin	5.5%
(54% of Cap'l)	42.3	43.4	42.8	41.8	46.2	63.4	76.0	68.5	99.6	98.3	105	105	Working Cap'l ($mill)	100
Leases, Uncapitalized Annual rentals $4.0 mill.	40.1	67.1	70.3	51.8	60.7	308.8	302.6	225.5	231.8	301.1	370	400	Long-Term Debt ($mill)	325
Pension Liability None	141.9	164.7	167.5	182.3	197.2	207.0	215.2	238.6	279.2	314.1	310	315	Net Worth ($mill)	435
	13.7%	12.2%	4.6%	4.8%	8.8%	4.4%	5.4%	9.6%	12.2%	10.0%	5.5%	5.0%	% Earned Total Cap'l	10.0%
Pfd Stock None	16.5%	15.9%	4.8%	4.7%	10.2%	7.6%	6.4%	13.2%	18.4%	15.2%	6.0%	6.5%	% Earned Net Worth	14.0%
	12.7%	12.2%	.8%	.7%	6.3%	3.6%	2.4%	9.3%	14.8%	10.7%	1.0%	2.0%	% Retained to Comm Eq	10.0%
Common Stock 20,508,644 shares (46% of Cap'l)	23%	24%	84%	85%	38%	53%	63%	30%	20%	29%	80%	72%	% All Div'ds to Net Prof	28%

CURRENT POSITION
($mill.)	1988	1989	9/30/90
Cash Assets	1.1	.5	.4
Receivables	75.0	88.8	98.9
Inventory (LIFO)	87.3	91.0	86.6
Other	2.0	3.3	6.6
Current Assets	165.4	183.6	192.5
Accts Payable	55.6	67.6	78.3
Debt Due	3.0	4.7	3.7
Other	7.2	13.0	5.3
Current Liab.	65.8	85.3	87.3

ANNUAL RATES
of change (per sh)	Past 10 Yrs.	Past 5 Yrs.	Est'd '87-'89 to '93-'95
Sales	13.0%	19.5%	7.5%
"Cash Flow"	11.5%	20.5%	7.5%
Earnings	11.5%	28.0%	6.0%
Dividends	9.0%	8.5%	7.0%
Book Value	8.0%	7.5%	8.0%

QUARTERLY SALES ($ mill.)
Cal-endar	Mar.31	Jun.30	Sep.30	Dec.31	Full Year
1987	155.5	175.0	179.4	165.8	675.7
1988	161.3	184.7	184.4	176.9	711.3
1989	188.0	213.4	205.7	206.0	813.1
1990	203.6	222.8	215.9	232.7	875
1991	215	225	235	250	925

EARNINGS PER SHARE A
Cal-endar	Mar.31	Jun.30	Sep.30	Dec.31	Full Year
1987	.18	.35	.32	.68	1.53
1988	.48	.58	.70	.75	2.51
1989	.63	.58	.60	.50	2.31
1990	.22	.36	.15	.17	.90
1991	.15	.20	.30	.35	1.00

QUARTERLY DIVIDENDS PAID B ■
Cal-endar	Mar.31	Jun.30	Sep.30	Dec.31	Full Year
1987	.11	.11	.12	.12	.46
1988	.12	.12	.14	.14	.52
1989	.14	.14	.18	.18	.68
1990	.18	.18	.18	.18	.72
1991					

BUSINESS: Chesapeake Corp. manufactures kraft paper, paper-board, corrugating medium, and bleached hardwood market pulp. Also produces commercial and industrial tissue products. Owns 368,000 acres of timberland near its West Point, Virginia, mill. Owns 11 converting plants that produce corrugated containers. Bought tissue and coated paper mills, 7/85. Sold coated paper mill, 12/87. Also sells lumber and plywood. 1989 depreciation rate: 5.4%. Estimated plant age: 7 years; labor costs: 20% of sales. Has 4,945 employees; 7,387 shareholders. Insiders control approxi-mately 18.2% of common. Chairman: Sture G. Olsson. President and C.E.O.: J. Carter Fox. Incorporated: Virginia. Address: 1021 East Cary Street, Richmond, VA 23218. Telephone: 804-697-1000.

Chesapeake shares are an above-average three- to five-year choice for risk-tolerant investors. Over the haul to 1993-95, we believe the company's efforts to upgrade its product mix toward higher value-added specialty grades will pay off in higher and more stable sales and earn-ings. The higher cash flows which result will enable Chesapeake to pay down debt to a more manageable level. For the pres-ent, however, the company's leveraged bal-ance sheet, higher-than-average beta, and low Financial Strength rating are all rea-sons for caution. In addition, the stock is trading at an abnormally high relative multiple which we doubt can be sustained. This equity is not a timely selection for the coming six to twelve months.
Although the first half of 1991 will be difficult, Chesapeake will probably report favorable second half com-parisons. Last year's performance was hampered by weakening prices for many products, recurring operating difficulties, a steep increase in non-cash charges and a higher effective tax rate. Accordingly, earnings declined about 60% despite a modest sales gain. This year, each busi-

ness line is feeling pressure from the weaker economic environment. In addi-tion, depreciation will rise again, as will interest expense. And prices for the com-pany's commodity kraft products may erode further. Nevertheless, we think the following factors will outweigh these nega-tives: First, last year's start-up of a new tissue and converting operation boosted Chesapeake's capacity of this relatively recession-resistant grade. Second, since the company now provides its own lower-cost tissue to the converting operation, segment margins ought to widen. Third, the company continues to improve its pro-duct mix by emphasizing specialty grades of bleached top linerboard, and point-of-sale displays. And finally, the company believes that the operating difficulties which plagued results last year are now behind it. All told, we think Chesapeake's earnings will advance about 10%.
Deborah Schondorf January 25, 1991

CASH POSITION
	5-Year Av'g	9/30/90
Current Assets to Current Liabilities	240%	220%
Cash & Equiv's to Current Liabilities	4%	.5%
Working Capital to Sales	13%	12%

(A) Primary earnings. Excludes nonrecurring gain: 1984, 16¢; loss from discontinued opera-tions: 1987, (6¢). Next earnings report due late April.

(B) Next dividend meeting about April 15th. Goes ex-dividend about April 30th. Approxi-mate dividend payment dates: 15th of Febru-ary, May, August, and November.

■ Dividend reinvestment plan available.
(C) Includes intangibles. In 1989: $37.5 million, $1.82/share.
(D) In millions, adjusted for stock splits.

Company's Financial Strength	C++
Stock's Price Stability	60
Price Growth Persistence	50
Earnings Predictability	40

Factual material is obtained from sources believed to be reliable, but the publisher is not responsible for any errors or omissions contained herein.

Source: *Value Line.*

Appendix • *Gaylord Container Corporation continued*

| GAYLORD CONTAINER ASE-GCR | RECENT PRICE 3.0 | P/E RATIO NMF | (Trailing: NMF / Median: NMF) | RELATIVE P/E RATIO NMF | DIV'D YLD Nil | VALUE LINE 954 |

			High:	22.0	15.8	9.3		Target Price Range
TIMELINESS 4 Below Average			Low:	12.0	7.3	2.5		1993	1994	1995

TIMELINESS 4 Below Average (Relative Price Performance Next 12 Mos.)
SAFETY 5 Lowest (Scale: 1 Highest to 5 Lowest)
BETA 1.35 (1.00 = Market)

1993-95 PROJECTIONS

	Price	Gain	Ann'l Total Return
High	20	(+565%)	60%
Low	10	(+235%)	35%

Insider Decisions

	A	M	J	J	A	S	O	N	D
to Buy	2	1	3	0	0	0	1	0	1
Options	0	0	0	0	0	0	0	0	0
to Sell	0	0	0	0	0	0	0	0	0

Institutional Decisions

	1Q'90	2Q'90	3Q'90
to Buy	8	3	4
to Sell	6	4	11
Hld's(000)	1916	1747	1629

Percent shares traded 6.0 / 4.0 / 2.0

In November '86, Gaylord Container formed its business through the acquisition of 3 containerboard/paper mills, 17 corrugated plants, a specialty chemicals facility and a cogeneration facility for roughly $260 million. (Operations formerly owned by Crown Zellerbach Corporation.) In March 1988, Gaylord acquired certain assets from Fibreboard Corp. for about $151 million. Next, in a pooling of interests, Gaylord merged with Mid-America Packaging, Inc. At its initial public offering in July 1988, Gaylord issued 3,277,500 shares of Class A Common stock at $20.50 per share.

CAPITAL STRUCTURE as of 9/30/90
Total Debt $766.9 mill. Due in 5 Yrs $180.0 mill.
LT Debt $733.7 mill.   LT Interest $77.0 mill.
Incl. $1.2 mill. capitalized leases.
(Interest not covered)   (83% of Cap'l)
Leases, Uncapitalized Annual rentals $4.4 mill.
Pension Liability $7.2 mill. in '90 vs. none in '89

Pfd Stock None
Common Stock 15,364,773 shs.D   (17% of Cap'l)

CURRENT POSITION

(SMILL.)	1988	1989	9/30/90
Cash Assets	71.8	107.5	13.3
Receivables	90.2	96.2	95.6
Inventory(LIFO)	46.6	43.3	50.7
Other	11.7	21.0	18.8
Current Assets	220.3	268.0	178.4
Accts Payable	49.6	61.2	53.8
Debt Due	11.8	12.0	33.2
Other	77.7	65.4	70.3
Current Liab.	139.1	138.6	157.3

ANNUAL RATES

of change (per sh)	Past 10 Yrs.	Past 5 Yrs.	Est'd '88-'90 to '93-'95
Sales	--	--	5.0%
"Cash Flow"	--	--	7.5%
Earnings	--	--	6.0%
Dividends	--	--	NMF
Book Value	--	--	1.5%

QUARTERLY SALES ($ mill.) A

Fiscal Year Ends	Dec.31	Mar.31	Jun.30	Sep.30	Full Fiscal Year
1987	48.4	121.2	128.7	139.5	437.8
1988	137.7	151.1	188.2	194.2	671.2
1989	182.7	178.0	193.5	191.8	746.0
1990	183	161.5	172.2	201.6	718.3
1991	190	180	190	210	770

EARNINGS PER SHARE A B

Fiscal Year Ends	Dec.31	Mar.31	Jun.30	Sep.30	Full Fiscal Year
1987	.04	.43	.53	.50	1.50
1988	.50	.78	.95	.83	3.06
1989	.57	.38	.69	.63	2.27
1990	.13	d.79	d.43	d.38	d1.47
1991	d.50	d.35	d.30	d.20	d1.35

QUARTERLY DIVIDENDS PAID

Calendar	Mar.31	Jun.30	Sep.30	Dec.31	Full Year
1987					
1988					
1989		NO COMMON DIVIDENDS			
1990		BEING PAID			
1991					

Statistical Array

	1980	1981	1982	1983	1984	1985	1986	1987	1988	1989	1990	1991	© VALUE LINE PUB., INC. 93-95	
Sales per sh A								36.48	43.93	48.90	46.75	50.35	59.50
"Cash Flow" per sh								3.44	5.03	5.61	2.13	3.45	5.95
Earnings per sh B								1.50	3.06	2.27	d1.47	d1.35	1.70
Div'ds Decl'd per sh								--	--	--	--	Nil	Nil
Cap'l Spending per sh								3.79	4.51	11.86	11.24	3.25	4.50
Book Value per sh								3.16	9.24	11.82	9.98	9.15	11.10
Common Shs Outst'g C								12.00	15.28	15.26	15.36	15.30	15.30
Avg Ann'l P/E Ratio								--	6.3	5.3	--		8.0
Relative P/E Ratio								--	.52	.41	--		.65
Avg Ann'l Div'd Yield								--	--	--	--		Nil
Sales ($mill) A								437.8	671.2	746.0	718.3	770	910
Operating Margin								18.4%	20.6%	20.7%	13.6%	14.0%	20.0%
Depreciation ($mill)								23.3	36.3	46.2	55.9	55.0	65.0
Net Profit ($mill)								19.3	41.9	36.1	d23.2	d20.5	26.0
Income Tax Rate								34.1%	27.9%	38.0%	NMF	38.0%	38.0%
Net Profit Margin								4.4%	6.2%	5.3%	NMF	NMF	2.9%
Working Cap'l ($mill)								31.7	81.2	129.4	21.1	25.0	30.0
Long-Term Debt ($mill)								303.1	472.1	623.5	733.7	750	700
Net Worth ($mill)								57.2	141.1	180.3	153.3	140	170
% Earned Total Cap'l								5.4%	10.4%	7.6%	1.7%	2.0%	7.0%
% Earned Net Worth								37.0%	29.7%	20.0%	NMF	15.5%	15.5%
% Retained to Comm Eq								47.5%	28.8%	20.0%	NMF	NMF	15.5%
% All Div'ds to Net Prof								7%	3%	--	--	Nil	Nil

BUSINESS: Gaylord Container Corp. is a major producer of paperboard and corrugated containers. 1989 production: Containerboard, 935,100 tons; Corrugated shipments, 10.2 billion square feet; Unbleached kraft paper, 251,800 tons; Multiwall bag shipments, 179.4 million. Also manufactures specialty chemicals. Has 3 containerboard and paper mills, 16 corrugated container plants, 5 corrugated sheet plants, 2 multiwall bag plants, 3 grocery bag and sack plants, a specialty chemicals facility and a cogeneration facility. '90 deprec. rate: 5.7%. Has about 4,100 empls.; 578 shrhldrs. of record. Insiders control about 55% of voting power; Grinnell College, about 32%. Chairman and CEO: M.A. Pomerantz. Inc.: DE. Address: 500 Lake Cook Road, Ste. 400, Deerfield, IL 60015. Tel.: 708-405-5500.

Gaylord's recovery is going to take longer than expected. The company is unlikely to post profits during any quarter of fiscal 1991 (began October 1st), although the largest losses probably occurred in the December interim. During this past three-month stretch, scheduled downtime for maintenance took place at Gaylord's two largest plants. Although each plant must routinely close down one week a year for upkeep, these two particular shutdowns usually don't occur in the same quarter. Our feeling is that Gaylord could have delayed one of these work stoppages if the additional capacity was needed. This, apparently, is not the case, since containerboard prices are still at depressed levels and have shown no clear signs of recovery. In addition, the company's largest linerboard machines will likely not be operating at peak efficiency for another six to nine months. And Gaylord is currently shouldering a heavy debt burden incurred to fund its recently completed $300 million modernization program. Add a U.S. economic recession to these company-specific and industry-wide problems and perhaps it's well that management elected to suffer the plant shutdowns sooner rather than later. We do expect that Gaylord's losses will moderate throughout the current fiscal year, but still think that it will post a $1.35 per share full-year loss followed by a smaller loss in fiscal 1992.

Gaylord's shares will likely lag the year-ahead market. This equity has fallen about 15% since our last report three months ago, while the market has risen roughly 5%. Until Gaylord turns profitable, most investors should look elsewhere. **Over a 3- to 5-year time horizon, however, these very risky shares have superior price appreciation potential.** The expected improvement in Gaylord's operating efficiencies should pave the way for an earnings and share-price recovery, provided that the economy resumes normal growth and containerboard prices rebound from their depressed levels.
Robert M. Egan   *January 25, 1991*

CASH POSITION

	5-Year Av'g	9/30/90
Current Assets to Current Liabilities:	NA	113%
Cash & Equiv's to Current Liabilities:	NA	8%
Working Capital to Sales:	NA	3%

(A) Fiscal year ends Sept. 30th. Fiscal 1987 was from Nov. 18, 1986 through Sept. 27, 1987. (B) Primary earnings. Excludes gain on asset sale: 1989, 21¢. Next earnings report due early Feb. (C) In mill. (D) Includes approx. 6 million shares of Class B Common stock; remainder is Class A Common Stock. Class B stockholders are entitled to 10 votes per share, and elect 75% of Gaylord's directors. Class A stockholders are entitled to one vote per share and elect 25% of Gaylord's directors.

Company's Financial Strength C+
Stock's Price Stability 15
Price Growth Persistence NMF
Earnings Predictability NMF

Factual material is obtained from sources believed to be reliable, but the publisher is not responsible for any errors or omissions contained herein.

Source: *Value Line.*

Appendix • *Gaylord Container Corporation continued*

GEORGIA-PACIFIC NYSE-GP | RECENT PRICE **38** | P/E RATIO **13.7** (Trailing: 7.1 Median: 12.0) | RELATIVE P/E RATIO **1.22** | DIV'D YLD **4.5%** | VALUE LINE **926**

TIMELINESS 3 Average	High:	30.4	34.9	32.4	31.9	25.8	27.4	41.3	52.8	62.0	52.1			Target Price Range
(Relative Price Performance Next 12 Mos.)	Low:	23.5	21.5	17.8	13.3	22.4	18.0	20.5	24.8	22.8	30.8	36.6	25.4	1993 1994 1995

SAFETY 3 Average (Scale: 1 Highest to 5 Lowest)
BETA 1.30 (1.00 = Market)

1993-95 PROJECTIONS
Ann'l Total
Price Gain Return
High 110 (+190%) 33%
Low 70 (+85%) 19%

Insider Decisions
	A	M	J	J	A	S	O	N	D
to Buy	0	1	1	0	0	0	0	0	0
Options	1	0	0	0	1	0	0	0	0
to Sell	0	0	0	1	0	1	0	1	0

Institutional Decisions
	1Q'90	2Q'90	3Q'90
to Buy	107	111	77
to Sell	115	117	142
Hld's(000)	55442	54193	55765

Percent shares traded: 9.0 6.0 3.0

Options: PHLE
© VALUE LINE PUB., INC.

1974	1975	1976	1977	1978	1979	1980	1981	1982	1983	1984	1985	1986	1987	1988	1989	1990	1991		93-95
26.14	25.07	29.59	35.77	42.84	52.81	50.77	54.72	53.31	63.72	65.17	65.06	67.29	82.14	100.27	117.35	149.20	164.00	Sales per sh	203.35
3.09	3.00	3.57	4.25	4.83	5.54	5.05	4.29	3.88	5.43	5.09	4.90	5.56	7.67	9.67	13.56	12.15	13.05	"Cash Flow" per sh	18.00
1.76	1.57	2.12	2.54	2.93	3.12	2.34	1.51	.48	1.81	2.28	1.83	2.51	3.86	4.76	7.42	4.05	2.95	Earnings per sh A	7.45
.48	.50	.70	.83	1.03	1.13	1.20	1.20	1.05	.60	.70	.79	.80	1.05	1.25	1.45	1.60	1.70	Div'ds Decl'd per sh B■	1.95
3.28	2.62	2.79	4.36	4.68	8.27	5.91	6.81	2.57	2.54	5.61	6.00	3.97	5.65	7.50	5.69	10.35	6.85	Cap'l Spending per sh	8.00
9.64	10.92	13.17	14.88	16.79	18.19	19.32	19.47	19.63	19.48	19.58	20.59	22.70	25.59	27.78	31.35	33.80	35.00	Book Value per sh	50.00
93.07	94.08	102.66	102.75	102.77	98.61	98.79	98.94	101.34	101.52	102.53	103.23	107.35	104.74	94.84	86.67	86.80	87.85	Common Shs Outst'g C	90.00
11.6	16.2	15.6	11.7	9.2	8.7	11.6	16.6	38.3	14.5	9.7	12.9	13.2	11.0	7.8	6.5	9.0		Avg Ann'l P/E Ratio	12.0
1.62	2.16	2.00	1.53	1.25	1.26	1.54	2.02	4.22	1.23	.90	1.05	.90	.74	.65	.52	.75		Relative P/E Ratio	1.00
2.4%	2.0%	2.1%	3.8%	3.8%	4.1%	4.4%	4.8%	5.7%	3.2%	3.3%	4.0%	2.4%	2.5%	3.4%	3.0%	3.9%		Avg Ann'l Div'd Yield	2.2%

CAPITAL STRUCTURE as of 9/30/90

Total Debt $6669.0 mill. Due in 5 Yrs $525.0 mill.
LT Debt $5790.0 mill. LT Interest $720.0 mill.
Incl. $129.0 mill. capitalized leases.
(LT interest earned: 2.0x; total interest coverage: 1.9x) (66% of Cap'l)

Pension Liability None
Pfd Stock None.
Common Stock 86,703,000 shs. (34% of Cap'l)

CURRENT POSITION 1988 1989 9/30/90
(SMILL)
	1988	1989	9/30/90
Cash Assets	62.0	23.0	42.0
Receivables	905.0	890.0	430.0
Inventory (LIFO)	892.0	876.0	1223.0
Other	33.0	40.0	60.0
Current Assets	1892.0	1829.0	1755.0
Accts Payable	404.0	394.0	585.0
Debt Due	318.0	210.0	879.0
Other	291.0	320.0	552.0
Current Liab.	1013.0	924.0	2016.0

5016.0	5414.0	5402.0	6469.0	6682.0	6716.0	7223.0	8603.0	9509.0	10171	12850	14400	Sales ($mill)	18300
13.9%	11.7%	9.9%	12.3%	12.2%	10.9%	12.9%	14.4%	15.0%	18.3%	14.5%	14.0%	Operating Margin	14.5%
267.0	277.0	356.0	371.0	282.0	310.0	339.0	387.0	450.0	514.0	705	890	Depreciation ($mill)	955
244.0	160.0	52.0	195.0	253.0	207.0	277.0	418.0	467.0	661.0	350	255	Net Profit ($mill)	605
30.9%	30.4%	22.4%		36.1%	33.0%	38.7%	42.9%	40.0%	39.2%	48.0%	48.0%	Income Tax Rate	44.0%
4.9%	3.0%	1.0%	3.0%	3.8%	3.1%	3.8%	4.9%	4.9%	6.5%	2.7%	1.8%	Net Profit Margin	3.6%
425.0	429.0	552.0	771.0	733.0	660.0	583.0	733.0	879.0	905.0	650	720	Working Cap'l ($mill)	915
1227.0	1487.0	1618.0	1453.0	1383.0	1257.0	893.0	1298.0	2514.0	2336.0	6100	6000	Long-Term Debt ($mill)	5000
2078.0	2129.0	2198.0	2228.0	2225.0	2303.0	2565.0	2680.0	2635.0	2717.0	2935	3080	Net Worth ($mill)	4345
8.7%	6.5%	3.4%	7.3%	9.0%	7.7%	9.9%	12.0%	11.0%	15.6%	7.0%	6.0%	% Earned Total Cap'l	10.0%
11.7%	7.5%	2.4%	8.8%	11.4%	9.0%	10.8%	15.6%	17.7%	24.3%	12.0%	8.5%	% Earned Net Worth	15.5%
6.0%	1.5%	NMF	6.0%	8.4%	5.4%	7.4%	11.3%	13.1%	19.5%	7.0%	3.5%	% Retained to Comm Eq	11.5%
53%	83%	NMF	39%	34%	41%	45%	35%	28%	26%	20%	40%	% All Div'ds to Net Prof	26%

ANNUAL RATES Past Past Est'd '87-'89
of change (per sh) 10 Yrs. 5 Yrs. to '93-'95
	10 Yrs.	5 Yrs.	to '93-'95
Sales	8.5%	5.0%	12.5%
"Cash Flow"	8.0%	8.0%	9.5%
Earnings	6.5%	15.5%	6.0%
Dividends	2.5%	5.0%	7.5%
Book Value	5.5%	5.0%	10.0%

QUARTERLY SALES ($ mill.)
Cal-endar	Mar.31	Jun.30	Sep.30	Dec.31	Full Year
1987	1855	2095	2424	2229	8603.0
1988	2115	2418	2404	2567	9509.0
1989	2447	2640	2646	2438	10171.0
1990	2659	3519	3430	3342	12850
1991	3500	3700	3700	3500	14400

EARNINGS PER SHARE A
Cal-endar	Mar.31	Jun.30	Sep.30	Dec.31	Full Year
1987	.68	1.01	1.10	1.07	3.86
1988	1.02	1.21	1.19	1.34	4.76
1989	1.65	1.90	2.03	1.84	7.42
1990	1.18	1.25	1.11	.51	4.05
1991	.50	.65	1.00	.80	2.95

QUARTERLY DIVIDENDS PAID B■
Cal-endar	Mar.31	Jun.30	Sep.30	Dec.31	Full Year
1987	.25	.25	.25	.30	1.05
1988	.30	.30	.30	.35	1.25
1989	.35	.35	.35	.40	1.45
1990	.40	.40	.40	.40	1.60
1991					

BUSINESS: Georgia-Pacific Corp. is the world's largest manufacturer of paper (pulp, containerboard, tissue, printing) and wood products (plywood, lumber, particleboard, gypsum). Controls 6.5 million acres of North American timberland (75% in Southeast). Also owns building products distribution centers. Acquired Great Northern Nekoosa (3/90). Amer. Forest Products and Brunswick Pulp & Paper ('88), U.S. Plywood ('87). Sold chemicals operations ('84); oil and gas op's ('85). 1989 deprec. rate: 6.3%. Est'd plant age: 7 years. Has 44,000 employees, 66,000 shareholders. Insiders own 2% of stock. Chairman and C.E.O.: T. Marshall Hahn Jr. President: Ronald P. Hogan. Incorporated: Georgia. Address: 133 Peachtree Street, N.E., Atlanta, Georgia 30303. Tel.: 404-521-5210.

Georgia-Pacific is certainly feeling the recession. The company has always been sensitive to economic fluctuations, due to the nature of its paper and building businesses. But that sensitivity was magnified last year because of the financial leverage that G-P took on in order to implement the $3.8 billion takeover of Great Northern Nekoosa. The company's building products — plywood, lumber and wallboard — have all been hit hard in the economic downturn, but its paper products — especially raw pulp and groundwood — are also suffering reduced demand. G-P's earnings are likely to fall to $2.90-$3.00 a share in 1991, more than 25% behind last year's pace and 60% below the record-high tally of 1989. **The company's cash flow is holding up comparatively well.** G-P will likely report more than $900 million in non-cash expenses this year, including depreciation, depletion, deferred taxes, and amortization of goodwill from the GNN acquisition. In fact, G-P's "cash flow" per share is likely to wind up within 5% of its record $13.56 level of 1989. With capital spending scheduled to be cut this year and with as-

set sales possible, G-P should be able to begin to work down its onerous debt. **G-P's prospects are bright.** The company is a low-cost producer. It is also largely self-sufficient in timber — especially in its Northwestern operations — giving it protection from future logging restrictions. G-P is positioned for a solid earnings recovery when the recession ends, and its stock — which is ranked to pace the market in the year ahead — should produce strong appreciation and an attractive total return over the pull to 1993-95. We note that G-P faces a risk (which we believe to be small) from a multi-billion dollar class action suit alleging that the company's kraft mill in New Augusta, Miss. dumped dioxin and other pollutants into three state rivers. G-P is currently appealing a $1 million verdict in a similar suit.
Ben Sharav *January 25, 1991*

Restated Sales (and Operating Profit Margins*) by Business Line
	1988	1989	1990	1991
Building Prod	8029 (7.1%)	6098 (9.8%)	6250 (7.5%)	6100 (7.0%)
Pulp/paper	3436 (17.9%)	4042 (22.7%)	6850 (14.7%)	6250 (11.5%)
Other	44 (22.7%)	41 (36.6%)	50 (20.0%)	50 (20.0%)
Company Total	9509 (11.1%)	10171 (14.4%)	12850 (11.7%)	14400 (9.5%)
*After depreciation; before corporate expenses.

(A) Primary earnings. Excludes nonrecurring losses: '83, 84¢; '84, $1.31; '85, 29¢; gains: '82, 96¢; '86, 18¢; '87, 44¢. Next earnings report due late January. (B) Next dividend meeting about Feb. 1. Goes ex about Feb. 15. Approx. dividend payment dates: Mar. 12, June 11, Sept. 10, Dec. 5. Plus stock: 2% semi-annually: '74-'77. ■ Dividend reinvestment plan available. (C) In millions, adj. for stock splits and dividends.

Company's Financial Strength B+
Stock's Price Stability 50
Price Growth Persistence 50
Earnings Predictability 55

Factual material is obtained from sources believed to be reliable, but the publisher is not responsible for any errors or omissions contained herein.

Source: *Value Line.*

Appendix • *Gaylord Container Corporation continued*

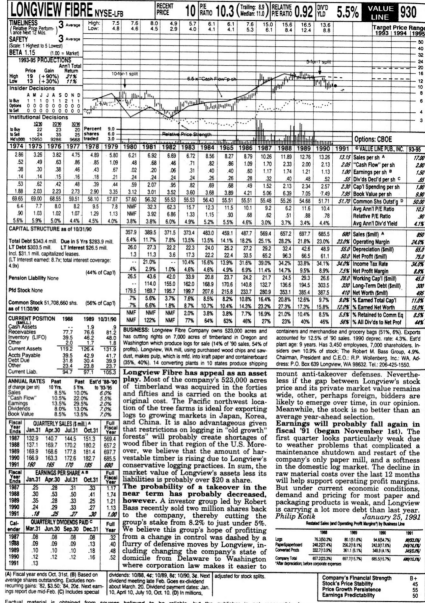

Appendix • *Gaylord Container Corporation continued*

STONE CONTAINER NYSE-STO	RECENT PRICE **9.0**	P/E RATIO **12.0** (Trailing: 3.6 Median: 10.0)	RELATIVE P/E RATIO **1.07**	DIV'D YLD **8.0 4.0 %**	VALUE LINE **939**

| TIMELINESS **4** Below Average (Relative Price Perform-ance Next 12 Mos.) | High: Low: | 5.3 1.9 | 4.8 3.1 | 7.5 3.8 | 8.1 4.2 | 15.0 6.8 | 14.4 8.6 | 39.8 8.0 | 20.0 11.3 | 39.8 15.3 | 39.5 20.7 | 36.4 22.1 | 25.3 8.1 | Target Price Range 1993 1994 1995 |

SAFETY **4** Below Average (Scale: 1 Highest to 5 Lowest)

BETA 1.70 (1.00 = Market)

1993-95 PROJECTIONS

	Price	Gain	Ann'l Total Return
High	55	(+510%)	60%
Low	35	(+290%)	44%

Insider Decisions

	A	M	J	J	A	S	O	N	D
to Buy	0	0	0	0	3	3	2	2	
Options	0	0	1	0	0	0	0	1	
to Sell	0	0	0	0	0	0	2	0	

Institutional Decisions

	1Q90	2Q90	3Q90
to Buy	43	40	30
to Sell	47	41	41
Hld's(000)	26274	25226	24308

| Percent shares traded | 15.0 10.0 5.0 | |

5.0 x "Cash Flow" p sh

3 for 2 split

2-for-1 split

50% div'd   25% div'd

Relative Price Strength

Options: PACE

© VALUE LINE PUB., INC. 93-95

1974	1975	1976	1977	1978	1979	1980	1981	1982	1983	1984	1985	1986	1987	1988	1989	1990	1991		93-95
7.20	7.71	8.88	9.44	10.09	11.47	13.15	14.12	14.59	16.00	30.27	29.54	42.37	54.16	62.42	88.98	95.85	96.65	Sales per sh	120.85
.65	.73	.77	.76	.69	1.03	1.26	1.41	1.22	.75	2.37	1.71	2.55	4.96	7.88	8.42	6.15	5.35	"Cash Flow" per sh	10.75
.50	.41	.43	.36	.24	.54	.74	.83	.49	d.10	.80	.08	.65	2.79	5.40	4.45	1.65	.45	Earnings per sh A	5.00
.05	.07	.09	.11	.11	.11	.13	.17	.20	.20	.20	.20	.20	.25	.36	.72	.72	.72	Div'ds Decl'd per sh B	.90
.35	.47	1.01	.55	.82	.89	1.34	2.33	2.16	.51	1.02	1.13	1.32	2.92	2.28	8.38	8.75	5.00	Cap'l Spending per sh	5.85
2.16	2.50	2.89	3.13	2.94	3.36	3.96	4.59	4.86	6.59	7.18	7.08	8.04	12.40	17.74	22.50	24.90	24.65	Book Value per sh C	33.65
28.20	28.20	28.24	28.32	28.43	28.62	28.83	29.10	29.25	40.99	41.11	41.61	47.96	59.69	59.96	59.90	60.00	60.00	Common Shs Outst'g D	60.00
2.6	3.3	5.7	6.4	9.1	7.8	5.3	6.5	11.0	--	14.1	NMF	24.5	10.2	5.7	6.5	9.8		Avg Ann'l P/E Ratio	9.0
.36	.44	.73	.84	1.24	1.13	.70	.79	1.21	--	1.31	NMF	1.66	.68	.47	.49	.75		Relative P/E Ratio	.75
4.2%	5.2%	3.5%	4.7%	4.9%	2.5%	3.2%	3.2%	3.7%	1.9%	1.8%	2.1%	1.3%	9%	1.2%	2.5%	4.4%		Avg Ann'l Div'd Yield	2.0%

CAPITAL STRUCTURE as of 9/30/90

Total Debt $4112.3 mill. Due in 5 Yrs $2225.0
LT Debt $3641.1 mill. LT Interest $434.0 mill.
Incl. $191.7 mill. capitalized leases; $409.1 mill. in non-recourse debt of affiliates. (LT and total interest coverage: 1.3x) (72% of Cap'l)

Leases, Uncapitalized Annual rentals $51.4 mill.

Pension Liability $70.1 mill in '89 vs. none in '88

Pfd Stock None

Common Stock 60,021,952 shs. (28% of Cap'l)

CURRENT POSITION ($MILL.)	1988	1989	9/30/90
Cash Assets	11.1	22.9	33.1
Receivables	440.6	684.8	723.7
Inventory (FIFO)	368.0	767.0	748.7
Other	46.0	212.3	190.6
Current Assets	865.7	1687.0	1696.1
Accts Payable	178.9	355.9	316.6
Debt Due	15.8	352.4	471.2
Other	231.3	364.3	374.2
Current Liab.	426.0	1072.6	1162.0

ANNUAL RATES of change (per sh)	Past 10 Yrs.	Past 5 Yrs.	Est'd '87-'89 to '93-'95
Sales	21.0%	27.5%	10.0%
"Cash Flow"	24.0%	37.5%	7.0%
Earnings	27.5%	66.5%	3.0%
Dividends	15.5%	17.5%	12.5%
Book Value	19.0%	23.0%	10.5%

Cal-endar	QUARTERLY SALES ($ mill.)				Full Year
	Mar.31	Jun.30	Sep.30	Dec.31	
1987	585.8	830.8	907.5	908.8	3232.9
1988	881.3	858.7	1022.2	980.3	3742.5
1989	1127.4	1379.9	1373.3	1449.1	5329.7
1990	1453.7	1429.8	1426.6	1437.9	5750
1991	1430	1440	1450	1480	5800

Cal-endar	EARNINGS PER SHARE A				Full Year
	Mar.31	Jun.30	Sep.30	Dec.31	
1987	.50	.55	.69	.97	2.79
1988	1.09	1.30	1.48	1.53	5.40
1989	1.45	1.06	.86	1.08	4.45
1990	.61	.49	.33	.22	1.65
1991	.10	.10	.10	.15	.45

Cal-endar	QUARTERLY DIVIDENDS PAID B				Full Year
	Mar.31	Jun.30	Sep.30	Dec.31	
1987	.05	.067	.067	.067	.25
1988	.09	.09	.09	.09	.36
1989	.18	.18	.18	.18	.72
1990	.18	.18	.18	.18	.72
1991					

379.2	411.1	426.6	655.9	1244.4	1229.2	2032.3	3232.9	3742.5	5329.7	5750	5800	Sales ($mill)	7250
14.0%	12.7%	9.6%	7.1%	13.8%	10.4%	11.1%	16.7%	20.6%	18.0%	15.0%	13.5%	Operating Margin	17.0%
15.1	17.3	21.6	34.2	64.4	67.8	92.3	138.7	148.1	237.1	270	295	Depreciation ($mill)	345
21.3	24.0	14.2	d2.9	33.7	3.8	35.4	158.3	324.5	267.1	100	25.0	Net Profit ($mill)	300
36.5%	22.7%	34.0%	--	39.2%	--	40.7%	43.1%	37.8%	40.6%	48.0%	50.0%	Income Tax Rate	43.0%
5.6%	5.8%	3.3%	NMF	2.7%	.3%	1.7%	4.9%	8.7%	5.0%	1.7%	.4%	Net Profit Margin	4.1%
42.4	52.3	53.8	147.9	158.9	155.1	327.1	384.0	439.7	614.4	575	625	Working Cap'l ($mill)	900
68.9	112.6	138.6	548.2	482.8	493.3	767.0	1070.5	765.2	3536.9	3700	3655	Long-Term Debt ($mill)	3000
114.2	133.5	149.6	277.9	303.7	302.7	483.3	741.8	1063.6	1347.6	1495	1480	Net Worth ($mill) C	2020
13.4%	11.5%	7.3%	1.1%	7.5%	4.1%	6.2%	12.0%	20.1%	9.1%	6.0%	5.0%	% Earned Total Cap'l	10.0%
18.7%	18.0%	9.5%	NMF	11.1%	1.2%	7.3%	21.3%	30.5%	19.8%	6.5%	1.5%	% Earned Net Worth	15.0%
15.5%	14.3%	5.9%	NMF	8.5%	NMF	5.4%	19.4%	28.5%	16.6%	4.0%	NMF	% Retained to Comm Eq	12.0%
17%	21%	41%	NMF	26%	NMF	41%	9%	7%	16%	43%	158%	% All Div'ds to Net Prof	18%

BUSINESS: Stone Container is a major producer of paperboard, corrugated containers, paper bags and sacks, newsprint, market pulp and groundwood specialty papers. '89 sales mix: paperboard and paper packaging, 76%; white paper and pulp, 21%; other, 3%. Acquired Consolidated-Bathurst, 3/89; Southwest Forest Industries, 4/87; Trinity Paper & Plastics Corp., 7/88. Has plants in U.S., Canada, Mexico, W. Germany, U.K., and Holland. Foreign operations accounted for 26% of '89 sales; 16% of pretax profits. '89 depreciation rate: 6.0%. Has about 32,600 employees; 5,300 shareholders. Stone family members own about 25% of stock. Chairman, C.E.O. & President: R.W. Stone. Incorporated: Illinois. Address: 150 North Michigan Avenue, Chicago, IL 60601. Telephone: 312-580-4639.

Stone Container's debt burden is coming into sharper focus. Due to worsening conditions in some key businesses, interest expense is now absorbing most of operating profits. What's more, Stone faces a $350 million principal payment in May. In our opinion, it won't be covered by cash flow and funds on hand. Stone might sell some timberland or peripheral assets. Most likely it will tap its credit lines, which had $366 million available as of this writing. The added interest burden, combined with an expected drop in operating profits this year, will make it even more difficult for Stone to dig its way out from under the mountain of debt.

The company is cutting back its capital program. Capital expenditures will fall to about $300 million a year in 1991-92 versus more than $500 million last year. If our earnings estimates and projections are on the mark, operating cash flow will cover these commitments. But Stone will need fresh borrowings to help meet principal obligations of $1.8 billion over the span 1991-94. We would also not rule out the possibility of a dividend cut.

Uncertainties about newsprint pric- ing complicate the '91 earnings picture. Despite sluggish demand and rising capacity, newsprint manufacturers were able to raise prices last June and again in January of '91 because several Canadian mills were on strike in the second half of 1990. Most of that capacity is back on line, however, and demand forecasts are still weak, so it's quite possible that price realizations will start to erode. With other major profit centers being squeezed by flat or falling prices and rising costs, a collapse in newsprint pricing might tip Stone into a loss position for the year.

This untimely equity is suitable only for high-risk accounts. Financial and operating leverage will help propel earnings sharply upward in the next cyclical upswing. But our 1993-95 projections assume Stone will maintain control of all of its assets until then, which is hardly a sure thing.

Philip Kotik   *January 25, 1991*

CASH POSITION	5-Year Av'g	9/30/90
Current Assets to Current Liabilities:	213%	146%
Cash & Equiv's to Current Liabilities:	4%	3%
Working Capital to Sales:	13%	9%

(A) Primary earnings. Excludes extraordinary gain: '84, 8¢. Excludes gain on asset sales: '87, 5¢; '88, 16¢; '89, 31¢. Next earnings report due early Feb. In '87, sum of quarterly earnings does not equal annual total due to change in capitalization. (B) Next dividend meeting May 9. Goes ex-dividend about June 5. Approximate dividend payment dates: March 15, June 15, Sept. 15, Dec. 31. (C) Includes intangibles. In '89: $1.089 billion, $18.18/sh. (D) In millions, adjusted for stock splits and dividends.

Company's Financial Strength	C+
Stock's Price Stability	20
Price Growth Persistence	75
Earnings Predictability	25

Factual material is obtained from sources believed to be reliable, but the publisher is not responsible for any errors or omissions contained herein.

Source: *Value Line.*

Appendix • *Gaylord Container Corporation continued*

TEMPLE-INLAND NYSE-TIN | RECENT PRICE **31** | P/E RATIO **9.1** (Trailing: 7.5 / Median: NMF) | RELATIVE P/E RATIO **0.81** | DIV'D YLD **2.7%** | VALUE LINE **940**

| | High: | 14.4 | 15.1 | 17.8 | 23.7 | 34.3 | 28.3 | 35.5 | 38.6 | | Target Price Range 1993 | 1994 | 1995 |
| Low: | 13.0 | 10.2 | 12.7 | 16.8 | 17.5 | 20.1 | 23.4 | 24.1 |

TIMELINESS 3 Average (Relative Price Perform-ance Next 12 Mos.)

SAFETY 3 Average (Scale: 1 Highest to 5 Lowest)

BETA 1.35 (1.00 = Market)

1993-95 PROJECTIONS

	Price	Gain	Ann'l Total Return
High	65	(+110%)	22%
Low	45	(+45%)	12%

Insider Decisions

	A	M	J	J	A	S	O	N	D
to Buy	0	0	0	0	0	0	0	0	0
Options	0	0	1	1	0	0	0	0	0
to Sell	0	0	0	0	0	0	0	0	0

Institutional Decisions

	1Q'90	2Q'90	3Q'90		
to Buy	59	79	64	Percent	6.0
to Sell	76	56	68	shares	4.0
Hld'g(000)	35929	37352	37467	traded	2.0

Temple-Inland Inc. was formed by Time, Inc. (now Time Warner) to hold the stock of two Time subsidiaries, Temple-Eastex and Inland Container Corp. 90% of Temple-Inland's common stock was spun off to Time shareholders in December 1983. All figures on this page for years prior to 1984, although based on actual data, are not necessarily indicative of Temple-Inland's performance as an independent company, since certain expenses are excluded.

	1980	1981	1982	1983	1984	1985	1986	1987	1988	1989	1990	1991	©VALUE LINE PUB., INC.	93-95
	--	--	--	19.30	20.94	20.56	21.35	28.96	32.15	34.53	*34.90*	*36.35*	Sales per sh A	46.35
	--	--	--	1.86	2.75	2.39	2.64	4.25	5.64	6.09	*6.65*	*5.80*	"Cash Flow" per sh	8.90
	--	--	--	.80	1.70	1.28	1.32	2.35	3.58	3.75	*4.20*	*3.10*	Earnings per sh B	5.50
	--	--	--	.20	.26	.29	.35	.42	.58	.80	*.85*	Div'ds Decl'd per sh C ■	1.40
	--	--	--	.88	2.15	3.04	1.69	2.50	3.97	4.74	*5.90*	*6.35*	Cap'l Spending per sh	5.00
	--	--	--	11.65	13.14	14.29	15.30	16.76	19.86	22.95	*26.25*	*28.55*	Book Value per sh	39.10
	--	--	--	60.19	60.30	60.46	60.70	55.34	55.17	54.85	*55.00*	*55.00*	Common Shs Outst'g D	55.00
	--	--	--	17.2	7.5	11.5	15.8	12.2	6.8	7.8	*7.5*		Avg Ann'l P/E Ratio	10.0
	--	--	--	1.45	.70	.93	1.07	.82	.56	.59	*.55*		Relative P/E Ratio	.85
	--	--	--	--	1.6%	1.7%	1.4%	1.2%	1.7%	2.0%	2.5%		Avg Ann'l Div'd Yield	2.5%

CAPITAL STRUCTURE as of 9/29/90 A

Total Debt $514.6 mill.   Due in 5 Yrs $300.0 mill.
LT Debt $511.4 mill.   LT Interest $43.5 mill.
Incl. $94.3 mill. capitalized leases.
(Total interest coverage: 9.7x)

(27% of Cap'l)

Leases, Uncapitalized Annual rentals $6.6 mill.

Pension Liability None

Pfd Stock None

Common Stock 54,984,114 shs.   (73% of Cap'l)

	1114.2	1096.4	1161.7	1262.9	1423.1	1295.8	1602.7	1773.5	1894.2	*1920*	*2000*	Sales ($mill) A	2550
	14.5%	10.4%	10.0%	16.7%	12.3%	12.7%	20.1%	23.8%	24.3%	*19.5%*	*17.0%*	Operating Margin	20.5%
	53.5	58.9	63.8	63.2	66.7	79.3	93.9	112.1	126.5	*135*	*150*	Depreciation ($mill)	185
	95.1	39.4	48.2	102.7	78.0	80.8	141.4	199.2	207.4	*230*	*170*	Net Profit ($mill)	305
	24.2%	43.3%	38.8%	38.0%	32.9%	28.7%	35.8%	34.0%	34.0%	*13.0%*	*19.0%*	Income Tax Rate	20.0%
	8.5%	3.6%	4.1%	8.1%	6.3%	6.2%	8.8%	11.2%	10.9%	*12.0%*	*8.5%*	Net Profit Margin	11.9%
	95.0	136.1	174.5	163.7	131.4	146.4	169.1	232.2	*220*	*200*	Working Cap'l ($mill)	275
	82.0	80.2	208.5	251.1	247.6	365.5	416.1	417.5	398.8	*560*	*685*	Long-Term Debt ($mill)	630
	784.0	822.8	701.0	792.7	863.7	928.9	927.5	1095.8	1258.9	*1445*	*1570*	Net Worth ($mill)	2150
	11.0%	4.7%	5.8%	9.9%	7.9%	7.1%	11.6%	14.3%	13.6%	*12.5%*	*8.5%*	% Earned Total Cap'l	12.0%
	12.1%	4.8%	6.9%	13.0%	9.0%	8.7%	15.2%	18.2%	16.5%	*16.0%*	*11.0%*	% Earned Net Worth	14.0%
	12.1%	4.8%	6.9%	11.4%	7.2%	6.8%	13.0%	16.1%	13.9%	*13.0%*	*8.0%*	% Retained to Comm Eq	10.5%
	--	--	--	12%	20%	22%	15%	12%	15%	*19%*	*27%*	% All Div'ds to Net Prof	25%

CURRENT POSITION

(\$MILL.)	1988	1989	9/29/90
Cash Assets	16.2	18.2	11.5
Receivables	182.0	200.0	224.4
Inventory (FIFO)	157.7	167.0	182.2
Other	27.2	22.4	19.5
Current Assets	383.1	407.6	437.6
Accts Payable	169.4	154.7	164.6
Debt Due	28.3	3.6	3.2
Other	16.3	17.1	18.5
Current Liab.	214.0	175.4	186.3

ANNUAL RATES

of change (per sh)	Past 10 Yrs.	Past 5 Yrs.	Est'd '87-'89 to '93-'95
Sales	--	9.5%	6.5%
"Cash Flow"	--	18.0%	9.0%
Earnings	--	21.0%	9.5%
Dividends	--	17.5%	21.0%
Book Value	--	10.0%	12.0%

QUARTERLY SALES ($ mill.) A

Cal- endar	Mar.31	Jun.30	Sep.30	Dec.31	Full Year
1987	390.6	395.1	419.1	397.9	1602.7
1988	425.7	448.5	454.6	444.7	1773.5
1989	462.6	476.6	479.9	475.1	1894.2
1990	477.0	475.3	475.0	492.7	*1920*
1991	*495*	*500*	*505*	*500*	*2000*

EARNINGS PER SHARE B

Cal- endar	Mar.31	Jun.30	Sep.30	Dec.31	Full Year
1987	.55	.59	.62	.59	2.35
1988	.82	.96	.95	.85	3.58
1989	.98	.96	1.01	.80	3.75
1990	1.12	1.18	1.02	*.88*	*4.20*
1991	*.75*	*.75*	*.80*	*.80*	*3.10*

QUARTERLY DIVIDENDS PAID C ■

Cal- endar	Mar.31	Jun.30	Sep.30	Dec.31	Full Year
1987	.072	.09	.09	.09	.34
1988	.105	.105	.105	.105	.42
1989	.145	.145	.145	.145	.58
1990	.20	.20	.20	.20	.80
1991					

BUSINESS: Temple-Inland Inc.'s mfg. group makes corrugated boxes, bleached paperboard, pulp, and bldg. mat'ls. Fin'l services group incl. S&Ls, mortgage banking, real estate devel. and insurance. Acq'd. control of Guarantee Federal Savings Bank, which owns 3 Texas S&Ls in FSLIC-assisted transaction, 9/88. Owns or leases 1.9 million acres of timberland in TX, LA, AL, and GA. Operates 6 containerboard mills, 1 bleached paperboard mill, 40 corrugated container plants, 5 lumber mills, and 6 bldg. prod. plants. '89 deprec. rate: 5.0%. Est'd plant age: 8 years. Employs 12,000. Has 10,162 stockholders; insiders own about 2.6% of stock. Chrmn.: A. Temple. Pres. & C.E.O.: C.J. Grum, Inc.: DE. Address: 303 South Temple Drive, Diboll, TX 75941. Tel.: 409-829-2211.

Temple-Inland is not your typical paper company. Since 1988, T-I has bought up 16 failed Texas thrifts (it owned one prior to '88) and it now owns institutions with over $5 billion in deposits. The S&Ls generated about $50 million, or 19%, of total pretax profits last year. Better yet, federal tax benefits arising from the acquisition of Guarantee Federal knocked the corporate tax rate down to 13% in '90, and will keep it at about 20% for the next five years. The acquired thrifts' asset quality is high because in all but one deal T-I assumed only a fraction of their loans, those judged to be of top quality. And in the one case involving some shaky credits, T-I is guaranteed a return on them by Uncle Sam. With much of the competition blown out of the water, these thrifts, which T-I says will concentrate on conservative, home mortgage lending, are well positioned to grow once the Texas real estate market climbs out of the doldrums. Meanwhile, tax benefits are cushioning the drop in paper and building products profits. **We estimate that share earnings will fall about 25% in '91.** We expect the weak economy to depress demand, leading to lower price realizations and profits in the paper and packaging businesses. Furthermore, increases in interest expense and the effective income tax rate will subtract about 35¢ a share from the bottom line. Looking out to 1993-95, we see T-I earning $5.50 a share based on capacity increases in 1992-93 and our assumption that a stronger economy will boost the currently depressed building products segment and stimulate growth in mortgage lending. The expected profit decline in '91, however, raises doubts about the stock's year-ahead performance. And at current price levels, its dividend yield and 3- to 5-year appreciation potential are below par. **T-I's financial condition is solid.** Long-term debt increased by about $160 million last year as a result of the acquisition of two corrugated box manufacturing companies and the need to inject $100 million in equity capital into the new thrift units. Even so, debt to total capital was below 30% at yearend, which is below average for the industry, and we expect the board of directors to approve a modest increase in the dividend at the February meeting. *Philip Kotik*   *January 25, 1991*

(A) Excludes financial service subsidiaries. (B) Primary earnings. Excludes nonrecurring gain: '85, 24¢. Next earnings report due Feb. 1. (C) Next dividend meeting Feb. 1. Goes ex-dividend about Feb. 25. Approximate dividend payment dates: the 15th of March, June, Sept., Dec. ■ Dividend reinvestment plan available. (D) In millions, adjusted for stock splits.

Company's Financial Strength	B+
Stock's Price Stability	55
Price Growth Persistence	80
Earnings Predictability	60

Factual material is obtained from sources believed to be reliable, but the publisher is not responsible for any errors or omissions contained herein.

Source: *Value Line.*

Appendix • *Gaylord Container Corporation continued*

WILLAMETTE INDS. OTC-WMTT | RECENT PRICE **41** | P/E RATIO **12.7** (Trailing: 6.2 / Median: 11.0) | RELATIVE P/E RATIO **1.13** | DIV'D YLD **3.9%** | VALUE LINE **945**

	High:	22.8	24.2	29.1	23.5	28.0	23.5	31.2	46.0	64.0	53.5	55.5	57.5
TIMELINESS **3** Average	Low:	15.8	15.0	14.9	9.6	18.9	13.9	20.2	29.4	30.8	38.5	41.0	29.8

Target Price Range 1993 1994 1995

TIMELINESS 3 Average (Relative Price Performance Next 12 Mos.)
SAFETY 3 Average (Scale: 1 Highest to 5 Lowest)
BETA 1.20 (1.00 = Market)

1993-95 PROJECTIONS
	Price	Gain	Ann'l Total Return
High	85	(+105%)	22%
Low	60	(+45%)	13%

5-for-3 split
5.0 x "Cash Flow" p sh

Insider Decisions
	A	M	J	J	A	S	O	N	D
to Buy	1	0	1	1	0	2	1	1	4
Options	0	0	0	0	0	0	0	0	0
to Sell	2	0	0	0	1	0	0	0	0

Institutional Decisions
	1Q'90	2Q'90	3Q'90
to Buy	41	32	31
to Sell	23	28	24
Hld's(000)	14632	14688	14497

Percent shares traded: 6.0 / 4.0 / 2.0

Options: NYSE
© VALUE LINE PUB., INC. 93-95

1974	1975	1976	1977	1978	1979	1980	1981	1982	1983	1984	1985	1986	1987	1988	1989	1990	1991		93-95	
15.90	17.78	22.34	25.66	30.38	33.99	37.00	38.40	36.56	41.16	46.52	45.35	47.24	56.34	67.52	74.42	74.80	78.75	Sales per sh	90.55
2.17	2.23	2.57	2.86	3.43	4.05	4.09	2.98	2.40	3.02	4.91	5.02	5.80	8.20	10.13	11.62	9.45	9.85	"Cash Flow" per sh	14.75
1.54	1.40	1.71	1.92	2.34	2.67	2.49	1.13	.21	.71	2.60	2.37	2.94	4.78	6.34	7.52	5.00	4.00	Earnings per sh A	7.25
.32	.37	.44	.52	.57	.70	.82	.88	.90	.90	.90	.99	1.02	1.08	1.20	1.45	1.60	1.80	Div'ds Decl'd per sh B	1.80
2.76	1.75	1.72	2.06	3.08	2.77	3.14	5.06	3.06	2.37	2.34	3.75	9.57	5.07	10.95	11.01	13.60	8.45	Cap'l Spending per sh	7.85
7.76	8.80	10.08	11.54	13.06	15.07	16.77	17.02	15.76	15.74	17.24	18.62	20.54	24.23	29.38	35.44	38.80	41.15	Book Value per sh	53.15
24.45	24.45	24.44	25.45	25.42	25.41	25.41	25.41	25.41	25.41	25.41	25.41	25.41	25.41	25.42	25.40	25.40	25.40	Common Shs Outst'g C	25.40
5.0	6.7	8.7	8.0	6.7	6.7	7.9	19.2	69.5	33.2	7.1	10.7	12.9	10.6	7.3	6.4	9.4		Avg Ann'l P/E Ratio	10.0
.70	.89	1.11	1.05	.91	.97	1.05	2.33	7.66	2.81	.66	.87	.87	.71	.61	.49	.70		Relative P/E Ratio	.85
4.2%	4.0%	3.0%	3.4%	3.7%	3.9%	4.1%	4.0%	6.2%	3.8%	4.9%	3.9%	2.7%	2.1%	2.6%	3.0%	3.4%		Avg Ann'l Div'd Yield	2.5%

CAPITAL STRUCTURE as of 9/30/90

Total Debt $556.5 mill. Due in 5 Yrs $124.8 mill.
LT Debt $551.1 mill. LT Interest $62.0 mill.
Includes $38.6 mill. capitalized leases.

(LT interest earned: 3.7x; total interest coverage: 3.6x) (36% of Cap'l)

Pension Liability None

Pfd Stock None

Common Stock 25,422,266 shares (64% of Cap'l)

1984	1985	1986	1987	1988	1989	1990	1991		93-95	
940.2	975.6	928.7	1045.7	1181.9	1152.1	1200.2	1431.6	1716.0	1891.8	Sales ($mill) 1900 2000 → 2300
15.0%	10.6%	9.0%	10.6%	15.9%	15.4%	17.3%	22.2%	22.2%	23.2%	Operating Margin 18.0% 18.5% → 22.0%
40.6	47.2	55.6	58.6	61.3	64.5	72.7	87.0	96.3	104.3	Depreciation ($mill) 115 150 → 190
63.4	28.6	5.4	18.2	66.2	60.2	74.7	121.3	161.1	191.1	Net Profit ($mill) 125 100 → 185
29.1%	8.6%	--	50.0%	34.6%	36.9%	33.2%	39.6%	36.7%	38.0%	Income Tax Rate 38.0% 38.0% → 38.0%
6.7%	2.9%	.6%	1.7%	5.6%	5.2%	6.2%	8.5%	9.4%	10.1%	Net Profit Margin 6.6% 5.0% → 8.0%
74.7	87.0	95.2	60.1	58.2	85.6	88.1	131.3	192.0	131.3	Working Cap'l ($mill) 155 175 → 345
227.1	246.9	295.9	238.4	183.4	186.0	313.8	293.9	391.5	387.7	Long-Term Debt ($mill) 500 620 → 510
426.0	432.4	400.4	399.8	438.0	473.1	521.8	615.8	746.6	901.0	Net Worth ($mill) 985 1045 → 1350
11.3%	6.5%	3.1%	5.0%	12.3%	10.8%	10.1%	15.0%	15.7%	16.3%	% Earned Total Cap'l 10.0% 8.0% → 10.5%
14.9%	6.6%	1.3%	4.5%	15.1%	12.7%	14.3%	19.7%	21.6%	21.2%	% Earned Net Worth 12.5% 9.5% → 13.5%
10.1%	1.5%	NMF	NMF	9.9%	7.4%	9.3%	15.2%	17.5%	17.1%	% Retained to Comm Eq 8.5% 5.5% → 10.5%
32%	78%	NMF	NMF	35%	42%	35%	23%	20%	19%	% All Div'ds to Net Prof 32% 40% → 25%

CURRENT POSITION ($MILL.)
	1988	1989	9/30/90
Cash Assets	33.2	11.4	6.0
Receivables	154.4	159.5	187.8
Inventory (LIFO)	132.2	153.5	168.9
Other	23.8	24.4	27.9
Current Assets	343.6	348.8	390.6
Accts Payable	57.9	64.5	166.7
Debt Due	3.3	3.6	5.4
Other	90.4	99.4	5.8
Current Liab.	151.6	167.5	177.9

ANNUAL RATES
of change (per sh)	Past 10 Yrs.	Past 5 Yrs.	Est'd '87-'89 to '93-'95
Sales	8.0%	8.0%	5.5%
"Cash Flow"	10.5%	23.5%	6.5%
Earnings	9.0%	47.0%	2.5%
Dividends	8.0%	4.5%	6.5%
Book Value	8.0%	10.0%	10.0%

QUARTERLY SALES ($ mill.)
Cal-endar	Mar.31	Jun.30	Sep.30	Dec.31	Full Year
1987	323.0	352.4	376.8	379.4	1431.6
1988	404.8	424.6	441.0	445.6	1716.0
1989	437.8	491.5	486.6	475.9	1891.8
1990	469.9	491.6	483.6	454.9	1900
1991	450	500	500	550	2000

EARNINGS PER SHARE A
Cal-endar	Mar.31	Jun.30	Sep.30	Dec.31	Full Year
1987	.90	1.10	1.25	1.53	4.78
1988	1.59	1.66	1.54	1.55	6.34
1989	1.57	1.85	2.08	2.02	7.52
1990	1.67	1.71	1.24	.38	5.00
1991	.65	.95	1.50		4.00

QUARTERLY DIVIDENDS PAID B
Cal-endar	Mar.31	Jun.30	Sep.30	Dec.31	Full Year
1987	.27	.27	.27	.27	1.08
1988	.30	.30	.30	.30	1.20
1989	.362	.362	.362	.362	1.45
1990	.40	.40	.40		1.60
1991					

BUSINESS: Willamette Industries, Inc. is an integrated forest products company. Manufactures containerboard, fine paper, bleached hardwood market pulp, corrugated containers, business forms, paper bags, lumber, plywood, particleboard and fiberboard. Owns or holds leases on 1.0 million acres of timberland in OR, LA, TX, TN, Arkansas, and the Carolinas, which provide 43% of log require- ments. Employee costs, 20% of sales. 1989 depreciation rate: 5.7%. Estimated plant age: 6 yrs. Has about 9,370 employees, 9,600 stockholders. Directors, management and families control 40% of common. Chairman and President: William Swindells Jr. Incorporated: Oregon. Address: 3800 First Interstate Tower, 1300 S.W. Fifth Ave., Portland, OR 97201. Telephone: 503-227-5581.

Willamette common has advanced nearly 40% from October's lows. The shares began their descent last fall, as wood products markets weakened, and bottomed out soon after the 40% decline in third quarter earnings was reported. Since then, the stock has recovered nicely. Because forest products equities tend to lead the economy, Willamette's recent trading history illustrates that investors believe this recession is almost over. We rank the shares to match the market in the coming year. Over the 3- to 5-year period, however, capital gains potential appears well below average. That's because at the current quotation, the stock's relative multiple is well above its historic range.

But the company's near-term prospects are dim. The depressed level of housing starts has shrunk demand for building materials to a mere trickle. And selling prices have plummeted. Willamette has been forced to curtail production at several plywood operations so that output does not exceed orders. Value Line's estimate for 1991 housing starts holds out little hope for any improvement in this segment. Meanwhile, pulp prices continue to erode, and are likely to remain weak all year. To date, the white paper markets are doing fairly well, but prices will probably weaken later this year because lots of new capacity is scheduled to come on-line then. Rising paper prices hurt Willamette's results in 1990; the company was buying paper on the open market in order to presell the output of its now-complete Bennettsville mill. The mill started up last month and we think it will be profitable by the June period. But the mill's lower production costs will be offset by higher depreciation charges and interest expense. All told, Willamette has some difficult months ahead. By the final period of the year, we think a positive comparison is possible: The year-ago quarter was burdened by start-up costs, a restructuring charge, and interest due on tax settlements.

Deborah Schondorf   *January 25, 1991*

Restated Sales (and Operating Profit Margins*) by Business Line

	1987	1988	1989	1990
Paper	952.2(19.0%)	1174.7(21.7%)	1295.0(21.0%)	1370(14.5%)
Building Mater.	479.4(10.6%)	541.3(5.4%)	596.8(9.5%)	530(5.5%)
Company Total	1431.6(16.1%)	1716.0(16.2%)	1891.8(17.5%)	1900(12.0%)
*After depreciation, before corporate expenses

(A) Based on average shares outstanding. Excludes extraordinary charges in 1982, 57¢; 1984, 20¢. Excludes nonrecurring gain: 1983, 16¢. Next earnings report due mid-April.

(B) Next dividend meeting about February 10th. Goes ex-dividend about February 20th. Approximate dividend payment dates: 15th of March, June, September, and December. Plus stock dividends: '74-'81, 3%.
(C) In millions, adjusted for stock split.

Company's Financial Strength	B+
Stock's Price Stability	55
Price Growth Persistence	70
Earnings Predictability	55

Factual material is obtained from sources believed to be reliable, but the publisher is not responsible for any errors or omissions contained herein.

Source: *Value Line.*

PART
7

Technical Note

The Business Environment:
A Retrospective, 1929–1993

The cases in this book cover a decade of doing business in this and other countries. Over this period, a number of things changed in the environment in which managers conducted business. For instance, managers of all kinds were affected by inflation at levels not experienced in most countries since the mid-1940s; the maturing of the baby-boom generation in the United States influenced the sale and advertising of products attractive to the young (e.g., soft drinks and fast foods); and worldwide product and capital market integration forced managers to face new competition in unfamiliar environments. These managers found the 1970s and 1980s confusing, frustrating, and, for some, bursting with opportunity.

Many of you were neither active participants nor interested bystanders in the world of business at the times of these cases. The easy approach to analyzing a case set in an unfamiliar period would be to use today's social, economic, and political environment as the context in which the decisions must be made. To do this is dangerous. Decisions based on a particular environment frequently are specific to that environment, and, as we all know, changes occur with surprising rapidity. Thus, confronted with the same problem, rational managers in different economic, political, and social environments could have made different decisions. This is as it should be. The job for the manager, as well as the student, is to gain an understanding of the environmental factors and the interrelationships among those factors that can have a major impact on the decisions he or she will make. To operate in the context of these cases, to understand how these managers made their decisions, and to put yourself in the position of making some of the decisions, you must recreate those environments. This note provides you with some perspective on the various environments in which the managers in these cases made their decisions.

Since most of these cases are set in the United States, this note describes the United States, but with international data added starting in for the 1980s as international product and capital markets became increasingly integrated. For the cases set outside the United States, the case itself or an appendix to it contains some of the pertinent contextual information, but space necessarily limits that information. The manager in each instance would have conducted and used extensive research and broad experience in his or her particular environment in making each decision. To be a good manager requires skill, talent, and insight based on as much information about the environment as can be learned.

While these cases are set in the 1970s, the 1980s, and the 1990s, the practice of management during those periods was conditioned by what had gone on before. Although one could go back to earliest recorded history and find events that profoundly affect the practice of management today, my choice was to begin with a period that has a recent and continuing impact on business and one for which there is easily obtainable statistical information—the 1930s.

The data used in this note come primarily from readily available sources and can be updated or expanded at most public and all university libraries. Much of the data is presented in graphic form to make casual inspection easy. For each exhibit, the data source is noted so more detailed information can be gathered if needed. The exhibits appear at the end of the note.

The 1930s

The 1930s was a period of shock to the United States both socially and economically. The period now known as the Great Depression affected every person and business in this country and around the world. Capital markets, lures for the speculator in the 1920s, destroyed the savings of many during the 1930s. Industrial production, which was stagnant for most of the previous decade, dropped precipitously in the early 1930s (Exhibit 1), and investment in new enterprises came to a virtual standstill. As production declined, interest rates dropped as a reaction to the lack of demand; the average work week, which had been declining since the turn of the century, reached a century-long low (Exhibit 2); breadlines became an everyday occurrence for many who had never been without a job and never dreamed they would be. Drought in the Midwest created the dust bowl. Movies and books chronicled the disaster, but not until years later—after the hurt and bewilderment had passed.

Population growth, steadily increasing by more than 1.5 percent per year before 1930, dropped below 0.8 percent, setting the stage for the baby boom of the late 1940s. President Franklin Roosevelt, in response to the crisis, put in place many of the institutions we still know today and many that are parts of our economic and political history—Social Security, Securities and Exchange Commission (SEC), Works Progress Administration (WPA), savings and loans, and laws governing the banking industry (the Glass Steagall Act).

TABLE 1 • Gross National Product, 1929–1940

	GNP (billions)	Year-to-Year Change
1929	$103.4	6.6%
1930	90.7	−12.3
1931	76.1	−16.1
1932	58.3	−23.4
1933	55.8	− 4.2
1934	65.3	17.0
1935	72.5	11.0
1936	82.7	14.1
1937	90.7	9.7
1938	85.0	− 6.4
1939	90.9	7.0
1940	100.0	10.0

During this period, the gross national product, the sum of goods and services in the whole economy, dropped from $103 billion in 1929 to $56 billion in 1934, before it began a gradual recovery, as shown in Table 1 and Exhibits 3A and 3B.[1]

To fuel the programs designed to pull the country out of the Depression, government spending increased. As a percentage of the GNP, the federal debt rose to a pre-WW II high of 45 percent (Exhibit 4), and the federal government operated at a previously unheard of deficit (Exhibits 5A and 5B). Up to that point, debt in the United States had increased in line with GNP growth (Exhibits 6A and 6B)—a process analogous to a firm financing part of its growth with debt. It was not until the mid-1920s that debt grew more rapidly than the economy itself, and in the early 1930s, the growth in debt significantly outstripped economic growth: the real level of debt financing had increased substantially. That growth in debt came largely from the public sector, and private sector debt decreased substantially (Exhibit 7).

As demand for money decreased, the cost of that money decreased as well. In 1929, short-term interest rates were just over 2 percent (Exhibit 8). By 1933, they were 0.5 percent, and in 1940, they reached a low for the decade of just over 0.14 percent. The prime rate, the rate charged by banks to their best customers, declined from 6.0 percent to 1.5 percent over the same period (Exhibit 9). Long-term corporate and government interest rates also declined over the same period (Exhibits 10A and 10B), with Aaa corporate bonds beginning the decade at almost 5 percent and ending it at

[1] The exhibits and tables in this note contain, for the most part, data from 1930 to 1992.

just over 3 percent. Nominal rates that included expected inflation declined, while real rates—rates net of inflation—first rose precipitously before finally declining, as shown in Exhibit 11. In 1930, the real interest rate was about 5 percent in spite of the fact that inflation, the underlying cause of the very high real rate of interest declined by 11.1 percent in 1932 alone, as shown in Table 2. Because of the disinflation that characterized the Great Depression, by 1932 the real rate was over 10 percent before it began to decline. The *real* interest rate has not been as high since.

Stock prices, always a part of the Great Depression lore, began declining in 1929, but that was only the beginning. Investors were heartened by the short periods of price recovery, shown in Figure 1, only to be hurt once again by the downtrend that continued well into 1932 when the market bottomed at under 60 (Exhibit 12), as measured by the Dow Jones Industrial Average. Volume rose and finally dropped along with price. In 1932 alone, the average investor in the stock market lost more than 40 percent of the value of his or her holdings (Exhibit 13). It was the single worst loss of capital in the history of the U.S. markets. From 1929 to 1933, the average market investor's stock portfolio had declined by more than 60 percent, and investors in small companies saw losses that made the decline in the Standard & Poor's 500 pale in comparison (Exhibit 14). Corporations that survived the decade did so with management embracing a "debt is dangerous—pay cash, extend no credit" philosophy.

The economic shocks of the 1930s led the United States and other governments around the world to try to protect their own economies, if they could. Trade protectionism became widespread. Import restrictions were imposed in an effort to build up the domestic economy, and currencies were devalued for competitive reasons. Currency devaluation led to a decrease in the cost of exported goods and an increase in the cost of imports—a concept called *beggar thy neighbor.* These efforts, instead of saving economies, had the effect of shrinking world wealth as nations struggled not to operate at their competitive advantages, but to insulate their economies.

In 1941, the United States entered World War II. Ending the deprivation of the 1930s, the war finished the economic reconstruction that Franklin Roosevelt had started during the decade, but it did so with a speed that could never have been achieved with peaceful solutions. The Japanese attack on the U.S. military installations at Pearl Harbor was a shock to the American people and both a shock and opportunity for American business. The era marked the beginning of many trends that are still affecting business in the 1980s. It was the era that saw women enter the work force in jobs that had never been held by women and would not again be easily open to them until the late 1970s, if then. It represented the first large group of women working by choice rather than from personal economic necessity, and they were the mothers of the working women of the

TABLE 2 • Changes in Gross National Product, 1929–1940

	GNP Deflator
1929	0.0%
1930	− 3.2
1931	− 9.2
1932	−11.1
1933	− 2.2
1934	8.5
1935	1.9
1936	0.5
1937	4.8
1938	− 2.4
1939	− 0.7
1940	2.5%

Source: *Federal Reserve Bulletin,* Board of Governors of the Federal Reserve System, Washington, D.C.

FIGURE 1 • Weekly Dow Jones Industrial Average, 1929–1933

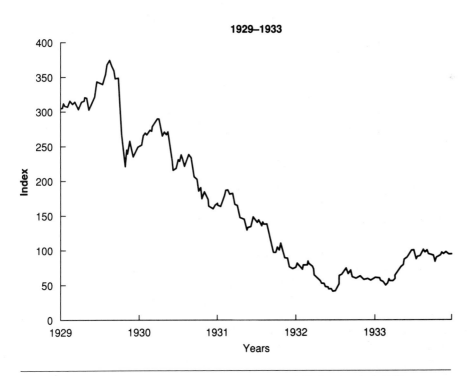

Source: Phyllis S. Pierce. ed.. *The Dow Jones Averages 1885–1980* (Homewood, Ill.: Dow Jones-Irwin, 1982).

1970s. It was also the era when the demand for production from industries spawned the defense industry's cost-plus contracts that have endured without real criticism up to the present time. It was a period of radical solutions to potential military defeat: the atom bomb was developed and used, leaving a legacy of nuclear fear and the danger of world annihilation that haunted us into the future.

The romance and danger of war that began in 1941 left us with legacies that influence our thinking and our ways of doing business today. Understanding that the events of 1941 had, and have, a profound effect on the way managers run their businesses allows one to understand the effect of even more recent events. Table 3 details the major events, economic and political, social and technological, that were important in the 1940s. To provide further perspective on the environment, there is a bit of information about the books, movies, and songs popular at this time.

1940 to 1949

Even before the United States entered the war in late 1941, industrial production had sped up to satisfy the demands of warring nations. Lend-lease, under which the United States lent war material to countries involved that could not afford outright purchase of the equipment, temporarily kept the United States out of the war while gearing up production. By 1940, industrial production had recovered to well above pre-1929 levels (Exhibit 1). The gross national product, as shown in Table 4 and Exhibit 3A, increased at a pace that, in the beginning, heartened the Depression-ravaged economy.

To fuel this upsurge in production, the federal government increased its debt. At first glance, the increase in debt during this period (Exhibit 4) bears no comparison with the increases that would follow, but as a percentage of the GNP, the debt burden was staggering. Debt increased faster than GNP could follow, and the federal government was the primary borrower. For the first time, the federal debt exceeded non-federal obligations (Exhibit 7). At the same time, deficit spending, a feature of the economic recovery programs of the 1930s, more than doubled (Exhibit 5A).

While the federal government raised debt to finance the increased production for the war, interest rates rose little (Exhibits 8, 9, 10A, and 10B). The 90-day Treasury bill rate, at a low of 0.014 percent at the beginning of the decade, rose to 0.375 percent in 1944 and did not change until 1947. The cause of the stability of interest rates obviously was not a lack of demand. Instead, it resulted because the federal government controlled—pegged—the rate of interest during the war. It was not until 1948 that short-term rates exceeded 1.0 percent, the prime rate rising from 1.5 to 2.0 percent by the end of the decade.

TABLE 3 • The Decade of the 1940s

	Economy	History and Politics	Science and Technology	Popular Culture and Daily Life
1941	Office of Price Administration (OPA) established. Supreme Court upholds federal wage and hour law.	Lend-Lease Bill signed. Pearl Harbor—U.S. enters WWII.	"Manhattan Project" atomic research begins.	Film: Citizen Kane F. Scott Fitzgerald, The Last Tycoon
1942	OPA freezes rents. War Production Board (WPB) and National War Labor Board (NWLB) established.	War Manpower Commission established with power over all essential workers. American forces land in French North Africa.	First automatic computer developed in U.S. Magnetic recording tape invented.	Popular song: "White Christmas" Gas, sugar, and coffee rationing
1943	Wage and price freeze. Start of income tax withholding.	Eisenhower named supreme commander. Race riots in several major U.S. cities.	Penicillin successfully used.	Film: Casablanca Popular dance: Jitterbug
1944	Cost of living in U.S. rises almost 30 percent.	D-Day landings in Normandy Roosevelt defeats Dewey.	Synthetic quinine developed. First eye bank established.	Film: Going My Way Tennessee Williams, The Glass Menagerie
1945	Wage Stabilization Board established	FDR dies; Truman becomes president. World War II ends.	First atomic bomb detonated.	"Bebop" comes into fashion. Catchword "Kilroy was here" spreads.
1946	Price and wage controls terminated except on rents, sugar, and rice.	U.S. General Assembly holds first session. Churchill gives Iron Curtain speech.	Xerography process invented.	John Hersey, Hiroshima "Ranch" homes become popular.
1947	Taft-Hartley Act passed.	Marshall Plan announced. Truman Doctrine for containment of Soviet expansion.	Transistor invented.	More than 1 million veterans enroll in colleges under G.I. Bill of Rights.
1948	Injunction prevents nationwide rail strike. GM–UAW contract has first cost-of-living clause.	Berlin airlifts begin. Israel comes into existence.	Long-playing record invented.	Alfred C. Kinsey, Sexual Behavior in the Human Male.
1949	U.S. Foreign Assistance Bill grants $5.43 billion to Europe.	NATO formed. Communist People's Republic proclaimed in China.	U.S.S.R. tests atomic bomb. U.S. launches guided missile.	George Orwell, Nineteen Eighty-Four Arthur Miller, Death of a Salesman

Source: Copyright © 1946, 1963 by F. A. Herbig Verlagsbuchhandlung. English Translation, Copyright 1975, 1979, 1991 by Simon & Schuster, Inc. Reprinted by permission of Simon & Schuster, Inc.

TABLE 4 • Gross National Product and Treasury Borrowing Rate, 1940–1949

	GNP (billions)	Annual Change	Change in GNP Deflator	90-Day Treasury Bill Rate
1940	$100.0	10.0%	2.5%	0.014%
1941	125.0	25.0	8.2	0.103
1942	158.5	26.7	10.6	0.326
1943	192.1	21.3	4.6	0.373
1944	210.6	9.6	2.0	0.375
1945	212.4	0.9	2.3	0.375
1946	209.8	−1.2	15.6	0.375
1947	233.1	11.1	13.1	0.594
1948	259.5	11.3	6.9	1.040
1949	$258.3	0.5%	−1.0%	1.102%

Source: *Federal Reserve Bulletin*, Board of Governors of the Federal Reserve System, Washington, D.C.

While these rates seem quite low by modern standards, they are in nominal terms. If we examine the rates in real terms, they are not low, but negative, meaning inflation exceeded interest rates, as shown in Exhibit 11. The inflation rate of the mid-1940s was high—so high that it would not be seen again until the 1970s. At one point just after the end of the war, the real rate of interest was more than a negative 13 percent.

Stock market prices increased steadily during this period (Exhibit 12A). Only the end of the war brought the Dow Jones Industrial average down, but even then it was nowhere near the level that had been reached in the previous decade. Volume, however, still had not recovered to pre-1930 levels. The returns that shareholders received during this period (Exhibit 13), with the exception of those in the period immediately following the end of the war, were all positive. Stock prices of smaller firms recovered with particular strength (Exhibit 14).

Business during the early 1940s boomed. Costs lost importance in the demand-driven wartime society. When the war was over, however, many firms found the shift from war to peacetime production difficult. Returning servicemen with pent-up demand created widespread shortages for consumer goods. Rationing of staples and nonstaple consumer goods, driven by wartime necessity and propaganda, exacerbated demand in the late 1940s. As servicemen returned home and lives began to become more normal, autos, homes, home furnishings, and consumer durables were in short supply. Demand drove the retooling of many industries, and the recovery of normal personal relationships created the baby boom—a population increase (shown in Figure 2) that did not taper off until 1960.

To stabilize world financial conditions after World War II, international financial leaders met at Bretton Woods, New Hampshire, and estab-

FIGURE 2 • Population Growth

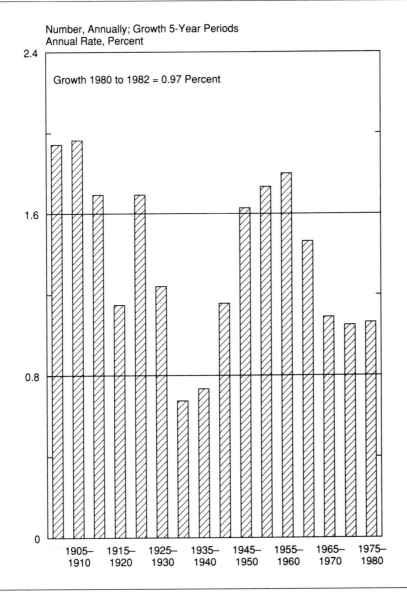

Number, Annually; Growth 5-Year Periods
Annual Rate, Percent

Growth 1980 to 1982 = 0.97 Percent

Source: *Federal Reserve Bulletin*, Board of Governors of the Federal Reserve System, Washington, D.C.

lished the World Bank to lend money to developing countries for building infrastructure, the International Monetary Fund as a lender of last resort for countries with balance-of-payments problems, a system of fixed exchange rates, and the gold standard for the United States.

The 1950s

By the end of the 1940s, Rosie the Riveter, the symbol of American working women during the war, was back at home. The United States successfully managed to airlift supplies into Berlin as the Soviet bloc tried to cut the isolated city off from the rest of West Germany; the first cost-of-living clause was written into a union contract; and the Korean "police action" was about to begin. Out of World War II had come radar, the transistor, and a host of useful and destructive inventions. During the 1950s came the oral contraceptive, the hydrogen bomb, color TV, and the polio vaccine, all of which would change American life for some time to come. In this era, the Supreme Court ruled that school segregation violated the Constitution. Joseph McCarthy began a series of congressional hearings on communist influence in the United States that would profoundly affect what we believed about communism and would adversely affect the lives of many prominent and not so prominent people. The McCarthy hearings would later be characterized by many as witch hunts. Table 5 provides more details of this retrospectively conservative decade.

After tapering off in the late 1940s, industrial production began to climb again (Exhibit 1). While the growth was not smooth, it was relentless. Real GNP fluctuated (Exhibits 3A and 3B) as inflation rose (Exhibit 15). These post-war highs would not be exceeded until the late 1960s. Even with the Korean conflict, federal debt leveled off. As a percentage of GNP (Exhibits 6A and 6B), it reached a post-war low of 50 percent by the decade's end. In fact, the government actually operated at a surplus (Exhibits 5A and 5B) for several periods during the decade—a balanced budget that politicians in the 1980s and 1990s would long to see again. Federal debt not only fell but did so relative to total debt in the United States (Exhibit 7). The increase in total debt even kept pace with the increase in the output of goods and services, the GNP. The worldwide economy was also expanding. Major countries' currencies, which had not been so before, became freely convertible and helped trade to flourish.

As spending for the Korean police action waned, national defense expenditures dropped, while benefit payments for individuals, much of it entitlement benefits to which the government was obliged (i.e., social security and pensions), began their inexorable climb (Exhibit 16).

Interest rates, which were pegged during the war years, began a rise that saw the prime rate in 1959 at 4.5 percent—the highest it had been since before the Depression (Exhibits 8, 9, 10A, and 10B). Treasury bills, long yielding less than 2 percent, reached 3.4 percent in 1959. In real terms, interest rates were positive again (Exhibit 11).

The stock market volume and prices (Exhibits 12A and 12B) rose, and investors had years when their returns from investing in common stocks were as high as 50 percent (Exhibit 13A). Earnings yields (earnings

TABLE 5 • The Decade of the 1950s

	Economy	History and Politics	Science and Technology	Popular Culture and Daily Life
1950	Defense Productions Act gives president power to stabilize wages and prices.	Start of Korean War.	Einstein: General Field Theory.	Film: *All about Eve*
1951	Office of Economic Stabilization established.	Internal Security Act restricts communists in United States.	Electric power produced from atomic energy. Color television introduced.	J. D. Salinger, *The Catcher in the Rye* Film: *A Streetcar Named Desire*
1952	Defense Productions Act extended.	Eisenhower elected president. Republicans capture both houses of Congress.	First hydrogen bomb exploded. Oral contraceptive produced.	Ernest Hemingway, *The Old Man and the Sea* John Steinbeck, *East of Eden*
1953	End of price controls. Margin requirements for stock purchases reduced from 75 to 50 percent.	Department of Health, Education, and Welfare created. Korean armistice signed.	Lung cancer reported attributable to cigarette smoking.	Film: *The Robe*—first Cinemascope B. F. Skinner, *Science and Human Behavior*
1954	3.7 million unemployed as result of recession.	*Brown v. Board of Education*— Supreme Court rules that segregation in public schools violates 14th Amendment. Army–McCarthy hearings.	First use of Salk antipolio serum.	Film: *On the Waterfront* First Newport Jazz Festival held.
1955	AFL and CIO merge; new president George Meany.	Montgomery, Alabama bus boycott begins.	Ultra-high frequency waves produced at MIT.	Popular song: "Rock around the Clock" Vladimir Nabokov, *Lolita*
1956	Economic expansion sparked by government defense spending.	Eisenhower reelected president; Congress is Democratic. Soviet troops march into Hungary.	Transatlantic cable telephone service inaugurated.	Elvis Presley gains popularity. Theater: *My Fair Lady*
1957	Teamsters Union expelled from AFL–CIO when Hoffa refuses to expel criminals.	Troops sent to Little Rock, Arkansas to enforce integration. Eisenhower Doctrine to protect Middle East from communists.	U.S.S.R. launches Sputnik I and II.	Jack Kerouac, *On the Road* Dr. Seuss, *The Cat in the Hat*
1958	1958 recession reaches trough in April; 7.7 percent unemployment.	European Common Market established. John XXIII becomes pope.	U.S. launches Explorer I satellite. Stereo recording comes into use. NASA established.	J. K. Galbraith, *The Affluent Society* Film: *Cat on a Hot Tin Roof*
1959	Four-month steel strike ended when Taft-Hartley Act invoked.	Alaska and Hawaii become states. Castro becomes Premier of Cuba; expropriates U.S.-owned sugar mills.	Nobel Prize for synthesis of RNA and DNA.	Popular song: "Mack the Knife" Philip Roth, *Goodbye Columbus*

Source: Copyright © 1946, 1963 by F. A. Herbig Verlagsbuchhandlung. English Translation, Copyright 1975, 1979, 1991 by Simon & Schuster, Inc. Reprinted by permission of Simon & Schuster, Inc.

per share/price per share) on common stocks, which began the decade at almost 15 percent, dropped to 2.5 percent. Price/earnings ratios which began at over 7 rose to an average of almost 40 (Exhibit 17). Real stock returns, net of inflation, rose from less than 30 in 1948 to over 50 during the decade (Exhibit 18). All these changes indicate that investors were willing to take more risks and take less in current income. By all accounts, confidence had returned to the stock market. Corporate profits (Exhibit 19) and returns on assets and equity showed significant declines before rising at the end of the decade: return on assets and equity dropped by 35 percent before rebounding. Investment in assets slowed, and internal funds generally kept pace with corporate needs (Exhibit 21). As a result, liquid assets declined, and notably in 1954, the ratio of long-term to short-term debt (Exhibit 22) was at a level that would never again be reached by U.S. corporations.

The 1960s

In 1960, the United States was in a recession. The president who ushered in the decade was a well-known WWII figure, Dwight D. Eisenhower. By year's end, John Kennedy was president, and perhaps as a portent of things to come, *Psycho* was the movie of the year. The 1960s marked the entry into the Vietnam war, the investment in the social programs of Lyndon Johnson's Great Society, and both manned and unmanned satellites in space. The Beatles came to the U.S. music scene, and riots came to many American cities. Civil rights came, if slowly; Vietnam escalated; and the killing of students at Kent State and Memphis State radicalized a generation. It was also a decade that saw some of the banking regulations that had been imposed during the aftermath of the stock market crash of 1929 began to crack, and that watched the environment become a matter of legislation and government regulation. Table 6 details some of the highlights of the decade.

Industrial production and gross national product increased (Exhibits 1, 3A, and 3B), resulting in a decrease in relative federal debt. The budget, at least in the pre-Vietnam half of the decade, was almost in balance. It wasn't until the later half of the decade that things began to change. The Great Society increased government spending for individual benefits at a dizzying pace (Exhibits 5A, 5B, and 16). While Americans at home watched the Vietnam war in living color on the 6 o'clock news, defense spending growth was transient (Exhibit 16).

The later part of the 1950s and early 1960s was a period of great growth and expansion of U.S. multinational corporations. Some became concerned that unfettered growth of U.S. multinational companies abroad could result in U.S. business dominance of some economies. As a result, some governments attempted to restrict the growth of these firms. In addi-

TABLE 6 • The Decade of the 1960s

	Economy	History and Politics	Science and Technology	Popular Culture and Daily Life
1960	Recession. Eisenhower cuts military staff abroad to slow gold drain; $4 billion lost since 1958.	U-2 airplane shot down over U.S.S.R. Kennedy elected president.	Laser device developed. First weather satellite.	Film: *Psycho* John Updike, *Rabbit Run*
1961	Business recovery; GNP up 4.1 percent from 1960.	Bay of Pigs invasion. Berlin Wall constructed.	First U.S. manned space flight.	Joseph Heller, *Catch-22* Film: *West Side Story*
1962	Kennedy forces steel companies to cancel price increases. Trade Expansion Act cuts some tariffs.	Cuban missile crisis. U.S. marshals and troops enforce James Meredith's admittance to Univ. of Mississippi.	Thalidomide causes birth defects.	Rachel Carson, *Silent Spring* Popular song; "Blowing in the Wind"
1963	$380 million U.S. wheat sale to Soviet Union. Congressional act requiring arbitration passed to avoid rail strike.	Nuclear test ban treaty signed by U.S. and U.S.S.R. Kennedy assassinated.	First use of an artificial heart during heart surgery.	John LeCarre, *The Spy Who Came in from the Cold* Film: *Dr. Strangelove*
1964	Tax Reduction Act: Personal income tax rates reduced from 20–91 percent scale to 14–70 percent; corporate from 52 percent to 48 percent over 2 years	Gulf of Tonkin Resolution, escalation of war in Vietnam. Civil Rights Law passed. Johnson defeats Goldwater in Democratic landslide.	Ranger VII takes close-up photographs of the moon's surface.	The Beatles become popular. Films: *Mary Poppins, Goldfinger.*
1965	Johnson's budget of $97.7 billion is less than 15 percent of GNP; lowest ratio in 15 years.	Johnson proclaims Great Society; Medicare bill signed. Riots in Watts, Los Angeles.	Momentum increases for antipollution laws on a national scale in United States.	Film: *The Sound of Music* Ralph Nader, *Unsafe at Any Speed*
1966	Rate of inflation doubles from 1965 to 3 percent.	International days of protest agains U.S. policy in Vietnam.	U.S. and U.S.S.R. spacecrafts make soft landing on moon.	William Manchester, *The Death of a President*
1967	Balance of payments deficit over $3.5 billion.	Six-Day War between Israel and Arabs. Riots in Cleveland, Newark, and Detroit.	China explodes first hydrogen bomb. First human heart transplant.	Film: *Bonnie and Clyde* J. K. Galbraith, *The New Industrial State* Miniskirts popular
1968	Tax surcharge passed. Gold crisis—London gold market closed at request of United States to halt heavy selling of gold; two-price system for gold adopted.	Navy intelligence ship Pueblo captured by North Korea. Martin Luther King and Robert Kennedy assassinated. Nixon defeats Humphrey.	James D. Watson: The double helix. AMA sets new standard of death—brain death.	Film: *2001: A Space Odyssey* Popular song: "Mrs. Robinson" Student unrest on university campuses.
1969	Inflation becomes worldwide problem. Prime bank rate at record high 8.5 percent.	Warren Burger appointed Chief Justice of Supreme Court. William Calley charged with murder of civilians at My Lai, Vietnam.	Apollo IX; first manned moon landing. Use of cyclamates and DDT restricted.	Film: *Midnight Cowboy* Popular song: "Aquarius," Woodstock Festival.

Source: Copyright © 1946, 1963 by F. A. Herbig Verlagsbuchhandlung. English Translation, Copyright 1975, 1979, 1991 by Simon & Schuster, Inc. Reprinted by permission of Simon & Schuster, Inc.

tion, the U.S. government attempted to stem the flow of U.S. investment abroad when it became clear that there were, for the first time, balance of payments deficits (Exhibit 23).

U.S. corporate profits rose faster and further than they had fallen in the 1950s (Exhibit 19). Corporate investment increased from the 1958 low of 8.7 percent of real GNP to 11 percent in 1966—the same year capacity utilization reached 91 percent. Not only did firms increase their investment in capital assets (Exhibit 21), but they invested heavily in research and development: 1963 research and development spending exceeded 2 percent of the real GNP.

As corporations increased their need for funds, they decreased their reluctance to go to the debt markets for capital (Exhibit 24). The markets responded with increased nominal rates of interest (Exhibits 8, 9, 10A, and 10B), and stock prices reacted to increased earnings and went up, thereby rewarding the risk taker (Exhibits 12A and 12B). Real returns from investing in common stocks rose (Exhibit 18), one indication of why the 1960s are often called the "go-go" or golden years of the stock market. From the late 1950s onward, many believed that it was hard not to pick winners (Exhibits 13 and 14). The euphoria of a long upward trend in the stock market, a bull market, led many into a position that the erratic 1970s demonstrated was not inviolate. Indeed, by 1974, many felt as if they had survived a period like the crash of 1929. But in the late 1960s, U.S. business appeared to be strong, the stock market a haven for the prudent investor, and it was believed little could change this inevitable course. The year 1970 itself gave some warning, but one that would not be heeded until after the disastrous oil embargo and price increases changed the sources and uses of capital in the world.

The 1970s

By 1971, wages and prices were frozen as President Nixon battled inflation that had reached an unacceptable 6 percent. The fixed exchange rate system for currency established at Bretton Woods was abandoned, the U.S. dollar was devalued in 1971 and again in 1973, and wage and price controls that were instituted to curb inflation continued until the year after the landslide reelection of Richard Nixon.

After the ice-cream era of the 1960s, the 1970s shocked, dislocated, and changed the face of business in the United States and around the world. This was the era in which the United States would ignominiously lose a war, would lose a vice president to accusations of graft, and would almost impeach a president. The word *stagflation* was coined as economies struggled to recover from simultaneous inflation and recession brought on by the meteoric rise in oil prices in 1973 and 1974. Table 7 shows some of the events of the 1970s.

TABLE 7 • The Decade of the 1970s

	Economy	History and Politics	Science and Technology	Popular Culture and Daily Life
1970	Dow Jones drops to 631 during recession. Regulation Q limiting interest rate banks can pay is suspended for 30–89-day CDs.	Killing of four students at Kent State by National Guard during Vietnam protest. Environmental Protection Agency created.	First complete synthesis of a gene. First Earth Day.	Film: *Catch-22* Popular song: "Raindrops Keep Falling on My Head"
1971	Nixon orders 90-day freeze on wages and prices. U.S. devalues dollar; Japan and most European countries revalue currencies upwards.	26th Amendment allowing 18-year-olds to vote ratified. Fighting in Indochina spreads to Laos and Cambodia. Prisoner uprising at Attica results in death of 42.	Mariner 9 orbits Mars.	Film: *A Clockwork Orange* Aircraft hijacking becomes major problem.
1972	Dow-Jones Stock Index over 1000 for first time. "Phase II" economic measures continue to control wages, prices, and profits.	Nixon visits China. Nixon defeats McGovern in landslide; Democrats retain majorities in Congress.	Discovery of a 2.5 million-year-old human skull in Kenya.	Film: *The Godfather* "All in the Family" leading TV show
1973	U.S. devalues dollar. Arab oil embargo. End of most wage-price controls. Regulation Q suspended for investments over 90 days.	Vietnam cease-fire agreement. Watergate investigation underway. Agnew resigns as vice president.	Congress authorizes trans-Alaska pipeline.	Film: *Last Tango in Paris* "The Waltons" leading TV show
1974	Worldwide inflation; dramatic increases in cost of fuel, food, and materials. Oil embargo lifted. Dow Jones Index at 12-year low.	Nixon resigns over Watergate. Gerald Ford becomes president. Patty Hearst kidnapped.	Mariner 10 sends pictures of Venus.	Film: *The Exorcist* "Streaking" craze on campus.
1975	Gold sales legal in U.S.; first time in 41 years. Electricity rates rise by 30 percent. Individual and corporate income taxes cut by $22.8 billion. Moratorium on grain sales to Russia.	South Vietnam falls to communists. American merchant ship Mayaguez seized by Cambodia.	First artificial animal gene created. U.S. prepares for voluntary conversion to metric system.	Film: *Jaws* Discos become popular.

Year				
1976	Decline in consumer spending owing to steep increases in retail prices. Lockheed payoffs lead to close scrutiny of business ethics. Prime rate goes below 7 percent. Budget deficit equals $65.6 billion.	Jimmy Carter elected president. Sec. of State Kissinger calls for policy of detente with Soviet Union.	Swine-flu immunization. Red Dye No. 2 banned.	CB radio craze. Bicentennial celebrated. Film: *Network*.
1977	Minimum wage increases from $2.30 to $3.35 per hour by 1981. Dollar weak in foreign exchange. Record trade deficit of $2.82 billion reported in June.	U.S. announces reduction in aid to nations with human rights violations. "Koreagate" scandal of influence buying.	GM introduces its first diesel-powered auto. Alaska pipeline opens.	"Roots" popular TV miniseries. Film: *Star Wars*. Punk rock popular.
1978	105-day United Mineworkers strike. Prime rate reaches 11¾ percent from 7¾ percent. Humphrey-Hawkins bill approved by Congress legislating 4 percent unemployment and 3 percent inflation by 1983.	Panama Canal treaty ratified. Proposition 13 initiative in California.	First test-tube baby born. Oil drilling begins in Baltimore Canyon region off New Jersey shore.	Films: *Coming Home, Animal House*
1979	Prime rate reaches 15¾ percent. Chrysler receives loan guarantee. Federal Reserve changes monetary policy to control member banks' reserves.	American hostages taken in embassy in Teheran, Iran. Salt II Treaty signed between U.S. and U.S.S.R. Egypt and Israel sign peace treaty.	Three Mile Island nuclear accident occurs.	Film: *Kramer* vs. *Kramer*. Gas shortages create long lines at gas stations.

Until 1973, most industrialized nations had operated as if fuel were inexhaustible and cheap. Typifying this faith was the all-electric home, with electric appliances for all but the simplest tasks, and automobiles that disregarded fuel consumption as they became more and more like mobile living rooms. The United States, mindful of the costs and relative success of exploring for domestic crude, had increased its dependence on imported oil (Table 8). This dependence on imports was expected to grow, and imports more often than not came from the Middle East, an area that had increasingly become the primary worldwide source of crude. The Organization of Petroleum Exporting Countries (OPEC) changed this way of thought and life almost overnight.

Crude oil prices, all below $4.50 a barrel in January 1973, rose fourfold by year's end. As shown in Table 9, by the beginning of 1975, the prices were up to a high of $15.00 a barrel, and the oil-exporting nations had become the new holders of the world's wealth. In 1974 alone, OPEC earned $95 billion, three times what it had earned in 1973. Of that, $60 billion found its way into capital markets as direct investments, primarily in short-term bank deposits and government securities. Oil importers became vassals to a new master, the countries that exported large amounts of crude. Borrowing to import oil, many nations would become the 1980s debtor nations. The United States' problems with its balance of payments and current account balance (Exhibit 23) were exacerbated by the increase in oil prices.

As a result, industrial production (Exhibit 1), which had leveled off in response to the recession in the early 1970s, nosedived. Gross national product increased (Exhibits 3A and 3B), but the increase was masked by the rate of inflation (Exhibit 15). Real GNP declined, although GNP had declined in only one year since 1947, in 1970. The impact of the change in oil prices on inflation is shown in Table 10.

Oil price rises hurt, and since exchange rates were no longer fixed, the unpredictability of exchange rate changes increased. While allowing exchange rates to float relative to each other better reflected supply

TABLE 8 • U.S. Foreign Trade: Fuel (billions of U.S. dollars)

	Exports	Imports	Balance
1958	$1.1	$1.6	$− 0.5
1960	0.8	1.6	− 0.9
1965	0.9	2.2	− 1.3
1970	1.6	3.1	− 1.5
1971	1.5	3.7	− 2.2
1972	1.6	4.8	− 3.2
1973	1.7	8.2	− 6.5
1974	$3.4	$25.4	$−21.9

Source: *International Economic Report of the President*, March 1975, 133.

TABLE 9 • Posted Price: Crude Oil by Origin (dollars per barrel, January 1[a])

	1973	1974	1975
Saudi Arabia	$2.591	$11.651	$11.251
Libya	3.770	15.768	15.768
Nigeria	3.561	14.690	14.691
Venezuela	3.094	13.776	14.312
Canada	$4.400	$ 6.600	$12.100

[a]42 U.S. gallons per barrel.

Source: *International Economic Report of the President,* March 1975, 157–159.

and demand, and the game of guessing when and how a currency would be devalued was made less profitable, a new set of problems were created for U.S. companies doing business abroad.

In response to the oil price-induced recession, unemployment began to rise (Exhibit 25). The decline in employment caused by the recession coincided with the coming to age of the majority of the boom babies, exacerbating a problem that would have arisen anyway.

Federal budget deficits (Exhibits 5A and 5B) renewed their climb to levels that in the 1980s would not only reach an all-time high, but would also become politicized. To finance oil imports, the United States increased its borrowing, even though in proportion to GNP, the level of debt did not rise as quickly (Exhibit 4).

The increase in inflation and the change in the structure of wealth worldwide had yet another effect—that of increasing uncertainty. The combined effect of inflation on interest rates could have been devastating. Only because the Federal Reserve Board of Governors policy was to manage interest rates rather than the amount of money available did interest rates remain relatively stable (Exhibits 8, 9, 10A, and 10B). When the policy was changed in 1978, interest rates destabilized and rose.

The effect that the rise in oil prices had on the stock market was profound. The Dow Jones Industrial Average, which had reached an all-time high in 1972, dropped by 200 points by early 1974 (Exhibits 12A and 12B), and real stock returns dropped to a level not realized since the 1930s (Exhibit 18). Some believed that we were on the cusp of a 1929-like depression. At the low point of the market, it was rumored that over 20 percent of all New York Stock Exchange stocks were selling for less than their net working capital.

The effect on the wealth of investors was devastating. Not since the beginning of the 1930s had investors been so affected: the return on the Standard & Poor's 500 was a loss of 14.7 percent in 1973 and 26.5 in 1947, for a two-year loss of 20.8 percent (Exhibit 13). The booming 1960s had done nothing to prepare investors for these losses, particularly since it had been believed that common stocks were inflation hedges. Not unexpect-

TABLE 10 • GNP and Inflation, 1969–1975 (billions of dollars)

	GNP	Constant GNP[a]	GNP Deflator
1969	$ 944.0	$1,087.6	5.0%
1970	992.7	1,085.6	5.4
1971	1,077.6	1,122.4	5.1
1972	1,185.9	1,185.9	4.1
1973	1,326.4	1,254.3	5.8
1974	1,434.2	1,246.3	9.7
1975	$1,549.2	$1,231.6	9.6%

[a]Constant 1972 dollars.

Source: *Federal Reserve Bulletin,* Board of Governors of the Federal Reserve System, Washington, D.C.

edly, at the same time that market prices dropped, the market for new equity issues was virtually nonexistent. Much of the financing done in 1974 and 1975 was debt (Exhibit 24).

In nominal terms, long-term corporate bondholders suffered less, with an average loss of 1 percent over the same period. Borrowers, in large measure because of the Federal Reserve Board's policy to control the level of interest rates, obtained what amounted to negative interest rates on the money they borrowed (Exhibit 11).

While the market was reacting to changes in the very structure of the world economic order, U.S. corporations began to feel the effect: the stock market's precipitous drop was a forecast of the real returns American corporations would soon earn. Return on assets and equity declined (Exhibit 20), and corporate capital expenditure programs were curtailed (Exhibit 21). In every way, corporate profits suffered, and shareholders suffered another loss as dividends were lowered. Exhibit 19 shows that 1974 to 1975 was the single worst period for corporations in more than 3 decades. Capacity utilization rates dropped to almost 70 percent, and real investment was as low as the period immediately following the Korean War (Exhibit 26). The effect on certain corporate liabilities and assets was clear. As shown in Table 11, cash dropped as inflation ate into assets, and short-term debt rose markedly throughout the decade (Exhibits 27 and 28) as managers sought to put off financing until more favorable circumstances prevailed.

In retrospect, many believe that the effort to control all controllable expenses led many corporations to cut their research and development programs, although the decline seems to have been underway since the early years of the decade, as shown in Figure 3.

As inflation increased the costs of doing business, corporations began to enter the capital markets with renewed interest. There was a substantial increase in borrowing (Exhibits 22 and 24), particularly of short-term capital.

TABLE 11 • Selected Items: Corporate Balance Sheets
(as a percentage of total assets and liabilities except as noted)

	1960	1970	1975	1979
Total assets and liabilities (billions)	$1,207	$2,635	$4,287	$6,835
Assets				
Cash	8.04%	6.72%	6.76%	6.75%
Notes and accounts receivable	20.05	22.58	23.82	25.91
Inventories	7.54	7.21	7.42	7.36
Mortgage and real estate loans	10.69	12.45	12.78	12.30
Capital assets	24.28	22.77	20.81	19.72
Liabilities				
Notes and accounts payable	9.28	12.14	12.50	13.65
Other current liabilities	30.24	33.85	36.32	37.79
Bonded debt and mortgages	12.76	13.78	13.69	12.95
Surplus and individual profits	22.29%	20.91%	19.66%	19.96%

Source: "Income Tax Returns of Active Corporations—Assets and Liabilities: 1960–1979," *Statistical Abstract of the U.S., 1982–1983,* 536.

In late 1979, Paul Volcker was appointed chairman of the Federal Reserve Board of Governors. Real and nominal rates of interest on borrowed funds rose dramatically; the average rates on new 90-day Treasury bills rose from 7.2 in 1978 to 10.0 percent in 1979 (Exhibit 8) and were poised for further rises in the early 1980s. In April 1980, the prime rate topped 20 percent; inflation was more than 11 percent (Exhibit 15) and was expected to go higher. Oil prices, the source of much of the dislocation in late 1973, doubled once again, but without the same crippling effect. The increase in oil prices was cushioned by the decrease in consumption that came from conservation policies and behavior worldwide—an unexpectedly large decrease.

The 1980s

By mid-1980, the growth in real GNP (Exhibits 3A and 3B) had dropped below its 1974 bottom. Industrial production (Exhibit 1) had flattened, and real stock returns had reached a decade low (Exhibit 18). Iran held members of the U.S. embassy staff hostage despite President Jimmy Carter's efforts to release them. To add to the difficulty, unemployment (Exhibit 25), which had dropped since its 1975 peak, began to increase. It was in this environment of economic uncertainty and political turmoil that Ronald Reagan was elected president, bringing with him a Republican majority to the Senate.

By July of 1981, President Reagan's controversial trickle-down, supply-side economics had become not just a catch phrase, but a reality. It had been enacted with the Economic Recovery Act of 1981 and was designed

FIGURE 3 • The Slump in Industrial R&D Spending

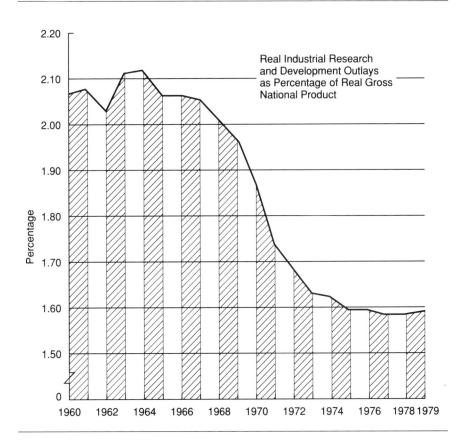

to put more capital into the hands of investors, to speed economic recovery, and thereby to increase tax revenues. By 1981, the budget deficit had reached almost $60 billion. Congress increased the debt ceiling and increased it once again; originally estimated in 1981 to reach $91.5 billion by 1983, the actual deficit was $195 billion. Table 12 lists some of the events of 1980 through 1987.

Interest rates, the bête noire of the late 1970s, continued to be both high and volatile (Exhibits 8, 9, 10A, and 10B). Figure 4 shows the level of interest rates and the major events that determined their course from 1979 onwards. Ninety-day Treasury bills reached a high of 16.3 percent in May 1981, and it was not until late 1981 that rates began to decline. By mid-1984, forecasters were divided on the direction the rates, then over 10 percent on 90-day Treasury bills, would go.

In this environment, stock prices languished until they made a whirlwind recovery in late summer 1982. Analysts, who were surprised at the

TABLE 12 • The Decades of the 1980s and the 1990s

	Economy	History and Politics	Science and Technology	Popular Culture and Daily Life
1980	Monetary Control Act approved. U.S. economy in recession. President Carter announces new anti-inflation program. Prime rate exceeds 20 percent: interest rates extremely volatile.	Abscam investigations of congressional influence buying. Reagan defeats Carter; Republican majority in Senate.	Virus-fighting substance made by gene splicing.	Film: *The Empire Strikes Back*
1981	Economy remains depressed. Interest rates remain high and volatile. Dollar strong in foreign exchange. Bankruptcies increase. Inflation falls. Economic Recovery Act of 1981. 1981 budget deficit = $57.9 billion.	Reagan cuts budget. Labor unrest in Poland. Iranian hostages returned. Equal Rights Amendment fails.	Columbia space shuttle in operation.	Film: *On Golden Pond* Baseball players strike.
1982	Prime rate falls to 11.5 percent, unemployment over 10 percent. International lending crisis—over $706 billion owed by troubled developing and Eastern bloc countries. Oil prices decline.	Israel invades Lebanon. Argentina and Great Britain go to war over the Falkland Islands.	First permanent artificial heart implanted into human.	Films: *E.T., Gandhi* More than 3 million personal computers sold.
1983	Inflation drops to 3.6 percent. Federal deficit reaches record $200 billion. WPPSS $2.25 billion is largest municipal bond default in U.S. history. Dow-Jones Industrial Average reaches 1287.	More than 200 U.S. Marines killed in Lebanon. Korean Air Lines jet shot down by Soviet Union. U.S. Marines invade Grenada.	Nuclear Magnetic Resonance (NMR) radiation-free X-ray scanner developed. Scientists search for cure for AIDS.	TV movie: *The Day After* Film: *Return of the Jedi* Rock videos become popular.
1984	Trade deficit hits $100 billion. Grace Commission proposes $424 billion in government savings over 3 years. Oil company mergers begin Texaco/Getty, Chevron/Gulf, and Mobil/Superior. Continental–Illinois Bank bailed out by FDIC.	Reagan/Bush reelected in landslide. Andropov dies, replaced by Chernenko. 2000+ killed in India by Union Carbide plant toxic fumes. Indira Gandhi killed. Marines pull out of Lebanon.	First baby from frozen embryo born. Next mass extinction forecasted in 15 million years.	Film: *The Killing Fields.* Olympics held in Los Angeles.
1985	Uninsured savings and loan crisis in Ohio. Discount rate falls to 7½ percent.	Gramm–Rudman–Hollings bill becomes law. Chernenko dies, replaced by Gorbachev. TWA plane hijacked, one American killed.	*Titanic* found. First septuplets born in United States. Anticancer drug tested.	New Coke introduced. "Live-Aid" concert held to feed hungry Africans. Professional wrestling makes it big.

Year				
1986	West Texas crude oil prices plummet from $30.90/bbl. in November 1985 to $11.30/bbl. in July 1986, then rebound to $18/bbl. in December 1986. Discount rate falls to 5½ percent. Producer prices fall in 1986 for first decline in 20 years. Unemployment falls to 6.6 percent.	One American killed when *Achille Lauro* cruise ship is hijacked. Mexican earthquake kills more than 5,000. U.S. bombs Libya, killing Qaddafi's daughter. Space Shuttle *Challenger* explodes, killing seven astronauts. Major tax reform becomes law. Reagan administration admits to having traded arms for hostages with Iran. Gramm–Rudman–Hollings ruled unconstitutional. President Marcos flees Philippines, Aquino becomes president.	AIDS drug AZT gets FDA approval. Halley's Comet returns on 76-year orbit. Chernobyl nuclear accident kills 23.	Film: *Out of Africa.*
1987	Volcker resigns as Chair of Fed. Stock market boom, followed by biggest one-day decline (over 500 points) on October 19. Brazil suspends interest on commercial debt.	INF agreement signed by United States and U.S.S.R. Boesky pleads guilty to insider trading and implicates others. Margaret Thatcher reelected UK prime minister for third time.	Average age in U.S. 32+. Population on earth reaches 5 billion.	Films: *Fatal Attraction, Wall Street* Madonna is queen of popular music. Oral Roberts raises $4.5 million after saying otherwise God would "call him home."
1988	Program trading curbs instituted. Canada and United States sign free trade agreements. Ownership battle over RJ Reynolds by leverage buyout firm Kohlberg Kravis and current top management. Philip Morris acquires Kraft. Art auctions reach all-time high. Tobacco company ordered to pay damages to lung cancer victim in New Jersey.	John Poindexter and Oliver North indicted in Iran-Contra scandal. SEC charges Drexel, Burnham, Lambert and Michael Milken of insider trading. George Bush reelected over Michael Dukakis, former governor of Massachusetts. USS Vincennes shoots down Iranian airliner. Widespread strikes by Solidarity in Poland. Soviet Union begins to destroy medium-range nuclear missiles. Mikhail Gorbachev President of USSR	Computer virus designed by student jams military computers in United States.	Film: *Rain Man,* a story of an autistic, wins an Oscar. Salman Rushie's "The Satanic Verses" attacked by Muslims. Findings show daily aspirin reduces heart attack risk. Ozone layer-damaging chemicals removed by some cosmetic manufacturers. Smoking banned on U.S. domestic flights of less than 2 hours.
1989	Eastern Airlines files for Chapter 11 protection. RTC created to implement thrift bailout. President Bush authorizes $300 billion to prevent collapse of thrift industry in United States. Hurricane Hugo devastates	Soviets withdraw from Afghanistan. German Democratic Republic allows its citizens to travel to West freely. Chinese demonstrations in Beijing.	Greenhouse effect becomes concern worldwide after warmest year on record.	Film: *Driving Miss Daisy* wins movie of the year. Ban on ivory trading worldwide ratified. Declaration to stop producing ozone-damaging fluorocarbons by year 2000 ratified by 80 nations.

Year			
1990	Caribbean Islands and Carolina coast. Time and Warner companies merge. Drexel, Burnham, Lambert liquidates. Dow Jones Industrial Average reaches 3000. Michael Milken sentenced to 10 years in prison.	Nelson Mandela, head of African National party in South Africa, freed. Iraq invades Kuwait. German Democratic Republic and West Germany unite. Margaret Thatcher, England's prime minister, resigns. President Noriega of Panama surrenders to U.S. troops in Panama.	*Dances with Wolves* wins Oscar. Rap music in vogue. Junk bond king, Milken, fined $600 million.
1991	Pan American Airlines files for bankruptcy. U.S. economy in recession. Soloman Brothers suspended for cornering U.S. treasury note auction. Exxon agrees to pay $1.03 billion for Alaska oil spill cleanup.	U.S. leader in Desert Storm, United Nations action against Iraq. Croatia and Slovenia declare independence from Yugoslavia. Gorbachev ousted and replaced by Boris Yelstin in U.S.S.R. Clarence Thomas confirmed U.S. Supreme Court Justice after bitter hearings over sexual harassment. Araknsas Governor, Bill Clinton, elected president.	Microsoft drops OS/2 and focuses on Windows. *Thelma and Louise,* movie of the year. Basketball star Magic Johnson retires after testing positive for the HIV virus.
1992	Stock market hits new highs in United States. United States sees beginnings of recovery; worldwide recession continues. Japanese stock market recovers to previous levels. Interest rates lowest in two decades. German central bank finally cuts rates. Japanese government implements stimulus plan.	Bill Clinton inaugurated as president of United States; Al Gore, vice-president. Police officers accused of beating Rodney King (in front of videotape witness), acquitted in Los Angeles. Riots breakout after verdict. Ethnic cleansing by Serbs in former Yugoslavia transfixes world and paralyzes world leaders. Yelstin gains "vote of confidence" after battle with opposition.	Disney has new hit movie, *Aladdin.*
1993	Somalia heats up. Worldwide, stock and bond markets rise.	L.A. police officers retried for depriving Rodney King of civil rights; found guilty on some charges. Second woman, Ruth Bader Ginsburg, confirmed to U.S. Supreme Court.	Michael Jordan retires from basketball. First African-American, Toni Morrison, wins Nobel Prize for literature.

FIGURE 4 • How Interest Rates Behaved during Volcker's Tenure

Carter orders Fed to
impose credit controls
to restrain borrowing.

Fed raises
discount rate
to record 14%

Treasury Secretary
Regan says low money
growth risks severe
recession.

Fed cuts discount
rate to 8.5%—seventh
cut in six months.

Fed focuses on
controlling money
growth and lets interest
rates fluctuate.

Reagan defeats
Carter; Fed begins
to tighten.

Volcker announces Fed
is no longer using basic
M1 money supply as a
guide to policy.

Credit
controls
abandoned.

Volcker
sworn in.

Volcker tells Congress
Fed is trying to foster
recovery.

Three-Month Treasury Bills

Percentage

16
14
12
10
8
6
4

J   J   D   J   D   J   D   J   D
       1979   1980   1981   1982

Source: "Washington Debate: Paul Volcker's Report Card," *Business Week,* May 2, 1983, 114; updated from *Economic Report of the President,* January 1987.

meteoric rise of stock prices—almost 25 percent in the last 6 months of the year—called the market a forecast of good things to come for corporate profits, even as the unemployment rate continued to climb and soup kitchens reappeared. Corporate profitability reached a low in 1982.

There was much to concern the alternately optimistic and pessimistic forecasters in late 1983 and early 1984. U.S. banks had lent many times their capital in some of the most uncertain areas of the world. Oil-price rises in the 1970s had begun the problem. OPEC loaned "petrodollars" short term to banks, and banks loaned money to less developed countries to buy oil from the oil-producing nations. The loans were largely at floating rates, and the less developed countries expected to repay them with income derived largely from commodity exports. Inflation (Table 13), interest rates, and decreased commodity prices, however, put the borrowers in difficult positions. The foreign debt was large (Table 14), and the ability of countries to pay it decreasing. For instance, Argentina's gross domestic product was $199.5 billion, and debt was $58.1 billion; Poland's debt was $80.8 billion, and GDP was $84.6 billion.

As borrowers struggled to find ways to pay the interest on their debts, international financial experts struggled to limit the interest payments that had been designed to increase when interest rates rose, as they did in mid-

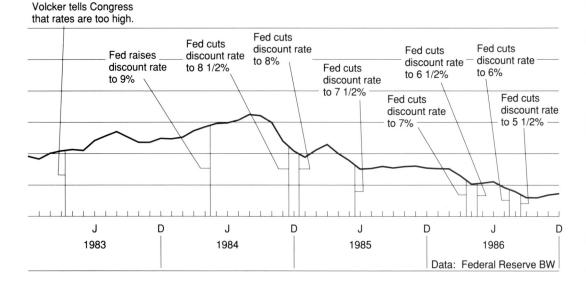

TABLE 13 • International Rates of Inflation (annual average rate)[a]

Country	1960–1969	1970–1973	1974–1975	1976–1978	1979–1980
Israel	5.2%	12.7%	39.5%	39.2%	103.0%
United States	2.3	4.9	10.1	6.6	12.4
United Kingdom	3.4	8.0	20.0	13.5	15.7
Italy	3.7	6.6	18.1	15.3	17.9
West Germany	2.4	5.3	6.5	3.6	4.8
Argentina	22.2	40.3	86.6	245.7	128.3
Chile	28.5[b]	89.5	436.1	103.1	34.3
Brazil	44.2	17.9	28.3	41.5	67.1
Industrial countries	2.9	5.8	12.2	8.0	10.6
Western hemisphere (excluding United States and Canada)	21.1	20.5	36.1	48.8	51.8
World	4.1%	6.8%	14.4%	10.8%	13.5%

[a]Based on rates of change for average yearly price levels.
[b]Computed for the 1964 to 1969 period.
Source: *Bulletin,* Federal Reserve Bank of St. Louis, August/September 1982.

1984. For example, a last-minute rescue by other Latin American countries allowed Argentina, where inflation was raging at 500 percent in the first

TABLE 14 • Largest Borrowers—Amount of Outstanding Debt

| Country | Foreign Debt (in billions) | 1985 Interest | | Debt Owed to U.S. Banks (in billions) |
		Amount (in billions)	Estimated Percentage of 1985 GNP	
Brazil	$103.5	$11.8	5.8%	$23.8
Mexico	97.7	10.0	6.3	25.8
Argentina	50.8	5.1	7.9	8.1
Venezuela	32.6	4.1	8.1	10.6
Philippines	27.4	2.1	6.2	5.5
Chile	21.9	2.1	12.9	6.6
Yugoslavia	20.0	1.7	3.6	2.4
Nigeria	18.0	1.8	1.9	1.5
Morocco	14.4	1.0	8.2	0.9
Peru	13.9	1.3	10.8	2.1
Colombia	13.9	1.3	3.3	2.6
Ecuador	7.9	0.7	6.0	2.2
Ivory Coast	6.3	0.6	8.7	0.5
Uruguay	4.9	0.5	9.8	1.0
Bolivia	4.2	0.4	10.0	0.2
Total	$437.4	$44.5	Average 7.3%	$93.8

Source: "Plan Has a Peck of Practical Problems," FORTUNE, December 23, 1985, p. 101. © 1985 Time Inc. All rights reserved. Reprinted with permission.

half of 1984, to keep the interest on its debt current for awhile, but by mid-July, many U.S. banks were finally writing off their Argentine loans as nonperforming, with an unwelcome effect on bank profitability.

Not only did less developed countries increase their debt, but U.S. government debt and accompanying interest payments had risen drastically, as shown in Figure 5. The U.S. current account balance was a distressing deficit of 41.6 billion in 1983.

At the same time, by many indications the economy and corporations were recovering. Real GNP (shown in Figure 6) had increased, and corporate profitability was up.

Along with the precarious position in which the international banking community found itself, the United States struggled with increasing deficits, an exchange rate that favored imports, and a stock market that favored pessimists. Whether the United States could recover from the shocks of the last two decades, as shown in Figure 7, remained to be seen.

A westward- and southern-moving population, aging as the baby-boom generation reached majority, presented new directions for the creative manager. For managers with vision, the integrated world economy offered a challenge, not just a longing for days when the world seemed to be made up of underdeveloped areas waiting for goods from the U.S. industrial machine.

FIGURE 5 • Federal Interest Payments

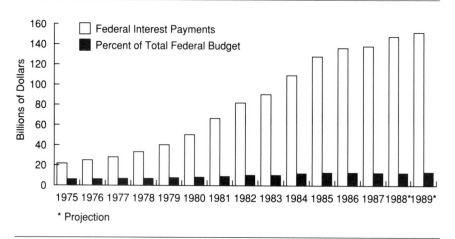

Source: *Economic Report of the President*, January 1988, 338–339.

FIGURE 6 • Quarterly Change in Real GNP (1982 dollars)

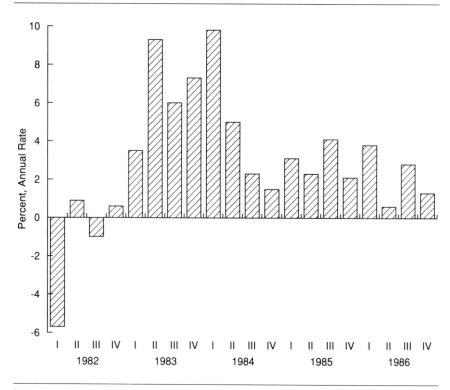

Source: Economic Indicators, February 1987, December 1986, December 1985, 3.

FIGURE 7 • Recovering from the Era of Shocks

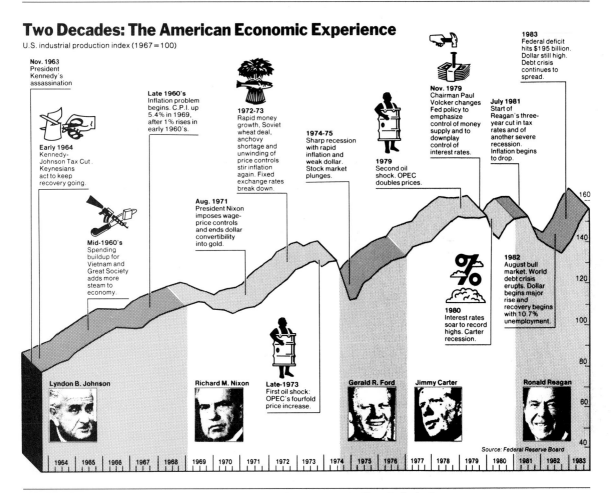

Two Decades: The American Economic Experience

U.S. industrial production index (1967 = 100)

Nov. 1963 President Kennedy's assassination

Early 1964 Kennedy-Johnson Tax Cut. Keynesians act to keep recovery going.

Mid-1960's Spending buildup for Vietnam and Great Society adds more steam to economy.

Late 1960's Inflation problem begins. C.P.I. up 5.4% in 1969, after 1% rises in early 1960's.

Aug. 1971 President Nixon imposes wage-price controls and ends dollar convertibility into gold.

1972-73 Rapid money growth, Soviet wheat deal, anchovy shortage and unwinding of price controls stir inflation again. Fixed exchange rates break down.

Late-1973 First oil shock: OPEC's fourfold price increase.

1974-75 Sharp recession with rapid inflation and weak dollar. Stock market plunges.

1979 Second oil shock. OPEC doubles prices.

Nov. 1979 Chairman Paul Volcker changes Fed policy to emphasize control of money supply and to downplay control of interest rates.

1980 Interest rates soar to record highs. Carter recession.

July 1981 Start of Reagan's three-year cut in tax rates and of another severe recession. Inflation begins to drop.

1982 August bull market. World debt crisis erupts. Dollar begins major rise and recovery begins with 10.7% unemployment.

1983 Federal deficit hits $195 billion. Dollar still high. Debt crisis continues to spread.

Lyndon B. Johnson   Richard M. Nixon   Gerald R. Ford   Jimmy Carter   Ronald Reagan

Source: Federal Reserve Board

160 140 120 100 80 60 40

1964 1965 1966 1967 1968 1969 1970 1971 1972 1973 1974 1975 1976 1977 1978 1979 1980 1981 1982 1983

Source: Leonard Silk, "Recovering from the Era of Shocks," *The New York Times,* January 8, 1984, p. F1, Section 3.
Copyright © 1984 by The New York Times Company. Reprinted by permission.

By 1985, the U.S. economy had rebounded. Industrial production was up, annualized real GNP approached 10 percent in some quarters (Figure 6), and Ronald Reagan had been elected to a second term by a landslide. The vote for Reagan did not, however, carry Republicans into the U.S. Congress as it had in 1980. Supply-side economics, based in the main on stimulative tax cuts rather than spending cuts, seemed to be working—contrary to its vigorous opponents' expectations.

Record employment growth had outstripped that of our major trading partners by 1985, as shown in Figure 8, and the proportion of the U.S. population that was employed showed its first real gains in two decades

FIGURE 8 • Cumulative Change in Employment since 1959,
           an International Comparison (annual data)

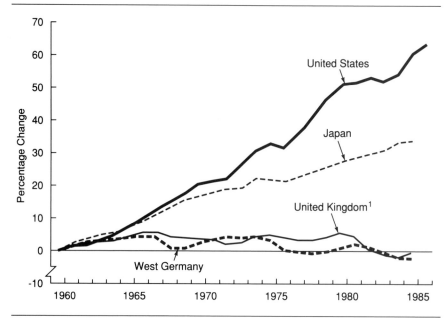

¹Excludes Northern Ireland.

Note: For United States, employment includes resident Armed Forces; data relate to persons 16 years of age and over. For other countries, data approximate U.S. concepts.

Source: *Economic Report of the President*, January 1987, 42.

(Figure 9). Coming out of the deep mid-1970s recession, with its concomitant unemployment increase, and the second round of oil-price increases in the early 1980s, employers were operating from strength and used that strength to trim wages: wage growth slowed from 10 percent in 1981 to 2 percent in 1986. Many of the new jobs were being found in a lower paying but growing sector of the economy, service industries. Manufacturing, long the partner of agriculture in U.S. productivity, began to wane (Figure 10), and as Figure 11 shows, employment in the goods-producing industries began to decline.

At the same time that the service sector was showing strong growth, agriculture was facing one of its worst periods. Commodity prices had been in decline for some time, and when they fell further (Figure 12), many farmers were forced into bankruptcy. While some believed that this decline was just the bottom of a long economic cycle, many banks, already reeling from problems with their loans to less developed countries, were hard hit by farm-loan losses and problems in the oil fields.

In 1986, worldwide oil prices suffered their first real decline ever. From November 1985 to April 1986, prices fell by $17.15 per barrel, from a high of $30.90. Some price recovery had stabilized prices at about $18.00

a barrel by December 1986. The price declines sorely affected oil-field loans by banks, which had forecast higher cash flows from their creditors, but the declines also pushed inflation down to its 20-year low (Exhibit 15).

Low inflation helped rescue interest rates. As shown in Figure 13, the Federal Reserve discount rate declined three times during 1986 alone, and in real terms, interest rates seemed to fall to their historic levels (Exhibit 11). Mortgage rates, long high enough to discourage home buying and building, descended to 8.5 percent for 30-year mortgages in some places. These rates encouraged rushes to refinance old, high-rate mortgages and stimulated home building.

Even as the interest rates declined, the dollar was dropping from its inflated high (Figures 13 and 14), a high that had spurred foreign travel and the budget deficit shown in Figure 15. While the president was focusing on a supply-side–driven recovery, little tangible evidence could be found that recovery would reduce U.S. government debt. Receipts were below average and, worse yet, expenditures were far outstripping reasonable forecasts for revenues (Figure 15). Interest alone was taking 13 per-

FIGURE 9 • Employment–Population Ratio, an International Comparison (annual data)

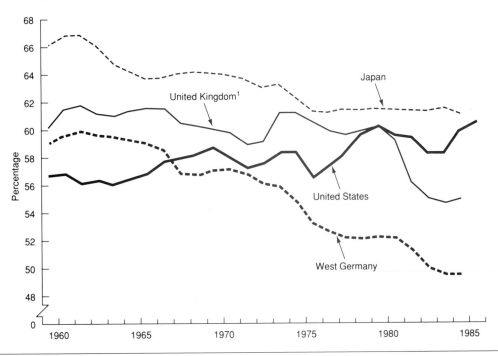

[1]Excludes Northern Ireland.

Note: For United States, employment as percent of noninstitutional population (both include resident Armed Forces); data related to persons 16 years of age and over. For other countries, data approximate U.S. concepts.

Source: *Economic Report of the President,* January 1987, 41.

FIGURE 10 • Employment Shares—Goods-Producing
and Service-Producing Industries

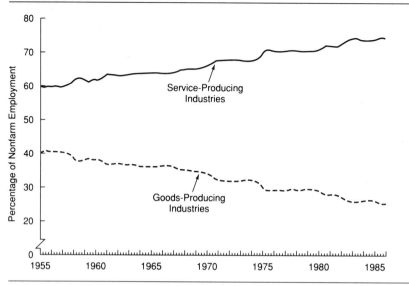

Note: Data relate to all employees on nonfarm payrolls (establishment data), seasonally adjusted.
Source: *Economic Report to the President*, January 1986, 45.

FIGURE 11 • Manufacturing Shares in Real GDP and Employment

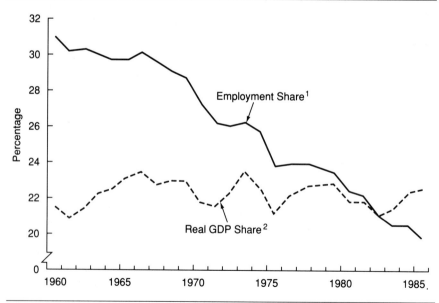

[1]Manufacturing as percent of nonfarm payroll employment.
[2]Manufacturing as percent of real gross domestic product less agriculture, forestry, and fisheries.
Source: *Economic Report of the President*, January 1986, 27.

FIGURE 12 • Commodity Prices: The Great Decline Returns

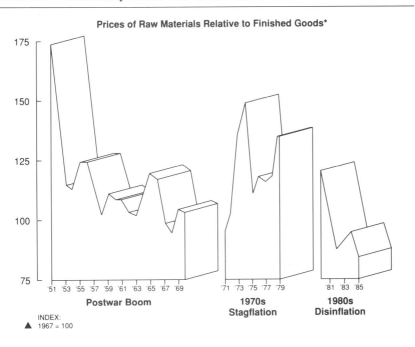

*Ratio of spot-market price index for raw industrial commodities to producer-price index for finished goods.

Source: Reprinted from May 5, 1986 issue of *Business Week* by special permission "Is the World Economy Riding a Long Wave to Prosperity?" p. 84. Copyright © 1993 by McGraw-Hill, Inc.

FIGURE 13 • U.S. Jawboning and Lower Interest Rates Push the Dollar Down

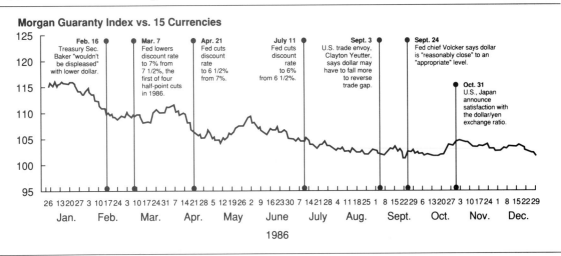

Source: "Dollar Appears Set for a Calm Year," *The Wall Street Journal,* January 2, 1987, 6B. Reprinted by permission of *The Wall Street Journal,* © Dow Jones & Company, Inc., 1987. All Rights Reserved Worldwide.

FIGURE 14 • Index of the Dollar's Value against 15 Industrial-Country Currencies (1980–1982 = 100)

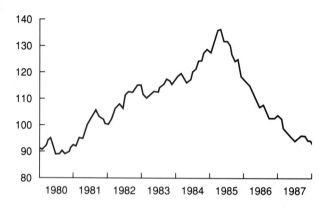

Source: "The Falling Dollar Isn't a Magic Cure," *The Wall Street Journal,* November 23, 1987. Reprinted by permission of *The Wall Street Journal,* © Dow Jones & Company, Inc., 1987. All Rights Reserved Worldwide.

cent of government expenditures in 1986, more than double the 1966 level (Figure 16). The deficit had boomed since Reagan had taken office in 1980 (Figure 17). Not since World War II had the U.S. endured large deficits, and never so large as those created in the 1980s.

FIGURE 15 • Federal Outlays and Receipts as Percent of GNP

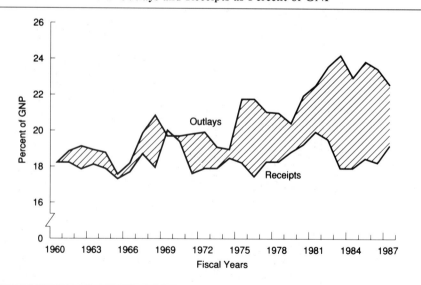

Note: Data for 1987 are estimates.

Source: *Economic Report of the President,* January 1986, 67.

FIGURE 16 • Government Expenditures, 1966–1986

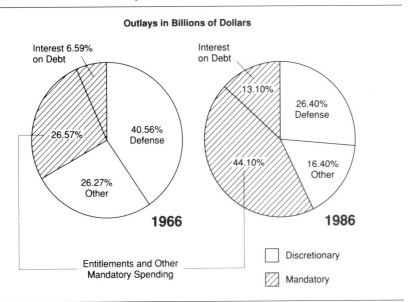

Source: Heidi Mack and Shirley Horn, "How the Government Spends Its Money," *The Christian Science Monitor,* October 27, 1987, 6. © 1987 TCSPS. Reprinted with permission.

FIGURE 17 • The Federal Budget Deficit

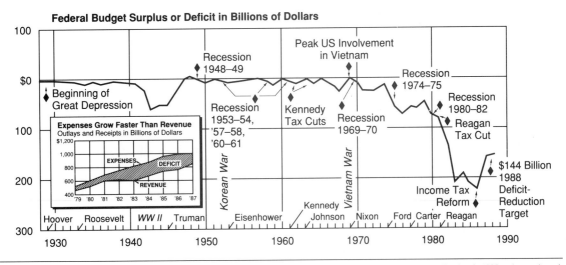

Note: All figures are for fiscal years. The government's budget years are similar to car model years. Fiscal year 1988 began October 2, 1987 and runs through September 30, 1988.

Source: Shirley Horn, "The Looming Budget Deficit," *The Christian Science Monitor,* October 27, 1987, 6. Copyright © 1987 TCSPS. Reprinted with permission.

TABLE 15 • Foreigners' Appetite for U.S. Securities, 1986

	Net Foreign Purchases (billions of dollars)		
	U.S. Treasurys and Agencies	U.S. Corporates (including Euro issues)	U.S. Equities
1981	7.0	13.2	5.8
1982	12.8	17.0	3.9
1983	16.9	11.0	5.4
1984	26.6	28.6	−3.0
1985	24.8	44.4	5.0
1986[a]	68.4	47.5	20.0
1987[b]	72.0	50.0	30.0

[a]Estimate

[b]Projection

Source: "U.S. Attracts Foreign Capital," *The Wall Street Journal,* January 2, 1987, p. 8B. Reprinted by permission of *The Wall Street Journal,* © Dow Jones & Company, Inc., 1987. All Rights Reserved Worldwide.

To fuel the deficits, massive Treasury financings were undertaken. Foreign purchases of these and other securities increased in spite of the declines in the dollar (see Figure 14 and Table 15). Despite these problems, by the end of 1986, industrial production had increased, durable goods orders had risen, employment was at a record high, interest rates had fallen, and the stock market bulls were raging.

Consumer confidence (Figure 18) had sparked the rebirth of the basic engines of the U.S. economy, especially the auto industry. By the end of 1986, the Dow Jones Industrial Average had almost doubled (Figure 19) and reached just under 2000 at year's end. The rapid rise in the Dow, and the considerable profits made and expected on Wall Street, brought out both the optimists and the pessimists. This longest and broadest sustained rise in the stock market, when coupled with worries about the budget deficit, the balance of payments, and the high degree of leverage of both companies and individuals—that is, the debtor status of the country and its people—gave rise to a number of market crash forecasts. Others who were more optimistic found reasons for the remarkable recovery that were rooted in forecasts for further economic progress. The bulls and the optimists won. Although looming and rising deficits were of concern, they did not affect the markets.

As debt continued to rise, interest rates began to climb. Spending was outstripping growth in disposable income, and imports contributed to the balance-of-trade deficit (Figures 20 and 21). In August 1987, the Dow Jones Industrial Average passed 2700. Then on Black Monday October 19, the markets reacted in the most dramatic one-day decline in Wall Street history. The Dow Jones Industrial Average dropped from just under 2300

FIGURE 18 • Strong Consumer Confidence in Economy

Consumer confidence has stabilized in recent years, compared to the dramatic swings that occurred with recessions in the past. Left scale: Consumer Confidence Index, 1985 equals 100. Right scale: Quarterly percentage changes in real GNP, at annual rates.

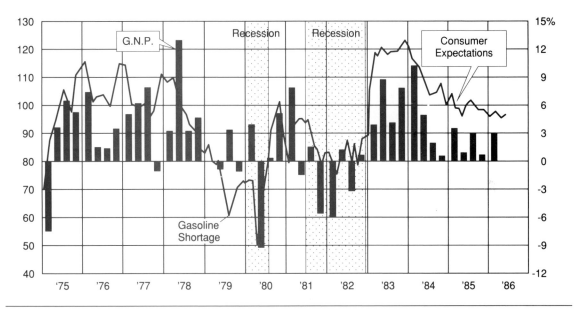

Source: *The New York Times Financial Planning Guide,* September 14, 1987, 12. Copyright © 1987 by The New York Times Company. Reprinted by permission.

to just over 1700. A variety of forces led to this severe decline. (See the appendix to this note for one commentary on the reasons.)

The impact of the shock was felt on all the major markets (Figure 22), and eventually in the political arena, as well. In fact, rules governing programmed trading, computerized trading that implemented trades based on stock market level changes, a kind of trading that was credited for at least part of the rapid decline in the stock market in October 1987, were implemented. While growth in the money supply had declined throughout 1986 and early 1987, the Federal Reserve Board had injected considerable cash into the struggling financial system. Parallels to 1929 immediately leaped to the minds of the press (Figure 23), and numerous pleas for political action, or at least support, were heard. In particular, the U.S. budget deficit was cited as the initial cause for Black Monday, and Congress and the president were urged to take immediate action. Interest rates were cut, and the dollar, which had been supported throughout early 1987 by the United States' trading partners, went into free fall (Figure 24).

By the end of 1987, some of the fear produced by the October 19 market decline seemed to have receded. The U.S. Congress and the presi-

FIGURE 19 • Year-End Review of Markets and Finance

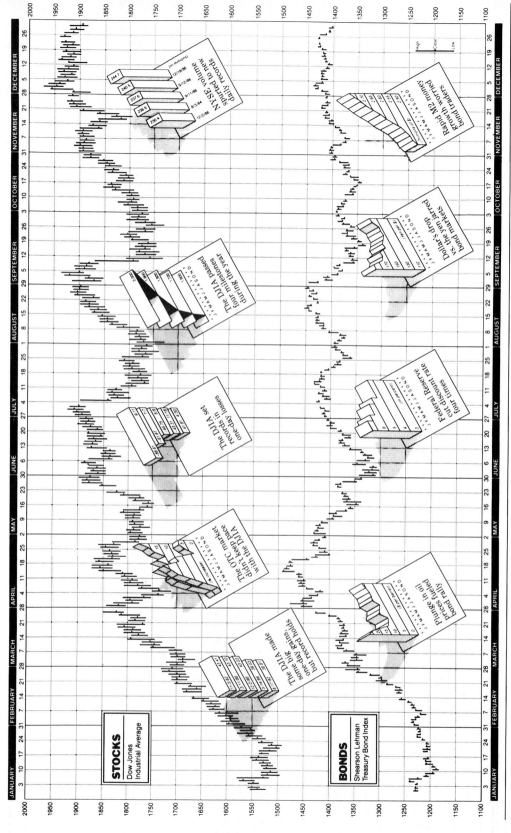

Source: Karl Hartig, "Year-End Review of Markets and Finance," *The Wall Street Journal*, January 2, 1987, p. 1B. Reprinted by permission of *The Wall Street Journal*. © Dow Jones & Company, Inc., 1987. All Rights Reserved.

FIGURE 20 • Spending Is Growing Faster Than Income

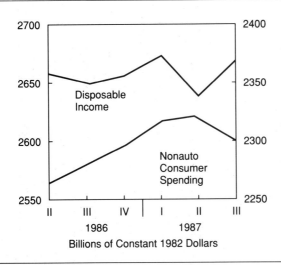

Billions of Constant 1982 Dollars

Source: Reprinted from November 9, 1987 issue of *Business Week* by special permission "Business Outlook," p. 26. Copyright © 1993 by McGraw-Hill, Inc.

dent seemed to be making some progress discussing the budget deficit, the country's major trading partners were cutting interest rates in order to stimulate their economies, and U.S. exporters were hopeful that the

FIGURE 21 • Imports Are Jumping Again

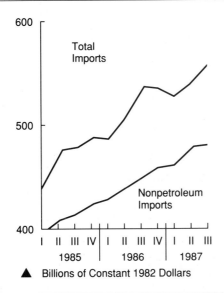

▲ Billions of Constant 1982 Dollars

Source: Reprinted from November 9, 1987 issue of *Business Week* by special permission "Business Outlook," p. 27. Copyright © 1993 by McGraw-Hill, Inc.

FIGURE 22 • Stock Market Averages, September–October 23, 1987

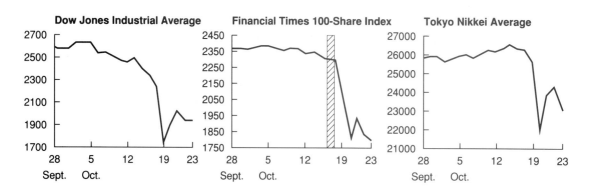

Source: "Big Bang Deregulation Helps London Survive the Burst of Market Turbulence," *The Wall Street Journal,* October 26, 1987, p. 36. Reprinted by permission of *The Wall Street Journal,* © Dow Jones & Company, Inc., 1987. All Rights Reserved Worldwide.

exchange-rate-driven export surge would continue and would support economic growth. Once again opportunities appeared to exist, but danger also seemed to be closer to hand than it had been since the late 1920s.

FIGURE 23 • The Crash: How Close an Economic Parallel?

Money Supply Growth Was Slowing...
M-2 year-end levels; 1922 and 1980 indexed to 100

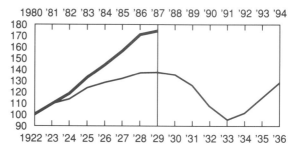

And Debt Was Climbing...
Private nonfinancial debt as a percentage of GNP

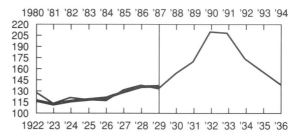

FIGURE 23 • *continued*

But Trade Showed a Surplus...
Balance on goods and services as a percentage of GNP

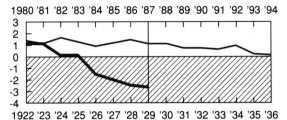

And the Federal Budget Was Balanced
Federal government surplus or deficit
as a percentage of GNP

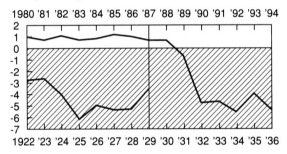

Weekly close of the Dow Jones Industrial Average,
indexed so that Dec. 31, 1928 and Dec. 31, 1986
are equal to 100

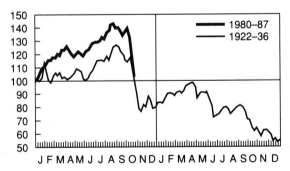

Source: "Avoiding the Economic Debacle: Comparing 1929 and 1987," *The Wall Street Journal*, October 26, 1987, p. 29.
Reprinted by permission of *The Wall Street Journal*, © Dow Jones & Company, Inc., 1987. All Rights Reserved Worldwide.

The 1990s

By 1989, the stock market had rebounded to its pre-October 1987 level, and those crying that the United States was on the brink of disaster

FIGURE 24 • U.S. Dollar

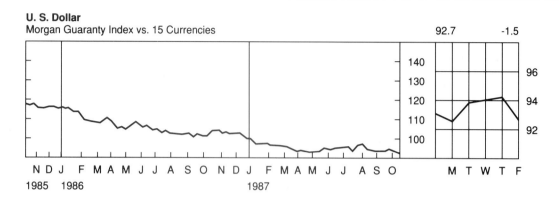

U. S. Dollar
Morgan Guaranty Index vs. 15 Currencies   92.7   -1.5

had quieted. While the stock market had stabilized, the excesses of the 1980s took a toll on the U.S. economy. The decade had been marked by leveraged buyouts, financial restructuring, and a takeover mania, in which large companies bought unrelated businesses in the name of corporate diversification. By the beginning of the 1990s, managements of many U.S. companies had begun to regret some of their earlier actions and had begun to focus on operations, not on financial wizardry. Still, a weak U.S. economy could not withstand the plunge in consumer confidence (see Figure 25) as corporations began to lay off workers and the United States and its allies began to prepare for war with Iraq under the umbrella of the United Nations.

Operation Desert Storm, as the war on Iraq was called, resulted in a defeat of the Iraqi troops, but a failure to remove the country's leader. As the war reached its conclusion, Americans regained their confidence, and the U.S. stock markets rose dramatically, as shown in Figure 26. The confidence was, however, short lived as the United States led the world into another recession. Workers were laid off by companies in increasing numbers, even at some of the country's best-known firms. Figure 27 shows the decline in jobs in the United States alone.[2] While some positive employment changes were emerging around the world (see Figure 28), the picture was not heartening. In addition, middle management, long a group that had been imperious to layoffs, joined the ranks of the unemployed. Housing markets in several regions of the country plunged. The recession gradually spread worldwide.

---

[2] Note there have been revisions of the job-creation data published in the late 1980s, thus calling into question the actual decline in jobs in the early 1990s.

FIGURE 25 • University of Michigan—Index of Consumer Confidence
(Index: 1966=100)

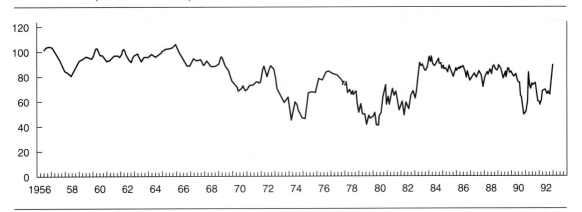

Source: *Survey of Current Business*, January 1993, p. C-10.

FIGURE 26 • Stock Market Level 1956–1993

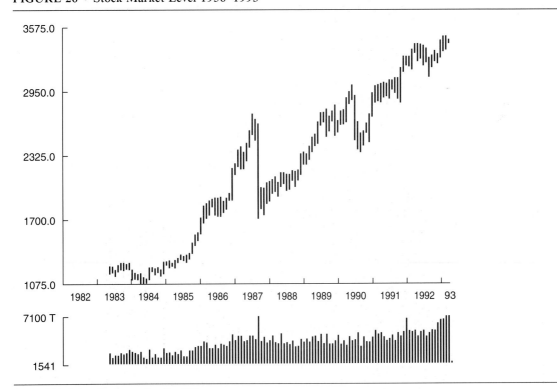

Source: *Bridge Information Systems, Inc.*, May 1993.

FIGURE 27 • Job and Benefit Loss: 1979–1991

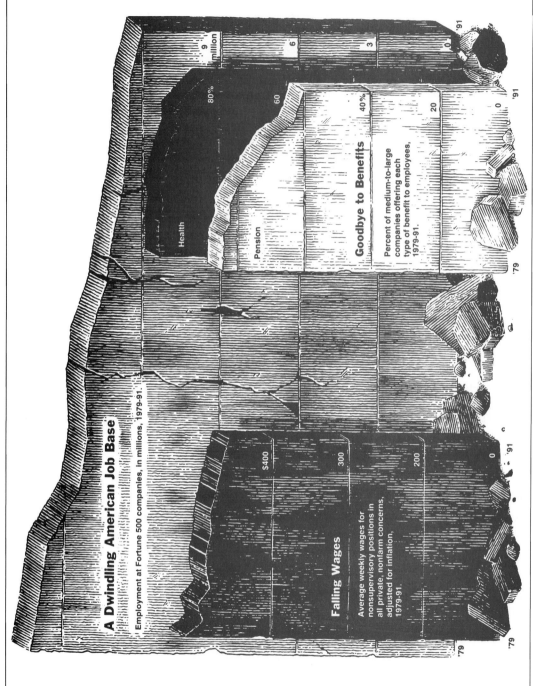

Note: 1991 data are preliminary. Sources for data: *Fortune* (employment); Bureau of Labor Statistics (wages); Employee Benefits Research Institute (benefits).

Source: *New York Times*, January 31, 1993. Section 3, p. 1. Copyright 1993 by the New York Times Company. Reprinted by permission.

FIGURE 28 • Cumulative Change in Employment

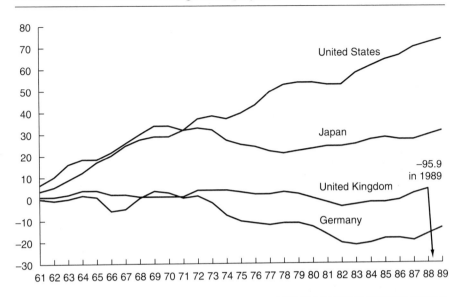

Source: *International Financial Statistics Yearbook*, 1991, pp. 112–113

At the same time, dramatic changes had been occurring in the world. borders had come down, alliances, like that of the Soviet Union, crumbled, and old alliances were recreated. The symbol of the Cold War between the East and West, the Berlin Wall, came down in dramatic fashion, and East and West Germany, separated since World War II, merged. The reuniting of the Germanies resulted in significant economic and political dislocations in both countries, and a staggering rebuilding bill for West Germany as the real cost of the combination became evident. These costs had, and continued to have, a profound impact on German political and economic policies, particularly German interest rates.

On the collapse of the Soviet Union, the United States declared a victory in the Cold War, and U.S. citizens relished the thought of the "peace dividend" that might be used to rebuild the crumbling infrastructure. Corporations around the world leaped at opportunities in the old Eastern block countries, only to be daunted by the crumbled infrastructure, outdated production facilities, and people without a real concept of free-market capitalism or the money to buy more readily available products. The early euphoria gave way to a more reasoned understanding of the real costs and challenges that were ahead. The elected president of Russia, a strong advocate of economic adjustment, ran into political problems with the moderate and hard-line opposition, and inflation and economic adjustment began to erode the lifestyles of those in the newly freed Eastern block countries. Long-standing ethnic and political divisions throughout the old Soviet block began to reemerge, and bloody conflicts broke out in a number of areas, and political differences resulted in open conflict in the Kremlin in late 1993.

At the same time, one part of the world where growth had long been absent, Latin America, had begun to grow and was attracting both the interest of corporate and portfolio investors. The stock markets of the better-known countries rose dramatically, and countries in severe economic straits, such as Peru and Bolivia, began to seek ways of attracting stock market investors. The return to democracy, economic liberalization, the decline in importance of debt outstanding, and the privatization of state-owned companies were credited for the renewed vigor of the economies and the heightened interest by outside investors. The only real concern seemed to be that capital inflows might have been too fast, and investors might be fickle, and that Brazil, the largest country and largest market, would not be able to join the move toward greater growth and prosperity.

By mid-1993, the end of the century had became a hot topic. The face of the United States, and of the world, had changed dramatically, and forecasters expected even more rapid change by the end of the century. In the United States

- Population had grown by 100 since 1950 but growth had slowed to 1 percent.

- More than half the population lived in cities.

- The population was aging.

- Service-sector employment was growing, and manufacturing-sector employment declining (in 1993 government jobs were equal to those in manufacturing).

- Debt as a percentage of GDP had risen to an all-time high of 55 percent, and GDP had only grown marginally (see Figure 29). At the same time, federal interest payments had increased (see Figures 30 and 31) in spite of significant declines in inflation around the world (Figure 32).

- Household debt had gone from less than 70 percent to more than 85 percent of personal income from 1979 to 1991, although consumer spending had leveled off from the 1980s' buying binge (Figure 33). Personal savings in the United States still lagged.

FIGURE 29 • Quarterly Change in Real GNP

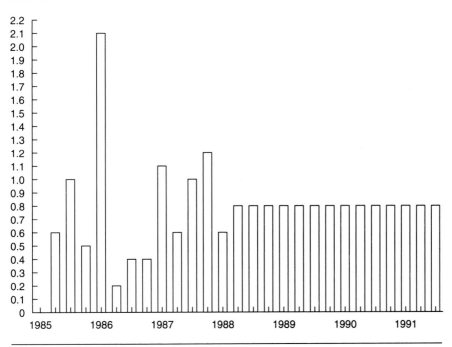

Source: *International Financial Statistics Yearbook*, 1991.

FIGURE 30 • Federal Interest Payments

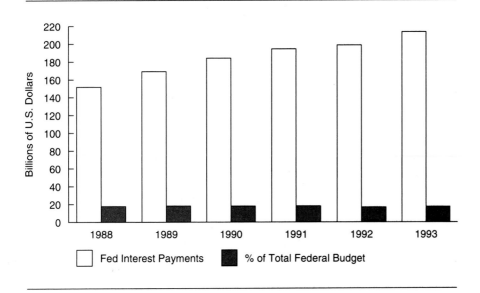

FIGURE 31 • Government Expenditures: 1986 and 1991

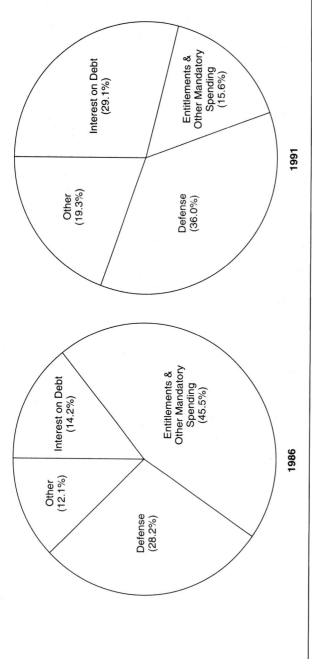

1986

1991

Source: Board of Governors of the Federal Reserve System.

FIGURE 32 • World Inflation Rates

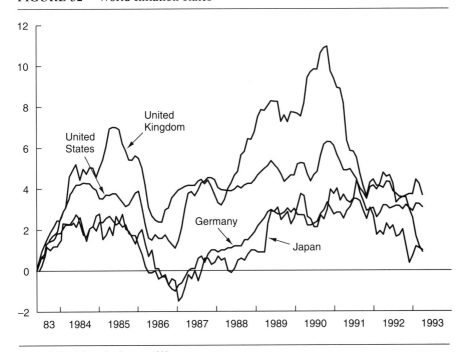

Source: Bridge Information Systems, 1993.

- The U.S. savings rate was low (5.4 percent relative to 14.1 percent in Japan and 12.7 percent in France).

- The majority of U.S. families were dual income.

- The costs of education and health care had grown faster than the rate of inflation, and health-care reform was part of the national agenda.

- The federal budget was still out of balance, and the deficit, a rallying cry during the 1992 national elections, continued its growth (see Figure 34).

- The value of the dollar continued to be low and dropped again in 1992 to a post-war low against the yen (Figure 35). In spite of this, imports into the United States grew (Figure 36), and a verbal trade war with Japan was underway.

- Interest rates in the United States and around the world had declined to their lowest points in two decades (Figures 37–39), and these low rates had a small but noticeable impact on GDP in the United States (Exhibit 40). Rate cuts in the United Kingdom had had a similar impact, while continental Europe remained hostage to inflation—fighting high rates in Germany.

FIGURE 33 • Spending Is Growing Faster Than Income

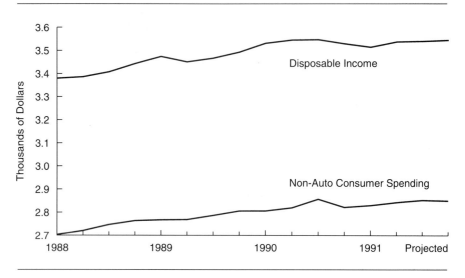

The end of the 20th century was clearly a time of change. Regional conflicts, economic and social reform, and economic realignment, all seemed to be part of the agenda for the final six years of the century. The

FIGURE 34 • Federal Outlays and Receipts as Percentage of GNP

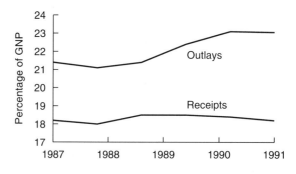

Source: *Economic Report of the President*, 1992.

FIGURE 35 • Index of the Dollar Against Ten Industrial Countries

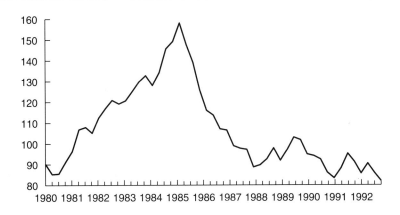

Source: Board of Governors of the Federal Reserve System.

fate of the North American Free Trade Agreement, the EEC, and the growing prosperity of Latin America remained to be determined. As for the success of the Eastern European countries, and other closed economies such as Viet Nam and Burma, speculators had high hopes. There was no doubt that the rest of the decade would determine the "new world order," in both political and economic terms.

FIGURE 36 • Imports Are Jumping Again

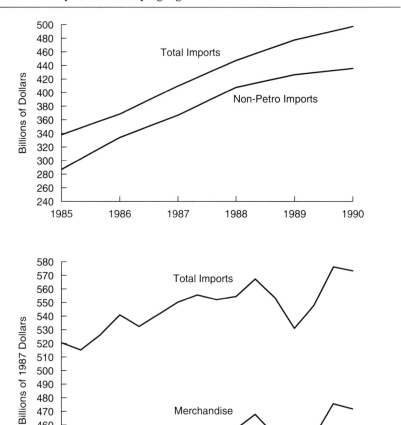

Quarterly data at seasonally adjusted annual rates; P = projected.
Source: *Economic Report of the President*, February 1992.

FIGURE 37 • U.S. Rates

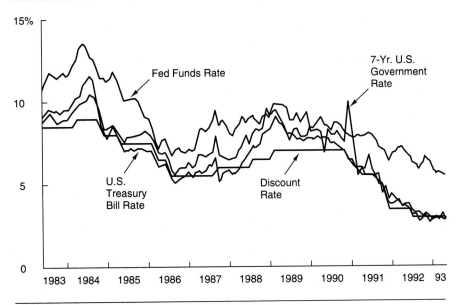

Source: Bridge Information Systems, Inc.

FIGURE 38 • U.S. Government Yield Curves, 1991–1993

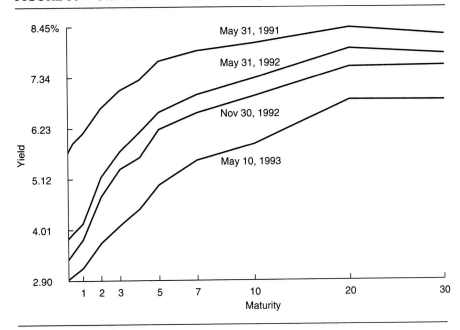

Source: Bridge Information Systems, Inc.

FIGURE 39 • International Intermediate Term Bond Yields, 1992–1993

Source: Bridge Information Systems.

FIGURE 40 • Nominal and Real Gross Domestic Product Change

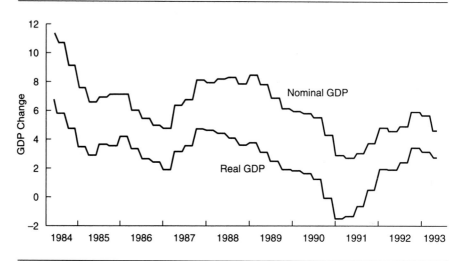

Source: Bridge Information Systems, Inc.

The Business Environment: A Retrospective, 1929–1993
EXHIBIT 1 • Industrial Production Total (seasonally adjusted, quarterly)

Ratio Scale, 1977 = 100

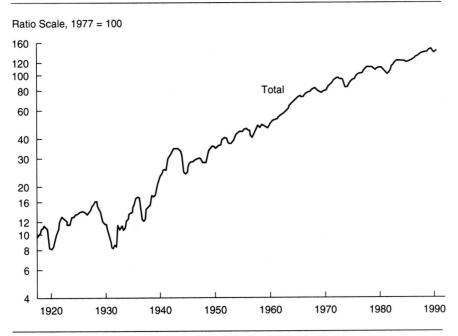

Source: Board of Governors of the Federal Reserve System, *1992 Historical Chart Book.*

The Business Environment: A Retrospective, 1929–1993
EXHIBIT 2 • Average Manufacturing Work Week

Ratio Scale, Number of Hours

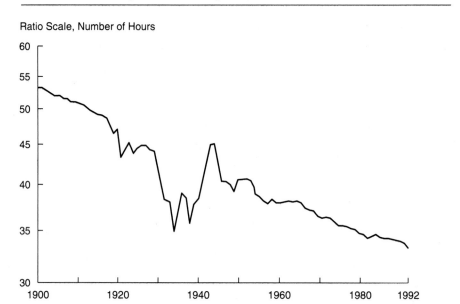

Source: *Economic Report of the President*, February 1992.

The Business Environment: A Retrospective, 1929–1993
EXHIBIT 3A • Gross National Product (GNP)[a] 1929–1992

Year	GNP (billions of US$)	Percent Change from Prior Period	GNP (in 1987 dollars)	GNP Deflator 1987=100	Percent Change from Prior Period
1959	497.0		1,942.1	25.6	
1960	516.6	3.9	1,985.1	26.0	1.7
1961	535.4	3.6	2,039.0	26.3	0.9
1962	575.8	7.5	2,145.0	26.8	2.2
1963	607.7	5.5	2,234.2	27.2	1.3
1964	653.0	7.5	2,360.8	27.7	1.7
1965	708.1	8.4	2,491.9	28.4	2.7
1966	774.9	9.4	2,639.4	29.4	3.3
1967	819.8	5.8	2,707.8	30.3	3.1
1968	895.5	9.2	2,819.8	31.8	4.9
1969	965.6	7.8	2,895.0	33.4	5.0
1970	1,017.1	5.3	2,893.5	35.2	5.4
1971	1,104.9	8.6	2,985.2	37.0	5.3
1972	1,215.7	10.0	3,128.8	38.9	5.0
1973	1,362.3	12.1	3,298.6	41.3	6.3
1974	1,474.3	8.2	3,282.4	44.9	8.8
1975	1,599.1	8.5	3,247.6	49.2	9.6
1976	1,785.5	11.7	3,412.2	52.3	6.3
1977	1,994.6	11.7	3,568.9	55.9	6.8
1978	2,254.5	13.0	3,739.0	60.3	7.9
1979	2,520.8	11.8	3,845.3	65.6	8.7
1980	2,742.1	8.8	3,823.4	71.7	9.4
1981	3,063.8	11.7	3,884.4	78.9	10.0
1982	3,179.8	3.8	3,796.1	83.8	6.2
1983	3,434.4	8.0	3,939.6	87.2	4.1
1984	3,801.5	10.7	4,174.5	91.1	4.5
1985	4,053.6	6.6	4,295.0	94.4	3.6
1986	4,277.7	5.5	4,413.5	96.9	2.7
1987	4,544.5	6.2	4,544.6	100.0	3.2
1988	4,908.2	8.0	4,726.1	103.9	3.9
1989	5,266.8	7.31	4,852.9	108.5	4.5
1990	5,542.9	5.24	4,895.8	113.2	4.3
1991	5,694.9	2.74	4,835.8	117.8	4.0
1992	5,920.4	3.96	4,911.1	120.6	2.4

Source: *Economic Report of the President,* February 1992.

The Business Environment: A Retrospective, 1929–1993
EXHIBIT 3B • Gross National Product (seasonally adjusted annual rates, quarterly)

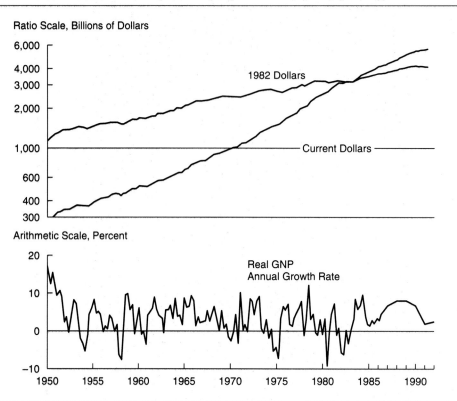

Source: Board of Governors of the Federal Reserve System, *1992 Historical Chart Book.*

The Business Environment: A Retrospective, 1929–1993
EXHIBIT 4 • Net Federal Debt, Amount Outstanding (end of year, 1929–1950; seasonally adjusted, end of quarter, 1950–1987)

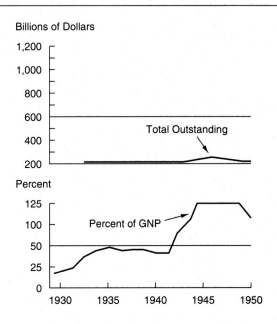

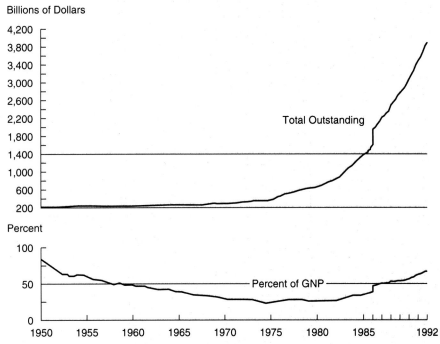

Source: Board of Governors of the Federal Reserve System, *1992 Historical Chart Book.*

The Business Environment: A Retrospective, 1929-1993
EXHIBIT 5A • Federal Receipts, Outlays, Surplus or Deficit, and Debt Selected Fiscal Years 1929-1993

Fiscal year or period	Total			On-budget			Off-budget			Gross Federal debt (end of period)		Addendum: Gross domestic product
	Receipts	Outlays	Surplus or deficit (−)	Receipts	Outlays	Surplus or deficit (−)	Receipts	Outlays	Surplus or deficit (−)	Total	Held by the public	
1929	3.9	3.1	0.7							¹ 16.9		
1933	2.0	4.6	−2.6							¹ 22.5		
1939	6.3	9.1	−2.8	5.8	9.2	−3.4	0.5	−0.0	0.5	48.2	41.4	87.8
1940	6.5	9.5	−2.9	6.0	9.5	−3.5	.6	−.0	.6	50.7	42.8	95.4
1941	8.7	13.7	−4.9	8.0	13.6	−5.6	.7	.0	.7	57.5	48.2	112.5
1942	14.6	35.1	−20.5	13.7	35.1	−21.3	.9	.1	.8	79.2	67.8	141.8
1943	24.0	78.6	−54.6	22.9	78.5	−55.6	1.1	.1	1.0	142.6	127.8	175.4
1944	43.7	91.3	−47.6	42.5	91.2	−48.7	1.3	.1	1.2	204.1	184.8	201.7
1945	45.2	92.7	−47.6	43.8	92.6	−48.7	1.3	.1	1.2	260.1	235.2	212.0
1946	39.3	55.2	−15.9	38.1	55.0	−17.0	1.2	.2	1.0	271.0	241.9	212.5
1947	38.5	34.5	4.0	37.1	34.2	2.9	1.5	.3	1.2	257.1	224.3	222.9
1948	41.6	29.8	11.8	39.9	29.4	10.5	1.6	.4	1.2	252.0	216.3	246.7
1949	39.4	38.8	.6	37.7	38.4	−.7	1.7	.4	1.3	252.6	214.3	262.7
1950	39.4	42.6	−3.1	37.3	42.0	−4.7	2.1	.5	1.6	256.9	219.0	265.8
1951	51.6	45.5	6.1	48.5	44.2	4.3	3.1	1.3	1.8	255.3	214.3	313.5
1952	66.2	67.7	−1.5	62.6	66.0	−3.4	3.6	1.7	1.9	259.1	214.8	340.5
1953	69.6	76.1	−6.5	65.5	73.8	−8.3	4.1	2.3	1.8	266.0	218.4	363.8
1954	69.7	70.9	−1.2	65.1	67.9	−2.8	4.6	2.9	1.7	270.8	224.5	368.0
1955	65.5	68.4	−3.0	60.4	64.5	−4.1	5.1	4.0	1.1	274.4	226.6	384.7
1956	74.6	70.6	3.9	68.2	65.7	2.5	6.4	5.0	1.5	272.7	222.2	416.3
1957	80.0	76.6	3.4	73.2	70.6	2.6	6.8	6.0	.8	272.3	219.3	438.3
1958	79.6	82.4	−2.8	71.6	74.9	−3.3	8.0	7.5	.5	279.7	226.3	448.1
1959	79.2	92.1	−12.8	71.0	83.1	−12.1	8.9	9.0	−.7	287.5	234.7	480.2
1960	92.5	92.2	.3	81.9	81.3	.5	10.6	10.9	−.2	290.5	236.8	504.6
1961	94.4	97.7	−3.3	82.3	86.0	−3.8	12.1	11.7	.4	292.6	238.4	517.0
1962	99.7	106.8	−7.1	87.4	93.3	−5.9	12.3	13.5	−1.3	302.9	248.0	555.2
1963	106.6	111.3	−4.8	92.4	96.4	−4.0	14.2	15.0	−.8	310.3	254.0	584.5
1964	112.6	118.5	−5.9	96.2	102.8	−6.5	16.4	15.7	.6	316.1	256.8	625.3
1965	116.8	118.2	−1.4	100.1	101.7	−1.6	16.7	16.5	.2	322.3	260.8	671.0
1966	130.8	134.5	−3.7	111.7	114.8	−3.1	19.1	19.7	−.6	328.5	263.7	735.4
1967	148.8	157.5	−8.6	124.4	137.0	−12.6	24.4	20.4	4.0	340.4	266.6	793.3
1968	153.0	178.1	−25.2	128.1	155.8	−27.7	24.9	22.3	2.6	368.7	289.5	847.2
1969	186.9	183.6	3.2	157.9	158.4	−.5	29.0	25.2	3.7	365.8	278.1	925.7
1970	192.8	195.6	−2.8	159.3	168.0	−8.7	33.5	27.6	5.9	380.9	283.2	985.4
1971	187.1	210.2	−23.0	151.3	177.3	−26.1	35.8	32.8	3.0	408.2	303.0	1,050.9
1972	207.3	230.7	−23.4	167.4	193.8	−26.4	39.9	36.9	3.1	435.9	322.4	1,147.8
1973	230.8	245.7	−14.9	184.7	200.1	−15.4	46.1	45.6	.5	466.3	340.9	1,274.0
1974	263.2	269.4	−6.1	209.3	217.3	−8.0	53.9	52.1	1.8	483.9	343.7	1,403.6
1975	279.1	332.3	−53.2	216.6	271.9	−55.3	62.5	60.4	2.0	541.9	394.7	1,509.8
1976	298.1	371.8	−73.7	231.7	302.2	−70.5	66.4	69.6	−3.2	629.0	477.4	1,684.2
Transition quarter	81.2	96.0	−14.7	63.2	76.6	−13.3	18.0	19.4	−1.4	643.6	495.5	445.0
1977	355.6	409.2	−53.7	278.7	328.5	−49.8	76.8	80.7	−3.9	706.4	549.1	1,917.2
1978	399.6	458.7	−59.2	314.2	369.1	−54.9	85.4	89.7	−4.3	776.6	607.1	2,155.0
1979	463.3	503.5	−40.2	365.3	403.5	−38.2	98.0	100.0	−2.0	828.9	639.8	2,429.5
1980	517.1	590.9	−73.8	403.9	476.6	−72.7	113.2	114.3	−1.1	908.5	709.3	2,644.1
1981	599.3	678.2	−79.0	469.1	543.1	−74.0	130.2	135.2	−5.0	994.3	784.8	2,964.4
1982	617.8	745.8	−128.0	474.3	594.4	−120.1	143.5	151.4	−7.9	1,136.8	919.2	3,122.2
1983	600.6	808.4	−207.8	453.2	661.3	−208.0	147.3	147.1	.2	1,371.2	1,131.0	3,316.5
1984	666.5	851.8	−185.4	500.4	686.0	−185.7	166.1	165.8	.3	1,564.1	1,300.0	3,695.0
1985	734.1	946.4	−212.3	547.9	769.6	−221.7	186.2	176.8	9.4	1,817.0	1,499.4	3,967.7
1986	769.1	990.3	−221.2	568.9	806.8	−238.0	200.2	183.5	16.7	2,120.1	1,736.2	4,219.0
1987	854.1	1,003.9	−149.8	640.7	810.1	−169.3	213.4	193.8	19.6	2,345.6	1,888.1	4,452.4
1988	909.0	1,064.1	−155.2	667.5	861.4	−194.0	241.5	202.7	38.8	2,600.8	2,050.3	4,808.4
1989	990.7	1,143.2	−152.5	727.0	932.3	−205.2	263.7	210.9	52.8	2,867.5	2,189.3	5,173.3
1990	1,031.3	1,252.7	−221.4	749.7	1,027.6	−278.0	281.7	225.1	56.6	3,206.3	2,410.4	5,467.1
1991	1,054.3	1,323.8	−269.5	760.4	1,082.1	−321.7	293.9	241.7	52.2	3,599.0	2,687.9	5,632.6
1992	1,091.6	1,381.8	−290.2	789.2	1,129.5	−340.3	302.4	252.3	50.1	4,002.7	2,998.6	5,868.6
1993 ²	1,147.6	1,474.9	−327.3	828.2	1,208.1	−379.9	319.4	266.8	52.6	4,410.5	3,309.7	6,164.4

¹ Not strictly comparable with later data.
² Estimates.

Note.—Through fiscal year 1976, the fiscal year was on a July 1–June 30 basis; beginning October 1976 (fiscal year 1977), the fiscal year is on an October 1–September 30 basis. The 3-month period from July 1, 1976 through September 30, 1976 is a separate fiscal period known as the transition quarter.

Refunds of receipts are excluded from receipts and outlays.

See *Budget Baselines, Historical Data, and Alternatives for the Future,* January 1993, for additional information.

Sources: Department of Commerce (Bureau of Economic Analysis), Department of the Treasury, and Office of Management and Budget.

Source: *Economic Report of the President,* February 1992.

The Business Environment: A Retrospective, 1929–1993
EXHIBIT 5B • Federal Budget, Fiscal Year Totals (seasonally adjusted annual rates, quarterly)

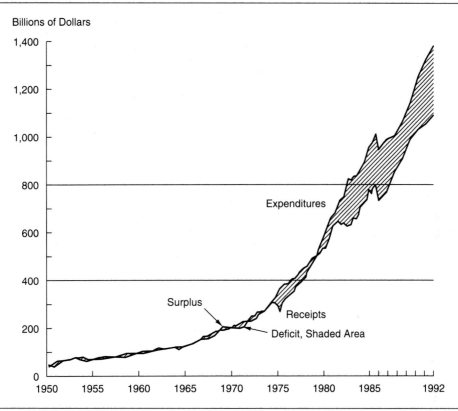

Source: Board of Governors of the Federal Reserve System, *1992 Historical Chart Book*.

The Business Environment: A Retrospective, 1929–1993
EXHIBIT 6A • Debt in the United States (amount outstanding; debt, end of year; GNP, annually)

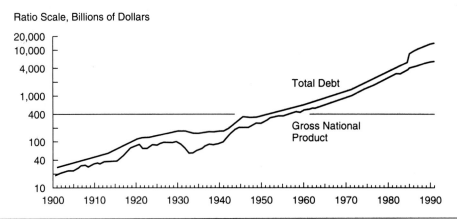

Ratio Scale, Billions of Dollars

Source: Board of Governors of the Federal Reserve System, *1991 Historical Chart Book.*

The Business Environment: A Retrospective, 1929–1993
EXHIBIT 6B • Net Federal Debt as Percentage of GNP; Net Public and Private Debt by Major Sectors, 1916 to 1970 (in billions of dollars, as of end of year)

| | | Public | | | | Private | | | | | Individual and Noncorporate | | | | | | |
| | | | | | | | Corporate | | | | Farm[d] | | Nonfarm Mortgage | | Other Nonfarm | | |
Year	Total	Total	Federal[a]	Federal Financial Agencies[b]	State and Local	Total	Total	Long-Term[c]	Short-Term[c]	Total	Production	Mortgage	1- to 4-family	Multifamily Residential and Commercial	Commercial	Financial[f]	Consumer
1970	$1,854.1	$484.7	301.1	$38.8	$144.8	$1,369.4	$793.5	$360.2	433.4	$575.9	$27.5	$31.2	$274.6	$46.3	$35.8	$33.3	$127.2
1969	1,735.0	452.4	289.3	30.6	132.6	1,282.6	734.2	323.5	410.7	548.4	26.0	29.5	261.5	42.4	35.6	32.3	121.1
1968	1,582.5	437.1	291.9	21.4	123.9	1,145.4	631.5	283.6	347.9	513.9	24.3	27.5	246.5	38.4	33.4	33.0	110.8
1967	1,438.7	408.8	286.5	9.0	113.4	1,029.9	553.7	255.6	298.1	476.2	22.8	25.5	232.0	34.9	31.1	29.1	100.8
1966	1,338.7	387.9	271.8	11.2	104.8	950.8	506.6	231.3	275.3	444.2	19.1	23.3	219.6	32.0	29.4	24.5	96.2
1965	1,234.6	373.7	266.4	8.9	98.3	870.0	454.3	209.4	244.9	415.7	18.1	21.2	208.7	28.1	27.0	22.7	89.9
1964	1,151.6	301.9	264.0	7.5	90.4	789.7	409.6	192.5	217.1	380.1	17.1	18.9	193.3	25.6	23.5	21.5	80.3
1963	1,070.9	348.5	257.5	7.2	83.9	722.3	376.4	174.8	201.7	345.8	16.4	16.8	177.1	21.5	21.5	20.8	71.7
1962	996.0	335.9	253.6	5.3	77.0	660.1	348.2	161.2	187.0	311.9	15.0	15.2	161.9	18.4	19.3	18.3	63.8
1961	930.3	321.2	246.7	4.0	70.5	609.1	324.3	149.3	174.9	284.8	13.6	13.9	148.9	15.6	17.9	16.9	58.0
1960	874.2	308.1	239.8	3.5	64.9	566.1	302.8	139.1	163.7	263.3	12.3	12.8	137.4	13.9	16.6	14.2	56.1
1959	833.0	304.7	241.4	3.7	59.6	528.3	283.3	129.3	154.0	245.0	11.7	12.1	127.3	13.7	15.8	13.4	51.5
1958	769.6	287.2	231.0	2.5	53.7	482.4	259.5	121.2	138.4	222.9	12.1	11.1	114.5	13.6	13.7	12.8	45.1
1957	728.3	274.0	223.0	2.4	48.6	454.3	246.7	112.1	134.6	207.6	9.8	10.4	105.2	12.9	13.2	11.1	45.0
1956	698.4	271.2	224.3	2.4	44.5	427.2	231.7	100.1	131.7	195.5	9.6	9.8	96.8	12.6	13.3	11.1	42.3

continued

		Public				Private											
							Corporate			Individual and Noncorporate							
											Farm[d]		Nonfarm Mortgage		Other Nonfarm		
	Total	Total	Federal[a]	Federal Financial Agencies[b]	State and Local	Total	Total	Long-Term[c]	Short-Term[c]	Total	Production	Mortgage	1- to 4-family	Multifamily Residential and Commercial	Commercial	Financial[f]	Consumer
1955	665.8	273.6	229.6	2.9	41.1	392.2	212.1	90.0	122.2	180.1	9.7	9.0	86.3	12.4	12.4	11.6	38.8
1954	605.9	265.9	229.1	1.3	35.5	340.0	182.8	82.9	100.0	157.2	9.3	8.2	74.1	12.3	10.4	10.4	32.5
1953	581.6	258.9	226.8	1.4	30.7	322.7	179.5	78.3	101.2	143.2	9.1	7.7	64.7	12.0	9.9	8.5	31.4
1952	550.2	249.8	221.5	1.3	27.0	300.4	171.0	73.3	97.7	129.4	8.0	7.2	57.1	11.8	10.3	7.5	27.5
1951	519.2	242.4	216.9	1.3	24.2	276.8	162.5	66.6	95.9	114.3	7.0	6.7	50.4	11.3	9.5	6.7	22.7
1950	486.2	239.8	217.4	0.7	21.7	246.4	142.1	60.1	81.9	104.3	6.2	6.1	43.9	10.9	8.9	6.9	21.5
1949	445.8	237.4	217.6	0.7	19.1	208.4	118.0	56.5	61.4	90.4	6.4	5.6	36.4	10.7	7.9	6.0	17.4
1948	431.3	232.9	215.3	0.6	17.0	198.4	117.8	52.5	65.3	80.6	5.5	5.3	32.0	10.4	7.8	5.1	14.4
1947	415.7	237.4	221.7	$ 0.7	15.0	178.3	108.9	46.1	62.8	69.4	3.5	5.1	27.1	10.1	7.1	4.8	11.6
1946	396.6	243.2	229.5	—	13.7	153.4	93.5	41.3	52.2	59.9	2.7	4.9	22.1	9.7	6.2	5.9	8.4
1945	405.9	265.9	252.5	—	13.4	140.0	85.3	38.3	47.0	54.7	2.5	4.8	17.7	9.3	4.4	10.3	5.7
1944	370.6	225.8	211.9	—	13.9	144.8	94.1	39.8	54.3	50.7	2.8	4.9	17.0	9.0	3.7	8.1	5.1
1943	313.2	168.9	154.4	—	14.5	144.3	95.5	41.0	54.5	48.8	2.8	5.4	16.9	9.2	3.8	5.7	4.9
1942	258.6	117.1	101.7	—	15.4	141.5	91.6	42.7	49.0	49.9	3.0	6.0	17.3	9.5	4.1	4.0	6.0
1941	211.4	72.4	56.3	—	16.1	139.0	83.4	43.6	39.8	55.6	2.9	6.4	17.4	9.7	5.0	5.0	9.2
1940	189.8	61.2	44.8	—	16.4	128.6	75.6	43.7	31.9	53.0	2.6	6.5	16.5	9.6	4.3	5.2	8.3
1939	183.3	59.0	42.6	—	16.4	124.3	73.5	44.4	29.2	50.8	2.2	6.6	15.5	9.5	3.8	6.0	7.2
1938	179.9	56.6	40.5	—	16.1	123.3	73.3	44.8	28.5	50.0	2.2	6.8	15.0	9.5	10.1		6.4
1937	182.2	55.3	39.2	—	16.1	126.9	75.8	43.5	32.3	51.1	1.6	7.0	14.7	9.6	11.3		6.9
1936	180.6	53.9	37.7	—	16.2	126.7	76.1	42.5	33.5	50.6	1.4	7.2	14.6	9.8	11.2		6.4

Year																
1935	175.0	50.5	34.4	—	16.1	124.5	74.8	43.6	31.2	49.7	1.5	7.4	14.7	10.1	10.8	5.2
1934	171.0	46.3	30.4	—	15.9	125.3	75.5	44.6	30.9	49.8	1.3	7.6	14.8	10.7	11.2	4.2
1933	168.5	40.6	24.3	—	16.3	127.9	76.9	47.9	29.0	51.0	1.4	7.7	14.6	11.7	11.7	3.9
1932	175.0	37.9	21.3	—	16.6	137.1	80.0	49.2	30.8	57.1	1.6	8.5	15.8	13.2	14.0	4.0
1931	182.9	34.5	18.5	—	16.0	148.4	83.5	50.3	33.2	64.9	2.0	9.1	17.2	13.7	17.6	5.3
1930	192.3	31.2	16.5	—	14.7	161.1	89.3	51.1	38.2	71.8	2.4	9.4	17.9	14.1	21.6	6.4
1929	191.9	30.1	16.5	—	13.6	161.8	88.9	47.3	41.6	72.9	2.6	9.6	18.0	13.2	22.4	7.1
1928	186.3	30.2	17.5	—	12.7	156.1	86.1	—	—	70.0	2.7	9.8	29.6		21.6	6.3
1927	177.9	30.3	18.2	—	12.1	147.6	81.2	—	—	66.4	2.6	9.8	26.9		21.8	5.3
1926	169.2	30.3	19.2	—	11.1	138.9	76.2	—	—	62.7	2.6	9.7	24.0		21.2	5.2
1925	162.9	30.6	20.3	—	10.3	132.3	72.7	—	—	59.6	2.8	9.7	21.3		21.1	4.7
1924	153.4	30.4	21.0	—	9.4	123.0	67.2	—	—	55.8	2.7	9.9	18.6		20.6	4.0
1923	146.7	30.4	21.8	—	8.6	116.3	62.6	—	—	53.7	3.0	10.7	16.3		20.0	3.7
1922	140.2	30.7	22.8	—	7.9	109.5	58.6	—	—	50.9	3.1	10.8	14.1		19.7	3.2
1921	136.3	30.1	23.1	—	7.0	106.2	57.0	—	—	49.2	3.3	10.7	12.8		19.4	3.0
1920	135.7	29.9	23.7	—	6.2	105.8	57.7	—	—	48.1	3.9	10.2	11.7		19.3	3.0
1919	128.3	31.1	25.6	—	5.5	97.2	53.3	—	—	43.9	3.5	8.4	10.1		$19.3	$2.6
1918	117.5	26.0	20.9	—	5.1	91.5	47.0	—	—	44.5	2.7	7.1	9.6		25.1	
1917	94.5	12.1	7.3	—	4.8	82.4	43.7	—	—	38.7	2.5	6.5	9.3		20.4	
1916	$82.2	$5.7	1.2	—	$4.5	$76.5	$40.2	—	—	$36.3	$2.0	$5.8	$8.4		$20.1	

[a] Net federal debt (public and agency) is the outstanding debt held by the public as shown in *The Budget of the United States Government, Fiscal Year 1974*.

[b] Comprised the debt of federally sponsored agencies, in which there is no longer any federal proprietary interest. Includes obligations of the Federal Land Banks, beginning 1947; debt of the Federal Home Loan Banks, beginning 1951; and debts of the Federal National Mortgage Association, Federal Intermediate Credit Banks, and Banks for Cooperatives, beginning 1963.

[c] Long-term debt has a maturity of one year or more; short-term debt, less than one year.

[d] Farm production loans and farm mortgages. Farmers' financial and consumer debt is included in the nonfarm categories.

[e] Financial debt is owed to banks for purchasing or carrying securities, customers' debt to brokers, and debt owed to life insurance companies by policyholders.

Source: U.S. Bureau of Economic Analysis, *Survey of Current Business*.

The Business Environment: A Retrospective, 1929–1993
EXHIBIT 7 • Debt in the United States (amount outstanding;
debt, end of year; nonfederal and federal)

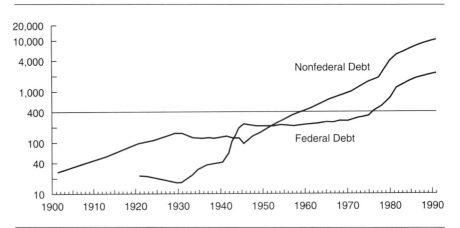

Source: Board of Governors of the Federal Reserve System, *1981 Historical Chart Book.*

The Business Environment: A Retrospective, 1929–1993
EXHIBIT 8 • Short-Term Interest Rates, Money Market (discount
rate, effective date of change; all others, quarterly averages)

Percent per Annum

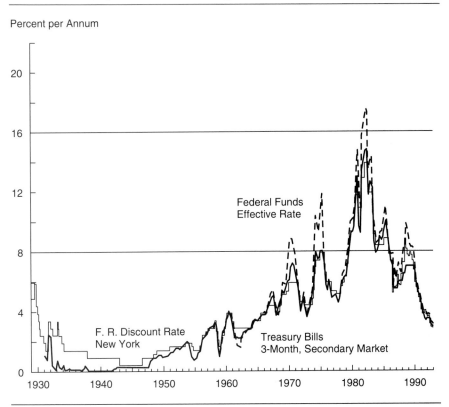

Source: Board of Governors of the Federal Reserve System, *1992 Historical Chart Book.*

The Business Environment: A Retrospective, 1929–1993
EXHIBIT 9 • Short-Term Interest Rates, Business Borrowing (prime rate,
effective date of change; commercial paper, quarterly averages)

Percent per Annum

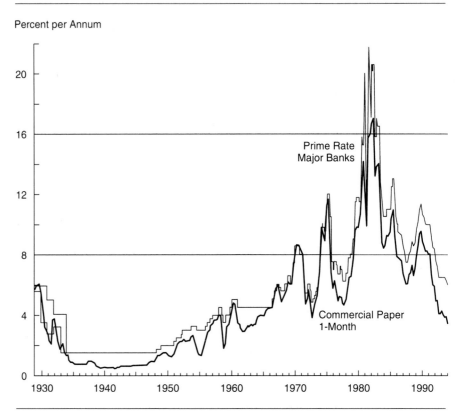

Third and fourth quarter data projected for 1993.

Source: Board of Governors of the Federal Reserve System, *1992 Historical Chart Book.*

The Business Environment: A Retrospective, 1929–1993
EXHIBIT 10A • **Long-Term Bond Yields** (quarterly averages)

Percent per Annum

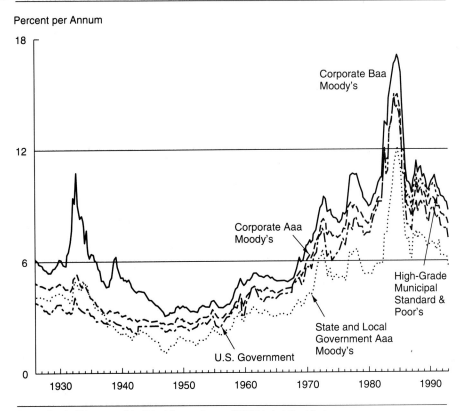

Source: Board of Governors of the Federal Reserve System, *1992 Historical Chart Book.*

The Business Environment: A Retrospective, 1929–1993

EXHIBIT 10B • Bond Yields and Interest Rates, 1929–1992

Year and month	U.S. Treasury securities				Corporate bonds (Moody's)		High-grade munici-pal bonds (Stand-ard & Poor's) yields [3]	New-home mort-gage yields [3]	Commer-cial paper, 6 months [4]	Prime rate charged by banks [5]	Discount rate, Federal Reserve Bank of New York [5]	Federal funds rate [6]
	Bills (new issues) [1]		Constant maturities [2]		Aaa	Baa						
	3-month	6-month	3-year	10-year								
1929					4.73	5.90	4.27		5.85	5.50–6.00	5.16	
1933	0.515				4.49	7.76	4.71		1.73	1.50–4.00	2.56	
1939	.023				3.01	4.96	2.76		.59	1.50	1.00	
1940	.014				2.84	4.75	2.50		.56	1.50	1.00	
1941	.103				2.77	4.33	2.10		.53	1.50	1.00	
1942	.326				2.83	4.28	2.36		.66	1.50	[7] 1.00	
1943	.373				2.73	3.91	2.06		.69	1.50	[7] 1.00	
1944	.375				2.72	3.61	1.86		.73	1.50	[7] 1.00	
1945	.375				2.62	3.29	1.67		.75	1.50	[7] 1.00	
1946	.375				2.53	3.05	1.64		.81	1.50	[7] 1.00	
1947	.594				2.61	3.24	2.01		1.03	1.50–1.75	1.00	
1948	1.040				2.82	3.47	2.40		1.4	1.75–2.00	1.34	
1949	1.102				2.66	3.42	2.21		1.49	2.00	1.50	
1950	1.218				2.62	3.24	1.98		1.45	2.07	1.59	
1951	1.552				2.86	3.41	2.00		2.16	2.56	1.75	
1952	1.766				2.96	3.52	2.19		2.33	3.00	1.75	
1953	1.931		2.47	2.85	3.20	3.74	2.72		2.52	3.17	1.99	
1954	.953		1.63	2.40	2.90	3.51	2.37		1.58	3.05	1.60	
1955	1.753		2.47	2.82	3.06	3.53	2.53		2.18	3.16	1.89	1.78
1956	2.658		3.19	3.18	3.36	3.88	2.93		3.31	3.77	2.77	2.73
1957	3.267		3.98	3.65	3.89	4.71	3.60		3.81	4.20	3.12	3.11
1958	1.839		2.84	3.32	3.79	4.73	3.56		2.46	3.83	2.15	1.57
1959	3.405	3.832	4.46	4.33	4.38	5.05	3.95		3.97	4.48	3.36	3.30
1960	2.928	3.247	3.98	4.12	4.41	5.19	3.73		3.85	4.82	3.53	3.22
1961	2.378	2.605	3.54	3.88	4.35	5.08	3.46		2.97	4.50	3.00	1.96
1962	2.778	2.908	3.47	3.95	4.33	5.02	3.18		3.26	4.50	3.00	2.68
1963	3.157	3.253	3.67	4.00	4.26	4.86	3.23	5.89	3.55	4.50	3.23	3.18
1964	3.549	3.686	4.03	4.19	4.40	4.83	3.22	5.83	3.97	4.50	3.55	3.50
1965	3.954	4.055	4.22	4.28	4.49	4.87	3.27	5.81	4.38	4.54	4.04	4.07
1966	4.881	5.082	5.23	4.92	5.13	5.67	3.82	6.25	5.55	5.63	4.50	5.11
1967	4.321	4.630	5.03	5.07	5.51	6.23	3.98	6.46	5.10	5.61	4.19	4.22
1968	5.339	5.470	5.68	5.65	6.18	6.94	4.51	6.97	5.90	6.30	5.16	5.66
1969	6.677	6.853	7.02	6.67	7.03	7.81	5.81	7.81	7.83	7.96	5.87	8.20
1970	6.458	6.562	7.29	7.35	8.04	9.11	6.51	8.45	7.71	7.91	5.95	7.18
1971	4.348	4.511	5.65	6.16	7.39	8.56	5.70	7.74	5.11	5.72	4.88	4.66
1972	4.071	4.466	5.72	6.21	7.21	8.16	5.27	7.60	4.73	5.25	4.50	4.43
1973	7.041	7.178	6.95	6.84	7.44	8.24	5.18	7.96	8.15	8.03	6.44	8.73
1974	7.886	7.926	7.82	7.56	8.57	9.50	6.09	8.92	9.84	10.81	7.83	10.50
1975	5.838	6.122	7.49	7.99	8.83	10.61	6.89	9.00	6.32	7.86	6.25	5.82
1976	4.989	5.266	6.77	7.61	8.43	9.75	6.49	9.00	5.34	6.84	5.50	5.04
1977	5.265	5.510	6.69	7.42	8.02	8.97	5.56	9.02	5.61	6.83	5.46	5.54
1978	7.221	7.572	8.29	8.41	8.73	9.49	5.90	9.56	7.99	9.06	7.46	7.93
1979	10.041	10.017	9.71	9.44	9.63	10.69	6.39	10.78	10.91	12.67	10.28	11.19
1980	11.506	11.374	11.55	11.46	11.94	13.67	8.51	12.66	12.29	15.27	11.77	13.36
1981	14.029	13.776	14.44	13.91	14.17	16.04	11.23	14.70	14.76	18.87	13.42	16.38
1982	10.686	11.084	12.92	13.00	13.79	16.11	11.57	15.14	11.89	14.86	11.02	12.26
1983	8.63	8.75	10.45	11.10	12.04	13.55	9.47	12.57	8.89	10.79	8.50	9.09
1984	9.58	9.80	11.89	12.44	12.71	14.19	10.15	12.38	10.16	12.04	8.80	10.23
1985	7.48	7.66	9.64	10.62	11.37	12.72	9.18	11.55	8.01	9.93	7.69	8.10
1986	5.98	6.03	7.06	7.68	9.02	10.39	7.38	10.17	6.39	8.33	6.33	6.81
1987	5.82	6.05	7.68	8.39	9.38	10.58	7.73	9.31	6.85	8.21	5.66	6.66
1988	6.69	6.92	8.26	8.85	9.71	10.83	7.76	9.19	7.68	9.32	6.20	7.57
1989	8.12	8.04	8.55	8.49	9.26	10.18	7.24	10.13	8.80	10.87	6.93	9.21
1990	7.51	7.47	8.26	8.55	9.32	10.36	7.25	10.05	7.95	10.01	6.98	8.10
1991	5.42	5.49	6.82	7.86	8.77	9.80	6.89	9.32	5.85	8.46	5.45	5.69
1992	3.45	3.57	5.30	7.01	8.14	8.98	6.41		3.80	6.25	3.25	3.52
										High-low	High-low	
1987												
Jan	5.45	5.47	6.41	7.08	8.36	9.72	6.63	9.51	5.76	7.50– 7.50	5.50–5.50	6.43
Feb	5.59	5.60	6.56	7.25	8.38	9.65	6.66	9.23	5.99	7.50– 7.50	5.50–5.50	6.10
Mar	5.56	5.56	6.58	7.25	8.36	9.61	6.71	9.14	6.10	7.50– 7.50	5.50–5.50	6.13
Apr	5.76	5.93	7.32	8.02	8.85	10.04	7.62	9.21	6.50	7.75– 7.50	5.50–5.50	6.37
May	5.75	6.11	8.02	8.61	9.33	10.51	8.10	9.37	7.04	8.25– 7.75	5.50–5.50	6.85
June	5.69	5.99	7.82	8.40	9.32	10.52	7.89	9.45	7.00	8.25– 8.25	5.50–5.50	6.73
July	5.78	5.86	7.74	8.45	9.42	10.61	7.83	9.41	6.72	8.25– 8.25	5.50–5.50	6.58
Aug	6.00	6.14	8.03	8.76	9.67	10.80	7.90	9.38	6.81	8.25– 8.25	5.50–5.50	6.73
Sept	6.32	6.57	8.67	9.42	10.18	11.31	8.36	9.37	7.55	8.75– 8.25	6.00–5.50	7.22
Oct	6.40	6.86	8.75	9.52	10.52	11.62	8.84	9.25	7.96	9.25– 8.75	6.00–6.00	7.29
Nov	5.81	6.23	7.99	8.86	10.01	11.23	8.09	9.30	7.17	9.00– 8.75	6.00–6.00	6.69
Dec	5.80	6.36	8.13	8.99	10.11	11.29	8.07	9.15	7.49	8.75– 8.75	6.00–6.00	6.77

[1] Rate on new issues within period; bank-discount basis.
[2] Yields on the more actively traded issues adjusted to constant maturities by the Treasury Department.
[3] Effective rate (in the primary market) on conventional mortgages, reflecting fees and charges as well as contract rate and assuming, on the average, repayment at end of 10 years. Rates beginning January 1973 not strictly comparable with prior rates.
See next page for continuation of table.

EXHIBIT 10B • *continued*

Year and month	U.S. Treasury securities Bills (new issues)[1] 3-month	6-month	Constant maturities[2] 3-year	10-year	Corporate bonds (Moody's) Aaa	Baa	High-grade municipal bonds (Standard & Poor's)	New-home mortgage yields[3]	Commercial paper, 6 months[4]	Prime rate charged by banks[5] High-low	Discount rate, Federal Reserve Bank of New York[5] High-low	Federal funds rate[6]
1988:												
Jan.....	5.90	6.31	7.87	8.67	9.88	11.07	7.81	9.10	6.92	8.75– 8.75	6.00–6.00	6.83
Feb.....	5.69	5.96	7.38	8.21	9.40	10.62	7.55	9.12	6.58	8.75– 8.50	6.00–6.00	6.58
Mar.....	5.69	5.91	7.50	8.37	9.39	10.57	7.80	9.15	6.64	8.50– 8.50	6.00–6.00	6.58
Apr.....	5.92	6.21	7.83	8.72	9.67	10.90	7.91	9.13	6.92	8.50– 8.50	6.00–6.00	6.87
May.....	6.27	6.53	8.24	9.09	9.90	11.04	8.01	8.95	7.31	9.00– 8.50	6.00–6.00	7.09
June.....	6.50	6.76	8.22	8.92	9.86	11.00	7.86	9.26	7.53	9.00– 9.00	6.00–6.00	7.51
July.....	6.73	6.97	8.44	9.06	9.96	11.11	7.87	9.17	7.90	9.50– 9.00	6.00–6.00	7.75
Aug.....	7.02	7.36	8.77	9.26	10.11	11.21	7.86	9.06	8.36	10.00– 9.50	6.50–6.00	8.01
Sept.....	7.23	7.43	8.57	8.98	9.82	10.90	7.71	9.26	8.23	10.00–10.00	6.50–6.50	8.19
Oct.....	7.34	7.50	8.43	8.80	9.51	10.41	7.54	9.10	8.24	10.00–10.00	6.50–6.50	8.30
Nov.....	7.68	7.76	8.72	8.96	9.45	10.48	7.58	9.43	8.55	10.50–10.00	6.50–6.50	8.35
Dec.....	8.09	8.24	9.11	9.11	9.57	10.65	7.66	9.39	8.97	10.50–10.50	6.50–6.50	8.76
1989:												
Jan.....	8.29	8.38	9.20	9.09	9.62	10.65	7.41	9.52	9.02	10.50–10.50	6.50–6.50	9.12
Feb.....	8.48	8.49	9.32	9.17	9.64	10.61	7.47	9.82	9.35	11.50–10.50	7.00–6.50	9.36
Mar.....	8.83	8.87	9.61	9.36	9.80	10.67	7.61	9.99	9.97	11.50–11.50	7.00–7.00	9.85
Apr.....	8.70	8.73	9.40	9.18	9.79	10.61	7.49	10.17	9.78	11.50–11.50	7.00–7.00	9.84
May.....	8.40	8.39	8.98	8.86	9.57	10.46	7.25	10.18	9.29	11.50–11.50	7.00–7.00	9.81
June.....	8.22	8.00	8.37	8.28	9.10	10.03	6.97	10.42	8.80	11.50–11.00	7.00–7.00	9.53
July.....	7.92	7.63	7.83	8.02	8.93	9.87	6.97	10.48	8.35	11.00–10.50	7.00–7.00	9.24
Aug.....	7.91	7.72	8.13	8.11	8.96	9.88	7.08	10.22	8.32	10.50–10.50	7.00–7.00	8.99
Sept.....	7.72	7.74	8.26	8.19	9.01	9.91	7.27	10.24	8.50	10.50–10.50	7.00–7.00	9.02
Oct.....	7.63	7.61	8.02	8.01	8.92	9.81	7.22	10.11	8.24	10.50–10.50	7.00–7.00	8.84
Nov.....	7.65	7.46	7.80	7.87	8.89	9.81	7.13	10.09	8.00	10.50–10.50	7.00–7.00	8.55
Dec.....	7.64	7.45	7.77	7.84	8.86	9.82	7.01	10.07	7.93	10.50–10.50	7.00–7.00	8.45
1990:												
Jan.....	7.64	7.52	8.13	8.21	8.99	9.94	7.13	9.91	7.96	10.50–10.00	7.00–7.00	8.23
Feb.....	7.76	7.72	8.39	8.47	9.22	10.14	7.21	9.88	8.04	10.00–10.00	7.00–7.00	8.24
Mar.....	7.87	7.83	8.63	8.59	9.37	10.21	7.29	10.03	8.23	10.00–10.00	7.00–7.00	8.28
Apr.....	7.78	7.82	8.78	8.79	9.46	10.30	7.36	10.17	8.29	10.00–10.00	7.00–7.00	8.26
May.....	7.78	7.82	8.69	8.76	9.47	10.41	7.34	10.28	8.23	10.00–10.00	7.00–7.00	8.18
June.....	7.74	7.64	8.40	8.48	9.26	10.22	7.22	10.13	8.06	10.00–10.00	7.00–7.00	8.29
July.....	7.66	7.57	8.26	8.47	9.24	10.20	7.15	10.08	7.90	10.00–10.00	7.00–7.00	8.15
Aug.....	7.44	7.36	8.22	8.75	9.41	10.41	7.31	10.11	7.77	10.00–10.00	7.00–7.00	8.13
Sept.....	7.38	7.33	8.27	8.89	9.56	10.64	7.40	9.90	7.83	10.00–10.00	7.00–7.00	8.20
Oct.....	7.19	7.20	8.07	8.72	9.53	10.74	7.40	9.98	7.81	10.00–10.00	7.00–7.00	8.11
Nov.....	7.07	7.04	7.74	8.39	9.30	10.62	7.10	9.90	7.74	10.00–10.00	7.00–7.00	7.81
Dec.....	6.81	6.76	7.47	8.08	9.05	10.43	7.04	9.76	7.49	10.00–10.00	7.00–6.50	7.31
1991:												
Jan.....	6.30	6.34	7.38	8.09	9.04	10.45	7.05	9.65	7.02	10.00– 9.50	6.50–6.50	6.91
Feb.....	5.95	5.93	7.08	7.85	8.83	10.07	6.90	9.57	6.41	9.50– 9.00	6.50–6.00	6.25
Mar.....	5.91	5.91	7.35	8.11	8.93	10.09	7.07	9.43	6.36	9.00– 9.00	6.00–6.00	6.12
Apr.....	5.67	5.73	7.23	8.04	8.86	9.94	7.05	9.60	6.07	9.00– 9.00	6.00–5.50	5.91
May.....	5.51	5.65	7.12	8.07	8.86	9.86	6.95	9.52	5.94	9.00– 8.50	5.50–5.50	5.78
June.....	5.60	5.76	7.39	8.28	9.01	9.96	7.09	9.46	6.16	8.50– 8.50	5.50–5.50	5.90
July.....	5.58	5.71	7.38	8.27	9.00	9.89	7.03	9.43	6.14	8.50– 8.50	5.50–5.50	5.82
Aug.....	5.39	5.47	6.80	7.90	8.75	9.65	6.89	9.48	5.76	8.50– 8.50	5.50–5.50	5.66
Sept.....	5.25	5.29	6.50	7.65	8.61	9.51	6.80	9.30	5.59	8.50– 8.00	5.50–5.00	5.45
Oct.....	5.03	5.08	6.23	7.53	8.55	9.49	6.59	9.04	5.33	8.00– 8.00	5.00–5.00	5.21
Nov.....	4.60	4.66	5.90	7.42	8.48	9.45	6.64	8.64	4.93	8.00– 7.50	5.00–4.50	4.81
Dec.....	4.12	4.16	5.39	7.09	8.31	9.26	6.63	8.53	4.49	7.50– 6.50	4.50–3.50	4.43
1992:												
Jan.....	3.84	3.88	5.40	7.03	8.20	9.13	6.41	8.49	4.06	6.50–6.50	3.50–3.50	4.03
Feb.....	3.84	3.94	5.72	7.34	8.29	9.23	6.67	8.65	4.13	6.50–6.50	3.50–3.50	4.06
Mar.....	4.05	4.19	6.18	7.54	8.35	9.25	6.69	8.51	4.38	6.50–6.50	3.50–3.50	3.98
Apr.....	3.81	3.93	5.93	7.48	8.33	9.21	6.64	8.58	4.13	6.50–6.50	3.50–3.50	3.73
May.....	3.66	3.78	5.81	7.39	8.28	9.13	6.57	8.59	3.97	6.50–6.50	3.50–3.50	3.82
June.....	3.70	3.81	5.60	7.26	8.22	9.05	6.50	8.43	3.99	6.50–6.50	3.50–3.50	3.76
July.....	3.28	3.36	4.91	6.84	8.07	8.84	6.12	8.00	3.53	6.50–6.00	3.50–3.00	3.25
Aug.....	3.14	3.23	4.72	6.59	7.95	8.65	6.08	8.00	3.44	6.00–6.00	3.00–3.00	3.30
Sept.....	2.97	3.01	4.42	6.42	7.92	8.62	6.24	7.93	3.26	6.00–6.00	3.00–3.00	3.22
Oct.....	2.84	2.98	4.64	6.59	7.99	8.84	6.38	7.90	3.33	6.00–6.00	3.00–3.00	3.10
Nov.....	3.14	3.35	5.14	6.87	8.10	8.96	6.35	8.07	3.67	6.00–6.00	3.00–3.00	3.09
Dec.....	3.25	3.39	5.21	6.77	7.98	8.81	6.24	....	3.70	6.00–6.00	3.00–3.00	2.92

[4] Bank-discount basis; prior to November 1979, data are for 4–6 months paper.

[5] For monthly data, high and low for the period. Prime rate for 1929–33 and 1947–48 are ranges of the rate in effect during the period.

[6] Since July 19, 1975, the daily effective rate is an average of the rates on a given day weighted by the volume of transactions at these rates. Prior to that date, the daily effective rate was the rate considered most representative of the day's transactions, usually the one at which most transactions occurred.

[7] From October 30, 1942, to April 24, 1946, a preferential rate of 0.50 percent was in effect for advances secured by Government securities maturing in 1 year or less.

Sources: Department of the Treasury, Board of Governors of the Federal Reserve System, Federal Housing Finance Board, Moody's Investors Service, and Standard & Poor's Corporation.

Source: *Economic Report of the President*, February 1992.

The Business Environment: A Retrospective, 1929–1993

EXHIBIT 11 • Real Interest Rates, 1933–1992 (Average 90-Day T-Bill − Change in CPI)

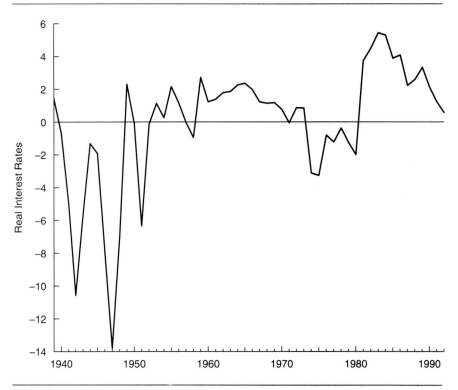

Source: *Economic Report of the President,* February 1992.

The Business Environment: A Retrospective, 1929–1993
EXHIBIT 12A • Stock Market Trading Volume and Prices (quarterly averages)

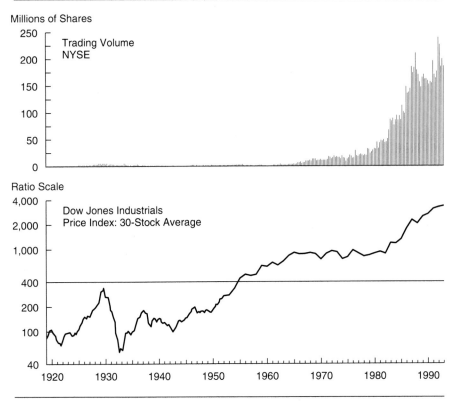

Source: Board of Governors of the Federal Reserve System, and *Economic Report of the President*, February 1992.

The Business Environment: A Retrospective, 1929–1993

EXHIBIT 12B • Common Stock Prices and Yields, 1955–1992

Year or month	Common stock prices [1]							Common stock yields (percent) [5]	
	New York Stock Exchange indexes (Dec. 31, 1965 = 50) [2]					Dow Jones industrial average [3]	Standard & Poor's composite index (1941–43 = 10) [4]	Dividend-price ratio [6]	Earnings-price ratio [7]
	Composite	Industrial	Transportation	Utility	Finance				
1955	21.54					442.72	40.49	4.08	7.95
1956	24.40					493.01	46.62	4.09	7.55
1957	23.67					475.71	44.38	4.35	7.89
1958	24.56					491.66	46.24	3.97	6.23
1959	30.73					632.12	57.38	3.23	5.78
1960	30.01					618.04	55.85	3.47	5.90
1961	35.37					691.55	66.27	2.98	4.62
1962	33.49					639.76	62.38	3.37	5.82
1963	37.51					714.81	69.87	3.17	5.50
1964	43.76					834.05	81.37	3.01	5.32
1965	47.39					910.88	88.17	3.00	5.59
1966	46.15	46.18	50.26	45.41	44.45	873.60	85.26	3.40	6.63
1967	50.77	51.97	53.51	45.43	49.82	879.12	91.93	3.20	5.73
1968	55.37	58.00	50.58	44.19	65.85	906.00	98.70	3.07	5.67
1969	54.67	57.44	46.96	42.80	70.49	876.72	97.84	3.24	6.08
1970	45.72	48.03	32.14	37.24	60.00	753.19	83.22	3.83	6.45
1971	54.22	57.92	44.35	39.53	70.38	884.76	98.29	3.14	5.41
1972	60.29	65.73	50.17	38.48	78.35	950.71	109.20	2.84	5.50
1973	57.42	63.08	37.74	37.69	70.12	923.88	107.43	3.06	7.12
1974	43.84	48.08	31.89	29.79	49.67	759.37	82.85	4.47	11.59
1975	45.73	50.52	31.10	31.50	47.14	802.49	86.16	4.31	9.15
1976	54.46	60.44	39.57	36.97	52.94	974.92	102.01	3.77	8.90
1977	53.69	57.86	41.09	40.92	55.25	894.63	98.20	4.62	10.79
1978	53.70	58.23	43.50	39.22	56.65	820.23	96.02	5.28	12.03
1979	58.32	64.76	47.34	38.20	61.42	844.40	103.01	5.47	13.46
1980	68.10	78.70	60.61	37.35	64.25	891.41	118.78	5.26	12.66
1981	74.02	85.44	72.61	38.91	73.52	932.92	128.05	5.20	11.96
1982	68.93	78.18	60.41	39.75	71.99	884.36	119.71	5.81	11.60
1983	92.63	107.45	89.36	47.00	95.34	1,190.34	160.41	4.40	8.03
1984	92.46	108.01	85.63	46.44	89.28	1,178.48	160.46	4.64	10.02
1985	108.09	123.79	104.11	56.75	114.21	1,328.23	186.84	4.25	8.12
1986	136.00	155.85	119.87	71.36	147.20	1,792.76	236.34	3.49	6.09
1987	161.70	195.31	140.39	74.30	146.48	2,275.99	286.83	3.08	5.48
1988	149.91	180.95	134.12	71.77	127.26	2,060.82	265.79	3.64	8.01
1989	180.02	216.23	175.28	87.43	151.88	2,508.91	322.84	3.45	7.41
1990	183.46	225.78	158.62	90.60	133.26	2,678.94	334.59	3.61	6.47
1991	206.33	258.14	173.99	92.66	150.82	2,929.33	376.18	3.24	4.81
1992	229.01	284.62	201.09	99.46	179.26	3,284.29	415.74	2.99	
1991: Jan	177.95	220.69	145.89	88.59	121.39	2,587.60	325.49	3.82	
Feb	197.75	246.74	166.06	92.08	141.03	2,863.04	362.26	3.35	
Mar	203.57	255.36	166.26	92.29	145.42	2,920.11	372.28	3.26	5.58
Apr	207.71	260.15	166.90	92.92	152.64	2,925.54	379.68	3.19	
May	206.93	260.13	170.77	90.76	151.32	2,928.42	377.99	3.23	
June	207.32	261.16	177.05	89.01	152.31	2,968.14	378.29	3.23	5.23
July	208.29	262.48	177.15	90.05	151.60	2,978.19	380.23	3.20	
Aug	213.33	268.22	178.52	92.38	157.70	3,006.09	389.40	3.10	
Sept	212.55	266.21	177.99	93.72	157.69	3,010.35	387.20	3.15	4.59
Oct	213.10	265.68	187.31	95.25	158.94	3,019.74	386.88	3.14	
Nov	213.25	264.89	188.52	96.78	159.78	2,986.12	385.92	3.15	
Dec	214.26	266.01	185.47	98.08	159.96	2,958.64	388.51	3.11	3.83
1992: Jan	229.34	286.62	201.55	99.31	174.50	3,227.06	416.08	2.90	
Feb	228.12	286.09	205.53	96.18	174.08	3,257.27	412.56	2.94	
Mar	225.21	282.36	204.07	94.16	173.49	3,247.42	407.36	3.01	4.01
Apr	224.55	281.60	201.28	94.92	171.10	3,294.08	407.41	3.02	
May	228.61	285.25	207.93	98.26	175.90	3,376.79	414.81	2.99	
June	224.68	279.54	202.02	97.23	174.82	3,337.79	408.27	3.06	4.18
July	228.17	281.90	198.36	101.18	181.00	3,329.41	415.05	3.00	
Aug	230.07	284.44	191.31	103.41	180.47	3,307.45	417.93	2.97	
Sept	230.13	285.76	191.61	102.26	178.27	3,293.92	418.48	3.00	4.32
Oct	226.97	279.70	192.30	101.62	181.36	3,198.70	412.50	3.07	
Nov	232.84	287.30	204.78	101.13	189.27	3,238.49	422.84	2.98	
Dec	239.47	294.86	212.35	103.85	196.87	3,303.15	435.64	2.90	

[1] Averages of daily closing prices, except New York Stock Exchange data through May 1964 are averages of weekly closing prices.
[2] Includes all the stocks (more than 1,500) listed on the New York Stock Exchange.
[3] Includes 30 stocks.
[4] Includes 500 stocks.
[5] Standard & Poor's series, based on 500 stocks in the composite index.
[6] Aggregate cash dividends (based on latest known annual rate) divided by aggregate market value based on Wednesday closing prices. Monthly data are averages of weekly figures; annual data are averages of monthly figures.
[7] Quarterly data are ratio of earnings (after taxes) for 4 quarters ending with particular quarter to price index for last day of that quarter. Annual data are averages of quarterly ratios.

Note.—All data relate to stocks listed on the New York Stock Exchange.

Sources: New York Stock Exchange, Dow Jones & Co., Inc., and Standard & Poor's Corporation.

Source: *Economic Report of the President,* February 1992.

The Business Environment: A Retrospective, 1929–1993
EXHIBIT 13 • Year-by-Year Total Returns on Common Stocks, 1926–1991

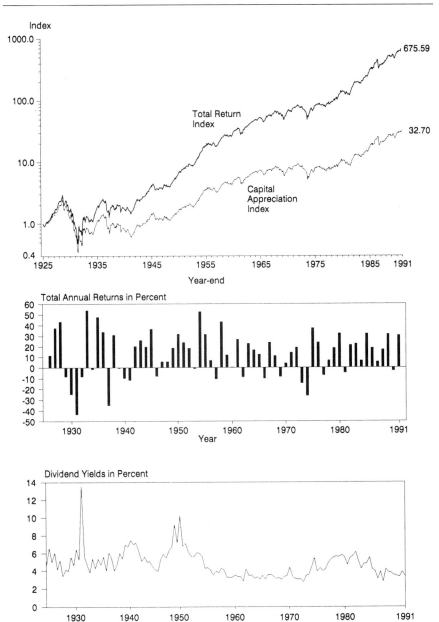

The Business Environment: A Retrospective, 1929–1993
EXHIBIT 14 • Wealth Indexes of Investments in the U.S. Capital Markets, 1925–1991

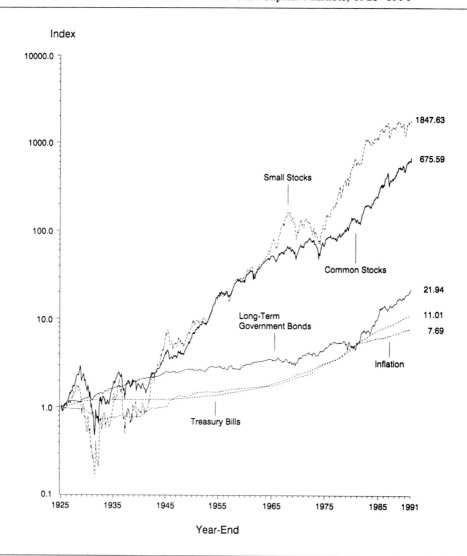

The Business Environment: A Retrospective, 1929–1993

EXHIBIT 15 • Three Measures of Inflation

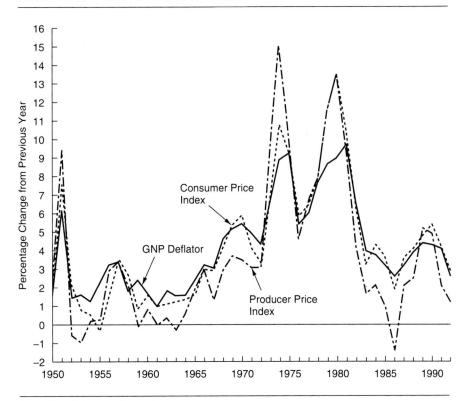

Source: Bridge Information Systems, Inc.

The Business Environment: A Retrospective, 1929–1993
EXHIBIT 16 • Federal Outlays as Percent of GNP

Percent

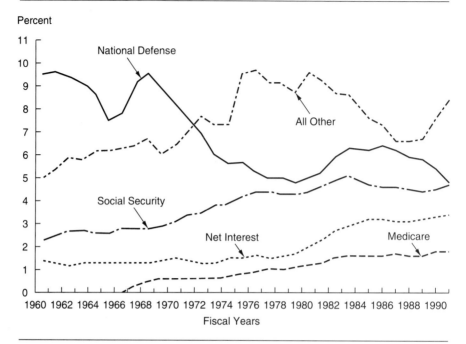

Source: *Economic Report of the President,* February 1992.

The Business Environment: A Retrospective, 1929–1993

EXHIBIT 17 • **Stock and Bond Yields (Earnings/Price Ratio: Annually, 1926–1935; End of Quarter, 1936; All Others, Quarterly)**

Percent per Annum

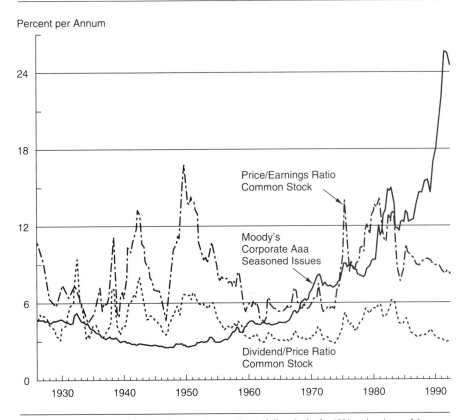

Source: Board of Governors of the Federal Reserve System, *Historical Chart Book,* after 1986, various issues of the *Federal Reserve Bulletin.*

The Business Environment: A Retrospective, 1929–1993
EXHIBIT 18 • Real Stock Returns, 1926–1992

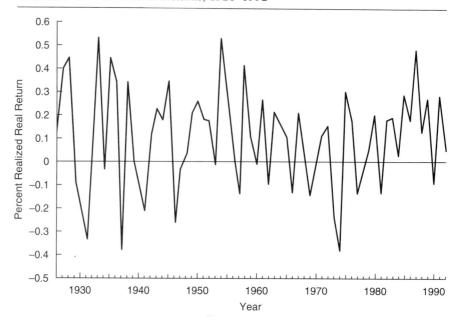

The Business Environment: A Retrospective, 1929–1993
EXHIBIT 19 • Corporate Profits (seasonally adjusted annual rates, quarterly)

Billions of Dollars

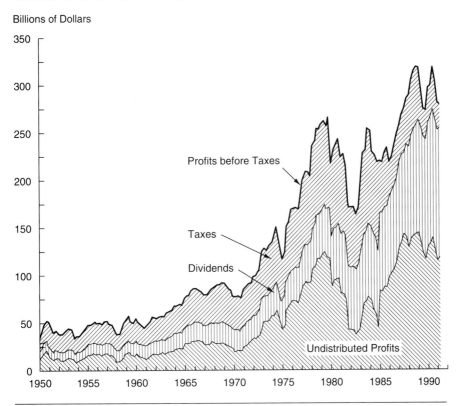

Source: Board of Governors of the Federal Reserve System, *1992 Historical Chart Book,* after 1986, various issues of the *Federal Reserve Bulletin.*

The Business Environment: A Retrospective, 1929–1993
**EXHIBIT 20 • Corporate Cash Flows, Capital Expenditures,
and New Orders, 1983–1993**

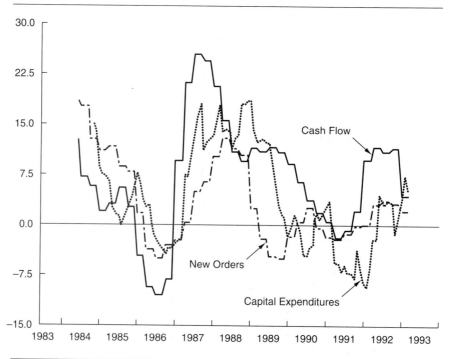

Source: Bridge Information Systems, Inc.

The Business Environment: A Retrospective, 1929–1993

EXHIBIT 21 • Capital Expenditures, External Funds Raised, Undistributed Profits*

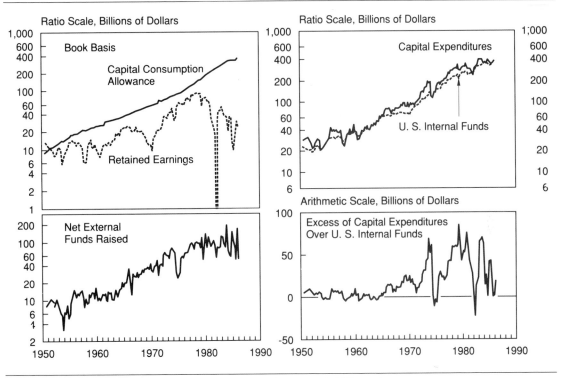

*Nonfinancial corporations; annually, 1950–1951; seasonally adjusted annual rates, quarterly 1952 onward.

Source: Board of Governors of the Federal Reserve System, *1987 Historical Chart Book*, 61.

The Business Environment: A Retrospective, 1929–1993
EXHIBIT 22 • Total Corporate Debt and Its Composition*

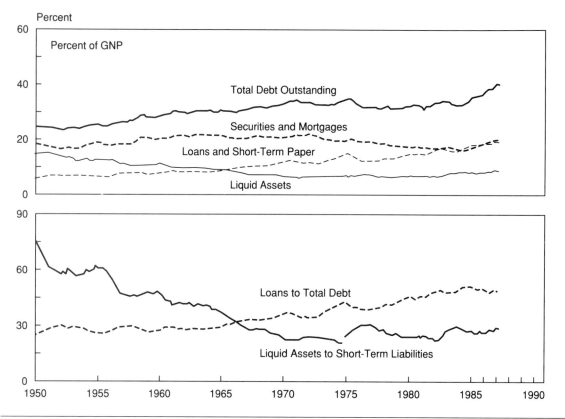

*Ratios for nonfinancial corporations; end of year, 1950–1951; seasonally adjusted, end of quarter, 1952-1986.

Source: Board of Governors of the Federal Reserve System, *1987 Historical Chart Book,* 64, and after 1986 various issues of the *Federal Reserve Bulletin.*

The Business Environment: A Retrospective, 1929–1993

EXHIBIT 23 • U.S. International Transactions (current account, 1959–1991)

Billions of Dollars

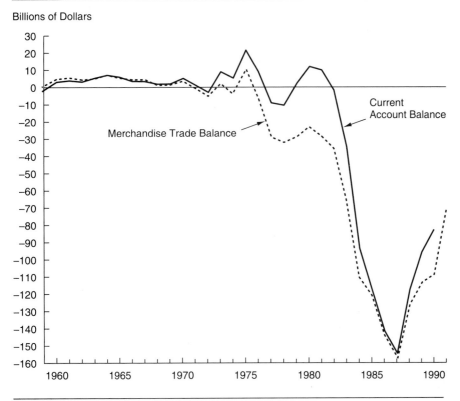

Source: *Economic Report of the President,* February 1992.

The Business Environment: A Retrospective, 1929–1993

EXHIBIT 24 • Corporate Security Issues: Gross Proceeds, Annual Totals

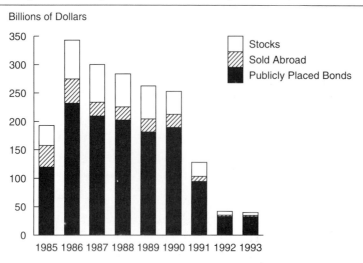

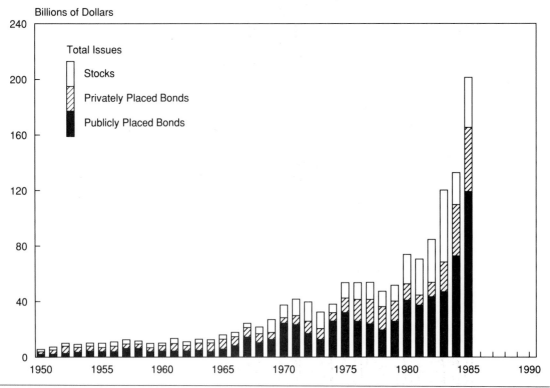

Source: Board of Governors of the Federal Reserve System, *1986 Historical Chart Book*, 59.

The Business Environment: A Retrospective, 1929–1993
EXHIBIT 25 • Labor Force, Employment, and Unemployment
(seasonally adjusted, quarterly)

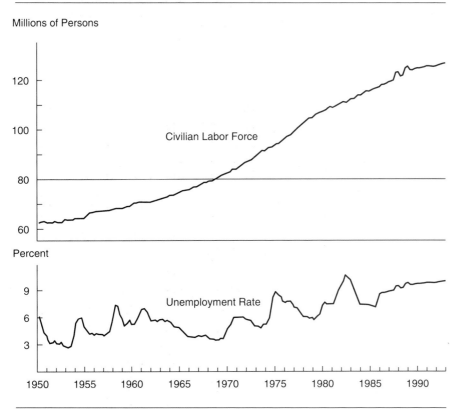

Source: Board of Governors of the Federal Reserve System, *1987 Historical Chart Book,* 20, after 1986, various issues of the *Federal Reserve Bulletin.*

The Business Environment: A Retrospective, 1929–1993
EXHIBIT 26 • Determinants of Business Fixed Investments 1955–1982
(percent, except as noted)

Year	Real investment as percent of real GNP	Capacity utilization rate in manufacturing [1]	Cash flow as percent of GNP [2]	Nonfinancial corporations				
				Rate of return on depreciable assets [3]		Rate of return on stockholders' equity [4]		Ratio of market value to replacement cost of net assets [5]
				Before tax	After tax	Before tax	After tax	
1955	9.3	87.1	9.3	19.8	9.8	13.1	6.2	1.112
1956	9.7	86.4	8.9	16.8	7.9	11.6	5.4	1.104
1957	9.7	83.7	8.9	15.2	7.4	10.5	5.0	1.018
1958	8.7	75.2	8.6	12.8	6.5	8.4	3.9	1.041
1959	8.8	81.9	9.3	16.4	8.5	10.5	5.1	1.252
1960	9.1	80.2	8.9	15.0	8.0	9.9	5.0	1.222
1961	8.8	77.4	8.8	15.1	8.2	9.5	4.6	1.350
1962	9.0	81.6	9.4	17.4	10.3	11.2	6.1	1.282
1963	9.0	83.5	9.7	18.8	11.2	12.1	6.7	1.419
1964	9.4	85.6	10.1	20.2	12.5	13.3	7.8	1.521
1965	10.5	89.6	10.6	22.1	14.0	15.5	9.6	1.621
1966	11.0	91.1	10.3	21.8	13.7	15.2	9.2	1.466
1967	10.4	86.9	10.0	19.3	12.4	13.4	8.2	1.480
1968	10.3	87.1	9.4	18.9	11.3	13.8	8.0	1.523
1969	10.7	86.2	8.6	16.5	9.7	12.5	7.1	1.353
1970	10.5	79.3	7.8	12.8	7.9	8.8	4.7	1.091
1971	10.0	78.4	8.3	13.5	8.5	9.9	5.7	1.176
1972	10.2	83.5	8.6	14.3	9.1	10.5	6.2	1.258
1973	11.0	87.6	8.0	14.3	8.7	12.8	8.3	1.157
1974	10.9	83.8	7.0	11.0	6.1	11.2	7.3	.827
1975	9.7	72.9	9.0	11.9	7.7	8.5	5.2	.811
1976	9.7	79.5	9.3	12.9	7.9	8.6	4.8	.911
1977	10.2	81.9	9.7	13.9	8.7	10.2	6.3	.797
1978	11.0	84.4	9.5	13.7	8.6	10.7	6.8	.761
1979	11.5	85.7	8.9	12.1	7.4	10.2	6.6	.709
1980	11.3	79.1	8.7	10.5	6.6	8.4	5.5	.666
1981	11.4	78.5	9.5	11.0	7.7	7.7	5.1	.694
1982 [p]	11.2	69.8	9.6	9.5	7.5	([6])	([6])	.690

[1] Federal Reserve Board index.
[2] Cash flow calculated as after-tax profits plus capital consumption allowance plus inventory valuation adjustment.
[3] Profits plus capital consumption adjustment and inventory valuation adjustment plus net interest paid divided by the stock of depreciable assets valued at current replacement cost.
[4] Profits corrected for inflation effects divided by net worth (physical capital component valued at current replacement cost).
[5] Equity plus interest-bearing debt divided by current replacement cost of net assets.
[6] Not available.

Sources: Department of Commerce (Bureau of Economic Analysis), Board of Governors of the Federal Reserve System, and Council of Economic Advisers.

Source: *Economic Report of the President*, February 1983, p. 263.

The Business Environment: A Retrospective, 1929–1993
EXHIBIT 27 • Basic Series: Summary Statistics of Annual Returns, 1926–1991

Series	Geometric Mean	Arithmetic Mean	Standard Deviation	Distribution
Common Stocks	10.4%	12.4%	20.8%	
Small Company Stocks	12.1	17.5	35.3	
Long-Term Corporate Bonds	5.4	5.7	8.5	
Long-Term Government Bonds	4.8	5.1	8.6	
Intermediate-Term Government Bonds	5.1	5.3	5.6	
U.S. Treasury Bills	3.7	3.8	3.4	
Inflation	3.1	3.2	4.7	

-90%   0%   90%

*1933 Small Company Stock Total Return was 142.9%.

Source: © *Stocks, Bonds, Bills, and Inflation 1993 Yearbook*™, Ibbotson Associates, Chicago (annually updates work by Roger G. Ibbotson and Rex A. Sinquefield). Used with permission. All rights reserved.

The Business Environment: A Retrospective, 1929–1993

EXHIBIT 28 • 400 Industrials[a] Per Share Data—Adjusted to Stock Price
Index Level; Average of Stock Price Indexes, 1941–1943=10

	Sales	Oper. Profit	Profit Margin (%)	Depr.	Income Taxes	Earnings		Dividends	
						Per Share	% of Sales	Per Share	% of Earn.
1956	54.73	8.36	15.27	2.04	2.96	3.50	6.40	1.84	52.57
1957	55.81	8.79	15.75	2.41	2.87	3.53	6.33	1.94	54.96
1958	53.48	7.70	14.40	2.38	2.40	2.95	5.52	1.86	63.05
1959	57.83	8.84	15.29	2.47	2.99	3.47	6.00	1.95	56.20
1960	59.47	8.73	14.68	2.56	2.87	3.40	5.72	2.00	58.82
1961	59.51	8.75	14.70	2.66	2.80	3.37	5.66	2.07	61.42
1962	64.63	9.81	15.18	2.89	3.16	3.83	5.93	2.20	57.44
1963	68.50	10.73	15.66	3.04	3.51	4.24	6.19	2.36	55.66
1964	73.19	11.67	15.94	3.24	3.70	4.85	6.63	2.58	53.20
1965	80.69	13.11	16.25	3.52	4.14	5.50	6.82	2.82	51.27
1966	88.46	14.48	16.37	3.87	4.35	5.87	6.64	2.95	50.26
1967	91.86	14.28	15.55	4.25	4.11	5.62	6.12	2.97	52.85
1968	101.49	16.08	15.84	4.56	5.14	6.16	6.07	3.16	51.30
1969	108.53	16.63	15.32	4.87	5.14	6.13	5.65	3.25	53.02
1970	109.85	15.54	14.15	5.17	4.23	5.41	4.92	3.20	59.15
1971	118.23	17.22	14.56	5.45	4.98	5.97	5.04	3.16	52.93
1972	128.79	19.39	15.06	5.76	5.90	6.83	5.30	3.22	47.14
1973	149.22	23.64	15.84	6.25	7.59	8.89	5.96	3.46	38.92
1974	182.10	27.97	15.36	6.86	10.22	9.61	5.28	3.71	38.61
1975	185.16	26.63	14.38	7.36	9.40	8.58	4.63	3.72	43.36
1976	202.66	29.23	14.42	7.58	10.21	10.69	5.27	4.22	39.48
1977	224.24	32.20	14.36	8.53	11.14	11.45	5.11	4.95	43.23
1978	251.32	36.19	14.40	9.64	12.14	13.04	5.19	5.37	41.18
1979	292.38	42.01	14.37	10.82	14.02	16.29	5.57	5.92	36.34
1980	327.36	43.08	13.16	12.37	13.67	16.12	4.92	6.49	40.26
1981	344.31	44.50	12.92	13.82	12.95	16.74	4.86	7.01	41.88
1982	333.86	42.67	12.78	15.30	10.95	13.20	3.95	7.13	54.02
1983	334.07	45.57	13.64	15.67	12.12	14.77	4.42	7.32	49.56
1984	379.70	51.50	13.56	16.31	14.15	18.11	4.77	7.51	41.47
R1985	398.42	53.23	13.36	18.19	13.68	15.28	3.84	7.87	51.51
P1986	388.44	52.36	13.48	19.44	10.95	14.57	3.75	8.15	55.94

Note: 1983 data include results of 'old' A.T.&T.; excls. $5.5 bil. charge; 1984 data reflect A.T.&T. divestiture.

[a]Based on 70 individual groups.

Stock Price Indexes for this group extend back to 1918.

Source: Standard & Poor's *1987 Analysts' Handbook,* 181.

Price 1941–1943=10		Price/Earn. Ratio		Div. Yields %		Book Value		Work-ing Capital	Capital Expend-itures
High	Low	High	Low	High	Low	Per Share	% Return		
53.28	45.71	15.22	13.06	4.03	3.45	26.35	13.28	13.91	4.14
53.25	41.98	15.08	11.89	4.62	3.64	29.44	11.99	13.50	4.84
58.97	43.20	19.99	14.64	4.31	3.15	30.66	9.62	14.27	3.58
65.32	57.02	18.82	16.43	3.42	2.99	32.26	10.76	14.93	3.65
65.02	55.34	19.12	16.28	3.61	3.08	33.74	10.08	15.29	4.23
76.69	60.87	22.76	18.06	3.40	2.70	34.85	9.67	15.84	3.97
75.22	54.80	19.64	14.31	4.01	2.92	36.37	10.53	16.85	4.41
79.25	65.48	18.69	15.44	3.60	2.98	38.17	11.11	17.64	4.41
91.29	79.74	18.82	16.44	3.24	2.83	40.23	12.06	18.07	5.71
98.55	86.43	17.92	15.71	3.26	2.86	43.50	12.64	18.80	6.87
100.60	77.89	17.14	13.27	3.79	2.93	45.59	12.88	19.48	8.26
106.15	85.31	18.89	15.18	3.48	2.80	47.78	11.76	20.74	8.35
118.03	95.05	19.16	15.43	3.32	2.68	50.21	12.27	21.08	8.65
116.24	97.75	18.96	15.95	3.32	2.80	51.70	11.86	21.05	9.70
102.87	75.58	19.01	13.97	4.23	3.11	52.65	10.28	20.70	10.25
115.84	99.36	19.40	16.64	3.18	2.73	55.28	10.80	22.61	9.96
132.95	112.19	19.47	16.43	2.87	2.42	58.34	11.71	24.41	10.08
134.54	103.37	15.13	11.63	3.35	2.57	62.84	14.15	26.49	11.65
111.65	69.53	11.62	7.24	5.34	3.32	67.81	14.17	28.47	14.65
107.40	77.71	12.52	9.06	4.79	3.46	70.84	12.11	30.47	14.43
120.89	101.64	11.31	9.51	4.15	3.49	76.26	14.02	31.89	14.92
118.92	99.88	10.39	8.72	4.96	4.16	82.21	13.93	33.28	17.02
118.71	95.52	9.10	7.33	5.63	4.53	89.34	14.60	34.88	19.70
124.49	107.08	7.64	6.57	5.53	4.76	98.71	16.50	36.32	26.44
160.96	111.09	9.99	6.89	5.84	4.03	108.33	14.88	36.52	29.86
157.02	125.93	9.38	7.52	5.57	4.46	116.06	14.42	35.98	33.03
159.66	114.08	12.10	8.64	6.25	4.47	118.60	11.13	34.41	31.30
194.84	154.95	13.19	10.49	4.72	3.76	122.32	12.07	36.55	25.24
191.48	167.75	10.57	9.26	4.48	3.92	123.99	14.61	38.94	30.08
235.75	182.24	15.43	11.93	4.32	3.34	125.89	12.14	39.32	31.42
282.77	324.88	19.41	15.43	3.62	2.88	124.53	11.70	40.61	29.24

The Business Environment: A Retrospective, 1929–1993
EXHIBIT 29 • Standard & Poor's 400 Per Share Data—Adjusted to Stock Price Index Level Average of Stock Price Indexes, 1941–1943 = 10 (millions of dollars except as noted)

Income Account	*1986*	*1985*	*1984*	*1983*	*1979*	*1978*	*1977*
Sales	$379.81	$398.42	$379.70	$334.00	$292.38	$251.32	$224.24
Costs and expenses	329.74	345.19	328.31	288.44	250.37	215.13	192.05
Operating income	50.07	53.22	51.50	45.56	42.01	36.19	32.30
Other income	4.09	3.64	6.13	5.12	4.14	2.84	2.48
Total income	54.15	56.87	57.63	50.69	46.15	39.02	34.67
Depreciation	19.17	18.19	16.31	15.67	10.82	9.64	8.53
Interest	9.59	9.24	8.54	7.62	4.58	3.84	3.25
Minority interest	0.17	0.16	0.18	0.21	0.29	0.23	0.20
Income taxes	10.74	13.68	14.15	12.12	14.02	12.14	11.14
Net income	14.48	15.60	18.45	15.07	16.45	13.17	11.56
Preferred dividends	0.27	0.35	0.36	0.34	0.19	0.16	0.14
Savings from common stock equivalents	0.02	0.03	0.03	0.03	0.03	0.03	0.03
Common earnings	14.23	15.28	18.11	14.76	16.29	13.04	11.45
Common dividends	8.94	7.87	7.51	7.32	5.92	5.37	4.95
Balance after dividends	$ 5.29	$ 7.41	$ 10.60	$ 7.45	$ 10.38	$ 7.67	$ 6.50

Financial Ratios =	*1986*	*1985*	*1984*	*1983*	*1979*	*1978*	*1977*
Current ratio	NA	NA	NA	NA	1.6%	1.7%	1.8%
Quick ratio	NA	NA	NA	NA	0.9	1.0	1.0
Debt to total assets (percent)	27%	26%	25%	23%	22	22	22
Times interest earned	3.6×	4.2×	4.8×	4.6×	7.7×	7.6×	8.0×
Inventory turnover	7.0	6.9	7.3	8.0	7.2	7.2	6.9
Total assets turnover	1.1×	1.2×	1.2×	1.2×	1.3×	1.3×	1.3×
Profit margin (percent)	13.18%	13.36%	13.56%	13.64%	14.37%	14.40%	14.36%
Return on total assets (percent)	3.97%	4.41%	5.80%	5.10%	7.24%	6.58%	6.49%

continued

Balance Sheet

Assets	1986	1985	1984	1983	1979	1978	1977
Cash and equivalent	$26.61	$22.76	$21.01	$20.52	$15.27	$15.34	$14.10
Receivables	47.58	47.78	47.39	45.36	38.80	33.39	28.71
Income tax refund	0.40	0.22	0.14	0.29	0.07	0.04	0.08
Inventories	54.51	57.85	51.68	41.89	40.42	35.09	32.35
Other current assets	8.27	7.95	6.18	4.99	3.19	2.68	2.36
Total current assets	NA	NA	NA	NA	97.65	86.44	77.53
Net property, plant, and equipment	152.26	150.20	138.79	142.26	106.89	94.15	83.64
Inventory and advertising to unconsolidated subsidiaries	17.13	16.44	16.62	13.13	10.03	8.89	7.96
Intangibles	14.56	9.63	5.94	3.98	2.69	2.22	1.68
Other assets	36.98	33.86	24.30	16.94	7.65	6.43	5.54
Total assets	$358.28	$346.68	$312.04	$289.35	$225.00	$198.24	$176.44

Note: Data presented in the above format reflect results for only those companies which have reported; no estimates are used. This holds true for all industry groups.

Source: Standard & Poor's *1987 Analyst Handbook*, 182.

Liabilities	1986	1985	1984	1983	1979	1978	1977
Notes payable	$25.56	$27.53	$19.90	$13.40	$8.01	$5.89	$5.63
Current portion of long-term debt	4.68	3.64	3.79	2.52	1.79	1.85	1.33
Accounts payable	32.62	34.47	30.07	27.41	23.75	19.88	17.14
Income tax payable	8.20	8.25	7.82	6.84	7.26	5.87	5.13
Accrued expenses	22.66	22.28	18.31	15.68	12.61	11.11	9.40
Other current liabilities	12.45	11.07	10.27	9.09	7.91	6.96	5.62
Total current liabilities	NA	NA	NA	NA	61.33	51.56	44.25
Long-term debt	65.83	59.22	53.25	50.08	39.22	36.23	32.09
Deferred income tax	21.00	19.99	17.85	18.49	10.83	8.93	7.41
Minority interest	1.71	1.56	1.47	1.84	2.06	1.83	1.54
Other liabilities	22.16	18.90	15.11	13.93	6.90	5.45	4.68
Preferred stock	2.89	3.51	3.56	3.21	2.19	1.82	1.49
Common stock	10.44	9.85	10.29	9.53	10.37	10.34	10.05
Capital surplus	20.49	20.30	17.30	20.71	11.90	11.29	10.75
Retained earnings	107.61	106.13	103.07	96.64	80.20	70.78	64.19
Total liabilities	$358.28	$346.68	$312.04	$289.35	$225.00	$198.24	$176.44